SPRINGER SERIES
IN PERCEPTION ENGINEERING

Series Editor: Ramesh Jain

Springer Series
in Perception Engineering

P.J. Besl: *Surfaces in Range Image Understanding*

J.L.C. Sanz (ed.): *Advances in Machine Vision*

Jorge L.C. Sanz
Editor

Advances in Machine Vision

With 190 Illustrations

Springer-Verlag
New York Berlin Heidelberg
London Paris Tokyo

Jorge L.C. Sanz
IBM Almaden Research Center
650 Harry Road
San Jose, CA 95120-6099
USA

Series Editor
Ramesh Jain
Electrical Engineering
and Computer Science Department
University of Michigan
Ann Arbor, MI 48105
USA

Library of Congress Cataloging-in-Publication Data
Advances in machine vision/Jorge L.C. Sanz, editor.
p. cm. — (Springer series in perception engineering)
Bibliography: p.
Includes index.
1. Computer vision. I. Sanz, J.L.C. (Jorge L.C.), 1955–
II. Series.
TA1632.A275 1988 88-12330
006.3'7—dc19 CIP

Printed on acid-free paper

Typeset by David Seham Associates, Metuchen, New Jersey.
Printed and bound by Quinn-Woodbine, Inc., Woodbine, New Jersey.
Printed in the United States of America.

9 8 7 6 5 4 3 2 1

ISBN 0-387-96822-9 Springer-Verlag New York Berlin Heidelberg
ISBN 3-540-96822-9 Springer-Verlag Berlin Heidelberg New York

Preface

In most industrial perception systems, some property in space is measured using a sensor, and then knowledge of the application and the environment is used to control a process. Though many different properties are useful in different applications, surfaces and their characteristics play a vital role in most industrial applications. Commonly used sensors for acquiring surface-related information obtain measurements on a two-dimensional grid. Since a 2-D function can be represented in the form of an image, the techniques used to analyze such measurements are commonly considered under *machine vision*.

The papers in *Advances in Machine Vision,* edited by Jorge L.C. Sanz, range from active optical imaging sensors to architectures and algorithms for image understanding. The first three papers present techniques for acquiring three-dimensional information using many different approaches. Besl's paper is an exceptionally thorough and exhaustive survey of optical range imaging sensors designed and implemented using many different techniques. This paper gives valuable information to those considering the use of a sensor for measurement of 3-D surface information. Aggarwal and Chien present a survey of techniques used to recover depth information using optical images. Poussart and Laurendeau discuss techniques for 3-D sensing in the industrial environment.

Inspection is the most common application of machine vision systems. Most analysts of the machine vision industry believe that in the next decade, more than half of the applications of machine vision systems will be in quality control using both in-process and product inspection. Hedengren presents a general methodology for inspection of industrial objects. There is an increasing trend in the direction of integrating CAD databases with machine vision systems for inspection applications. An inspection system that uses a design database is the topic of the paper by Silvén, Virtanen, Westman, Piironen, and Pietikäinen. Jeong and Musicus describe their approach to extracting masks from optical images of VLSI circuits.

Special architectures for implementing compute-intensive machine vision tasks in real time are essential to the applications of machine vision. Five papers in this volume address architectures for machine vision systems. Blanz, Sanz, and Petkovic discuss their approach to control-free low-level image segmentation.

They present their theory, discuss its implementation in hardware, and finally describe their experiments. Guerra and Levialdi describe algorithms and architectures for connectivity analysis, stereo, and Hough transform. Shu, Nash, and Weems present an architecture for image understanding. Sasaki, Gotoh, and Yoshida describe a reconfigurable video-rate image processor. Finally, Lougheed, McCubbrey, and Jain present an architecture and algorithms for iconic processing using morphology.

Advances in Machine Vision presents state-of-the-art sensing techniques, architectures, and inspection systems. Sanz has collected eleven excellent papers in this book. These papers address many aspects of a machine perception system. The emphasis in all these papers is industrial application. I am pleased to have this book in the series on *Perception Engineering*.

Ann Arbor, Michigan RAMESH JAIN

Contents

Contributors

J.K. Aggarwal Computer and Vision Research Center, The University of Texas at Austin, Austin, Texas 78712-1084, USA.

P.J. Besl Computer Science Department, General Motors Research Laboratories, Warren, Michigan 48090-9055, USA.

W.E. Blanz Computer Science Department, IBM Almaden Research Center, San Jose, California 95120-6099, USA.

C.H. Chien Computer Science Department, Carnegie-Mellon University, Pittsburgh, Pennsylvania 15213, USA.

T. Gotoh Pattern Information Processing Laboratory, Fujitsu Laboratories Ltd., Kawasaki 211, Japan.

C. Guerra Department of Computer Sciences, Purdue University, West Lafayette, Indiana 47907, USA.

K.H. Hedengren General Electric Company, Schenectady, New York 12301, USA.

R. Jain Electrical Engineering and Computer Science Department, University of Michigan, Ann Arbor, Michigan 48109, USA.

H. Jeong Department of Electrical Engineering and Computer Science, Massachusetts Institute of Technology, Cambridge, Massachusetts 02139, USA.

D. Laurendeau Department of Electrical Engineering, Université Laval, Quebec G1K 7P4, Canada.

S. Levialdi Dipartimento di Matematica, Universita di Roma, Rome 1-00185, Italy.

R.M. Lougheed Environmental Research Institute of Michigan, Ann Arbor, Michigan 48107-8618, USA.

D.L. McCubbrey Environmental Research Institute of Michigan, Ann Arbor, Michigan 48107-8618, USA.

B.R. Musicus Department of Electrical Engineering and Computer Science, Massachusetts Institute of Technology, Cambridge, Massachusetts 02139, USA.

G. Nash Hughes Research Laboratories, Malibu, California 90265, USA.

D. Petkovic Computer Science Department, IBM Almaden Research Center, San Jose, California 95120-6099, USA.

M. Pietikäinen Department of Electrical Engineering, University of Oulu, SF-90570 Oulu 57, Finland.

T. Piironen Electronics Laboratory, Technical Research Centre of Finland, SF-90101 Oulu, Finland.

D. Poussart Department of Electrical Engineering, Université Laval, Quebec G1K 7P4 Canada.

J.L.C. Sanz Computer Science Department, IBM Almaden Research Laboratory, San Jose, California 95120-6099, USA.

S. Sasaki Pattern Information Processing Laboratory, Fujitsu Laboratories Ltd., Kawasaki 211, Japan.

D.B. Shu Hughes Research Laboratories, Malibu, California 90265, USA.

O. Silvén Department of Electrical Engineering, University of Oulu, SF-90570 Oulu 57, Finland.

I. Virtanen Department of Electrical Engineering, University of Oulu, SF-90570 Oulu 57, Finland.

C. Weems Computer and Information Science Department, University of Massachusetts, Amherst, Massachusetts 01003, USA.

T. Westman Department of Electrical Engineering, University of Oulu, SF-90570 Oulu 57, Finland.

M. Yoshida Pattern Information Processing Laboratory, Fujitsu Laboratories Ltd., Kawasaki 211, Japan.

1
Active Optical Range Imaging Sensors

PAUL J. BESL

ABSTRACT: Active, optical range imaging systems collect three-dimensional coordinate data from object surfaces. These systems can be useful in a wide variety of automation applications, including shape acquisition, bin picking, assembly, inspection, gauging, robot navigation, medical diagnosis, cartography, and military tasks. The range-imaging sensors in such systems are unique imaging devices in that the image data points explicitly represent scene surface geometry in a sampled form. At least six different optical principles have been used to actively obtain range images: (1) radar, (2) triangulation, (3) moire, (4) holographic interferometry, (5) lens focusing, and (6) diffraction. The relative capabilities of different sensors and sensing methods are evaluated using a figure of merit based on range accuracy, depth of field, and image acquisition time.

1 Introduction

Range-imaging systems collect large amounts of three-dimensional (3-D) coordinate data from visible object surfaces in a scene. These systems can be used in a wide variety of automation applications, including object shape acquisition, bin picking, robotic assembly, inspection, gauging, mobile robot navigation, automated cartography, medical diagnosis (biostereometrics), and automated military applications. The range-imaging sensors in such systems are unique imaging devices in that the image data points explicitly represent scene surface geometry as sampled surface points. The inherent problems of automatically interpreting 3-D structure from the output of other types of imaging sensors, such as video cameras, are not encountered with range-imaging sensors although most low-level problems, such as image segmentation and edge detection, remain.

Range images are known by many other names depending on context: range map, depth map, depth image, range picture, rangepic, 3-D image,

2.5-D image, digital terrain map (DTM), topographic map, 2.5-D primal sketch, surface profiles, *xyz*-point list, surface distance matrix, contour map, and surface height map. The number of techniques for obtaining range images outnumbers this list of synonyms by a wide margin, but most active optical techniques are based on one of six principles: (1) radar, (2) triangulation, (3) moire, (4) holographic interferometry, (5) lens focusing, and (6) Fresnel diffraction. This chapter addresses each of these fundamental categories by presenting tutorial material on each range-measuring principle and then surveying representative sensors in that category. To make comparisons between different sensors and different sensing techniques, a performance figure of merit is defined and computed for each representative sensor. This measure combines image acquisition speed, depth of field, and range accuracy into a single number. Other application-specific factors, such as sensor cost, field of view, and standoff distance are not evaluated.

No claims are made regarding the completeness of the survey, and the inclusion of commercial sensors should not be interpreted in any way as an endorsement of a vendor's product. Moreover, if the figure of merit ranks one sensor better than another, this does not necessarily mean that it is better than the other for any given application.

Jarvis [1983b] wrote a survey of range-imaging methods that has served as the classic reference in range imaging for computer vision researchers. An earlier survey was done by Kanade and Asada [1981]. Strand [1983] covered range-imaging techniques from an optical engineering viewpoint. Several other surveys have appeared since then (e.g., Kak [1985]; Nitzan et al. [1986]; Svetkoff [1986]; Wagner [1987]). This survey is different from previous work in that it provides an example of a simple methodology for quantitative performance comparisons between different sensing methods which may assist system engineers in performing evaluations for their applications. In addition, the state of the art in range imaging advanced rapidly in the past few years and is not adequately documented elsewhere.

This survey is structured as follows. Definitions of range images and range-imaging sensors are given first. Two different forms of range images and the generic viewing constraints and motion requirements for range imaging are discussed next, followed by an introduction to sensor performance parameters that are common to all types of range-imaging sensors. These parameters are then used to define a figure of merit for comparison purposes. The main body sequentially addresses each of the fundamental ranging methods. The figure of merit is computed for each sensor if documented results are available. The conclusion consists of a sensor comparison section and a final summary. An introduction to laser eye safety is given in an appendix, as this is an important concern with active optical sensors.

2 Preliminaries

A *range-imaging sensor* is any combination of hardware and software capable of producing a range image of a real-world scene under appropriate operating conditions. Thus, a range-imaging sensor is only defined by the property that it produces range images of scenes. A *range image* is a large collection of distance measurements from a known reference coordinate system to surface points on object(s) in a scene. If *scenes* are defined as collections of physical objects and if each *object* is defined by its mass density function, then *surface points* are defined as the 3-D points in the half-density level set of each object's normalized mass density function [Koenderink and VanDoorn 1986].

If the distance measurements are listed relative to three orthogonal coordinate axes, the range image is in *xyz* form. If the distance measurements indicate range along 3-D direction vectors indexed by two integers (i,j), the range image is in r_{ij} form. Any range image in r_{ij} form can be converted directly to *xyz* form, but the converse is not true. As no ordering of points is required in the *xyz* form either, this is the more general form, but it is also more involved to process than the r_{ij} form. Range images in the *xyz* form require low-level processing algorithms not found in previous computer vision or image-processing literature.

If the surface-point sampling-intervals are consistent in the horizontal and vertical directions of an *xyz* range image, the image can be represented in the form of a large matrix of scaled, quantized range values r_{ij} where the corresponding x,y,z coordinates are determined implicitly by the row and column position in the matrix and the range value. The term "image" is used because any r_{ij} range image can be displayed on a video monitor; it is identical in form to a digitized video image from a TV camera. The only difference is that the pixel (matrix element) values in a range image represent distance whereas the pixel values in a video image represent brightness (the number of photons with visible frequencies falling on a camera pixel).

The term "large" used in the previous definition is relative, of course, but for this survey, a range image must specify more than 100 (x,y,z) sample points. Anything less is referred to as *sparse range data* as compared to the *dense range data* in a range image. For example, the 20 × 20 matrix of heights of surface points measured above a plane (shown in Figure 1.1) is a range image. If r_{ij} is the pixel value at the i-th row and the j-th column of the matrix, then the 3-D coordinates would be given as

$$x = a_x + s_x i \tag{1.1a}$$

$$y = a_y + s_y j \tag{1.1b}$$

$$z = a_z + s_x r_{ij} \tag{1.1c}$$

171	160	163	163	166	166	168	166	168	166	163	160	163	163	160	163	166	163	166	163
168	166	166	163	166	163	168	166	166	166	163	163	166	163	166	163	166	160	163	163
168	168	166	166	166	163	160	166	166	171	166	168	168	166	160	163	166	160	160	166
166	163	166	166	163	163	160	163	179	174	185	177	185	179	212	196	185	204	196	185
163	166	160	166	163	163	166	190	174	168	168	182	185	190	201	196	199	182	196	199
166	163	163	163	168	160	163	166	166	163	168	177	190	188	199	188	190	196	193	185
163	166	166	157	160	160	160	171	160	168	168	182	199	199	199	193	199	188	193	193
160	160	160	166	157	160	168	166	166	163	163	182	201	199	190	188	190	190	193	193
163	166	157	163	160	157	160	177	166	160	171	201	215	199	196	201	190	190	188	188
155	160	160	163	160	163	160	166	166	163	163	204	207	207	190	185	193	190	196	196
157	155	163	160	157	157	168	166	168	163	177	188	201	199	196	196	201	182	210	196
157	157	155	157	160	157	163	171	163	157	155	204	185	196	193	188	196	188	193	201
157	160	155	155	157	157	168	168	163	166	166	190	201	201	196	188	190	193	185	193
157	155	160	160	157	157	163	157	157	160	157	182	204	190	185	190	190	188	185	188
157	157	157	160	157	157	152	166	160	163	166	193	196	193	199	190	190	185	190	185
155	157	160	160	160	152	166	152	163	152	168	171	212	212	193	190	188	182	188	185
152	157	155	155	152	155	149	163	160	155	157	185	210	210	212	215	210	185	204	193
155	155	157	152	152	155	155	171	174	166	171	188	188	199	188	204	188	185	215	207
155	157	152	157	149	157	157	168	179	204	182	221	174	193	182	179	212	188	201	182
155	155	155	155	152	149	146	174	188	193	168	185	168	179	171	190	190	193	190	179

FIGURE 1.1. 20 × 20 matrix of range measurements: r_{ij} form of range image.

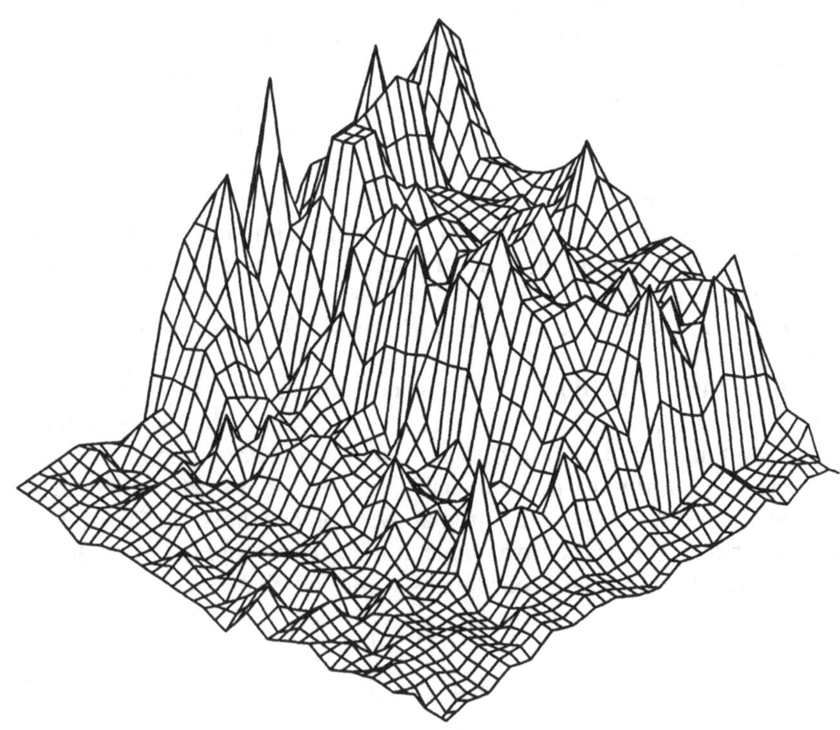

FIGURE 1.2. Surface plot of range image in Figure 1.

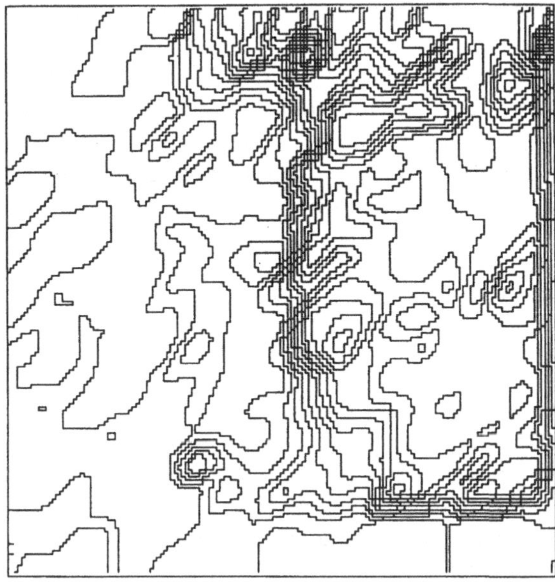

FIGURE 1.3. Contour plot of range image in Figure 1.

where the $\vec{s}$-values are distance increments (scale factors) and the $\vec{a}$-values are coordinate offsets. The matrix of numbers can be graphed as a surface net viewed obliquely (as shown in Figure 1.2), interpolated and plotted as a contour map (as shown in Figure 1.3), displayed as a black-and-white or color image (a gray level image is shown in Figure 1.4), or simply listed on a terminal or printer as shown in Figure 1.1. Each representation is equally valid.

The affine transformation in Equations (1.1 a–c) is an appropriate form for orthographic r_{ij} range images, where the term *orthographic* signifies

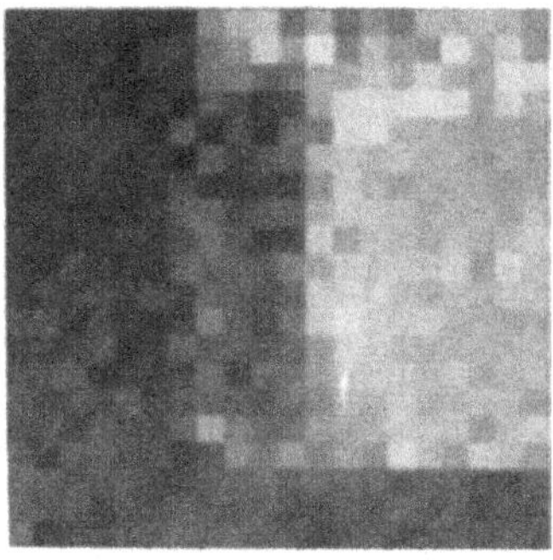

FIGURE 1.4. Gray-level representation of range image in Figure 1.

that depths are measured along parallel rays orthogonal to the image plane. Nonaffine transformations of (i,j,r_{ij}) coordinates to Cartesian (x,y,z) coordinates are more common in active, optical range-sensing methods. In the commonly used spherical coordinate system shown in Figure 5, the (i,j) indices correspond to angular increments in the vertical (latitude, elevation) and horizontal (longitude, azimuth) directions. The spherical-to-Cartesian transformation is given by

$$x = a_x + s_r r_{ij} \cos(is_\phi) \sin(js_\theta) \tag{1.2a}$$

$$y = a_y + s_r r_{ij} \sin(is_\phi) \tag{1.2b}$$

$$z = a_z + s_r r_{ij} \cos(is_\phi) \cos(js_\theta) \tag{1.2c}$$

where the s_r, s_ϕ, s_θ, values are the scale factors in range, elevation, and azimuth and the $\vec{a}$-values are the offsets.

A closely related angular coordinate system is the two orthogonal-axis angular coordinate system. This coordinate system is also shown in Figure 1.5 where the alternate elevation angle ϕ is used with the normal azimuth definition θ. Using the same notations for the scale factors and offsets, the transformation to Cartesian coordinates is given by [Besl 1986]:

$$x = a_x + s_r r_{ij} \tan(js_\theta)/\sqrt{1 + \tan^2(is_\theta) + \tan^2(js_\phi)} \tag{1.3a}$$

$$y = a_y + s_r r_{ij} \tan(is_\phi)/\sqrt{1 + \tan^2(is_\theta) + \tan^2(js_\phi)} \tag{1.3b}$$

$$z = a_z + s_r r_{ij}/\sqrt{1 + \tan^2(is_\theta) + \tan^2(js_\phi)}. \tag{1.3c}$$

Note the symmetry of the azimuth and alternate elevation angles in the x and y coordinates, which is not present in spherical coordinates. Azimuth depends only on x and z, and the alternate elevation angle depends only on y and z. The differences in transformed Cartesian coordinates (x,y,z)

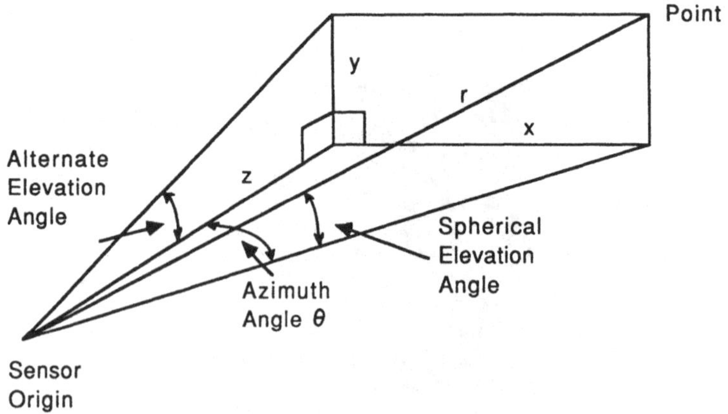

FIGURE 1.5. Cartesian, spherical, and orthogonal-axis coordinates.

between these coordinates and spherical coordinates for the same values of azimuth and elevation are less than 4% in x and z and less than 11% in y even when both angles are as large as ± 30 degrees (a 60×60 degree field of view).

2.1 Viewing Constraints and Motion Requirements

The first question to be addressed in range imaging sensor requirements is sensor viewing constraints. Is a single view sufficient, or are multiple views of a scene necessary for the given application? What types of range sensors are compatible with these needs? For example, a mobile robot at an instant in time is constrained to acquire data from its on-board sensors at its current location. An automated modeling system may acquire multiple views of an object with many sensors at different viewpoints such that every accessible, exterior surface of the object is imaged. Four basic types of range sensors are distinguished, based on the viewing constraints, scanning mechanisms, and object movement possibilities:

1. A *point sensor* measures the distance to a single visible surface point from a single viewpoint along a single ray. A point sensor can create a range image if (1) the scene object(s) can be satisfactorily "scanned" in two orthogonal directions in front of the point-ranging sensor, or (2) the point-ranging sensor can be scanned in two directions over the scene, or (3) the scene object(s) are stepped in one direction and the point sensor is scanned in the other direction.
2. A *line* or *circle sensor* measures the distance to visible surface points that lie in a single 3-D plane or cone that contains the single viewpoint or viewing direction. A line or circle sensor can create a range image if (1) the scene object(s) can be satisfactorily "scanned" in the direction orthogonal to the sensing plane or cone, or (2) the line- or circle-ranging sensor can be scanned over the scene in the orthogonal direction.
3. A *field-of-view sensor* measures the distance to many visible surface points that lie within a given field of view relative to a single viewpoint or viewing direction. This type of sensor creates a range image directly. No scene motion is required.
4. A *multiple-view sensor* locates surface points relative to more than one viewpoint or viewing direction because all surface points of interest are not visible or cannot be adequately measured from a single viewpoint or viewing direction. Scene motion is not required.

These sensor types form a natural hierarchy: a point sensor may be scanned (with respect to a sensor axis) to create a line or circle sensor, and a line or circle sensor may be scanned (with respect to the orthogonal sensor axis) to create a field-of-view sensor. Any combination of point, line/circle, and field-of-view sensors can be used to create a multiple-view sensor by (1) rotating and translating the scene in front of the sensor(s),

(2) maneuvering the sensor(s) around the scene with a robot, (3) using multiple sensors in different locations to capture the appropriate views, or (4) any combination of these methods.

The specified viewing constraints may or may not require scene movement depending upon the type of sensor used. For example, an expensive coordinate-measuring machine (CMM) can be used to digitize surface points from almost the entire 4π solid angle around an object without requiring object movement, whereas a relatively inexpensive line-scan structured-light range sensor can digitize the same points with slightly less accuracy if the object can be placed on a precision rotation table. Since movement requirements are a significant factor in the characterization of range-image-sensing techniques, the following checklist is given:

- Motion of scene object(s)

1. No mechanical motion. Scene stationary relative to sensor.
2. Limited translation of scene object(s) along specified axes allowed (e.g., place scene object(s) on precision *xy*-table for *x* or *y* translation).
3. Limited rotation of scene object(s) around specified axes allowed (e.g., place scene object(s) on precision rotation table for single-axis rotation).
4. Full 3-D motion of scene object(s) in front of sensor needed (e.g., use robot arm to manipulate scene object(s)).

- Sensor motion

1. No mechanical motion. Sensor housing and all sensor components fixed.
2. Sensor housing fixed, internal scan motion for one direction needed (e.g., use internal rotating polygon mirror or translation stage).
3. Sensor housing fixed, internal scan motion for two orthogonal directions needed (e.g., use internal rotating mirror and galvanometer nodding mirror).
4. Limited translation of complete sensor along specified axes needed (e.g., place sensor on precision *xy*-table for *x* or *y* translation).
5. Limited rotation of complete sensor around specified axes needed.
6. Full 3-D motion of sensor around object in scene needed (e.g., mount sensor on robot to move sensor around scene object(s)).

A given range-imaging system might combine any scene motion with any sensor motion to achieve its goals.

Accurate sensor and/or scene object positioning is achieved via commercially available translation stages, *xy*-tables, and $xy\theta$-tables (translation repeatability in submicron range, angular repeatability in microradians or arc-seconds). Such methods are preferred to mirror-scanning methods for very high precision applications because these mechanisms can be controlled more tightly than scanning mirrors. Accurate, controlled 3-D motion of sensor and/or object via gantry, slider, or revolute joint robot arms is also possible, but is generally more expensive than table motion for the same locating accuracy. Scanning motion internal to sensor housings must be as accurate as possible and is usually rotational, but may also be translational using a precision translation stage. Optical scanning of laser beams may be achieved via (1) rotating polygon mirrors, (2) galvanometer-driven mirrors, (3) acousto-optic (AO) modulators, (4) rotating holographic scanners, or (5) stepper-motor-driven mirrors [Marshall 1985; Gottlieb 1983]. However, AO modulators and holographic scanners significantly attenuate laser power and AO modulators have a very narrow angular field of view (about 10×10 degrees), making them less desirable for many applications.

2.2 Sensor Performance Parameters

Any measuring device is characterized by its measurement resolution or precision, its measurement repeatability, and its measurement accuracy. For this discussion, the following definitions are adopted. *Range resolution* or *range precision* is the smallest change in range that a ranging sensor can report. *Range repeatability* measures statistical variations as a range sensor makes repeated measurements of the exact same distance over time. *Range accuracy* measures relative statistical variations as a range sensor makes repeated measurements of a known true value. An accuracy figure should be an indication of the largest possible deviation of a measurement from the actual true value. For our purposes, a range sensor is characterized by its resolution and its accuracy. If a sensor has good repeatability, it is assumed that it can also be calibrated to be accurate. Loss of calibration over time (drift) is a big problem for some sensors, but this is not regarded as a system parameter and is not addressed here. Since range sensors can improve accuracy by averaging multiple measurements, sensor accuracy should be quoted with measurement time to be meaningful for comparison purposes.

A range-imaging sensor measures point positions (x,y,z) within a specified accuracy or error tolerance. The method of specifying accuracy varies with different applications, but the accuracy specification should include one or more of the following: (1) the mean absolute error (MAE) $\pm\ (\delta_x,\delta_y,\delta_z)$ for N observations where

$$\delta_x = (1/N) \sum_{i}^{N} | x_i - \mu_x | \tag{1.4a}$$

$$\mu_x = (1/N) \sum_{i}^{N} x_i; \tag{1.4b}$$

(2) the RMS (root-mean-square) error $\pm(\sigma_x, \sigma_y, \sigma_z)$ where

$$\sigma_x = 1/(N - 1) \sum_{i}^{N} (x_i - \mu_x)^2 \tag{1.5a}$$

$$\mu_x = (1/N) \sum_{i}^{N} x_i; \tag{1.5b}$$

or (3) the maximum error $\pm(\varepsilon_x, \varepsilon_y, \varepsilon_z)$ where

$$\varepsilon_x = \max_{i=1,N} |x_i - \mu_x| \tag{1.6a}$$

$$\mu_x = (1/N) \sum_{i}^{N} x_i. \tag{1.6b}$$

It is always true that $\delta \leqslant \sigma \leqslant \varepsilon$ for each direction regardless of the probability distribution of the measurement process. Other specifications are possible. Some specify range accuracy (σ) with $\pm\sigma$ for RMS error, others specify $\pm 3\sigma$, others specify the positive width of the normal distribution as 2σ, and others don't say which of these they mean, if any. Whatever specification is used, the sensor should meet the specified error tolerance on each point in the working volume V of size $L_x \times L_y \times L_z$.

The above parameters specify the spatial properties of the sensor. The pixel dwell time T is the time required for a single pixel range measurement. For points acquired sequentially, the total time to take N_p points in an image frame will be N_pT. The frame rate of the imaging sensor is then $1/N_pT$, whereas the pixel data rate is $1/T$ pixels per second. If all image points are acquired simultaneously (in parallel) in time T, the frame rate is $1/T$ and the pixel rate N_p/T.

A system figure of merit maps several system parameters to a single number that can be used to compare different systems. An application-independent performance figure of merit M is defined to measure the spatial and temporal performance of range-imaging sensors. For example, an airborne sensor and printed circuit board sensor can have the same figure of merit (same level of performance), but each sensor is only useful for its application. For xyz- form range imaging, the figure of merit M is defined as

$$M = \frac{1}{\sqrt{T}} \left(\frac{L_x L_y L_z}{\sigma_x \sigma_y \sigma_z} \right)^{1/3}. \tag{1.7}$$

For r_{ij}-form range imaging, there is usually very little relative uncertainty in the direction of a ray specified by the integer i and j indices compared to the uncertainty in the measured range r. Thus, the uncertainty in the resulting x-,y-, and z-coordinates is dominated by the uncertainty in the r_{ij}-values. The working volume is a portion of a pyramid cut out by spherical surfaces with the minimum distance and the maximum distance radius. Therefore, the figure of merit for r_{ij}-form range-imaging sensors is given by the simpler expression

$$M = \frac{L_r}{\sigma_r \sqrt{T}}, \tag{1.8}$$

where L_r is the depth of field and σ_r is the RMS range accuracy. Both quantities are defined along rays emanating from the sensor. The factors of standoff distance, angular field of view, and field of view are other important parameters for range sensors that do not enter into the figure of merit calculations directly, but should be considered. These parameters are shown in Figure 1.6.

The dimensions of M may be thought of roughly as the amount of good-quality range data per second, and of course, the higher the number the better. A doubling of the depth-of-field-to-range-accuracy ratio is reflected by a doubling of the figure of merit. However, a quadrupling of image-acquisition speed is required to double the figure of merit. This expresses a bias for accurate over fast measurements. However, suppose a given system does internal averaging of normally distributed measurement errors over the pixel dwell time T. If the time is quartered, the σ-value should only double in theory. If the square root of the time T were not used, the figure of merit would double as the data became noisier and the sensor got faster. This seems to be an undesirable trait for a figure of merit, and therefore, the square root is used to maintain an invariant figure of merit under such averaging changes.

It might seem that $\pm 3\sigma$-values should be used instead of just σ. However, it is clear that $\pm 3\sigma$ performance is not always being quoted as accuracy in the literature. Besides, it is difficult to know the actual accuracy for a given application without actually testing a sensor. For lack of a better approach, we have equated accuracy and σ for evaluating figures of merit. As a result, several sensors, especially sensors from commercial companies whose main products are ranging sensors, will be underrated by this scheme. They know the big difference between measurements in the lab and measurements in the customer's plant and prefer to avoid customer disappointment. In fact, some commercial sensors are conser-

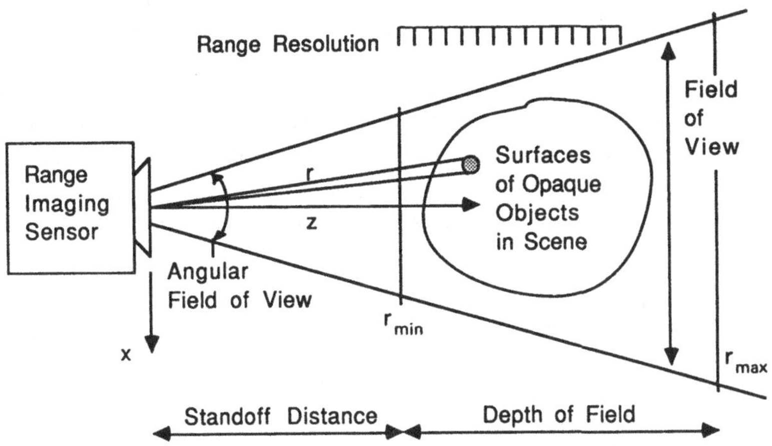

FIGURE 1.6. Range-imaging sensor with angular scan.

vatively rated ten to twenty times less accurate than they would be in the lab. To make matters worse, other literature (commercial vendors included) overrates sensor accuracy or only specifies resolution. Therefore, the figure of merit values should be taken as examples of the rough order of magnitude of sensor performance, not as exact numbers.

The sensor cost C is combined with the performance figure of merit to create a cost-weighted figure of merit $M' = M/C$ where the dimensions are roughly range data per second per unit cost. Cost estimates are not included here because actual costs can vary significantly from year to year depending upon technical developments and market forces, not to mention customized features that might be needed for a given application. Cost estimates were also not available for many sensors.

It is likely that these figures of merit M and M' may place no importance on factors that dominate decisions for a particular application. The figures of merit given here represent an example of measures for comparing different range-imaging sensors. No figure of merit can represent all factors for all applications. As discussed later in the triangulation section, triangulation-based range-imaging sensors may suffer from the missing parts problem (or shadowing problem) for large separations of source and detector. The figure of merit does not reflect this limitation, although this aspect might be unacceptable for a given application. Also, if an application needed to acquire the surface geometry of a mirrored polyhedral object, most optical methods would be inappropriate; indeed, highly specular objects are usually a problem for active, optical sensors.

The specularity problem is just an example of a scene "materials" problem that cannot easily be factored into a figure of merit for sensor performance. For example, some materials almost completely absorb the infrared beam from a laser radar causing interpretation problems. In contrast, glass is transparent to optical radars and is not detected at all. In this sense, the physical and chemical composition of the matter in a scene, which determines the reflection, transmission, and absorption properties of surfaces, is as important as the mass density function of the matter in a scene, which determines the geometric properties of surfaces. Even though range-imaging sensors are designed for determining scene surface geometry directly, physical models of the materials in the scene are needed for interpreting the range images. This discussion also leads to the question of what materials are used in performing accuracy tests of various sensors. Sensor performance is usually quoted under the most favorable conditions.

3 Imaging Radars

Bats [Griffin 1958] and porpoises [Kellogg 1961] are equipped by nature with ultrasonic "radars." Mankind's use of radar dates back to 1903 when Hulsmeyer [1904] experimented with the detection of radio waves reflected from ships. The basic time/range equation for radars is

$$v\tau = 2r = \text{roundtrip distance} \tag{1.9}$$

where v is the speed of signal propagation, r is the distance to a reflecting object, and τ is the transit time of the signal from the radar transmitter to the reflecting object and back to the radar receiver.

In order to measure the transit time τ (time of flight (TOF)), a sufficient percentage of the transmitted energy must be detected by the receiver so that the received signal can be adequately discriminated from noise sources. The energy or power in a radar system can be analyzed in general terms regardless of the signal type or frequency of operation. Herein, the subscript X refers to the transmitter properties and the subscript R refers to the receiver properties. If $P_x(t - \tau)$ is the total instantaneous transmitted power in the direction $\hat{l}$ at the time $t - \tau$; G_X is the directional "antenna gain" of the transmitter, which is approximately $4\pi/\phi^2$ where ϕ is the angular beam width of the "main lobe" of transmitted signal; T_X is transmission coefficient for the transmitter optics or antenna (ideally 1.0); T_R is transmission coefficient for the receiver optics or antenna (ideally 1.0); and A_R is the effective capture area of the receiver; then the received power $P_R(t)$ at the radar transmitter/receiver at the time t from a small diffusely reflecting (Lambertian) surface patch of area A (that lies within the transmitted beam width) with an average surface normal $\hat{n}$ and a diffuse surface reflection coefficient (or albedo) ρ_d at a distance r from the source is given by

$$P_R(t) = (G_X T_X P_X(t - \tau))\,(T_R A_R)(A\rho_d\,\hat{l} \cdot \hat{\mathrm{n}})\left(\frac{e^{-2\alpha r}}{16\pi^2 r^4}\right), \tag{1.10}$$

where α is the atmospheric attenuation coefficient for the medium between the radar unit and the reflecting object and $\tau = 2r/v$. The first grouping of terms is completely dependent upon the radar transmitter subsystem, the second grouping of terms is completely dependent upon the radar receiver subsystem, the third grouping of terms is the "radar cross section" of the diffusely reflecting surface, and the fourth (final) grouping of terms expresses the spatial propagation attenuation for the round trip through the intervening medium and includes the classical r^{-4} radar dependence. This is the fundamental signal-power radar equation for a diffuse (Lambertian) reflector.

Of course, not all surfaces of interest reflect light diffusely. One way to model specular reflection from shiny surfaces is to augment the radar cross section term with a specular term: $A(\rho_d\hat{l}\cdot\hat{\mathrm{n}} + \rho_s(\hat{l}\cdot\hat{n})^m)$ where ρ_s is the specular reflection coefficient and m is a phenomenological constant that models the beam spreading in the specular reflection due to finite surface roughness. For large m, the model represents perfect specular reflection. For specular reflection to occur in radar, the surface normal must align closely with the incident direction of the radar beam. This does happen, but not in most scenes viewed from randomly selected viewpoints.

If the radar beam enters the relatively large ($\approx\pi/2$ steradians) reflecting solid angle of a retroreflector in a scene (a specularly reflecting (mirrored), concave, cube corner surface), the radar cross section term must be augmented further to include a high directional gain retroreflection term as in Kawata et al. [1985]. Some ranging sensors rely on the placement of retroreflectors at the appropriate positions in the scene. Such methods might be termed "cooperative target" methods. Many commercial measurement sensors are based on such techniques (e.g., Namco [1986]). Scenes consisting only of "noncooperative" objects are considered here.

Noise sources can obscure the radar return if the signal is not strong enough relative to the noise. Hence, the maximum range for a radar r_{max} is limited by the minimum detectable signal power P_{min} that meets the probability of detection and false alarm requirements for a given application. Range accuracy σ_r is also limited by noise. One way to characterize the noise in a radar system is via the noise equivalent power (NEP), which is the signal power required to produce a signal-to-noise ratio (SNR) of one. Detailed noise calculations may involve the actual receiver design, operating frequency, and application-dependent detectability requirements. In general, the NEP may depend on [Yariv 1976]: (1) thermal noise (Johnson noise, Nyquist noise); (2) shot noise (with Poisson statistics) from the signal, the ambient background radiation, or the detector dark current; (3) semiconductor flicker noise ($1/f$ noise); (4) generation-recombination noise in photoconductive detectors; (5) laser source noise; (6) surface roughness noise; and (7) speckle noise [Goodman 1986; Leader 1986] in coherent laser systems. Shot noise dominates other noise sources at optical frequencies owing to the underlying Bose-Einstein quantum statistics of photons and the dominance of the $h\nu$ photon energy over kT thermal energy.

Several different radar principles have been used to measure range. Pulsed, time-of-flight radars emit energy in short pulses of oscillating energy, wait for an echo, and then use the transit time as determined by a counter to determine range. Continuous-wave (CW) radars emit energy continuously during the time that range is being measured. CW radars usually emit either amplitude-modulated (AM) or frequency-modulated (FM) signals. AM CW radars measure phase differences to determine range, whereas FM CW radars use beat frequencies to measure range. Detection techniques in radars [Keyes 1986] are either coherent heterodyne detection [Teich 1968] or direct detection. These concepts are discussed in more detail later.

Range resolution and accuracy are major concerns in range imaging, but lateral resolution and accuracy are also key factors for imaging purposes. The Rayleigh criterion for (laterally) resolving two point sources is that the angular separation θ_{sep} in radians of the two points must be greater than 1.22 times the ratio of the signal wavelength λ to the diameter D of the aperture receiving the signal [Marion 1965]:

$$\theta_{sep} \geqslant 1.22\frac{\lambda}{D}. \tag{1.11}$$

For a 3-GHz (10-cm) S-band radar, a 14-m (46-ft) diameter antenna is needed to achieve a 0.5-degree angular resolution similar to the beam spread of a good laser diode. Small radar units at normal radar frequencies are not useful for range-imaging applications.

For narrow laser beams reflected from macroscopic objects, the area A in the radar cross section term is almost always determined by the beam spread ϕ, not by scene object parameters. That is, the projected area along the beam that reflects energy back to the radar receiver is approximately $(r\phi)^2$. This cancels out the beam spread dependence of the directional transmitter gain G_X and part of the r^{-4} dependence in the propagation term to yield

$$P_R(t) = \left(\frac{1}{4\pi}A_R T_R e^{-2\alpha r} T_X P_X(t - \tau)\right)\left(\frac{\rho_d\, \hat{l} \cdot \hat{n}}{r^2}\right). \tag{1.12}$$

The unknown parameters are the range r, the diffuse surface reflection coefficient (albedo) ρ_d, and the object surface normal orientation $\hat{n}$ (relative to the optical axis $\hat{l}$ of the radar beam). All other parameters can be lumped into a single function $K_X(t) = A_R T_R T_X P_X(t)/4_\pi$, which depends only on the radar transceiver hardware:

$$P_R(t,\theta_{\hat{n}},\rho_d,r) = K_X(t - \tau)\rho_d \cos\theta_{\hat{n}}/r^2, \tag{1.13}$$

where $\cos\theta_{\hat{n}} = \hat{n} \cdot \hat{l}$. This simpler form tells us that if ten bits of range resolution are required on surfaces that may tilt away from the sight line by as much as 60 degrees, and if a moderate range of surface reflection coefficients from 1 to 0.002 are possible on scene surfaces, then a radar receiver with a dynamic range of 90 dB is required to meet the specifications.

3.1 Time of Flight, Pulse Detection

In this section, several pulse-detection imaging laser radars are mentioned. A figure of merit M is assigned to each sensor.

Lewis and Johnston [1977] built an imaging laser radar beginning in 1972 for the Mars rover (a mobile robot). Their best range resolution was 20 mm over a three-meter depth of field and the maximum data rate possible was 100 points per second. It took about 40 seconds to obtain 64×64 range images ($M = 1{,}520$).

Jarvis [1983a] built a similar sensor capable of acquiring a 64×64 range image with ± 2.5 mm range resolution over a 4-m field of view in 40 seconds ($M = 16{,}160$).

Heikkinen et al. [1986] and Ahola et al. [1985] developed a pulsed time-of-flight range sensor with a depth of field of 1.5 meters at a standoff of-

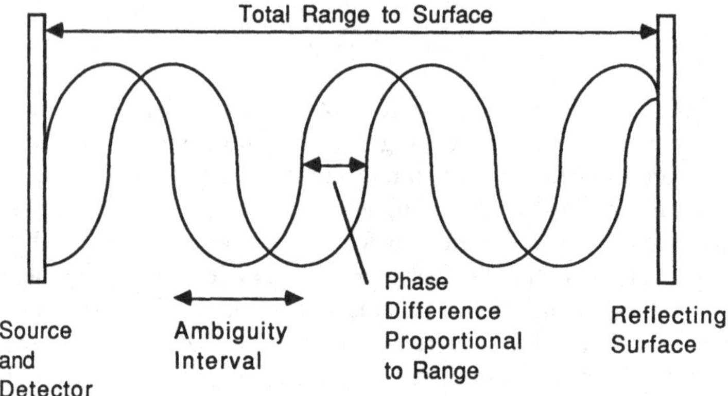

FIGURE 1.7. Phase and range ambiguity with AM CW radar.

2.5 meters. The range resolution is about 20 mm at its maximum data rate (10,000 points/sec) at a range of 3.5 m ($M = 7{,}500$).

Ross [1978] patented a novel, pulsed time-of-flight imaging laser radar concept that uses several fast camera shutters instead of mechanical scanning. For a range sensor with 30 cm resolution over a 75-meter depth of field, the least significant range-bit image is determined by a 2-ns shutter (the fastest shutter required). Assuming a conservative frame rate of 15 Hz and eight 512 $\times$ 512 cameras, $M = 500{,}000$ if it can be built.

An imaging laser radar is commercially available for airborne hydrographic surveying [Banic et al. 1987]. The system can measure water depths down to 40 m with an accuracy of 0.3 meters from an aerial standoff of 500 m. Two hundred scan lines were acquired covering 2,000 square kilometers with 2,000,000 "soundings" in 30 hours ($M = 596$). This number is low because application-specific capabilities are not included.

3.2 Amplitude Modulation

Rather than sending out a short pulse, waiting for an echo, and measuring transit time, a laser beam can be amplitude-modulated by varying the drive current of a laser diode at a frequency $f_{AM} = c/\lambda_{AM}$. An electronic phase detector measures the phase difference $\Delta\phi$ (in radians) between the transmitted signal and the received signal to get the range:

$$r(\Delta\phi) = \frac{c}{4\pi f_{AM}}\Delta\phi = \frac{\lambda_{AM}}{4\pi}\Delta\phi. \tag{1.14}$$

Since relative phase differences are only determined modulo 2π, the range to a point is only determined within a range ambiguity interval r_{ambig} (see

Figure 1.7). In the absence of any ambiguity-resolving mechanisms, the depth of field of an AM laser radar is the ambiguity interval:

$$L_r = r_{ambig} = \frac{c}{2f_{AM}} = \frac{\lambda_{AM}}{2}, \tag{1.15}$$

which is divided into $2^{N_{\text{bits}}}$ range levels where N_{bits} is the number of bits of quantization at the output of the phase detector.

Finer depth resolution and smaller ambiguity intervals are achieved by using higher modulating frequencies. The RMS range accuracy σ_r depends on the properties of the phase detection circuit and the signal-to-noise ratio (SNR). Under ideal low-signal conditions, the noise at the detector is dominated by the signal photon shot noise, and the signal-to-noise ratio is given by the square root of the average number of photoelectrons n_e released within a pixel dwell time T:

$$\text{SNR} = \sqrt{n_e} = \sqrt{P_R T\eta/h\nu}, \tag{1.16}$$

where η is the quantum efficiency of the photon detector, h is Planck's constant, and ν is the optical frequency. Nitzan et al. [1977] derived an approximate expression for the RMS range error (assuming 100 percent modulation index) yielding

$$\frac{L_r}{\sigma_r} = \sqrt{2}\pi\text{SNR}. \tag{1.17}$$

Therefore, the figure of merit is proportional to the signal-to-noise ratio and to the square root of the received signal power.

The ambiguity interval problem in AM CW radars can be resolved either via software or more hardware. If the imaged scene is limited in surface gradient relative to the sensor, it is possible in software to unwrap the phase ambiguity because the phase gradient will always exceed the surface gradient limit at phase wraparound pixels. This type of processing is done routinely by moire sensors discussed later [Halioua and Srinivasan 1987]. In hardware, a system could use multiple modulation frequencies simultaneously. In a simple approach, each range ambiguity is resolved by checking against lower modulation frequency measurements. Other methods are also possible, but none are commercially available at the current time.

Nitzan et al. [1977] built one of the first nonmilitary AM imaging laser radars. It created high-quality registered range and intensity images. With a 40-dB SNR, a range accuracy of 4 cm within an ambiguity interval of 16.6 m was obtained. With a 67-dB SNR, the range accuracy improved to 2 mm. The pixel dwell time was variable: 500 ms per pixel dwell times were common and more than two hours were needed for a full 128 × 128 image. The system insured image quality by averaging the received signal until the SNR was high enough ($M = 3{,}770$ at 67 dB).

The Environmental Research Institute of Michigan (ERIM) developed three AM imaging laser radars: (1) the Adaptive Suspension Vehicle (ASV) system (128 × 128 image), (2) the Autonomous Land Vehicle (ALV) system (256 × 64), and (3) the Intelligent Task Automation (ITA) system (programmable up to 512 × 512). Zuk and Dell'Eva [1983] described the ASV sensor. The range accuracy is about 61 mm over 9.75 m at a frame rate of two 128 × 128 images per second ($M = 28{,}930$).

The ERIM ALV sensor generates two 256 × 64 image frames per second. The ambiguity interval was increased to 19.5 m, but $M = 28{,}930$ is identical to the ASV sensor since pixel dwell time and depth-of-field-to-range-accuracy ratios stayed the same. The new ERIM navigation sensor [Sampson 1987] uses lasers with three different frequencies and has 2-cm range resolution ($M = 353{,}000$, assuming depth of field is doubled).

The ERIM ITA sensor is programmable as described in Svetkoff et al. [1984]. The depth of field can change from 150 to 900 mm. As an inspection sensor, the laser diode is modulated at 720 MHz. The sensor then has a range accuracy of 100 microns at a standoff of 230 mm in a 76-mm × 76-mm field of view over a depth of field of 200 mm. The latest system of this type claims a 100-kHz pixel rate ($M = 632{,}500$).

A commercially available AM imaging laser radar is built by Odetics [Binger and Harris 1987]. Their sensor has a 9.4-m ambiguity interval with a nine-bit range resolution of 18 mm per depth level. The pixel dwell time is 32 microseconds ($M = 71{,}720$). This sensor features an auto-calibration feature that calibrates the system every frame, avoiding thermal drift problems encountered in other sensors of this type. It is currently the smallest (9 × 9 × 9 in.), lightest weight (33 lb), and least power-hungry (42 W) imaging laser radar. Class I CDRH eye-safety requirements (see appendix) are met, except within a 0.4-m radius of the aperture.

Another commercially available AM imaging laser radar was built by Boulder Electro-Optics [1986]. The ambiguity interval is 43 m with an 8-bit resolution (about 170 mm). The frame rate was 1.4 256 × 256 frames/sec ($M = 27{,}360$).

Perception [1987] reports that it is developing an AM imaging laser radar for the factory with a 360-kHz data rate, a 1.87-m ambiguity interval, a 3-m standoff, and a 0.45-mm (12-bit) range resolution ($M = 153{,}600$ assuming 8-bit accuracy).

Cathey and Davis [1986] have designed a system using multiple laser diodes, one for each pixel, to avoid scanning. They obtained a 15-cm range accuracy in bright sunlight at a range of 13 meters for a two-diode system. For N^2 laser diodes fired four times a second, $M = 512N$. If the cost of the sensor is dominated by N^2 laser diode cost, the cost-weighted figure of merit M' would decrease as $1/N$. A full imaging system has not been built.

Miller and Wagner [1987] have built an AM radar unit using a modulated infrared LED. The system scans 360 degrees in azimuth, digitizing about 1,000 points in a second. The depth of field is about six meters with a range accuracy of about 25 mm ($M=7{,}590$). This system is very inexpensive to build and is designed for mobile robot navigation.

The Perkin-Elmer imaging airborne laser radar [Keyes 1986] scans 2,790 pixels per scan line in 2 ms ($M=302{,}360$ assuming eight-bit range accuracy). Aircraft motion provides the necessary scanning motion in the flight direction of the aircraft.

Wang et al. [1984] and Terras [1986] discussed the imaging laser radar developed at General Dynamics. The 12 × 12 degree angular field of view is scanned by dual galvanometers. It ranges out to 350 meters, but the ambiguity interval is 10 m, yielding lots of phase transition stripes in uncorrected range images.

Other work in AM imaging laser radars has been done at Hughes Aircraft, MIT Lincoln Labs [Quist et al. 1978], and Raytheon [Jelalian and McManus 1977], as well, as at United Technologies, Rockwell, and other defense contractors.

3.3 Frequency Modulation, Heterodyne Detection

The optical frequency of a laser diode can be tuned thermally by modulating the laser diode drive current [Dandridge 1982]. If the transmitted optical frequency is repetitively swept linearly between ($\nu \pm \Delta\nu/2$ to create a total frequency deviation of $\Delta\nu$ during the period $1/f_m$ (f_m is the linear sweep modulation frequency) as shown in Figure 1.8, the reflected return signal can be mixed coherently with a reference signal at the detector to create a beat frequency f_b signal that depends upon the range to the object r [Skolnick 1962]. This detection process is known as FM coherent heterodyne detection. Range is proportional to the beat frequency in an FM CW radar:

$$r(f_b) = \frac{cf_b}{4f_m\Delta\nu}. \tag{1.18}$$

One method for measuring the beat frequency is counting the number of zero crossings N_b of the beat signal during a ramp of the linear sweep frequency modulation. This zero-crossing count must satisfy the relationship $2N_b = \lfloor f_b/f_m \rfloor$, which yields the range equation

$$r(N_b) = \frac{c}{2\Delta\nu}N_b. \tag{1.19}$$

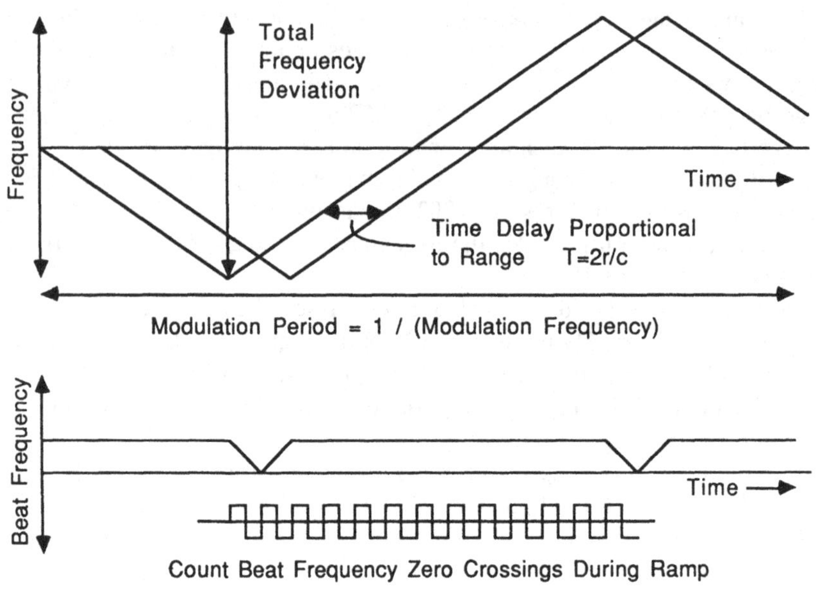

FIGURE 1.8. FM CW radar principles.

The range values in this method are determined to within $\delta r = \pm c/4\Delta\nu$ since N_b must be an integer. The maximum range of an FM radar should satisfy the constraint that $r_{\max} << c/f_m$. Since it is difficult to insure the exact optical frequency deviation $\Delta\nu$ of a laser diode, it is possible to measure range indirectly by comparing the N_b-value with a known reference count N_{ref} for an accurately known reference distance r_{ref}:

$$r(N_b) = \frac{r_{ref}}{N_{ref}} N_b. \tag{1.20}$$

Hersman et al. [1987] reported results for two commercially available FM imaging laser radars: a vision system and a metrology system. The vision system measures a one-meter depth of field with an 8-bit resolution at four 256 × 256 range image frames per second ($M = 3{,}770$ using a quoted value of 12 mm for RMS depth accuracy after averaging 128 frames in 32 seconds). A new receiver is being developed to obtain this performance in a quarter of a second. The metrology system measures to an accuracy of 50 microns in 0.1 seconds over a depth of field of 2.5 m ($M = 30{,}430$). Better performance is expected when electronically tunable laser diodes are available.

Beheim and Fritsch [1986] reported results with an in-house sensor. Points were acquired at a rate of 29.3 per second. The range accuracy varied with target-to-source distance. From 50 to 500 mm, the range accuracy was 2.7 mm; from 600 to 1,000 mm, $\sigma_z = 7.4$ mm, and from 1,100 to 1,500 mm, $\sigma_z = 15$ mm (approximately $M = 1{,}080$).

3.4 Heterodyne versus Nonheterodyne Issues

Keyes [1986] states that "Within the scientific community, it is commonly assumed that the direct detection of laser radiation is vastly less sensitive than coherent detection. This fallacy has its origin in the radio and microwave fields where, because of the small energy of the photon $h\nu$, it is extremely difficult to make receivers whose thermal kT noise is small compared to $h\nu$." He shows that, for realistic existing detector parameters, coherent detection has no benefit for SNRs greater than 23 dB in longer-wave optical radars (1.6 to 10.6 microns) and 10 dB in shorter wave optical radars (0.3 to 1.06 microns). For strong, clean return signals, sensor performance may actually be degraded by using heterodyne detection instead of direct detection. However, operating at lower SNRs may allow further ranging, better eye safety, or cheaper laser diodes. One can conservatively conclude from Keyes' statements that laser radars must be carefully compared to determine performance differences, and that optical coherent heterodyne detection does not necessarily offer the significant benefits of coherent heterodyne radars at lower radio frequency (RF) and microwave frequencies.

4 Active Triangulation

Triangulation is certainly the oldest method for measuring range to remote points and is probably also the most common. The law of sines states that if the length B (the baseline) of one side and two interior angles ∠AB and ∠BC of the triangle ABC are known, then the other lengths, A and C, and the remaining angle ∠AC must satisfy

$$\frac{\sin(\angle AB)}{C} = \frac{\sin(\angle BC)}{A} = \frac{\sin(\angle CA)}{B}. \tag{1.21}$$

Thus, instead of measuring picosecond time intervals, detecting one-degree phase differences, or counting zero crossings as in imaging radars, triangulation-based imaging systems measure angles and baseline distances as accurately as possible in order to do accurate ranging. All triangulation systems can have the missing parts (shadowing) problem if occlusion prevents measurement of the second angle because a point is only visible along side A or C in the ABC triangle.

A simple geometry for an active triangulation system is shown in Figure 1.9. A single camera is aligned along the z-axis with the center of the lens located at (0,0,0). At a baseline distance b to the lert of the camera (along

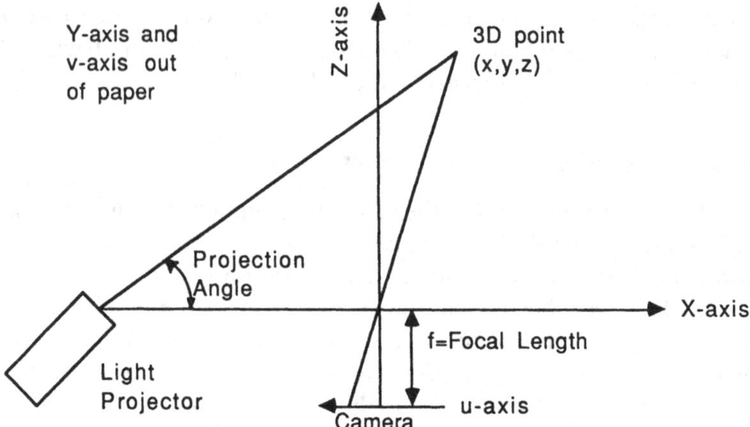

FIGURE 1.9. Camera-centered active triangulation geometry.

the negative x-axis) is a light projector sending out a beam or plane of light at a variable angle θ relative to the x-axis baseline. The point (x,y,z) is projected into the digitized image at the pixel (u,v) so $uz = xf$ and $vz = yf$ by similar triangles where f is the focal length of the camera in pixels. The measured quantities (u,v,θ) are used to compute the (x,y,z) coordinates:

$$x = \frac{b}{f \cot \theta - u} \cdot u \tag{1.22a}$$

$$y = \frac{b}{f \cot \theta - u} \cdot v \tag{1.22b}$$

$$z = \frac{b}{f \cot \theta - u} \cdot f. \tag{1.22c}$$

4.1 Structured Light: Point

It is commonly believed that a large baseline distance b separating the light source and detector is necessary for accurate ranging. However, for any fixed focal length f and baseline distance b, the range resolution of a triangulation system is only limited by the ability to accurately measure the angle θ and the horizontal position u.

Rioux [1984] has patented a synchronized scanner concept for active triangulation in which the horizontal position detector and beam projector are both scanned. The angle θ is coupled with the u measurement, yielding high-range resolution with a small baseline by making more efficient use of the finite resolution of the horizontal position detector. The basic concept is that if one uses the available resolution to measure differences rather than mean quantities, the effective resolution can be much greater.

Rioux [1984] implemented a range-imaging sensor using this concept. A laser diode and a lateral effect photodiode are positioned opposite to each other around a double-sided scanning mirror. As shown in Figure 1.10, the beam leaves the source, hits the mirror currently rotated at a position θ, bounces off a fixed mirror M_S, and impinges on an object surface. The illuminated bright spot is viewed via the opposite side of the mirror (and a symmetrically positioned fixed mirror M_D separated by the baseline distance b from the other fixed mirror). The focal length of the detector's lens is f and the average range to object surface points is r_0. The value r_0 is determined by the angular positioning of the mirrors M_S and M_D. The horizontal position p of the bright spot at the detector is determined by the lateral effect photodiode. The effective horizontal position $u(p)$ is given by

$$u(p) = w \cdot \frac{p + w \tan \theta}{w - p \tan \theta} \tag{1.23}$$

where the distance from the center of the focusing optics to the position detector surface is given by $w = r_0 f / r_0 - f$. Hence, θ leverages the detected value of p to obtain an effective value of $u(p)$. A vertical nodding mirror is rotated by an angle ϕ whose rotational axis is located a distance h from the baseline between the fixed mirrors. The 3-D coordinates of scene points

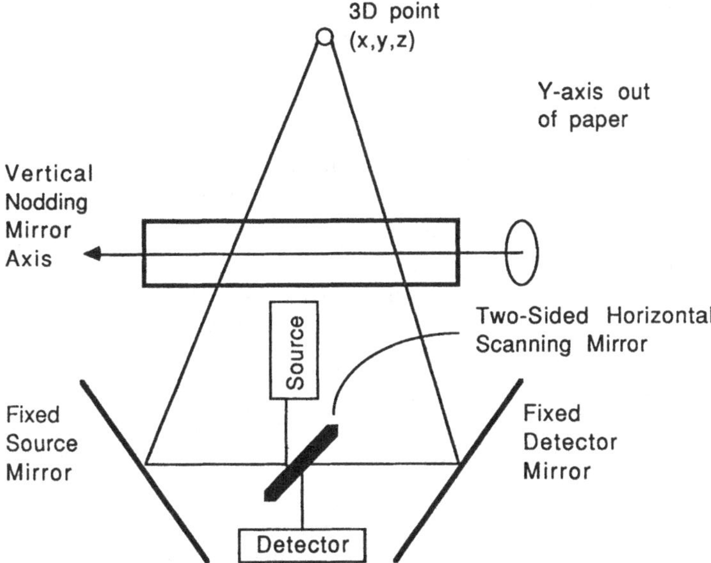

FIGURE 1.10. Synchronous scanning of source and detector.

are determined by the horizontal scanning mirror angle θ, the vertical nodding mirror angle ϕ, and the horizontal position detector value p:

$$x = \frac{bu(p)}{u(p) + wa(\theta)} \tag{1.24a}$$

$$y = \left(\frac{bw}{u(p) + wa(\theta)} - h\right) \sin(2\phi) \tag{1.24b}$$

$$z = \left(\frac{bw}{u(p) + wa(\theta)} - h\right) \cos(2\phi), \tag{1.24c}$$

where the angular function of horizontal scanning pyramid mirror is given by

$$a(\theta) = \frac{b + 2r_0 \tan\theta}{b \tan\theta - 2r_0}. \tag{1.25}$$

If the vertical nodding mirror is positioned such that $h = (r_0^2 - b^2/4)/(2r_0)$, then the reference surface of optimal focus for the sensor is spherical. Rioux [1984] documents a 128 × 256 range image is created in less than 1 second. The angular separation of the fixed mirrors is about 10 degrees. For a total working volume of 250 mm × 250 mm × 100 mm, the spatial resolutions in the x,y, and z-directions were 1, 2, and 0.4 millimeters, respectively ($M = 45{,}255$).

Servo-Robot [1987] manufactures the Saturn and Jupiter line-scan range sensors. Both are based on synchronous scanning. The Saturn system measures a 60-mm × 60-mm × 60-mm working volume from a distance of 80 mm. The volume-center resolution is 0.06 mm in y and 0.05 mm in z ($M = 32{,}860$ for 3,000 points/sec). The Jupiter system measures a 1-m × 1-m × 1-m volume from a standoff of 0.1 m. The volume-center resolution is 1 mm in y and 0.3 mm in z ($M = 91{,}290$ for 3,000 points/sec).

Hymarc [1987] also has a line-scan sensor based on synchronous scanning. The sensor is accurate to 0.25 mm in a 500-mm × 500-mm × 500-mm working volume at a 600-mm standoff with a 3000 point per second data rate ($M = 109{,}540$).

Photonic Automation, Inc. [Juha and Donahue 1987] made a commercially available range-imaging sensor for high-precision ranging in a shallow depth of field. Their sensor had a range accuracy of 25 microns over a depth of field of 6.25 mm at a speed of 10,000,000 pixels per second ($M = 790{,}570$). The angular separation between source and detector was about 5 degrees. Synthetic Vision Systems of Ann Arbor, Michigan, has a competing unit in production.

Bickel et al. [1984] independently developed a mechanically coupled deflector arrangement for spot scanners similar in concept to the Rioux [1984] design. Bickel et al. [1985] address the depth of focus problems inherent in triangulation systems for both illumination and detection. They claim that a tele-axicon lens and a laser source can provide a 25-micron spot that is in focus over a 100-mm range at a 500-mm standoff. The detection optics should be configured to satisfy the Scheimpflug (tilted detector plane) condition [Slevogt 1974]:

$$\tan \theta_{tilt} = \frac{1}{M} \tan \theta_{sep} \tag{1.26}$$

where θ_{sep} is the separation angle of the illumination direction and the detector's viewing direction, θ_{tilt} is the tilt angle of the photosensitive surface in the focusing region of the lens relative to the viewing direction, and $M = (w_c - f)/w_c$ is the on-axis magnification of the lens where w_c is the distance from the center of the lens to the center of the detector plane and f is the focal length of the lens. The Scheimpflug configuration is shown in Figure 1.11. All points in the illumination plane are in exact focus in the detector plane. Using a 4,000-element linear array detector without subpixel computations, they get 25-micron range resolution and 13-micron lateral resolution over a depth of field of 88 mm. No timing information is given, so $M = 17{,}530$ using a rate of 30 points/sec. Tilted detector planes are used by some commercial vendors. Hausler and Maul [1985] have examined the implications of using telecentric scanning configurations for triangulation point scanners. A telecentric system positions optical components at the focal length of the lens (or mirror) so that points at infinity are in focus.

Faugeras and Hebert [1986] use an in-house laser scanner. Their sensor uses a laser spot projector and two horizontal position detectors. Objects

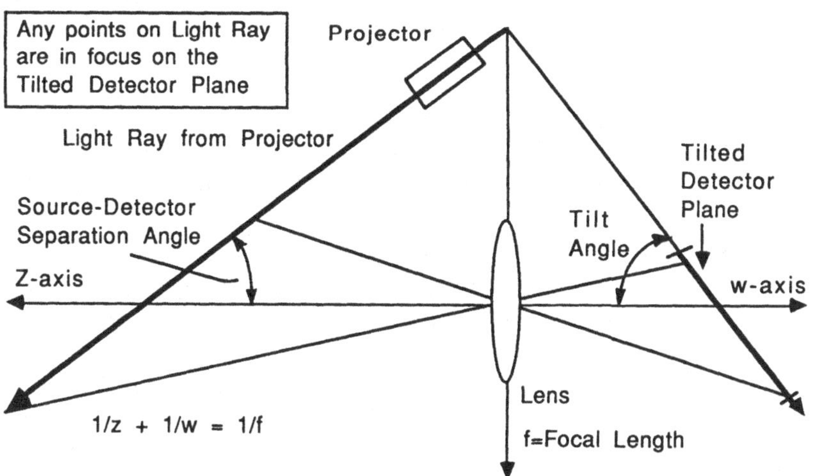

FIGURE 1.11. Scheimpflug condition: Tilted detector to maintain focus for all depths.

are placed on a turntable, and points are digitized as the object rotates. Scans are taken at several different heights to define object shape. No numbers were available to compute the figure of merit.

CyberOptics Corporation [1987] manufactures a series of point range sensors. For example, the PRS-30 measures a 300-micron depth of field from a standoff of 5 mm with 0.75-micron accuracy (one part in 400). A precision *xy*-table (0.25 microns) can be combined with these units to provide object scanning under a stationary sensor head at a rate of 15 points/sec ($M = 1{,}550$).

Diffracto [1987] also makes a series of range sensors. Their Model 300 LaserProbe measures a depth of field of 2 mm from a standoff of 50 mm with an accuracy of 2.5 microns in 5 ms ($M = 11{,}300$). The detector handles a 50,000:1 dynamic range of reflected light intensities and works well for a variety of surfaces.

Kern Instruments [Gottwald and Berner 1987] has developed the System for Positioning and Automated Coordinate Evaluation (SPACE) using two automated Kern theodolites. This system measures points in a 3-m × 3-m × 3-m working volume to an accuracy of 50 microns (one part in 60,000) at a rate of about 7.5 seconds per point ($M = 21{,}910$).

Lorenz [1986] has designed an optical probe to measure range with a repeatability of 2.5 microns over a depth of field of 100 mm (one part in 40,000). He uses split-beam illumination and optimal estimation theory. The probe was tested on the *z*-axis of a CNC machining center. Even at one point per second, $M = 40{,}000$.

The Selcom Opticator [Selcom 1987] series contains some of the highest performing commercially available ranging probes. They measure with one part in 4,000 resolution at 16,000 points per second ($M = 126{,}490$ assuming one part in 1,000 accuracy). The resolution of different models ranges from 2 to 128 microns in powers of two as the depth of field ranges from 8 to 512 mm.

Harding and Goodson [1986] implemented a prototype optical guillotine system that uses a high-precision translation stage with 2-micron resolution to obtain an accuracy of one part in 16,000 over a range of 150 mm. The system generates a scan in about one second ($M = 256{,}000$ assuming a 256-point scan).

Pipitone and Marshall [1983] documented their experience in building a point scanning system. They measured with an accuracy of about one part in 400 over a depth of field of about 7.6 meters ($M = 8{,}940$ for 500 points per second).

Haggren and Leikas [1987] have developed a photogrammetric machine-vision system with accuracy of better than one part in 10,000. The system generates one 3-D point every 1.5 seconds with subpixel accuracy of 1/20 of pixel using four cameras ($M = 8{,}160$). Earlier photogrammetry work of this sort is found in Pinckney [1978] and Kratky [1979].

4.2 Structured Light: Line

Passing a laser beam through a cylindrical lens creates a line of light. Shirai and Suwa [1971] and Will and Pennington [1972] were some of the first researchers to use light striping for computer vision. Nevatia and Binford [1973], Rocker [1974], and Popplestone et al. [1975] also used light striping. The General Motors Consight System [Holland et al. 1979] was one of the first industrial systems to use light stripe principles.

Technical Arts Corp. [1987] produces the 100X White Scanner. The camera and laser are typically separated by 45 degrees or more. The system can measure up to a range of 2.4 m with a resolution of about 0.5 mm ($M = 87{,}640$ for 3,000 points per second and accuracy of 1.5 mm).

The IMAGE Laboratory at ENST in France developed a light stripe laser ranging system [Schmitt et al. 1985], commercially available from Studec. Schmitt et al. [1986] shows a range image of a human head sculpture obtained with this sensor.

Ozeki et al [1986] developed a light stripe system that could create a 48 × 50 range image representing a 60-cm × 60-cm field of view with a range accuracy of 20 mm with a frame time of 490 ms ($M = 1{,}732$ assuming a 50-cm depth of field).

Cotter and Batchelor [1986] describe a depth map module (DMM) based on light striping techniques that produces 128 × 128 range images in about four seconds ($M = 8{,}192$ assuming seven-bit resolution).

Silvaggi et al. [1986] describe a very inexpensive triangulation system (less than $1,000 in component cost) that is acccurate to 0.25 mm over a 50-mm depth of field at a standoff of 100 mm. A photo-sensitive RAM chip is used instead of a video camera.

CyberOptics Corporation [1987] also manufactures a series of line range sensors. The LRS-30-500 measures a 300-micron depth of field and an 800-micron field of view from a standoff of 15 mm with 0.75-micron range accuracy (one part in 400). A precision *xy*-table (0.25 microns) can be combined to provide object scanning under the stationary sensor head at a rate of five lines per second ($M = 7{,}155$ for 64 points per line).

Landman and Robertson [1986] describe the capabilities of the Eyecrometer system available from Octek. This system is capable of 25-micron 3σ accuracy in the narrow view mode with a 12.7 mm depth of field. The time for a high-accuracy scan is 9.2 seconds. With 256 pixels in a scan line, $M = 2{,}680$.

The APOMS (Automated Propeller Optical Measurement System) built by RVSI (Robotic Vision Systems, Inc.) uses a high-precision point range sensor mounted on the arm of a five-axis inspection robot arm. The working volume of the sensor is larger than 3.2 m × 3.5 m × 4.2 m. The accuracy of the local sensor (x,y,z) coordinates is 64 microns in an 81-mm field of view. The three linear axes of the robot are accurate to 2.5 microns.

The two pitch and roll axes are accurate to 2 seconds of arc. The system covers 5.6 square meters per hour. Assuming four points per square millimeter, the data rate is about 6,000 points per second ($M = 3{,}485{,}700$). RVSI makes other triangulation ranging systems. The Ship Surface Scanner is a portable tripod-mounted unit that has a maximum 70-degree by 70-degree field of view. The line scanner scans at an azimuthal rate of eight degrees a second in automatic mode. The range accuracy is about one part in 600 of the range or about 5.7 mm at 3.66 m. The RVSI RoboLocator sensor can measure depths to an accuracy of 50 microns in a 25-mm × 25-mm field of view and a 50-mm depth of field. The RVSI RoboSensor measures about one part in 1,000 over up to a one-meter depth of field in a 500-mm × 500-mm field of view. Assuming 3,000 points per second, $M = 54{,}000$.

Perception [1987] makes a contour sensor that uses light striping and the Scheimpflug condition to obtain 25-micron accuracy over a 45-mm depth of field at a rate of 15 points per second ($M = 6{,}970$).

Diffracto [1987] also manufactures a Z-Sensor series of light stripe range sensors. Their Z-750 can measure a depth of field of 19 mm with an accuracy of 50 microns from a standoff of 762 mm (M-6,100 assuming one 256-point-line per second).

4.3 Structured Light: Multiple Points

Kanade and Fuhrman [1987] developed an 18-LED light-source optical proximity sensor that computes 200 local surface points in one second with a precision of 0.1 mm over a depth of field of 100 mm ($M = 14{,}140$). Damm [1987] has developed a similar but smaller proximity sensor using optical fibers.

Labuz and McVey [1986] developed a ranging method based on tracking the multiple points of a moving grid over a scene. Lewis and Sopwith [1986] used the multiple-point-projection approach with a static stereo pair of images.

4.4 Structured Light: Multiple Lines

Jalkio et al. [1985] use multiple light stripes to obtain range images subject to ambiguity constraints. The field of view is 60 mm × 60 mm with at least a 25-mm depth of field. The range resolution is about 0.25 mm with a lateral sampling interval of 0.5 mm. The image-acquisition time is currently dominated by software processing of two minutes ($M = 1{,}170$).

Mundy and Porter [1986] and Porter and Mundy [1982] describe a system designed to yield 25-micron range resolution within 50-micron by 50-micron pixels at a pixel rate of 1 MHz while tolerating a 10-to-1 change in surface reflectance. The goals were met, except for the data-acquisition speed, about 16kHz ($M = 32{,}380$ assuming an eight bit depth of field).

4.5 Structured Light: Grid

Range measurements can be extracted from a single projected grid image, but if no constraints are imposed on the surface shapes in the scene, range ambiguities can arise.

Will and Pennington [1972] discussed grid-coding methods for isolating planar surfaces in scenes based on vertical and horizontal spatial frequency analysis. Methods for removing the inherent ambiguities were discussed, but range resolution, depth of field, and frame time were not discussed.

Hall et al. [1982] describe a grid-pattern method for obtaining sparse range images of simple objects. Results for thirty coordinates in a 6×5 array show an accuracy of a few percent. Potmesil [1983] used a projected grid method to obtain range data for automatically generating surface models of solid objects. Stockman and Hu [1986] have examined the ambiguity problem using relaxation labeling. Wang et al. [1985] have used projected grids to obtain local surface orientation.

4.6 Structured Light: Circle

Wei and Gini [1983] proposed a structured light method using circles. They propose using a spinning mirror assembly to create a converging cone of light that projects to a circle on a flat surface and an ellipse on a sloped surface. The ellipse parameters determine the distance to the surface as well as the surface normal within a sign ambiguity.

4.7 Structured Light: Cross

If the light source projects two intersecting lines (X), it is easier to achieve subpixel accuracy at the point. The cross can be achieved with a laser by using a beamsplitter and two cylindrical lenses. Pelowski [1986] discusses a commercially available Perceptron sensor that guarantees $\pm 3\sigma$ accuracy in (x,y,z) of 0.1 mm over a depth of field of 45 mm in a quarter of a second or less. Nakagawa and Ninomiya [1987] also use the cross structure.

4.8 Structured Light: Thick Stripes

Asada et al. [1986] project thick stripes on an object to obtain from a single image a denser map of surface normals than what is possible using grid projection. The thickness of the stripes limits ambiguity because of the signed brightness transitions at thick stripe edges.

4.9 Structured Light: Coded Binary Patterns

Rather than scan a light stripe over a scene and process N separate images or deal with the ambiguities possible in processing a single multistripe on grid image, it is possible to obtain the equivalent information using $N' = \lceil \log_2 N \rceil$ images where the scene is illuminated with binary patterns of the type shown in Figure 1.12. The first pattern establishes the least significant bit in the final range value using a square wave mask with a small period. The next mask uses a pattern with twice the period and so on until the most significant bit pattern which contains only a single square wave period, is used. In an appropriate configuration, the output range image can be computed from intensity images using lookup tables. This method is potentially very fast and relatively inexpensive.

Solid Photography, Inc. [1977] made the first use of Gray-coded binary patterns for range imaging. A gantry mounted system with several range cameras could acquire range data from a 2π solid angle around an object. The system was equipped with a special-purpose milling machine so that a person could sit down inside the gantry, have their range picture taken, and then have a 3-D bust machined in a matter of minutes. The point accuracy of the entire multisensor system was about 0.75 mm in a 300-

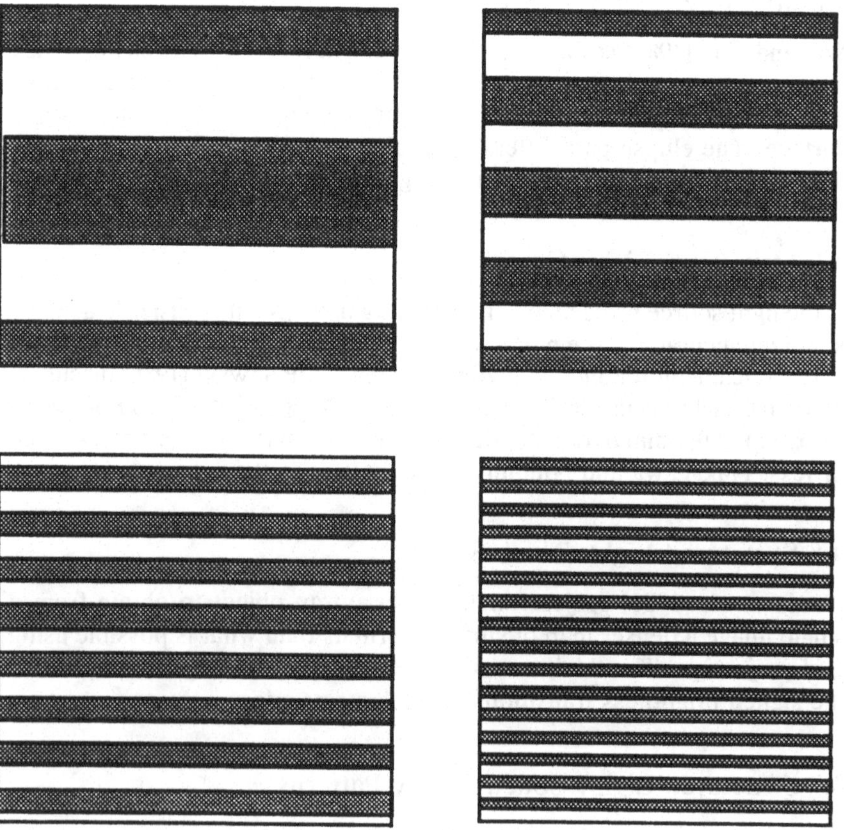

FIGURE 1.12. Four binary patterns for coded pattern triangulation ranging.

mm × 300-mm × 300-mm volume ($M = 100{,}000$ assuming 64K points per second).

Altschuler et al. [1981] and Potsdamer and Altschuler [1982] developed a numerical stereo camera consisting of a laser and an electro-optic shutter synchronized to a video camera. They used standard binary patterns and performed experiments using two crossed electro-optic shutters (grid patterns).

Inokuchi et al. [1984] and Sato and Inokuchi [1985] showed results from their system based on the Gray-code binary pattern concept. More recently, Yamamoto et al. [1986] reported another approach based on binary image accumulation. A variation on the binary pattern scheme is given in Yeung and Lawrence [1986].

Rosenfeld and Tsikos [1986] at RCA built a prototype range camera using 10 Gray code patterns on a 15.2-cm-diameter disk that rotates at five revolutions per second. Cylindrical and projection lenses are used to create straight lines from the curved lines on the disk. Besides the electronics needed to lock the projector rotation to the camera's vertical retrace signal, the rest of the system requires only commercially available image-processing hardware and a camera. Their system was able to create a 256 × 256 eight-bit range image with 2-mm resolution in about 0.7 seconds ($M = 78{,}330$).

Vuylsteke and Oosterlinck [1986] developed another binary coding scheme. They project a specially formulated binary mask in which each local neighborhood of the mask has its own signature. The ambiguities of simple multistripe methods do not arise. A 64 × 64 range image was computed from a 604 × 576 resolution intensity image in about 70 CPU seconds on a VAX 11/750. ($M = 1{,}260$ assuming 7-bit accuracy).

4.10 Structured Light: Color-Coded Stripes

Boyer and Kak [1987] developed a real-time light striping concept that requires only one image frame from a color video camera and no mechanical operations. If many stripes are used to illuminate a scene and only one black and white image is used, ambiguities arise at depth discontinuities because it is not clear which image stripe corresponds to which projected stripe. However, when stripes are color coded with unique color subsequences embedded in the color stripe sequence, the unique color subsequences can be used to establish the correct correspondence for all stripes. Although no figures are given, 128 × 128 images with 8-bit accuracy at a 7.5-Hz frame rate would yield $M = 89{,}000$.

4.11 Structured Light: Intensity Ratio Sensor

The intensity ratio method, invented by Schwartz [1983], prototyped by Bastuschek and Schwartz [1984], researched by Carrihill [1986] in his thesis work, and documented by Carrihill and Hummel [1985], determines range unambiguously using the digitization and analysis of only three images. The method requires a light projector with two filters that can be mechanically switched, a camera with a digitizer, and a computer (with fast image-processing hardware). One of the filters must have a very linear transmittance profile for this method to work. The implemented sensor was tested with a standoff of 80 cm. The depth of field was 860 mm with a range resolution of 12 bits, but an overall range repeatability of 2 mm, almost 9 bits. The total acquisition and computation time on a VICOM image processor was about 40 seconds ($M = 33{,}700$).

4.12 Structured Light: Random Texture

Schewe and Forstner [1986] have developed a precision photogrammetry system based on a random texture projection technique. A stereo pair of metric cameras are mounted on a tripod with a high-resolution texture projector. The scene is illuminated by the texture projector and photographed on high-resolution glass plates. The developed plates are placed in a modified stereo comparator, and registered pairs of subimages are digitized. A single starting point is manually selected to start the processing. An 8×8 window in one image is matched to an 8×8 window in the other image to create a single range point via a least squares method. The range accuracy of the points is about 0.1 mm over about a one-meter depth of field and a several-meter field of view. A complete wireframe model for the imaged surface is created requiring a few seconds per point on a microcomputer ($M = 10{,}000$).

5 Moire and Holographic Interferometry

The trigonometric identity $2 \cos A \cos B = \cos(A - B) + \cos(A + B)$ is a key ingredient to understanding interference phenomena. It is used to introduce moire techniques and holographic interferometry herein.

In moire techniques, one amplitude-modulated spatial signal (reflected light from a scene) is multiplied by another amplitude-modulated spatial signal (the viewing grating) to create an output signal $A(x)$:

$$A(x) = A_1(1 + m_1 \cos(\omega_1 x + \phi_1(x))) \cdot A_2(1 + m_2 \cos(\omega_2 x + \phi_2(x)), \quad (1.27)$$

where the A_i are the amplitudes, the m_i are the modulation indices of the amplitude modulation, the ω_i are the spatial frequencies, and the $\phi_i(x)$ are the phases that vary slowly over the scene. Using the trignometric identity given above, this product can be expanded into terms with spatial frequencies $\omega_1 - \omega_2$, ω_1, ω_2, and $\omega_1 + \omega_2$. When this signal is low-pass filtered (LPF) (blurred) with a cutoff frequency less than the minimum of ω_1 and ω_2, only the difference frequency term and the constant is passed:

$$A'(x) = \mathrm{LPF}(A(x)) = A_1A_2(1 + m_1m_2 \cos((\omega_1 - \omega_2)x + \phi_1(x) - \phi_2(x))). \quad (1.28)$$

For equal spatial frequencies, only the phase difference term remains. In moire range-imaging sensors, surface depth information is encoded in the phase difference term.

In holographic interferometry, coherent light is used. Suppose two laser beams (with the same polarization) meet at a surface point $\vec{x}$, and the electric field from the two beams are added together to create the net electric field:

$$E(\vec{x},t), = E_1 \cos(\omega_1 t - \vec{k}_1 \cdot \vec{x} + \phi_1(\vec{x})) + E_2 \cos(\omega_2 t - \vec{k}_2 \cdot \vec{x} + \phi_2(\vec{x})), \quad (1.29)$$

where the $\vec{k}_i$ are the wave vectors representing the wavelengths λ_i and directions of the propagating light such that $\|\vec{k}\| = 2\pi/\lambda$, the $\omega_i = \|\vec{k}\| c$ are the optical frequencies of the beams, and $\phi_i(\vec{x})$ are the phases, which may vary slowly over a surface. Detectors of light respond to the intensity of the radiation (the square of the electric field). Hence, the detectable intensity (irradiance) is given by $I(\vec{x},t) = E^2(\vec{x},t)$. Using the trignometric identity given earlier in this section, this E^2 product can be expanded into terms with optical frequencies $\omega_1 - \omega_2$, $2\omega_1$, $2\omega_2$, and $\omega_1 + \omega_2$. The detectors of light cannot respond to optical frequency variations and thus act as low-pass filters of the irradiance function I. The detectable interference signal is given by $I'(\vec{x},t) = \mathrm{LPF}(I(\vec{x},t))$ or

$$I'(\vec{x}, t) = \frac{E_1^2 + E_2^2}{2}\left(1 + \frac{2E_1E_2}{E_1^2 + E_2^2}\cos(\Delta\omega t + \Delta\vec{k} \cdot \vec{x} + \Delta\phi(\vec{x}))\right), \quad (1.30)$$

where $\Delta\omega = \omega_1 - \omega_2$ is the difference frequency, $\Delta\vec{k} = \vec{k}_2 - \vec{k}_1$ is the difference wave vector, and $\Delta\phi(\vec{x}) = \phi_1 - \phi_2$ is the phase difference. This equation is of the exact same form as the equation given above for $A'(x)$, except that vector notation has been explicitly used for the wave vectors (vector spatial frequencies), the constants have a slightly different form, and a time-varying term is included. Since phase changes are proportional to optical path differences in holographic interferometry, distances that are fractions of a wavelength of light can be measured. For equal optical frequencies and equal (vector) spatial frequencies, only the phase-difference term remains. In holographic interferometric range-imaging sensors, surface depth information is encoded in the phase difference term.

These descriptions are intended to illustrate the common principles of two distinctly different interference phenomena that are useful for measuring relative surface height (depth) using images of interference fringes.

5.1 Moire Techniques

Reviews and bibliographies of moire methods may be found in Pirodda [1982], Sciammarella [1982], and Oster [1965]. Theocaris [1969] provides some of the history of moire techniques. A moire pattern is defined as the low spatial frequency interference pattern created when two gratings with regularly spaced patterns of higher spatial frequency are superimposed on one another. Figure 1.13 shows two linear gratings overlaid at a slight angle to create a low-frequency pattern. The angular separation of source and detector is critical to range measurements and therefore, moire can be considered another type of triangulation method [Perrin and Thomas 1979]. However, moire techniques exhibit many similarities to holographic interferometry as indicated in the interference analysis earlier.

Moire range-imaging methods are useful for measuring the relative distance to surface points on a smooth surface $z(x,y)$ that does not exhibit depth discontinuities. The magnitude of surface slope as viewed from the sensor direction should be bounded by a maximum value that is not too large: $\| \nabla z \| < K$. Under such constraints, absolute range for an entire moire image can be determined if the distance to one or more reference image points is known.

Moire methods for surface measurement usually involve line gratings of alternating opaque and transparent bars of equal width (Ronchi gratings). The pitch P of a grating is specified by the number of opaque/transparent line pairs per millimeter (LP/mm). The period $p = 1/P$ of the grating is the distance between the centers of two opaque lines.

5.1.1 Projection Moire. Khetan [1975] gives a theoretical analysis of projection moire. In a projection moire system, a precisely matched pair of gratings is required. The projector grating is placed in front of the projector (a focused light source), and the camera grating is placed in front of the camera. The projector light source is located at an angle θ_l relative to the z-axis as shown in Figure 1.14. The viewing camera (or detector) is located

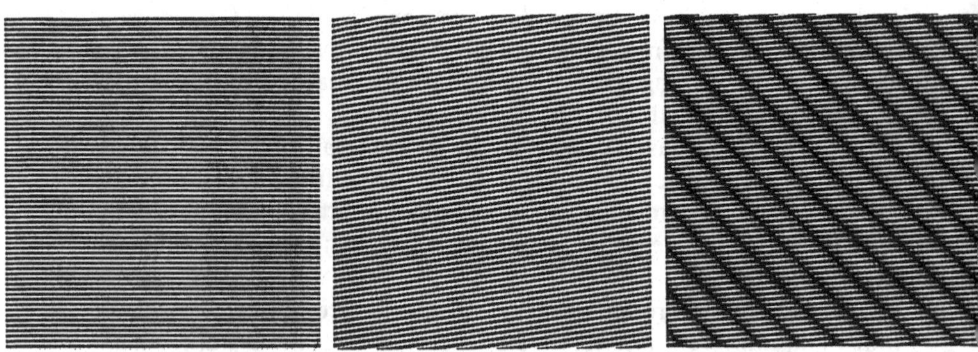

FIGURE 1.13. Grating A, grating B, and moire pattern.

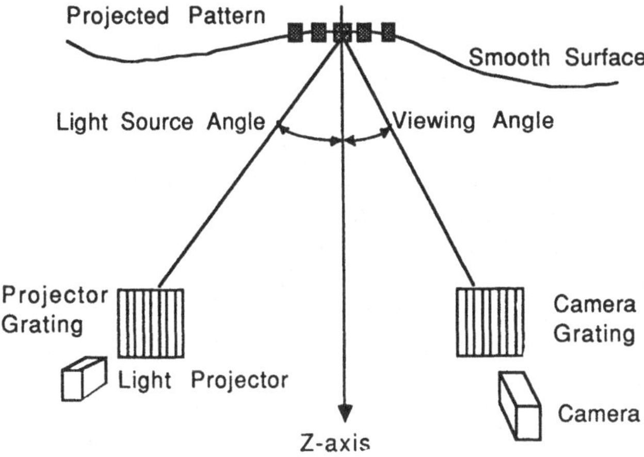

FIGURE 1.14. Projection moire configuration.

at an angle θ_v relative to the z-axis. The projected beam of light is spatially amplitude-modulated by the pitch of the projector grating. In communication theory terms, a spatial "carrier" image is generated. When the projected beam falls on the smooth surface, the shape of the surface modulates the phase of the spatial carrier. By viewing these stripes through a camera grating a identical pitch, interference fringes are created at the camera. The camera grating "demodulates" the modulated carrier yielding a "baseband" image signal whose fringes carry information about surface shape. If p_0 is the period of the projected fringes at the object surface, then the change in z between the centers of the interference fringes viewed by the camera is given by

$$\Delta z = \frac{p_0}{\tan(\theta_l) + \tan(\theta_v)}. \tag{1.31}$$

It is relatively inexpensive to set up a moire system using commercially available moire projectors, moire viewers, matched gratings, and video cameras [Newport Corp. 1987]. The problem is accurate calibration and automated analysis of moire fringe images. Automated fringe analysis systems are surveyed in Reid [1986]. The limitations of projection moire automated by digital image processing algorithms are addressed by Gasvik [1983]. The main goal of such algorithms is to track the ridges or valleys of the fringes in the intensity surface to create one-pixel-wide contours. Phase unwrapping techniques can be used to order the contours in depth, assuming adequate spacing between the contours. It is not possible to correctly interpolate the phase (depth) between the fringes because beween-fringe gray level variations are a function of local contrast and local surface reflectance as well as of phase due to distance.

5.1.2 Shadow Moire. If the depth of field of the object surface is small, the shadow moire method can be used. A single grating of large extent is positioned near the object surface. A light source projects light through the grating, which is then reflected and viewed through the same grating. This avoids needing two exactly matched gratings as in projection moire. The pitch of a shadow moire grating should be much coarser than projection moire gratings because the grating is positioned much closer to the surface. The interference fringe images and analysis methods are the same for shadow moire as they are for projection moire. Cline et al. [1982, 1984] show experimental results where 512 × 512 range images of several different surfaces were obtained automatically using shadow moire methods.

5.1.3 Single-Frame Moire with Reference. The projected grating on a surface can be imaged directly by a camera without a camera grating, digitized, and "demodulated" via computer software, provided that a reference image of a flat plane is also digitized. As a general rule of thumb, single-frame systems of this type are able to resolve range proportional to about 1/20 of a fringe spacing. Idesawa et al. [1976,1977] and Idesawa and Yatagia. [1980] did early work in automated moire surface measurement.

Electro-Optical Information Systems, Inc. [1987] has a commercially available range-imaging sensor of this type. On appropriate surfaces, the system creates a 480 × 512 range image in about two seconds using two array processors and has a one-part-in-4,000 resolution ($M = 350{,}540$, assuming accuracy of one part in 1,000). The system uses gratings of two to ten line pairs per millimeter.

5.1.4 Multiple-Frame Phase-Shifted Moire. Multiple-frame (N-frame) phase-shifted moire is similar to single-frame moire except that after the first frame of image data is acquired, the projector grating is precisely shifted laterally in the projector by a small distance increment that corresponds to a phase shift of $360/N$ degrees and subsequent image frames are acquired. This method, very similar to quasi-heterodyne holographic interferometry, allows for an order of magnitude increase in range accuracy compared to more conventional methods.

Halioua and Srinivasan [1987] have patented this general concept for moire (see also Srinivasan et al. [1985]). Range accuracies on the order of ten microns are possible with this approach. This N-frame sensor technique works as follows. The nth frame ($n = 1,2. . . ,N$) of image data $I^{obj}_n(x,y)$ for the object surface is acquired with a grating of pitch P_p at the location $(n - 1)P_p/N$, which corresponds to the phase $\phi_n = (N - 1)(2\pi/N)$. The effective projected pitch at the object is $P_o = 1/p_o$. The camera and projector are separated by an angle θ. It is assumed that N frames of reference images $I^{ref}_n(x,y)$ for a flat reference surface have been acquired during a calibration procedure. The object surface images and reference images are modeled as

$$I^{obj}_n = a(x,y) + b(x,y)\cos(\phi_{obj}(x,y) + \phi_n) \quad (1.32)$$

$$I^{ref}_n = a(x,y) + b(x,y)\cos(\phi_{ref}(x,y) + \phi_n). \quad (1.33)$$

The reflected ambient light level in the images is $a(x,y)$, the reflected fringe contrast is $b(x,y)$, $\phi_{obj}(x,y)$ is the phase function of the first image of the object surface prior to grating shifts, and $\phi_{ref}(x,y)$ is the phase function of the first image of the reference surface prior to grating shifts. After the N image frames have been acquired, the averaged object phase image $\Phi_{obj}(x,y)$ is computed:

$$\tan \Phi_{obj}(x, y) = \frac{\sum_{n=1}^{N} I_n^{obj} \sin(2\pi n/N)}{\sum_{n=1}^{N} I_n^{obj} \cos(2\pi n/N)}. \quad (1.34)$$

The object phase image is then unwrapped to yield a smooth phase image Φ^s_{obj} without any rapid 2π transitions: $\Phi^s_{obj} = \Phi_{obj} + 2\pi m$. It is also assumed that the N image frames of the reference surface were similarly processed to yield a phase image for the reference surface $\Phi_{ref}(x,y)$ and the unwrapped smooth phase image $\Phi^s_{ref} = \Phi_{ref} + 2\pi m$. The phase difference image $\Delta\Phi^s(x,y)$ is computed as the image difference: $\Delta\Phi^s(x,y) = \Phi^s_{obj}(x,y) - \Phi^s_{ref}(x,y)$. If the rays of light are approximately parallel when they impinge on the object and reference surfaces, the range image of the smooth surface is given approximately by

$$z(x, y) = \frac{p_0}{\tan\theta} \frac{\Delta\Phi^s(x, y)}{2\pi}. \quad (1.35)$$

Diverging light rays are handled with a slightly different algorithm. Srinivasan et al. [1985] show experimental results for a mannequin head using $N = 3$. They obtained 0.1-mm range accuracy over a 100-mm depth of field ($M=46{,}740$ assuming two minute computation time for 512×512 images). Other research in this area has been reported by Andresen [1986].

Boehnlein and Harding [1986] implemented this algorithm on special hardware. The computations take less than 3.5 seconds for a 256×256 image, but the high-accuracy phase-shifting translation device (accurate to 0.1 microns) limited them to about 10 seconds for complete range-image acquisition. The range resolution of the system is 11 microns over a 64-mm depth of field, which is almost one part in 6,000 ($M= 121{,}430$, assuming an accuracy of one part in 1,500).

5.2 Holographic Interferometry

Holography was introduced in 1961 by Leith and Upatnieks [1962]. The principles of holographic interferometry were discovered soon after [Vest 1979; Schuman and Dubas 1979]. Holographic interferometers use coherent light from laser sources to produce interference patterns due to the optical-frequency phase differences in different optical paths. Just as the z-depth spacing of moire interference fringes is proportional to the period of grating lines, the z-depth spacing of holographic interference fringes is proportional to the wavelength of the light being used. Measured object surfaces must be very flat and smooth.

5.2.1 Conventional Holography. In conventional interferometry, the optical frequencies of the interfering beams are exactly equal i.e., $\omega_1 = \omega_2$. There are three types of conventional holographic interferometry that are used most often in industrial applications:

- Real-time holography allows the observer to see instantaneous changes in an object surface. A hologram of the object is made off line, and the observer views a holographic image of the object superimposed on the object. Fringes appear as the object's surface varies from the shape of the surface when the hologram was made.
- Double-exposure holographic systems expose a hologram once to capture object surface shape in one state and then the hologram is exposed again to the same field of view to capture it in a second state, e.g., after applying stress to the object. The hologram provides a permanent record of the object surface shape change.
- Time-average holography produces a hologram while an object is vibrated. A vibration mode map is obtained, which is useful for verifying finite element analyses.

Conventional holographic interferometry is used to visualize stress, thermal strains, pressure effects, erosion, microscopic cracks, fluid flow, and other physical effects in nondestructive testing. Tozer et al. [1985], Mader [1985], Wuerker and Hill [1985], and Church et al. [1985] provide a sampling of industrial use of holographic interferometry. The Holomatic 8000 from Laser Technology, Norristown, Pennsylvania, and the HC1000 Instant Holographic Camera (ten-second development time on erasable thermoplastic film) from Newport Corporation [1987] are commercially available holographic cameras.

5.2.2 Heterodyne Holography. Heterodyne holographic interferometers cause two coherent beams of slightly different optical frequencies (less than 100 MHz generates RF beat frequencies) to interfere, creating time-varying holographic fringes in the image plane. Optical frequency shifts can be achieved by rotating quarter wave plates, rotating gratings, acousto-optic modulators, and other methods. Optical phase measurements corresponding to optical path differences can be made at each point by electronically measuring the phase of the beat frequency signal relative to some reference using a phasemeter. The time-varying interference fringe image must be mechanically scanned using a high-speed detector in order to obtain a range image. Heterodyne holographic interferometers can make out-of-plane surface measurements with nanometer resolution over several microns, but they are typically slow. The general rule of thumb is that $\lambda/1{,}000$ range resolution is possible using heterodyne methods.

Pantzer et al. [1986] built a heterodyne profilometer that has a mechanical-vibration-limited range resolution of 5 nm and a lateral resolution of 3 microns. A 15-mW He-Ne laser beam is split and acousto-optically modulated at 75 MHz and 75.025 MHz. The theoretical resolution of this method is 0.4 nm if mechanical instabilities are removed. It takes about 20 seconds to linearly scan 1 mm to get 330 points ($M = 2{,}450$, assuming a three-micron depth of field).

Dandliker and Thalmann [1985] obtained 0.2-nm range resolution over a depth of field of 3 microns at a rate of 1 point per second over a lateral range of 120 mm using a double-exposure heterodyne interferometer ($M = 7{,}500$ assuming 0.4-nm accuracy).

Pryputniewicz [1985] used heterodyne interferometry to study the load-deformation characteristics of surface mount components on a printed circuit board. The reported 3σ range accuracy was 2 nm.

Sasaki and Okazaki [1986] developed a variation on frequency-shift heterodyne methods. The mirror for the reference path is mounted on a piezo-electric transducer (PZT), which is modulated at about 220 Hz. The reference wave is sinusoidally phase modulated to obtain the needed small frequency shift for heterodyne accuracy. This is slow enough that CCD image sensors can be used to collect the video signals. They obtained repeatable range measurements at less than 1-nm resolution. Over a 250 × 250 micron field of view, the lateral resolution is about five microns.

5.2.3 Quasi-Heterodyne (Phase-Shifted) Methods. Phase-shifted holographic interferometers are referred to as quasi-heterodyne since $\lambda/100$ range resolution is not quite heterodyne-performance, but much better than conventional. Quasi-heterodyne systems can be much simpler, cheaper, and faster than heterodyne systems by trading off some range resolution. Standard video cameras can be used to image several frames of holographic fringes. Phase-shifts can be achieved at every pixel in parallel in real-time using a piezo-electric translator to move a mirror as opposed to the lateral shifting of a grating in front of a projector, as in phase-shifted moire. Other phase-shifting methods are possible. The computations are very similar to those described in the section on multiple-frame phase-shifted moire.

Hariharan [1985] used a 100 × 100 camera to digitize the holographic fringes needed to compute the range image. The measurement cycle for each fringe image was about 150 ms, and the total computation time was ten-seconds using a machine-language program. They used the same formulas used by Boehnlein and Harding [1986]. Results are shown for a large 50-mm × 100-mm field of view ($M = 8{,}095$, assuming eight-bit accuracy).

Thalmann and Dandliker [1985] and Dandliker and Thalmann [1985] examine two-reference beam interferometry and two-wavelength contouring for quasi-heterodyne and heterodyne systems.

Chang et al. [1985] did experiments in digital phase-shifted holographic interferometry to eliminate the need to calibrate the phase shifter as in Hariharan et al. [1983]. They claim an accuracy of 2 nm over a 300-nm depth of field.

5.2.4 Microscopic Interferometry. Peterson et al. [1984] measured VHS video tape surfaces with an interferometer, obtaining 1-micron lateral resolution and 1-nm range repeatability.

Matthews et al. [1986] describe a phase-locked loop interferometric method wherein the two arms of a confocal interference microscope are maintained in quadrature by using an electro-optic phase modulator. Results are shown where the system scanned a 3-micron by 3-micron field of view over a depth of field of 300 nm in two seconds with a range accuracy of 1 nm (estimate $M = 27{,}150$).

6 Focusing

Horn [1968], Tenenbaum [1970], Jarvis [1976], and Krotkov [1986] have discussed focusing for range determination. The Gauss thin lens law states that a thin lens of focal length f focuses a point light source in a scene at a distance z from the center of the lens onto a focal plane behind the lens at a distance ω from the lens center:

$$\frac{1}{w} + \frac{1}{z} = \frac{1}{f}. \tag{1.36}$$

Figure 1.15 shows basic focusing relationships. The thin lens law may be expressed as $z(w) = wf/(w - f)$ (what depth z is in focus for w setting) or $w(z) = zf/(z - f)$ (what setting is needed to focus points of depth z). It is easy to see that as w varies from its minimum value of f to some maximum value w_{max}, points at depths from $z = \infty$ to the corresponding minimum value $z_{min} = w_{max}f/w_{max} - f)$ are focused.

A camera lens has a finite aperture of diameter D, and light passing through a finite aperture always experiences diffraction, hence images are blurred. The radius of the blur of a point at range z is a minimum when the point is in focus at $w = w(z)$. The blur increases as w varies away from $w(z)$, or similarly, as the point distance z varies away from $z(w)$ (in either direction). If a point blur is modeled as a 2-D Gaussian intensity distribution of diameter σ for a fixed focal plane distance w, the range to that point is given as

$$z_{\pm}(\sigma) = \frac{wf}{w - f \pm \sigma F}, \tag{1.37}$$

where $F = f/D$, the so-called f-number of the lens aperture. If the blur characterized by σ is small enough to maintain adequate focus, the depth

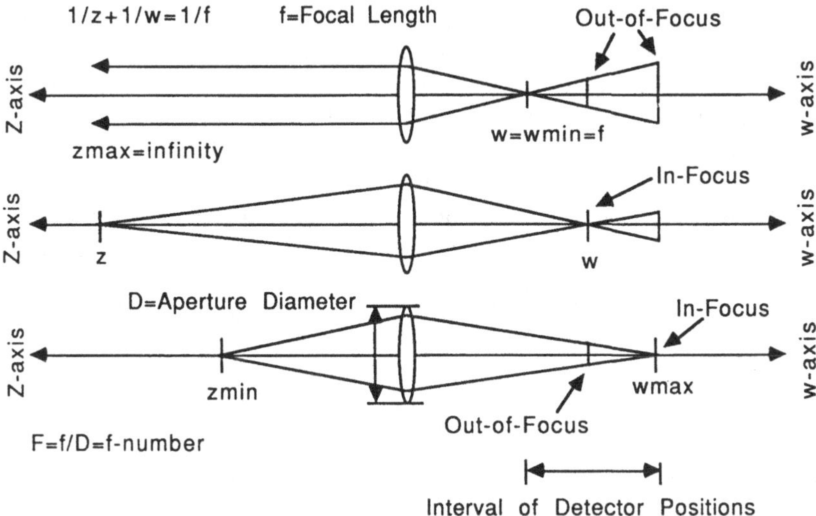

FIGURE 1.15. Thin lens relationships.

of field L_z of the camera in which all points are in adequate focus is given by

$$L_z = z_-(\sigma) - z_+(\sigma) = \frac{2wf\sigma F}{(w - f)^2 - \sigma^2 F^2} . \tag{1.38}$$

This makes it clear that the depth of field increases with increasing f-number F. Pentland [1987], Grossman [1987], Krotkov and Martin [1986], Schlag et al. [1983], Jarvis [1976], and Harvey et al. [1985] discuss passive methods to determine range from focus.

The autofocus mechanisms in cameras act as range sensors [Goldberg 1982] [Denstman 1980], but most commercially available units do not use focusing principles to determine range. The Canon "Sure-Shot" autofocusing mechanism is an active triangulation system that uses a frequency-modulated infrared beam (Jarvis [1982] used this Canon sensor module to create a 64 × 64 range image in 50 minutes). The Honeywell Visitronic module for Konica, Minolta, and Yashica cameras is a passive triangulation system that correlates photocell readouts to achieve a binocular stereo match and the corresponding distance. The Polaroid autofocusing mechanism is a broad-beam sonar unit.

Rioux and Blais [1986] developed two techniques based on lens-focusing properties to design a compact range-imaging sensor. In the first technique, a grid of point sources is projected onto a scene. The range to each point is determined by the radius of the blur in the focal plane of the camera. The system was capable of measuring depths to 144 points with 1-mm resolution over a 100-mm depth of field. The second technique uses a multistripe illuminator. If a line is not in focus, the camera is set up to see split lines where the splitting distance between the lines is related to the distance to the illuminated surface. Special-purpose electronics process the video signal [Blais and Rioux 1986] and detect peaks to obtain line splitting distances and hence range, on each scan line. The system creates a 256 × 240 range image in less than 1 second by analyzing 10 projected lines in each of 24 frames. The projected lines are shifted slightly between each frame. A resolution of 1 mm over a depth of 250 mm is quoted (8 bits) at a 1-m standoff for a small robot-mountable unit ($M = 63{,}450$).

Kinoshita et al. [1986] developed a point range sensor based on a projected conical ring of light and focusing principles. A lens is mechanically focused to optimize the energy density in a photodiode. The prototype system measured range with a repeatability of 0.3 mm over a depth of field of 150 mm (9 bits) with a standoff distance of 430 mm.

Corle et al. [1987] measured distances with accuracies as small as 40 nm over a 4-micron depth of field (1:100) using a type II confocal scanning optical microscope.

7 Fresnel Diffraction

Any wave experiences diffraction when it passes through a finite aperture. The diffraction effects of light are well described by the scalar Fresnel-Kirchhoff diffraction integral when polarization effects can be ignored. Let $\psi(x,y,z)$ be the wave amplitude at the point $\vec{r} = (x,y,z)$ after a single frequency plane wave described by $\psi_0 e^{i\vec{k}\cdot\vec{r}}$ passes through an aperture transmission function $T(x,y)$ located in the plane $z = 0$. The wave vector k has (1) magnitude $\|\vec{k}\| = k = 2\pi/\lambda$ where λ is the optical wavelength and (2) direction pointed along the $\hat{n}$ unit vector direction. The diffracted wave $\psi(x,y,z)$ is computed by integrating the effects of an infinite number of point sources in the aperture emanating spherical waves (e^{ikr}/r) [Born and Wolf 1975; Marion 1965]:

$$\varphi(x, y, z) = \frac{-i\varphi_0}{2\lambda}\int_{-\infty}^{\infty}\int_{-\infty}^{\infty} T(x', y')\frac{e^{ikr(x',y')}}{r(x', y')}(1 + \cos\theta(x', y'))dx'dy', \tag{1.39}$$

where the distance function r is given by $r^2 = (x - x')^2 + (y - y')^2 + z^2$ and the angle function is given by $\cos(\theta) = \hat{n}\cdot\vec{r}/r$. Talbot [1836] first observed that if a periodic optical grating $T(x,y) = T(x + p,y)$ with period p is illuminated with coherent light, exact in-focus images of the grating are formed at regular periodic intervals D:

$$I(x,y,z = nD) = |\psi(x,y,z = nD)|^2 = T(x,y), \tag{1.40}$$

where n is an integer. This is the self-imaging property of a grating. Lord Rayleigh [1881] first deduced that $D = 2p^2/\lambda$ when $p >> \lambda$. Moreover, the grating images are out of focus in a predictable manner between the endpoints of the Talbot interval. Local contrast depends upon the depth z. The Talbot effect has been analyzed by Cowley and Moodie [1957] and Winthrop and Worthington [1965]. Figure 1.16 shows the basic configuration for measuring distance with the Talbot effect.

Chavel and Strand [1984] and Leger and Snyder [1984] have developed range-imaging sensors based on the Talbot effect for square wave or cosine gratings. The transmittance function for a cosine grating may be written as

$$T(x,y) = a(1 + m\cos(2\pi x/p)) \quad \text{if } (x,y) \in A, \tag{1.41}$$

where A is the aperture area, a is the contrast of the grating, and m is the modulation index. In this case, the grating images are reproduced at $D/2$ intervals with a 180-degree phase shift. Thus, the ambiguity interval for such a range sensor is given by

$$L_r = \frac{p^2}{2\lambda} = \frac{D}{4}, \tag{1.42}$$

which is one fourth of the Talbot spacing D. Ambiguity resolving techniques are needed for larger depths of field.

The Chavel and Strand [1984] method illuminates an object with laser light that has passed through the cosine grating. A camera views the object through a beam-splitter so that the grating image is superimposed on the returned object image that is modulated by (1) the distance to object surface points and (2) the object surface reflectivity. The contrast ratio of the power in the fundamental frequency p^{-1} to the average (dc) power can be determined via analog means in real-time by video electronics that

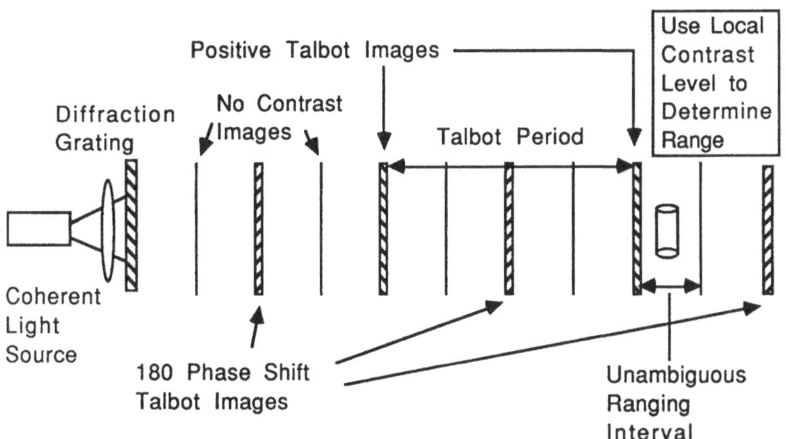

FIGURE 1.16. Talbot effect or self-imagine property of gratings for ranging.

filters the voltage versus time signals for each scan line in the camera image. This analog contrast ratio signal is proportional to depth. The analog range-image signal was digitized to create an 8-bit 512 × 512 image representing a 20-mm × 20-mm field of view approximately. The ambiguity interval was 38 mm. The digitizer averaged 16 frames so that the frame time is about 0.5 seconds ($M = 92{,}680$, assuming 7-bit accuracy).

Leger and Snyder [1984] developed two techniques for range imaging using the Talbot effect. The first method used two gratings crossed at right angles to provide two independent channels for depth measurement. The second method uses a modulated grating created by performing optical spatial filtering operations on the original signal emanating from a standard grating. Two prototype sensors were built to demonstrate these methods. The ambiguity intervals were 7.3 mm and 4.6 mm. The figure of merit is similar to the Chavel and Strand sensor. Speckle noise [Goodman 1986] is a problem with coherent light in these methods and high resolution is almost impossible to achieve from a local contrast measure. Other research in this area has been pursued by Hane and Grover [1985].

8 Sensor Comparisons

The key performance factors of any range-imaging sensor are listed in the following table:

Depth of field	L_r
Range accuracy	σ_r
Pixel dwell time	T
Pixel rate	$1/T$
Range resolution	N_{bits}
Image size	$N_x \times N_y$
Angular field of view	$\theta_x \times \theta_y$
Lateral resolution	$\theta_x/N_x \times \theta_y/N_y$
Standoff distance	L_s
Nominal field of view	$(L_s + L_r/2)\theta_x \times (L_s + L_r/2)\theta_y$
Frame time	$T \times N_x \times N_y$
Frame rate	$1/(T \times N_x \times N_y)$

The figure of merit M used to evaluate sensors in this survey only uses the first three values. A full evaluation for a given application should consider all sensor parameters.

Different types of range imaging sensors are compared by showing the rated sensors in the survey in two scatter plots. In Figure 1.17, range-imaging sensors are shown at the appropriate locations in a plot of (log) figure of merit M versus (log) range accuracy σ. In Figure 1.18, range-imaging sensors are shown at the appropriate locations in a plot of (log) depth-of-field-to-range-accuracy ratio (number of accurate range bits) as

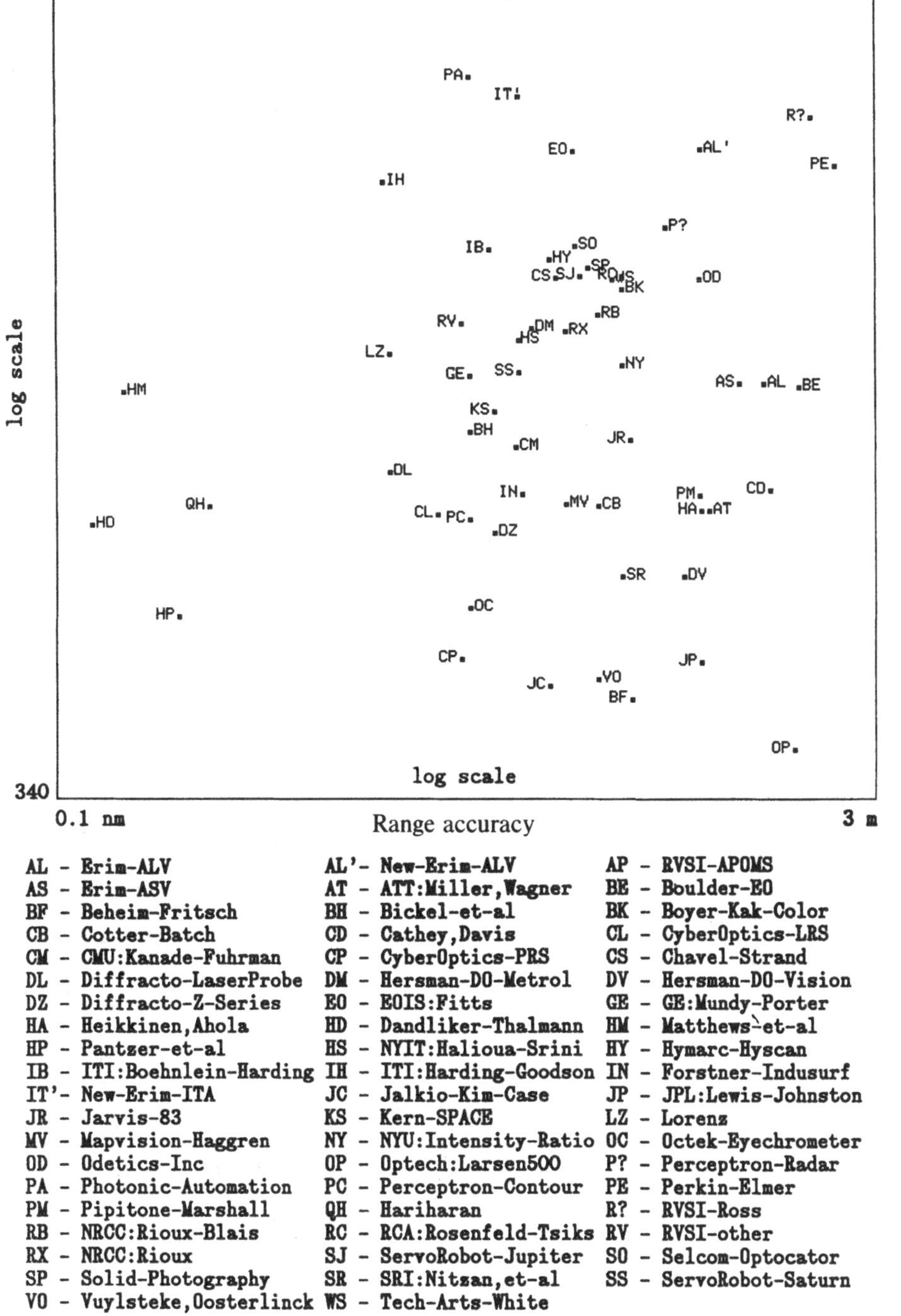
3.3e6
340
Figure of merit
log scale
0.1 nm
3 m
Range accuracy
log scale
AP
PA
IT'
R?
EO
AL'
PE
IH
P?
IB
SO
HY
SP
CS
SJ
RC
WS
BK
OD
RV
RB
DM
RX
HS
LZ
NY
GE
SS
HM
AS
AL
BE
KS
BH
CM
JR
DL
IN
CD
QH
MV
CB
PM
CL
PC
HA
AT
HD
DZ
SR
DV
HP
OC
CP
JP
JC
VO
BF
OP
AL - Erim-ALV
AL'- New-Erim-ALV
AP - RVSI-APOMS
AS - Erim-ASV
AT - ATT:Miller,Wagner
BE - Boulder-EO
BF - Beheim-Fritsch
BH - Bickel-et-al
BK - Boyer-Kak-Color
CB - Cotter-Batch
CD - Cathey,Davis
CL - CyberOptics-LRS
CM - CMU:Kanade-Fuhrman
CP - CyberOptics-PRS
CS - Chavel-Strand
DL - Diffracto-LaserProbe
DM - Hersman-DO-Metrol
DV - Hersman-DO-Vision
DZ - Diffracto-Z-Series
EO - EOIS:Fitts
GE - GE:Mundy-Porter
HA - Heikkinen,Ahola
HD - Dandliker-Thalmann
HM - Matthews-et-al
HP - Pantzer-et-al
HS - NYIT:Halioua-Srini
HY - Hymarc-Hyscan
IB - ITI:Boehnlein-Harding
IH - ITI:Harding-Goodson
IN - Forstner-Indusurf
IT'- New-Erim-ITA
JC - Jalkio-Kim-Case
JP - JPL:Lewis-Johnston
JR - Jarvis-83
KS - Kern-SPACE
LZ - Lorenz
MV - Mapvision-Haggren
NY - NYU:Intensity-Ratio
OC - Octek-Eyechrometer
OD - Odetics-Inc
OP - Optech:Larsen500
P? - Perceptron-Radar
PA - Photonic-Automation
PC - Perceptron-Contour
PE - Perkin-Elmer
PM - Pipitone-Marshall
QH - Hariharan
R? - RVSI-Ross
RB - NRCC:Rioux-Blais
RC - RCA:Rosenfeld-Tsiks
RV - RVSI-other
RX - NRCC:Rioux
SJ - ServoRobot-Jupiter
SO - Selcom-Optocator
SP - Solid-Photography
SR - SRI:Nitzan,et-al
SS - ServoRobot-Saturn
VO - Vuylsteke,Oosterlinck
WS - Tech-Arts-White

FIGURE 1.17. Figure of merit versus range accuracy.

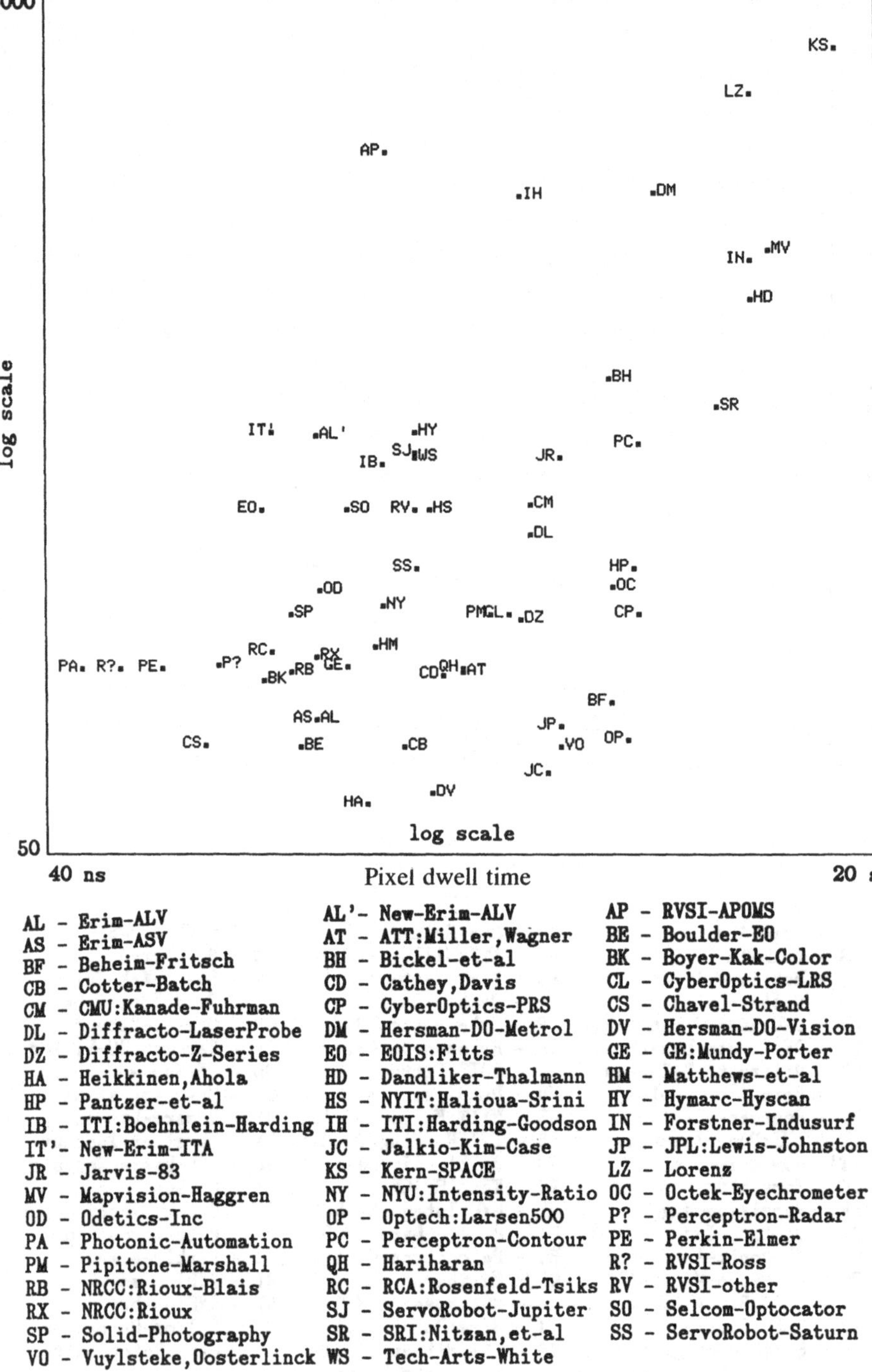

FIGURE 1.18. Depth-of-field/range-accuracy ratio versus pixel dwell time.

a function of the (log) pixel dwell time. The two plots in Figures 17 and 18 display the quantitative comparisons of rated sensors and show a wide range of sensor performance.

8.1 General Method Comparisons

At this point, the reader has been exposed to many range-finding methods and many sensor implementations. The six optical ranging principles are briefly summarized.

Imaging laser radars are capable of range accuracies from about 50 microns to 5 meters over depths of field 250 to 25,000 times larger. They benefit from having very small source-to-detector separations and operate at higher speeds than many other types of range-imaging sensors because range is determined electronically without much computation. They are also quite expensive, with commercially available units starting at around $100,000. Existing laser radars are sequential in data acquisition (they acquire one point at a time), although parallel designs have been suggested.

Triangulation sensors are capable of range accuracies beginning at about 5 microns over depths of field from 250 to 40,000 times larger. In the past, some have considered triangulation systems to be inaccurate or slow. Many believe that large baselines are required for reasonable accuracy. However, triangulation systems have shown themselves to be accurate, fast, and compact, mainly owing to the advent of synchronous scanning approaches. Simple triangulation systems start between $1,000 and $10,000, depending on how much you put together yourself and how much relevant equipment you already have. Commercially available turnkey systems can easily run upwards of $50,000, and fancier systems can run into the hundreds of thousands of dollars if there are requirements for fine accuracy over large working volumes. Triangulation systems go from totally sequential, as in point scanners, to almost totally parallel, as in the intensity ratio scheme or the color encoded stripe scheme. Triangulation systems have been the mainstay of range imaging, and promise to remain so.

Moire systems are limited to about the same accuracies as triangulation sensors (a few microns), and are not applicable unless surface slope constraints are satisfied. The depth of field of a moire system depends on the camera resolution and the object grating period p_o. For a 512 × 512 camera and a minimum of about 5 pixels per fringe, 100 phase transitions can be unwrapped, yielding a depth of field on the order of $100p_o$. Optical moire components are reasonably priced, but because digital computations are required to obtain range images, the system cost and speed of range image acquisition depends largely on the computer hardware. Image array processors have been used and vary in cost, but a complete moire system with reasonable speed will probably run more than $50,000. Moire techniques are inherently parallel and will benefit from the development of reasonably priced parallel computing hardware.

Holographic interferometer systems can measure with accuracies of less than half a nanometer over as many wavelengths of light as can be disambiguated. Surface slope and smoothness constraints must be met before holographic methods are valid. The most accurate heterodyne methods are the slowest and most expensive. The quasi-heterodyne methods are faster and cheaper, but give up about an order of magnitude in accuracy compared to heterodyne. Holographic techniques are also inherently parallel and should benefit from the development of parallel computing hardware. Holographic systems are generally much more specialized than other

TABLE 1.1. General comments on fundamental categories.

Category	ACC/DOF	Notes
Radar (pulse,AM,FM)	0.1 mm 100 km	Detect time, phase, or frequency differences. RF, microwave, IR, optical ultrasonic. Signal depends on range, surface normal, reflectance. Beam scanning usually required, no computation. History: since 1903, popular since 1940s. Cost: inexpensive to extremely expensive.
Triangulation	1 μm 100 m	Active or passive, one or more cameras. Scanned point, scanned stripe, multistripe, grid binary pattern, color, texture, intensity ratio. Terms: synchronous scan, Scheimpflug condition. History: since 200 B.C., most popular method. Cost: inexpensive to very expensive.
Moire techniques	1 μm 10 m	Projector, grating(s), camera, computer. Fringe tracking: projection, shadow. Reference: single-frame, multiframe (phase-shifted) surface slope constraint, noncoherent light no scanning; computation required. History: since 1859, used since 1950s in Mech. Eng. Cost: inexpensive (excluding computer).
Holographic interferometry	0.1 nm 100 μm	Detector, laser, optics, electronics, computer. Conventional: real-time, 2–exposure, time average. Quasi-heterodyne (phase-shifted), heterodyne. Surface slope constraint, coherent light. No scanning; computation/electronics required. History: not practical until laser 1961, big in NDT. Cost: inexpensive to expensive.
Focusing	1 mm 10 m	Active or passive, measure contrast or displacement limited depth-of-field-to-accuracy ratio. History: since 1800s. No scanning; computation/electronics required. Potential for inexpensive systems.
Fresnel diffraction (Talbot effect)	0.1 mm 10 m	Laser, grating, camera/not explored by many. Video rates, limited accuracy, electronics required, no scanning. History: discovered 1836, used 1983. Potential for inexpensive systems.

TABLE 1.2. Methods and applications of range-imaging sensors.

Application	Radar	Trian	Moire	Holog	Focus	Diffr
Cartography	X	X				
Navigation	X	X			X	
Medical	X	X	X			
Capture shape	X	X	X	X		
Bin picking	X	X			X	X
Assembly	X	X	X	X	X	X
Inspection	X	X	X	X		X
Gauging	X	X	X	X		X
Military	X	X				

optical techniques, and are applicable to fine grain surface inspection and nondestructive testing.

The Fresnel diffraction techniques based on the Talbot effect offer video frame rate range images using some special video processing hardware. The range resolution of these systems is limited by the resolution of local contrast measures; it appears to be difficult to get more than seven or eight bits of range. Diffraction ranging is also inherently parallel.

Active focusing methods have great potential for inexpensive range-imaging sensors, but high-range-resolution systems (more than 8-bits) are not likely.

Tactile methods still dominate many potential range-imaging applications where industry needs to exactly specify the shape of a prototype object. The reliability and accuracy of coordinate measuring machines (CMMs) over very large working volumes are hard to beat, but they are inherently slow and very expensive. If flexible noncontact optical methods can provide similar performance and be reliable and easy to use, then a significant cost savings can be realized in applications currently requiring CMMs. At very fine scales, the (nonoptical) scanning tunneling microscope [Binnig and Rohrer 1985] is the state of the art in very accurate surface studies. It is clear that active, optical ranging sensors have competition from other techniques.

Some of the comments of this section and the survey are summarized in Table 1.1. The first range value for each method in this table (ACC) is a good nominal accuracy rounded to the nearest power of ten, whereas the second value is the maximum nominal depth of field (DOF). Table 1.2 indicates in a brief format the types of applications wherein the different ranging methods are being used or might be used.

9 Emerging Themes

As in any field, people always want equipment to be faster, more accurate, more reliable, easier to use, and less expensive. Range-imaging sensors are no exception. Compared to the state of the art ten years ago, range imaging has come a very long way. An image that took hours to acquire before takes less than a second today. It is now reasonable to begin thinking about automating many tasks that might have been considered impossible ten years ago. The sensors are only one part of the technology needed for practical automated system functionality though; algorithms and software play the biggest role in application systems. Research in range-image analysis and object recognition using range images [Besl and Jain 1985] has come a long way in the last ten years, but there is still a lot further to go to achieve desired levels of performance in many applications.

Image-acquisition speed is a critical issue in many range-imaging applications. Since photons are quantized, the speed of data acquisition is limited by the number of photons that can be gathered by a pixel's effective photon collecting area during the pixel dwell time. The higher the energy of the projected beam, the higher the number of photons collected in a given time interval. This allows for greater accuracy or shorter dwell times. Hence, higher energy levels are needed to speed up sensors and make them more accurate. but higher power laser diodes are difficult to focus to a small point size because of irregularities in the beams from today's laser diodes and they are a greater threat to eye safety. Lower energy levels are needed to meet eye safety requirements in many planned applications where people will be working close to the range-imaging sensors (see appendix). Longer wavelengths (1.3 to 1.55 microns) are sought for better eye safety. However, not enough power is available from today's laser diodes at these wavelengths to obtain reasonable quality range images. The fiber optics communications industry is driving the development of longer wavelength laser diodes, and hopefully this situation will be remedied.

Another issue in the speed of data acquisition is scanning mechanisms. Many sensors are limited by the time for a moving part to move from point A to point B. Image dissector cameras are being explored by several investigators to avoid mechanical scanning. Mechanical scanning is a calibration and a reliability problem because moving parts do eventually wear out or break. However, today's mechanical scanners can offer years of reliable service.

The accuracy of many range sensors is limited by the depth of focus of the lenses used. Triangulation systems benefit from using tilted detectors according to the Scheimpflug condition. More optical engineering could go into many of today's range-imaging sensors.

Once considered state of the art, 8-bit resolution sensors are giving way to sensors with 10 or 12 bits or more of resolution and, possibly, accuracy. Processing this information is difficult with inexpensive image processing hardware designed for 8-bit images. Several commercial vendors do provide 16-bit image-processing hardware, but it is generally more expensive.

The performance of current range-imaging hardware (commercially available or otherwise) is not yet meeting with any fundamental physical limits in range-imaging performance. More optical, electrical, mechanical, and computer engineering is needed to build faster, cheaper, more accurate, more reliable, more maintainable, and less expensive range-imaging systems.

Reliable subpixel image location is being achieved in many light stripe triangulation sensors. It is commonly accepted that a fourth, fifth, eighth, or tenth of a pixel accuracy can realistically be obtained with intensity-weighted averaging techniques. Moreover, Kalman filtering (recursive least squares) algorithms [Smith and Cheeseman 1987] are beginning to be used in vision algorithms for optimally combining geometric information from different sensing viewpoints or different range sensors. Such efforts will continue to increase the accuracy of sensors and systems.

Although not specifically mentioned, most range sensors also acquire perfectly registered intensity images at the same time. Although there is no 3-D metrology information in these images, there is a great deal of other useful information that is important for automated systems. Only a few researchers have addressed methods for using this additional information. Commercially available software solutions are more than a few years away.

Range-imaging sensors are the data-gathering components of range-imaging systems, and ranging-imaging systems are the machine-perception components of application systems. Algorithms, software, and hardware are typically developed in isolation and brought together later, but hardware can incorporate programmability features that expedite operations that many applications perform. This is another of many problems in range-imaging research and development that have yet to be resolved in a widely applicable manner.

Appendix: Eye Safety

Lasers are used in imaging radars, active triangulation schemes, interferometers, active focusing methods, and diffraction techniques. If people are exposed to laser radiation, eye safety must be considered. An understanding of eye safety issues is important to the range-imaging-application engineer.

Concerning the sale of laser products across state lines in the United States, vendors of end user equipment containing lasers must comply with the requirements of the Food and Drug Administration's Center for Devices and Radiological Health (CDRH). If laser devices are sold for a system being integrated by another organization, then the CDRH regulations do not apply to the vendor. Concerning the use of laser products, most organizations follow the ANSI Z136.1 standard regulations. The ANSI and CDRH regulations are essentially the same except for some fine points. A very simplified version of the regulations is given here to introduce the terminology. The applications engineer should consult the CDRH [1985] regulations or the ANSI [1986] regulations for complete details.

Lasers emit electromagnetic radiation that is either visible (light) or invisible (infrared or ultraviolet). When laser radiation is received by the human eye, damage may occur in the retina or cornea depending upon the wavelength, if the radiation levels exceed the maximum allowable exposure. Visible light regulations are specified separately from invisible regulations because people have an aversion response such that they will blink or look away in less than one quarter of a second when exposed to intense visible radiation. With invisible light, no such aversion response occurs, although broad spectrum near-infrared laser diodes are visible to many people. Even though they are not listed separately in the official documents, the regulations may be viewed as two distinct sets of safety classes, one set for visible and another set for invisible. Within each class, there are two requirements that must be met: (1) the average power through a standard aperture (usually 7-mm diameter) must be less than the maximum average power for that class laser at every point in the field of view of the laser accessible to people, and (2) the energy in any pulse received by the standard aperture must be less than the maximum energy level for that class. One subtlety that should be considered for most range-imaging sensors is that the pulse repetition frequency (PRF) is included in the ANSI regulations, but not in the CDRH regulations.

For visible light (400–700 nm wavelengths), there are really five classes of lasers to indicate the danger level for laser powers within the given limits. The actual ratings are wavelength dependent, but the following list gives a reasonable indication of allowable average powers through the standard 7-mm diameter aperture with a 5-diopter lens.

- Class I (no risk, eye safe) average power $< 0.4\ \mu W$.
- Class II (low power, caution) $0.4\ \mu W <$ average power < 1 mW.
- Class IIIa (medium low power, caution) 1 mW $<$ average power < 5 mW.
- Class IIIb (medium power, danger) 5 mW $<$ average power < 500 mW.
- Class IV (high power, danger) average power > 500 mW.

Pulse requirements are more complicated and must be computed from equations and tables listed in the CDRH and ANSI regulations based on wavelength.

For invisible lasers (UV:200–400nm, IR:700nm–1mm wavelengths), there are only three classes to indicate the danger level for laser powers less than the given limits:

- Class I (no risk, eye safe) wavelength-dependent regulations.
- Class IIIb (medium power, danger) average power < 500 mW, not class I.
- Class IV (high power, danger) average power > 500 mW.

Pulse requirements are more complicated and must be computed from equations and tables listed in the CDRH and ANSI regulations based on wavelength. Note that there are no low or medium low power categories here. However, the ANSI regulations vary slightly from the CDRH regulations in that they allow a Class IIIa (caution) for infrared lasers with powers that exceed the class I limit by less than a factor of five (sec. 3.3.3.2 [ANSI 1986]).

New lasers are being developed in the 1.3- to 1.55-micron region that will be eye safe (class I) at powers that are rated class IIIb for 800–900 nm lasers. The retina is not as sensitive at the lower wavelengths and more energy is absorbed in the cornea. Sufficient power lasers for laser range finders are not yet commercially available, but prototype lasers in this spectral region have been tested in research laboratories. It may mean that eye-safe laser range finders can be built to replace current noneye-safe designs, possibly widening the applicability of range, imaging sensors.

Acknowledgments. The author would like to express his appreciation to R. Tilove and W. Reguiro for their thorough reviews, and to G. Dodd, S. Walter, R. Khetan, J. Szczesniak, M. Stevens, S. Marin, R. Hickling, W. Wiittanen, T. Sanderson, M. Delleva, H. Stern, R. Drap, and J. Sanz.

References

Agin G.J., and Highnam, P.T. 1983. Movable light stripe sensor for obtaining 3D coordinate measurements. In *Proceedings of SPIE Conference on 3-D Machine Perception* Vol. 360, p. 326.

Ahola, R., Heikkinen, T., and Manninen, M. 1985. 3D image acquisition by scanning time of flight measurements. In *Proc. Intl Conf. on Advances in Image Processing and Pattern Recognition* (Dec. 10–12, Pisa, Italy).

Altschuler, M.D., Altschuler, B.R., and Toboada, J. 1981. Laser electro-optic system for rapid 3D topographic mapping of surfaces. *Opt. Engrg.* **20,** 6, 953–961.

Andresen, K. 1986. The phase shift method applied to moire image processing. *Optik* **72,** 115–119.

ANSI. 1986. American National Standard for the safe use of lasers. *ANSI Z136.1-1986*. American National Standards Institute, New York.

Asada, M., Ichikawa, H., and Tsuji, S. 1986. Determining surface property by projecting a stripe pattern. In *Proc. Intl Conference on Pattern Recognition* (Oct., Paris, France) IEEE-CS, IAPR, New York, 1162–1164.

Banic, J., Sizgoric, S., and O'Neill, R. 1987. Airborne scanning lidar bathymeter measures water depth. *Laser focus/Electro-optics*. Feb., 48–52.

Bastuschek, C.M., and Schwartz, J.T. 1984. Preliminary implementation of a ratio image depth sensor. *Robotics Research Report No. 28,* Courant Institute of Mathematical Sciences, New York University, New York.

Beheim, G., and Fritsch, K. 1986. Range finding using frequency-modulated laser diode. *Appl. Opt.* **25,** 9, (May), 1439–1442.

Besl, P.J. 1986. Surfaces in early range image understanding. Ph.D. dissertation, Electr. Eng. Comp. Sci. Dept. *(RSD-TR-10-86),* University of Michigan, Ann Arbor, Mich. (Mar.); also Springer-Verlag, 1988.

Besl, P.J., and Jain, R.C. 1985. Three dimensional object-recognition. *ACM Computing Surveys* **17,** 1 (Mar.), 75–145.

Bickel, G., Hausler, G., and Maul, M. 1984. In *Optics in modern science and technology,* Conf. Dig. ICO-13, p. 534.

Bickel, G., Hausler, G., and Maul, M. 1985. Triangulation with expanded range of depth. *Opt. Engrg.* **24,** 6 (Nov.–Dec.), 975–979.

Binger, N., and Harris, S.J. 1987. Applications of laser radar technology. *Sensors* **4,** 4,42–44.

Binnig, G., and Rohrer, H. 1985. The scanning tunneling microscope. *Sci. Amer.* **253,** 2 (Aug.), 50–69.

Blais, F., and Rioux, M. 1986. Biris: A simple 3D sensor. In *Proc. SPIE Conference on Optics, Illumination, and Image Sensing for Machine Vision* (D.J. Svetkoff, Ed.), Vol. 728 (Oct. 30–31, Cambridge, Mass.), 235–242.

Boehnlein, A.J., and Harding, K.G. 1986. Adaptation of a parallel architecture computer to phase-shifted moire interferometry. In *Proc. SPIE Conference on Optics, Illumination, and Image Sensing for Machine Vision* (D.J. Svetkoff, Ed.), Vol. 728 (Oct. 30–31, Cambridge, Mass.), 132–146.

Born, M., and Wolf, E. 1975. *Principles of optics,* 5th ed. Pergamon Press, New York.

Boulder Electro-Optics. 1986. Product information, Boulder, Col. (now Boulder Melles Griot).

Boyer, K.L., and Kak, A.C. 1987. Color encoded structured light for rapid active ranging. *IEEE Trans. Pattern Analysis Machine Intell.* PAMI-9, 1 (Jan.), 14–28.

Bumbaca, F., Blais, F., and Rioux, M. 1986. Real-time correction of 3D nonlinearities for a laser rangefinder. *Opt. Engrg.* **25,** 4 (Apr.), 561–565.

Carrihill, B. 1986. The intensity ratio depth sensor. Ph.D. dissertation. Courant Institute of Mathematical Sciences, New York University, New York.

Carrihill, B., and Hummel, R. 1985. Experiments with the intensity ratio depth sensor. *Computer Vision, Graphics, Image Processing* **32,** 337–358.

Case, S.K., Jalkio, J.A., and Kim, R.C. 1987. 3D vision system analysis and design. In *Three-dimensional machine vision* (T. Kanade, Ed.), Kluwer Academic, Boston, Mass., 63–96.

Cathey, W.T., and Davis, W.C. 1986. Vision system with ranging for maneuvering in space. *Opt. Engrg.* **24,** 7 (Jul.), 821–824. [See also Imaging system with range to each pixel. *J. Opt. Soc. Amer.* **A 3,** 9 (Sept.), 1537–1542.

CDRH. 1985. Federal register. Part III, Dept. of Health and Human Services, 21 CFR Parts 1000 and 1040 [Docket No. 80N-0364], Laser Products; Amendments to Performance Standard; Final Rule. [For further information, contact Glenn Conklin, Center for Devices and Radiological Health (HFZ-84), U.S. Food and Drug Administration, 5600 Fishers Lane, Rockville, MD 20857.]

Chang, M., Hu, C.P., Lam, P., and Wyant, J.C. 1985. High precision deformation measurement by digital phase shifting holographic interferometry. *Appl. Opt.* **24,** 22, 3780–3783.

Chavel, P., and Strand, T.C. 1984. Range measurement using Talbot diffraction imaging of gratings. *Appl. Opt.* **23,** 6, 862–871.

Church, E.L., Vorburger, T.V., and Wyant, J.C. 1985. Direct comparison of mechanical and optical measurements of the finish of precision machined optical surfaces. *Opt. Engrg.* **24,** 3 (May–June), 388–395.

Cline, H.E., Holik, A.S., and Lorenson, W.E. 1982. Computer-aided surface reconstruction of interference contours. *Appl. Opt.* **21,** 24, 4481–4489.

Cline, H.E., Lorenson, W.E., and Holik, A.S. 1984. Automated moire contouring. *Appl. Opt.* **23,** 10, 1454–1459.

Corle, T.R., Fanton, J.T., and Kino, G.S. 1987. Distance measurements by differential confocal optical ranging. *Appl. Opt.* **26,** 12, 2416–2420.

Cotter, S.M., and Batchelor, B.G. 1986. Deriving range maps at real-time video rates. *Sensor Rev.* **6,** 4 (Oct.), IFS Publication, Ltd., 185–192.

Cowley, J.M., and Moodie, A.F. 1957. Fourier images: I—The point source. *Proc. Phys. Soc.* **70,** 486–496.

Cunningham, R. 1986. Laser radar for the space conscious. *Lasers and Applications*. July, 18–20.

Cyberoptics Corporation. 1987. Product information. Minneapolis, Minn.

Damm, L. 1987. A minimum-size all purpose fiber optical proximity sensor. In *Proc. Vision'87 Conference* (June 8–11, Detroit, Mich.), SME, 6-71–6-91.

Dandliker, R. 1980. (Review paper on heterodyne holography.) *Progress in Optics* 17, 1.

Dandliker, R., and Thalmann, R. 1985. Heterodyne and quasi-heterodyne holographic interferometry. *Opt. Engrg* **24,** 5 (Sep.–Oct.), 824–831.

Dandliker, R., Ineichen, B., and Mottier, F. 1973. (Paper first introducing heterodyne holography.) *Opt. Commun.* **9,** 412.

Dandridge, A. 1982. Current induced frequency modulation in diode lasers. *Electron. Letters* **18,** 302.

Denstman, H. 1980. State-of-the-art optics: Automated image focusing. *Indust. Photog.,* July, 33–37.

Dereniak, E.L., and Crowe, D.G. 1984. *Optical radiation detectors*. Wiley, New York.

Diffracto. 1987. Laser probe digital ranging sensor. *Product literature*. Diffracto, Ltd., Windsor, Ontario, Canada.

Dimatteo, P.L., Ross, J.A., and Stern, H.K. 1979. Arrangement for sensing the geometric characteristics of an object. (RVSI) U.S. Patent 4175862.

Electro-Optical Information Systems. 1987. Product information. EOIS, Santa Monica, Calif.

Faugeras, O.D., and Hebert, M. 1986. The representation, recognition, and locating of 3-D objects. *Inst. J. Robotic Res.* **5,** 3 (Fall), 27–52.

Froome, K.D., and Bradsell, R.H. 1961. Distance measurement by means of a light ray modulated at a microwave frequency. *J. Sci. Instrum.* **38,** 458–462.

Gasvik, K.J. 1983. Moire technique by means of digital image processing. *Appl. Opt.* **22,** 23, 3543–3548.

Goldberg, N. 1982. Inside autofocus: How the magic works. *Pop. Photog.* Feb., 77–83.

Goodman, J.W. 1986. A random walk through the field of speckle. *Opt. Engrg.* **25,** 5, 610–612.

Gottlief, M. 1983. *Electro-optic and acousto-optic scanning and deflection*. Marcel-Dekker, New York.

Gottwald, R., and Berner, W. 1987. The new kern system for positioning and automated coordinate evaluation; advanced technology for automated 3D coordinate determination. *Product Information*. Kern Instruments, Brewster, N.Y., and Aarau, Switzerland.

Griffin, D.R. 1958. Listening in the dark: the acoustic orientation of bats and men. Yale University Press, New Haven, Conn.

Grossman, P. 1987. Depth from focus. *Pattern Recognition Lett.* **5,** 1 (Jan.), 63–69.

Haggren, H., and Leikas, E. 1987. Mapvision—The photogrammetric machine vision system. In *Proc. Vision'87 Conference* (June 8–11, Detroit, Mich.), 10-37–10-50.

Halioua, M., and Srinivasan, V. 1987. Method and apparatus for surface profilometry. New York Institute of Technology, Old Westbury, NY. U.S. Patent 4,641,972.

Halioua, M., Krishnamurthy, R.S. Liu, H., and Chiang, F.P. 1983. Projection moire with moving gratings for automated 3D topography. *Appl. Opt.* **22,** 6, 850–855.

Hall, E.L., Tio, J.B.K., McPherson, C.A., and Sadjadi, F.A. 1982. Measuring curved surfaces for robot vision. *Computer* **15,** 12 (Dec.), 42–54.

Hane, K., and Grover, C.P. 1985. Grating imaging and its application to displacement sensing. *J. Opt. Soc. Am.* **A** 2, 13, P9.

Harding, K.G. 1983. Moire interferometry for industrial inspection. *Lasers and Applications* (Nov.), 73.

Harding, K.G., and Goodson, K. 1986. Hybrid high accuracy structured light profiler. In *Proc. SPIE Conference on Optics, Illumination, and Image Sensing for Machine Vision,* (D.J. Svetkoff, Ed.), Vol. 728 (Oct. 30–31, Cambridge, Mass.), 132–145.

Harding, K.G., and Tait, R. 1986. Moire techniques applied to automated inspection of machined parts. In *Proc. Vision'86 Conference* (May, Detroit, Mich.,), SME, Dearborn, Mich.

Hariharan, P. 1985. Quasi-heterodyne hologram interferometry. *Opt. Engrg.* **24,** 4 (July–Aug.), 632–638.

Hariharan, P., Oreb, B.F., and Brown, N. 1983. *Appl. Opt.* **22,** 6, 876.

Harvey, J.E., MacFarlane, M.J., and Forgham, J.L. 1985. Design and performance of ranging telescopes: Monolithic vs. synthetic aperture. *Opt. Engrg.* **24,** 1 (Jan.–Feb.), 183–188.

Hausler, G., and Maul, M. 1985. Telecentric scanner for 3D sensing. *Opt. Engrg.* **24,** 6 (Nov.–Dec.), 978–980.

Heikkinen, T., Ahola, R., Manninen, M., and Myllyla, R. 1986. Recent results of the performance analysis of a 3D sensor based on time of flight. In *Proc. SPIE Quebec Int'l Symp. on Optical and Optoelectronic Applied Sci. and Engrg.*

Hersman, M., Goodwin, F., Kenyon, S., and Slotwinski, A. 1987. Coherent laser radar application to 3D vision and metrology. In *Proc. Vision'87 Conf.* (June 8–11, Detroit, Mich.), 3-1–3-12.

Holland, S.W., Rossol, L., and Ward, M.R. 1979. Consight-1: A vision controlled robot system for transferring parts from belt conveyors. In *Computer Vision and Sensor-Based Robots* (G.G. Dodd and L. Rossol, Eds.), Plenum Press, New York, 81–97.

Horn, B.K.P. 1968. Focusing. Project MAC, AI Memo 160. M.I.T., Cambridge, Mass.

Hulsmeyer, C. 1904. Hertzian wave projecting and receiving apparatus adapted to indicate or give warning of the presence of a metallic body, such as a ship or a train, in the line of projection of such waves. *U.K. Patent 13,170,* United Kingdom.

Hymarc 1987. Product Information. Ottawa, Ontario, Canada.
Idesawa, M., and Kinoshita, G. 1986. New type of miniaturized optical range sensing methods RORS and RORST. *J. Robotic Sys.* **3,** 2, 165–181.
Idesawa, M., and Yatagai, Y. 1980. 3D shape input and processing by moire technique. In *Proc. 5th Intl. Conf. Pattern Recognition* (Dec., Miami, Fla.) IEEE-CS, New York, 1085–1090.
Idesawa, M., Yatagai, Y., and Soma, T. 1976. A method for the automatic measurement of 3D shapes by new type of moire topography. In *Proc. 3rd Intl. Conference Pattern Recognition* (Nov. 8–11, Coronado, Calif), 708.
Idesawa, M., Yatagai, Y., and Soma, T. 1977. Scanning moire method and automatic measurement of 3D shapes. *Appl. Opt.* **16,** 8, 2152–2162.
Inokuchi, S., Sato, K., and Matsuda, F. 1984. Range imaging system for 3-D object recognition. In *Proc. 7th Intl. Conference Pattern Recognition* (Montreal, Canada, July 30–Aug. 2), 806–808.
Jalkio, J., Kim, R., and Case, S. 1985. 3D inspection using multi-stripe structured light. *Opt. Engrg.* **24,** 6 (Nov.–Dec.), 966–974.
Jalkio, J., Kim, R., and Case, S. 1986. Triangulation based range sensor design. In *Proc. SPIE Conference on Optics, Illumination, and Image Sensing for Machine Vision* (D.J. Svetkoff, Ed.), Vol. 728 (Oct. 30–31, Cambridge, Mass.), 132–146.
Jarvis, R. A. 1976. Focus optimization criteria for computer image processing. *Microscope* **24,** 2, 163–180.
Jarvis, R.A. 1982. Computer vision and robotics laboratory. *IEEE Computer* **15,** 6 (June), 9–23.
Jarvis, R.A. 1983a. A laser time-of-flight range scanner for robotic vision. *IEEE Trans. Pattern Analysis Mach. Intell.* **PAMI-5,** 5 (Sep.), 505–512.
Jarvis, R.A. 1983b. A perspective on range finding techniques for computer vision. *IEEE Trans. Pattern Analysis Mach. Intell.* **PAMI-5,** 2 (Mar.), 122–139.
Jelalian, A.V., and McManus, R.G. 1977. AGARD Panel Proceeding No. 77. June, Sec. 2.1, 1–21.
Johnson, M. 1985. Fiber displacement sensors for metrology and control. *Opt. Engrg.* **24,** 6, 961–965.
Juha, M., and Donahue, J. 1987. Improving automated SMT inspection with 3D vision. *Product literature.* Photonic Automation, Inc., Santa Ana, Calif.
Kak, A.C. 1985. Depth perception for robot vision. In *Handbook of Industrial Robotics* (S. Nof, Ed.), Wiley, New York., pp. 272–319.
Kanade, T., and Asada, H. 1981. Noncontact visual 3D range-finding devices. In *Proc. SPIE 283, 3D Machine Perception* (B.R. Altschuler, Ed.), pp. 48–53.
Kanade, T., and Fuhrman, M. 1987. A noncontact optical proximity sensor for measuring surface shape. In *Three-Dimensional Machine Vision* (T. Kanade, Ed.), Kluwer Academic, Boston. 151–194.
Karara, H.M. 1985. Close-range photogrammetry: Where are we and where are we heading? *Photogramm. Engrg. and Remote Sensing* **51,** 5, 537–544.
Kawata, H., Endo, H., and Eto, Y. 1985. A study of laser radar. In *Proc. 10th Intl. Tech. Conf. on Experimental Safety Vehicles* (July 1–4, Oxford, U.K.), 16 pp.
Kellogg, W.N. 1961. Porpoises and sonar. University of Chicago Press, Chicago, Ill.
Keyes, R.J. 1986. Heterodyne and nonheterodyne laser transceivers. *Rev. Sci. Instrum.* **57,** 4 (Apr.), 519–528.

Khetan, R.P. 1975. The theory and application of projection moire methods. Ph.D. dissertation. Department of Engineering Mechanics, State University of New York, Stony Brook, N.Y.

Kingslake, R. 1983. Optical System Design, Academic Press, New York.

Kinoshita, G., Idesawa, M., and Naomi, S. 1986. Robotic range sensor with projections of bright ring pattern. *J. Robotic Systems* **3,** 3 (Mar.), 249–257.

Koenderink, J.J., and VanDoorn, A.J. 1986. Dynamic shape. *Biological Cybernetics* **53,** 383–396.

Kratky, V. 1979. Real-time photogrammetric support of dynamic 3D control. *Photogrammetric Engrg. and Remote Sensing* **45,** 9, 1231–1242.

Krotkov, E.P. 1986. Focusing. Ph.D. Dissertation, University of Pennsylvania, Philadelphia, Pa.

Krotkov, E., and Martin, J.P. 1986. Range from focus. *Proc. IEEE Intl. Conference on Robotics and Automation* (Apr. 7–10, San Francisco, Calif.) IEEE-CS, New York, 1093–1098.

Kurahashi, A., Adachi, M., and Idesawa, M. 1986. A prototype of optical proximity sensor based on RORS *J. Robotic Sys.* **3,** 2, 183–190.

Labuz, J. and McVey, E.S. 1986. Camera and projector motion for range mapping. In *Proc. SPIE Conference on Optics, Illumination, and Image Sensing for Machine Vision* (D.J. Svetkoff, Ed.). Vol. 728 (Oct. 30–31, Cambridge, Mass.), 227–234.

Lamy, F., Liegeois, C., and Meyrueis, P. 1981. 3D automated pattern recognition using moire techniques. In *Proc. SPIE* **360,** 345–351.

Landman, M.M., and Robertson, S.J. 1986. A flexible industrial system for automated 3D inspection. In *Proc. SPIE Conference on Optics, Illumination, and Image Sensing for Machine Vision* (D.J. Svetkoff, Ed.), Vol. 728, (Oct. 30–31, Cambridge, Mass.), 203–209.

Leader, J.C. 1986. Speckle effects on coherent laser radar detection efficiency. *Opt. Engrg.* **25,** 5, 644–650.

Leger, J.R., and Snyder, M.A. 1984. Real-time depth measurement and display using Fresnel diffraction and white-light processing. *Appl. Opt.* **23,** 10, 1655–1670.

Leith, E., and Upatnieks, J. 1962. Reconstructed wavefronts and communication theory. *J. Opt. Soc. Amer.* **54,** 1123–1130.

Lewis, J.R.T., and Sopwith, T. 1986. 3D surface measurement by microcomputer. *Image and Vision Computing* **4,** 3 (Aug.), 159–166.

Lewis, R.A., and Johnston, A.R. 1977. A scanning laser rangefinder for a robotic vehicle. In *Proc. 5th Intl. Joint Conference on Artificial Intelligence* (Cambridge, Mass., Aug. 22–25), 762–768.

Livingstone, F.R., and Rioux, M. 1986. Development of a large field of view 3D vision system. In *Proc. SPIE* **665** (Cambridge, Mass.).

Livingstone, F.R., Tulai, A.F., and Thomas, M.R. 1987. Application of 3-D vision to the measurement of marine propellers. In *Proc. Vision'87 Conference* (June 8–11, Detroit, Mich.), 10-25–10-36.

Lord Rayleigh (J.W. Strutt). 1874. On the manufacture and theory of diffraction gratings. *Phil. Mag.* **47,** 81, 193.

Lord Rayleigh (J.W. Strutt). 1881. *Phil. Mag.* **11,** 196.

Lorenz, R.D. 1984. Theory and design of optical/electronic probes for high performance measurement of parts. Ph.D. dissertation. Univ. of Wisconsin-Madison, Madison, Wisc.

Lorenz, R.D. 1986. A novel, high-range-to-resolution ratio, optical sensing technique for high speed surface geometry measurements. In *Proc. SPIE Conference on Optics, Illumination, and Image Sensing for Machine Vision* (D.J. Svetkoff, Ed.), Vol. 728 (Oct. 30–31, Cambridge, Mass.), 152–156.

Macy, W.W. 1983. Two-dimensional fringe pattern analysis. *Appl. Opt.* **22,** 22, 3898–3901.

Maider, D.L. 1985. Holographic interferometry of pipes: Precision interpretation by least squares fitting. *Appl. Opt.* **24,** 22, 3784–3790.

Marion, J.B. 1965. Classical electromagnetic radiation. Academic Press, New York.

Marshall, G. 1985. *Laser beam scanning,* Marcel-Dekker, New York.

Matsuda, R. 1986. Multifunctional optical proximity sensor using phase modulation. *J. Robotic Sys.* **3,** 2, 137–147.

Matthews, H.J., Hamilton, D.K., and Sheppard, C.J.R. 1986. Surface profiling by phase-locked interferometry. *Appl. Opt.* **25,** 14, 2372–2374.

Mersch, S.H., and Doles, J.E. 1985. Cylindrical optics applied to machine vision. In *Proc. Vision'85 Conference* (Mar. 25–28, Detroit, Mich.), SME, 4-53–4-63.

Mertz, L. 1983. Real-time fringe pattern analysis. *Appl. Opt.* **22,** 10, 1535–1539.

Miller, G.L., and Wagner, E.R. 1987. An optical rangefinder for autonomous robot cart navigation. In *Proc. SPIE* Industrial Electronics, Cambridge, Mass. (Nov.).

Moore, D.T., and Traux, B.E. 1979. Phase-locked moire fringe analysis for automated contouring of diffuse surfaces. *Appl. Opt.* **18,** 1, 91–96.

Mundy, J.L., and Porter, G.B. 1987. A three-dimensional sensor based on structured light. In *Three-dimensional machine vision* (T. Kanade, Ed.), Kluwer Academic, Boston, 3–62.

Nakagawa, Y., and Ninomiya, T. 1987. Three-dimensional vision systems using the structured light method for inspecting solder joints and assembly robots. In *Three-dimensional machine vision* (T. Kanade, Ed.), Kluwer Academic, Boston, 543–565.

Namco, 1986. Product literature. Namco, Cleveland, Ohio.

Nevatia, R., and Binford, T.O. 1973. Structured descriptions of complex objects. In *Proc. 3rd International Joint Conference on Artificial Intelligence* (Stanford, Calif., Aug. 20–23), 641–647.

Newman, W.M., and Sproull, R.F. 1979. *Principles of interactive computer graphics,* 2nd Ed. McGraw-Hill, New York.

Newport Corp. 1987. Design and testing with holography. Machine vision components. *Product Information.* Fountain Valley, Calif.

Nitzan, D., Brain, A.E., and Duda, R.O. 1977. The measurement and use of registered reflectance and range data in scene analysis. *Proc. IEEE* **65,** 2 (Feb.), 206–220.

Nitzan, D., Bolles, R., Kremers, J., and Mulgaonkar, P. 1986. 3D vision for robot applications. *NATO Workshop on Knowledge Engineering for Robotic Applications.* (May 12–16, Maratea, Italy).

Oboshi, T. 1976. *Three-dimensional imaging techniques.* Academic Press, New York.

Oster, G. 1965. Moire optics: A bibliography. *J. Opt. Soc. Amer.* **55,** 1329.

Ozeki, O., Nakano, T., and Yamamoto, S. 1986. Real-time range measurement device for 3D object recognition. *IEEE Trans. Pattern Analysis Mach. Intell.* **PAMI-8,** 4, 550–553.

Pantzer, D., Politch, J., and Ek, L. 1986. Heterodyne profiling instrument for the angstrom region. *Appl. Opt.* **25,** 22, 4168–4172.

Parthasarathy, S., Birk, J., and Dessimoz, J. 1982. Laser rangefinder for robot control and inspection. In *Proc. SPIE* **336**—*Robot Vision* (May 6–7, Arlington, Va.), 2–11.

Pelowski, K.R. 1986. SME, 3D measurement with machine vision. In *Proc. Vision'86 Conference* (May, Detroit, Mich.), 2-17–2-31.

Pentland, A.P. 1987. A new sense of depth of field. *IEEE Trans. Pattern Analysis Mach. Intell.* **PAMI-9,** 4 (July), 523–531.

Perceptron. 1987. Product information. Farmington Hills, Mich.

Perrin, J.C., and Thomas, A. 1979. Electronic processing of moire fringes: Application to moire topography and comparison with photogrametry. *Appl. Opt.* **18,** 4, 563–574.

Peterson, R.W., Robinson, G.M., Carlsen, R.A., Englund, C.D., Moran, P.J., and Wirth, W.M. 1984. Interferometric measurements of the surface profile of moving samples. *Appl. Opt.* **23,** 10, 1464–1466.

Pinckney, H.F.L. 1978. Theory and development of an on-line 30 Hz video photogrammetry system for real-time 3D control. *Int. Archives of Photogrammetry* **XXII,** V.2, 38 pp.

Pipitone, F.J., and Marshall, T.G. 1983. A wide-field scanning triangulation rangefinder for machine vision. *Intl. J. Robotics Res.* **2,** 1 (Spring), 39–49.

Pirodda, L. 1982. Shadow and projection moire techniques for absolute and relative mapping of surface shapes. *Opt. Engrg.* **21,** 640.

Popplestone, R.J., Brown, C.M., Ambler, A.P., and Crawford, G.F. 1975. Forming models of plane-and-cylinder faceted bodies from light stripes. In *Proc. 4th International Joint Conference on Artificial Intelligence* (Tbilisi, Georgia, USSR, Sept.), 664–668.

Porter, G.B., and Mundy, J.L. 1982. A noncontact profile sensing system for visual inspection. In *Proc. Workshop on Industrial Applications of Machine Vision,* (May, Research Triangle Park, N.C.), IEEE, New York, 119–129.

Potmesil, M. 1983. Generating models of solid objects by matching 3D surface segments. In *Proc. 8th International Joint Conference on Artificial Intelligence* (Karlsruhe, West Germany, Aug. 8–12), 1089–1093.

Potsdamer, J., and Altschuler, M. 1982. Surface measurement by space-encoded projected beam system. *Computer Graphics Image Processing* **18,** 1–17.

Pryputniewicz, R.J. 1985. Heterodyne holography applications in studies of small components. *Opt. Engrg.* **24,** 5 (Sept.–Oct.), 849–854.

Quist, T.M., Bicknell, W.E., and Bates, D.A. 1978. ARPA Semi-annual report: Optics research. Lincoln Laboratory, M.I.T., Cambridge, Mass.

Reid, G.T. 1986. Automatic fringe pattern analysis: A review. *Opt. and Lasers in Engrg.* **7,** 37–68.

Rioux, M. 1984. Laser range finder based upon synchronized scanners. *Appl. Opt.* **23,** 21, 3837–3844.

Rioux, M., and Blais, F. 1986. Compact 3-D camera for robotic applications. *J. Opt. Soc. Amer.* **A 3,** 9 (Sept.), 1518–1521.

Robotic Vision Systems, Inc. 1987. Product literature. RVSI, Hauppage, N.Y.

Rocker, F. 1974. Localization and classification of 3D objects. In *Proc. 2nd Intl. Conference Pattern Recognition,* (Aug., Copenhagen, Denmark), 527–528.

Rosenfeld, J.P., and Tsikos, C.J. 1986. High-speed space encoding projector for 3D imaging. In *Proc. SPIE Conference on Optics, Illumination, and Image Sensing for Machine Vision* (D.J. Svetkoff, Ed.), Vol. 728 (Oct. 30–31, Cambridge, Mass.), 146–151.

Ross, J.A. 1978. Methods and systems for 3D measurement. U.S. Patent 4,199,253. (RVSI).

Sampson, R.E. 1987. 3D range sensor via phase shift detection. (Insert). *IEEE Computer* **20,** 8 (Aug.), 23–24.

Sasaki, O., and Okazaki, H. 1986. Sinusoidal phase modulating interferometry for surface profile measurements; and Analysis of measurement accuracy in sinusoidal phase modulating interferometry. *Appl. Opt.* **25,** 18, 3137–3140; and 3152–3158.

Sato, K., and Inokuchi, S. 1985. 3D surface measurement by space encoding range imaging. *J. Robotic Systems* **2,** 1, 27–39.

Sato, Y., Kitagawa, H., and Fujita, H. 1982. Shape measurement of curved objects using multiple-slit ray projection. *IEEE Trans. Pattern Analysis Mach. Intell.* **PAMI-4,** 6 (Nov.), 641–649.

Schewe, H., and Forstner, W. 1986. The program PALM for automatic line and surface measurement using image matching techniques. In *Proc. Symposium Intl. Soc. for Photogrammetry and Remote Sensing,* Vol. 26, Part 3/2, From Analog to Digital, 608–622.

Schlag, J.F., Sanderson, A.C., Neumann, C.P. and Wimberly, F.C. 1983. Implementation of automatic focusing algorithms for a computer vision system with camera control. *CMU-RI-TR-83-14* (Aug.).

Schmitt, F., Barsky, B., and Du, W. 1986. An adaptive subdivision method for surface-fitting from sampled data. *Computer Graphics* **20,** 4 (Aug.), 179–188.

Schmitt, F., Maitre, H., Clainchard, A., and Lopez-Krahm, J. 1985. Acquisition and representation of real object surface data. *SPIE Proc. Biostereometrics Conference,* Vol. 602 (Cannes, Frances, Dec. 2–6).

Schulman, W., and Dubas, M. 1979. *Holographic interferometry.* Springer-Verlag, Berlin, Germany.

Schwartz, J. 1983. Structured light sensors for 3D robot vision. *Robotics Research Report No. 8,* Courant Institute of Mathematical Sciences, New York University, New York.

Sciammarella, C.A. 1982. The moire method—A review. *Exp. Mech.* **22,** 418–433.

Selcom. 1987. Optocator product information. Valdese, N.C., Partille, Sweden; Krefeld, West Germany.

Servo-Robot. 1987. Product information. Boucherville, Quebec, Canada.

Shirai, Y. 1972. Recognition of polyhedra with a range finder. *Pattern Recognition* **4,** 243–250.

Shirai, Y., and Suwa, M. 1971. Recognition of polyhedra with a range finder. In *Proc. 2nd International Joint Conference on Artificial Intelligence* (London, U.K., Aug.), 80–87.

Silvaggi, C., Luk, F., and North, W. 1986. Position/dimension by structured light. *Exper. Tech.* (Oct.), 22–25.

Skolnick, M.I. 1962. *Introduction to radar systems.* McGraw-Hill, New York.

Slevogt, H. 1974. *Technische Optik.* Walter de Gruyter, Berlin, Germany 55–57.

Smith. R. C., and Cheeseman, P. 1987. On the representation and estimation of spatial uncertainty. *Intl. J. Robotics Res.* **5,** 4, 56–68.

Solid Photography, Inc. 1977. (now Robotic Vision Systems, Inc. (RVSI), Product information. (Hauppage, N.Y.).

Srinivasan, V., Liu, H.C., and Halioua, M. 1985. Automated phase measuring profilometry: A phase-mapping approach. *Appl. Opt.* **24,** 2, 185–188.

Stockman, G., and Hu, G. 1986. Sensing 3D surface patches using a projected grid. In *Proc. Computer Vision Pattern Recognition Conference* (June 22–26, Miami, Fla.), 602–607.

Strand, T. 1983. Optical three dimensional sensing. *Opt. Engrg.* **24,** 1 (Jan.–Feb.), 33–40.

Svetkoff, D.J. 1986. Towards a high resolution, video rate, 3D sensor for machine vision. In *Proceedings of SPIE Conference on Optics, Illuminations, and Image Sensing for Machine Vision,* Vol. 728 (D.J. Svetkoff, Ed.), (Oct. 30–31, Cambridge, Mass.), pp. 216–226.

Svetkoff, D.J., Leonard, P.F., Sampson, R.E., and Jain, R.C. 1984. Techniques for real-time feature extraction using range information. In *Proc. SPIE* **521**—Intelligent Robotics and Computer Vision (Nov. 5–8, Cambridge, Mass.), 302–309.

Talbot, H. 1836. Facts relating to optical science. No. IV. *Phil. Mag.* **9,** 401–407.

Technical Arts Corp. 1987. Product literature. Redmond, Wash.

Teich, M.C. 1968. Infrared heterodyne detection. *Proc. IEEE* **56,** 1 (Jan.), 37–46.

Tenenbaum, J. 1970. Accomodation in computer vision. Ph.D. dissertation. Stanford University, Stanford, Calif.

Terras, R. 1986. Detection of phase in modulated optical signals subject to ideal Rayleigh fading. *J. Opt. Soc. Am.* **A 3,** 11 (Nov.), 1816–1825.

Thalmann, R., and Dandliker, R. 1985. Holographic contouring using electronic phase measurement. *Opt. Engrg.* **24,** 6 (Nov.–Dec.), 930–935.

Theocaris, P.S. 1969. *Moire fringes in strain analysis.* Pergamon Press, New York.

Tozer, B.A., Glanville, R., Gordon, A.L., Little, M.J., Webster, J.M., and Wright, D.G. 1985. Holography applied to inspection and measurement in an industrial environment. *Opt. Engrg.* **24,** 5 (Sep.–Oct), 746–753.

Tsai, R. 1986. An efficient and accurate camera calibration technique for 3D machine vision. In *Proc. Computer Vision Pattern Recognition Conference* (June 22–26, Miami, Fla.), IEEE-CS, New York, 364–374.

Vest, C.M. 1979. *Holographic interferometry.* Wiley, New York.

Vuylsteke, P., and Oosterlinck, A. 1986. 3D perception with a single binary coded illumination pattern. In *Proc. SPIE Conferences on Optics, Illumination, and Image Sensing for Machine Vision* (D.J. Svetkoff, Ed.), Vol. 728 (Oct. 30–31, Cambridge, Mass.), 195–202.

Wagner, J.F. 1987. Sensors for dimensional measurement. In *Proc. Vision '87 Conference* (June 8–11, Detroit, Mich.), 13-1–13-18.

Wagner, J.W. 1986. Heterodyne holographic interferometry for high-resolution 3D sensing. In *Proc. SPIE Conference on Optics, Illumination, and Image Sensing for Machine Vision* (D.J. Svetkoff, Ed.), Vol. 728 (Oct. 30–31, Cambridge, Mass.), 173–182.

Wang, J.Y. 1984. Detection efficiency of coherent optical radar. *Appl. Opt.* **23,** 19, 3421–3427.

Wang, J.Y. 1986. Lidar signal fluctuations caused by beam translation and scan. *Appl. Opt.* **25,** 17, 2878–2885.

Wang, J.Y., Bartholomew, B.J., Streiff, M.L., and Starr, E.F. 1984. Imaging CO_2 laser radar field tests. *Appl. Opt.* **23,** 15, 2565–2571.

Wang, Y.E., Mitiche, A., and Aggarwal, J.K. 1985. Inferring local surface orientation with the aid of grid coding. In *IEEE Workshop on Computer Vision: Representation and Control* (Oct., Bellaire, Mich.), IEEE, New York, 96–104.

Wei, D., and Gini, M. 1983. The use of taper light beam for object recognition. In *Robot Vision* (R. Pugh, Ed.), IFS Publications, U.K., Springer-Verlag, Berlin, Germany, 143–156.

Will, P.M., and Pennington, K.S. 1972. Grid coding: A novel technique for image processing. *Proc. IEEE* **60,** 6 (June), 669–680.

Winthrop, J.T., and Worthington, C.R. 1965. Theory of Fresnel images I. Plane periodic objects in monochromatic light. *J. Opt. Soc. Amer.* **55,** 4 (Apr.), 373–381.

Wuerker, R. F., and Hill, D.A. 1985. Holographic microscopy. *Opt. Engrg.* **24,** 3 (May–June), 480–484.

Yamamoto, H., Sato, K., and Inokuchi, S. 1986. Range imaging system based on binary image accumulation. *Proc. Intl. Conference on Pattern Recognition* (Oct., Paris, France) IEEE, New York, 233–235.

Yariv, A. 1976. Introduction to optical electronics. Holt Rinehart Winston, New York.

Yatagai, T., Idesawa, M., Yamaashi, Y., and Suzuki, M. 1982. Interactive fringe analysis system: Applications to moire contourogram and interferogram. *Opt. Engrg.* **21,** 5, 901.

Yeung, K.K., and Lawrence, P.D. 1986. A low-cost 3D vision system using space-encoded spot projections. In *Proc. SPIE Conference on Optics, Illumination and Image Sensing for Machine Vision* (D.J. Svetkoff, Ed.), Vol. 728 (Oct. 30–31, Cambridge, Mass.), 160–172.

Zuk, D.M., and Dell'eva, M.L. 1983. Three-dimensional vision system for the adaptive suspension vehicle. *Final Report No. 170400-3-F,* ERIM, DARPA 4468, Defense Supply Service, Washington, D.C. (Jan.).

2
3-D Structures from 2-D Images

J.K. AGGARWAL AND C.H. CHIEN

ABSTRACT: In recent years, an important area of research in computer vision has been the recovery or inference of the 3-D information about a scene from its 2-D image. In light of the fascinating power of humans in inferring the 3-D structure of objects from visual images, a great deal of effort has been directed towards the understanding of each module in the human visual system. The results of these efforts have yielded mathematical models for most of these modules. In this chapter, we survey results of a variety of research work conducted in this area using different depth cues, including depth from stereopsis; structure from motion parallax and optical flow, shape from shading, texture, and surface contours; and shape from occluding contours. Also included are two nonanthropomorphic approaches, i.e., structure from volume intersection and shape from spatial encoding, which are closely tied to cues used in the human visual system for inferring 3-D structure from 2-D images. We present the strengths and shortcomings of each approach, and briefly discuss the possibility of combining different approaches in order to obtain more robust and reliable results, and suggest the direction of future research.

1 Introduction

Computer vision researchers have found it extremely frustrating to attempt to duplicate the ease with which a small child is able to discriminate between items in a picture, like, say, people or objects. This capability of the child is all the more impressive since the components of the picture may in reality have constantly changing attributes. For example, people are growing old, or may be in different clothes; objects may have different shapes, or various sizes; a comprehensive definition of trees would require a description of every conceivable variant. While the most sophisticated programs still have great difficulty in solving simple vision tasks, the human visual system can quickly "understand" the labyrinth of vision identification with little effort. Even more fascinating, the world surrounding us is three-dimensional and the images projected onto the retinas of human eyes are essentially two-dimensional. In theory, a single two-dimensional image can be the projection of any three-dimensional scene. This is to say that the problems such as those posed by visual perception tasks constitute a subset of what are called "random problems": problems whose solution requires knowledge of essentially every possible state of a system [Abu-Mostafa and Psaltis 1987]. How can the human visual system interpret perceived images as three-dimensional scenes in times of the order of hundreds of mini-seconds [Ballard 1986]? How can we casually recognize objects even when they are occluded, or in poor illumination conditions? Can we build a machine that can perform certain visual tasks at level no worse than the human visual system? Even though there has been no full-fledged attempt in the computer vision community to duplicate the human visual system in machines, the consensus is that understanding how the human visual perception mechanism works can guide the development of computer vision systems.

A certain amount of progress has been made in the search to identify and isolate particular modules of the human visual system. These include Land and McCann's [1971] demonstration of the computation of lightness, Julesz's [1960, 1967] demonstration of stereoscopic fusion without monocular cues, Horn's [1975] illustration of the highly developed human ability to infer shape from shading, Steven's [1979b] study on the three-dimensional interpretation of surface contours by humans, Marr's [1982] observation of our ability of perceiving silhouettes in terms of three-dimensional shapes, and Ullman's [1979] demonstration of the interpretation of the motion of random dots in two cylinders.

Julesz [1960] devised computer-generated random-dot stereograms to demonstrate stereoscopic fusion without monocular cues. The image for the left eye is a matrix of randomly generated black and white squares. The image for the right eye is made by copying the left image, shifting a square-shaped region at its center slightly to the right, and then providing a new random pattern to fill the gap that the shift creates. If each of the eyes sees only one matrix, the result is the sensation of a square floating in space. Such perceptions are caused solely by the stereo disparity between matching elements in the images.

In more general cases, three-dimensional shapes can also be perceived by the human visual system through motion parallax. In Ullman's [1979] rotating cylinders demonstration, dots painted on the two cylinders were projected orthographically onto a screen as a sequence of frames. Each single frame had the appearance of random dots and was by itself uninterpretable. Only when shown as a continuous sequence did the movement of the dots create the perception of two counterrotating cylinders. This demonstration strongly suggests that both the decomposition of a scene into objects and the recovery of their three-dimensional shapes can be accomplished through their changing appearances as they move.

In some cases, while a single image does not have a unique 3-D interpretation, it often presents a striking appearance of three-dimensionality. Stevens [1979b] suspected that much of the apparent three-dimensionality of single images is due to perceived surface orientation. Three theories on (relative) "depth cues" have been developed. Ittelson [1960] hypothesized that depth cues in the image are unconsciously interpreted in terms of prior visual experience. For instance, it is well known that ellipses appear to be slanted circles, trapezoids appear to be perspective rectangles. Attneave and Frost [1969] postulated that the rules of perspective are implicit in an analog medium representing physical space, within which the representation of an object moves towards a stable state characterized by figural goodness or minimum complexity. For example, the lengths of two intersected contours strongly suggests a spatial orientation. Gibson [1950] introduced a stimulus-response theory of surface perception in which distance, surface orientation, and size constancy are specified by higher-order variables in the image. For example, texture gradients suggest surfaces that appear to slant out of the image plane.

Another source of relative depth cues is shading. It is well known, in the context of facial makeup, that by darkening certain slopes of human faces, those slopes can be made to appear steeper. This is due to the relationship between the surface orientations and reflected light intensity, and could be how the human vision system is based to infer the 3-D structure of the viewed surface, as suggested by Horn [1975].

More fascinating is the ability of our human perceptual system to interpret occluding contours (or silhouettes) in terms of three-dimensional shapes, as pointed out by Marr [1982]. An illustration of this ability is the shadow graph, where an appropriate arrangement of a person's hands may produce shadows of different 3-D shapes, like public figures or a variety of animals.

A considerable amount of work in computer vision has been concentrated on topics corresponding to identifiable modules in the human visual system. For example, substantial progress has been made in depth from stereopsis [Julesz 1960, 1971; Barnard and Fishler 1982; Marr and Poggio 1976, 1976, 1979; Grimson 1981a, 1981b, 1985; Mayhew and Frisby 1981; Kak 1983; Arnold 1978; Arnold and Binford 1980; Baker 1980; Baker and Binford 1981; Moravec 1979, 1980, 1981; Thorpe 1984; Barnard and Thompson 1980; Lucas and Kanade 1981; Ohta and Kanade 1986; Kim and Aggarwal 1985; Barnard 1986; Terzopoulos et al. 1987; Hoff and Ahuja 1986]; structure from motion [Ullman 1979; Roach and Aggarwal 1979, 1980; Webb and Aggarwal 1982, 1983; Chen 1985; Nagel 1979, 1981a, 1981b, 1986; Tsai and Huang 1981, 1984; Tsai et al. 1982; Huang and Tsai 1981; Longuet-Higgins 1984; Mitiche et al. 1985a; Yen and Huang 1983a, 1983b; Aggarwal and Mitiche 1985b] and optical flow [Prazdny 1980, 1983; Ballard and Kimball 1983; Mitiche 1984a, 1984b, 1986; Kanatani 1985a, 1985b, 1985c; Waxman 1984; Wohn and Waxman 1985; Subbarao and

Waxman 1985; Blostein and Huang 1984; Horn and Schunk 1981; Mitiche et al. 1987; Bottema and Roth 1979; Aggarwal et al. 1981; Aggarwal and Mitiche 1985a]; shape from shading [Horn 1975, 1977; Horn and Sjoberg 1979; Woodham 1979, 1981; Brooks 1979; Strat 1979; Ikeuchi and Horn 1979, 1981; Bruss 1981; Coleman and Jain 1981, 1982; Pentland 1984a, 1984b; Ikeuchi 1984, 1987; Grankot and Chellappa 1987], texture and surface contours [Stevens 1979a, 1979b, 1981; Attneave and Frost 1969; Gibson 1950; Bajcsy and Lieberman 1976; Kender 1978, 1979, 1980; Ikeuchi 1980; Witkin 1981; Ohta et al. 1981; Davis et al. 1983; Sugihara 1985], and line drawings [Guzman 1986; Huffman 1971, 1977a, 1977b; Clowes 1971; Waltz 1975; Thorpe and Shafer 1983; Mackworth 1973, 1977; Kanade 1980, 1981; Falk 1972; Sugihara 1982, 1986; Barnard and Pentland 1983]; and shape from occluding contours (including model-based vision) [Marr 1982; Marr and Nishihara 1978; Barrow and Tenenbaum 1981; Brady and Yuille 1984; Giblin 1987; Brooks 1981; Besl and Jain 1985; Mulgaonkar et al. 1982; Wallace and Wintz 1980; Fischler and Bolles 1981; Fisher 1983; Lee and Fu 1983; Goad 1986; Ben-Arie and Meiri 1986; Lowe 1986; Chien 1986; Chien and Aggarwal 1987; Thompson and Mundy 1987]. Efforts have also been directed toward the study of two nonanthropomorphic approaches, namely, structure from volume intersection [Martin and Aggarwal 1983; Martin et al. 1983; Chien and Aggarwal 1984, 1985, 1986a, 1986b, 1986c; Kim and Aggarwal 1986a, 1986b], and shape from spatial encoding [Pennington and Will 1970; Will and Pennington 1971, 1972; Potmesil and Freeman 1972; Frobin and Hierholzer 1981, 1982a, 1982b; McPherson et al. 1982; Tio et al. 1982; Hall et al. 1982; Posdamer and Altschuler 1982; Potmesil 1983; Le Moigne and Waxman 1984; Stockman and Hu 1986; Wang et al. 1985, 1987; Wang and Aggarwal 1987]. These two approaches are closely tied to cues used in the human visual system for inferring the 3-D structure from 2-D images. The volume intersection technique is primarily used in model construction. It can be likened to a learning process in which people try to understand an unfamiliar object by observing the object from different viewpoints and piecing together all this information to infer the 3-D structure of the object. The shape from the spatial encoding process is a restricted form of the shape from surface contours methodology. By projecting structured light onto a 3-D scene and observing the distortion of the structured pattern (e.g., grid), the shape of the object can be inferred from a single view.

In this chapter, we will survey results of a variety of research work on these topics. As recovery of 3-D information from 2-D images is the most active research area in computer vision, it is neither our intent nor is it possible to include all the research work in this area in a single chapter. Instead, we present some sections reflecting the current status of each of the following topics: depth from stereopsis, structure from motion, structure from optical flow, shape from shading, shape from texture and surface contours, shape from line drawings, shape from occluding contours, structure from volume intersection, and shape from spatial encoding, in that order. We will also briefly discuss the possibility of combining different approaches in order to obtain more robust and reliable results, and we will suggest future research direction.

2 Depth from Stereopsis

Stereo vision is one of the most extensive areas of research in computer vision. The process of stereo vision essentially measures the disparities of two images of a (3-D) scene, and uses them to recover the depth information of surfaces in the scene. Disparity is measured over each pair of corresponding points or features (in the two images), and different disparities indicate different relative depths. A paradigm of the stereo vision process involves (1) camera modeling, (2) feature extraction, (3) feature matching, (4) depth computation, and (5) interpolation. [Grimson 1981a,b]

Shown in Figure 2.1 is the configuration of a nonconvergent binocular imaging system, a typical camera model used by most researchers working

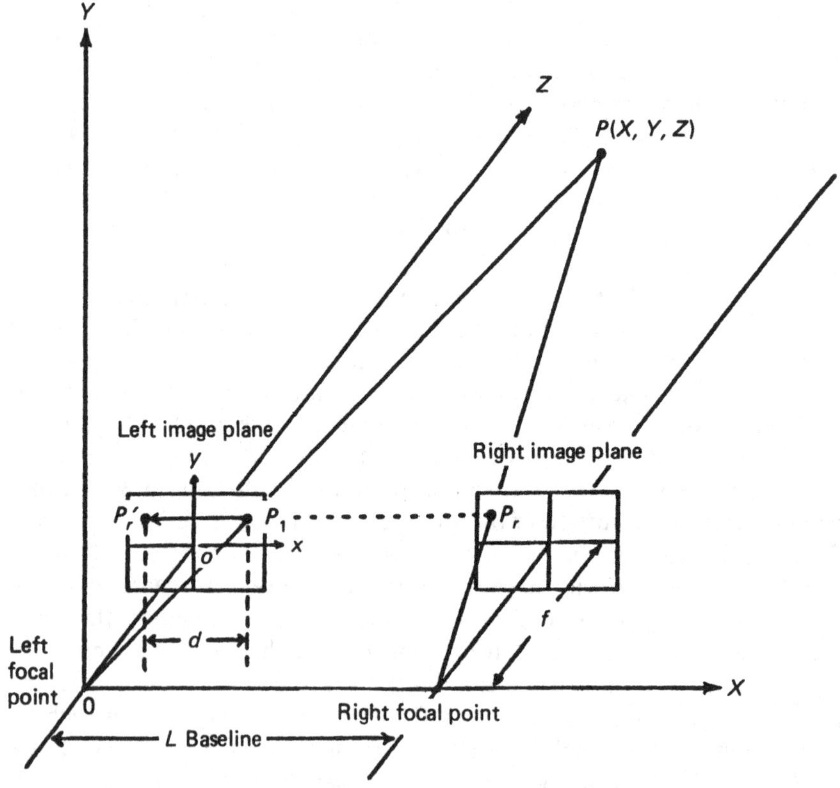

FIGURE 2.1. The configuration of a nonconvergent binocular imaging system.

on stereo vision. The two cameras are separated by a baseline L, with both optical axes parallel to the z-axis and image coordinate systems aligned with the x- and y-axes. The images of a point P in the 3-space are P_l and P_r in the two image planes, respectively, with the disparity equal to $| P_l - P_r |$. Any point in 3-space, together with the centers of projection of two camera systems, defines an epipolar plane. The intersection of an epipolar plane with an image plane (e.g., $\overline{P_l P_r}$) is called an epipolar line.

While stereo vision allows us to recover information about the location of surfaces in 3-space, establishing correspondences between points in the two images in order to recover depth information is not a trivial task. A computation theory of the stereo process for the human visual system was proposed by Marr and Poggio [1976, 1979]. According to this theory, the algorithm by which the human visual processor solves the stereo matching problem consists of five steps: (1) The left and right images are each filtered at different orientations with bar masks of four sizes that increase with eccentricity, the shape of these masks is given by $\nabla^2 G$, the Laplacian of a Gaussian function Marr and Hildreth 1980; (2) zero-crossings in the filtered images are found along horizontal scan lines; (3) for each mask size, matching takes place between zero-crossing segments of the same sign and roughly the same orientation in the two images, for a range of disparities up to about the width of the mask's central region; (4) the output of the wide masks can control vergence movements, thus causing smaller masks to come into correspondence; and (5) when a correspondence is achieved, it is stored in a dynamic buffer, called the 2½ -D sketch [Marr 1982; Marr and Nishihara 1978].

The Marr–Poggio model of human stereo vision was implemented by Grimson [1981a,b]. It is found that the performance of the implementation coincides well with that of human subjects over a broad range of random dot test cases obtained from the literature, including defocusing, compression, and the introduction of various kinds of masking noise to one image of a random dot stereo pair. When stereo pairs of natural images were tested, they provide some difficulty for the implementation. For example, the regular pattern of the windows provides a strong false-targets problem. If the optical axes were aligned at the level of the building, the zero-crossings corresponding to the windows were all assigned a correct disparity; if the optical axes were aligned with trees in front of the building, the windows were assigned an incorrect disparity due to the regular pattern of zero-crossings associated with them [Grimson 1981a]. The same problem is encountered by human observers, though. It is argued that other visual information besides disparity (such as texture boundaries) may drive eye convergence movements to avoid the false-targets problem. In the implementation, the module finds all acceptable stereo matchings and writes them into the 2½-D sketch, the content of which may be altered based on more global information.

Later, Mayfew and Frisby [1981] proposed the so-called BRPS (binocular raw primal sketch) conjecture:

> The process of human binocular combination integrally relates the extraction of disparity information with the construction of raw primal sketch assertions.

Based on this conjecture, a stereo algorithm called STEROEDGE was developed. By exploiting figural continuity, the algorithm demonstrates that curvilinear grouping rules can successfully disambiguate zero-crossings and peak matches in both natural and random dot stereograms. The algorithm returns edge-segment and angle assertions to which disparity assignment is tied. Figural continuity was implemented as the piecewise local binocular grouping of adjacent peaks or zero-crossing matches of the same contrast sign. The type of figural grouping employed is similar to the process of curvilinear aggregation described by Marr and Poggio [1976].

The notion of figural continuity was also included in the Marr-Poggio-Grimson algorithm [Grimson 1985], a modified version of the original Marr-Poggio stereo algorithm, which embodies the modifications suggested by a number of psychophysical experiments. In the modified algorithm, a figural continuity constraint was applied to distinguish correct matches from random feature matches by restricting the accepted matches to those extended contour segments whose length is sufficiently large. The algorithm was tested on a laboratory scene with many of the characteristics of industrial robotics situations and aerial photographs of natural and artificial terrain.

While all of these studies address the psychophysical and biological aspects of the human visual system, there is another line of studies that is not biologically motivated and which examines computational aspects in various application domains.

Baker [1980] presented an algorithm for stereo matching. It used an edge-based line-by-line stereo correlation scheme. The processing consists of (1) extracting edge descriptions for a stereo pair of images, (2) linking these edges to their nearest neighbors to obtain the edge connectivity structure, and then (3) cooperatively removing those edge correspondences determined to be in error. Later, this algorithm was modified by adding an intensity correlation step, which correlates the edge descriptions on the basis of local edge properties (such as contrast, image slope and intensity to either side), in order to fill the gaps between matched edges [Baker and Binford 1981].

Moravec [1979, 1980, 1981] developed a vision system for a Stanford Cart. The cart used several kinds of stereo to locate objects around it in 3-D and to plan an obstacle-avoiding path to a desired destination. It moved one meter every ten to fifteen minutes in lurches. At each pause, it took nine pictures and used features extracted by the interest operator [Moravec 1977] in the fifth image to match features from previous positions. In the case of correct matches, the estimated distance to the feature was inversely proportional to its displacement from one image to another. Next, in order to model the distance uncertainty, it considered each of the thirty-six image pairings as a stereo baseline, of which the corresponding estimated distance added a little normal curve to the histogram. The standard deviation of the normal curve is inversely proportional to the baseline, and the area under the curve scaled by the correlation and shift of the feature in the direction orthogonal to the baseline. The distance to the feature was then determined by the largest peak in the resulting histogram. This approach provides an efficient way of finding the strongest cluster of mutually agreeing measurements, and thus a very reliable distance measurement.

A similar approach was taken by Thorpe [1984] in his FIDO algorithm, but using only two cameras. The FIDO algorithm is summarized as follows: (1) A pair of stereo images are taken of the environment, and certain features are extracted from the two images; (2) features in the right image are matched to the old (previous) right image in order to identify objects in the scenes and calculate the vehicle motion; (3) features in the two images are matched in order to obtain "depth" information; (4) the locations of all the features are examined, and a path is planned that does not go through the feature points; and (5) the robot is then instructed to move, and the next pair of images is taken.

Kim and Aggarwal [1985] have developed an efficient algorithm for recovering range information of 3-D objects from stereo intensity images. First, feature points (i.e., zero-crossing points) are extracted from the two images. The corresponding feature points in the two images are matched based on the vertical connectivities of their zero-crossing patterns (Figure 2.2). A relaxation process is used to reduce or eliminate ambiguities that may arise in matching zero-crossing points in the two images. The initial weight to each candidate matched point is assigned according to the similarities of the zero-crossing pattern and the intensity gradients. The relaxation process then proceeds based on the figural continuity, the disparity continuity, and the certainty of matches of the connected zero-crossing points. The use of the similarities of the zero-crossing patterns and the intensity gradients in the initial weight assignment yields fairly reliable initial weights, which in turn result in fast convergence and accurate matches. The authors report that about 90% and 98% of the feature points are matched after the fourth and seventh iterations, respectively.

Once correspondence between each pair of matched feature points is established, the disparity values are measured and used to compute (3-D coordinates of the feature point) as follows:

$$(X, Y, Z) = \frac{L}{d}(x, y, f), \tag{2.1}$$

where L is the length of the base line, f is the focal length, and (X, Y, Z) and (x, y) are 3-D and 2-D coordinates of the feature point, respectively.

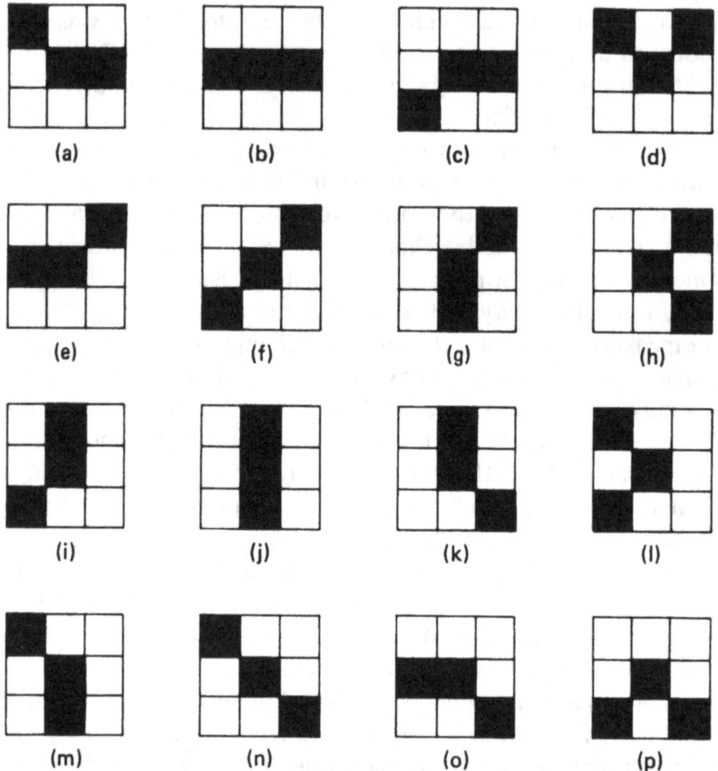

FIGURE 2.2. Zero-crossing patterns used in Kim and Aggarwal's stereo matching algorithm. Reprinted with permission from Kim and Aggarwal [1985], © 1985 IEEE.

Barnard [1986] proposed a stochastic optimization approach to stereo matching. First, the stereo matching problem is defined in terms of finding a disparity map that satisfies two competing constraints: (1) Matched points should have similar image intensity, and (2) the disparity map should be smooth. These constraints are expressed in the form of an energy function

$$E = \sum_{k} \| I_L(k) - I_R(i, j + D,(K)) \| \lambda \| \delta D(K) \| , \tag{2.2}$$

where I_L and I_R are the intensities in the left and right images, and $D(k)$ is the disparity between the kth lattice point and (i, j). This function is similar to the nonquadratic Tikhonov stabilizer proposed for stereo by Poggio et al. [1985], and can be evaluated locally. A simulated annealing algorithm was used to find a disparity that may have very low energy. They claimed that their approach provides a dense array of disparities, eliminating the need for interpolation. Results were shown for a sparse random-dot stereogram, a vertical aerial stereogram, and an oblique ground-level scene with occlusion boundaries.

A slightly different approach has been taken by Terzopoulos et al. [1987], which is based on matching multiple, multidimensional signals that have been deformed with respect to one another. The problem is formulated as the minimization of an energy measure that combines a similarity functional with a controlled continuity constraint, and solved by a deterministic dynamic system governed by a set of coupled, first-order differential equations (see Terzopoulos et al. [1987] for details). The system finds an optimal approximation at a coarse scale, then tracks it continuously to a fine scale, thus avoiding bad local minima. This continuation approach to finding and tracking good local minima offers an efficient deterministic alternative to the stochastic optimization technique proposed by Barnard [1986]. Experimental results on images of natural scenes are provided to demonstrate the effectiveness of the approach.

Hoff and Ahuja [1986] have presented an integrated approach to extracting surfaces from stereo images. The approach integrates feature matching, contour detection, and surface interpolation into one process. Along with performing matching and interpolation, depth and ridge contours are extracted so as to enforce surface smoothness everywhere except across these contours. The authors claim that the computational effort in their approach is relatively uniform in its distribution across various integrated processes as a consequence of integration, and the approach lends itself to a parallel implementation and does not require any major iterative steps. As a result, the errors occur mainly around the occluding boundaries and are usually within a pixel of disparity.

3 Structure from Motion

The problem of determining the structure and motion of objects in space from images is currently a topic of major interest in computer vision for its theoretical and practical challenges. Research in computer vision has produced numerous papers on various facets of the problem. The overall approach consists of the two obvious and logical steps: (1) Compute observables in the images, and (2) relate these to structures and events in space. Various observables have been considered: points, lines, occluding contours, optical flow, etc.

In principle, the observation of a number of points in two or more views can yield the position of these points in space and the relative displacement between the viewing systems. This line of reasoning using points as observables has been pursued by Ullman [1979], Roach and Aggarwal [1979, 1980], Webb and Aggarwal [1982, 1983], Chen [1985], Nagel [1979, 1981a, b], Tsai and Huang [1981, 1984], Tsai et al. [1982], Huang and Tsai [1981], Longuet-Higgins [1981, 1984], and Mitiche et al. [1985], among many other researchers.

The basic equations used in Roach and Aggarwal [1979, 1980] are the ones that relate the 3-D coordinates (X, Y, Z) of a space point to its 2-D projective coordinates (x, y)

$$x = F\frac{a_{11}(X - X_0) + a_{12}(Y - Y_0) + a_{13}(Z - Z_0)}{a_{31}(X - X_0) + a_{32}(Y - Y_0) + a_{33}(Z - Z_0)} \tag{2.3}$$

$$y = F\frac{a_{21}(X - X_0) + a_{22}(Y - Y_0) + a_{23}(Z - Z_0)}{a_{31}(X - X_0) + a_{32}(Y - Y_0) + a_{33}(Z - Z_0)} \tag{2.4}$$

where F is the focal length, (X_0, Y_0, Z_0) are the 3-D coordinates of the lens center, and $a_{11}, a_{12}, \ldots, a_{33}$ are functions of (Θ, Φ, Ψ), which specify the orientation of the camera in the global reference system.

Five points in two views yielded 27 unknowns and 20 nonlinear equations [Roach and Aggarwal 1979, 1980]. The number of unknowns was reduced to 20 by setting the six parameters of the first camera position and choosing one positive constant for fixing the scaling factor. The nonlinear equations were then solved by an iterative finite difference Levenberg-Marguardt algorithm [Levenberg 1944]. The procedure typically converged to the correct answer within 15 seconds on a Cyber 170/50 and hence is reasonably efficient. It is suggested that a considerably overdetermined system of equations is needed in a noisy environment to attain good accuracy of the results. For example, two views of twelve or even fifteen points and three views of seven or eight points are usually needed in noisy cases.

Webb and Aggarwal [1982] presented a method for recovering the 3-D structure of moving rigid and jointed objects from several single camera views. The fixed-axis assumption is adopted to interpret images of moving objects. The fixed-axis assumption asserts that every rigid object movement consists of a translation plus a rotation about an axis which is fixed in direction for a short period of time. It is shown that, under the fixed-axis assumption, fixing any point on a rigid moving object causes the other points to trace out circles in planes normal to the fixed axis. Under parallel projection, these circles project into ellipses in the image plane. The structure of the rigid object can be recovered to within a reflection by finding the equation describing the ellipses.

Unlike Roach and Aggarwal [1979, 1980], who solve the motion parameters at once, thus creating a large search space, Nagel [1979] has proposed a technique that reduces the dimension of the search space through the elimination of unknown variables. The important observation Nagel made was that the translation vector can be eliminated and the rotation matrix can be solved separately. A rotation matrix is completely specified by three parameters, namely, the orientation of the rotation axis and the rotation angle around this axis. It is shown that if measurements of five points in two views are available, then three equations can be written and the three rotation parameters can be solved for separately from the translation parameters. The distance of the configuration of points from the view is arbitrarily fixed and the translation vector can then be determined.

Ullman [1979] in his highly acclaimed thesis proved the following theoretical result:

Given three distinct orthographic projections of four non-coplanar points in a rigid configuration, the structure and motion compatible with the three views are uniquely determined up to a reflection about the image plane.

The assumption of parallel projection makes it possible to find surface structure in closed form when four noncoplanar points are seen in three distinct views. However, also as a consequence of the parallel projection assumption, the structure deduced could be reflected in depth and produce the same image, and the absolute distance from the camera to an object cannot be determined uniquely.

Tsai and Huang [1981] take an approach significantly different from this approach. Instead of considering the motion of individual points, they consider the motion of a planar patch ($AX + BY + CZ = 1$) characterized by eight points. By exploiting the projected geometrical constraints and the notion of rigid motion, equations can be written to relate the coordinates of the image points in the two frames

$$x' = \frac{a_1x + a_2y + a_3}{a_7x + a_8y + 1} \tag{2.5}$$

$$y' = \frac{a_4x + a_5y + a_6}{a_7x + a_8y + 1}, \tag{2.6}$$

where a_1–a_8 are the eight pure parameters and can be expressed in terms of the focal length, the structure parameters (A,B,C), and the motion parameters $N_x,N_y,N_z,\Theta,T_x,T_y$, and T_z (N specifies the rotation axis, Θ is the rotational angle, and **T** is the translational vector). After a tedious algebraic manipulation a sixth-order polynomial may be formulated, such that its coefficients are expressed in terms of pure parameters and its solution yields (together with additional manipulation) the motion and structure parameters in terms of scale. Although potentially six real roots may result from solving a sixth-order polynomial, the authors reported that aside from a scale factor for the translation parameters, the number of real solutions never exceeds two in their simulation.

Later, the problem of a curved surface patch in motion was investigated in Tsai and Huang [1984]. The equations that relate the coordinates of the image points in two successive frames for points on a curved surface patch are very similar to the ones obtained for a planar surface patch. The corresponding mapping is given by

$$x' = \frac{(r_1x + r_2y + r_3)Z + T_X}{(r_7x + r_8y + r_9)Z + T_Z} \tag{2.7}$$

$$y' = \frac{(r_4x + r_5y + r_6)Z + T_Y}{(r_7x + r_8y + r_9)Z + T_Z} \tag{2.8}$$

where r_is are the entries in the rotation matrix **R**. It can be shown that by equating Z in Equations (7) and (8), we obtain

$$[x'y'1]\,\mathbf{E}\,[xy1]^T = 0, \tag{2.9}$$

where $\mathbf{E} = [e_{ij}]$, and e_is are called essential parameters. Here, two main results were established concerning the existence and uniqueness of the solutions. First, the actual 3-D motion parameters can be determined uniquely given **E**, and can be computed by taking the singular value decomposition of **E** without having to solve nonlinear equations. Furthermore, given the image correspondences of eight object points in general positions, the eight essential parameters can be determined uniquely by solving eight linear equations. The proofs of the claims are quite lengthy and involved and will not be discussed here.

Longuet-Higgins [1981, 1984] worked independently to obtain results similar to those just described. He derived the **E** matrix and presented a method to recover **R** from **T** and **E** using tensor and vector analysis. Interested readers are referred to Longuet-Higgins [1981, 1984].

Mitiche et al. [1985] developed a different formulation to solve the structure and motion problem by exploiting the principle of conservation of distance with respect to rigid motion. The principle of conservation of distance simply states that distance between points on an object does not change as a result of rigid motion. A scenario of a static scene with a mobile viewing system was chosen. Let each point P_i be described by:

$$X_i = \lambda_i x_i \tag{2.10a}$$

$$X'_i = \gamma_i x'_i \tag{2.10b}$$

$$Y_i = \lambda_i y_i \tag{2.11a}$$

$$Y'_i = \gamma_i y'_i \tag{2.11b}$$

$$Z_i = (1 - \lambda_i)f \tag{2.12a}$$

$$Z'_i = (1 - \gamma_i)f', \tag{2.12b}$$

where λ_i and γ_i are the unknown parameters that determine the distance of the point P_i to the two image frames S and S', and f and f' are the focal length of the two camera systems. Note that the coordinate system may be chosen so that the values of λs and γs are greater than 1. It can be proved that based on the principle of conservation of distance between two points P_i and P_i in space,

$$\begin{aligned}(\lambda_i x_i - \lambda_j x_j)^2 + (\lambda_i y_i - \lambda_j y_j)^2 + (\lambda_j - \lambda_i)^2 f^2 \\ = (\gamma_i x'_i - \gamma_j x'_j)^2 + (\gamma_i y'_i - \gamma_j y'_j)^2 + (\gamma_j - \gamma_i)^2 f'^2.\end{aligned} \tag{2.13}$$

It may be that each point P_i contributes two unknowns λ_i and γ_i, and each pair of points (P_i, P_j) produces one second-order equation. Therefore, five points yield ten equations in nine unknowns with one variable chosen to fix the scaling factor. Note that each equation involves only four of the unknowns. Note also that the formulation so far does not involve the parameters of the displacement between the two cameras. Because these motion parameters do not appear in the equations and because only some of the unknowns in position appear in each equation, the authors reported that the resulting system of equations can be solved quite efficiently using existing numerical iterative algorithms.

Once the position of the points in space has been computed, determining the relative position of the cameras becomes a simple matter. Take four noncoplanar points and let **A** and **A**$'$ be the matrices of homogeneous coordinates of these points in S and S' respectively. If **M** is the transformation matrix in the homogeneous coordinate system we have

$$\mathbf{A}' = \mathbf{M}\,\mathbf{A}. \tag{2.14}$$

The rotation axis direction, rotational angle, and translation vector can then be recovered directly from **M**.

Mitiche et al. presented a method that uses the principle of invariance of angular configuration (between each pair of lines) with respect to rigid motion. Based on this principle,

$$\left[\frac{L_1 \cdot L_2}{|L_1||L_2|}\right]^2 = \left[\frac{L_1' \cdot L_2'}{|L_1'||L_2'|}\right]^2, \tag{2.15}$$

where L_1, L_2, and L_1', L_2' are the vector representations of the two lines in frames S and S', respectively. In their formulation, each line contributes one unknown (per view) to the system of equations, which accounts for the inability to recover the line orientation in space from a single view. With n views, $n - 1$ constraints on the orientation of lines for each possible pairing in the set of observed lines can be obtained. For example, if we consider four lines in space (therefore six possible different pairs of lines) and three views, then simple enumeration gives us twelve equations in twelve unknowns over the three views. The equations have the following properties: (a) The equations are of second order in each of the variables, (b) only four of the twelve unknowns appear in every equation, and (c) the motion parameters are not involved in the equations. The authors reported that the system of equations is numerically well behaved. Once the orientation of the lines in space is solved, the rotational components of motion between the viewing systems are then readily recovered from these orientations. The translation components of motion may also be recovered after this step.

Unlike the use of point correspondences, which usually requires the correspondence relationships to be specified between two adjacent image frames, it was shown that determining the structure and motion parameters using line correspondences from two views is in general a highly underconstrained problem [Aggarwal and Mitiche 1985b]. Various restrictions have to be imposed on the 3-D line configuration for the existence of a unique solution [Yen and Huang 1983b]. Also, we notice that the two approaches [Yen and Huang 1983b] and [Mitiche et al. (submitted for publication)] are different in the sense that Yen and Huang solve for the motion parameters first and then for the configuration of lines in space, while Mitiche et al. solve for the configuration of lines (the orientation of lines in space) and then for the motion parameters.

4 Structure from Optical Flow

Optical flow is the field of instantaneous apparent velocities of points on the surface of objects moving in space. Psychological and neurophysiological evidence has long demonstrated the importance of optical flow in human and animal visual perceptual mechanisms. In this section, we will discuss the recent developments in incorporating optical flow information in the computation of structure and motion.

Prazdny [1980, 1983] has discussed the possibility of using optical flow information to recover the relative depth of points in space and local surface orientation. Here, optical flow is defined to be the instantaneous distribution of the angular velocity of the projection ray passing though an object point P. The angular velocity, $\mathbf{a}_s$, comprises two components, a translational component $\mathbf{a}_t$ and a rotational component $\mathbf{a}_r$. The rotational component, $\mathbf{a}_r$, of the angular velocity is a property of the moving object and does not vary from point to point on the object. The translation component $\mathbf{a}_t$, however, is affected by the distance from the point to the projection center O. Or

$$\mathbf{a}_s = \mathbf{a}_r + \mathbf{a}_t = \mathbf{a}_r + \frac{\mathbf{TP}}{\sin \beta} \tag{2.16}$$

and

$$|a_t| = \frac{T \sin \beta}{S}, \tag{2.17}$$

where $\mathbf{T}$ is the 3-D translation vector, $\mathbf{P}$ is the positional vector of point P, β is the angle between $\mathbf{P}$ and $\mathbf{T}$, and S is the distance between the object point P and the origin O. This equation is a manifestation of the fact that although all points on an object undergo the same translation $\mathbf{T}$, the portion of the translation that is perceived as motion in the image plane depends on both the distance between the object point and the origin as well as the direction of translation. Only the translation components perpendicular to the positional vector show on the image plane as motion, whereas velocity components parallel to the projection direction are lost in the process of image formation.

One can then exploit the difference in the translation component, $\mathbf{a}_t$, of the angular velocity of two points to discern the relative depth between the two points. The rotational component is the same for all points on the same object and is factored out when angular velocities of two points are subtracted; we therefore have

$$\frac{(\mathbf{a}_{s1} - \mathbf{a}_{s2}) \cdot \mathbf{p}_1}{(\mathbf{a}_{s1} - \mathbf{a}_{s2}) \cdot \mathbf{p}_2} = \frac{S_1}{S_2} \tag{2.18}$$

where $\mathbf{a}_{s1}$ and $\mathbf{a}_{s2}$ denote the optical flow created by points P_1 and P_2, respectively; $\mathbf{P}_1$ and $\mathbf{P}_2$ are the unit vectors in the direction of P_1 and P_2, respectively; and S_1 and S_2 are the distances from the object points p_1 and p_2 to the origin. It has also been shown that the local surface orientation relative to the viewing direction can be recovered.

Ballard and Kimball [1983] have proposed a method that combines depth and optical flow to recover rigid body motion. The 3-D motion is represented by three sets of parameters in this research: (1) three positional parameters that specify the displacement of the origin of the local coordinate system centered on the rigid body with respect to the origin of the global reference system, (2) three translational parameters that describe the translation velocity of the local origin, and (3) three parameters to specify the rotational velocity. The algorithm for recovering rigid body motion is partitioned into two steps.

First, 3-D velocity is computed from the 2-D optical flow field and the depth map. The authors recommend the gradient-based method developed in Horn and Schunk [1981] for computing the 2-D flow field. The Z component of the 3-D velocity $\mathbf{V} = (u, v, V_z)$ can then be obtained (assuming that the depth map $Z(X, Y)$ is available) by

$$V_Z \approx \frac{1}{\Delta t}[Z(X + u\Delta t,\ Y + v\Delta t,\ t + \Delta t) - Z(X, Y, t)], \tag{2.19}$$

where u and v are the 2-D flow velocities.

Next, the motion parameters are derived from the 3-D velocity. The positional parameters (the position of the origin of local coordinate in the global reference system) can be found directly from the knowledge of 3-D velocity. Assuming that at reference time $t = 0$, the origin of the local coordinate system coincides with that of the global reference system, then at time t greater than 0, the position of the origin of the local coordinate system is

$$P_o(t + \Delta t) = \mathbf{P}_o(t) + \mathbf{V}\Delta t. \tag{2.20}$$

For determining the other motion parameters, the authors suggest a Hough transform approach. The search space is reduced by partitioning the search into two stages: First, find the rotation axis N and then the rotational angle Θ and the translation vector $\mathbf{T}$. The observation that the rotational axis N is perpendicular to the direction of acceleration, A, at any point in the body, provided that the body is not subjected to large external forces, is used for finding the direction of the rotational axis. Since the 3-D velocity has been derived from the optical flow field and the depth map, two accelerations can be determined from three successive measurements of $\mathbf{V}$. Or

$$\mathbf{A}_1 = \frac{\mathbf{V}_2 - \mathbf{V}_1}{\Delta t}, \tag{2.21}$$

$$\mathbf{A}_2 = \frac{\mathbf{V}_3 - \mathbf{V}_2}{\Delta t}, \tag{2.22}$$

and

$$\mathbf{N} = \frac{\mathbf{A}_1 \times \mathbf{A}_2}{|\mathbf{A}_1 \times \mathbf{A}_2|}. \tag{2.23}$$

The direction of $\mathbf{N}$ can be determined using the voting mechanism embedded in the Hough transform if more than one pair of acceleration vectors is available. The rotational angle Θ and the translation vector $\mathbf{T}$ can also be found through a similar Hough process using the following constraint

$$\mathbf{V} = \mathbf{T} + \Theta \cdot \mathbf{N} \times \mathbf{P}, \tag{2.24}$$

where $\mathbf{P}$ is the positional vector of the point P under consideration. Here only $\mathbf{T}$ and Θ are unknown. A Hough transform process similar to the one used for recovering the direction of the rotational axis can be employed here for recovering these parameters.

Furthermore, the authors have suggested a top-down refinement process to locate the optical flow boundaries. The basic assumption is that flow parameters can be used to find the 3-D motion parameters as demonstrated herein. If adjacent neighbors in the image plane cease to predict similar 3-D motion parameters, then it is highly likely that a boundary exists in the neighborhood under consideration and multiple 3-D objects, each moving with a different translation and rotation velocity, are present in the viewing field. Finally, the concept of parallel computation of the optical flow and rigid body motion was proposed. The justification for parallel computation is that optical flow computation in the interior of a region (which is not affected by the underconstrained situation occurring at boundaries) can be used in estimating the 3-D motion parameters. The availability of the 3-D velocity can then be used to locate the optical flow boundaries. A parallel implementation can facilitate both the top-down location of the flow boundaries and the bottom-up computation of the 3-D motion parameters.

Some theoretical results were obtained by Mitiche [1984a,b, 1986] concerning the recovery of the 3-D motion from the 2-D point position and optical flow field. In Mitiche [1984a], it was established that under the parallel projection model, the structure and motion of a rigid structure of four points can be found provided that the points' image positions and optical velocities are given. The observation that the distance between any two points on an object that undergoes a rigid motion does not change with time is exploited. It can be shown that the following equation always holds in rigid motion:

$$(\mathbf{V}_P - \mathbf{V}_Q)\cdot\mathbf{L} = 0 \tag{2.25}$$

where $\mathbf{V}_P$ and $\mathbf{V}_Q$ stands for the instantaneous velocities at points P and Q, respectively; and $\mathbf{L}$ is the vector connecting these two points. Also notice that the 3-D motion can be related to 2-D motion (i.e., optical flow) by the following equations:

$$V_X = uZ + xV_Z \tag{2.26}$$

$$V_Y = vZ + yV_Z. \tag{2.27}$$

These equations directly relate the 3-D motion (V_X, V_Y, V_z) to the 2-D point position (x,y) and optical flow velocity (u,v). Combining all these facts, it can be shown that four points P_1,P_2,P_3, and P_4 produce six unknown structure and motion parameters, namely, Z_2,Z_3,Z_4, which are the depths of the space points (Z_1 being arbitrarily chosen to fix the scaling factor); T_Z, which represents the translation component ni the Z-direction (translation in the X- and Y-directions being identical to the optical flow components u and v in a viewer-centered, parallel projection configuration); and (N_X,N_Y,N_Z), which denote the direction of the rotational axis with $N_X^2 + N_Y^2 + N_Z^2 = 1$. All possible pairings of these four points give rise to six equations. Thus, it is possible to solve for the motion parameters using four point correspondences over two successive frames with the aid of optical flow.

Furthermore, the formulation using the central projection model and a stereoscopy setup was investigated in Mitiche [1984b, 1986]. It was shown that if the correspondence relationship is established and the displacement between the binocular views is specified, the motion of points in space can be uniquely recovered.

Mitiche noted the difficulty in computing optical flow reliably in real situations. He also suggested a gradient-based method for optical flow computation. Gradient-based techniques rely on an equation that relates optical flow to the spatial and temporal changes in images:

$$\frac{\partial f}{\partial x}u + \frac{\partial f}{\partial y}v + \frac{\partial f}{\partial t} = 0. \tag{2.28}$$

Here f is the image function, t is time, x and y are the image coordinates, and u and v are the flow velocities. A single equation alone is of course not sufficient to determine the two unknowns u and v. The possibility of using image functions other than illuminance for specifying other equations was investigated. Equations can be specified using pictures sensed in different spectral bands or by using various feature images computed from the intensity image using different spatial operators. This multiconstraint technique was later successfully implemented [Mitiche et al. 1987]. Results show that if the flow magnitude is reasonably small, the flow velocity can be reliably estimated using multiple sets of images.

If the surface of the 3-D object can be decomposed into a collection of planar patches ($Z = px + gy + r$), Kanatani [1985a] has shown that under perspective projection, the motion of a point on a plane induces optical flow, which can be written analytically as

$$u = u_0 + Ax + By + (Ex + Fy)x \tag{2.29}$$

$$v = v_0 + Cx + Dy + (Ex + Fy)y, \tag{2.30}$$

where the eight "flow parameters" (u_0,v_0,A,B,C,D,E,F) are functions of the focal length and twelve structure and motion parameters. The structure and motion parameters are p, q, and r, which specify the surface orientation in space, (T_X,T_Y,T_Z), which is the translation vector and (N_x,N_y,N_z), which is the instantaneous rotation velocity.

The procedure to recover the structure and motion parameters through the observed flow parameters is divided into two stages. First the flow parameters are detected from a given image sequence. The structure and motion parameters can then be computed from these flow parameters. The second stage, computation of the structure and motion parameters from the flow parameters, is performed by solving some complicated nonlinear simultaneous equations. To solve for the flow parameters, a multiconstraint method similar to the one proposed in Mitiche et al. [1987] was used. The idea is that if we can find a sufficient number of independent feature functions on the image sequence (eight or more), then the flow parameters can be obtained by solving a linear set of equations. Kanatani has suggested feature functions such as various line integrals along a closed image curve or the surface integrals over the area enclosed by a closed image curve.

Waxman [1984] has proposed an image flow paradigm which takes an image sequence as input and deduces a variety of information relating to the structure and motion of objects in space. The central theme of this paradigm analyzes the motion of a small but finite textured surface patch (either planar or quadric) moving in space. Contours that usually correspond to texture edges on the surface patch are extracted using edge detection and tracking routines. The evolution of these contours over time can then be used to derive the deformation parameters, which relate closely to the local optical flow. Finally, a kinematic analysis, which interprets these deformation parameters as one or more possible surface structures in rigid body motion, is brought in to obtain the 3-D interpretation of motion.

The overall paradigm addresses the problem in a more general setting, that is, an entire scene composed of several objects and background executing relative rigid body motions with respect to the observer. The segmentation process must be brought in at this stage to partition the images into regions. Contours are extracted from each image, and the sequence of evolving contours is stacked to form a stream tube. The normal flow component around each contour over several frames can be estimated and the deformation parameters for the neighborhood can be derived from a stream tube. The analysis is then extended over a larger neighborhood to obtain the second-order approximation to the flow. The compatibility of the deformation parameters is used as the criterion to merge adjacent neighborhoods into analytic regions. The kinematic analysis is then performed for each analytic region to obtain one or more 3-D interpretations of the structure of the surface patch and its relative spatial motion.

5 Shape from Shading

Shape from shading refers to a photometric approach to determining surface orientation from image brightness. The image of a three-dimensional object depends on its shape, its reflectance properties, and the distribution of light sources. The reflectance properties of the surface of an object are described by a BRDF (bidirectional reflectance distribution function) $f(\Theta_i\Phi_i;\Theta_e,\Phi_e)$ [Nichodemus et al. 1977], which relates brightness of a surface to the viewing direction (Θ_e,Φ_e) and the direction (Θ_i, Φ_i) of the light source. (see Figure 2.3). For example, the BRDF of an ideal Lambertian surface, which appears equally bright from all viewing directions, is a constant $1/\pi$. On the other hand, an ideal specular reflector reflects all of the light arriving from the direction (Θ_i, Φ_i) into the direction $(\Theta_i, \Phi_i + \pi)$, and therefore has the BRDF proportional to the product of two impulses, $\delta(\Theta_e - \Theta_i)$ and $\delta(\Theta_e - \Theta_i - \pi)$.

While the BRDF is of fundamental importance for understanding reflectance from a surface, what we really need to understand in the image formation is the reflectance map [Horn 1977]. The reflectance map makes explicit the relationship between surface orientation and brightness (see Figure 2.4). It encodes information about surface reflectance properties and light-source distributions.

The reflectance map is defined in gradient space [Huffman 1977a]. Let us assume that the viewing direction is parallel to the z-axis. The shape of a 3-D object can then be described by its height, z, above the xy-plane. Let p,q denote the first partial derivatives of z with respect to x and y:

$$p = \delta z/\delta x \tag{2.31}$$

$$q = \delta z/\delta y \tag{2.32}$$

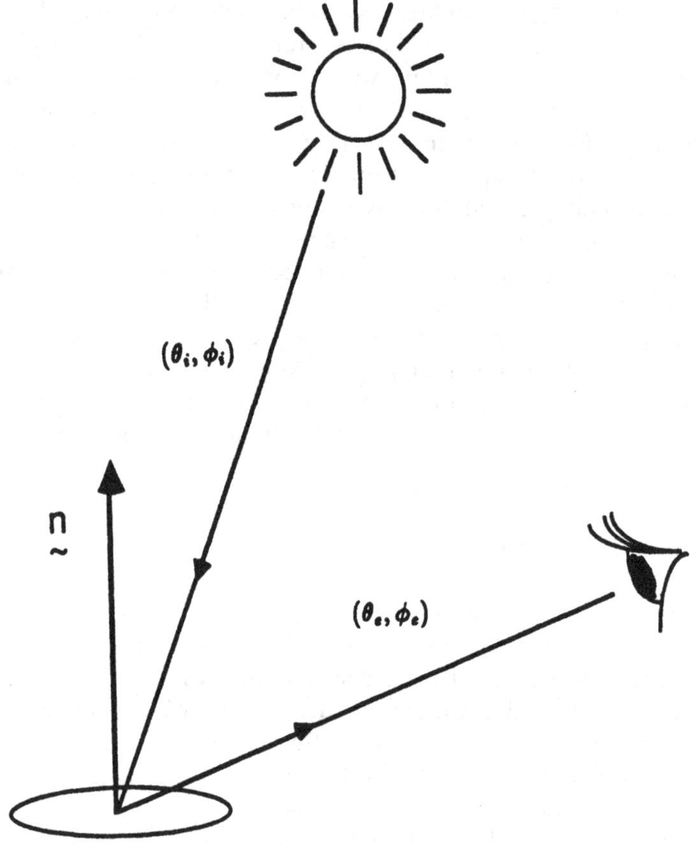

FIGURE 2.3. The configuration for the analysis of shape from shading.

The reflectance map $R(p,q)$ is then defined by associating with each point (p,q) in gradient space the brightness of a surface patch with the specified orientation, and is usually depicted by means of iso-brightness contours. $R(p,q)$ can be obtained experimentally using a test object or a sample mounted on a goniometer stage. It can also be computed if the BRDF and the distribution of light sources are known [Horn and Sjoberg 1979].

The reflectance map provides a simple constraint for recovering 3-D shape from shading information. The constraint is expressed by the image-irradiance equation

$$R(p,q) = E(x,y), \tag{2.33}$$

where (p,q) denotes possible orientations, and $E(x,y)$ is the brightness (intensity) at the point (x,y). Since one constraint is not enough for de-

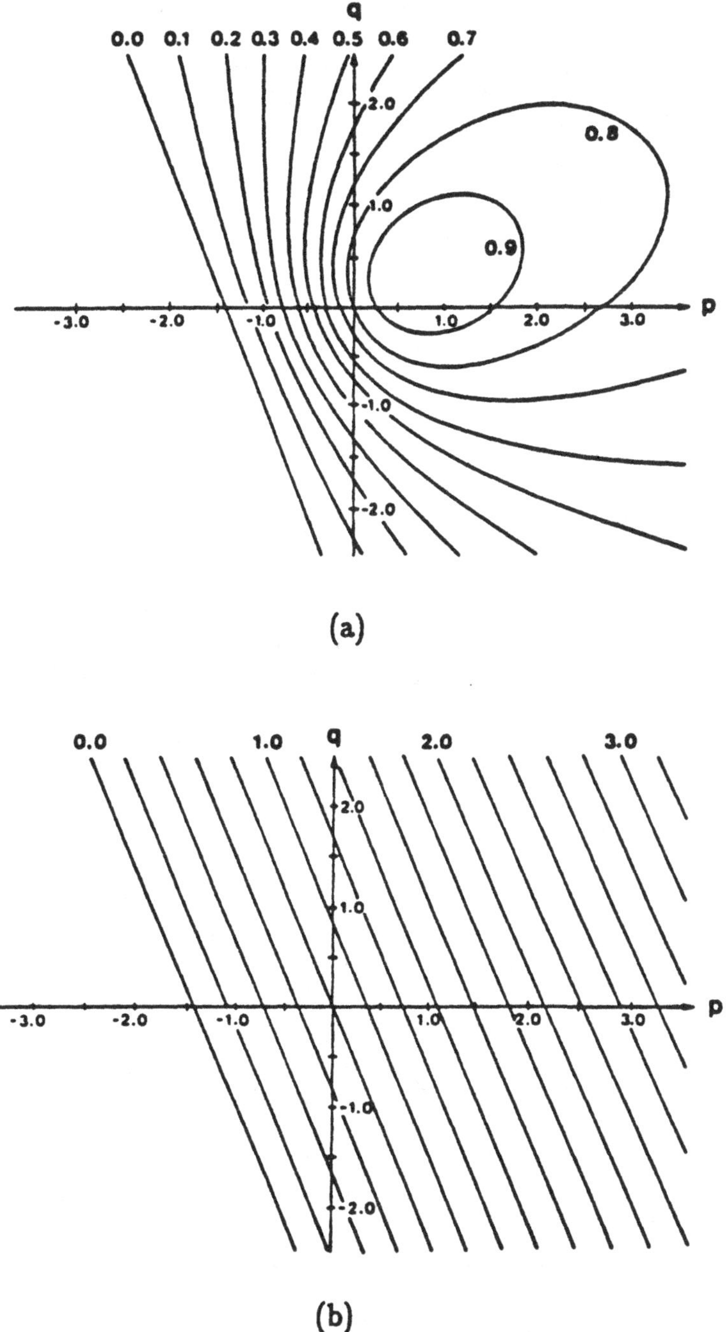

FIGURE 2.4. The reflection maps of (a) a Lambertial surface, and (b) a surface similar to that of the maria of the moon. Reprinted with permission from [Woodham 1981], © 1981 North Holland Elsevier Science Publishers.

termining a unique solution, additional constraints are required to recover shape information.

Determining shape from shading was first formulated in the form of a nonlinear first-order partial differential equation in two unknowns [Horn 1975]. A useful method of dealing with this first-order nonlinear partial differential equation is to solve an equivalent set of five ordinary differential equations:

$$dx/ds = R_q \tag{2.34}$$

$$dy/ds = R_q \tag{2.35}$$

$$dz/ds = pR_p + qR_q \tag{2.36}$$

$$dp/ds = E_x \tag{2.37}$$

$$dq/ds = E_y \tag{2.38}$$

where subscripts indicate partial derivatives. These equations can be solved using a modified characteristic strip-expansion method [Garabedien 1964]. In this method, the parameter s varies monotonically along a particular characteristic strip (starting near a so-called singular point [Horn 1977]. When the characteristic strip is expanded, the corresponding point in the image and that in the reflectance map move in certain directions constrained by the differential equations. The orientation of the surface is known at the end of the strip. It should be noted that the directions of motion will be computed incorrectly in the presence of noise in the image. One way to reduce this effect is to expand neighboring strips simultaneously and to adjust the solution using the assumption that the surface is smooth between strips.

One can also employ relaxation (or cooperative computation methods) to recover shape from shading using the information encoded in the reflectance map; in which the local constraints are propagated to determine global solutions [Brooks 1979; Strat 1979; Woodham 1979]. For example, if the surface is elliptical or hyperbolic at a point, one can guarantee the sign of the change to the view angle or the sign of the change to the direction of steepest ascent by choosing the small step (dx,dy) from the current image point P_1 to the neighboring point P_2 appropriately. As a result, local assumptions about surface shape provide monotonicity relations between selected image points in the shape from shading process [Woodham 1979].

Alternatively, the smoothness constraint can be formulated in a somewhat different way. Let us assume that the second partial derivatives of the surface height z exist and are continuous, then

$$\partial p/\partial y = \partial^2 z/\partial y \partial x = \partial^2 z/\partial x \partial y = \partial q/\partial x. \tag{2.39}$$

For any simply connected region R with contour C, we have

$$\int\int_R \{\partial p/\partial y - \partial q/\partial x\} = 0 \tag{2.40}$$

Since the integrand is zero at every point. By Green's theorem, we have

$$\oint \{pdx + qdy\} = 0. \tag{2.41}$$

This approach has been taken by Brooks [1979] and Strat [1979]. Brooks showed that he could restrict attention to integrals around small loops in the image plane. The possible orientations at each point were listed, and those conflicting with the loop integral criterion were eliminated. This process is carried out using a relaxation method.

Strat minimized the weighted sum of the errors in integrals around small loops and the errors in the image-irradiance equations. A large, sparse set of equations due to this minimization formulation were solved using an iterative procedure [Strat 1979]. Strat's method used the gradient space projection in which occluding contour information cannot be expressed since the associated great circle in the Gaussian sphere is mapped to infinity in the gradient space. As a result, his method could not deal with occluding boundaries.

One solution to this problem is the use of the stereographic projection [Sohon 1941]. If the coordinate axes of the stereographic plane are f and g, then

$$f = \frac{2p[\sqrt{1 + p^2 + q^2} - 1]}{(p^2 + q^2)} \tag{2.42}$$

$$g = \frac{2q[\sqrt{1 + p^2 + q^2} - 1]}{(p^2 + q^2)}. \tag{2.43}$$

Let $R_s(f,g)$ be the reflectance expressed in stereographic coordinates. Then the smoothness constraint can be reformulated as a mimimization problem, i.e., the solution minimizes the departure from smoothness (in the discrete case)

$$\sum_i \sum_j s_{ij} = \sum_i \sum_j [(F_{i+1,j} - f_{i,j})^2 + (f_{i,j+1} - f_{i,j})^2$$

$$+ (g_{i+1,j} - g_{i,j})^2 + (g_{i,j+1} - g_{i,j})^2]/4; \tag{2.44}$$

$$e = \sum_i \sum_j (s_{i,j} + \lambda r_{i,j}). \tag{2.45}$$

In the presence of errors in both the measurements of the irradiance and the determination of the reflectance map, we would also like to minimize the error

$$\sum_i \sum_j r_{ij} = \sum_i \sum_j [E(ij) - R_s(f_{ij}, g_{ij})]^2. \tag{2.46}$$

Overall we are to minimize

$$e = \sum_i \sum_j (s_{ij} + \lambda r_{ij}), \tag{2.47}$$

where λ is a parameter that weights the errors in the image irradiance equation relative to the departure from smoothness. This parameter should be made large if brightness measurements are very accurate and small if they are very noisy [Horn 1986]. An iterative algorithm is employed to solve this minimization problem using the following equations:

$$f_{ij}^{n+1} = f_{ij}^{*n} + \lambda[E_{ij} - R_s(f_{ij}^{*n}, g_{ij}^{*n})]\,\partial R_s/\partial f \tag{2.48}$$

$$g_{ij}^{n+1} = g_{ij}^{*n} + \lambda[E_{ij} - R_s(f_{ij}^{*n}, g_{ij}^{*n})]\,\partial R_s/\partial g \tag{2.49}$$

where * denotes the local average (over a 2 × 2 window), and n denotes the iteration number. Note that the computations for a given iteration are local. Global consistency is achieved by the propagation of constraints over many iterations.

Note that most of the shape from shading techniques discussed so far require a priori knowledge of the scene, and infer surface information by propagating certain constraints (such as smoothness) from the boundary (e.g., occluding contours). These techniques may fail in cases where unfamiliar scenes need to be analyzed, i.e., where local shading analysis is required. Shape from local shading analysis was first addressed by Bruss [1981], and later by Pentland [1984]. Bruss dealt mostly with the limitation of local shading analysis. A detailed discussion of what can be accomplished with a local analysis of shading was presented in Pentland [1984]. Under the assumptions that the illumination and albedo of the surface change very little (in a small, homogeneous region of a surface), it can be proven that the second (first) derivative of image intensity depends upon the second (first) derivative of the surface normal. Therefore, each surface point can be classified as one of the five surface types (i.e., plane, cylinder, convex, concave, and saddle surface) based on the second derivative of associated image intensity.

One problem with the photometric stereo approach is that it cannot recover the absolute depth information. This problem is solved by combining the photometric stereo and binocular stereo approaches together [Ikeuchi 1984]—the combined approach is called binocular photometric stereo or dual photometric stereo. In a dual photometric stereo approach proposed by Ikeuchi [1984], a pair of surface orientation maps were first generated and segmented into isolated regions with respect to surface orientations, using a geodesic dome for grouping surface orientations. The resulting left and right regions were compared to pair corresponding regions, based on the following three kinds of constraints: a surface orientation constraint, an area constraint, and an epipolar constraint. Region matching was done iteratively, starting from a coarse segmented result and proceeding to a fine segmented one, using a parent-children constraint. The horizontal difference in the position of the center of mass of a region pair determines the absolute depth value for the physical surface patch imaged onto that pair. The system was later used by the author as an input device for a bin-picking system [Ikeuchi 1987a].

6 Shape from Texture and Surface Contours

While the depth cues in contours in an image are often weak, there are usually strong cues to surface orientation. The spatial orientation of a point on a surface has two degrees of freedom, which can be described in terms of tilt τ and slant σ. Given a unit vector as an example, the orientation of the projected vector (on the image plane) corresponds to the tilt $0 \leq \tau < 180°$, and the length of the projected vector determines the slant $0 \leq \sigma \leq 90°$. There is evidence that surface orientation is analyzed to a large extent prior to object recognition [Stevens 1979a], with some implicit assumptions about the viewed surface (e.g., the ratio of lengths and the angle of intersection). For example, the simple intersection of two contours (as shown in Figure 2.5) strongly suggests a spatial orientation. The subjective spatial orientation shown in Figure 2.5 is a function of the relative line lengths and their angle of intersection [Attneave and Frost 1969]:

$$\sin \sigma = (\cot \alpha \cot \beta)^{1/2} \tag{2.50}$$

Another source of cues to surface orientation (under perspective projection) is texture (see Figure 2.6). An image with a texture gradient is often interpreted as that of a surface receding in depth. Recovering the surface information based on texture was first investigated by Gibson [1950]. He observed that the gradient of texture density provides information of surface orientation under the assumptions of planarity and uniform distribution. A texture gradient can be described by the partial derivatives of some texture measures in two directions: the direction of the gradient (corresponding to the tilt of the surface), and the perpendicular to the gradient (of which the partial derivative is zero). Five texture measures used to describe texture gradients are: width (w) and height (h) of the texture element; its eccentricity ($e = h/w$), area ($a = hw$), and density (p). It can be shown [Stevens 1979a] that

$$\Delta w/w = -\tan \sigma, \tag{2.51}$$

$$\Delta h/h = -2 \tan \sigma, \tag{2.52}$$

$$\Delta e/e = -\tan \sigma, \tag{2.53}$$

$$\Delta a/a = -3 \tan \sigma, \tag{2.54}$$

$$\Delta \rho/\rho = 3 \tan \sigma. \tag{2.55}$$

The ratios in equations (2.51)–(2.55) are called normalized texture gradients. They allow the computation of local surface slant for arbitrary surfaces with only qualitative assumptions concerning the surfaces (i.e., that they are locally planar and locally uniform). The image orientation perpendicular to r corresponds to the orientation on the surface of points that are locally equidistant from the viewer, and the image orientation r

FIGURE 2.5. The intersection of two contours strongly suggests a spatial orientation.

corresponds to the direction of the surface of steepest descent from the view [Stevens 1979a].

Kender [1979] presented an elegant approach to recover the orientation of a plane "painted" with a network of parallel lines; in the image, these lines were usually perspectively distorted. A Hough-like transform was initially designed to group texture elements (lines in this case) according to the two or more vanishing points towards which they orient. Let each edge vector be denoted by $\vec{E} = (E_x, E_y)$, and its position vector by $\vec{P} =$

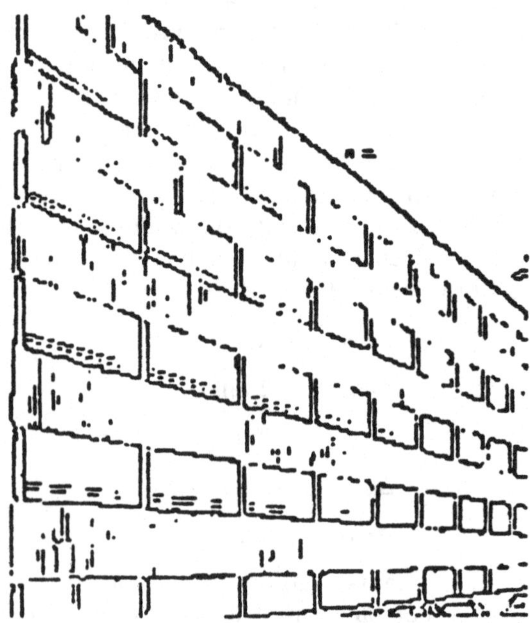

FIGURE 2.6. An image with a texture gradient is interpreted as that of a surface receding in depth.

(P_x, P_y). Then the transformed point, represented as a vector, $\vec{T} = (T_x, T_y)$ was defined as

$$\vec{T} = \frac{(\vec{E} \cdot \vec{P})}{\|\vec{E}\|^2}\vec{E}. \tag{2.56}$$

It can be shown [Kender 1979] that the transform maps mutually converging line segments into accumulation points that lie on a circle (or a line for parallel line segments) passing through the origin. The vanishing point is represented by that point on the circle farthest from the origin. A second transform was defined such that

$$\vec{T} = \frac{K}{\vec{E} \cdot \vec{P}}\vec{E} \tag{2.57}$$

for some constant K. This transform has even more desirable effects. A set of parallel lines (in the image) is mapped into accumulation points that lie along a straight line. The distance to the vanishing point of the line from the origin (of the second transform space) is inversely proportional to the distance to the vanishing point of the line set. A normal to the straight line is parallel to the direction of the vanishing point.

While both transforms allow efficient methods for recovering surface orientation of a plane painted with a network of parallel lines, they fail when a surface has different orientations everywhere. For example, they will not be able to decode surface orientation from the distortion of the small circles on the golf ball. Ikeuchi [1980] proposed a constraint propagation approach to handle this problem. In his approach, two perpendicular axis vectors were used to describe a texture element. When a pattern is distorted, the two vectors will also be distorted in a similar fashion. It can be shown that the magnitude of the cross product of two axis vector projections is proportional to $\cos \omega$, and the sum of the squares of their lengths is proportional to $1 + \cos^2 \omega$, where ω is the angle between the direction of the viewer and the direction of the surface orientation. The ratio of these two items

$$I = \frac{\cos \omega}{1 + \cos^2 \omega} \tag{2.58}$$

is defined as the distortion measure for the regular-pattern gradient map. Since the distortion measure I depends only on the angle ω, constant distortion values are mapped into circles on the Gaussian sphere. This is analogous to a situation in the shape-from-shading problem where the surface is known to be a Lambertian reflector and the light source is known to be near the viewer, and therefore a constraint propagation approach used in the photometric stereo can be exploited in this case to uniquely determine the orientation of a surface from three different vantage points.

This technique is referred to as texture stereo. If there is one regular pattern, it can be observed from several different vantage points; if the surface is planar and contains more than three regular patterns, the problem can be solved from a single vantage point.

While the distorting effects due to projection can be used to infer orientations of surfaces with regular patterns, the same technique is not applicable to the case of natural textures, which are usually not regular and unpredictable. Witkin [1981] suggested that to recover the 3-D structure of a surface, the distorting effects of projection must be distinguished from properties of texture on which the distortion acts. He argued that the constraints imposed by projective geometry are not sufficient to determine "shapes from natural textures," but must be augmented by assumptions about texture geometry (i.e., textures do not mimic projective, and the nonuniformities observed in images of some textured surfaces are due mostly to the projection). In his paper [Witkin 1981], the interpretation of variations observed in an image is chosen for which the textures, prior to projection, are made as uniform as possible. He related the texture of a surface to the distributions of surface marks, and posed the problem of shape from texture based on observing the distribution of edge directions in an image as a maximum likehood problem. This statistical approach was implemented and applied successfully to geographic contours and to natural images as reported in Witkin [1981]. The authors noted that the estimation strategy in Ohta et al. [1981] responds to foreshortening distortion, and thus fails for textures that are themselves systematically compressed or elongated (such as wood grain). Witkin suggested that incidence of these failures may be reduced by recourse to additional sources of information in the image, such as size gradients, and shading.

7 Shape from Line Drawings

A line drawing can be viewed as the minimal representation of intensity discontinuities in an image corresponding to discontinuities of surface orientation, range, reflectance, and illumination [Barrow and Tenenbaum, 1981]. Due to such a rich amount of information contained in it, even a fledgling visual system is capable of inferring three-dimensional structure of a scene from a line drawing. This is evident from the fact that even three-year-old children are able to interpret street scenes from coloring books.

The first extensive use of heuristics for interpreting line drawings was by Guzman [1968]. He made the important observation that different junction types in a line drawing suggested different (possible) associations of regions into objects. In his program SEE, junctions were classified into L, FORK, ARROW, T, K, X, PEAK, and MULTI. An analysis of the regions around junctions suggested heuristics for assigning regions to one body or another. Although SEE was designed to recognize three-dimensional objects, its heuristics were related to the two-dimensional image domain only. There was no explicit treatment of three-dimensional scene features. In addition, the heuristics were very *ad hoc* and there was little physical basis for them [Cohen and Feigenbaum 1981].

A more systematic approach was taken by Huffman [1971] and Clowes [1971] independently. They emphasized the important distinction between the scene domain and image domain. Junctions, lines, and regions in the image domain correspond to vertices, edges, and surfaces in the scene domain, respectively. Huffman and Clowes observed that lines in an image could have different physical meanings; they could be convex edges, concave edges, or occluding edges (as shown in Figure 2.7). Possible combinations of line labels could be categorized in a junction dictionary. Any line drawing could then be interpreted as an object in the trihedral world (in which exactly three plane surfaces can come together at a vertex) according to the junction dictionary. Recognizing an object was simply a matter of finding a consistent label for a line drawing of the object. However, their search for consistent interpretations was exhaustive [Cohen and Feigenbaum 1981].

The idea of junction dictionaries was extended further by Waltz [1975] to include shadows, cracks, and separably concave edges, and the types of junctions were increased accordingly. The procedure used by Waltz to label a line drawing is based on the Huffman-Clowes principle, but is

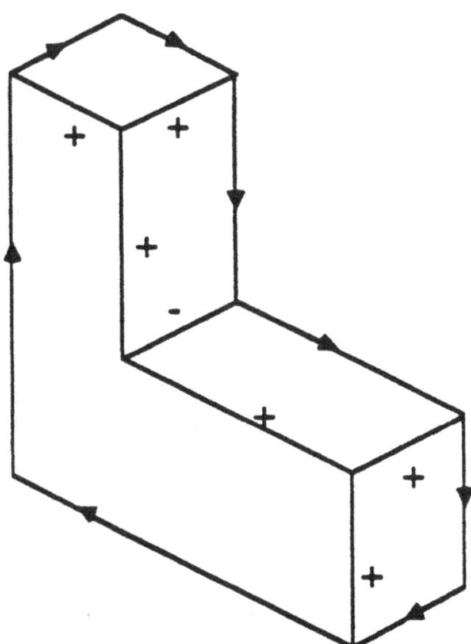

FIGURE 2.7. An example showing the interpretation of a line drawing with "+", "−", and arrow denoting convex, concave, and occluding edges, respectively.

more efficient. A constraint satisfaction algorithm was used to determine the possible labels for each junction in the context of the entire line drawing. It is called the *Waltz filtering algorithm* since it removes inconsistent labels as it proceeds. An interesting outcome of Waltz's research is that the inclusion of more detailed information does not complicate interpretation, rather it constrains and facilitates interpretation [Cohen and Feigenbaum 1981].

Instead of using table look-up, vertex types of 3-D objects can be derived by inference as shown by Thorpe and Shafer [1983]. He observed that each junction type usually results from only one kind of vertex, except for L-junctions, which may correspond to a limited number of vertex types due to the positions of the hidden third edges. He also analyzed the topological constraints on the changing appearance of line drawings as the objects or the camera moved, and derived three constraints on the changing in appearance of the objects: conservation of vertices, conservation of vertex types, and conservation of adjacencies. Conservation of vertices implies that the same vertices (of an object) must be present in different images even if they may not be visible. The conservation of vertex types is used as a constraint in node formation of the correspondence graph in the matching algorithm. Links in the graph connect nodes that are consistent, and consistency is defined using the conservation-of-adjacency constraint.

Whereas the Huffman-Clowes labeling scheme and the Waltz filtering algorithm are powerful tools for interpreting line drawings, they yield only a qualitative description of the objects in the scene. In addition, their algorithms sometimes assign legal labels to unrealizable polyhedra. The problem of unrealizable labels can only be solved by a quantitative analysis. Mackworth's [1973] POLY is a program to interpret line drawings as three-dimensional scenes by reasoning about surface orientations based on the properties of the gradient space introduced by Huffman [1977]. They pointed out that if two surfaces meet along a concave or convex edge, their gradients lie along a line in the gradient space that is "perpendicular to" that edge in the image. Based on this principle, first it searches in a given image for a coherent interpretation in which the gradients of planes can have consistent relationships and where as many edges as possible are connected edges. Next, it interprets occluding edges (nonconnected edges). Finally, it determines which surface of the line is in front of the other.

Using gradients, Kanade [1980, 1981] demonstrated multiple interpretation (from different viewing angles) and quantitative shape recovery from line drawings. He also extended the scene domain from the trihedral world to the origami world, which is composed of both planar surfaces and solids (see Figure 2.8). It is assumed that no more than three surfaces meet at a vertex. The junction dictionary for the origami world is augmented by constraints in the gradient space that must be satisfied by the surface

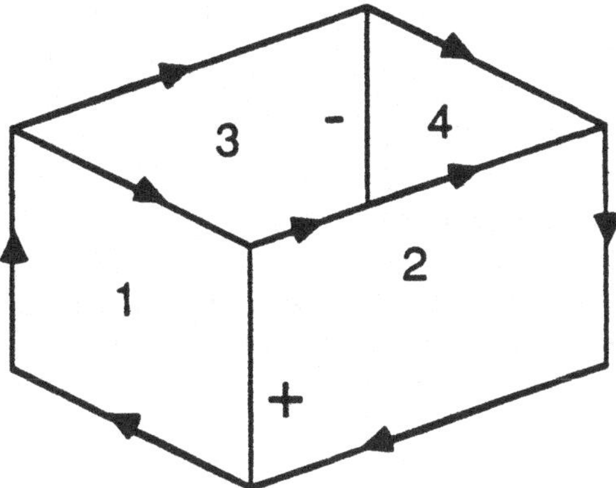

FIGURE 2.8. An example showing an interpretation of a line drawing in the Origami world.

incident at the junction. The labeling procedure tests the consistency of surface orientations by using the instantiated gradient space constraints [Kanade 1980]. The test can be performed systematically with an iterative operation that filters out possible relative positions for the gradient of each surface.

Labeling a line drawing does not quantitatively specify the shape of an object. Kanade developed a method for mapping image properties into shape constraints for recovering three-dimensional quantitative shapes. He introduced the idea of regularity heuristics—a parallel-line heuristic and a skew-symmetry heuristic, in particular. These heuristics were transformed into constraints in the gradient space to limit the possible interpretation of a line drawing. For example, the gradient of the plane contains a region of skewed symmetry in the gradient space to limit the possible interpretation of a line drawing. For example, the gradient of the plane containing a region of skewed symmetry is constrainted to a hyperbola. The two vertices of the hyperbola correspond to the least-slanted orientation that can produce the skewed symmetry in the image from the real symmetry in the scene [Kanade 1981]. With these additional constraints, a cubic block can be easily distinguished from a trapezoidal block, as described in Kanade [1981].

Alternatively, line drawings can also be analyzed using line algebra. Falk [1972] pointed out that a line drawing describing a polyhedron must satisfy a certain set of linear equations. More recently, Sugihara [1982, 1986] derived necessary and sufficient conditions in terms of linear algebra for a line drawing to represent a polyhedral scene. Based on these conditions, combinatorial structures were investigated and practical solutions were obtained to such problems as how to discriminate between correct and incorrect line drawings. As a result, the problem of judging the correctness of a line drawing is reduced to the problem of checking the existence of a solution to a certain system of linear equations and linear inequalities. However, the author observed that in practice many pictures were judged incorrectly only because the vertices were slightly deviated from the correct position. This difficulty is probably due to the fact that the system contains redundant equations, and can be solved by a counting theorem, which allows the extraction of a subset of equations for solving the problem. Based on this idea, Sugihara proposed a method for the interactive reconstruction of a polyhedron from a line drawing. The details of the method can be found in Sugihara [1982].

8 Shape from Occluding Contours

We have presented different techniques to recover 3-D information from 2-D images using a variety of cues. Each technique has its advantages and disadvantages, and is suitable for a particular class of images. One problem they have in common is that a small amount of noise in the given 2-D image may cause significant errors in the recovery of 3-D information, i.e., they are relatively noise-sensitive. For example, determination of the junction dictionary may depend on subtle variations in geometry that are difficult to distinguish in practice [Barrow and Tenebaum 1981]. The problem may be alleviated, if not eliminated, by using only the information contained in occluding contours, which is relatively easier to extract from the images, and thus is more reliable. Even though occluding contours usually provide insufficient information for reconstructing the 3-D structure of objects, their ability to depict shape has long been recognized. An illustration of this ability is the shadow graph, where an appropriate arrangement of a person's hands may produce shadows of different 3-D shapes, like public figures or a variety of animals.

Attempts have been made to infer surface orientation from occluding contours by imposing constraints on the geometry of the viewed surface. For example, Barrow and Tenenbaum [1981] use smoothness constraints that require that the curvatures of a space curve be as smooth as possible, and the space curve be as planar as possible. An obvious measure of the smoothness of a space curve is uniformity of curvature; a measure of the planarity is inversely proportional to the integral of the torsion. Both the smoothness and planarity of a space curve can be expressed in terms of a single, locally computed differential measure $d(KB)/ds$:

$$\int (\frac{d(kB)}{ds})^2 ds = \int (k')^2 + k^2 t^2) ds \tag{2.59}$$

where k and t are differential curvature and torsion of the space curve, respectively, and $'$ denotes the spatial derivative. Brady and Yuille [1984] pointed out that there are two problems with the measures used in Barrow and Tenenbaum's approach. First, the measure of the smoothness is overly dependent on small-scale behavior and therefore is highly noise-sensitive. Second, the measure of the planarity has a bias towards planes that correspond to the side-on viewing position.

On the contrary, Brady and Yuille [1984] employ an extremum principle to determine 3-D surface orientation from a 2-D contour, based on the following observations:

1. Contours that are the projection of curves in planes with large slant are most effective for eliciting a three-dimensional interpretation.
2. A curve is foreshortened by projection by the cosine of the slant angle in the tilt direction, and not at all in the orthogonal direction. The measure they suggested is the ratio of the area to the square of the perimeter (i.e., the compactness)

$$M = \frac{\text{Area}}{(\text{Perimeter})^2} \tag{2.60}$$

In general, given a contour, the extremum principle will choose the orientation in which the deprojected contour maximizes M.

However, the difficulties encountered in the implementation have forced Barrow and Tenenbaum [1981] to take an alternative approach based on a simple assumption that an ellipse in the image corresponds to a circle in 3-D space. The limitation of using geometric constraints (e.g., smoothness, planarity, or compactness) is that they allow one to infer only the 3-D structure of simple objects such as circles, squares, triangles (in the 3-space), or symmetric objects, but not of complex man-made objects. It is argued that one is able to infer an ellipse to be a projection of a circle, since one is "familiar" with the projection of a circle. Familiarity is one of the most crucial characteristics in recognizing a shadow graph.

In fact, this view is shared by many researchers. They have attempted the identification of unknown objects (from their 2-D silhouettes) by comparing them with the models in a data base. The one frequently referred to in the literature is ACRONYM, a rule-based scene-interpretation system [Brooks 1981]. ACRONYM searches in a given image for instances of object models in terms of ribbons and ellipses, which are the 2-D projections of the elongated bodies and the ends of the generalized cone models, respectively. A nonlinear constraint manipulation system (CMS) is used during interpretation. As pointed out in Besl and Jain [1985], despite the detailed 3-D considerations in the ACRONYM design, no 3-D interpretation results have ever been published to our knowledge. Many system difficulties have been blamed on the quality of output from the ribbon-finding mechanism [Nevatia and Binford 1973]. However, some assumptions made in Brooks [1981] may be valid only for aerial images and difficult to extend for more general viewing positions.

The same difficulty was encountered by Mulgaonkar et al. [1982] They developed a scene-analysis system using geometric and relational reasoning. Generalized blobs (sticks, plates, and blobs) are used to represent 3-D objects. All objects are assumed to be in an upright position. Only a 67% success rate in recognition was reported. This is probably due to the fact that the class of objects that can be described by generalized blobs is limited.

Wallace and Wintz [1980] have used normalized Fourier descriptors of 2-D silhouettes to recognize a 3-D aircraft. The normalized Fourier descriptor of an unknown view of an observed object is matched against those of all the possible views of each model stored in the database. Each normalized Fourier descriptor is compressed to reduce the storage requirement and to increase the computational efficiency. Experimental results are shown only for determining the orientation of an observed aircraft. No result is presented for recognition, which may limit the degree of data compression. Since different aircraft may look similar from the same viewing direction, it requires most components of their Fourier descriptors to be retained in order to distinguish them. As a consequence, both the storage requirement and the processing time will increase.

Fischler and Bolles [1981] introduce a paradigm, called Random Sample Consensus (RANSAC), for fitting a model to experimental data. The RANSAC procedure is opposite to that of conventional smoothing techniques. Rather than using as much of the data as possible to obtain an initial solution and then attempting to eliminate the invalid data points, RANSAC uses as small an initial data set as feasible and enlarges this set with consistent data when possible. They derived the results on minimum number of landmarks needed to obtain a solution to Location Determination Problem (LDP), and presented algorithms for computing these minimum-landmark solutions in closed form.

Fisher [1983] has implemented a data-driven object recognition program called IMAGINE. Surface boundaries are used to describe object models, and all the surfaces of the models are restricted to planar or have only a single axis of revolution. Lee and Fu [1983] propose a computer vision system that uses a set of regularity constraints and the least-slant-angle-preference rule to compute the 3-D surface orientations of the selected target regions. Experimental results are shown for a car and a machine tool, which have planar surfaces. No methodology for handling curved surfaces has been indicated.

Goad [1986] observed that in many practical vision applications it is necessary to recognize objects of the same shape in a sequence of images, and the exact shape of the objects is known in advance. As a result, object recognition tasks can be carried out based on special purpose automatic programming. In his approach, the computation is split into two stages: a time-consuming precomputation stage in which useful information about the model is compiled off-line; and an execution (running) stage, in which the precomputed information is exploited for the rapid recognition of the object in individual images. The author reports that the implementation provides recognition times of a few seconds on a MC 68000 for typical industrial applications. The practical impact of this work is that 3-D model-based vision becomes available at a speed and cost suitable for industrial use.

Ben-Arie and Meiri [1986] have developed algorithms for estimating imaging parameters using primitives such as edge orientations and area ratios (of image/object planar regions). Partial matches between primitive subsets of the image and of the object are hypothesized, and a geometric cost, which reflects the error in estimating observation parameters, is assigned to each hypothesized partial match. The so-called optimal matching of the object and the image is sought by a cost-guided ordered search algorithm. Experimental results are shown for complex (curved) objects such as aircraft. However, it is not clear how one could approximate curved surfaces by planar patches so that partial matches can be hypothesized, and edge orientations or area ratios calculated.

Lowe [1986] designed a system, called SCERPO, for the recognition of objects from single gray-scale images. The recognition task is accomplished through three processes. First, a process of perceptual organization is used to form groupings and structures in the image. Then, evidential reasoning is used to combine evidence from these groupings and other sources of information to reduce the size of the search space. Finally, a process of spatial correspondence is used to bring the projections of 3-D models into direct correspondence with the image by solving for unknown viewpoint and model parameters. The primitives used in SCERPO are line segments. The system is able to handle multiple objects with occlusion. However, object classes are restricted somewhat to the ones with well-defined straight line edges.

Chien [1986] and Chien and Aggarwal [1987] designed a system that is capable of recognizing 3-D objects using a limited amount of information such as corners and the occluding contours of single silhouettes. In their system, the location of the 3-D feature points, and the occluding contours and the quadtrees of three primary views of each model are stored in the database (as shown in Figure 2.9). The recognition task is carried out in two processes: a hypothesis and verification process and a 2-D contour-matching process. In the hypothesis and verification process, 2-D feature points of the given single silhouette are extracted and four-point correspondences between the 2-D feature points of the silhouette and the 3-D feature points of each model are hypothesized, and then verified by applying a variety of constraints to their associated viewing parameters. For example, the transformation matrix (between the model and the image plane) must be orthogonal:

$$R_{11}^2 + R_{12}^2 + R_{13}^2 = s^2, \tag{2.61a}$$

$$R_{21}^2 + R_{22}^2 + R_{23}^2 = s^2, \tag{2.61b}$$

$$R_{11}R_{21} + R_{12}R_{22} + R_{13}R_{23} = 0, \tag{2.61c}$$

where s is a scaling factor. The problem of solving the viewing parameters (i.e., R_{ij} for each hypothesized four-point correspondence) is formulated as a set of linear equations to ensure the efficiency. At the end of this process, a small set of valid four-point correspondences is selected; the associated viewing parameters are then used to extract the occluding contours of the likely candidate models.

In the 2-D contour matching process, the extracted contours are then matched against the occluding contour of the given silhouette to determine the viewing direction and identity of the unknown object based on a function called DRS (distance-ratio-standard-deviation), which measures the similarity between the two occluding contours [Chien 1986; Chien and Aggarwal 1987]. This approach allows for a method of handling both planar and curved objects in a uniform manner. Furthermore, it provides a solution to the recognition of multiple objects with occlusion as well, since only four points are required for the initial estimation, and occluding contours are used for final recognition as demonstrated by experimental results. Shown in Figure 2.10(a) are the silhouettes of two aircraft (the MIG-23 and the Yakolev) that occlude each other (Figure 2.10(b)). In the experiment, the MIG-23 was identified first (Figure 2.10(c)), and the 2-D feature points corresponding to 3-D feature points of the MIG-23 were

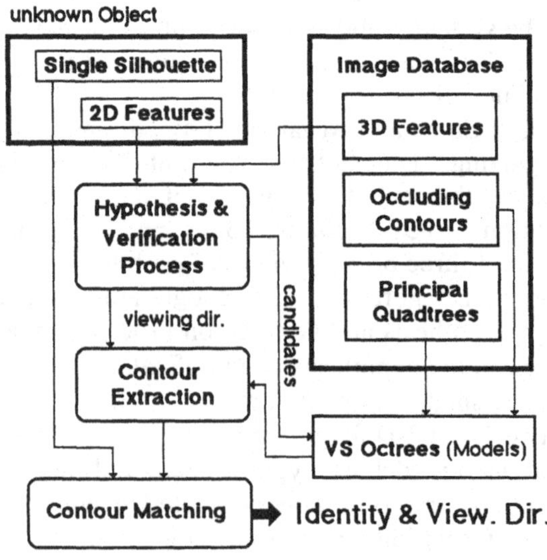

FIGURE 2.9. The block diagram of a system for recognizing single silhouettes.

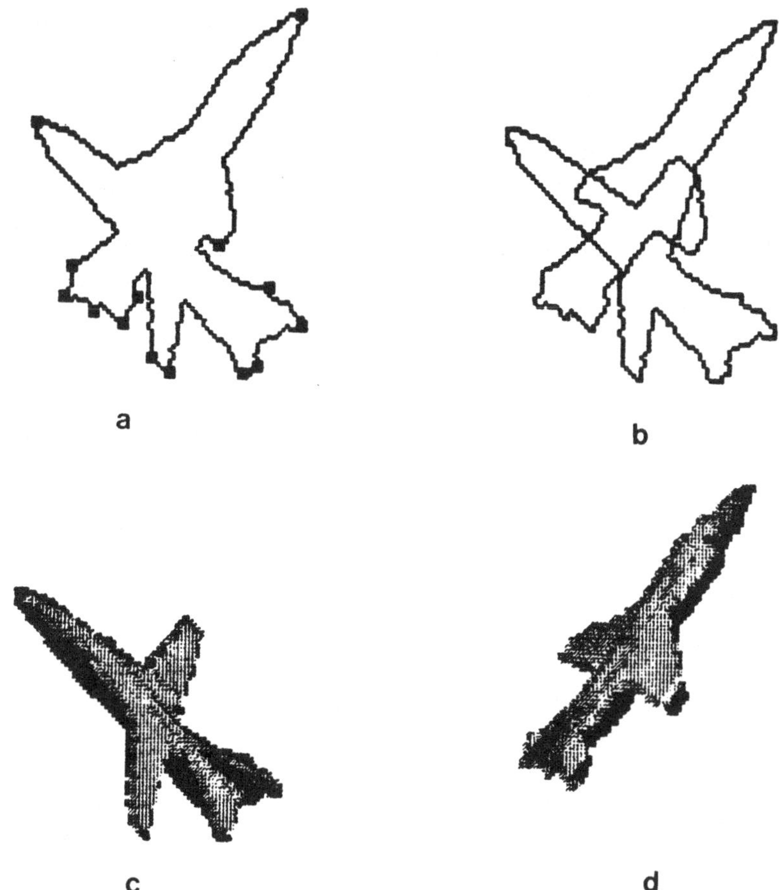

FIGURE 2.10. An input silhouette in (a) was identified as the silhouettes of two aircraft that occluded each other as shown in (b); the first aircraft was identified as MIG-23 (c); and the second, as Yakolev (d).

removed from the list of the 2-D feature points. The hypothesis and verification process was then applied to the remaining 2-D feature points, which matched 3-D feature points of the Yakolev (Figure 2.10(d)).

In general, the 2-D contour matching process takes less than one second in computation time, as opposed to the hypothesis and verification process, which is usually time-consuming. This process may be speeded up using an ordered search based on certain heuristics. For example, 2-D feature points with higher curvatures are most likely the projections of 3-D feature points with higher curvatures. This idea has been shared by many researchers in this area. While the processing time for object recognition tasks may be drastically reduced by using ordered searches, it is still far away from meeting the requirements for real-time applications. The consensus for the solution to this problem is parallel processing, in which independent subtasks in the recognition process can be executed concurrently to obtain a significant speedup.

Instead of corner points (or vertices), a new feature, the vertex-pair, was introduced by Thompson and Mundy [1987] as a feature for establishing correspondences between the (polyhedral) models and the scene, and thus determining the affine transformation. The vertex-pair is a group of model edges and vertices. The vertex associated with each pair of two edges is called the base vertex. The line between each pair of two vertices is called the spine (the authors note that the spine does not actually have to correspond to an edge in the model or in the image). The vertex-pair defines enough constraints so that all of the parameters of an affine transformation between a model vertex-pair and a scene vertex-pair can be computed. Each computed affine transformation yields a point in six-dimensional transform parameter space. A potential object is then defined by a tight cluster in transform space through a combination of histogramming and a form of the nearest-neighbor clustering algorithm.

9 Structure from Volume Intersection

The silhouette of an object usually conveys insufficient 3-D information about the object. When the silhouette of an object is extended into 3-space along the corresponding viewing direction to form a cylinder, one may only infer that the object is bounded by the cylinder. This problem is resolved by intersecting the bounding cylinders from different views (as shown in Figure 2.11). Martin and Aggarwal [1983] and Martin et al. [1983] derived the volume segment representation of a 3-D object from the occluding contours of its multiple views.

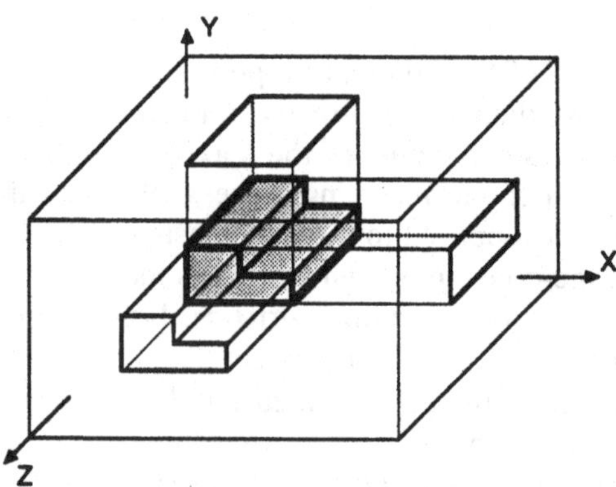

FIGURE 2.11. An example of volume intersection.

The volume segment representation is a generalization to three dimensions of the rasterized area description [Newman and Sproull 1973]. In addition to grouping collinear segments into lists (as in the rasterized area description), the set of segment lists is partitioned so that the subsets contain lists having coplanar segments. Given the occluding contours of two views of a 3-D object and the two viewing directions, the initial volume segment representation of the object is generated as follows:

1. Determine line common to the two image planes.
2. Rasterize each occluding contour along the scan line direction perpendicular to the common line.
3. Merge mutual constraints from corresponding scan line segments to form the parallelogram description of the object.
4. Define the coordinate axis system for the volume segment representation having the z-axis in the direction of the common line and the y-axis in the direction of the line of sight for the first frame.
5. Rasterize the parallelograms in each z-plane of the new axis system to define the segments of the volume representation.
6. Add the linkage structure to complete the volume segment representation.

This initial structure can be refined as each additional view is available. A detailed description of the refinement process can be found in Martin and Aggarwal [1983].

Alternatively, the structure from volume intersection approach can also be implemented in tree structures. Chien and Aggarwal [1986b, 1986c] derived a technique to generate the generalized octree of an object from the silhouettes of its multiple views. An octree is a hierarchical data structure used for describing the 3-D structures of objects. It is an extension of the well-known quadtree structures. In the regular octree structure, each node in the tree corresponds to a cubic block in 3-space; in the generalized octree structure, the block associated with each node is a rectangular parallelepiped. If a generalized octree is generated from three noncoplanar views, the three sides of each rectangular parallelepiped are parallel to the three viewing directions. In addition, a generalized coordinate system is specified by the three viewing directions in order to speed up the computation of geometric properties of the object [Chien and Aggarwal 1986b].

Given three noncoplanar views, each of them is projected onto an image plane determined by the two remaining viewing directions, which specify the two coordinate axes of the image plane. A quadtree is generated for each projected image. Each quadtree is then copied along the associated viewing direction to obtain a pseudo-octree describing the (oblique) cylinder, which is the sweeping volume of the projected image along the viewing direction. This is done by assigning two numbers to each node in the corresponding quadtree (as shown in Figure 2.12). With the three

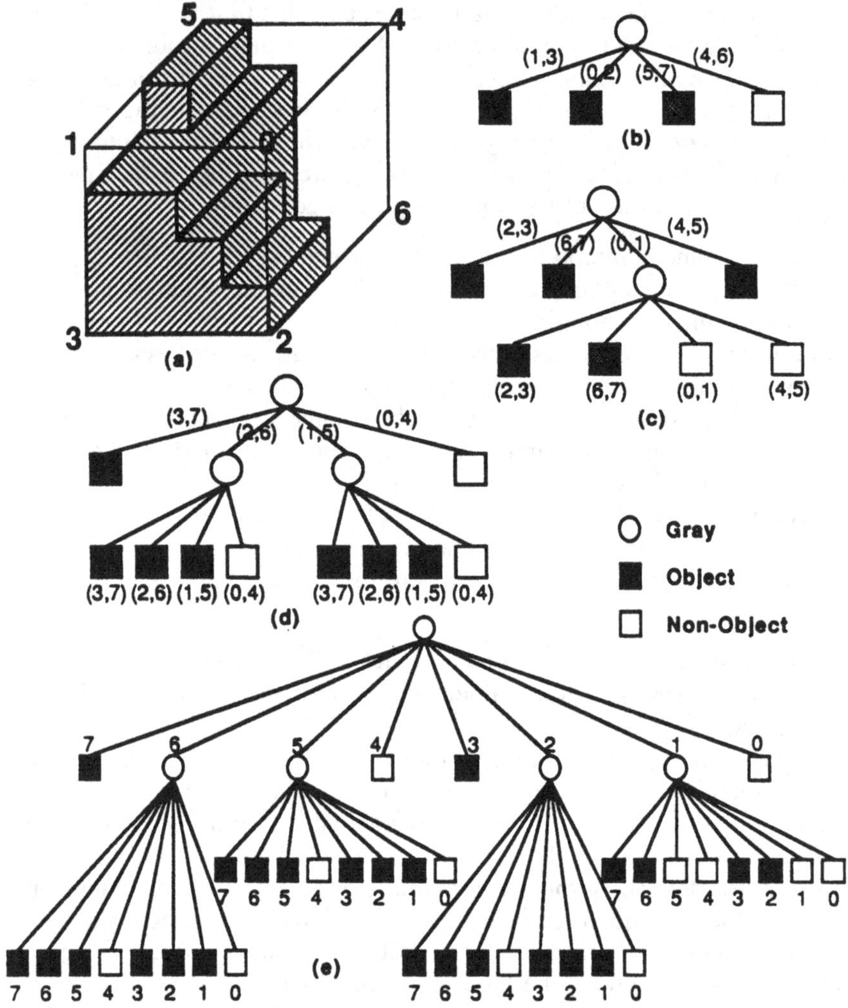

FIGURE 2.12. The generation of the octree (e) of the object in (a) from the quadtrees of its three views: (b) second view, (c) third view, and (d) first view.

pseudo-octrees generated, the (generalized) octree of an object is then generated through the intersection of the three-pseudo-octrees.

The octree generation algorithm described earlier can be modified to compute both volumetric and surface information directly from multiple silhouettes of the object. The key idea is to encode contour information into the quadtrees of the associated silhouettes. The contour information is then propagated during the volume intersection process to obtain the surface information. In order to obtain more accurate contour information, each occluding contour is fitted with a tension-spline. This curve-fitting process allows better approximations of the contour normals, and hence provides more accurate surface information. A generalized octree generated from three views yields the initial approximation of the structure of the object. As in Martin and Aggarwal [1983], this initial structure can be refined as additional views are available [Chien and Aggarwal 1986b].

One more alternative for inferring structure from volume intersection has been proposed by Kim and Aggarwal [1986a, 1986b]. They use rectangular coding for describing 2-D binary images [Kim and Aggarwal 1983], and rectangular parallelepiped (RP) coding for 3-D structure of objects. Similar to the previous two approaches, the 3-D structure of an object is reconstructed as follows: Given three orthogonal views of the object, 2-D rectangular codes are constructed for each of the three views at first. Next, these 2-D rectangular codes are converted to three sets of rectangular parallelepipeds. Finally, the RP codes of the object are generated using the volume intersection method.

The rectangular code of a 2-D object region is a set of rectangles that partition the object region. Each of these rectangles is described by a quadruple (x,y,W,H), where (x,y), W, and H are the corner coordinates, the width, and height of the rectangle, respectively. Figure 2.13 shows an example of the rectangular code of an object region. An extension of the 2-D rectangular coding is RP coding for describing the 3-D structure of an object. The RP code of an object is a set of rectangular parallelepipeds, each of which is described by a quintuple (x,y,W,H,D) with D coding the depth. The algorithm for generating the RP code of an object from a set of rectangular codes is similar to that for generating the octree from a set of quadtrees, and the details of the algorithm can be found in Kim and Aggarwal [1986a].

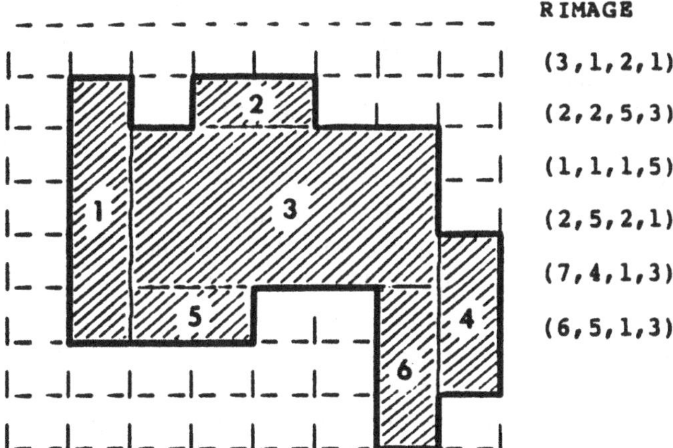

FIGURE 2.13. An example showing the rectangular code of an object region. Reprinted with permission from [Kim and Aggarwal 1986a], © 1986 IEEE.

It has been shown that RP coding is more efficient than octree coding in terms of storage requirements and processing time (for generation) [Kim and Aggarwal 1986a]. However, the regularity of the tree structures allows tree traversal procedures to be easily mapped onto any parallel architecture. In addition, RP coding is more noise sensitive. A small amount of noise may drastically change the RP code of an object. In other words, the RP coding is not suitable for model construction for recognition purposes.

10 Shape from Spatial Encoding

Shape from spatial encoding (also known as structured lighting) refers to a technique that involves illuminating the scene with controlled lighting and interpreting the pattern of the projection in terms of the surface geometry of the objects. This technique is applicable to controlled environments such as laboratories. The use of spatial encoding is aimed at reducing the computational complexity and improving the reliability of the 3-D object recognition process. Whereas the passive sensing techniques, such as shape from shading and stereoscopy, gather information from ambient light reflection, structured lighting methods cast modulated light (light cast through a plane masked with spatially variant patterns) onto the scene to obtain a "spatial encoding" for analysis.

The spatial encoding method was first proposed by Pennington and Will [1970] and Will and Pennington [1971, 1972] to extract surfaces of polyhedra. They argued that if the information to be extracted can be "coded" as the modulation of a suitable chosen "grid," then the desired information in the space domain will have a Fourier spectrum exhibiting the coding of the information as the distribution of a delta function array; thus they called this approach grid coding. For example, a planar area coded with crossed grids has a two-dimensional Fourier transform, which is a crossed set of harmonically related delta functions in the frequency domain. Separation of the delta functions in order to identify the individual planes is equivalent to band-pass filtering. The inverse transform can then reconstruct the image of the plane. However, they observed that a plane surface in a general scene is not uniquely coded in angle or spatial frequency carrier shift. They suggested a grid structure in which the code carried positional information by using a shift register derived code plate or the grid known as a linear zone plate in optics.

Later, the approach using grid coding was used to recover depth information using stereoscopic pairs of grid-coded images. However, using grid coding for depth reconstruction under the stereopsis principle poses some nontrivial difficulties. Indeed, it is difficult, if not impossible, to find the correspondence between the grid intersections in a stereo pair of grid-coded images. Heuristic search [Potmesil and Freeman 1972], time modulation [Posdamer and Altschuler 1982], spatial labeling [Le Moigne and Waxman 1984], and relaxation [Stockman and Hu 1986] have been proposed to alleviate this problem of correspondence.

Potmesil and Freeman [1972] presented a method for constructing surface models of 3-D objects by spatially matching 3-D surface segments describing the objects. In this method, projected grid patterns are used to recover the surface structure from multiple viewpoints. The surface segments from different viewpoints are imaged in such a way that they partially overlap to allow their alignment by matching the common surface areas. A heuristic search algorithm has been used, which determines the spatial registration of two partially or completely overlapped surface elements by maximizing their shape similarity. The criteria that have been used are the minimization of the differences in position, orientation, and curvature between two surface elements. However, the heuristic search is usually a time-consuming process.

Posdamer and Altschuler [1982] have presented a time modulation technique for assigning a unique "space code" or address to the grid junctions using a laser shutter/space encoding system. A single laser beam is converted into an array of projected rays by means of interference techniques. A high-speed computer-controlled shutter system is designed, which can selectively block rays at particular positions. A reference image is created by shining all laser rays simultaneously. Images are generated with different rays deleted through proper shutter control. The effect of the presence or absence of the laser ray at a particular position is equivalent to the assignment of a binary space code to that position. The space code thus specifies the correspondence between the grid junctions in the image plane and those in the grid plane. Hence, the 3-D coordinates of the illuminated points can again be computed via triangulation after the space code of the laser beam is determined. One potential problem of this approach is that it requires images to remain sufficiently registered over a long period of time.

Another possibility in assigning a unique space coding to the grid junctions (thus resolving the correspondence relationship) is through the use of a spatial labeling technique [Le Moigne and Waxman 1984]. The grid patterns are augmented with a few black dots of known positions. The black dots are detected in the image and a counting procedure that measures the offset of a junction to the black dots is used to determine the space code of the junction. Note that the discontinuities of the grid lines and missing intersections will mislead the address labeling process. A global relaxation process is incorporated to resolve the inconsistency in labeling. However, as pointed out in Wang et al. [1985], this spatial labeling fails when abrupt changes in depth cause a break of the observed stripe patterns because the grid intersections are used directly in stereo matching.

Stockman and Hu [1986] used geometric constraints (such as uniqueness, projection property, and general position) and topological constraints (such as neighborhood connectivity and unique intersection) to solve the grid labeling problem. Using geometric constraints from camera and projector calibration, a small set of grid label possibilities was assigned to each grid point. Neighborhood constraints in the 2-D grid network were used to select most of the grid label possibilities from each set through a constraint propagation (relaxation) process. Grid label assignments in separate surface patches were then related and ambiguities were reduced further. This method has been applied to both regular and irregular objects. However, the authors reported that a unique correspondence relationship between the grid junctions in the grid plane and those in the image plane cannot always be established using relaxation. Also, errors in preprocessing and camera calibration can propagate and yield inaccurate 3-D point coordinates.

A more elegant approach has been proposed by Wang et al. [1985, 1987]. Their approach exploits the orientation of the projected stripes and does not require any correspondence relationship between either the grid junctions or the grid lines to be specified. Two orthogonal stripe patterns are used for spatial encoding. Each set comprises a collection of equally spaced parallel stripes marked on a glass pane. The spatially encoded object is observed on an image plane through a video camera (see Figure 2.14).

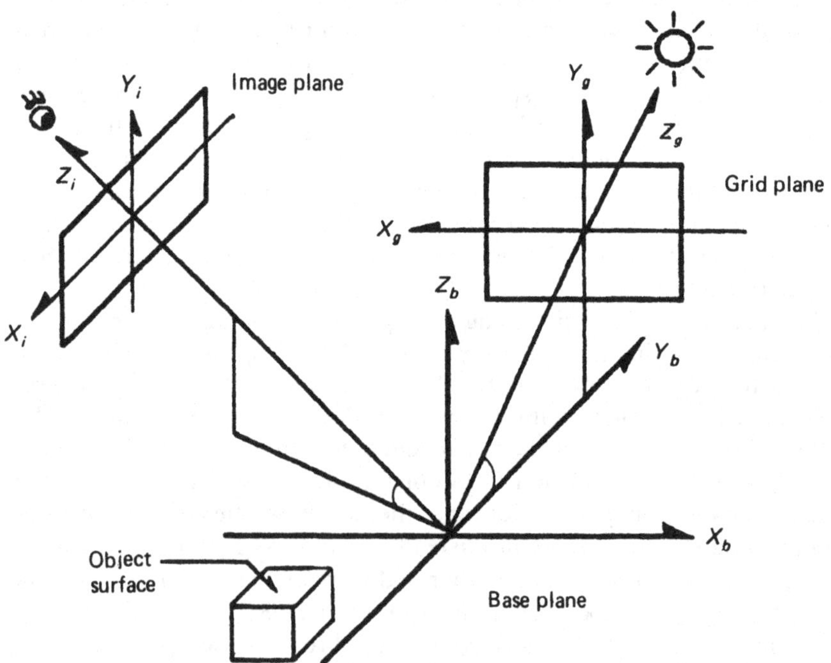

FIGURE 2.14. The system configuration of spatial encoding used in Wang et al. [1987]. © 1987 IEEE.

Inference of surface structure from a single view is accomplished in four steps: (1) A global coordinate system is defined with respect to the grid plane; (2) the orientation of the image plane in this global system is deduced by examining the observed base plane encoding; (3) the local surface orientation of visible portions of the object is determined from the observed object surface encoding, the orientation of the image plane, and the orientation of the grid plane; and (4) the surface structure is reconstructed if the object's surfaces obey certain smoothness constraints. The image plane registration and determination of surface orientation are formulated in terms of geometric constraints. The observed orientation of each set of stripes yields a constraint curve on the Gaussian sphere. Points along this curve denote the orientations that satisfy the constraint imposed by the observed encoding. The intersection of the constraint curves from two orthogonal stripes gives the orientation of the image plane and the object surface. Furthermore, if the surface is smooth and spacing between stripes small, a dense orientation map can be obtained through interpolation. Surface structure can then be reconstructed.

Later, Wang and Aggarwal exploited both the actively sensed partial surface structures as described in Wang et al. [1985], and the occluding contours, which were obtained through passive sensing, to construct the surface description of an object. Inferred surface structures represent pieces of strong evidence that should be incorporated in the surface description. Occluding contours delimit the projective range of the invisible surface structures from which the 3-D bounding volume can be constructed. Furthermore, occluding contours obtained from one view delimit the range in which surfaces inferred (via spatial encoding) from another view can lie. Partial surface structures inferred via spatial encoding provide local surface information, while occluding contours represent an estimate of the bounding volume structure. Exploiting these sources of information thus minimizes the number of views needed for accurate object reconstruction.

11 Concluding Remarks

In this chapter, we have surveyed a variety of techniques for the recovery of 3-D information from 2-D images. We began with binocular stereo, and extended the presentation to a more general form, i.e., structure from motion. Then, we focused our discussion on inferring shape from shading, shape from surface contour and texture, and shape from grid coding, and described a methodology to infer 3-D structures from multiple silhouettes. Finally, we presented the techniques for recognizing 3-D objects from single silhouettes using the principle of familiarity (also known as model-based vision).

Each of these approaches has its strengths and drawbacks, and is suitable for certain classes of objects, or for certain environments. For example, while the binocular stereo method is robust and yields (absolute) depth information, it usually takes a significant amount of time to solve the correspondence problem in computing the depth information. In addition, it determines depth only at the place where features (in the two images) are matched, and thus requires interpolation to obtain a continuous depth map.

The area of structure from motion has been sedulously explored for more than a decade. However, most of the research work in this area usually starts with the assumption that correspondences between a sequence of images have been solved. In this vein, it can be said that the motion and correspondence problems are not isolated from each other. It is encouraging that attempts have been made to derive structure from motion without correspondences. Increased efforts should be directed in dealing with the correspondence problem together with motion analysis, though. Furthermore, motion analysis usually requires solving a system of nonlinear equations, and the convergence problem of nonlinear solvers in turn relies on good initial guesses. The choice of the initial conditions and avoiding singularity are two crucial problems to be solved before the structure from motion method can be successfully applied to natural scenes.

One problem with most techniques based on shape from methods is that the absolute depth cannot be directly computed. A combination of any of these methods with other approaches (e.g., motion and binocular stereo) may be the answer to this problem. Moreover, the shape from methods usually require assumptions of certain regularities. For example, the techniques based on shape from shading are suitable in environments where incident illumination can be controlled and surface reflectance can be accurately modeled; this is next to impossible in complex natural scenes where the image formation parameters change in fairly arbitrary ways from point to point. On the other hand, the limitations of the shape from texture technique are that it requires statistical regularity of the textural elements, and is not suitable for nontextured objects. The same is true for shape from surface contour and for shape from occluding contour, which use the smoothness constraint or the extremum principle.

The volume intersection technique has been extensively employed in solid modeling. In most cases, a good approximation to the 3-D structure of an object may be reconstructed from its three primary views using the volume intersection technique. However, the inherent limitation of this technique is that it cannot not take care of certain kinds of concavities, such as the interior volume of a coffee cup. What are the classes of objects that can be reconstructed using the volume intersection technique? This is still an open problem, as is the problem of determining minimum number of views necessary for exact reconstruction. These two problems deserve careful study.

The shape from single silhouettes method is somewhat more robust than the other approaches due to the fact that it relies less on the information extracted from 2-D images than on the data stored in the database, which can be obtained under strictly controlled environments. Yet, there are two potential problems associated with this method:

1. It assumes that the objects in the given image have been successfully extracted; however, segmentation is not a trivial problem, especially in a highly noisy and textured image.
2. When the number of models stored in the data base increases, the recognition process becomes less efficient, unless the model can be carefully grouped into an object hierarchy.

It has been reported in the psychological literature [Jarvis 1983] that humans use a variety of cues or combinations of them to obtain depth information. This suggests that a computer vision system probably needs to include many modules, each of which implements a particular visual cue, so that vision tasks can be solved by using combinations of different modules with different weighting factors depending on the visual environments. It is encouraging to see that current research has been directed to the combinations of different approaches to obtain more robust and reliable results [Ikeuchi 1987; Wang and Aggarwal; Aloimos et al. 1987; Bulthoff and Mallot 1987]. For example, Ikeuchi [1987] has reported that more accurate depth information can be obtained through the binocular photometric stereo approach; Wang and Aggarwal [1985] have successfully recovered depth information by exploiting the volume intersection technique in the spatial encoding approach; Aloimonos et al. [1987] investigated the possibility of combining the binocular stereo method with the approaches using structure from motion and shape from contour.

One thing worth mentioning is the so-called "Active Vision" proposed by Aloimonos [1986], in which an observer may move around with a known or unknown motion, or rotate his/her eyes and track environmental objects. Aloimonos et al. [1987] have shown that some problems that are ill-posed for a passive observer become well-posed for an active one, and problems that are unstable become stable. We believed that Active Vision is a very promising approach to the solutions of otherwise ill-posed vision tasks, and deserves detailed investigation.

As mentioned in the introduction to this chapter, it is neither our intent nor is it possible to include all the research in the area of inferring 3-D structures from 2-D images, as this research area is the most active one in computer vision. The interested readers are directed to the extensive list of references at the end of the paper.

Acknowledgments. The authors would like to thank Dr. Y.C. Kim and Dr. Y.F. Wang for their help in preparing the manuscript. This research was supported by the National Science Foundation under grant ECS-8513123 and by the U.S. Army Research Office under contract DAAL03-87-K-0089.

References

Abu-Mostafa, Y.S., and Psaltis, D. 1987. Optical neural computers. *Sci. Amer.* **256,** 3 (Mar.) 88–95.

Aggarwal, J.K., and Mitiche, A. 1985a. Structure and motion from images: Fact and fiction. In *Proc. 3d Workshop on Computer Vision: Representation and Control.* (Bellaire, Mich., Oct. 13–16), IEEE Computer Society Press, Washington, D.C., 127–128.

Aggarwal, J.K., and Mitiche, A. 1985b. Structure and motion from images. In *Proc. Image Understanding Workshop,* (Miami Beach, Fla., Dec. 9–10), Science Applications, Inc., McLean, Va., 89–95.

Aggarwal, J.K., Davis, L.S., and Martin, W.N. 1981. Correspondence processes in dynamic scene analysis. In *Proc. IEEE* **69,** 5 (May), 562–572.

Aloimonos, J. 1986. Computing intrinsic images. Ph.D. thesis, University of Rochester, Rochester, N.Y.

Aloimonos, J., Weiss, I., and Bandyopadhyay, A. 1987. Active vision. In *Proc. 1st Intl. Conference on Computer Vision.* (London, England, June 8–11), IEEE Computer Society Press, Washington, D.C., 35–54.

Arnold, R.D. 1978. Local context in matching edges for stereo vision, In *Proc. Image Understanding Workshop* (Cambridge, Mass., May 3–4), Science Applications, Inc., McLean, Va., 65–72.

Arnold, R.D., and Binford, T.O. 1980. Geometrical constraints in stereo vision. In *Proc. SPIE,* **238,** San Diego, Calif., 281–292.

Attneave, F., and Frost, R. 1969. The determination of perceived tridimensional orientation by minimum criteria. *Perception and Psychophysics,* **6,** 6B, 391–396.

Bajcsy, R., and Lieberman, L. 1976. Texture gradient as a depth cue. *Computer Graphics and Image Processing* **5,** 1 (Mar.), 52–67.

Baker, H.H. 1980. Edge based stereo correlation." In *Proc. Image Understanding Workshop* (College Park, MD., Apr. 30.) Science Applications, Inc., McLean, Va., 168–175.

Baker, H.H., and Binford, T.O. 1981. Depth from edge and intensity based stereo. in *Proc. 7th IJCAI* (Vancouver, British Columbia, Canada, Aug. 24–28), IJCAI, 631–636.

Ballard, B.H., and Kimball, O.A. 1983. Rigid body motion from depth and optical flow. *Computer Vision, Graphics, and Image Processing* **22,** 1 (Apr.), 95–115.

Ballard, D.H. 1986. Cortical connections and parallel processing: Structure and function. *Behav. and Brain Sci.* **9,** 1 (Mar.), 67–90.

Barnard, S.T. and Pentland, A.P. 1983. Three dimensional shape from line drawings. In *Proc. 8th IJCAI* (Karlsruhe, West Germany, Aug. 8–12), IJCAI, 1062–1064.

Barnard, S.T. 1986. A stochastic approach to stereo vision. In *Proc. National Conference on AI* (AAAI-86). (Philadelphia, Pa., Aug. 11–15), Kaufmann, Los Altos, Calif., 676–680.

Barnard, S.T., and Fishler, M.A. 1982. Computational stereo. *ACM Computing Survey* **14,** 4 (Dec.), 553–572.

Barnard, S.T., and Thompson, W.B. 1980. Disparity analysis of images. *IEEE Trans. on PAMI.* **PAMI-2,** 4, 333–340.

Barrow, H.G., and Tenenbaum, J.M. 1981. Interpreting line drawings as three-dimensional surfaces. *Artificial Intell.* **17** (Aug.), 75–116.

Ben-Arie, J., and Meiri, A.A. 1986. 3-D objects recognition by state space search: Optimal geometric matching. In *Proc. CVPR-86.* (Miami Beach, Fla. June 22–26), IEEE Computer Society Press, Washington, D.C., 456–461.

Besl, P.J., and Jain, R.C. 1985. Three-dimensional object recognition. *Computing Surveys* **17,** 1 (Mar.), 75–145.

Blostein, S.D., and Huang, T.S. 1984. Estimating 3-D motion from range data. In *Proc. 1st Conference on Artificial Intelligence Applications.* (Denver, Colo., Dec. 5–7), IEEE Computer Society Press, Washington, D.C., 246–250.

Bottema, O., and Roth, B. 1979. *Theoretical kinematics.* North Holland Publishing Co., New York.

Brady, M., and Yuille, A. 1984. An extremum principle for shape from contour. *IEEE Trans. on PAMI.* **PAMI-6,** 3 (May), 288–301.

Brooks, M.J. 1979. Surface normals from closed paths. In *Proc. 6th IJCAI* (Tokyo, Japan, (Aug. 20–23), IJCAI, 98–101.

Brooks, R.A. 1981. Symbolic reasoning among 3-D models and 2-D images. *Artificial Intell.* **17** (Aug.), 285–348.

Bruss, A. 1981. Shape from shading and bounding contour. Ph.D. dissertation. Department of Electrical Engineering and Computer Science, Cambridge, Mass.

Bulthoff, H.H., and Mallot, H.A. 1987. Interaction of different modules in depth perception. In *Proc. 1st Intl. Conference on Computer Vision.* (London, England, June 8–11), IEEE Computer Society Press, Washington, D.C., 295–305.

Chen, S. 1985. Structure-from-motion without the rigidity assumption. In *Proc. 3rd Workshop on Computer Vision: Representation and Control.* (Bellaire, Mich., Oct. 13–16), IEEE Computer Society Press, Washington, D.C., 105–112.

Chien, C.H. and Aggarwal, J.K. 1986b. Identification of 3D objects from multiple silhouettes using quadtrees/octrees. *Computer Vision, Graphics, and Image Processing* **36,** 2–3 (Nov.–Dec.), 256–273.

Chien, C.H. and Aggarwal, J.K. 1986c. Volume/surface octrees for the representation of 3D objects. *Computer Vision, Graphics, and Image Processing* **36,** 1 (Oct.), 100–113.

Chien, C.H. 1986. Reconstruction and recognition of 3-D objects from occluding contours and silhouettes. Ph.D. dissertation. Department of Electrical and Computer Engineering, The University of Texas at Austin, Austin, Tex., May.

Chien, C.H., and Aggarwal, J.K. 1984. A volume/surface octree representation. In *Proc. 7th ICPR.* (Montreal, Canada, Jul. 30–Aug. 2), IEEE Computer Society Press, Silver Spring, MO., 817–820.

Chien, C.H., and Aggarwal, J.K. 1985. Reconstruction and matching of 3D objects using quadtrees/octrees. In *Proc. 3d Workshop on Computer Vision.* (Bellaire, Mich., Oct. 13–16), IEEE Computer Society Press, Washington, D.C., 49–54.

Chien, C.H., and Aggarwal, J.K. 1986a. Computation of volume/surface octrees from contours and silhouettes of multiple views. In *Proc. CVPR-86.* (Miami Beach, Fl., June 22–26), IEEE Computer Society Press, Washington, D.C., 250–255.

Chien, C.H., and Aggarwal, J.K. 1987. Shape recognition from single silhouettes. In *Proc. 1st Intl. Conference on Computer Vision*. (London, England, June 8–11), IEEE Computer Society Press, Washington, D.C., 481–490.

Chien, C.H., and Aggarwal, J.K. Model construction and shape recognition. *IEEE Trans. on PAMI*. To be published.

Clowes, M.B. 1971. On seeing things, *Artificial Intell.* **2,** 1, 79–116.

Cohen, P., and Feigenbaum, E.A. 1981. *The handbook of artificial intelligence*. Volume 3, William Kaufmann, Inc., Los Altos, Calif.

Coleman, Jr., E.N. and Jain, R. 1981. Shape from shading for surfaces with texture and specularity. In *Proc. 7th IJCAI*. (Aug. 24–28) University of British Columbia, Vancouver, British Columbia, Canada, 652–657.

Coleman, Jr., E.N. and Jain, R. 1982. Obtaining 3-dimensional shape of textured and specular surfaces using four-source photometry. *Computer Graphics and Image Processing* **18,** (Apr.) 309–328.

Davis, L.S., Janos, L., Dunn, S.M. 1983. Efficient recovery of shape from texture. *IEEE Trans. on PAMI*. **PAMI-5,** 5 (Sept.), 485–492.

Falk, G. 1972. Interpretation of imperfect line data as a three-dimensional scene. *Artificial Intell.* **3,** 2 101–144.

Fischler, M.A., and Bolles, R.C. 1981. Random sample consensus: A paradigm for model fitting with applications to image analysis and automated cartography. *Comm. ACM* **24,** 6, 381–395.

Fisher, R.B. 1983. Using surfaces and object models to recognize partially obscured objects. In *Proc. 8th IJCAI*. (Karlsruhe, West Germany, Aug. 8–12), IJCAI, 989–995.

Frobin, W., and Hierholzer, E. 1981. Rasterstereography: A photogrammetric method for measurement of body surfaces. *Photogramm. Engrg. Remote Sensing* **47,** 12 (Dec.), 1717–1724.

Frobin, W., and Hierholzer, E. 1982a. Calibration and model reconstruction in analytical close-range stereophotogrammetry part I: Mathematical fundamentals. *Photogramm. Engrg. Remote Sensing* **48,** 1 (Jan.), 67–72.

Frobin, W., and Hierholzer, E. 1982b. Calibration and model reconstruction in analytical close-range stereophotogrammetry part II: Special evaluation procedures for rasterstereography and moire topography. *Photogramm. Engrg. Remote Sensing* **48,** 2 (Feb.), 215–220.

Garabedien, P.R. 1964. *Partial differential equations*. Wiley, New York.

Giblin, P. 1987. Reconstruction of surfaces from profiles. In *Proc. 1st Intl. Conference on Computer Vision*. (London, England, June 8–11), IEEE Computer Society Press, Washington, D.C., 136–144.

Gibson, J.J. 1950; *The perception of the visual world*. Houghton Mifflin, Boston, Mass.

Goad, C. 1986. Fast 3D model-based vision. In *From pixels to predicates*. (A.P. Pentland, Ed.), Ablex, Norwood, N.J. 371–391.

Grankot, R.T., and Chellappa, R. 1987. A method for enforcing integrability in shape from shading algorithms. In *Proc. 1st Intl. Conference on Computer Vision* (London, England, June 8–11), IEEE Computer Society, Washington, D.C., 118–127.

Grimson, E.L. 1981b. *From images to surfaces*. MIT Press, Cambridge, Mass.

Grimson, W.E.L. 1981a. A computer implementation of a theory of human stereo vision. *Phil. Trans. Roy. Soc. London,* **B292,** 217–253.

Grimson, W.E.L. 1985. Computational experiments with a feature based stereo algorithm. *IEEE Trans. on PAMI,* **PAMI-7,** 1, 17–34.

Guzman, A., 1968. Computer recognition of three dimensional objects in a visual scene. *Technical Report MAC-TR-59.* M.I.T., Cambridge, Mass.

Hall, E.L., Tio, J.B.K., McPherson, C.A. and Sadjadi, F.A. 1982. Measuring curved surfaces for robot vision. *Computer* **15,** 12 (Dec.), 42–54.

Hoff, W., and Ahuja, N. 1986. Surfaces from stereo. *Proc. 8th Intl. Conference Pattern Recognition.* (Paris, France, Oct. 27–31) IEEE Computer Society Press, 516–518.

Horn, B.K.P. 1975. Obtaining shape from shading information. in *The psychology of computer vision* (P.H. Winston, Ed.) McGraw-Hill, New York, 115–155.

Horn, B.K.P. 1977. Understanding image intensities. *Artificial Intell.* **8,** 2 (Apr.), 201–231.

Horn, B.K.P. 1986. *Robot vision.* The MIT Press, Cambridge, Mass.

Horn, B.K.P., and Schunk, B.G. 1981. Determining optical flow. *Artificial Intell.* **17,** (Aug.), 185–203.

Horn, B.K.P., Sjoberg, R.W. 1979. Calculating the reflectance map. *Appl. Opt.* **18,** 11, 1770–1779.

Huang, T.S., and Tsai, R.Y. 1981. Image sequence analysis: Motion estimation. In *Image sequence processing and dynamic scene analysis.* (T.S. Huang, Ed.) Springer-Verlag, Berlin, Germany.

Huffman, D.A. 1971. Impossible objects as nonsense sentences. In *Machine Intelligence.* (B. Meltzer and D. Michie, Eds.), Vol. 6, Edinburgh University Press, Edinburgh, Scotland, 295–323.

Huffman, D.A. 1977b. Realizable configurations of lines in pictures of polyhedra. In *Machine Intelligence.* (E.W. Elcock and D. Michie, Eds), Vol. 8, Ellis Horwood, Chichester, England, 279–311.

Huffman, D.A. 1979a. A duality concept for the analysis of polyhedral scenes. *In Machine Intelligence.* (E.W. Elcock and D. Michie, Eds.) Vol. 8, Ellis Horwood, Chichester, England, 475–492.

Ikeuchi, K. 1980. Shape from regular patterns. *Technical Report A.I. Memo 567.* M.I.T. AI Lab, Cambridge, Mass., Mar.

Ikeuchi, K. 1984. Reconstructing a depth map from intensity maps. In *Proc. 7th ICPR* (Montreal, Canada, July 30–Aug. 2), IEEE Computer Society Press, Silverspring, Md., 736–738.

Ikeuchi, K. 1987. Determining a depth map using a dual photometric stereo. *Int. J. Robotics Res.* **6,** 1 (Spring) 15–31.

Ikeuchi, K. 1987. Precompiling a geometrical model into an interpretation tree for object recognition in bin-picking tasks. *Proc. Image Understanding Workshop.* (Los Angeles, Calif., Feb. 23–25). Science Applications, Inc., McLean, Va., 321–339.

Ikeuchi, K., and Horn, B.K.P. 1979. An application of the photometric stereo method. In *Proc. 6th IJCAI.* (Tokyo, Japan, Aug. 20–27), IJCAI, 413–415.

Ikeuchi, K., and Horn, B.K.P. 1981. Numerical shape from shading and occluding boundaries. *Artificial Intell.* **17,** (Aug.) 141–184.

Ittelson, W.H. 1960. *Visual space perception.* Springer-Verlag, Berlin, Germany.

Jarvis, A. 1983. A perspective on range finding. *IEEE Trans. Pattern Analysis and Machine Intell.* **PAMI-5,** 2 (Mar.), 122–139.

Julesz, B. 1960. Binocular depth perception of computer-generated pattern. *Bell System Tech. J.* **39,** 5, (Sept.), 1125–1162.

Julesz, B. 1971. *Foundation of cyclopean perception.* University of Chicago Press, Chicago, Ill.

Kak, A.C. Depth perception for robots. *TR-EE 83–44,* Purdue University, West Lafayette, Ind.

Kanade, T. 1980. A theory of origami world. *Artificial Intell.* **13,** 3 (May), 279–311.

Kanade, T. 1981. Recovery of the three-dimensional shape of an object from a single view. *Artificial Intell.* **17,** (Aug.) 409–460.

Kanatani, K.-i. 1985a. Detecting the motion of planar surface by line and surface integrals. *Computer Vision, Graphics, and Image Processing* **29,** 1 (Jan.), 13–22.

Kanatani, K.-i. 1985b. Structure from motion without correspondence: General principle. In *Proc. Image Understanding Workshop.* (Miami Beach, Fla., Dec. 9–10), Science Applications, Inc., McLean, Va., 107–116.

Kanatani, K.-i. 1985c. Tracing planar surface motion from a projection without knowing the correspondence. *Computer Vision, Graphics, and Image Processing* **29,** 1 (Jan.), 1–12.

Kender, J.R. 1978. Shape from texture: A brief overview and a new aggregation transform. In *Proc. Image Understanding Workshop.* (Pittsburgh, Pa., Nov. 14–15), Science Applications, McLean, Va., 79–84.

Kender, J.R. 1979. Shape from texture: An aggregation transform that maps a class of texture into surface orientation. In *Proc. 6th IJCAI* (Tokyo, Japan, Aug. 20–27), Vol. 1, 475–480.

Kender, J.R. 1980. Shape from texture. Ph.D thesis. Department of Computer Science, Carnegie-Mellon University, Pittsburgh, Pa.

Kim, Y.C., and Aggarwal, J.K. 1983. Rectangular coding for binary images. In *Proc. CVPR-83.* (Washington, D.C., June 19–23), IEEE Computer Society Press, Washington, D.C., 108–113.

Kim, Y.C., and Aggarwal, J.K. 1985. Finding range from stereo images. *Proc. IEEE Conference on Computer Vision and Pattern Recognition.* (San Francisco, Calif., June (19–23), IEEE, New York 289–294.

Kim, Y.C., and Aggarwal, J.K. 1986a. Rectangular parallelepiped coding: A volumetric representation of 3-D objects. *IEEE J. Robotics and Automation* **RA-2,** 3 (Sept.), 127–134.

Kim, Y.C., and Aggarwal, J.K. 1986b. Rectangular parallelepiped coding for solid modeling. *Intl. J. Robotics and Automation* **1,** 3, 77–85.

Land, E.H., and McCann, J.J. 1971. Lightness and retinex theory. *J. Opti. Soc. Amer.* **61,** 1 (Jan.), 1–11.

Le Moigne, J., and Waxman, A.M. 1984. Projected light grids for short range navigation of autonomous robots. In *Proc. 7th ICPR.* (Montreal, Canada, Jul. 30–Aug. 2), 203–206.

Lee, H.C., and Fu, K.S. 1983. Generating object descriptions for model retrieval. *IEEE Trans. on PAMI.* **PAMI-5,** 5 (Sept.) 462–471.

Levenberg, K. 1944. A method for the solution of certain non-linear problems in least squares. *Quart. Appl. Math.* **2,** 2 (July), 164–168.

Longuet-Higgins, H.C. 1981. A computer algorithm for reconstructing a scene from two projections. *Nat.* **293,** (Sep.) 133–135.

Longuet-Higgins, H.C. 1984. The reconstruction of a scene from two projections—

Configurations that defeat the 8-point algorithm. In *Proc. 1 Conference on Artificial Intelligence Applications*. (Denver, Colo., Dec. 5–7) 395–397.

Lowe, D.G. 1986. Three-dimensional object recognition from single two-dimensional images. *TR-202*. Computer Science Division, Courant Institute of Mathematical Sciences, New York University, New York, Feb.

Lucas, B.D., and Kanade, T. 1981. An iterative image registration technique with an application to stereo vision. In *Proc. Image Understanding Workshop*. (Washington, D.C., Apr. 23), 121–131.

Mackworth, A.K. 1973. Interpreting pictures of polyhedral scenes. *Artificial Intell.* **4,** 2 121–137.

Mackworth, A.K. 1977. How to see a simple world: An exegesis of some computer programs for scene analysis. In *Machine Intelligence*. (E.W. Elcock and D. Michie, Eds.), Vol. 8, Edinburgh University Press, Edinburgh, Scotland, 510–537.

Marr, D. 1982. *Vision*. W.H. Freeman and Company, San Francisco, Calif.

Marr, D., and Hildreth, E. 1980. Theory of edge detection. In *Proc. Roy. Soc. London* **B207,** 1167 (Feb.), 187–217.

Marr, D., and Nishihara, H.K. 1978. Representation and recognition of the spatial organization of three dimensional shapes. In *Proc. Roy. Soc. London* **B 200** (Mar.), 269–294.

Marr, D., and Poggio, T. 1976. Cooperative computation of stereo disparity. *Sci.* **194,** (Sept.) 283–287.

Marr, D., and Poggio, T. 1979. A theory of human stereo vision. in *Proc. Roy. Soc. London,* **B204,** 301–328.

Martin, W.N., and Aggarwal, J.K. 1983. Volumetric descriptions of objects from multiple views. *IEEE Trans. on PAMI*. **PAMI-5,** 2 (Mar.) 150–158.

Martin, W.N., Gil, B., and Aggarwal, J.K. Volumetric representation for object model acquisition. In *Proc. NASA Symposium on Computer Aided Geometry Modeling*. NASA Conference Publication, Washington, D.C., Apr. 87–94.

Mayhew, J.E.W., and Frisby, J.P. 1981. Psychophysical and computational studies towards a theory of human stereopsis. *Art. Intell.* **17,** (Aug.), 349–385.

McPherson, C.A., Tio, J.B.K., Sadjadi, F.A., and Hall, E.L. 1982. Curved surface representation for image recognition. In *Proc. PRIP-82* (Las Vegas, Nev., June 14–17), IEEE Computer Society Press, Washington, D.C., 363–369.

Mitiche, A. 1984a. Computation of optical flow and rigid motion. In *Proc. 2 Workshop on Computer Vision: Representation and Control*. (Annapolis, MD., Apr. 30–May 2), IEEE Computer Society Press, Washington, D.C., 63–71.

Mitiche, A. 1984b. On combining stereopsis and kineopsis for space perception. In *Proc. Artificial Intelligence Applications*. (Denver, Colo., Dec. 5–7), IEEE Computer Society Press, Washington, D.C., 156–160.

Mitiche, A. 1986. One kineopsis and computation of structure and motion. *IEEE Trans. on PAMI* **PAMI-8,** 1 (Jan.) 109–111.

Mitiche, A., Seida, S., and Aggarwal, J.K. 1985a. Determining position and displacement in space from images. In *Proc. of Conference on Computer Vision and Pattern Recognition*. (San Francisco, Calif., June 19–23), IEEE Computer Society Press, Washington, D.C., 504–509.

Mitiche, A., Seida, S., and Aggarwal, J.K. Interpretation of structure and motion from line correspondences. *IEEE Trans. on PAMI*. Submitted for publication.

Mitiche, A., Wang, Y.F., and Aggarwal, J.K. 1987. Experiments in computing optical flow with the gradient-based, multiconstraint method. *Pattern Recognition,* **20,** 2, 173–179.

Moravec, H.P. 1977. Towards automatic visual obstacle avoidance. In *Proc. 5th IJCAI.* (Cambridge, Mass., Aug. 22–25), IJCAI, 584.

Moravec, H.P. 1979. Visual mapping by a robot rover. In *Proc. 6th IJCAI* (Tokyo, Japan, Aug. 20–23), IJCAI, 598–600.

Moravec, H.P. 1980. Obstacle avoidance and navigation in the real world by a seeing robot rover. Ph.D. thesis, Stanford University, Stanford, Calif.

Moravec, H.P. 1981. Rover visual obstacle avoidance. In *Proc. 7th IJCAI* (Aug. 24–28), University of British Columbia, Vancouver, British Columbia, Canada, 785–790.

Mulgaonkar, P.G., Shapiro, L.G., and Haralick, R.M. 1982. Recognizing three-dimensional objects from single perspective views using Geometric and relational reasoning. In *Proc. PRIP-82.* (Las Vegas, Nev., June 14–17), IEEE Computer Society Press, Washington, D.C., 479–484.

Nagel, H.H. 1979. Image sequence analysis: What can we learn from applications? *Technical Report, IfI-HH-M-79/80.* Fachbereich Informatik, der Universitaet Hamburg, Hamburg, Germany, Sept.

Nagel, H.H. 1981a. On the derivation of 3D rigid point configuration from image sequences. In *Proc. Conference on Pattern Recognition and Image Processing.* (Dallas, Tex., Aug. 2–5), IEEE Computer Society Press, Washington, D.C., 103–108.

Nagel, H.H. 1981b. Representation of moving rigid objects based on visual observations. *Computer* **14** (Aug.) 29–39.

Nagel, H.H. 1986. Image sequences—Ten (octal) years—From phenomenology towards a theoretical foundation. In *Proc. 8th Intl. Conference on Pattern Recognition.* (Paris, France, Oct. 27–31), IEEE Computer Society Press, Washington, D.C., 1174–1185.

Nevatia, R. and Binford, T.O. 1973. Structured descriptions of complex objects. In *Proc. 3d IJCAI.* (Stanford, Calif., Aug. 20–23), IJCAI, 641–647.

Newman, W.M., and Sproull, R.F. 1973. In *Principles of interactive computer graphics.* McGraw-Hill, New York.

Nichodemus F.E., Richmond, J.C., Hsia, J.J., Ginsverg, I.W., and Limperis, T. 1977. *Geometrical considerations and nomenclature for reflectance.* NBS Monograph 160. U.S. Department of Commerce, National Bureau of Standards, Washington, D.C.

Ohta, Y.-I., Maenobu, K., and Sakai, T. 1981. Obtaining surface orientation from texels under perspective projection. In *Proc. 7th IJCAI,* (Vancouver, British Columbia, Canada, Aug. 24–28), IJCAI, 746–751.

Ohta, Y., and Kanade, T. 1985. Stereo by intra- and interscanline search using dynamic programming." *IEEE Trans. on PAMI,* **PAMI-7,** 2, (Mar.), 139–154.

Pennington, K.S., and Will, P.M. 1970. A grid-coded technique for recording 3-dimensional scenes illuminated with ambient light. *Opt. Comm.* **2,** 4 (Sep.), 167–169.

Pentland, A.P. 1984a. Local shading analysis. *IEEE Trans. on PAMI.* **PAMI-6,** (Mar.) 170–187.

Pentland, A.P. 1984b. Shading into texture. In *Proc. AAAI-84* (Austin, Texas, Aug. 6–10), Kaufmann, Los Altos, Calif., 269–273.

Poggio, T., Torre, V., and Koch, C. 1985. Computational vision and regularization theory. *Nature* **317,** (Sept.), 314–319.

Posdamer, J.L., and Altschuler, M.D. 1982. Surface measurement by space-encoded projected beam systems. *Computer Graphics and Image Processing* **18,** 1 (Jan.), 1–17.

Potmesil, M. and Freeman, H. 1972. Curved surface representation utilizing data extracted from multiple photographic images. *Workshop on the Representation of Three-Dimensional Objects.* (Philadelphia, Pa., May 1–2), University of Pennsylvania, Philadelphia, H1–H26.

Potmesil, M. 1983. Generating models of solid objects by matching 3D surface segments. In *Proc. 8th IJCAI.* (Karlsruhe, West Germany, Aug. 8–12), IJCAI, 1089–1093.

Prazdny, K. 1980. Egomotion and relative depth map from optical flow. *Biol. Cybernetics.* **36,** 2, 87–102.

Prazdny, K. 1983. On the information on optical flows. *Computer Vision, Graphics, and Image Processing* **22,** 2 (May), 239–259.

Roach, J.W., and Aggarwal, J.K. 1979. Computer tracking of objects moving in space. *IEEE Trans. on PAMI.* **PAMI-1,** 2 (Apr.), 127–135.

Roach, J.W., and Aggarwal, J.K. 1980. Determining the movement of objects from a sequence of images. *IEEE Trans. on PAMI.* **PAMI-2,** 6 (Nov.), 554–562.

Sohon, F.W. 1941. *The stereographic projection.* Chelsea, New York.

Stevens, K. 1979b. Surface perception from local analysis of texture and contour. Ph.D thesis, Department of Electrical Engineering and Computer Science, M.I.T., Cambridge, Mass.

Stevens, K.A. 1979a. Representing and analyzing surface orientation. In *Artificial intelligence: An MIT perspective.* (P.H. Winston and R.H. Brown, Eds.), Vol. 2, The MIT Press, Cambridge, Mass.

Stevens, K.A. 1981. The visual interpretation of surface contours. *Artificial Intell.* **17** (Aug.), 47–74.

Stockman, G., and Hu, G. 1986. Sensing 3-D surface patches using a projected grid. *IEEE Computer Society Conference on Computer Vision and Pattern Recognition.* (Miami Beach, Fla., June 22–26), IEEE, New York, 602–607.

Strat, T.M. 1979. A numerical method for shape from shading from a single image. Masters thesis. Department of Electrical Engineering and Computer Science, Cambridge, Mass.

Subbarao, M., and Waxman, A.M. 1985. On the uniqueness of image flow solutions for planar surfaces in motion. in *Proc. 3d Workshop on Computer Vision: Representation and Control.* (Bellaire, Mich., Oct. 13–16), IEEE Computer Society Press, Washington, D.C., 129–140.

Sugihara, K. 1982. Mathematical structures of line drawings of polyhedrons—Toward man-machine communication by means of line drawings. *IEEE Trans. on PAMI.* **PAMI-4,** 5 (Sept.), 458–468.

Sugihara, K. 1986. *Machine interpretation of line drawings.* The MIT Press, Cambridge, Mass.

Sugihara, K., Okazaki, K., Feng, K., and Sugie, N. 1985. Regular pattern projection for surface measurement. In *The second international symposium on robotics research.* (H. Hanafusa and H. Inoue, Eds.) MIT Press, Cambridge, Mass., 17–24.

Terzopoulos, D., Witkin, A., and Kass, M. 1987. Stereo matching as constrained optimization using scale continuation methods. In *Proc. SPIE Conference on Optical and Digital Pattern Recognition*. (Los Angeles, Calif. Jan. 13–15), SPIE, Bellingham, Wash.

Thompson, D.W., and Mundy, J.L. 1987. Model-directed object recognition on the connection machine. In Proc. Image Understanding Workshop. (Los Angeles, Calif., Feb. 23–25), Science Applications, Inc., McLean, Va., 98–106.

Thorpe, C.E. 1984. FIDO: Vision and navigation for a robot rover. Ph.D. thesis. Department of Computer Science, Carnegie-Mellon University, Pittsburgh, Pa.

Thorpe, C., and Shafer, S., 1983. Correspondence in line drawings of multiple views of objects. In *Proc. 8th IJCAI* (Karlsruhe, West Germany, Aug. 8–12), 959–965.

Tio, J.B.K., McPherson, C.A., and Hall, E.L. 1982. Curved surface measurement for robot vision. In *Proc. PRIP-82*. (Las Vegas, Nev., June 14–17), IEEE Computer Society Press, Washington, D.C., 370–378.

Tsai, R.Y. and Huang, T.S. 1984. Uniqueness and estimation of three-dimensional motion parameters of rigid objects with curved surface. *IEEE Trans. on PAMI*. **PAMI-6,** 1 (Jan.) 13–26.

Tsai, R.Y., and Huang, T.S. 1981. Estimating 3-D motion parameters of a rigid planar patch, I. *IEEE Trans. on ASSP*. ASSP-29, 6 (Dec.), 1147–1152.

Tsai, R.Y., Huang, T.S., and Zhu, W.L. 1982. Estimating three-dimensional motion parameters of a rigid planar patch, II: Singular value decomposition. *IEEE Trans. on ASSP*. ASSP-30 (Aug.), 525–534.

Ullman, S. 1979. *The interpretation of visual motion*. The MIT Press, Cambridge, Mass.

Wallace, T.P., and Wintz, P.A. 1980. An efficient three-dimensional aircraft recognition algorithm using normalized Fourier descriptors. *Computer Graphics and Image Processing*. **13,** 2 (June), 99–126.

Waltz, D. 1975. Generating semantic descriptions from drawings of polyhedral scenes. In *The psychology of computer vision* (P. Winston, Ed.), McGraw-Hill, New York, 19–92.

Wang, Y.F., and Aggarwal, J.K. 1987. On modelling 3-D objects using multiple sensory data. In *Proc. Intl. Conference on Robotics and Automation*. (Raleigh, N.C., Mar. 31–Apr. 3), IEEE Computer Society Press, Washington, D.C., 1098–1103.

Wang, Y.F., and Aggarwal, J.K. Integration of active and passive sensing techniques for representing three-dimensional objects. *IEEE J. Robotics and Automation*. To be published.

Wang, Y.F., Mitiche, A., and Aggarwal, J.K. 1987. Computation of surface orientation and structure of objects using grid coding. *IEEE Trans. on PAMI*. **PAMI-9,** 1 (Jan.), 129–137.

Waxman, A.M. 1984. An image flow paradigm. In *Proc. and Workshop on Computer Vision: Representation and Control*. (Annapolis, Md., Apr. 30–May 2), IEEE Computer Society Press, Washington, D.C., 49–57.

Webb, J.A., and Aggarwal, J.K. 1982. Structure and motion of rigid and jointed objects. *Artificial Intelli.* **19,** 1 (Sept.), 107–130.

Webb, J.A., and Aggarwal, J.K. 1983. Shape and correspondence. *Computer Vision, Graphics, and Image Processing* **21,** 1 (Jan.), 145–160.

Will, P.M., and Pennington, K.S. 1971. Grid coding: A preprocessing technique for robot and machine vision. *Artificial Intell.* **2,** 3–4, 319–329.

Will, P.M., and Pennington, K.S. 1972. Grid coding: A novel technique for image processing. *Proc. IEEE* **60,** 6 (June), 669–680.

Witkin, A.P. 1981. Recovering surface shape and orientation from texture. *Artificial Intell.* **17** (Aug.) 17–45.

Wohn, K., and Waxman, A.M. 1985. Contour evolution, neighborhood deformation and local image flow: Curved surfaces in motion. *Technical Report, CAR-TR-134*. Center for Automation Research, University of Maryland, College Park, Md.

Woodham, R.J. 1979. A cooperative algorithm for determining surface orientation from a single view. In *Proc. 5th IJCAI* (Cambridge, Mass., Aug. 22–25), IJCAI, 635–641.

Woodham, R.J. 1981. Analyzing images of curved surfaces. *Artificial Intell.* **17,** (Aug.) 117–140.

Yen, B.L. and Huang, T.S. 1983b. Determining 3-D motion/structure of a rigid body over 3 frames using straight line correspondences. In *Proc. Conference on Computer Vision and Pattern Recognition*. (Washington, D.C., June 19–23), 267–272.

Yen, B.L., and Huang, T.S. 1983a. Determining 3-D motion and structure of a rigid body using straight line correspondences. In *Image Sequence Processing and Dynamic Scene Analysis*. (T.S. Huang, Ed.), Springer-Verlag, Berlin, Germany, 365–394.

3
3-D Sensing for Industrial Computer Vision

DENIS POUSSART AND DENIS LAURENDEAU

ABSTRACT: Computer vision is becoming an important issue in many industrial applications such as automatic inspection of manufactured parts, robotic manipulations, autonomous vehicle guidance, and automatic assembly. Since these applications are performed in a three-dimensional world, it is imperative to gather reliable information on the 3-D structure of the scene. Rangefinder cameras are usually used to collect 3-D data. This chapter presents a review of various rangefinding techniques. Early designs and more recent developments are discussed along with a critical assessment of their performances. Purely optical techniques are not covered.

1 Introduction

The basic purpose of computer vision is to extract useful information from an image automatically and efficiently. The information can then be used to guide various processes such as robotic manipulation, automatic inspection, autonomous vehicle control, surveillance, etc. The image processing strategy in a computer vision application depends on the type of image data available. In many industrial applications, only grey-level (2-D) data is needed to provide useful information on a scene (e.g., aerial photography, pick-and-place manipulations). However, in numerous applications, the 3-D structure of the scene must be known and a 3-D range-sensing method must be implemented.

Three-dimensional acquisition must cover a wide spectrum of needs. For example, the detailed shape of an object in the scene might be needed instead of the mere range value of its surface elements. If a full 3-D description is required, view integration must be performed on multiple partial views of the object. In some cases, sparse 3-D data are all that is needed to understand a scene, while in others, dense 3-D data are required. Industrial processes often impose tight constraints on range-image acquisition time, so the choice must be made between static or dynamic rangefinding techniques. Environmental constraints must also be considered.

Generally speaking, currently available rangefinding techniques usually belong to either the active or the passive type. In the latter case, scene illumination is provided by the ambient light, while in the former case, a special lighting device illuminates the scene. Passive techniques are particularly appropriate for military or industrial applications where security or environmental constraints preclude the use of light sources such as lasers or powerful incandescent projectors. However, in many situations, environmental constraints can be relaxed and active techniques can be used.

This chapter reviews the recent developments in 3-D acquisition and sensing. Both passive and active techniques are covered along with an assessment of their advantages and drawbacks. The problems of rangefinding from motion and optical flow, Fourier techniques, and purely optical techniques will not be addressed. The chapter is organized as follows: passive techniques such as photometric stereo and shape form shading, are addressed in Section 2. The concept of range or shape from texture is also introduced, followed by a review of passive stereo techniques such as classical stereopsis, structural stereopsis, and the recent "one-eyed stereo" approach. Difficulties associated with the passive stereo approach are discussed. Section 2 ends with a review of several techniques allowing the recovery of range from a single grey-level or binary image. The problem of camera calibration is also discussed briefly.

Active techniques are covered in Section 3. Conventional striped lighting methods are reviewed first, followed by a description of the Moiré approach. Ultrasonic and laser time-of-flight techniques are then presented along with a discussion on recent designs. Classical triangulation rangefinders are described, and the concept of synchronized triangulation is introduced. It is followed by a review of the range-from-defocusing approach and ends on the subject of intensity-guided rangefinding.

2 Passive Techniques

The first two techniques reviewed, photometric stereo and shape from shading, are concerned with the recovery of surface orientation from one or multiple grey-level pictures. The remainder of Section 2 covers other passive rangefinding techniques.

2.1 Photometric Stereo

Common experience demonstrates that image intensity carries a great deal of information on a scene. The intensity recorded at a particular pixel results from the interaction of aspects that combine geometry and radiometry considerations: position and surface properties of the light sources, surface properties of the material, and surface position and orientation.

Consider the geometry of Figure 3.1. A patch of the surface with area δO and radiance L is seen as surface δI on the image plane after a perspective projection. The irradiance E in (W/m^2) of the image patch δI located at (x, y) is known to be [Horn 1986]

$$E(x, y) = \frac{\pi}{4} \left(\frac{d}{F}\right)^2 \cos^4(\alpha)\, L, \tag{3.1}$$

where parameters d and F are defined in Figure 1. Thus, for patches located near the optical axis, where $\cos^4\alpha \cong 1$, the image irradiance is proportional to the scene brightness L.

2.1.1 Surface Reflectance. The radiance of the object patch, as seen from the camera, results from the irradiance generated by the illuminating source and transformed by the optical characteristics of the surface. A convenient casting of these characteristics is through the bidirectional reflectance distribution function (BDRF) [Horn 1986]:

$$f(\theta_i, \phi_i, \theta_e, \phi_e) = \frac{\partial L(\theta_e, \phi_e)}{\partial E(\theta_i, \phi_i)}, \tag{3.2}$$

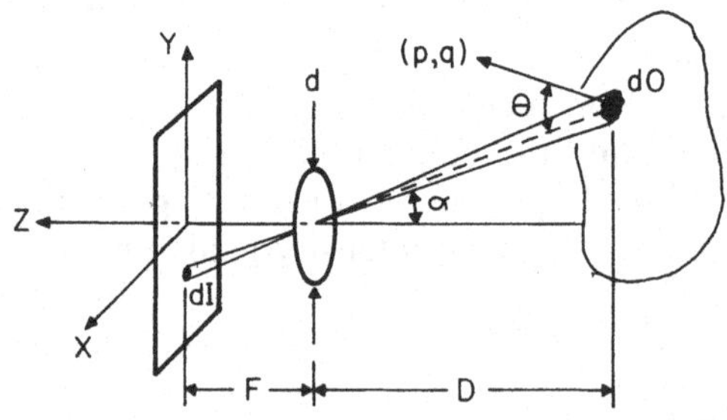

D : distance between object patch and lens
F : effective focal length of the camera
d : diameter of the lens
α : angle between the object patch and the optical axis
θ : object patch orientation relative to α
δI : area of image patch
δO : area of object patch

FIGURE 3.1. Image formation geometry (redrawn from Horn [1986]).

where θ_i, ϕ_i, θ_e, ϕ_e are defined in Figure 3.2. Useful cases of the BDRF include the Lambertian surface, which appears equally bright from all viewing directions (for a given constant illuminating angle):

$$f_{lambert} = \frac{1}{\pi}. \tag{3.3}$$

2.1.2 Surface Orientation. Given the explicit equation of a target surface with the geometry of Figure 3.1:

$$z = g(x, y). \tag{3.4}$$

A surface normal vector has elements

$$[-\frac{\partial g(x,y)}{\partial x}, \; -\frac{\partial g\,(x,y)}{\partial y}, \; 1]. \tag{3.5}$$

Defining the gradients components

$$p = \frac{\partial g(x,y)}{\partial x} \tag{3.6a}$$

and

$$q = \frac{\partial g(x,y)}{\partial y}, \tag{3.6b}$$

the surface normal can be written as $[-p, -q, 1]$. The gradient space of all points $(-p, -q)$ is viewer-centered and represents surface orientation. For a faraway source, rays appear to be coming from a single direction, which is specified in gradient space as $(-p_0, -q_0)$.

2.1.3 The Reflectance Map. The reflectance map folds surface orientation with brightness. It takes into account the properties of the light source

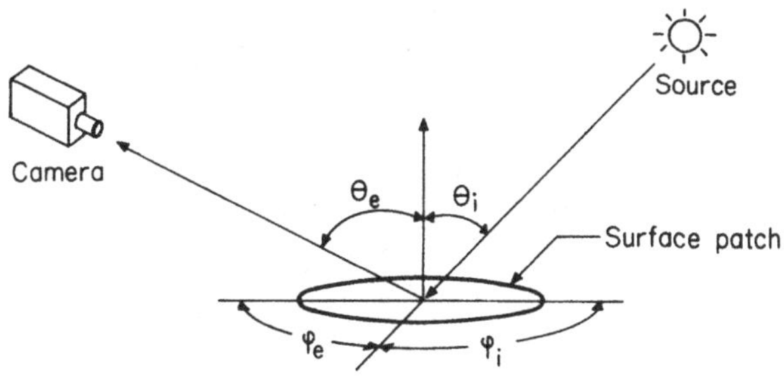

FIGURE 3.2. Angular geometry for the definition of the BDRF.

distribution and the specific reflectance characteristics of the target surface. For instance, consider a Lambertian patch with orientation $[-p, -q, 1]$ that is illuminated by a source providing irradiance E. Its radiance L, as seen from the viewing position, is:

$$L = \left(\frac{E}{\pi}\right) cos(\theta_i), \tag{3.7}$$

where θ_i corresponds to the angle between the impinging light and the orientation of the patch. Thus in equation (3.7):

$$cos(\theta_i) = \frac{1 + p_0 p + q_0 q}{\sqrt{1 + p^2 + q^2}\sqrt{1 + p_0^2 + q_0^2}} . \tag{3.8}$$

Equation (3.7) is known as Lambert's law of radiation [De Vriendt 1984] in which $cos(\phi_i)$ accounts for the foreshortening of the radiating surface as seen from the source. The reflectance map $R(p, q)$ displays (within a constant) how target radiance varies with surface orientation for a given source distribution. For the Lambertian case of equation (3.7),

$$R(p, q) = \frac{1 + p_0 p + q_0 q}{\sqrt{1 + p^2 + q^2}\sqrt{1 + p_0^2 + q_0^2}} . \tag{3.9}$$

It is convenient to display R as contours of equal radiance on the (p, q) gradient space. An example of a reflectance map presented by Woodham [1984] for a Lambertian surface and a source orientation of (0.7, 0.3) is shown in Figure 3.3.

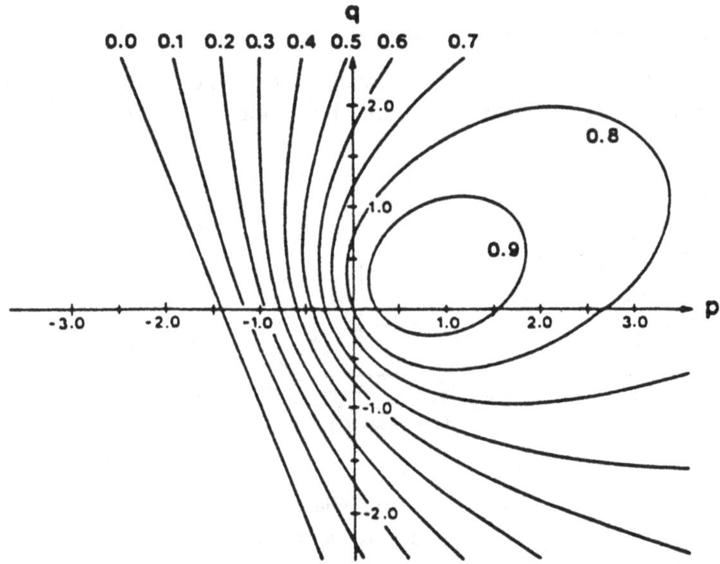

FIGURE 3.3. Reflectance map for a Lambertian surface with source orientation (0.7,0.3) (reproduced from Woodham [1981]).

From equations (3.1) and (3.9), the image irradiance can be related to the reflectance map:

$$E(x, y) = R(p, q). \tag{3.10}$$

Inferences about 3-D shape can be drawn from equation (3.10). Given a specific object shape, its gradient (p, q) is known at each point. $R(p, q)$ therefore maps orientation to reflectance. This provides means to compute the distribution of surface brightness required to produce synthesized images [Horn 1986]. However, the inverse mapping is not unique since $E(x, y)$ is a scalar and $[-p, -q, 1]$ is a vector with two degrees of freedom [Marr 1981]. The ambiguity of the inverse mapping can be resolved by photometric stereo, which correlates several distinct irradiance images obtained for identical viewing direction but with different illumination conditions. Since there is no change in the camera position, each picture element at location (x, y) corresponds to a specific target patch. Note that using a fixed viewing position eliminates the correspondence encountered with the classical stereo approach discussed later in Section 2.4.2. The two unknowns p and q are determined by locating the point in gradient space that simultaneously satisfies the reflectance maps corresponding to the set of illuminating conditions. The number of maps required depends on the type of surface reflectance. For instance, three views are sufficient to determine surface orientation for a Lambertian surface, provided that the three directions of illumination are not coplanar.

In practice, the rapid computation of surface orientation from several reflectance maps lends itself to techniques of lookup tables that are constructed (analytically or experimentally) from surface prototypes with the same surface properties as the scene of interest.

2.2 Shape from Shading

It is possible, under certain constraints, to recover surface orientation from a single image. For example, the smoothness characteristic of target objects may provide a useful reconstruction constraint [Ikeuchi and Horn 1981]. Moreover, in some special cases, an inverse solution can be found. More specifically, the cases of linear and rotationally symmetric reflectance maps are well described in Horn [1986]. The solution for the general case is quite involved mathematically and will not be discussed here. Interested readers are referred to Horn [1970, 1975, 1985] and Woodham [1979, 1981, 1984] for details.

Since they both rely on a solid theoretical framework, photometric stereo and shape from shading are two very interesting 3-D shape sensing techniques. However, they are still difficult to apply to complicated industrial scenes. For instance, photometric stereo would fail to produce reliable results when applied to an industrial environment containing objects with different surface characteristics (e.g., non-Lambertian surface, specular reflection, etc. and spurious light sources of unknown orientation. Future developments in specialized hardware processors should lower the computational cost and open new areas of application for these sophisticated techniques.

2.3 Range or Shape from Texture

When a smooth 3-D surface covered with a repetitive pattern is projected (perspective projection assumed) on a 2-D image plane, the size of the pattern images decreases with depth and thus provides valuable depth clues [Witkin 1981]. In order to estimate depth from texture; the texture gradient (i.e., the increasing fineness of texture with depth) must be computed. Gibson [1966] studied the special cases of horizontal planes (parallel to the optical axis) and vertical planes (normal to the optical axis). Bajcsy and Lieberman [1976] designed a texture operator based on Fourier descriptors.

Shen and Wong [1983] observed the fact that texture characteristics are highly resolution-dependent. To render a more meaningful representation (and comparison) of texture, they adopted the concept of observation windows (also called blocks) of different resolution. The texture is defined in terms of frequency diagrams of line features (e.g., mean grey-level, gradient amplitude) and circular features (e.g., gradient direction) over a block of given resolution. A measure is defined for the evaluation of texture similarity involving the unfolded frequency diagrams, which allows the comparison of frequency diagrams of adjacent blocks and the "event distance" between salient features of the diagrams. This chapter reports an interesting analysis of the performance of the metrics on various patterns. In some cases, the method can identify texture patterns that are not detected by the human eye.

If the absolute size of the texture pattern is not known *a priori,* only relative range values can be inferred from the textured scene. Fortunately, in industrial applications, it is often possible to use calibrated patterns. This is especially true in mobile robot guidance where calibrated patterns can be painted on the floor and used as milestones. McVey et al. [1986] used a straight-edged line (which is a degenerated pattern) of known width as a floor pattern in a robot navigation experiment.

Most of the past work on range or shape from texture was based on a smoothness constraint of surfaces to relate neighboring points. Even though such a constraint is acceptable in a man-made environment, it is no longer valid in natural scenes (often encountered in military applications) made of complex and rough surfaces. Pentland [1986] recently suggested a more general approach to the problem of texture and adopted a fractal model to describe rough-textured surfaces. Texture is defined as the 3-D structure of the surface in opposition to the concept of texture pattern described earlier.

It is a well-known fact that fractals look like natural surfaces [Mandelbrot 1982]. Moreover, fractals are a generalization of Brownian motion and have two important properties:

1. Each segment is similar to others.
2. Segments at different scales are statistically indistinguishable.

This means that the most important variable feature in a fractal surface is the ratio between the number of large features and the number of middle- and small-sized features. Within a mathematical framework based on fractal Brownian functions, Pentland suggests a texture measure and a method for estimating surface tilt and slant angles. A conclusion is that the estimates obtained are more reliable when the fractal technique is performed on textured surfaces (rough surfaces) rather than on shaded (or smooth) surfaces. Another interesting conclusion is that shape from texture evolves into shape from shading when 3-D texture decreases.

From an industrial point of view, texture is often used as an "artificial feature" added to the scene to speed up segmentation and range computation. According to current literature, natural texture analysis for range measurement is still absent from the factory environment. This situation should prevail in the near future since the segmentation of complex textured images is still computationally expensive.

2.4 Range from Passive Stereo

One of the functions of the human visual system is to reconstruct a 3-D representation of the world through stereopsis, i.e., the process of combining a pair of 2-D images obtained from two different view points, to establish the depth of surrounding surfaces. Because it only uses natural illumination and because it performs so well in humans, passive stereo is an attractive method of 3-D sensing.

2.4.1 Basic Principle of Stereopsis. A basic arrangement for stereopsis is shown in Figure 3.4. Let the scene reference frame be the reference frame of camera 1, centered at O_1, and let the origin O_2 of the reference frame of camera 2 be located at L_y in frame 1. From simple Euclidean geometry, one can write from Figure 3.4.

$$\frac{y_1}{f} = \frac{Y_1}{z + f} \tag{3.11a}$$

$$\frac{y_2}{f} = \frac{Y_2}{z + f} \tag{3.11b}$$

with

$$Y_2 = Y_1 - L_y \,. \tag{3.12}$$

In equations (3.11a,b), f is the effective focal length of the pinhole model adopted for the camera. Replacing Y_2 in equation (3.11b) with its value

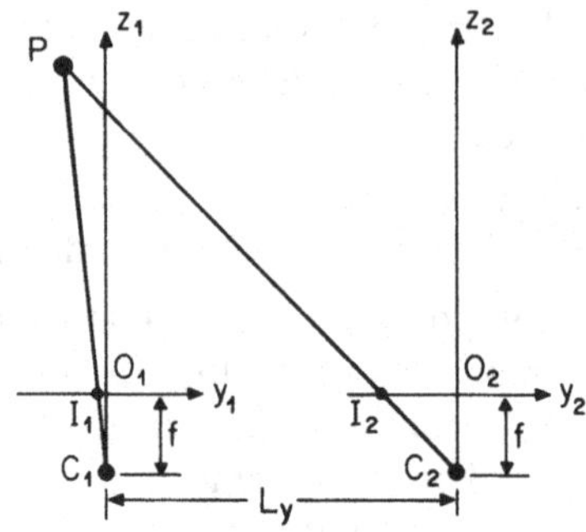

P : 3D point
O_1, O_2 : origins of camera coordinate systems
C_1, C_2 : centers of projection for camera 1 and 2
I_1, I_2 : images of point P
L : baseline separation (i.e. distance between cameras)
f : focal distance of the cameras

FIGURE 3.4. Geometry for stereopsis.

in equation (3.12) and eliminating Y_1 allows us to find the range z of point P:

$$z = \frac{-f[(y_2 - Y_1 - L_y]}{(y_2 - y_1)}. \tag{3.13}$$

In equation (3.13) $(y_2 - y_1)$ is the stereo disparity between the images of the same point taken from two different locations and shows that the accuracy on range is directly related to the separation L_y between the cameras. On sampled images, the range effort as a percent of range versus range-to-baseline ratio has a sawtooth shape with an increasing amplitude with the range-to-baseline ratio [Duda and Hart 1973].

2.4.2 Problems Related to Stereopsis. Despite its simple geometrical aspects, passive stereo is confronted with several significant difficulties:

1. Since it is necessary to establish the correspondence between joints, there may not be sufficient visual information at the points of interest to establish a unique pairing relationship, for instance, because of lack of intensity or color identifiers.
2. Some part of the scene may appear in only one view of the stereo pair, due to occlusion (or shadow) effects. Occlusion diminishes when the baseline L_y is reduced, but so does the accuracy in range.

3. Several candidate points may satisfy the matching operation with the resulting identification of false targets.

2.4.3 Solving the Correspondence Problem. There is a critical interplay between the type of feature selected and the complexity of the subsequent matching. Features might be high level (e.g., specific shape), therefore difficult to recognize in 2-D images but easy to match once recognized. Or, they may be low level, e.g., dots, edges, or local texture, relatively easy to detect but subject to more ambiguous matching.

There have been many instances of optical "busyness" indicators. Levine et al. [1973] has used the cross correlation between rectangular windows with hierarchical searches at coarse and fine resolutions. Yakimovsky and Cunningham [1978] compute cross correlation over cross- or diamond-shaped areas with the search for match being conditioned by a sufficient magnitude of the variance of the local masked region.

The remarkable work of Julez [1964], based on random dot stereograms, has suggested that human vision is capable of inferring depth perception even when each monocular image of a stereo pair, by itself, does not provide any high-level cue for disparity. This observation argues that stereovision can operate on low-level, primitive features. Marr and Poggio [1979], Marr and Hildreth [1980], and Grimson [1981] have convincingly proposed that disparity can be computed by comparing symbolic descriptions of features that arise from local changes in physical properties of the target and can be detected as changes in the 2-D image irradiance.

In the Marr-Poggio-Grimson (MPG) approach, the symbolic description of each image is obtained from the intensity edges detected by the zero-crossings produced by a nondirectional operator. The raw image $E(x, y)$ is first convolved with a Gaussian $G_\sigma(x, y)$

$$G_\sigma(x, y) * E(x, y) \tag{3.14}$$

with

$$G_\sigma(x,y) = \sigma^2 e^{-(x^2 + y^2)/2\sigma^2} \tag{3.15}$$

and then submitted to the Laplacian operator ∇^2:

$$\nabla^2 = \frac{\partial^2}{\partial x^2} + \frac{\partial^2}{\partial y^2}\,. \tag{3.16}$$

The application of the linear operators in equations (3.14) and (3.15) can be interchanged and the expression for the processed image may be written as

$$f(x, y, \sigma) = \nabla^2 (G_\sigma * E(x, y)). \tag{3.17}$$

The overall operator (called the primal sketch operator) is rotationally symmetric and is given by

$$\nabla^2 G_\sigma(r) = \frac{r^2 + 2\sigma^2}{\sigma^4} e^{-r^2/2\sigma^2} \tag{3.18}$$

with

$$r = \sqrt{x^2 + y^2} . \tag{3.19}$$

The central width of the operator is

$$w_{2D} = 2\sqrt{2}\sigma . \tag{3.20}$$

The shape of this operator can also be approximated as the difference of two properly selected Gaussian distributions (DOG), a realization that can be exploited towards real-time processing. Some hardware processors capable of convolving a DOG with a 512 × 512 grey-level image in one image frame are already available. Speed can be enhanced by using a DOG shape that is roughly quantized to three amplitudes over a 63 × 63 window.

Marr and Poggio have observed that the difficulties of correspondence and false targets could be reduced by lowering the range and/or resolution of the disparities being considered, and they proposed a vernier hierarchical strategy. A coarse filtered image (large w in equation (3.20)) is first used to bring the position of a feature point in coincidence. The coincidence is then refined by the contribution of a fine filtered image (small w). In each case, the search for a match is limited to disparity change that is consistent with w and false matches are substantially avoided.

The application of the primal sketch operator to find disparities may result in a sparse array of candidate points. Grimson [1981] has addressed the problem of reconstructing appropriate shapes from such data. The central principle is that the estimated surface should be the most conservative, i.e., should vary as little as possible between control points. For approximating the surface that most closely matches the sparse data points, the problem consists of solving for the minimum in the expression:

$$\int\int (s_{xx}^2 + s_{yy}^2 + 2\, s_{xy}^2)\, dx\, dy + \beta \sum [s(x,y) - c(x,y)]^2, \tag{3.21}$$

which combines a constraint for the most conservative surface s and mean-square distance to the set of data points $c(x, y)$. A possible solution for equation (3.21) is a spline function [Reinsch 1967].

A few conclusions can be derived from the preceding discussion:

1. The Marr-Poggio approach to the problem of correspondence is a very elegant computational model. Its theoretical framework is centered on observations of the first processes of human stereo vision.
2. The vernier hierarchical strategy is computationally expensive and is still difficult to implement in industrial applications.
3. Disparity measurements may result in a sparse array of points. That may not be sufficient (unless equation (3.21) is solved) in the factory environment.

2.4.4 Other Approaches to Stereopsis. The Marr-Poggio-Grimson algorithm for stereo is a global approach to the 3-D vision problem and makes little use of *a priori* knowledge of the scene. When the vision problem is more specific, as is often the case in robot vision, it is possible to impose restrictions leading to valuable results within a reasonable time on currently available hardware.

For instance, Luh and Klaasen [1985] designed a multicamera 3-D vision system for collision avoidance in a robotic application. A schematic of the camera arrangement is shown in Figure 3.5. A CID (charge injection device) camera is mounted on each axis of a cartesian coordinate system. The orthogonality of the optical axes of the cameras is essential since 3-D coordinates computation is based on this assumption. A binary image is obtained for each camera and is analyzed by an offshelf 2-D vision system based on the SRI technical approach [Nitzan et al. 1977]. The binary image processing was chosen to speed up the execution time. The method relies on sets of six numbers computed by the vision systems: x-min, x-max, y-min, y-max, x-centroid, and y-centroid for each blob found in each of the images. The system analyzes the blobs of an image, computes the six parameters and searches for a match with the centroids of the blobs of the other two images. If a match is found, the 3-D coordinates of the corners of the worst-case bounding box enclosing the objects of the scene are computed from the coordinates associated with the blobs in each binary image contributing to the match. This worst-case bounding box is used by a collision avoidance program for a robot.

Although only two cameras are needed to compute the 3-D coordinates of a point, a three-camera setup can help to avoid the problem of false targets due to the fact that, with only two cameras, some of the workspace may not be detected. It is assumed that two (or more) overlapping objects will be considered as a single object and the resulting bounding box will enclose all the overlapping objects. A typical execution time of between 100 ms and 1 s is reported. This figure is data-dependent and depends

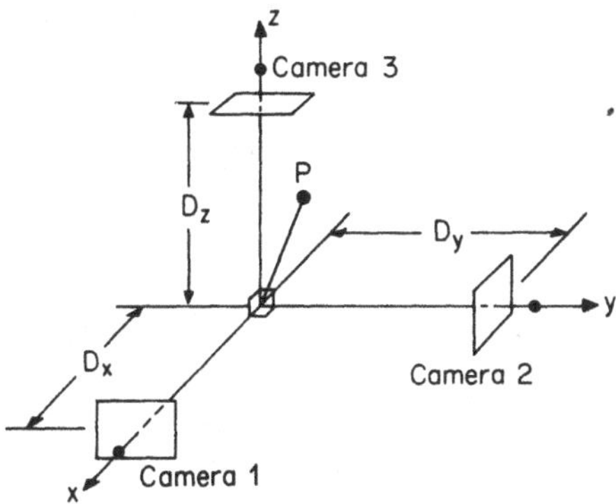

FIGURE 3.5. Multicameras 3-D vision setup (redrawn from Luh and Klaasen [1985]).

more specifically on the following: (1) the time required by the vision system to process the raw image data; (2) the "busyness" of the scene; and (3) the time required to transfer data between the vision system and the host computer. No absolute figure is given on the accuracy of the 3-D coordinates of the bounding box but the principal sources of error are described: image resolution (a 128 × 128 image array was used) and initialization of system parameters (e.g., position of the cameras in the reference frame).

A very interesting solution to the problem of stereopsis in a robot vision application is proposed by Boyer et al. [1986]. The approach is called structural stereopsis and relies on the observation that in many applications, a priori knowledge of the scene is available and could be used to speed up the stereo matching operation and the computation of 3-D coordinates while reducing the matching errors.

Structural stereopsis works as follows: a pair of stereo binary images of the scene is taken and analyzed. A structural description of the scene is built for each one. This description is used to represent, in a symbolic form, the information contained in the scene. The description is based on a set of primitives P and the relations between primitives R. The primitives are extracted from a radial-valued skeleton obtained from the binary images. The skeleton is divided in segments (called primitives) and each segment is described by a set of parameters (e.g., length, orientation, mass, loop). The structural description also includes how primitives are linked to one another: X left of Y; X above Y: X touching Y.

The structure of the left and right images of the stereo pair are symbolized by

$$D_l = (P_l, R_l) \tag{3.22a}$$

$$D_r = (P_r, R_r) \; . \tag{3.22b}$$

Each primitive is characterized by a set of features that comes in attribute-value pairs. The attribute is the name of the feature and the value is the "importance" of the given attribute. The relation between primitives is also parameterized by a mapping function. The solution of the stereo matching problem is thus an attempt to pair each primitive of the left image structural description D_l to at most one corresponding primitive from the right image structural description D_r. The quality of the pairing between primitives is computed using an information-theoretic interprimitive distance measure along with a measure of relational consistency defined in terms of parametric relations.

Structural stereopsis seek to minimize the distance between two structural descriptions. In the paper, stereopsis is taken in a more general sense than in the MPG approach and the parallax effect is used to locate objects. The parallax effect is illustrated in Figure 3.6. The height h of an object point is proportional to the Euclidean distance d between its coordinates

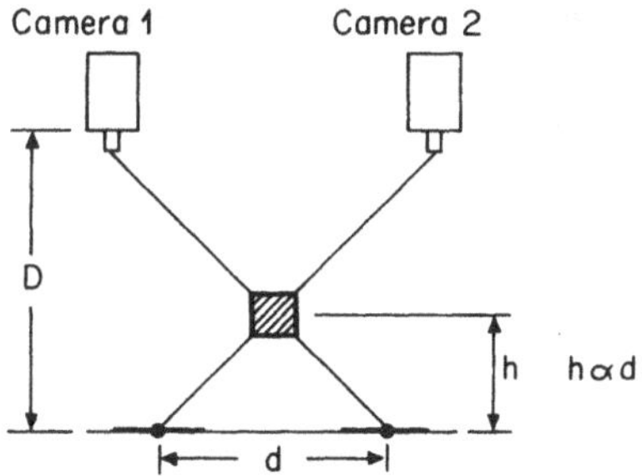

FIGURE 3.6. Parallax effect.

in the work table plane as computed by inverse perspective projection for each camera. This inverse perspective transformation is possible because the distance between each camera and the work table is known.

It is reported that the structural stereopsis method has been applied successfully to a "rod sorting" robotic experiment: rods of different length but identical diameter have to be sorted by the robot by order of decreasing length. The orientation and crossing of the rods is random on the work table. No accuracy or execution time figures are reported. The authors argue that the structural stereopsis approach is general and can be tailored to a wide variety of industrial computer vision and artificial intelligence applications.

Finally, Strat and Fischler [1986] recently introduced the concept of one-eyed stereo (OES). The OES approach is based on the idea that, even though a 2-D image is an ambiguous representation of a 3-D scene, it often contains strong 3-D clues. The OES paradigm is a five-step process. At step 1, the original 2-D image is segmented in order to find regions that are individually in conformance with a single model for image formation, for example, the uniform grid projection model discussed later in Section 3.1.1. At step 2, a model for image formation is chosen for each image partition. This is a very difficult task since it requires an accurate interpretation of the image. At step 3, a second image is generated from the original image and the chosen model. It is assumed that the second image is virtually obtained from an orthographic projection of the 3-D scene on the image plane. This virtual image and the original image are used to determine stereo correspondences (step 4) from which depth is computed (step 5). The OES method is general and could be applied to a broad spectrum of situations.

2.5 Range from a Single Grey-Level Image

A problem connected to rangefinding is the location-determination problem (LDP), which can be described as the determination of the position and orientation of an autonomous robot vehicle (or any other device) relative to a given reference frame. In this type of problem, the position of the robot in 3-D space must be computed quickly. Stereopsis, and even structural stereopsis, might be too slow to provide sufficient response time.

A common approach to LDP is to use a well-defined landmark of known dimensions as a target for data capture by a single camera. Geometrical constraints imposed on the perspective projection of the landmark on the image plane are then sufficient to recover the position and orientation of the camera relative to the landmark.

For example, Courtney and Aggarwal [1983] use a dark diamond-shaped landmark painted on a contrasting background as the target for LDP, as shown in Figure 3.7 (a). It is assumed that the height z_c of the camera relative to the landmark is known, which is an acceptable assumption since the landmark position is fixed and the camera is mounted rigidly on the robot (a horizontal floor must also be assumed, even though it is not mentioned in the paper). The optical axis of the camera is aimed at the center of the landmark. From Figure 3.7 (a),

$$z_c = D \sin(\beta); \tag{3.23}$$

also

$$\frac{\cos(\beta)}{\tan(\psi)} = \frac{\cos(\rho)}{\tan(\theta)}, \tag{3.24}$$

$$\cos(\beta) = \frac{(D^2 - w^2)\tan(\psi)}{2Dw}, \tag{3.25}$$

and

$$\cos(\rho) = \frac{(D^2 - w^2)\tan(\theta)}{2Dw}. \tag{3.26}$$

Equations (3.23)–(3.26) are all that is needed to compute D, β and ρ since ψ and θ can be found from the image of the landmark and w, the diagonal length of the landmark, is known. A computer simulation for error analysis shows that for special cases (e.g., ψ and $\theta \sim 0°$), small variation in the measured quantities result in large variation in position.

Another paper by Magee and Aggarwal [1984] proposes a landmark made of two great circles (one vertical, the other horizontal) painted on the surface of a sphere. With the use of the projected sphere on the image plane and points P_v and P_h on the great circles closest to its center, the

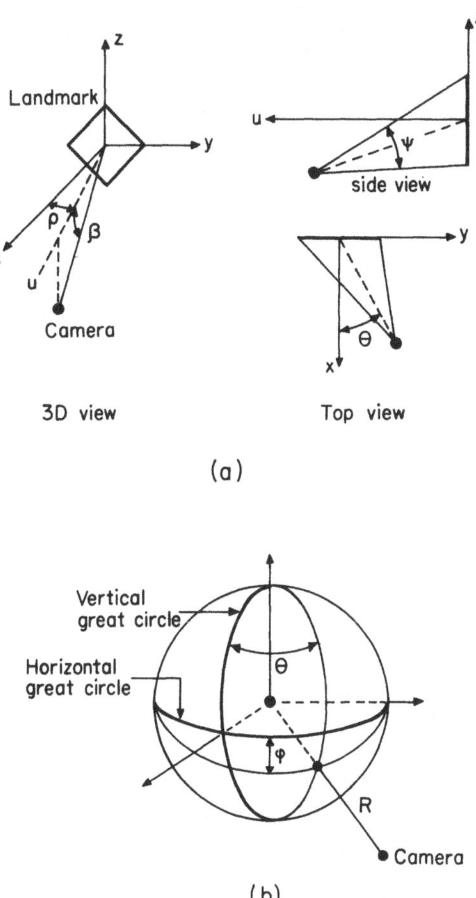

FIGURE 3.7. Various geometries for LDP: (a) diamond-shaped landmark (redrawn from Courtney and Aggarwal [1983]; (b) great circles landmark (redrawn from Magee and Aggarwal [1984].

camera-to-sphere distance R and the orientation (θ, ϕ) can be derived analytically. The geometry of the problem and the various parameters are depicted in Figure 3.7 (b). It is reported that for six tests made on experimental data, the results were within 5° for (θ, ϕ) and within 5% for the radial distance R for four of the six cases. The spherical landmark approach is less restrictive than the diamond-shaped landmark, since it relieves the obligation to know the height of the camera relative to the landmark.

Finally, a paper by Lessard et al. [1986] used the four coplanar vertices of the rectangular end of a crossarm (see box in Figure 3.8) as a landmark to find the position and orientation of a robot in its working environment.

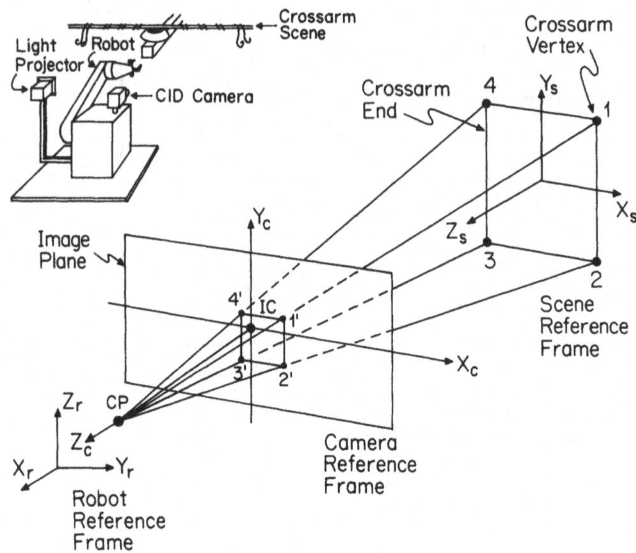

FIGURE 3.8. LDP with four coplanar points (redrawn from Lessárd et al. [1986]).

The robot is used to execute live line maintenance on a power distribution structure. Figure 3.8 shows the geometry adopted to solve the LDP. The position of the four vertices of the crossarm end are known in the crossarm reference frame. Segmentation of the image of the crossarm scene allows us to find the coordinates of the image of each vertex. The position (x_c, y_c, z_c) and orientation (tilt, pan, swing) of the camera in the crossarm reference frame is found with the perspective-4-point (P-4-P) algorithm proposed in Fischler and Bolles [1981]. Tests performed on an experimental setup show an accuracy of 3% on the position (x_c, y_c, z_c) estimate and an error within 2° for the orientation. The position data is obtained in less than two seconds. The principal sources of error are: (1) lens distorsion was not considered; (2) inaccuracy in the estimation of the focal distance of the pinhole camera model; and (3) errors caused by the segmentation of the image of the crossarm end (i.e., error in correspondences between vertices and their images).

2.6 Camera Calibration versus Range Measurements

In all the range measurement approaches discussed in Section 2, the camera parameters are used either explicitly or implicitly in the equations. Camera parameters are of two types: extrinsic and intrinsic. Extrinsic parameters describe the 3-D position and orientation of the camera frame relative to a given "world" reference frame (e.g., baseline separation in a stereo pair of cameras) while intrinsic parameters describe the internal geometric and optical characteristics of the camera (e.g., focal distance, lens distortion, image origin). If a range measurement experiment is to be successful, accurate estimation of the camera parameters is of paramount importance.

Several calibration techniques are reported in the literature. Since the purpose of this survey is not to discuss calibration techniques, we will limit ourselves to refer the reader to the following papers dealing with this important issue: Martins et al. [1981], Taylor and Inigo [1984], Ballard and Brown [1982], and Tsai [1986]. Tsai [1986] comprises an exhaustive review of calibration techniques and proposes a new approach that yields very accurate results.

3 Active Techniques

Most of the active ranging techniques have little to do with the human visual system. Their purpose is neither to model nor to imitate biological visual processes but rather to provide an accurate range image to be used in a given application involving 3-D operations.

3.1 Structured Light

3.1.1 Striped Lighting and Active Stereo. The stereo correspondence problem discussed in Sections 2.4.2–2.43. is avoided by tagging suitable points, in object space, by means of specific illumination patterns such as dots, lines, or grids. Once these points have been recognized in image space, they can be mapped back to object space by the same inverse perspective projection equations (see equations (3.11)–(3.13) and Figure 3.4).

The use of a slit projector as the illumination source is a very common approach to active range sensing [Shirai 1972]. A light beam is projected through a vertical slit in a projector placed a known distance from the camera, as shown in Figure 3.9. While the projector is rotated, images of the scene are acquired at predetermined time intervals and the information related to each picture and the slit beam orientation is stored. The position of the slit, in picture space, is determined, and its 3-D position is computed by triangulation. In Figure 3.9,

$$\tan(\theta) = \frac{x}{F}, \tag{3.27}$$

$$d_1 = z \tan(\phi), \tag{3.28}$$

$$d_2 = z \tan(\theta), \tag{3.29}$$

$$d = d_1 + d_2 + x. \tag{3.30}$$

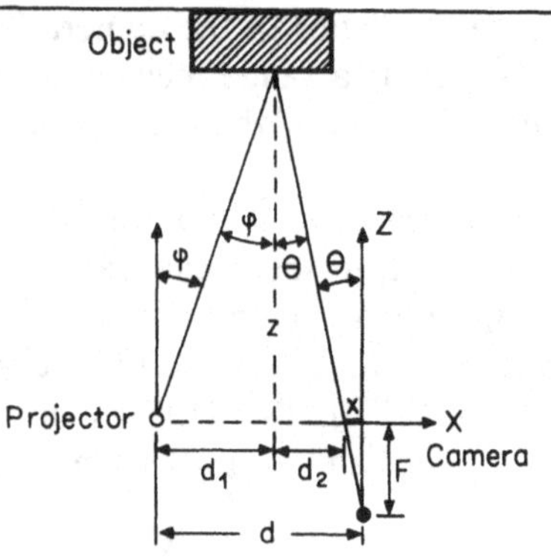

FIGURE 3.9. Slit projection geometry (top view).

Combining equations (3.27)–(3.30), we find for z

$$z = \frac{d - x}{\tan(\phi) + \dfrac{x}{f}}. \tag{3.31}$$

As in equation (3.13), the accuracy in range, computed from equation (3.13), is directly related to the baseline separation d. The timing between the slit scanning mechanism and the image sampling interval (i.e., $\phi(t)$ must also be synchronized. The acquisition time associated with this type of device is a major inconvenience. Agin and Binford [1973] reported an acquisition time of 5–10 minutes for a striped lighting arrangement conceptually similar to Shirai's. Acquisition time can be lowered if a set of stripes is projected onto the scene. For instance, Yachida used a cross-stripe pattern instead of a single sheet of light [Yachida et al., 1982]. However, this approach requires stripe identification.

The image acquisition time can be lowered when space encoding is used [Posdamer and Altshuler 1982]. Inokuchi et al. [1984] used a Gray-coded pattern projector to encode object space. A set on n masks can encode 2^n wedge-shaped regions when projected in sequence with the geometric arrangement shown in Figure 3.10. A stack of n images must be acquired compared to the 2^n for the slit projector without the need for a scanning mechanism. A Gray code is chosen, since it has the property that the Hamming distance between two adjacent numbers is always one. Thus, if a given mask is slightly misaligned with the others, the space code of

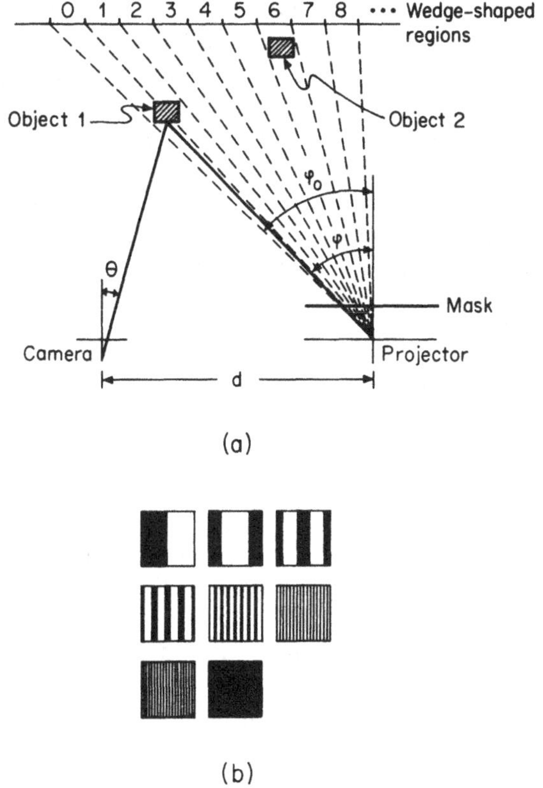

FIGURE 3.10. Space encoding with Gray-coded masks (redrawn from Inokuchi et al. [1984]): (a) geometry for space encoding; (b) gray-code masks.

encoded points is only affected by +/− 1 LSB. This is not the case for a simple set of binary masks (see [Posdamer and Altshuler 1982]). Range is computed by triangulation with an expression like equation (3.31). The problem with this technique is that the wedge-shaped regions become wider with range as shown in Figure 3.10 for objects 1 and 2. Furthermore, since the method is essentially discrete, information on projection orientation is only known at the boundary of wedge-shaped regions and interpolation (for ϕ) is needed to limit the quantization error. A similar approach based on the projection of a binary-coded light pattern is reported in Vuylsteke and Oosterlinck [1986].

A more practical active stereo arrangement is the one proposed by Hall et al. [1982]. A regular grid is projected on the scene, which is viewed by a TV camera from a different viewpoint. The image of the pattern is analyzed and correspondence between grid vertices and their images is simply solved with a given grid vertex defined as a reference. The grid pattern presents many advantages: (1) sharp discontinuities indicate jump boundaries at objects points; (2) the grid image can be used to segment the scene into simple surfaces; (3) a surface can be fitted to detected grid points, allowing measurement of the object location, orientation, and type (this method is well documented in the paper); and (4) a single image is needed to collect all the grid points. This is not the case for point or line patterns that must be scanned over the entire field of view in order to gather information on the whole scene. Each scan position of the pattern (or Gray-coded mask projection) requires the sampling of an image. For experiments conducted on a 6 × 5 grid pattern projected on a coffee cup, the accuracy in the *X, Y,* and *Z* coordinates is within a 10% margin for most of the 30 points. The baseline separation between the projector and the camera is not mentioned in the paper. The method works especially well on featureless objects like a football.

3.2 Moiré Shadows

When a 3-D scene is illuminated with a linear light source passing through an optical grating of constant pitch δ, distorted shadows, separated by bright fringes, appear on the surface of the objects in the scene. Each shadow is produced by a single element of the grating, preventing transmission of the light source. If the scene is also observed through an optical grating by a camera separated from the source by a distance *d*, interference of the distorted shadows with the regular observation grating causes contour curves to appear as virtual images on the object's surface. The elements of a given contour are located at equal range from the camera-source system [Duncan et al. 1980]. A typical Moiré setup is shown in Figure 3.11(a). Range can be computed by considering the geometry in Figure 3.11 (b). Let Y_s and Y_e be the respective positions of the source *S* and camera *E*, and let *P* be a point on a bright fringe at the surface of the object. Let Z_e be the distance between the camera and the grid and Z_s the distance between the source and the grid. From similar triangles $Y_u - P - Y_f$ and $Y_f - O - E$;

$$\frac{h}{Z_e} = \frac{Y_u - Y_f}{Y_f}. \tag{3.32}$$

From similar triangles $P - Y_u - Y_p$ and $Y_s - Y_{p-s}$,

$$\frac{h}{Z_s} = \frac{Y_s - Y_p}{Y_p - Y_u}. \tag{3.33}$$

Furthermore,

$$Y_p = Y_f + n\delta , \tag{3.34}$$

where n (0,1,2,...) is the fringe order, fringe $n = 0$ being associated with $h = 0$. Combining equations (3.32)–(3.34) yields the range value h_n associated with the *nth* order fringe:

$$h_n = \frac{Z_e Z_s n\delta}{(Z_s - Z_e)\, Y_f + Z_e\,(Y_s - n\delta)} \,. \tag{3.35}$$

If $Z_e = Z_s$ equation (3.35) becomes simply

$$h_n = \frac{n\, Z_e}{\dfrac{Y_s}{\delta} - n} \,, \tag{3.36}$$

where Y_s is the baseline separation between the source and the camera. The range difference $(h_n - h_{n-l})$ between two adjacent fringes depends on the fringe order. Different sets of quantized range values could be obtained by varying the grid pitch δ.

For equation (3.36) to be useful, the fringe order n of each fringe in the image must be identified and the ambiguity in the sign of the slopes of the observed surface must be resolved. This is the major problem with Moiré contourography. A possible solution to the problem of fringe indentification is to place a reference wire in front of the projection grid at a suitable location on the normal between the camera lens and the grid [Duncan et al. 1980]. A shadow associated with the wire is projected on

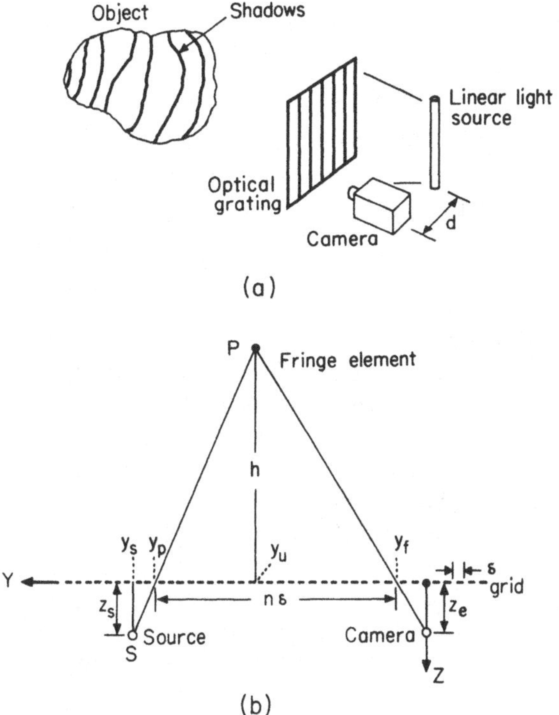

FIGURE 3.11. Depth from Moiré contour: (a) setup; (b) geometry.

the surface of the scene and appears on the Moiré pattern. By measuring the distance between the image of the wire and its shadow on the Moiré photograph, a particular fringe is identified and serves as a reference. The slope of the surface near the reference fringe can be determined by various techniques: moving the objects between two consecutive Moiré measurements; using mismatched gratings or moving the projection grating with respect to the detection grating (called "phase-shifted interferometry") [Idesawa et al. 1977]. The Moiré fringes move in different directions depending on the slope of the surface. A system based on phase-shifted Moiré interferometry is described in Boehnlein and Harding [1986]. Three 256 × 256 Moiré images are recorded and analyzed by a parallel computer in order to extract range and slope information. A 200-line-per-inch grating is used and the translation between gratings is 0.00125 inch. The time required to shift the gratings is approximately two seconds. It is reported in the paper that fringe analysis, excluding image acquisition, is performed in approximately 3.4 seconds.

Finally, a CAD/CAM system, described by Duret and Blouin [1986], uses a Moiré-based technique to measure the inside of the human mouth and then build a crown of a tooth. The miniaturized Moiré acquisition probe and a digitally controlled mill are interfaced to a computer. The 3-D shape of a tooth measured with the Moiré sensor is used to build the crown. The total operation including data acquisition, data reduction, data analysis, and crown fabrication takes less than an hour.

3.3 Time-of-Flight Techniques (TOF)

3.3.1 Ultrasonic TOF. When a short ultrasonic pulse is transmitted towards an object, some of its energy is reflected back to the transmitter. If the time interval between the transmitted and received pulses is measured, the distance d between the source and the object is obtained from

$$2d = v_s \, t_f, \tag{3.37}$$

where v_s is the speed of sound under given pressure conditions and t_f is the time of flight of the pulse. In order to avoid signal attenuation in a practical system, it is not a single pulse but rather a set of pulses at different frequencies that is transmitted [Jarvis 1983]. Commercial systems also provide a correction factor for speed-of-sound fluctuation under varying pressure conditions [Miller 1984].

An interesting property of ultrasonic rangefinders is that baseline separation between emission and reception is null since they are performed by the same unit. This eliminates the shadow effects encountered in all the systems with nonzero baseline separation. Furthermore, the need for segmentation is avoided, which is a very significant factor in real-time applications.

However, it is difficult to obtain a well-focused ultrasonic beam pattern.

This results in a poor resolution "ultrasonic image." According to Jarvis [1983], a 30° solid angle beam pattern can lead to a resolution of about 4 × 4 over a 90° solid angle field (for a Polaroid ultrasonic ranging kit). Resolutions of 10 × 10 can be obtained with acoustic focusing devices but these resolutions are still not suitable for the range acquisition of complex scenes [Jarvis 1980]. Another drawback of ultrasonic ranging is that for some incidence angle of the pulse on the object's surface, very little energy is reflected and the return pulse is lost in detector noise. This phenomenon is similar to specular reflection of light on a mirror-like surface.

A recent paper by Brown [1985] discuss a method using three ultrasonic sensors to compute the range and orientation of a plane surface in a robot guidance application. Thre three sensors are arranged in a general position (i.e., they are not colinear) and each radiates in a direction normal to the plane defined by their position. The method is interesting since it does not depend on the beam pattern and works well even with a wide beam pattern.

3.3.2 Laser TOF. A time-of-flight rangefinder can be constructed with a laser source instead of an ultrasonic source [Jarvis 1983]. Since a laser beam is well focused compared to an ultrasonic beam, better resolutions are achieved. A typical arrangement for a laser time-of-flight rangefinder is shown in Figure 3.12. A laser pulse is transmitted through a semitransparent mirror towards the scene. An electronic sync pulse is also generated and fed to a coincidence analyzer. The reflected pulse is collected by the same mirror and redirected towards a light-sensitive surface (such as a photomultiplier), which generates an arrival electronic pulse. The time interval Δt between the sync and arrival pulses, measured by the coin-

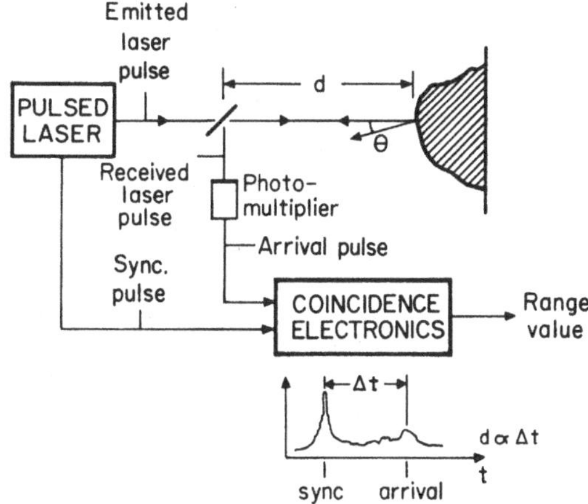

FIGURE 3.12. Laser time-of-flight rangefinder.

cidence electronics, is proportional to the range between the source and the scene. A complete range image is obtained by scanning the mirror over the scene. Here again, baseline separation is null and the missing part problem is avoided.

Despite their apparent simplicity, laster time-of-flight systems are not easy to design in practice. First, the coincidence electronics must accurately measure very short time intervals. For an object at three-meter range, the time of flight Δt is approximately 20 ns. If a $\pm$ 0.5-cm accuracy in range is required, the accuracy on Δt must be $\pm$ 20 ps. Such accuracies can be obtained only with the fast electronic coincidence systems in use in nuclear physics instrumentation, such as anticompton spectrometers for the detection of gamma-ray radiation.

Second, the power received from the target surface may be very low, which means that the electronic signal generated by the photomultiplier may be affected by photomultiplier noise. Assuming a Lambertian surface, the radiance L of an illuminated patch of the surface is given by equation (3.7). The solid angle sustended by the photomultiplier of photosensitive area A_r is

$$\Omega = \frac{A_r}{d^2} . \tag{3.38}$$

If the attenuation of the various optical components (e.g., filters, etc.) is neglected, the energy received by the photomultiplier is (in W/unit projected area)

$$L\Omega = \frac{E \cos(\theta) A_r}{\pi d^2} . \tag{3.39}$$

Thus, surface property and orientation along with range d affect the energy collected by the light detector. For a given beam orientation, good accuracy can be achieved if time interval measurements are averaged over many pulses. Jarvis [1983] reports that an accuracy of 0.5 cm in the range of 1–4 m is obtained in 40 seconds for a 64 × 64 image. A comparatively noisier 64 × 64 image is acquired in 4 seconds.

An alternative approach to the time-of-flight range sensor is the phase detector rangefinder shown in Figure 3.13 [Nitzan et al. 1977]. The laser beam transmitted is amplitude modulated with a sinusoidal waveform. The beam is directed towards the scene by a mirror M_t. A fraction of the light diffused at the surface of an object is collected by a second mirror M_r, at right angle with M_t, and deflected towards a photomultiplier tube. The electronic signal at the output of the photomultiplier is a sinusoid at the modulation frequency. The phase of this signal relative to the transmitted signal is proportional to the time required by the signal to travel from the transmitter to the scene and back, and thus provides twice the range value. The amplitude of the detected signal is proportional to the

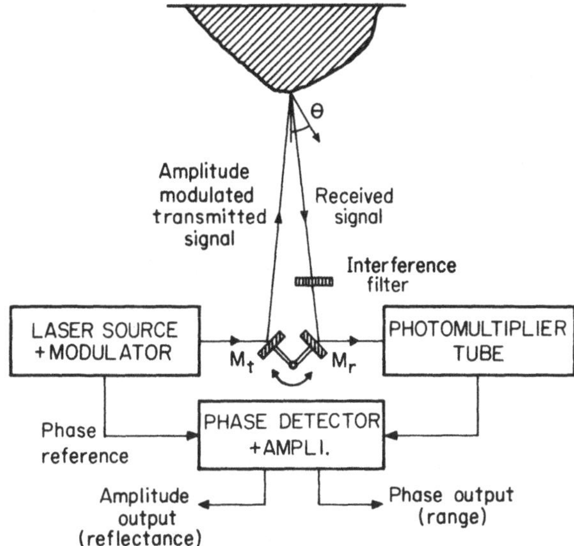

FIGURE 3.13. Phase detection rangefinder.

reflectance at the object patch once the inverse square-law effect in equation (3.39) is corrected. The phase detector rangefinder thus provides two registered images—range and intensity—which is a major advantage over simple rangefinders. However, the acquisition is very slow (two hours for a 128 × 128 image).

An amplitude-modulated CW-laser source phase detection rangefinder of the same generic type as the one described by Nitzan but working at much higher speed is described by Bair et al. [1986]. An avalanche photodiode is used as a light sensor instead of a photomultiplier and a pipelined cellular array processing system analyzes the 3-D data in real time. Two rangefinders are described in the paper. The first one is an optical radar used for road following. It performs the acquisition of two frames per second, 64 lines per frame 3-D (and reflectance) images with a resolution of 7.62 cm at a 19.4-m working distance. The second rangefinder is used for a bin-picking application. The frame rate is at one image each 2–10 seconds for a 20° × 20° field of view and a working distance between 8 and 32 inches. The scan pattern is computer controlled. Various resolutions are achieved (along with various working distances) by simply varying the modulation frequency.

3.4 Conventional Triangulation Rangefinders

The most straightforward approach to rangefinding is probably the single spot laser scanner. A typical design is made of the three components shown in Figure 3.14: (1) a low-power laser source; (2) a scanning mechanism,

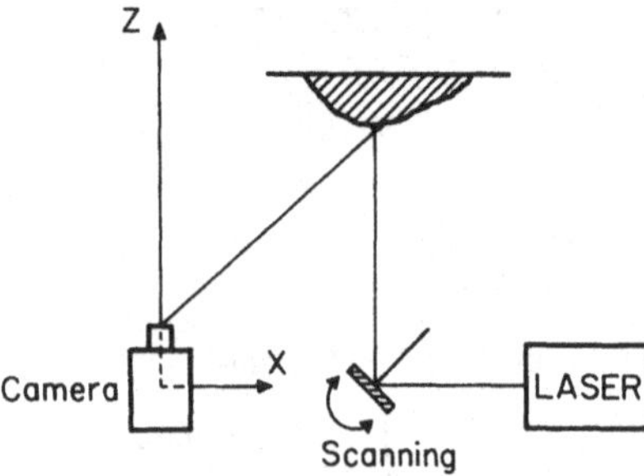

FIGURE 3.14. Basic configuration for active triangulation rangefinder.

usually a set of orientable mirrors; and (3) a camera with a light sensor. The laser beam is projected on the scene and the diffused spot is seen by the camera from a different viewing position. The orientation of the laser beam is known and the image of the diffused spot is easily detected without the need for involved image analysis, especially if an interference filter is used to prevent ambient light from reaching the sensor. The 3-D coordinates of a point are then computed with simple triangulation.

The differences between triangulation systems are often encountered at the camera level. Many systems use a custom camera design instead of a conventional TV camera in order to keep segmentation as simple and fast as possible.

For example, Ishii and Nagata [1976] used an image dissector camera to collect the image of a laser spot. The 2-D position of the imaged spot on the photosensitive surface is converted to two voltages by the dissector camera, each voltage being respectively proportional to the x- and y-coordinates of the spot. The voltages are digitized and fed to a computer. Three-dimensional coordinates are obtained by triangulation.

An installation for automatic acquisition of the 3-D shape of the human foot used a custom camera based on a linear CCD photosensor as its light-collecting element [Maldague et al. 1986]. The setup, shown in Figure 3.15 (a), consists of a fixed support and a mobile part. The foot is placed on the fixed support. A laser, a custom linear CCD camera, and the scanning mechanism are mounted on the mobile part, which is free to rotate around the foot. The mechanical setup was designed so it could stop at 64 equal angular positions during its rotation around the fixed support. For each angular position, the laser beam is scanned vertically over the foot and 64 points are measured by the camera. A total of 4,096 3-D points is acquired in less than three minutes. Figure 3.15 (b) shows the geometry of the camera and its various parameters. The position of the image of the laser spot is detected electronically. This position and the geometry of the apparatus are used to compute the cylindrical coordinates (R, Z, θ) of a given point by triangulation. From Figure 3.15 (b),

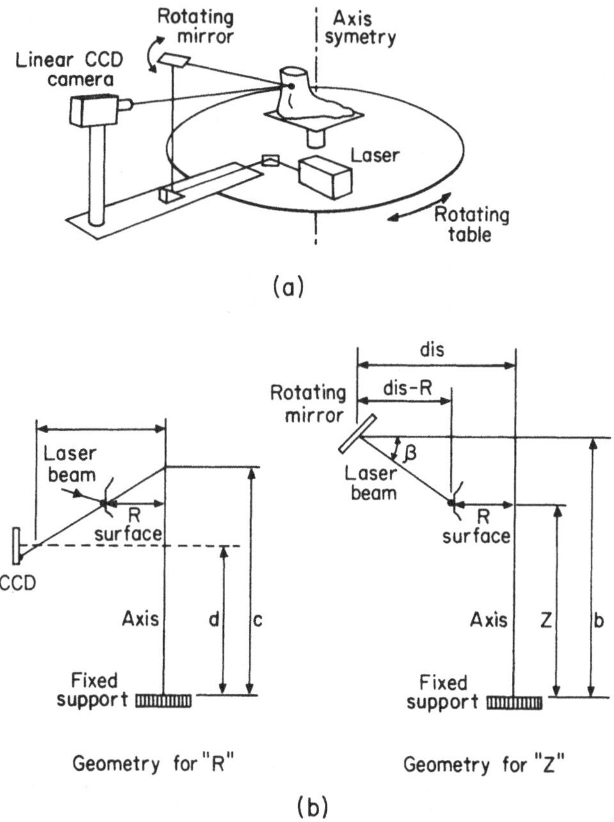

FIGURE 3.15. Human foot 3-D acquisition system: (a) basic system; (b) geometry for R and Z computations.

$$z = b + \tan(\beta)\,(R - \text{dis})\,, \tag{3.40}$$

$$\mathrm{R} = \mathrm{F}\left[\frac{c + \text{dis}\tan(\beta) - b}{c + F\tan(\beta) - d}\right]. \tag{3.41}$$

The accuracy on R and Z is approximately 1 mm. The value of θ is implicit since it is known a priori from the encoded position of the rotating table.

3.5 Synchronized Triangulation

As in the case of active and passive stereo, conventional triangulation by a laser scanner provides good accuracy only for a large baseline separation between the source and the camera. In addition to increased shadow effects, a large baseline means a large optical head for the camera that can be inconvenient in an industrial environment.

An interesting scanning mechanism proposed by Rioux [1984] allows the implementation of a compact camera head without reducing resolution and field of view. The design is based upon the angular synchronization of the projection and the detection of a laser beam. Synchronization can be obtained using two scanners instead of one. Figure 3.16 (a) shows the detailed geometry of a conventional scanner. The laser source is located at (d, O). For an angle θ_0, the beam defines a reference point at $(d/2, l)$ that is used for calibration. A lens of focal length f, located at the origin, is used to collect and focus the diffused light on a position sensor in focus at $-fl/(l-f)$ (thin lens formula) along the Z-axis. For a rotation of θ of the scanner, the position of the imaged point moves from the reference

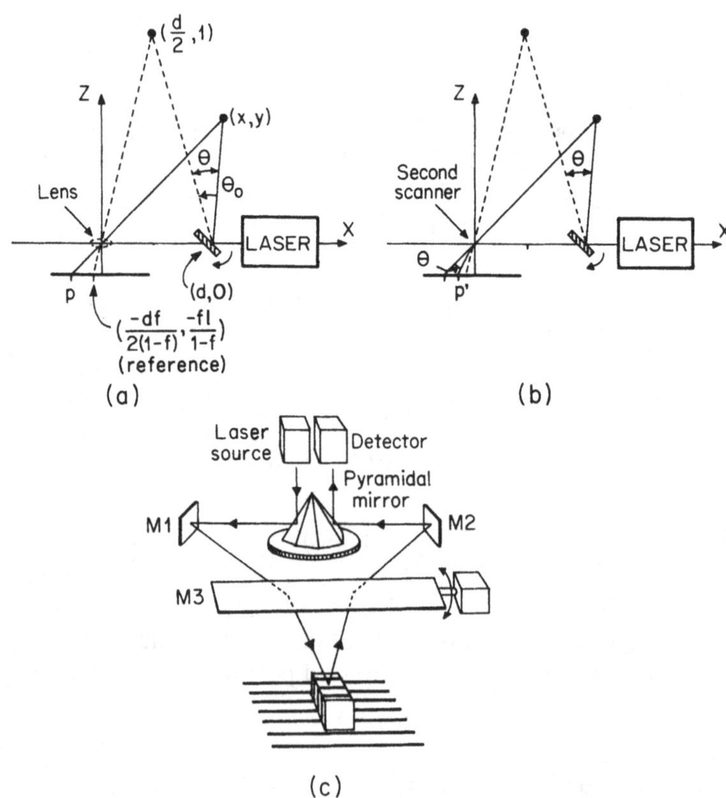

FIGURE 3.16. Synchronized geometry rangefinder (redrawn from Rioux [1984]): (a) conventional triangulation geometry; (b) synchronized triangulation geometry; (c) typical arrangement for synchronization.

image $df/2\,(l-f)$ on the position sensor to a new location p. Using trigonometry, the position (x, z) of the point is found to be

$$x = \frac{d\,p}{p + \dfrac{f\,l\,(2\,l\tan(\theta) + d)}{(l - f)(d\tan(\theta) - 2\,l)}}, \tag{3.42}$$

$$z = \frac{-d}{\dfrac{p\,(l - f)}{f\,l} + \dfrac{2\,l\tan(\theta) + d}{d\tan(\theta) - 2\,l}}, \tag{3.43}$$

assuming the camera parameters d, l, and f are known.

Now, suppose that a second scanner is placed at (0, 0), its axis of rotation being normal to the X-Z-plane. This second scanner moves synchronously with the one at $(d, 0)$, thus canceling its angular movement. The resulting effect of synchronization is that the position of the imaged spot on the sensor is brought to p', a point that is closer to the reference point $df/2(l-f)$, as shown in Figure 3.16 (b). The point p is related to p' by the following expression:

$$p = p' + \frac{\dfrac{f\,l\tan(\theta)}{(l - f)}}{1 - \dfrac{p'(l - f)\tan(\theta)}{f\,l}}, \tag{3.44}$$

Equations (3.42) and (3.43) still hold for the synchronized geometry if the value of p is computed from equation (3.44). Considering the geometries in Figures 3.16 (a) and (b), it can be seen that a change in the position of the spot along Z causes an equivalent angular shift for both the conventional and synchronized scanners. On the other hand, a change along X produces a smaller shift in the case of the synchronized geometry. This means that the position sensor (i.e., the light-sensitive area) is mainly used to measure range instead of lateral displacement. This also means that, for a given sensor, the focal length of the lens could be increased to obtain a better resolution in range without reducing the field of view.

Another difference between the synchronized and conventional geometries is that, for the synchronized case, a single point on the position sensor defines a locus in target space, i.e., a circle of radius

$$R = \frac{(l^2 + \frac{d^2}{4})}{2\,l} \tag{3.45}$$

centered at

$$\left(\frac{d}{2}, \frac{(l^2 - \frac{d^2}{4})}{2\,l}\right) \tag{3.46}$$

while in the conventional case, a single point on the sensor maps to a single point in 3-D space. The circular trajectory associated with a single image point can be used directly in inspection applications where profile measurement of spherically or near spherically shaped objects has to be done.

In practice, synchronization is obtained from a typical arrangement like the one shown in Figure 3.16 (c). Horizontal scanning of the laser spot is achieved by a rotating pyramidal (or polygonal) mirror while vertical scanning is done with a flat orientable mirror (M_3 in Figure 3.16 (c)). Synchronization is accomplished using two opposite facets of the rotating pyramidal mirror for deflecting the transmitted light beam S and collecting the diffused spot (which is directed on the position sensor D). Since the two opposite facets rotate in phase, perfect synchronization is ensured. The short distance between the two facets, each facet having a 5-cm^2 area, also reduces shadow effects.

While conventional triangulation systems require a 2-D light sensor to perform profile measurements, synchronized triangulation only requires a linear sensor. This greatly increases bandwidth (from 10 Khz to 1 Mhz). Rioux mentions in his paper that two different sensor types were tested: an analog lateral effect photodiode (LEP) and a CCD linear array. Light impinging on the LEP surface produces a current I_0 that is split by a resistive layer in two currents I_1 and I_2. Position p' of the spot is thus simply obtained from

$$\frac{I_1 - I_2}{I_1 + I_2}, \tag{3.47}$$

while reflectance data in perfect registration with range is obtained from

$$I_1 + I_2. \tag{3.48}$$

With a CCD sensor, higher resolution is achieved (subpixel accuracy can be obtained with proper signal processing, see [Blais and Rioux 1986a] for details) but at a much slower rate since the CCD does not allow a direct measurement of the light spot position.

Rioux reports that for an LEP arrangement with the geometry of Figure 16 (c), angular speed of the pyramidal mirror ranges from 60 to 1,800 rad/s. The field of view is 20° (focal length of the lens is 10 cm) and the X, Y, and Z resolutions for a 128×256 image are respectively 1, 2, and 0.4 mm for a field of view of $250 \times 250 \times 100$ mm. Image acquisition takes less than one second and equations (3.47) and (3.48) are computed in real time.

With the speed and resolution mentioned here, the synchronized scanning rangefinder is particularly appropriate for inspection of manufactured parts and general machine vision where acquisition speed is an important requirement.

3.6 Range from Defocusing

Except for active stereo, all the active techniques reviewed in Section 3 need a scanning mechanism made of mobile parts of some sort (mirrors, slit rotator, . . .). Such mechanisms are often prone to fall out of adjustment, especially in a robotic environment where shocks and vibration are very likely to happen. These rangefinders are thus more suitable for non-contacting inspection tasks rather than for robot manipulation applications. Furthermore, even for the small camera head of the synchronized geometry, it may be difficult to mount these rangefinders on or near the end effector of a robot because of weight or available space.

Robotic manipulation guided with a 3-D sensor thus calls for a sturdy and compact, yet accurate, 3-D camera. The BIRIS 3-D sensor described by Blais 1985 Blais and Rioux [1986], and Rioux et al. [1986] seems particularly appropriate for such situations. The BIRIS camera is based on the defocusing principle shown in Figure 3.17 (a). A mask with two small apertures is mounted in front of a standard CCD camera. The camera is focused such that a 3-D point A on a reference plane is in focus at A' on the CCD sensor. A point B on an object placed above the reference plane

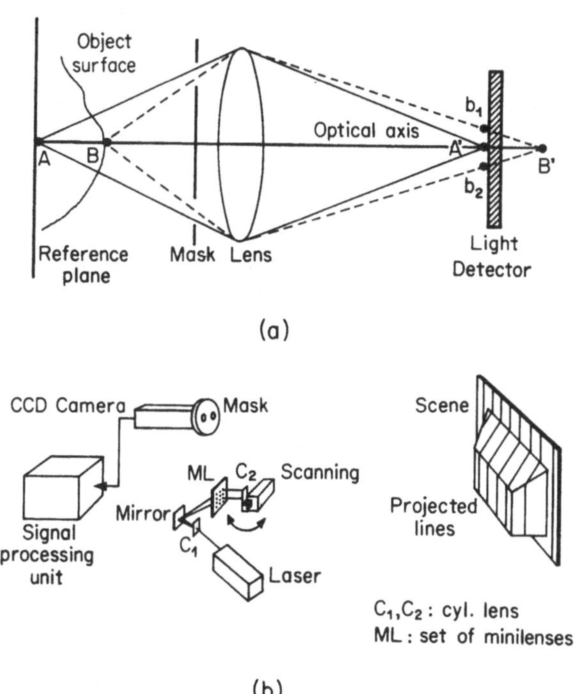

FIGURE 3.17. Range from defocusing (redrawn from Blais and Rioux [1986b]).

is in focus at B' behind the CCD sensor and is thus out of focus in the image plane. Furthermore, because of the mask, two points b_1 and b_2 are imaged in the sensor. The distance $(b_1 - b_2)$ is a function of the Z-coordinate of point B while the geometrical center of b_1 and b_2 gives the X- and Y-coordinates of B in 3-D space. If b_1 and b_2 can be detected efficiently in the image plane, the (x, y, z) coordinates of B can be found from the following expressions:

$$z = \frac{1}{\frac{1}{L} + b\frac{(L - f)}{(f\,D\,L)}}, \tag{3.49}$$

$$x = \frac{-X_0\,z\,(L - f)}{f\,l}, \tag{3.50}$$

$$y = \frac{-Y_0\,z\,(L - f)}{f\,l}, \tag{3.51}$$

where $b = (b_1 - b_2)$, f is the focal length of the lens, L is the distance between the reference plane and the lens, d is the distance between the two apertures in the mask, and $(X_0 Y_0)$ is the geometrical center of the $b_1 - b_2$ pair.

Thus, as shown in Figure 3.17 (b), the measurement of 3-D coordinates only requires a CCD camera with a mask, a light source to project a point (or pattern) on the scene, and a processing unit to extract the $b_1 - b_2$ pairs. The unit required to process the video signal at video rate is described in Blais and Rioux [1986b]. Extraction of the $b_1 - b_2$ pairs must be performed at subpixel accuracy in order to obtain good resolution in range. The main difficulty with the defocusing approach is that the separation between the two apertures of the mask, and therefore the separation between b_1 and b_2, is generally small, an upper limit being the lens aperture itself. It is possible to artificially increase this separation with the use of mirrors or prisms [Jalkio et al. 1985] but this leads to a more complicated and less sturdy design.

3.7 Intensity-Guided Rangefinding

In some applications, a complete range image of the scene is not required and a 2-D intensity image may be used to guide the acquisition of a sparse range image. For instance, Duda et al. [1979] used a grey-level image to detect planes and the range image to compute their 3-D parameters in space. More recently, Magee et al. [1985] described a system that used an intensity image to select feature points or objects (lines, circles, . . .) in the scene and then find their 3-D coordinates in a range image.

With a rangefinder having a random-access scanning mechanism, Magee's approach could be used to acquire the 3-D coordinates of only those regions of the scene associated with the features extracted from the grey-level image. Intensity-guided rangefinding can speed up the process of 3-D data acquisition without requiring a sophisticated range sensor as long as range accuracy is suitable for the application.

4 Conclusion

All the rangefinding techniques reviewed in this chapter present their specific advantages and drawbacks and none can be considered an overall "optimal" choice. The 3-D vision system designer must chose the technique best suited for his needs. The accuracy and acquisition time are two important issues that a designer has to consider. The physical dimensions of the rangefinder is often of importance, particularly in robotics applications. The building cost of a rangefinder is also a major element in the design of a system. Clearly, low-cost/high-performance 3-D range sensing is still not available to the factory environment. The lack of standardization between the various cameras, compared to the standard 2-D TV cameras, is a serious problem that should be addressed in order to facilitate industrial system integration. The missing part or shadow effect problem is also a very important issue. Finally, all the rangefinding techniques discussed here face the same major problem: the 3-D data provided conveys information only for the "visible" part of the scene. If a full 3-D image of an object is required, several images must be acquired from different positions and view integration must be performed. This is a rather complicated and time-consuming process.

Despite these various drawbacks, it is to be expected that rangefinders will become more present in the factory environment in the near future, since the manipulation of 3-D objects requires an accurate knowledge of their 3-D structure. New algorithms and dedicated computer achitectures for 3-D image segmentation and analysis will also become available and should promote a more widespread acceptance of 3-D rangefinding as an element of solution to many industrial computer vision applications.

References

Agin, G.J., and Binford, T.O. 1973. Computer description of curved objects. In *Proc. Intl. Joint Conference on Artificial Intelligence* (Stanford, Calif., Aug. 20–23), IJCAI, 629–640.

Bair, M.E., Sampson, R., and Zuk, R. 1986. Three-dimensional imaging and applications. In *Proc. SPIE 1986 Cambridge Symposium on Optics and Opto-electronics Advances in Intelligent Systems,* vol. 726 (Cambridge, Mass., Oct. 28–31), 264–274.

Bajcsy, R., and Lieberman, L. 1976. Texture gradient as a depth cue. *Computer, Graphics and Image Processing* **5,** 52–67.

Ballard, D.H., and Brown, C. 1982. *Computer vision*. Prentice-Hall, Englewood Cliffs, N.J., 481–483.

Blais, F., and Rioux, M. 1986a. "Real-time numerical peak detector," *Signal Processing* **11,** 145–155.

Blais, F., and Rioux, M. 1986b. BIRIS: A simple 3D sensor. In *Proc. SPIE 1986 Cambridge Symposium on Optics and Optoelectronics Advances in Intelligent Systems,* vol. 728 (Cambridge, Mass., Oct. 30–31), 235–242.

Blais, F., Rioux, M., and Poussart, D. 1985. A very compact 3-D camera for robotic application. In *Proc. 1985 Optical Society of America Topical Meeting on Machine Vision.*

Boehnlein, A.J., and Harding, K.G. 1986. Adaptation of a parallel architecture computer to phase shifted Moiré interferometry. In *Proc. SPIE 1986 Symposium on Optics and Optoelectronics Advances in Intelligent Systems, vol. 728,* (Cambridge, Mass., Oct. 30–31), 183–194.

Boyer, K.L., Vayda, A.J., and Kak, A.C. 1986. Robotic manipulation experiments using structural stereopsis for 3D vision. *IEEE Expert* **1,** 3 (Fall), 73–94.

Brown, M.K. 1985. Feature extraction techniques for recognizing solid objects with ultrasonic range sensor. *IEEE J. Robotics and Automation* **RA-1,** 4 (Dec.), 191–205.

Courtney, J.W., and Aggarwal, J.K. 1983 Robot guidance using computer vision. In *Proc. IEEE Conference on Trends and Applications* (Gaithersburg, Md., May 25–26), IEEE, New York, 57–62.

De Vriendt, A.B., 1984 Heat Transfer. *An introduction to thermal radiation* **2** (in French), Gaëtan Morin Ed., Canada, 15–16.

Duda, R.O., and Hart, P.E. 1973 *Pattern classification and scene analysis*. Wiley, New York, 401–402.

Duda, R.O., Nitzan, D., and Barrett, P. 1979. Use of range and reflectance data to find planar surface regions. *IEEE Trans. on Pattern Analysis and Machine Intelligence*. **PAMI-1,** 3 (Jul.) 259–271.

Duncan, J.P., Dean, D.P., and Pate, G.C. 1980. Moiré contourography and computer aided replication of human anatomy. *Engrg. in Medicine* **9,** 1, 29–36.

Duret, F., and Blouin, J.L. 1986. De l'empreinte optique à la conception et la fabrication assistées par ordinateur d'une couronne dentaire. *J Dentaire du Québec* **XXIII** (Apr.), 177–180.

Fischler, M.A., and Bolles, R.C. 1981. Random sample consensus: A paradigm for model fitting with applications to image analysis and automated cartography. *Communications of the ACM* **24,** 6 (June), 381–395.

Gibson, J.J. 1966. The senses considered as perceptual systems. Houghton-Mifflin, Boston, Mass.

Grimson, W.E.L. 1981. *From images to surfaces—A computational study of the human visual system*. MIT Press, Cambridge, Mass, 15–61.

Hall, E.L., Tio, J.B.K., McPherson, C.A., and Sadjadi, F.A. 1982. Measuring curved surfaces for robot vision. *Computer* **15,** 12, 42–54.

Horn, B.K.P. 1970. Shape from shading: A method for obtaining the shape of a smooth opaque object from one view. *MIT Project MAC Technical Report,* MAC TR-79, M.I.T., Cambridge, Mass.

Horn, B.K.P. 1975. Obtaining shape from shading information. In *The psychology of computer vision* (P.H. Winston, Ed.), McGraw-Hill, New York, 115–155.

Horn, B.K.P. 1985. The variational approach to shape from shading, *MIT AI Laboratory Memo 813,* Mar. M.I.T., Cambridge, Mass.

Horn, B.K.P. 1986. *Robot vision.* MIT Press, McGraw-Hill, Cambridge, Mass., 248–250.

Idesawa, M., Yatagi, T., and Soma. T. 1977. Scanning Moiré method and automatic measurement of 3-D shapes. *Appl. Opt.* **16,** 8 (Aug.), 2152, 2162.

Ikeuchi, K., and Horn, B.K.P. 1981. Numerical shape from shading and occluding boundaries. Artificial Intell. **17,** 141–184.

Inokuchi, S., Sato, K., and Matsuda, F. 1984. Range imaging system for 3D object recognition. In *Proc. 7th Intl. Conference on Pattern Recognition* (Montréal, Canada, Jul. 30–Aug. 2) IAPR, IEEE, New York, 806–808.

Ishii, M., and Nagata, T. 1976. Feature extraction of three-dimensional objects and visual processing in a hand-eye system using a laser tracker. In *Pattern Recognition,* Vol. 8. Pergamon Press, New York, 227–237.

Jalkio, J.A., Kim, R.C., and Case, S.K. 1985. Three-dimensional inspection using multistripe structured light. *Opt. Engrg.* **24,** 6, 966–974.

Jarvis, R.A. 1980. A mobile robot for computer vision research. In *Proc. 3rd Australian Computer Science Conference,* (Canberra, Australia, Jan. 31–Feb. 1), A.N.U. Canberra, A.C.T., 39–51.

Jarvis, R.A. 1983. A perspective on range finding techniques for computer vision. *IEEE Trans. on Pattern Analysis and Machine Intell.* **PAMI-5,** 2 (Mar.), 122–139.

Julesz, B. 1964. Binocular depth perception without familiarity clues. *Sci.* **145,** 356–362.

Lessard, J., Laurendeau, D., and Girard, P., 1986. Computer-vision based estimation of the position of a robot in its working environment. In *Proc. IEEE Conference on Power Industry Computer Application PICA'87* (Montréal, Canada, May 18–22), IEEE Power Engineering Society, New York, 94–100.

Levine, M.D., O'Handley, D.A., and Yagi, G.M., 1973. Computer determination of depth maps. *Computer, Graphics and Image Processing* **2,** 134–150.

Luh, J.Y.S., and Klaasen, J.A. 1985. A three-dimensional vision by off-shelf system with multi-cameras. *IEEE Trans. on Pattern Analysis and Machine Intell.* **PAMI-7,** 1 (Jan.) 35–45.

Magee, M.J., and Aggarwal, J.K. 1984. Determining the position of a robot using a single calibration object. In *Proc. IEEE Conference on Robotics* (Atlanta, Ga., Mar. 13–15), IEEE Computer Society, Silver Springs, Md., 140–149.

Magee, M.J., Boyter, B.A., Chien, C.H., and Aggarwal, J.K. 1985. Experiments in intensity guided range sensing recognition of three-dimensional objects. *IEEE Trans. on Pattern Analysis and Machine Intell.* **PAMI-7,** 6 (Nov.), 629–637.

Maldague, X., Poussart, D., Laurendeau, D., and April, R. 1986. Tridimensional form acquisition apparatus. In *Proc. SPIE Intl. Symposium on Optical and Optoelectronic Applied Sciences and Engineering,* vol. 665 (Quebec, Canada, June), 200–208.

Mandelbrot, B.B. 1982. *The fractal geometry of nature.* Freeman, San Francisco, Calif.

Marr, D. 1981. *VISION: A computational investigation in the human representation and processing of visual information.* W.H. Freeman, San Francisco, Calif., 240–250.

Marr, D., and Hildreth, H. 1980. *Theory of edge detection. Proc. Roy. Soc. London* **B207,** 187–217.

Marr, D., and Poggio, T. 1979. *A theory of human stereo vision. Proc. Roy. Soc. London* **B204,** 301–328.

Martins, H.A., Birk, J.R., and Kelley, R.B., 1981. Camera models based on data from two calibration planes. *Computer, Graphics and Image Processing* **17,** 173–180.

McVey, E.S., Drake, K.C., and Inigo, R.M. 1986. Range measurements by a mobile robot using a navigation line. *IEEE Trans. on Pattern Analysis and Machine Intel.* **PAMI-8,** 1 (Jan.), 105–109.

Miller, R.K. 1984. 3D machine vision. *SEAI Technical Publication and Technical Insight,* SEAI, Madison, Ga.

Nitzan, D., Brain, A.E., and Duda, R.O. 1977. The measurement and use of registered reflectance and range data in scene analysis. *Proc. IEEE* **65,** 2, 206–220.

Pentland, A.P. 1986. Shading into texture. *Artificial Intell.* **29,** 147–170.

Posdamer, J.L., and Altshuler, M.D. 1982. Surface measurement by space-encoded projected beam systems. *Computer, Graphics and Image Processing* **18,** 1.

Reinsch, C.H. 1967. Smoothing by spline functions. *Numerische Mathematik* **10,** 177–183.

Rioux, M. 1984. Laser range finder based on synchronized scanners. *Appl. Op.* **23,** 21 (Nov.), 3837–3844.

Rioux, M., and Blais, F. 1986. Compact three-dimensional camera for robotic applications. *J. Op. Soc. Amer.* **3** (Sept.), 1518–1521.

Shen, H.C., and Wong, K.C., 1983. Generalized texture representation and metric. *Computer Vision, Graphics and Image Processing* **23,** 187–206.

Shirai, Y. 1972. Recognition of polyhedrons using a range finder. *Pattern Recognition* **4,** 243–250.

Strat, T.M., and Fischler, M.A. 1986. One-eyed stereo: A general approach to modeling 3D scene geometry. *IEEE Trans. on Pattern Analysis and Machine Intell.* **PAMI-8,** 6 (Nov.), 730–741.

Taylor, J.P., and Inigo, R.M. 1984. Camera calibration for binary vision systems. *Proc. 3rd Canadian Conference on CAD/CAM and Robotics.* (Toronto, Canada, June 19–21), CASA-SME, 4.1–4.6.

Tsai, R.Y. 1986. An efficient and accurate camera calibration technique for 3D machine vision. In *Proc. IEEE Conference on Computer Vision and Pattern Recognition,* (Miami, Fla. June), IEEE Computer Society, Washington, D.C., 364–374.

Vuylsteke, P., and Oosterlinck, A., 1986. 3-D perception with a single binary coded illumination pattern. In *Proc. SPIE 1986 Cambridge Symposium on Optics and Optoelectronics Advances in Intelligent Systems,* vol. 728 (Cambridge, Mass., Oct. 30–31), 195–202.

Witkin, A.P. 1981. Recovering surface shape and orientation from texture. *Artificial Intell.* **17,** 17–45.

Woodham, R.J. 1979. Relating properties of surface curvature to image intensity. In *Proc. Intl. Joint Conference on Artificial Intelligence.* (Tokyo, Japan, Aug. 20–23), IJCAI, 971–977.

Woodham, R.J. 1981. Analysing images of curved surfaces. *Artificial Intell.* **17,** 117–140.

Woodham, R.J. 1984. Photometric method for determining shape from shading. *Image understanding* (S. Ullman and W. Richards, Eds.), Ablex, N.J., Chapter 4, 97–125.

Yachida, M., Tsuji, S., and Huang, X.-Q. 1982. WIRESIGHT—A computer vision system for 3D measurement and recognition of flexible wire using cross-stripe light. In *Proc. 6th IEEE Intl. Conference on Pattern Recognition* (Munich, W. Germany, Oct. 19–22), IEEE Computer Society, Silver Spring, Md., 220–222.

Yakimovsky, Y., and Cunningham, R. 1978. A system for extracting three-dimensional measurements from a stereo pair of TV cameras. *Computer, Graphics and Image Processing* **7**, 195–210.

4
Methodology for Automatic Image-Based Inspection of Industrial Objects

KRISTINA HEDENGREN

ABSTRACT: Many articles have been written dealing with applications of automated inspection for industry. These articles typically describe the application as well as selected algorithms and a specific proposed or implemented inspection system but do not describe the methodology of how the system was developed. This chapter attempts to describe basic concepts and general requirements for automation of an inspection application and suggests a methodology that might simplify algorithm development efforts for new applications. A systematic, general approach, which was originally developed for automatic real-time X-ray inspection of industrial objects with intricate internal structures, is described. Software-based functions for the automatic inspection are addressed, from geometric modeling of image content, through development of high-level process filters, creation of inspection process plans, and final simulation of system performance. An interactive development and simulation software environment that was designed and implemented to provide the necessary tools for automating an image-based inspection process is also described.

1 Introduction

Industry is increasingly using machine vision systems to aid in the manufacturing and quality-control processes. As examples, images are created and processed to assist with recognition of parts for robotic assembly and manipulation or inspection of parts for quality control. Many robotic applications involve recognition of known objects in unknown orientations and often become three-dimensional pattern recognition and classification challenges. Industrial quality control, however, deals with inspection of well-defined objects for specific types of defects that must be detected and accurately measured if they exist.

Images provide a suitable interface between computers and people—they are much easier to analyze than strip charts or oscilloscope traces. Additionally, imaging systems are used so that image-processing techniques may be applied to the data to enhance the capability to detect and characterize flaws.

Machine vision implies that the image is created by an optical system and most applications indeed use some type of camera to create an image. However, many other types of imaging modalities, based on specific physical parameters, are in use by industry. Vision systems measure either reflectance of an object or distance (range) to the object. Ultrasound systems [Gilmore et al. 1986] measure sonic echo amplitudes at structure boundaries in the object, while X-ray systems [Oliver et al. 1986] measure integrated absorption of X-rays through the object. Eddy-current systems [Joynson et al. 1986] measure the change in impedance of a coil as it is moved across a conducting surface.

The particular inspection problem dictates which type of imaging system is appropriate. Vision systems are suitable for external inspection of objects but are also used to digitize X-ray films or photographs to enable further analysis. Data from vision systems are, therefore, widely used for anything from analysis of medical images [Harlow and Eisenbeis 1973; Sankar and Sklansky 1982] to inspection of wood [Conners et al. 1983] and printed circuit boards [Antonsson et al. 1979]. However, if an inspection application requires detection of very fine surface cracks in a smooth metallic object, vision systems will not be able to provide adequate resolution and eddy-current inspection will be a likely choice. For penetration into an object to characterize a specific material, ultrasound inspection might be preferred as eddy-currents can not penetrate very deeply into metals and not at all into nonconducting materials. When detection and measurements of internal structures of a metallic object of some thickness are required, the only available option today is X-ray inspection. Figures 4.1–4.4 show examples of industrial images created by different types of imaging systems that have been developed and are in use at the General Electric Corporate Research and Development Center.

In today's competitive industrial world, quality is a *requirement* for survival—improved quality results in increased productivity. Strong motivations for automating the quality inspection process through the use of machine vision systems have been documented [Chin and Harlow 1982]. A major reason is to remove the variability of the inspection results due to subjective and inconsistent processing by human inspectors. Automated systems can potentially perform functions beyond the capability of the human inspector with remarkable consistency. The ultimate goal is automatic accept/reject decisions about objects. An object will be accepted if no abnormalities are detected, but rejection of an object requires that defects are both detected and characterized. Systems may, therefore, be used with partial automation for preliminary screening to accept objects with flawless images while all other images will be manually interpreted. With such routine screening, the inspection results improve because inspectors are relieved of the monotonous task of examining numerous good

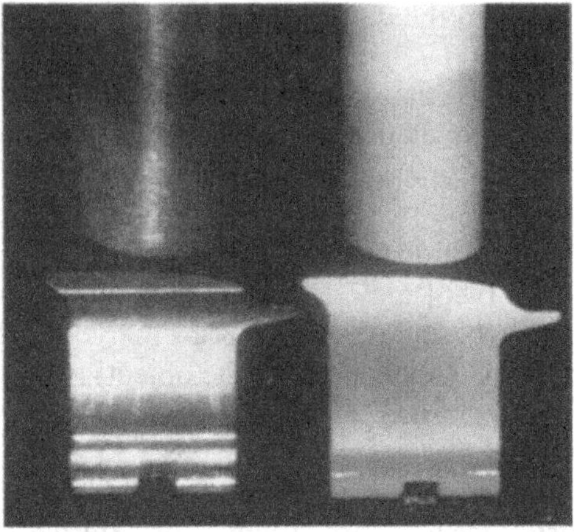

FIGURE 4.1. Images using vision system (courtesy of General Electric CR&D 3-D Vision Program). To the left is the *reflectance* image and to the right is the *range* image of an aircraft engine turbine blade.

images and are instead presented with challenging images that they will pay attention to because they are likely to contain defects.

Because automatic inspection systems are computer-based, they provide a convenient means of gathering statistical information from the inspections. Such information can be analyzed and fed back to design and manufacturing engineers to be used for modifications that will reduce the occurrence of future defects, as shown by Figure 4.5. As more sophisticated or reliable inspection systems become available, additional freedoms may

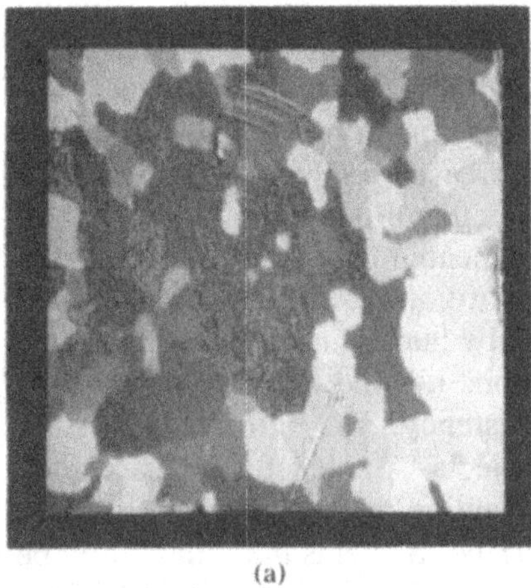

(a)

(b)

FIGURE 4.2. Images using Ultrasound microscope (courtesy of R. S. Gilmore, General Electric CR&D): (a) surface wave image showing copper grain structure and (b) direct reflection image showing relief design on face of coin.

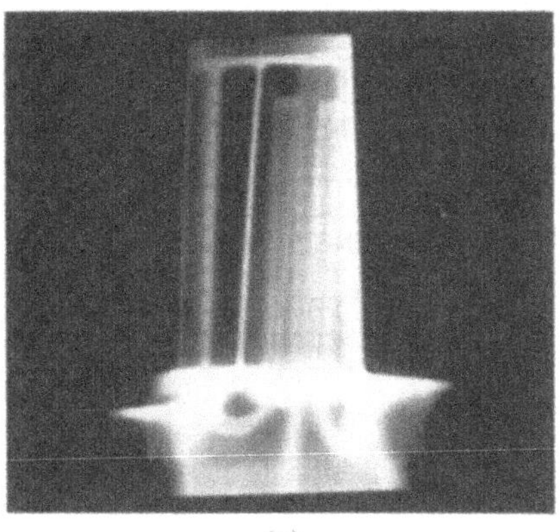
(a)

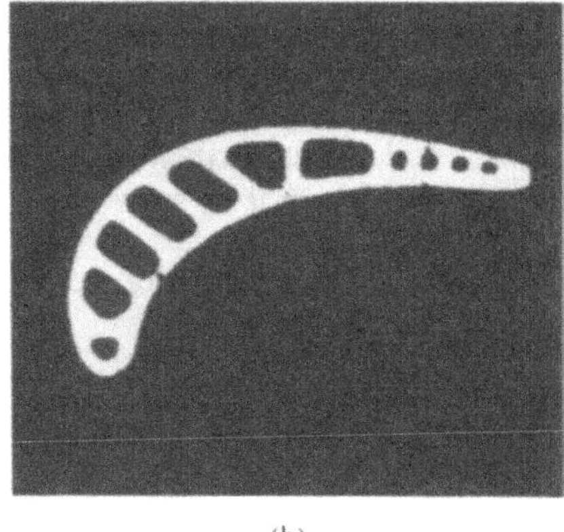
(b)

FIGURE 4.3. X-ray images using XIM inspection system (Automatic X-ray Inspection Module, courtesy of General Electric CR&D): (a) ordinary chest X-ray–type image of turbine blade and (b) computerized tomography (cross-sectional) image of turbine blade.

be permitted in the future part design and manufacturing processes as previously uninspectable designs may become inspectable.

The difficulty of automating a reasonably complex inspection problem should not be underestimated—it involves subtle interactions of processing, interpretation, and decision-making. In spite of their limitations, human inspectors perform complicated functions very fast when they inspect

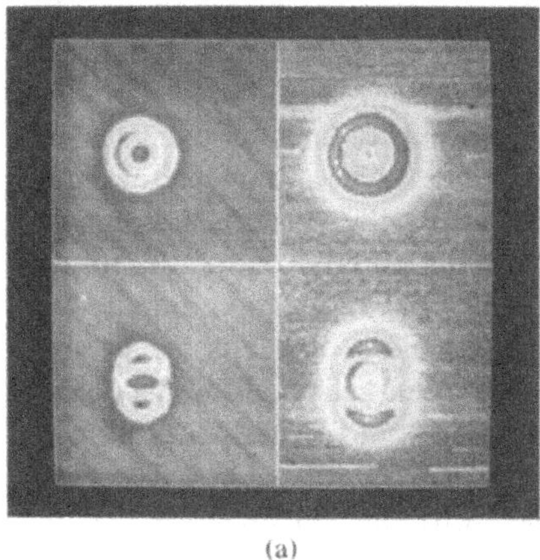
(a)

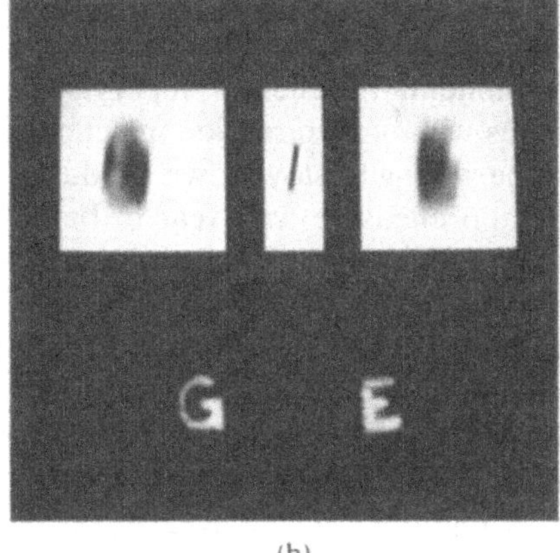

(b)

FIGURE 4.4. Images using Eddy Current laboratory system (courtesy of Quality Technology Branch, General Electric CR&D. For further explanations, see Joynson et al. [1986]): (a) images of small hole (top) and slot (bottom) in surface of alloy, (b) blurred images of characters G and E stamped into aluminum with point response image between them (top) and restored images after Wiener filtering (bottom).

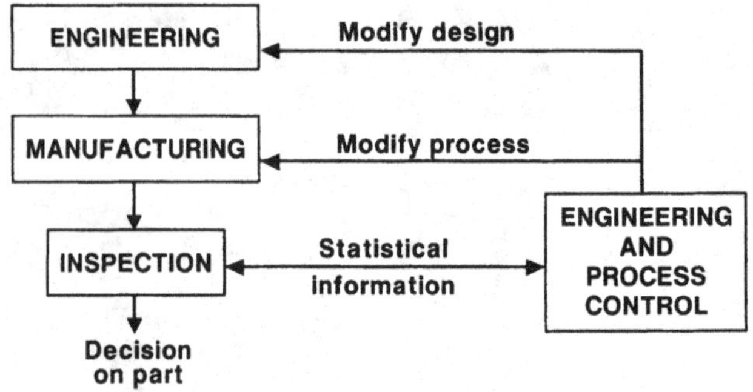

FIGURE 4.5. Inspection quality circle.

an object, and it is exceedingly difficult to substitute computer logic for human judgment. Not all inspection problems are suitable for automation, in fact, surprisingly few applications have been successfully automated today. If specified inspection throughput rates are met, the only criterion for success of an automated system is that it yields reliable, repeatable, and robust results. If the system does not perform to specifications, it cannot be used in a production environment. It is, therefore, of crucial importance that the feasibility of the inspection be established before a complex hardware system is built. Much of the current literature, in fact, deals with inspection feasibility studies [Don et al. 1984; Antwerpen et al. 1986]. Even if it is demonstrated that a system performs to specifications, there may be some reluctance to accept it in a production environment. Production supervisors, who follow well-established procedures with proven results, may not trust the results of an automated system or be willing to slow down production to install them, and inspectors may be apprehensive with fear of being replaced by the system. A common strategy to ease the transition into the production environment is to use the system in parallel with previous proven procedures and compare the results. If the performance of the system equals or exceeds the performance of the human inspector, the system eventually will be accepted. Inspectors may find that they still are needed, but for new, less monotonous tasks.

A high level of complexity of both software and hardware is usually required of production-type automated inspection systems—this results in long development times at substantial cost. Such development efforts are justified for large volume parts of economic benefit or for parts requiring high precision if the cost of failure of the part is high. The end result must be improved performance or reduced cost or both. Because most implementations are tailored to specific applications [Porter and Mundy 1980; Okamoto et al. 1984], previous work often is reinvented for new applications. Development costs and times could be substantially reduced if the automation process were partitioned into generic components, wherever possible, to be used again directly as new applications are addressed. In dynamic environments where new inspection applications are continuously addressed, each new application typically builds on work done for previous applications, not just in experience but also in actual functional software or hardware or both. Though hardware usually must be tailored to the specific application in order to meet requirements on accuracy and throughput, it can be developed for specific classes of applications. For example, an X-ray system can be designed to inspect arbitrary metal objects within a specified dimensional range. Similarly, algorithms that are invented for a specific application can also be generalized and used for new applications with parameters that are tuned to each application.

This chapter formulates a systematic, general approach to partition an image-based inspection problem into application-independent processing and application-dependent specification and classification. The focus is on methodology and development of software to provide the automatic image analysis capability rather than on hardware design—automatic inspection requires high-quality data and automation should not be considered unless a hardware system will be available to provide such data. The approach was developed for an X-ray inspection system, which currently is used in production at a General Electric factory. It was applied to factory inspection problems to demonstrate the automatic image-analysis capability of the system and to validate the inspection performance. The results met or exceeded specifications, as has been reported in the literature [Oliver et al. 1986]. Though the approach is independent of imaging modality, it was designed to deal with the challenging image-processing tasks that are inherent to X-ray applications: detection and measurement of faint structures in highly structured images that exhibit great dynamic range. However, the same approach could certainly be used for medical applications or any type of application in which image content can be geometrically described.

2 Inspection Process

The general problem of inspection of an object may be simply formulated as follows:

Given an object, determine if the object satisfies given conditions of acceptability.

No matter how simple or complex the inspection problem is, a conceptual approach always includes object manipulation, image creation, image processing, and object classification, as described by Figure 4.6.

The simply defined problem of inspection is performed at vastly different

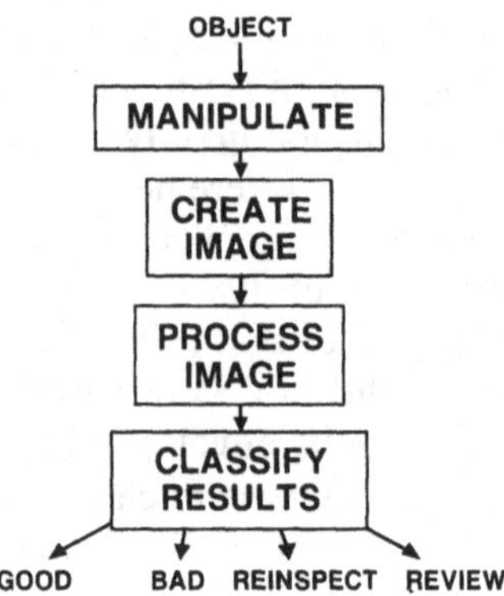

FIGURE 4.6. Inspection process.

levels of automation, from manual to fully automated. During manual inspection, a human might simply rotate the object in his hand, look for specific features on it, compare what he sees to some criteria, and decide if the comparison is good enough. At the most automated level, there is no human interaction. A robot places the object in a system with some sensing mechanism, a computer automatically initiates imaging and constructs an image from the sensor output, and computer logic processes the image data and classifies the object as good or bad. As the inspection process moves from manual towards automatic, trade-offs are made between the required training of the human inspector and the necessary complexity of the automated computer logic.

The most common form of inspection today is manual. Manual inspection requires that a human inspects an object or an image of an object following some predetermined procedure. He uses his judgment to determine whether the object is good or bad. He may use some physical aid, such as a measuring device, to resolve questionable situations. The manual method of inspection involves specialized inspector training and is prone to variability due to subjective judgments by the inspector.

The accuracy of conventional manual inspection may be improved by computer-aided processing of the images before they are analyzed. Such processing might be done by built-in hardware functions of a display device to enhance image contrast, or it might be accomplished by computer software. An inspector may interactively, using a display device and a "mouse," select regions of interest in the image and look at statistics of the regions, or he may trace boundaries around interesting structures and take measurements, as is done with nodules in medical images. A low level of automation is introduced into the inspection process if computer logic is used to extract and trace boundaries in the image. However, the inspector still must be trained to interpret the processed image.

A fully automated system uses computer logic to select regions of interest, to automatically process within these regions, and to interpret results of the processing for a final disposition of the object. An inspector is no longer required, so an operator or a robot positions the object to be imaged automatically. The image is then processed by the computer, and the decision as to whether the object is good or bad is made by computer logic. As the processing operations performed by computer logic usually must equal or exceed those of a human operator during manual inspection, the level of complexity of the required computer software becomes exceedingly high. If, in addition, the system must operate in real time, the automatic processing must keep up with data-collection rates, which strongly influence algorithm selection and often requires specially built hardware. To maximize the throughput of the system, a new object might be imaged while image data from the previous object are processed.

2.1 Requirements for Automation

An automated inspection system emulates the complicated functions performed by a human inspector when he examines an object. These functions were separated into the well-defined tasks that were shown in Figure 4.6. In the automated system, these functions are translated into an inspection plan that drives the system and synchronizes the sequence of operations performed by different modules, all without user intervention. Such a plan includes object orientations for manipulator control, parameters for imaging system control, a process plan to supervise the automatic image processing, and specific information needed for classification, as shown by Figure 4.7. The identical sequence of actions is executed for all nominally identical objects. Inspection plans are created in advance off line, during interactive sessions with typical images, and must be carefully tested and validated before they can be used in a hardware system.

As a potential automatic inspection application is developed, it is often evaluated at different stages to determine the likelihood of success. The success or failure of the system is intimately tied to such factors as the imaging technique, system resolution, and physics of the sensors, as well as to heuristic information that can be provided by experts and designers. The first development stage must establish basic feasibility and the second stage validates robustness. At the final stage, the speed or throughput of the inspection system is optimized to meet specifications.

A flexible software environment is required in order to address the complete development process for automatic inspection, from early feasibility experiments through simulation of automated system performance before final installation of software in the hardware system. The software must also provide a convenient environment for experimentation with image-processing algorithms and creation of process plans. Such a system was designed and implemented and is described later in Section 5.

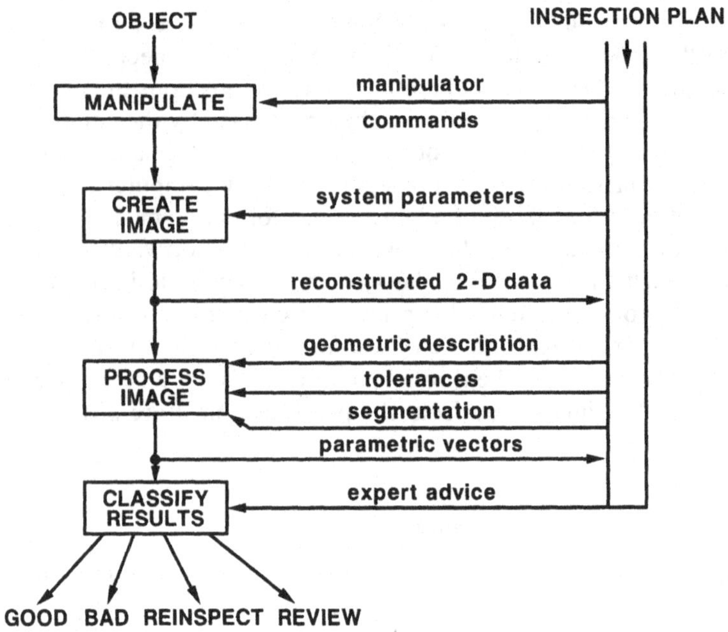

FIGURE 4.7. Automated inspection process.

2.2 Inspection System

The tasks of an automated inspection process, which were described earlier, are independent of imaging modality and application. These tasks can be directly mapped into a structure block diagram of an inspection system, as shown by Figure 4.8.

The master inspection plan, which is highly dependent on imaging modality and application, controls the whole system and synchronizes the sequence of operations performed by different system modules. The manipulator rapidly and accurately positions the object so that it can be imaged. The sensors (detectors) collect the data, which are digitized and stored in memory. Once all the image data are collected, the reconstructor processes, normalizes, and formats the data to produce a two-dimensional image. These image data then are sent to the flaw detector to be processed. Parametric vectors are output from the flaw dectector and sent to the classifier, decisions are made as to the quality of the object, and the report generator issues an inspection report.

Collecting the image data for the object is the first step in the inspection process. It is a crucial step, because the success of the final system is limited by the quality of the collected data. Specifics of hardware design will not be addressed in this chapter, however, as the objective is to formulate a system-independent approach to image-based inspections. With

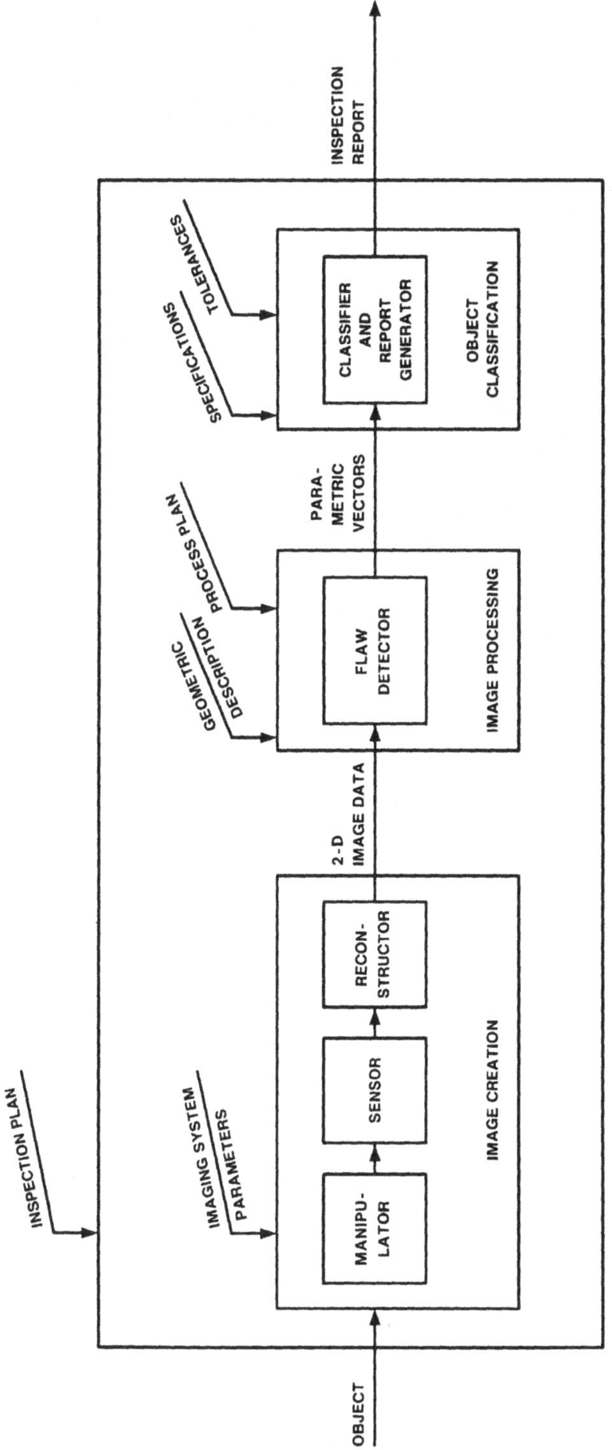

FIGURE 4.8. Automatic inspection system.

the assumption of availability of quality data, the real challenge in automatic inspection lies in the selection of algorithms and the creation of the overall process plan that drives the flaw detector. Ultimately, the solutions to these challenges determine the success of the system.

At the heart of the inspection system is the flaw detector. This is where image processing is done automatically through execution of a sequence of tasks on selected regions of object images as defined by a preselected process plan. As was mentioned earlier, industrial inspection applications often involve detection and measurement of a particular defect, such as a broken connection, in a well-defined image. The same inspection must be performed on numerous image instances that are not exactly identical and the process plan must be robust enough to deal with all images. A functional diagram of the flaw detector is shown in Figure 4.9. The input to the flaw detector is two-dimensional image data. The first tasks of the flaw detector are to register the image data to some reference position and orientation, to normalize the data to some desired dynamic range, and to segment the images according to the process plan directives. Preprocessing also may be done to reduce noise and artifacts that the imaging system is known to have contaminated the image data with. Preselected high-level image-processing primitives (process-filters or P-filters) then operate on geometric and topological descriptions of the image content to perform generic functions, such as FIND-THE-HORIZONTAL-BOUNDARY. The results from different operations are combined and formatted to describe geometric features in the image through parametric vectors that are the output from the flaw detector.

Images are examined for missing or additional structures as well as for incorrectly positioned or dimensioned structures. Detection of deviations

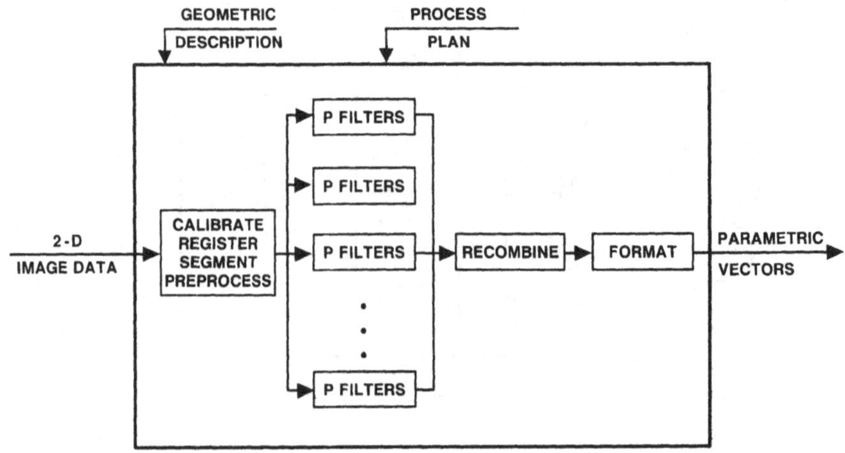

FIGURE 4.9. Flaw detection module.

and abnormalities in the uniformity of the image background regions also may be required. No fixed set of procedures or high-level primitives can find flaws of arbitrary types. Possible flaws, as well as image content, must be described geometrically (by a person that understands the specific application) for computer processing. Because flaw detection is still an art, there is no straightforward method of selecting processing schemes that are guaranteed to work. However, a methodical attack on the problem is described in the following sections.

3 General Approach

The general problem of inspection may be restated as follows:

Given an object and questions about the object, answer the questions.

To address the problem, the object image must be described and criteria for the analysis established. Industrial inspection applications are usually constrained. They involve detecting and measuring possible defects, which may have been introduced through a particular processing step, to ensure that the objects are acceptable before they are processed further. These objects and defects usually can be modeled by geometric descriptions. Inspection applications are identical to general image-analysis applications in that they require interpretation and analysis of image components. But they differ from general image-analysis applications in that they are constrained—objects may be positioned in very accurate orientations in the inspection system, lighting may be carefully controlled, and the objects may be represented by known models. However, performance requirements on accuracy and throughput rates are usually very strict and often more than cancel out advantages due to the constraints.

Several general questions must be answered before a specific application can be addressed:

- How do we describe image content so that meaningful questions can be asked?
- How do we process images to extract significant information?
- How do we format information for interpretation?
- How do we process automatically and in real time?
- How do we implement algorithms in systems and validate performance?
- What do we use for the development and simulation work?

Many of these questions have been analyzed in depth for specific problems. Several excellent books [Duda and Hart 1973; Rosenfeld and Kak 1976; Gonzalez and Wintz 1987] discuss basic image processing and pattern recognition techniques and the literature abounds with articles on scene descriptions, image processing algorithms, and special hardware designs. For most applications, the hardware components are chosen from available options but new and specific algorithms are often developed. These algorithms usually cannot be applied directly to other applications, but can often be modified for further use. Structured algorithm development should be encouraged, just as structured programming and development of modular software or hardware have been, to minimize algorithm development and testing effort. The questions listed earlier are addressed in the following sections to suggest a systematic integrated approach to image-based inspection applications. The use of high-level structured algorithms are proposed to operate on geometrically modeled images in a simulation environment that can be directly embedded in the final run time system.

3.1 Geometric Modeling of Image Content

Image data represent spatially collected physical measurements of an object—reflection, sound echo, X-ray attenuation, and so on—without any interpretation of the meaning of these measurements. Images can be processed without knowledge of how the data were collected, but in order to analyze images, the image data must be sorted into some kind of meaningful representation of the object.

Consider the industrial X-ray image of Figure 4.10, where lighter areas indicate more metal and darker areas indicate less metal. Very faint structures must be automatically detected and measured accurately in this image—a difficult problem. This image may be described by natural language sentences as follows:

The image appears, on the average, to be changing from lighter to darker across the image from left to right. Two clearly distinct regions exist in the image, a light region at the top with fairly uniform appearance and a dark region below with lighter and darker structures of various sizes and shapes. Several darker vertical lines of varying intensities appear in the uniform region at top. An irregularly shaped boundary separates the light and dark regions.

This image description, which is not at all unique, provides a basis for asking meaningful questions about the image. We have already described the image by geometric components (such as regions, lines, and boundaries), associated attributes (light, dark, uniform, irregular), and interrelational topology (across, top, below). To answer a question such as: "How many dark, vertical lines exist in the light region of the image?" a person would quickly scan the image, find the region that contains the structures he or she is interested in, focus on specific structures, and disregard everything in the surrounding background. This sequence of steps forms the basis for a new and simple geometric description of image content. The preliminary step is to conceptually segment or partition the image into one or more regions as was done by the natural language description. Each region may contain structures of interest and interfering background. What is called structure and what is called interfering background depends

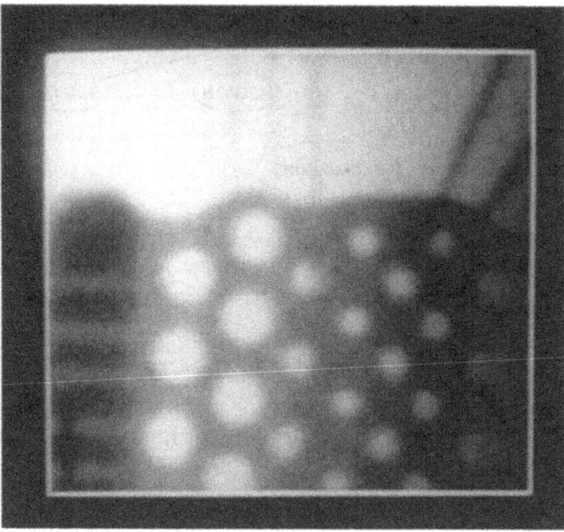

FIGURE 4.10. X-ray image of object with complex internal structures.

totally on the inspection application; structure is what we try to process in some way and interfering background is everything that makes that processing difficult. The partitioning can only be done by a person that understands the specific inspection problem, but the geometric primitives and their interrelations are generic. To answer the question about the lines, the structures would be the "lines" and the interfering background would be the "light region," which is a very natural separation. No further partitioning is required in this case. But if the question is: "Do any of the horizontal lines extend into the structured region below the boundary?" the structures of interest would again be "dark lines," but the interfering background would be the "light and dark shapes" in the region below the boundary. In order to detect the lines, processing to remove all other shapes may be necessary. This may require further partitioning of the background image to remove first the light circular shapes and then the dark striped shape to the left. For the first case, the structures of interest would be "light circular shapes" and the interfering background would be "dark uniform region." The object of partitioning the image as described is to gradually remove or neutralize all interfering background structures in the image so that, in the end, the structures of interest stand out against a homogeneous (or neutral) background, as is shown by Figure 4.11. In very difficult images, this may result in partitioning the image into numerous small subimages, removing the background in each subimage, and combining the results to recreate an image of the original size.

The structures of interest are described by geometric primitives that have relational descriptors and relative attributes associated with them,

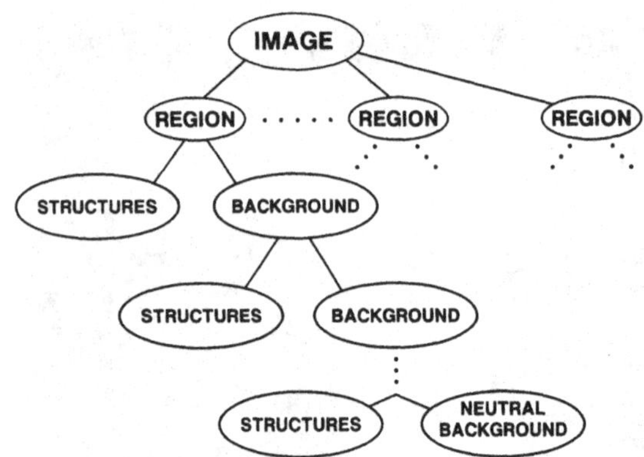

FIGURE 4.11. Partitioning of image.

as shown by Figure 4.12. Examples of geometric primitives are holes (structures with small areas compared to the containing region), cavities (structures with large areas compared to the containing region), lines (straight segments in region), boundaries (irregularly shaped connected line segments around structures or between regions), trends (large segments with slowly varying intensities), or masks (user-defined primitives represented by binary arrays of numbers that define specific shapes).

Some relational descriptors are horizontal, diagonal, below, middle, and right. These can be thought of as connections that define the relative positions and orientations of the components, as well as their interrelations. The relational descriptors also define where processing is to be done in the image.

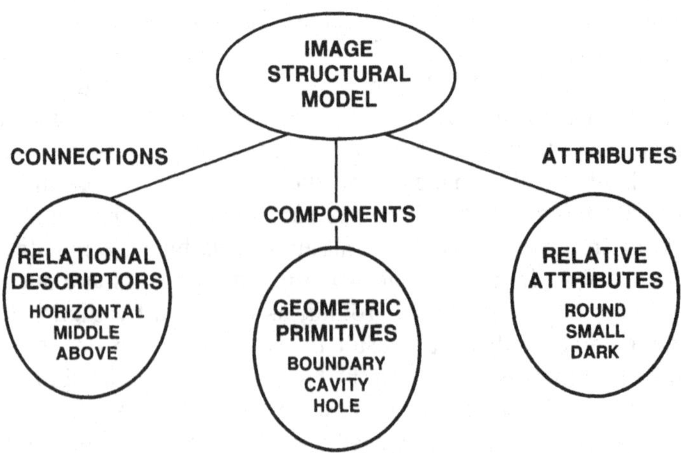

FIGURE 4.12. Geometric description of image structures.

Relative attributes, such as small, dark, light, wide, round, and pointed, describe the geometric primitives further. Exact or relative tolerances (or boundary values) may be imposed on the attributes to modify the shapes of the primitives. For example, a dark hole may be defined as having intensity values less than 65, or it may be defined as having intensity values that are at least 20% lower than the average background intensity value.

In spite of its simplicity, the geometric model that has been defined can deal with surprisingly complex images. Geometric primitives, parameterized by specific values, provide a feature-based description of object images that may be used by computer algorithms. The same simple geometric description can be applied to images from totally different applications; parameterized attributes provide application-specific values of tolerances and imaging system-specific information about the system point-spread-function, etc. The model base (list of geometric primitives) will continue to grow as new applications are addressed—this naturally leads to the idea of processing geometrically defined images with generic, high-level primitives.

3.2 P-Filters: Generic Primitives for High-Level Processing

Image processing involves performing one or more operations on image data. Context-independent processing modifies or transforms one image to another by subjecting the whole image to the same processing, independent of spatial location. Common image-processing primitives that perform edge detection, thresholding, convolution, or image-to-image transformations fall into this category. Context-dependent processing transforms the image content into a description of features in the image rather than into a modified image. Operators that segment the image, extract boundaries in the image, or do region growing belong to this category. Image analysis requires highly context-dependent processing algorithms which, invariably, are built from context-independent primitives. A particular set of primitive operators, thus, might be grouped together as a P-filter (Process-filter) to solve a general high-level image-processing problem without being tied to a specific application or imaging system in functionality.

A natural language sentence, such as FIND-THE-SMALL-DARK-ROUND-HOLES, describes the function of a particular P-filter as it is applied to image data. This functional description of the P-filter is a natural extension of the geometric description of image content that was given in the previous section.

Two-dimensional image data and parameters are the inputs to a P-filter; parametric vectors with geometric descriptions of image features and their properties, such as positions, orientations, widths, and lengths, are the outputs. Entries in the input parameter list tune the P-filter to a specific application. Quantitative values, which must be determined from images that are representative of the application, are entered to specify relative attributes, such as dark, or to define allowable deviations on relational descriptors, such as horizontal. Tolerances determine which particular primitive algorithms the P-filter will invoke: dark with a low contrast will probably require different processing from dark with a high contrast.

High-level P-filters are created from combinations of lower-level P-filters to form a simple process plan, similar to one that a person intuitively would follow if he or she were to look at the image and answer a question about the image directly.

Figure 4.13 (a) shows an X-ray image of an industrial object with a region of interest, containing a dark, vertical cavity and dark, horizontal lines, enclosed by a light border (or window). The objective of the inspection is to measure the widths of the horizontal lines and to determine if the lines intersect or penetrate through the vertical cavity. To extract the required information, the following P-filters are created:

- FIND-DARK-HORIZONTAL-LINES (parameter-list), and
- OUTLINE-DARK-VERTICAL-CAVITY (parameter-list).

Figures 4.13 (a) and (b) show the original image and the processed image after application of the P-filters. Parametric vectors with properties of the detected horizontal lines, such as positions, orientations, widths, and lengths, are output from the first P-filter while the second P-filter yields a list of coordinates to define the cavity outline.

A functionally high-level P-filter, such as the P-filter that finds the horizontal lines, is built from several lower-level P-filters or primitive functions:

(a)

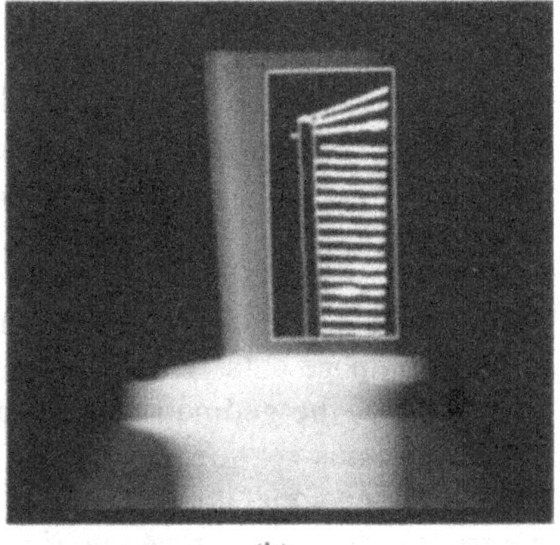

(b)

FIGURE 4.13. (a) X-ray image of metal object with window selected for processing; (b) dark lines defined, and cavity boundary outlined.

- FIND-ENTRY-INTO-DARK-LINES-FROM-ABOVE (parameter-list),
- FIND-ENTRY-INTO-DARK-LINES-FROM-BELOW (parameter-list),
- COMBINE-ENTRIES (parameter-list), and
- MERGE-INTO-CONNECTED-REGIONS (parameter-list).

The first two primitives find the outer boundaries of the lines, which then are combined by the third primitive. Finally, each line is identified as a connected region by the last primitive operator. The fact that the image was created using an X-ray system did not affect the algorithm development. Hierarchical image-processing operators that are independent of imaging system and application in concept can thus be developed. Quantitative values are then selected for the parameter list to tune them to specific applications. For instance, the sharpness of an edge (transition width) varies with different applications and may be specified by a parameter. This example demonstrates a method of structural algorithm development by combining previously validated primitive components into high-level P-filters and thus reducing the development time for new algorithms.

3.3 Parametric Vectors for Classification

Interpretation of image structures often begins with image processing that produces a binary image. To be analyzed, the contents may be grouped into connected geometric shapes. Specific criteria are then used to evaluate the interrelations of the shapes or their topologies. Each pixel in the image must be accessed once to define the boundaries of the structures. For further processing or analysis, the pixels often are accessed again, a time-consuming process. Line-segment boundary encoding is suggested to provide a powerful method of describing image content so that subsequent processing can be done efficiently on encoded data rather than on image data. In line-segment boundary encoding (which is similar to run-length encoding), the sequence of pixels of interest (binary or gray-level) along an image row is mapped into coordinate pairs, where each coordinate pair defines the starting and ending position of the data run. An associated vector contains the number of line segment pairs for each row. Connection analysis can then be done directly on the line segment coordinate pairs for region growing, and geometric properties, such as centroid positions, can be efficiently calculated from the encoded data rather than from the image data. Parametric vectors to describe image features may thus be created very fast from the line-segment encoded image data and may then be used for final interpretation of the processing.

A P-filter with the function FIND-THE-LARGE-ROUND-HOLES might have parametric vectors with the following components as its output:

$$< \text{primitive, type, tolerance, position, area, intensity} > \quad (4.1)$$

Examples of plausible vector entries are given by the following table:

Primitive	Type	Tolerance	Centroid position	Area	Intensity
Hole	Round	1	20,15	19	692
Hole	Round	0	16,18	20	694
Hole	Round	1	19,21	19	693
Hole	Round	1	15,24	19	694
Hole	Round	0	18,27	20	692
Hole	Round	1	14,30	21	694
Hole	Round	3	17,32	17	693

The information in the parametric vectors is geometric in content and similar to the information used to model image content. In the example, the values for the areas vary between 19 and 21 with the exception of the last entry, which has an area of 17. Tolerances to round are 0s or 1s, with the exception of the last entry of 3, which indicates a greater distortion. Here, tolerance to round is the maximum deviation in diameter through the centroid at several angles (in pixels).

The parametric vectors contain geometric information about the image features. The specific application then must evaluate the contents of these vectors and determine whether the values for the areas and the deviations

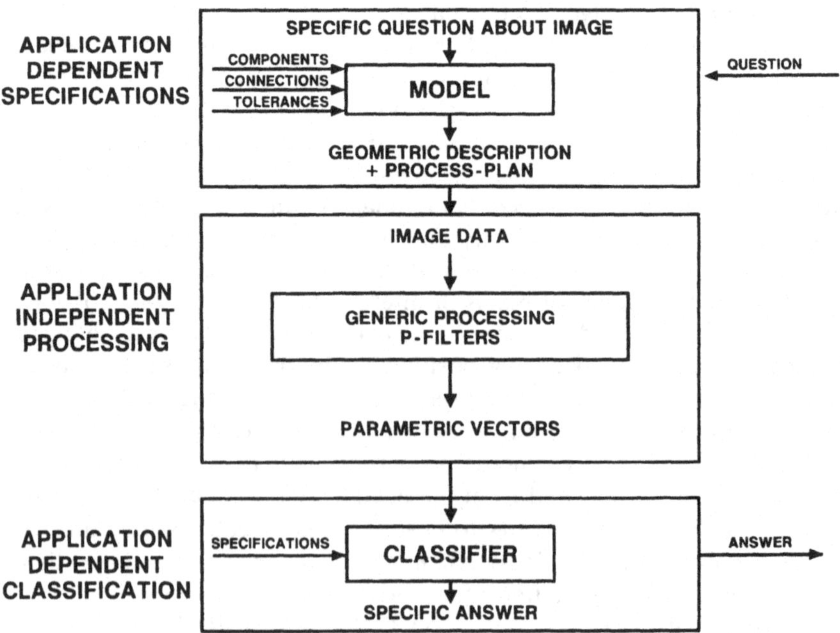

FIGURE 4.14. General approach to image analysis.

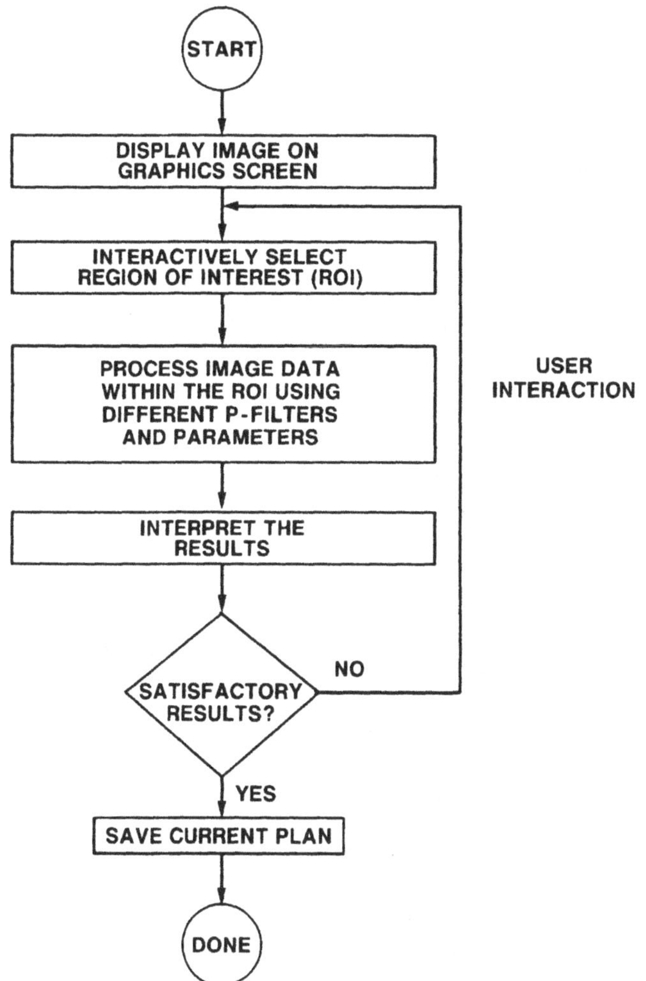

FIGURE 4.15. Interactive process plan development.

in shapes of the primitives are acceptable or not. This might be done by comparing the parametric vectors to a lookup table with acceptable entries or by list processing against acceptance criteria. For complicated classifications, a rule-based expert system may provide a powerful alternative.

3.4 Process Plan Development for Automatic Processing

Specifications for the inspection and evaluation of inspection results are highly dependent on the specific application, but a general group of image-processing filters may be suitable for widely different applications. The approach we have proposed to address an arbitrary image-based inspection

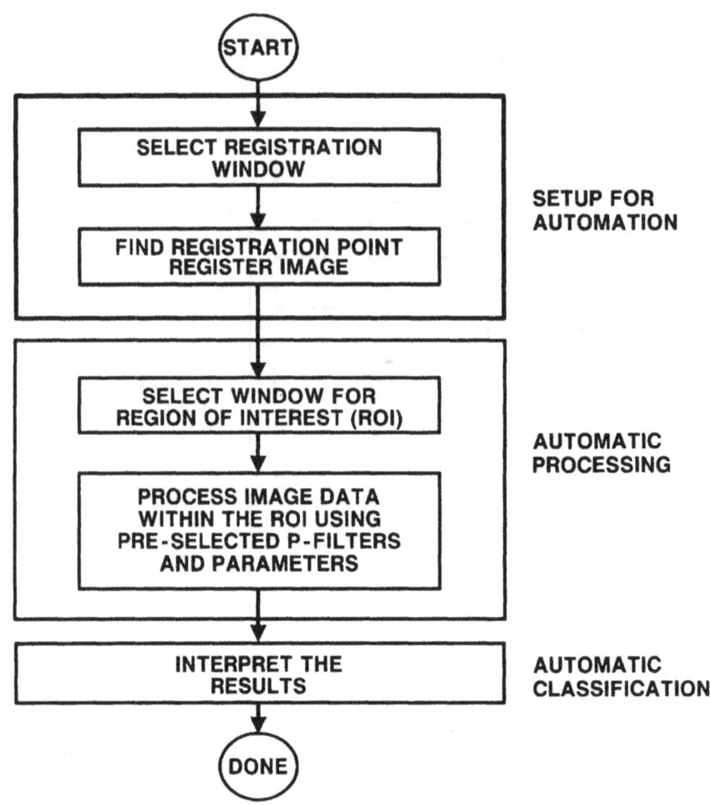

FIGURE 4.16. Structure of automatic process plan.

problem, therefore, separates the problem into application-independent processing and application-dependent specification and classification, as shown by Figure 4.14.

Just as an inspection plan drives the automated system, a process plan guides the automatic processing. A strategy for the automatic processing, which must be robust, i.e., it must yield accurate and reliable results for image instances that are not exactly identical, is developed off line in interactive sessions with representative object images. Typically, the position and orientation of objects vary in images of different object instances and prominent features in the image must be chosen for registration with respect to some reference position. Windows are selected for image processing to include the region of interest but to exclude interfering structures as much as possible. Application-independent P-filters are then selected and tuned to produce optimum results by specifying tolerances to attributes such as round or dark. Figure 4.15 shows how a process plan is generated interactively using typical images until satisfactory results are achieved. Figure 4.16 shows the functional structure of a plan when it is embedded

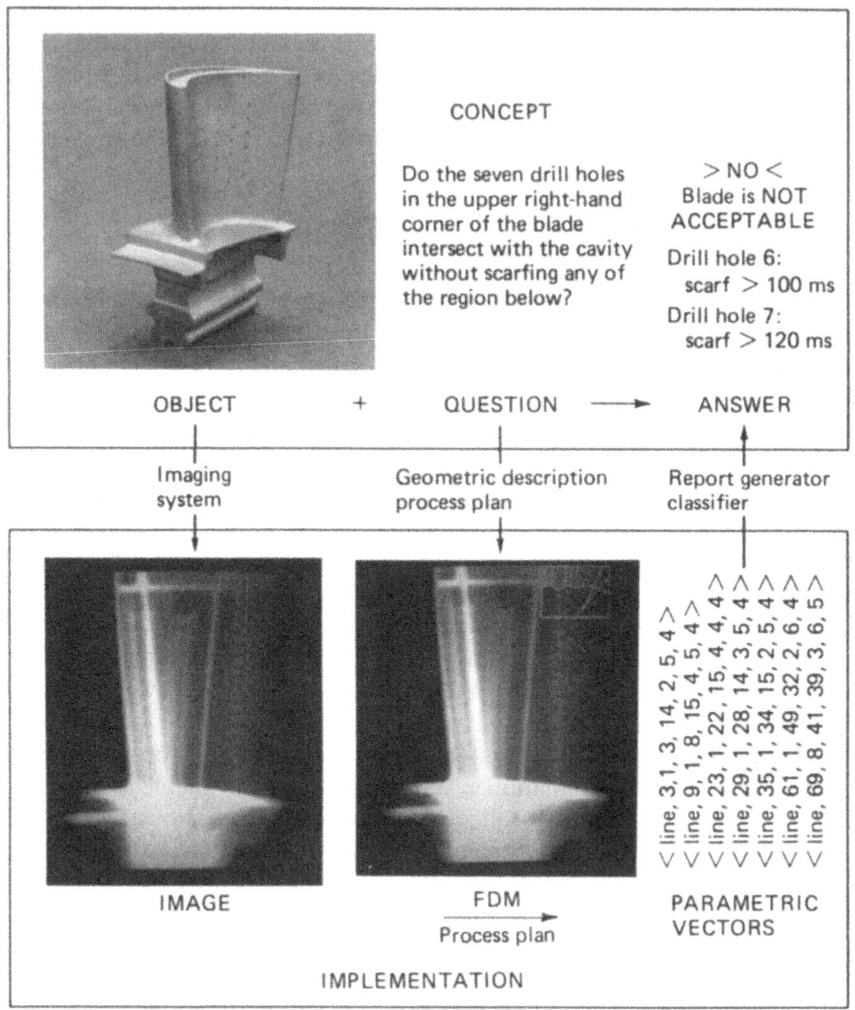

FIGURE 4.17. Inspection example and illustration of approach.

in an automatic system and user interaction no longer is possible. The process plan consists of a string of P-filters and typically begins by registering the image by REGISTER-IMAGE (parameters), where the parameters are the corner coordinates of the registration window and reference positions.

A strategy for the automatic inspection process has now been described and is illustrated by a specific example in Figure 4.17. At the top is the conceptual approach, which shows an object, a question about the object, and the answer to the question. The implementation is shown at the bottom. An image of the object has been created by the imaging system, and the question has been transformed into a process plan with the aid of a geometric model of the image. The image has then been processed in the flaw detector module (FDM) and the processed image is shown. Finally, parametric vectors have been created from the processed image and have been sent through the classifier and report generator to produce the answer.

4 Development, Testing, and Validation

Inspection problems addressed in a research environment may involve designing and building prototype systems to establish the feasibility of a particular imaging modality or specific new inspection problem. This in an expensive undertaking because the hardware might depend on components that represent the latest technological advances. Final development and tuning of a production-type system may not be done by the research staff; they will address the next challenging problem instead. Because the time window for introduction of a new technological development often is narrow in the industrial world, inspection system hardware and software frequently must be developed in parallel. When this is the case, images that are representative of the application will not be available for early algorithm development and reasonable test images must be created for experimentation. Additionally, when the hardware system is capable of creating images, there will not be much time allocated for software development using the actual system, as the hardware must be tested and validated. A software simulation system must then be available to process and evaluate images that are collected offline using the hardware system. A schedule must be carefully planned for the development work.

Figure 4.18 shows the development and testing approach that was created and used for a real-time automatic inspection application that required concurrent development of system software and hardware. To maximize the possibility of success when the software finally is installed in the hardware system, the software development is separated into four phases:

1. definition of initial strategy,
2. feasibility study,
3. algorithm tuning and process plan development, and
4. final validation.

During the preliminary phase, the problem should be defined as accurately as possible. Specifications must be included for throughput rates as those greatly affect later algorithm selection. During the feasibility stage, algorithms are developed using test data that reflect properties expected in the real system data. Once feasibility is established and satisfactory algorithms have been selected, they are evaluated using data that have been collected with the hardware system. At this time, the process plan that drives the automatic processing also is developed through interactive ses-

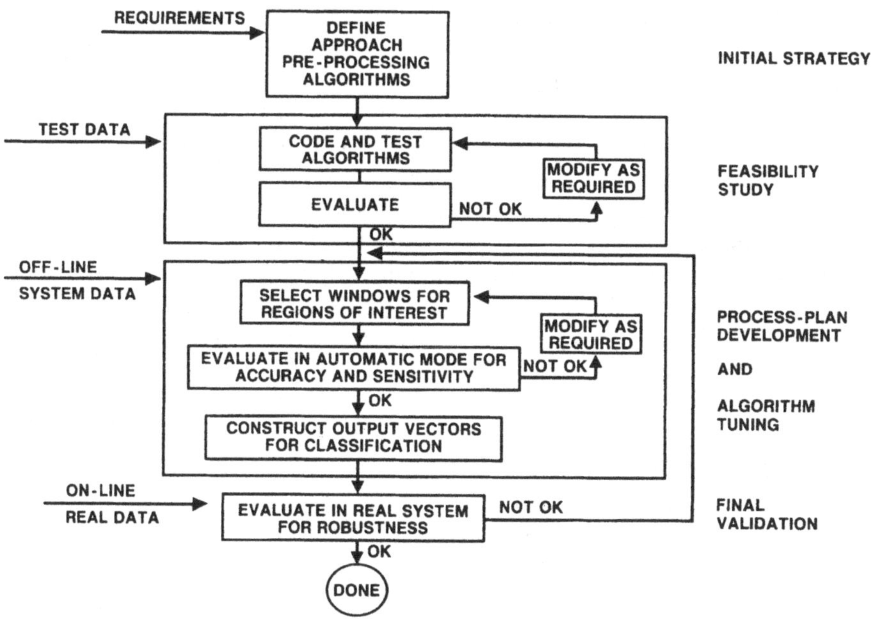

FIGURE 4.18. Systematic method of development, testing, and validation.

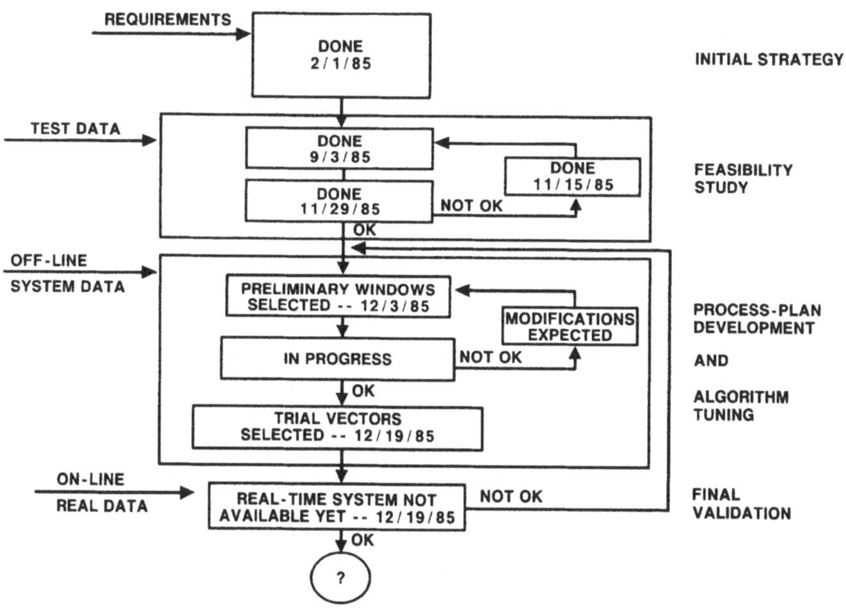

FIGURE 4.19. Overlay of Figure 4.18 for reporting status of development.

sions with "real" image data. Candidate plans are tested and tuned in an automatic mode through experimentation with several images from the hardware system. Finally, the selected process plan is incorporated into the overall system inspection plan and executed in the imaging system with image data that are collected on line in real time. The final classification parameters are adjusted using data from the real system runs.

The shell that describes the approach can be used to monitor progress during the development of algorithms and process plans. Each separate inspection problem of the application can be monitored separately for project status reports. If this is done, any bottleneck in the total systems development effort stands out quite clearly. Figure 4.19 shows an example of how the monitoring is done.

5 Development and Simulation System

In order to do the necessary research and development work for a complex image analysis application, it is important to have flexible and powerful software tools available. The image-processing part of an automated inspection application can be successful only if the selected processing schemes and inspection plans are accurate and robust. The manner in which algorithms are selected and evaluated also influences the ultimate success or failure of an application as projects can be abandoned if progress is too slow. A necessary requirement to support a systematic inspection approach is a flexible software system that allows general experimentation with image data. Until recently, there were no tools generally available for two-dimensional image processing. A prototype system called IPADS (image processing algorithm development and simulation system) was, therefore, designed and implemented and is briefly described.

5.1 Design Considerations

IPADS was designed to allow generic image processing of any type of 2-D images, independent of imaging system (such as visual, X-ray, eddy-current, or ultrasound). The main objective was to implement a totally self-contained system that can be used from early experimentation with algorithms on test data through final validation of selected algorithms in an automatic mode. IPADS, therefore, operates in an interactive mode as well as in an automatic mode, as selected by switches.

The system is driven by commands that perform desired functions. Sequences of interactive operations can be performed and recorded (through the command structure) to be executed again at a later time. This provides convenient generation of plans to drive the automated processing. User interaction takes place through a keyboard, graphics tablet, or file. The user may manipulate data in memory, perform image-processing functions, interact with the display screen, or set switches to change the operating mode or select diagnostic capabilities during the processing. All interactive functions are executed conveniently and with fast response.

Functionally, IPADS provides a complete set of software tools to deal with general image processing and analysis. Data files can be read and written in different formats and data can be displayed on a graphics screen. Test data can be generated and images can be degraded with controlled levels of noise. Regions of interest (ROI) can be selected so that data within them can be manipulated mathematically. Several ROIs can be selected and data can be combined from the different regions according to some function. Rectangular regions of interest are defined by windows and irregularly shaped subwindows are defined by line-segment endpoints, as shown by Figure 4.20. Selected parameters of the data, such as histogram or statistics, can be computed and displayed.

5.2 Implementation

Because all image-processing needs for an arbitrary application cannot be anticipated, flexibility and ease of implementation and modification of algorithms were given a high priority in the software system design.

The hierarchical modular structure consists of a high-level test executive module, lower-level functional modules, and lowest-level utility module.

FIGURE 4.20. Image with rectangular window and irregular subwindow defining regions of interest.

Each module has its own easily modifiable command structure and can access data that have been manipulated by commands from any other module. The test executive selects operating mode and communicates with the functional modules that handle generation of model data and noise, extraction of features in the data, processing of the image data, interaction with the display screen, and processing or classification for specific applications. The utility module can be accessed from any of the modules.

A common area for data permits communication between the different modules. Three large memory buffers allow access to image data in different stages of processing. A region of interest (ROI) can be selected in any of the data buffers. The window associated with the selected ROI applies to all three memory buffers. Data in the three buffers can be combined according to selected functions within the ROI and processing results can be displayed where they occur in the image, as shown by Figure 4.21.

The software was written in standard FORTRAN to run on a VAX 11/780 computer under the VMS operating system. A LEXIDATA graphics system with an interactive tablet serves as the display device. Figure 4.22 shows a block diagram of the hardware implementation.

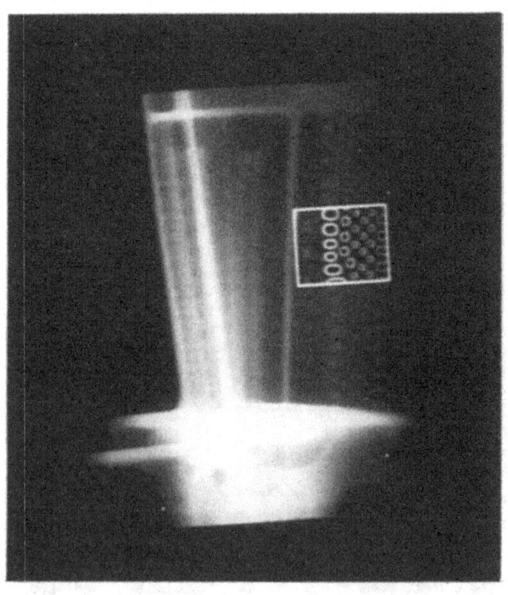

FIGURE 4.21. Processing result in region of interest.

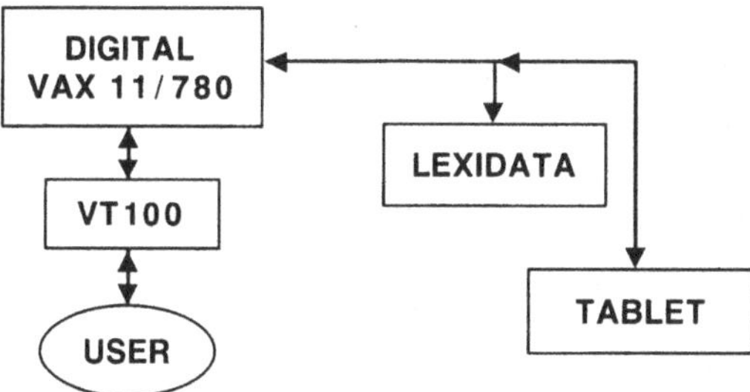

FIGURE 4.22. Hardware implementation of development and simulation system.

5.3 Image-Processing Operators

Image-processing functions are separated into low-level primitives and high-level operators that are built from the low-level primitives.

Many primitive operators are needed to provide the building blocks for sophisticated functions. Some basic operators combine the data in several buffers according to some function, or they return statistics of the buffer data. They invert, threshold, or correlate the buffer data. Simple image-processing functions such as edge detection or convolution also are classified as primitive operations.

High-level operators (P-filters) are derived to handle general image-processing tasks, such as finding the boundary between a light and dark region or neutralizing some trend in the data in a region. These tasks can be quite complicated and may require a substantial number of processing steps. The P-filters may exist as permanent commands when they have been evaluated enough to prove successful, or they may exist as temporary files (emulation files) while they are being developed.

The commands that perform the high-level functions represent permanent algorithms. They may be parameterized and require inputs or they may use preselected parameters. They may be very general, as when all the dark holes in an image are to be found, or they may be quite specific, as when two similar images are to be matched.

Emulation files are generated during interactive image-processing sessions. A special mode allows the image-processing steps to be saved in a file that can be executed at a later time to repeat the previous processing steps, either in the same or a different region of interest. This is how the P-filter commands generally are developed and evaluated. An emulation file can be extended and used as the plan that drives the automatic processing all the way from receiving the original image data to returning the final inspection results.

IPADS was demonstrated to be a powerful self-contained system that could be used effectively to evaluate algorithms and simulate system performance. It stimulated the develoment of a large General Electric–supported image-processing development environment (IPDE (Copyright of the General Electric Company 1986)), which now runs on VAX family computers, including the Micro VAX GPX workstation, and is used in several production inspection systems.

6 Comments and Developmental Experiences

The methodology described was defined and used for development of the automatic image analysis capability required for a production prototype X-ray inspection system currently in operation at a General Electric factory. An inspection plan directs the system in manipulating parts, in making the images, in analyzing them, and in forming a report of the results. Algorithms that were developed were successfully transitioned into the hardware system and embedded in the inspection plans in the form of high-level image-processing commands. To validate the system, numerous parts were loaded by an operator in grippers held to a conveyor, delivered to the inspection location inside the X-ray lead shielded chamber, manipulated and imaged, and returned on the conveyor. Part images were processed, results were evaluated, and parts were classified—all automatically. As a part emerged from the chamber, panel lights informed the operator of the correct disposition of the part. No modifications to the algorithms were necessary for the hardware system, but some classification parameters were modified to improve the final results. Performance of the automated system met or exceeded the system requirements. Previous publications describe the hardware and software systems [Oliver et al. 1986, Hedengren 1986] and some of the algorithms [Hedengren 1986].

Even though no special hardware was built for the image analysis, the system throughput requirements were met. As only one flaw condition was addressed at a given time, the system throughput was limited by the data acquisition, rather than by the image-processing time. However, as more flaws are added to the inspection plan, special hardware will probably be required to meet throughout requirements. This is true for most applications.

The software development and simulation system is of crucial importance in solving an inspection problem. Though many image-processing workstations or software packages now exist [Tamura et al. 1982], the ability to address the complete inspection problem, from experimentation through automation, in one environment is invaluable. Of special merit is the ability to generate high-level image-processing operators interactively from low-level primitives and to execute them directly with selected parameters. Selection of optimum parameters requires understanding of the imaging system characteristics and how they affect the images. The software environment permits experimentation to evaluate different preprocessing methods to reduce system-imposed effects. This is important because superior preprocessing produces clean images and thus simplifies final classification of the processing results.

7 Suggested Future Enhancements

The work described herein has dealt with industrial image analysis. A priori information has been used for specification and classification, as well as for tolerances imposed on the image-processing P-filters. Still, the processing has been based on the geometric content of the image. If the industrial objects were represented by solid models, much additional information would be available for the processing. Expected images could be produced of the object from the orientations that are specified for the inspection by simulating inspection of the solid models. Considerable preprocessing of the images could be avoided if the model representation is good enough to permit subtraction of the model image from the real image as a means of removing nominal backgrounds. Models also could be used for path planning for those systems that require a scan plan for the inspection. Additionally, models could be used to evaluate or improve inspectability of complex parts [Eberhard and Hedengren 1988] or to determine what hardware characteristics are required for inspection systems for such parts.

Interpretation of inspection results must be tailored to the specific application and is often done by very specific list processing. A generic rule-based expert system could be developed to simplify implementation of classification software for evaluation of the parametric vectors.

One cannot avoid human involvement in structuring the solution to a specific automatic inspection application; someone must define what the problem is and what the boundary conditions are. The current approach is built on a foundation of structured common sense. In the future lies the possibility of developing an artificial intelligence inspection system—high-level operators could be used to automatically evaluate image content and describe the image in geometric terms. The user might then be informed by the computer that the image contains certain structures and be queried as to which structures he wishes to examine. Finally, computer logic would select and proceed with the required processing.

Sensor fusing, combining different imaging modalities in the same inspection system, is an approach that should be explored for difficult inspection applications. It presents the new challenge of how to merge data from multiple images of different resolution and information content.

Acknowledgments. The author wishes to acknowledge the many people at the General Electric Corporate Research and Development Center who worked on the automatic imaging system. The support of Professor M. Savic at RPI during the course of this work is also much appreciated. Special thanks to Dr. L.W. Bauer for numerous helpful suggestions.

References

Antonsson, D., Danielsson, P.E., Kruse, B., Ohlsson, T., and Pääbo M. A system for automatic visual inspection of printed circuit boards. *LiTH-ISY-I-0264*. University of Linkoping Internal Publication, Linköping, Sweden.

Antwerpen, G. van, et al. 1986. Automatic recognition of asbestos and other mineral fibres. *Proc. 8th In. Conference on Pattern Recognition*. IEEE, 555–557.

Chin, R.T., and Harlow, C.A., 1982. Automated visual inspection: A survey. *IEEE Trans. on PAMI* **PAMI-4,** 6, 557–573.

Conners, R.W., McMillin, C.W., Lin, K., and Vasquez-Espinosa, 1983. Identifying and locating surface defects in wood: Part of an automated lumber processing system. *IEEE Trans. on PAMI* **PAMI-5,** 3, 573–583.

Don, H.S., Fu, K.S., Liu, C.R., and Lin, W.C. 1984. Metal surface inspection using image processing techniques. *IEEE Trans. on Systems, Man, and Cybernetics* CMC-14, 1, 139–146.

Duda, R.O. and Hart, P.E. 1973. *Pattern classification and scene analysis*. Wiley, New York.

Eberhard, J.W., and Hedengren, K.H. 1988. Use of a priori information in incomplete data X-ray CT. In *Review of progress in quantitative nondestructive evaluation,* vol. 7A (D.O. Thompson and D.E. Chimenti, eds.), Plenum, New York, 723–730.

Gilmore, R.S., Tam, K.C., Young, J.D., and Howard, D.R. 1986. Acoustic microscopy from 10 to 100 MHz for industrial applications. *Phil. Trans. Roy. Soc., London,* **A320,** 215–235.

Gonzalez, R.C., and Wintz, P. 1987. *Digital image processing*. Addison-Wesley, Reading, Mass.

Harlow, C.A., and Eisenbeis, S.A. 1973. The analysis of radiographic images. *IEEE Trans. on Computers* **C-22,** 7, 678–689.

Hedengren, K.H. 1986. Automatic image analysis for inspection of complex objects—a systems approach. *Proc 8th Int. Conference on Pattern Recognition,* IEEE, New York, 919–921.

Hedengren, K.H. 1986. Automatic analysis of complex object images—A systems approach. *Proc Int. Conference on Systems, Man, and Cybernetics,* IEEE, New York, 1548–1553.

Joynson, R.E., McCary, R.O., Oliver, D.W., Silverstein-Hedengren, K.H., and Thumhart, L.L. 1986. Eddy current imaging of surface breaking structures. *IEEE Trans. on Magnetics,* Mag-22, (Sept.).

Okamoto, K., et al. 1984 An automatic visual inspection system for LSI photomasks. *Proc. 7th Int. Conference on Pattern Recognition,* IEEE, New York, 1361–1364.

Oliver, D.W., et al. 1986. XIM: X-ray inspection module for automatic high-speed inspection of turbine blades and automatic flaw detection and classification. In *Review of progress in quantitative nondestructive evaluation*. Vol. 5A (D.O. Thompson and D.E. Chimenti, eds.), Plenum, New York, 817–823.

Porter, G.B., and Mundy, J.L. 1980. Visual inspection of metal surfaces. IEEE *Proc. 5th Int. Conference on Pattern Recognition*. IEEE, New York, 232–237.

Rosenfeld, A., and Kak, A.C. 1976. *Digital picture processing. Academic, New York.*

Sankar, P.V., and Sklansky, J. 1982. A Gestalt-guided heuristic boundary follower for X-ray images of lung nodules. *IEEE Trans. on PAMI* PAMI-4, 3 (May), 326–331.

Tamura, H., Tomita, F. Sakane, S., Yokoya, N., Sakaue, K., and Kaneko, M. 1982. A transportable image processing software package: SPIDER. IEEE *Proc. 6th Int. Conference on Pattern Recognition*. IEEE, New York, 75–78.

5
A Design Data-Based Visual Inspection System for Printed Wiring

OLLI SILVÉN, ILKKA VIRTANEN, TAPANI WESTMAN, TIMO PIIRONEN, AND MATTI PIETIKÄINEN

ABSTRACT: Until very recently, printed wiring board (PWB) fabrication relied on electrical testing and visual inspection by humans to provide feedback for process control. The low efficiency of visual inspection is often a severe problem for printed wiring board manufacturers. During the past few years, considerable work has been done both in industry and research institutions to solve inspection problems with image-analysis techniques. However, many of these efforts have focused on satisfying the needs of a limited set of users. This makes them vulnerable to changes in fabrication technology and the geometrics of wiring patterns. In the factories of the future, computer-aided design (CAD) data will be the source of all the control information for the fabrication processes. Accordingly, the primary goal of the work presented here has been to devise an approach that can be integrated to CAD data-driven production environments. The main result is the CAD data-based verification of wiring patterns. Other important objectives have been high throughput, low cost, and compact implementation. From the developmental point of view, the goal has been to build a functionally complete experimental system that can be upgraded to run at the speed of image acquisition by adding standard hardware.

1 Introduction

Printed wiring boards (PWBs) are rigid or semirigid dielectric sheets that carry patterns of copper or other conductive material. The purpose of printed wiring boards is to replace wires and components in electrical devices and, as such, they are the basic part of most electronic assemblies.

The advances in component technology demand more contacts per package and have increased the complexity and density of printed wiring. As a result, the need for automatic visual inspections is especially acute in the PWB industry.

Much interest in the past has concentrated on the prelamination visual inspection of inner layers of multilayer PWBs. Due to the high cost of multilayer boards, it is important to spot the defects at an early stage of the fabrication process.

The wiring patterns on the inner layers are typically simple and regular. Usually only one trace width and one or two pad sizes are present. These properties provide a good starting point for designing fast defect-detection methods with reasonable hardware implementations. Incidentally, most existing inspection systems are based on the idea of detecting defects, regardless of what the basic functional principle is called [Sanz and Jain 1986].

The current PWB inspection systems attain high defect detection and low false-alarm rates. However, these rates tend to be valid for only a limited set of patterns at a time [Silven et al. 1984a]. If the design rules change, these defect-detection devices may fall short of being fully automatic systems. A human operator may then be needed for screening the defect candidates and to make pass/fail decisions.

The outer layers of printed wiring boards are difficult inspection targets because several trace widths and types of pads are present. The coexistence of older and newer component packaging technologies complicate the situation because the same board is likely to carry patterns with conflicting design rules. In such cases, information about the underlying patterns is important for determining the nature of the detected discrepancy.

Clearly, the capability of detecting possible defects is not sufficient criterion for inspection methodology selection. The value of reliable and fast defect evaluation should not be underestimated.

Automatic error analysis is difficult to implement on top of plain defect-detection methods. In practice, the analytic functions may be most conveniently realized as an independent reevaluation stage that starts its work from the raw image data. A printed wiring board inspection system based on this approach is described in Thibadeau et al. [1982].

With high-speed implementation these kinds of analysis stages can also be applied to initial defect detection. Then no separate defect-detection scheme is needed. One of the early printed wiring board inspection systems was based on this solution [Sterling 1981]. The operation was based on the evaluation of lengths of runs of substrate and conductor material on successive scan lines. A region growing process generated conductor and substrate blobs that were analyzed. Defect detection was based on the knowledge of topological and localized constraints on the blobs, such as the maximum and minimum width and the manner in which they may change. Newer analysis-oriented approaches [Mandeville 1985; Lloyd-Doyle Ltd. 1984] are based on morphology.

The analysis-oriented methods can be used either with or without reference data that need not be detailed. Information about the approximate placements of the traces and other major features, such as pads and junctions, is a sufficient support for analysis. However, an automatic procedure does not exist for generating the inspection algorithms as a function of patterns and defects to be detected. Nevertheless, this is not a serious drawback with fixed design rules. In fact, any patterns, not just printed wiring, can be inspected with proper algorithms and reference data.

2 CAD Data-Based Inspection

Computer aided design (CAD) data-driven manufacturing environments require production machinery that can be rapidly adapted to product changes. Changes are frequent in printed wiring board fabrication because the production batches are typically rather small.

Most schemes devised for CAD data-based visual inspection of printed wiring deal with integrated circuit photomasks. Some of these methods can also be applied to printed wiring boards. The most straightforward approach is the pixel-by-pixel verification against the image of a perfect product created from the CAD data. This method works with integrated circuit photomasks [Automatic 1983] but has problems with the frequent permissible variations of printed wiring board patterns. A PWB inspection system based on a refined pixel level comparison scheme avoids these difficulties by using tolerance zones and considers the deviations from the model harmless unless the tolerance zones are violated [DIT-MCO Corp. 1984].

A variant of pixel-by-pixel comparison is employed in a CAD data-supported LSI photomask inspection system [Okamato et al. 1984]. This scheme compares the local features extracted from both the synthesized model image and the mask undergoing inspection. The comparison method allows alignment errors to some extent [Hara et al. 1980]. Also the method described in Tsujiyama et al. [1980] tolerates a small alignment error. This approach is based on comparing sums of the coordinates of the pattern edges found during each linear scan. As this method is most suitable for locating missing parts, a parallel rule-based inspection looks for micro defects.

An early design data-based PWB inspection system, which does not require extensive modification of the CAD data, is described in West et al. [1983]. The approach is based on an image dissector camera and a precision *xy*-table that separately scan every conductor, pad, and hole of the printed wiring. The scanning strategy exploits a priori knowledge of the types of probable defects, and only the regions considered critical are checked. Also the method presented in Chin et al. [1978] is a relatively early attempt to use a higher-level reference data in PWB inspection. During inspection the reference data is consulted for edge coordinates that are used for controlling a scanner to find the corresponding locations in the test image. Although this system obtained the reference through an interactive model-formation stage, it could have used CAD data.

3 An Inspection System Based on CAD Data-Based Pattern Verification

The experimental visual inspection system presented here is targeted for the automatic design data-based verification of printed wiring [Silven et al. 1984b]. The choice has been to use fairly high-level reference data because of the large storage needs of pixel-level models. Compact high-level reference data also simplify automatic defect analysis and the design of data paths of the inspection system.

The reference data is derived from photoplotter files that are created at the end of the computer aided design process. These files are usually

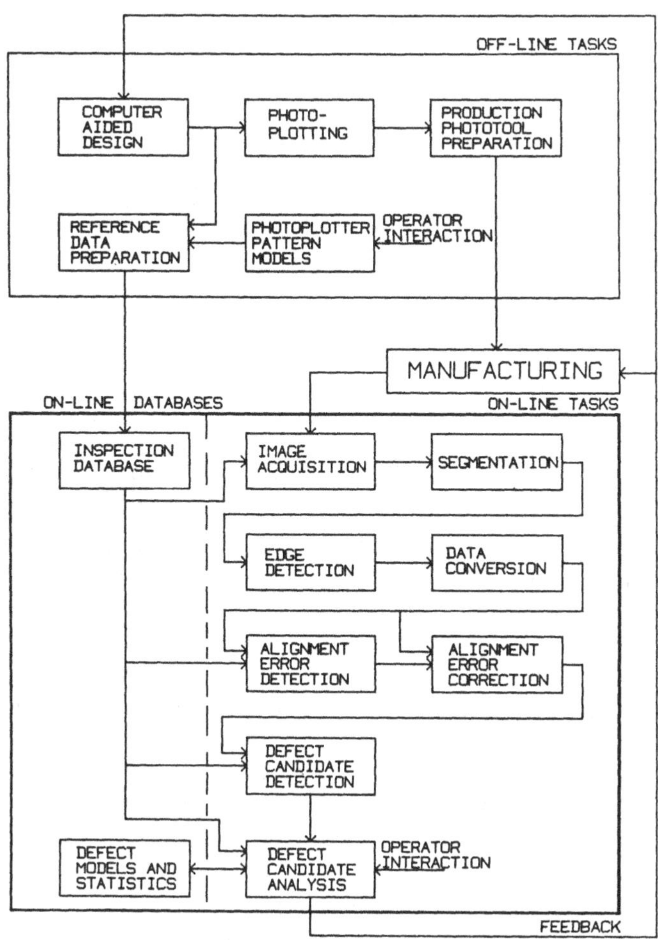

FIGURE 5.1. Framework of the CAD data-based inspection system.

used for producing artwork masters by photoplotters that expose film material with moving and stationary light patterns. For the inspection system, the photoplotter files are converted into descriptions of pattern borders. Each border description is assigned a tolerance zone that determines the deviations allowed for the patterns to be inspected.

A compact and low-cost system implementation has been pursued with a hierarchical approach that reduces the number of data items at each processing stage while the computational complexity increases. At the same time the control strategy is shifted from a data-driven to a model-based one.

The inspection methodology is the following: First the edges of the wiring patterns are detected and approximated by line segments at the data-conversion stage. After alignment error correction, the line segments are compared to the reference data and the differences found are delivered to the error-analysis stage for defect classification. Both the defect-detection and analysis stages use the same reference data base. The functional structure of the inspection system is depicted in the lower half of Figure 5.1.

The experimental inspection system consists of a scanner and a dedicated hardware unit that is connected to a minicomputer [Silven et al. 1985]. The dedicated hardware unit is used for preprocessing, while the minicomputer implements the later processing stages. A color graphics terminal is used for the human interface.

4 Reference Data

Photoplotter control files are used to generate reference data because they have a de facto standard: the Gerber format (ANSI standard, printed board description in digital form, *ANSI/IPC-D-350,* differs from this format.). This format describes the wiring patterns by aperture definitions, exposure, and movement commands. However, the photoplotter files do not contain all the information needed for inspection because hole descriptions and tolerance data are missing. The hole data can be obtained from the drill control file, but as most of the test boards lacked holes we chose to add them to the pad definitions when necessary. Because of the simplicity, the tolerance zones were assigned to be proportional to the pattern dimensions.

The primitives of the reference data generated from the photoplotter file are arcs and straight lines that describe the edges of the patterns. Arcs are necessary to keep the reference data file compact, although straight lines are computationally simpler to use at later stages.

The reference data base is organized into pages, i.e., blocks that describe 2,048-by-2,048 pixel areas of the wiring. Adjacent pages overlap by 24 pixels in order to avoid edge effects. Consequently, the line segments supplied by the data conversion processor are aligned and inspected 2,000-by-2,000 pixel areas at a time. This is necessary because the permissible fixture and printing variations prevent perfect simultaneous alignment of the whole board with the reference data.

The data in each page is organized for rapid access by dividing it into 64-by-64 (or 128-by-128) pixel subpages that overlap by 8 pixels. For each subpage there is a pointer bucket that contains the addresses of model edges that reside on the subpage. The addresses of the pointer buckets are in turn stored in an index table that contains an entry for each subpage.

Figures 5.2 (a) and (b) portray photoplotter control data and the corresponding photoplotted patterns, respectively. Figure 5.2 (c) shows the edge descriptions with subpage division and Figures 5.2 (d) presents the reference data. For clarity, the scaling factor for data is unity. Note that each edge description has two labels, namely, the edge and photoplotter stroke numbers. The latter is important for width measurements and the error analyzer. The last parameter for each description is tolerance.

In most cases the amount of storage needed for the reference data is almost equivalent to the original ASCII-coded photoplotter file. This ratio may change if a large number of complex special patterns are present.

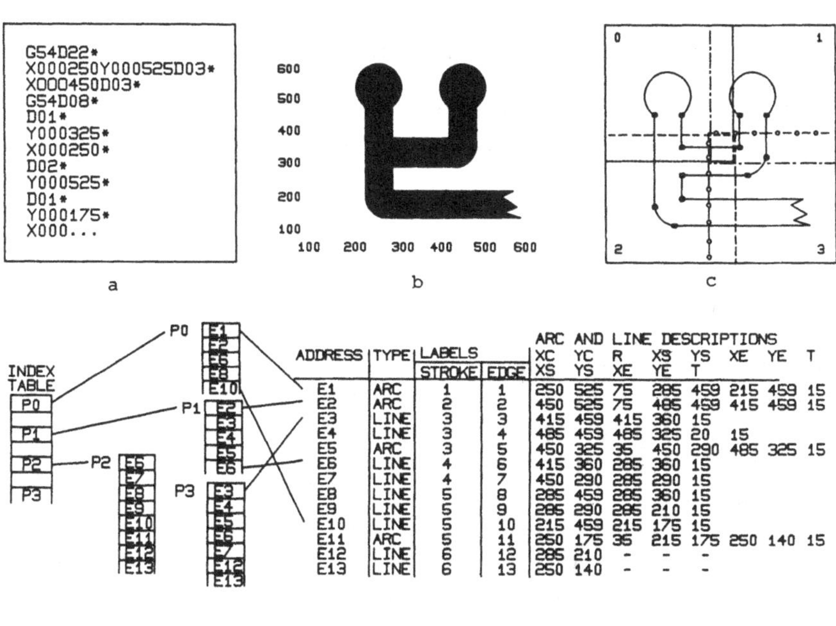

ADDRESS	TYPE	LABELS STROKE	EDGE	ARC AND LINE DESCRIPTIONS XC / XS	YC / YS	R / XE	XS / YE	YS / T	XE	YE	T
E1	ARC	1	1	250	525	75	285	459	215	459	15
E2	ARC	2	2	450	525	75	485	459	415	459	15
E3	LINE	3	3	415	459	415	360	15			
E4	LINE	3	4	485	459	485	325	20	15		
E5	ARC	3	5	450	325	35	450	290	485	325	15
E6	LINE	4	6	415	360	285	360	15			
E7	LINE	4	7	450	290	285	290	15			
E8	LINE	5	8	285	459	285	360	15			
E9	LINE	5	9	285	290	285	210	15			
E10	LINE	5	10	215	459	215	175	15			
E11	ARC	5	11	250	175	35	215	175	250	140	15
E12	LINE	6	12	285	210	-	-	-			
E13	LINE	6	13	250	140	-	-	-			

FIGURE 5.2. (a) Photoplotter control data; (b) photoplotted patterns; (c) reference edges; (d) reference data.

5 Image Acquisition

Inspection algorithms alone do not make a complete inspection system. The performance, cost, and reliability depend greatly on the mechanics, optics, illumination, and sensors.

The image-acquisition unit of the experimental inspection device is a rather conventional solution based on an *xy*-table and a CCD-line-scan camera that produces a 2,000-pixel wide image. This system was preferred to laser scanners because of cost and the expected better scan linearity needed by the comparison method. The imaging resolutions, 10 or 25 μm, are selected by changing the camera lens.

Special attention was paid to the illumination arrangements because the image signal is segmented by thresholding. For most materials, sufficient contrast is achieved by exploiting specular reflection and carefully selected combinations of lights and optical filters. However, this approach fails with reflowed solder-coated patterns as they are clearly three-dimensional. For these materials, a combination of an integrating sphere and beam-splitter shown in Figure 5.3 (a) was developed. The inside of the sphere is coated with barium sulphate (Eastman White Reflectance Coating CAT. No. 6080) to produce diffuse illumination on the conductor patterns. The relatively large holes needed for image acquisition at the top and bottom of the sphere are compensated for by a small amount of coaxial illumination added with a beamsplitter [Piironen 1987].

The achieved image-acquisition speed for printed wiring boards is 5,000,000 pixels/second at 10 μm resolution. The highest speed for back-lighted mask films at the same resolution is approximately 7,000,000 pixels/second. The image-acquisition part of the experimental inspection system is shown in Figure 5.3 (b).

6 Data Conversion

The purpose of the data-conversion step is to reduce the number of data items enough to enable further processing by a general purpose micro-computer. The principle involved is to approximate the pattern borders in the acquired binary image by line segments during one raster scan, which resembles the generation of a raster-scan-chain-code [Cederberg 1979; Danielsson 1982].

In order to keep the hardware simple, a straightforward conversion algorithm was developed. First the edges of the patterns in the binary image are detected, because the nonedge pixels can be rapidly skipped over when the image consists of only edge pixels and background. The following linear approximation algorithm is based on an extremely simple interpolation error-evaluation scheme: The approximating line segments are terminated when the edge ends: two or more line segments meet or the

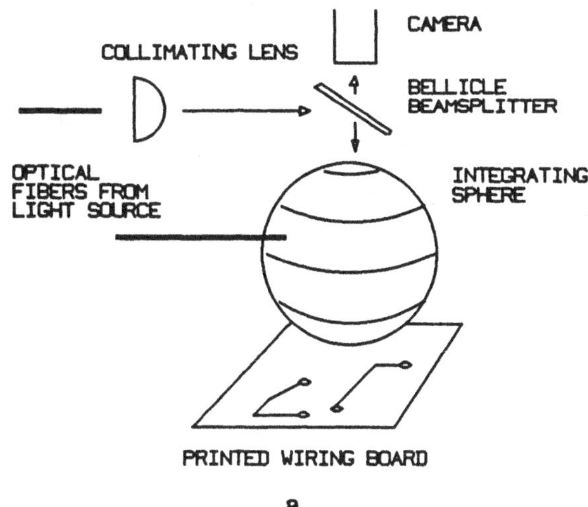

a

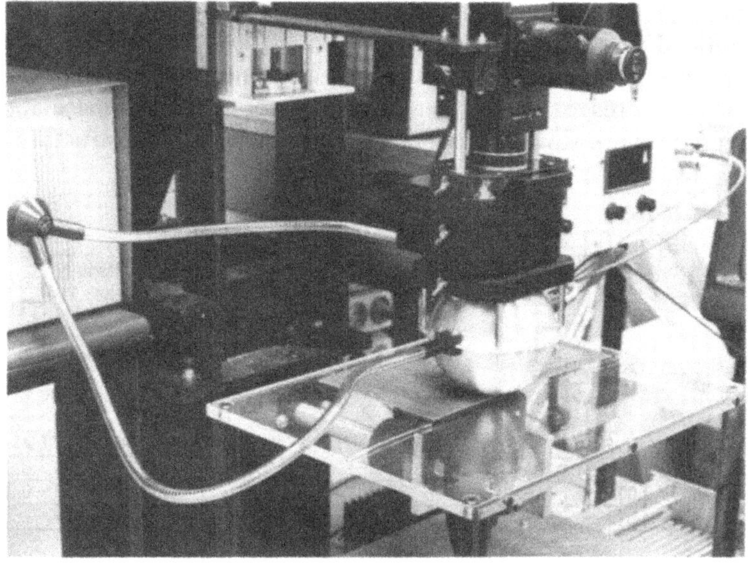

b

FIGURE 5.3. (a) Lighting arrangement for solder coated wiring; (b) image-acquisition system.

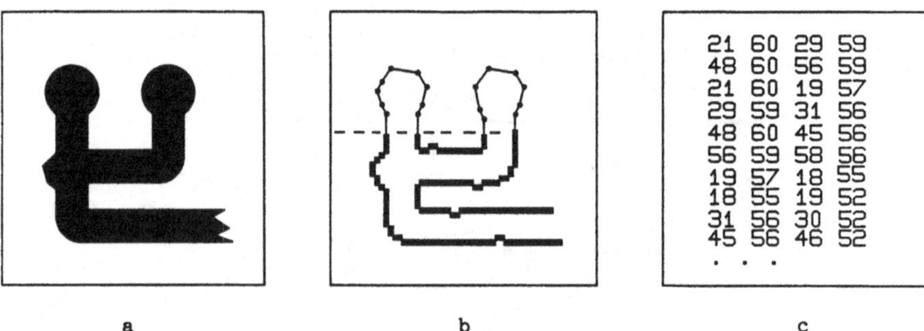

FIGURE 5.4. (a) Pattern on the board; (b) edge approximation; (c) generated line segment data.

line segment orientation departs from 0, 45°, 90°, or 135° that dominate in printed wiring.

Figure 5.4 presents the steps of data conversion, the pattern on the printed wiring board is shown in Figure 5.4 (a); Figure 5.4 (b) demonstrates the raster-scan linear approximation of the edges and Figure 5.4 (c) displays the generated data.

Due to raster scanning, several unterminated linear approximating segments may be present at the same time. The parameters of these active approximations are stored in a data structure that has a substructure for

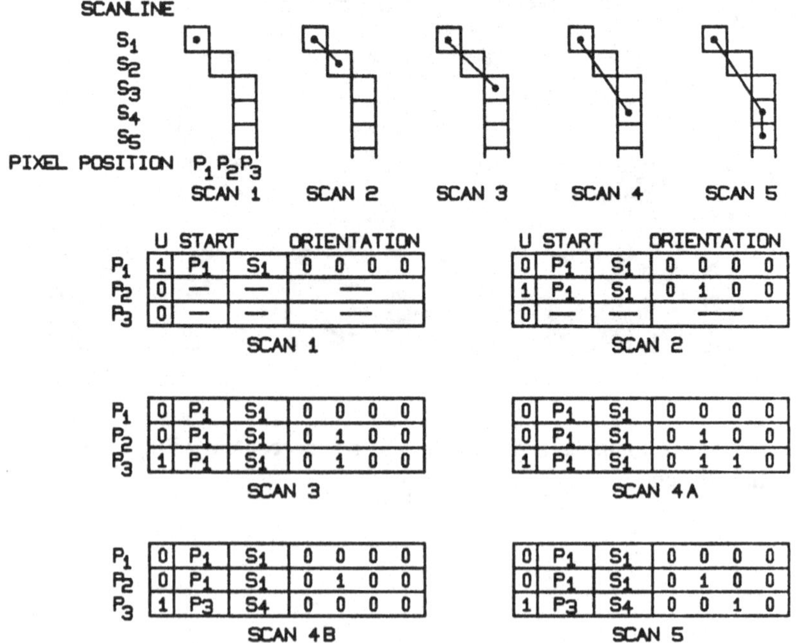

FIGURE 5.5. Manipulation of temporary data during linear approximation.

each horizontal pixel position. Figure 5.5 shows the approximation result and the corresponding "parent" data fields for an edge after each horizontal scan. The data for scan number 4 is shown both before terminating the first approximating segment and after the creation of the second one.

The data conversion is based on three basic actions, in other words, creation, continuation, and termination of the approximating line segment. A new active approximation is created by storing the column and row coordinates in the START-field of the parent structure of the current pixel position and by setting the usage-flag U. When the approximation is continued, the contents of the parent structure are moved to the location that again corresponds to the current pixel. Finally, the formation of the line segment is terminated and its START-coordinates are output with the current column and row coordinate values. More complicated cases, such as junctions and isolated pixels, are handled with combinations of the basic actions.

The four orientation flags, for 0, 45°, 90°, and 135°, are cleared when a new line segment approximation is started, and updated and tested when it is being continued. The orientation flag to be set is determined by the direction of the transition from the previous pixel in the border to the current one. The approximation is no longer errorless when more than one orientation flag is set. This condition causes the termination of the current line segment and the creation of a new one that starts from the previous termination point.

The data-conversion algorithm is implemented by dedicated microprogrammed hardware that consists of three Multibus I boards. The compact implementation is due to the raster-scan algorithm that needs to store only a few lines of the pixel level image at a time [Virtanen and Silven 1986].

7 Alignment Error Determination

The reference data and the line segment approximations must be precisely aligned because the position-sensitive comparison used cannot detect defects smaller than the alignment error. The size of the areas aligned at one time is 2,000-by-2,000 pixels.

The alignment method [Silven and Hakalahti 1985] resembles the approach described in Kahl et al. [1980]. During the generation of reference data, a number of conductors, at most eight, with differing orientations, are selected to be used for alignment error determination. Conductors are used instead of pads because their dimensions were found to vary less with respect to the design parameters. The positions of the edges of the selected conductors are assumed to be known to an accuracy of half of the trace width in an unaligned board. This assumption is realistic because the guidance holes or alignment markers required by automatic assembly machines can be exploited for initial positioning.

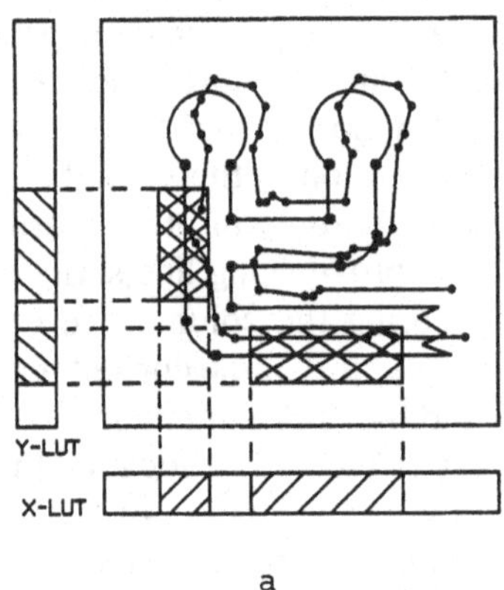

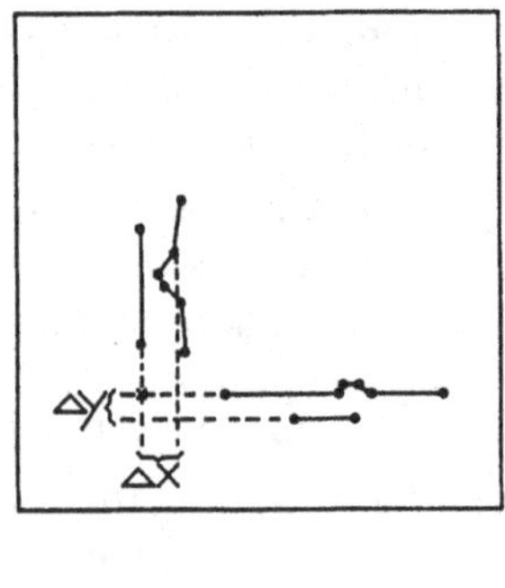

FIGURE 5.6. (a) Finding data of interest with table look-up; (b) alignment error determination.

During inspection the line segments produced by the data-conversion step are searched for approximations of the selected edges. This search is supported by look-up table hardware that points out the line segments originating from the areas of interest as shown in Figure 5.6 (a). The hardware that occupies a Multibus I board supports sixteen of these sampling windows, half of which are diagonally oriented. Two sampling windows are allocated for each selected conductor, one for each edge.

Alignment determination is based on calculating the position differences of intersections of pairwise selected model edges and corresponding approximating line segments. The principle is demonstrated by Figure 5.6 (b). The translation values obtained are used to address small translation space neighborhoods that are incremented. The incrementation results in a local maximum at the translation space element that corresponds to the alignment error.

So far, the accuracy of the alignment procedure has been better than 1.5 pixels when measured as the average absolute distance between approximating segments and the corresponding reference edges. This distance is about 0.6 pixels for the narrowest conductors that have the smallest dimensional variations.

8 Defect Detection

The defects of printed wiring are usually open and shorted conductors, violations of spacings and trace widths, and spurious conductor material. The size of the defects may vary from very small to massive. Tests do suggest that both comparison- and width measurement–based inspection methods are needed for reliable defect detection [Silven et al. 1984a].

Position-sensitive comparison is the only defect-detection method currently implemented in the experimental system. Figure 5.7 (a) illustrates this method by showing the line segments obtained from the board together with the tolerance zones of the reference edges. Figure 5.7 (b) shows the line segments that belong to the detected tolerance violation.

The position-sensitive comparison also serves as the basis for other defect-detection methods as it finds the correct reference edges for the approximating line segments. The comparison procedure is presented in Figure 5.8.

The inspection of each line segment starts with the consultation of a hash table to find out whether the result is already available for either end of the line segment. In a positive case a pointer to a probable correct reference is obtained and used as the first candidate in testing the other end of the line segment.

In a negative case more computational effort is needed. The index table entries for the ends of the segment are determined and the intersection of the sets of pointers in the corresponding pointer buckets is determined. The reason for this is that both ends of a linear segment are assumed to represent the same model edge. If the computed index table addresses are equal, then we proceed with the pointers in the corresponding bucket.

The edge descriptions addressed by the obtained pointers are tested to find out whether the line segment is inside the tolerance zone of any one of them. If a match is found for an end point, its coordinates and the pointer to the reference data are stored in the hash table for possible later use.

If the test fails, the segment is divided into two new segments that are tested in a similar way. The division and test operations are repeated re-

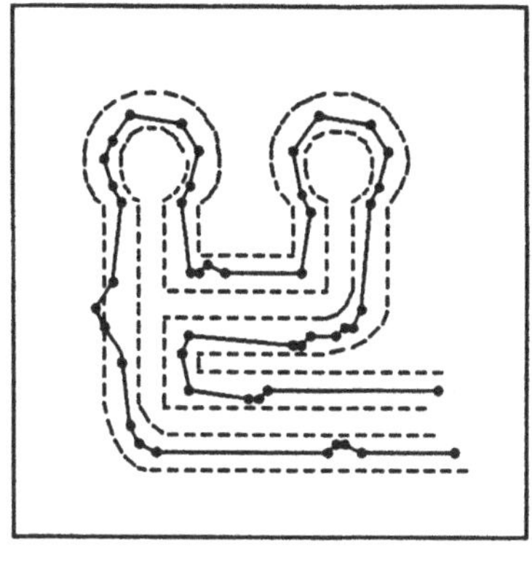

a

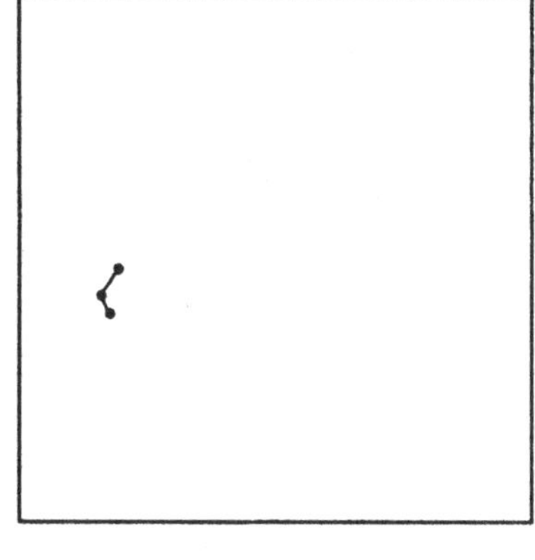

b

FIGURE 5.7. (a) Tolerance zones and aligned approximated patterns; (b) detected deviation.

```
    Hash_table[].key:     key in hash table
    Hash_table[].edge:    reference to the model edge in hash table
    Line = {C1,C2} = {(x1,y1),(x2,y2)}: line segment
    e, e.Tolerance:       reference edge and its tolerance
    Index():              function, computes the pointer
                          bucket address
    Bucket():             returns the pointers in the pointer bucket
    Distance():           distance from point to the reference edge
    Update():             updates the hash table and match list
                          of the reference edge

procedure Compare(Line)
do;
    e = NIL;
    /* check if the reference edge is already known
       for either end of the line segment        */
    if Hash_table[hash_address(C1)].key = C1
    do;
        C = C2; e = Hash_table[hash_address(C1)].edge;
    end;
    if Hash_table[hash_address(C2)].key = C2
    do;
        C = C1; e = Hash_table[hash_address(C2)].edge;
    end;
    /* check if the reference matches also the other end */
    if e ≠ NIL AND Distance(C,e) < e.Tolerance
    do;
        Update(C,e); return(TRUE);
    end;
    /* the reference edge is identified from among the candidates
       obtained from the pointer buckets */
    {e0,...,en} = Bucket(Index(C1)) ∩ Bucket(Index(C2));
    for e = ei, i = 0...n;
    do;
        if (d1 = Distance(C1,e)) < e.Tolerance then Update(C1,e);
        if (d2 = Distance(C2,e)) < e.Tolerance then Update(C2,e);
        if d1 < e.Tolerance AND d2 < e.Tolerance then return(TRUE);
    end;
    /* if no match, split the line segment and try again unless
       the line segment is too short to be splitted */
    if Length(Line) = 1 return(NIL);
    Line1 = {C1,C12} = {(x1,y1),((x1+x2)/2,(y1+y2)/2)};
    Line2 = {C12,C2};

    return(Compare(Line1) AND Compare(Line2));
end;
```

FIGURE 5.8. Position-sensitive comparison algorithm.

cursively until the line segments are one pixel long or every piece matches a single model. This division scheme ensures that linear segments with two or more models are handled correctly. An example is shown in Figure 5.9 where the edges of a pad and a conductor are collinear and are approximated by a single line segment. The division scheme verifies that

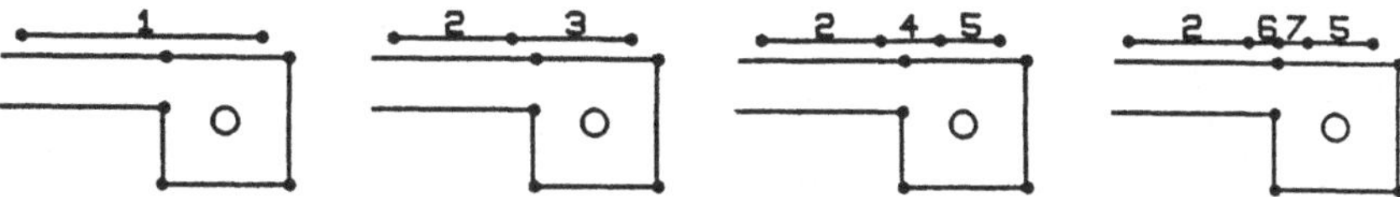

FIGURE 5.9. Connectivity test by splitting the approximating line segment.

connectivity exists in the design data by testing the parts of the line segment in the order shown. The tolerance zones are not shown for clarity.

For each match the distance of the tested point to the model is stored for possible additional inspection procedures. The line segment proceeds to the error analyzer if no match is found.

9 Defect Analysis

The ultimate purpose of defect analysis is to eliminate a human operator in classifying products into the acceptable or rejectable category. To accomplish this, the defect analyzer must reliably recognize the defect candidates. Both statistical and structural approaches can be used for this purpose. In our experiments a statistical analysis has performed well for simple, tightly controlled wiring patterns, while a structural analysis seems to work better with complex situations.

The first step of the analysis is similar for both statistical and structural methods: The detected suspicious line segments are sorted into continuous chains, called defect candidates. Each defect candidate is given pointers to possibly associated nearby edges found in the reference data.

In the statistical approach a set of numeric features are computed for each defect candidate and the feature vectors obtained are classified. This solution appears to be powerful, as most defect classes have simple descriptions, for instance, a short circuit is a defect that is connected to two different conductors.

The experiments with the statistical approach were initially based on six features of the defect candidate (closed/open chain of line segments, inside/outside of conductor, parallel/not parallel with the model edge, number of model edges connected to, maximum distance to the nearest model edge, and minimum distance to the next nearest model edge). The defect classes used were shorted, open, too wide and too narrow conductors, spurious copper, and holes. The classification accuracy for test material consisting of over 250 simulated defects on an artwork was over 85%. Unfortunately, the performance is not so good for the printed wiring boards of the test material, but additional features are needed to recognize certain special contexts. For example, the types of edges and their angles are needed as features to avoid false alarms from some additional copper at sharp turns of conductors. Approximately twenty features are needed to achieve 80% classification accuracy.

Structural analysis was found to be more flexible in handling many contexts [Silven et al. 1986]. Initially, the structural relations between the defect candidate and the reference edge descriptions and certain attributes are determined. Most of these descriptions are used with the statistical analysis, too. The major difference is that the relations among the associated reference edges themselves are also determined and used to form an attributed relational graph.

A defect candidate is recognized by finding the best match for it from among the defect models. Matching is performed by means of a depth-first search approach similar to the one described in Eshera and Fu [1984]. The state space searching starts with two sets of primitives, one for the defect candidate and the other for the model. The primitives are generated by decomposing the attributed relational graphs into simple "trees" that consist of a root node, the links emanating from it, and the nodes that terminate the links. Empty (NIL) primitives are added to the smaller set if the initial sizes are not equal. The graph of the simple case in Figure 5.7 is shown in Figure 5.10 (a) and its graph primitives in Figure 5.10 (b). The defect candidate graphs generally consist of less than ten nodes.

To achieve high speed the matching process starts by first matching nodes labeled "alarm" that exist in every defect candidate graph. This ordered matching scheme reduces the search trees significantly. When the search is terminated the matches are described by paths from the initial to the final states. Each state carries a weight that depends on the similarity between the associated primitives. The total weight of a path is normalized by the number of nodes in the model.

The defect candidate graph is compared with each model, one at a time, and is classified in the class for which the minimum normalized weight is obtained. The result is considered unreliable if the minimum weight is larger than a threshold value. In such a case the operator can either modify the threshold or give a new class name to the defect candidate and add it to the defect data base as a model.

Several instances of each defect may exist in the defect data base because separate models are needed for each context and both permissible and fatal variations of the same defect type. Due to speed constraints a practical implementation has first used the statistical method with six features to get a hint of the defect type for the structural analysis. The defect candidate is tested against every defect model only if the first match is not perfect. The structural analysis stage on a Symbolics 3645 workstation uses about one second for comparing a graph with five nodes to twenty models of the same size. The classifications agree with the human classifications for over 85% of the defects.

The shortcomings of the structural analysis are the experimentally determined quantizations of attributes such as angles and distances. These

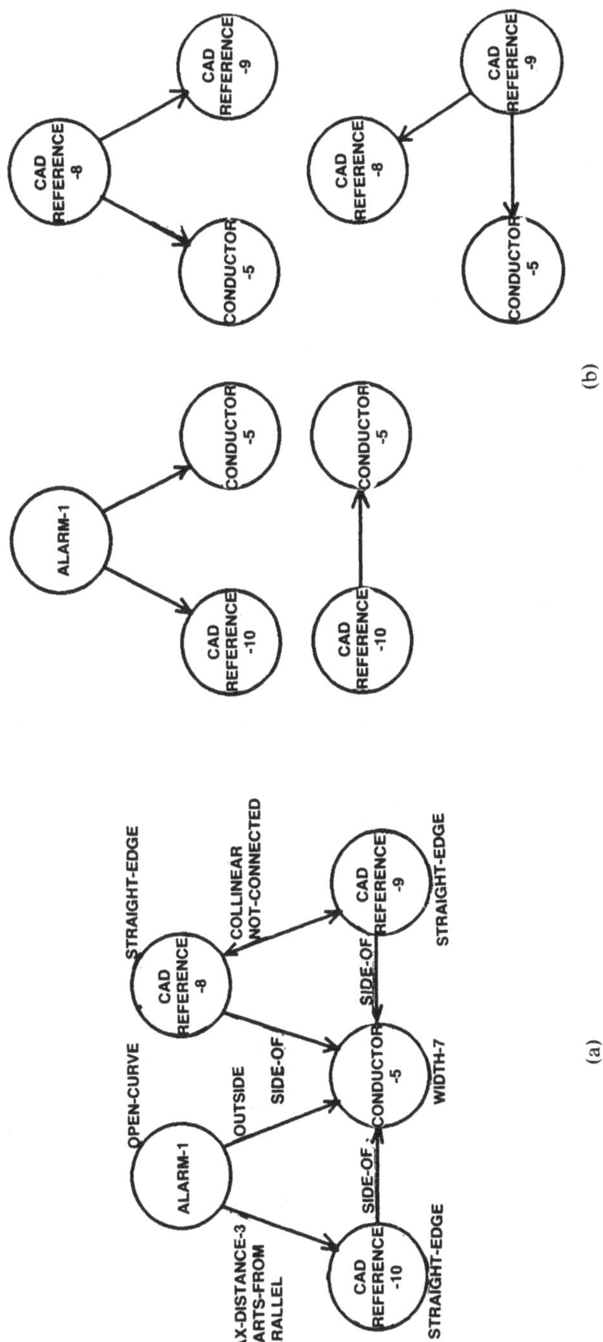

FIGURE 5.10. (a) Attributed relational graph of a protrusion; (b) primitives of the graph.

TABLE 5.1. Characteristics of test boards.

Board	Type	Size (cm)	Boards (N)	Minimum trace width (μ)	Minimum spacing (μ)	Defects (N)
A	Single-sided	14 × 25	7	75	120	47
B	4-layer	4 × 20	4	125	100	11

quantizations are likely to require modification if the inspection criteria change.

10 Test Material

The test material consists of several types of boards and masks rejected in visual or electrical inspection at printed wiring board factories. Most of the test boards have been designed for surface-mounted components.

The performance examples presented here were produced using the boards presented Table 5.1. The test material for board B consists of four $30 \times 30\ cm^2$ laminates, each carrying one layer repeated four times. Samples of the layouts are shown in Figures 5.11 (a) and (b) with defects flagged by the inspection system. The defects in Figure 5.11 (a) are a protrusion and spurious copper and the defect in Figure 5.11 (b) is an open conductor.

Most of the defects in the test boards are random intrusions and protrusions at conductor edges. There are also several short circuits caused by spurious copper and a few open conductors.

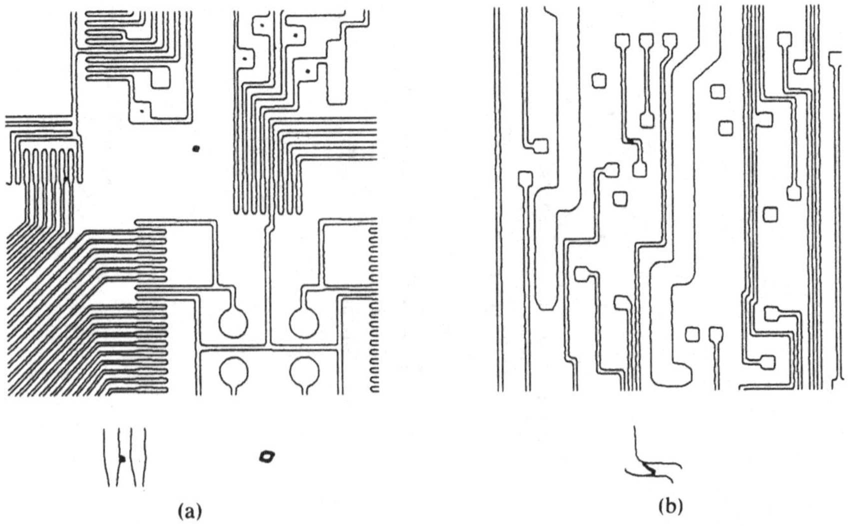

FIGURE 5.11. Examples of wiring and defects on test boards.

TABLE 5.2. The size of data files.

Board	Photoplotter file (kB)	Inspection reference (kB)
A	662	734
B	370	382

11 System Performance

The generation of the reference data from the photoplotter files takes approximately two hours on a VAX-11/730 for both of the test boards. This process is needed only once for each layout. Table 5.2 shows the sizes of the photoplotter files and corresponding reference data bases.

Table 5.3 shows the volume of line segment descriptions of pattern edges generated at the data-conversion stage. It should be noted that each line segment consumes eight bytes. The average segment length is longer for board B because of its more regular patterns and strictly obeyed 45° orientation division.

The performance of defect detection and analysis steps for the test material is shown in Table 5.4. The results in the defect columns of board A are averages obtained by inspecting each board twice. The false alarm rate is clearly not adequate for an industrial tool but can be considered satisfactory for an experimental system. Almost all of the false alarms are caused by dust particles that are difficult to eliminate in our laboratory. The false alarms are most often classified as spurious copper.

Very good performance is achieved in the inspection of backlighted printed wiring board mask films because of the simple lighting scheme and strict inspection criteria.

The throughput of the experimental system for boards A and B are approximately 0.25 and 0.8 Mpixels/second, respectively. This is only a fraction of the speed of image acquisition. The bottleneck is the general-

TABLE 5.3. The performance of the data conversion step.

Board	Line segments (N)	Average length of segments (pixels)	Maximum % of edge pixels for 2,000 × 2,000 area
A	490,000	10	5%
B	185,000	18	1.3%

TABLE 5.4. Defect detection and analysis performance.

Board	Tolerance	Defect candidates	Defects after analysis structural (statistical)	False alarms after analysis
A	2 pixels or 20%	87	53 (58)	6 (11)
B	3 pixels or 20%	28	14 (14)	3 (3)

purpose minicomputer (VAX-11/730) used to implement a number of stages of the inspection process. The most critical parts, namely, data conversion and alignment determination, execute in real time.

The experimental inspection system can obviously be enhanced to a real-time prototype. The most straightforward solution is to implement the minicomputer resident processing with multiple-powerful off-the-shelf microcomputers.

12 Summary and Conclusions

A printing wiring board inspection system is a mixture of mechanics, optics, illumination, sensors, architectures, and algorithms. The delicate balance of the solutions in these areas determine the speed, throughput, cost, and reliability of the system.

The basic objective of the experimental printed wiring board inspection system described is to provide good opportunities for defect analysis instead of concentrating only on defect detection. The solution supports both defect detection and defect analysis with a relatively high-level model derived from the design data. The approach has been tested with material that cannot be inspected by conventional-design rule-based methods.

The implementation of the experimental system is based on a fairly small amount of special hardware and a minicomputer. The dedicated hardware unit contains the early stages of the inspection process that are most critical for real-time operation. It should also be possible to achieve the speed of image acquisition for the remaining processing steps by adding programmable off-the-shelf components.

The performance obtained so far is not adequate for industrial use. However, most of the problems originate from the image-acquisition stage. Relatively small improvements in this respect could result in a significantly higher reliability.

Acknowledgments. We would like to thank Mr. Martti Elsilä and Dr. Hannu Hakalahti from the Technical Research Centre of Finland for their contributions. This work was supported by the Technology Development Center of Finland.

References

Automatic reticle/mask inspection system for VLSI. 1983. *Solid State Tech.* **26,** 1, 45–46.

Cederberg, R.L.T. Chain-link coding and segmentation for raster scan devices. *Computer Graphics and Image Processing*. Academic Press, New York, **10,** 3, 224–234.

Chin, R., Harlow, C., and Dwyer, S. 1978. Automatic visual inspection of printed circuit boards. In *Image Understanding Systems & Industrial Applications,* (R. Nevatia, Ed.) *Proc. SPIE* **155,** San Diego, Calif., 199–213.

Danielsson, P.-E. 1982. Encoding of binary images by raster-chain-coding of cracks. In *Proc. 6th Int. Conference on Pattern Recognition* (Munich, West Germany), IEEE Computer Society Press, Washington, D.C., 335–338.

DIT-MCO Corp. 1984. *P-SEE, general description,* DIT-MCO International Corporation, Kansas City, Mo.

Eshera, M.A., and Fu, K.S. 1984. A graph distance measure for image analysis. *IEEE Trans. on Systems, Man and Cybernetics*. **SMC-14,** 3, 398–408.

Hara, Y., Akiyama, N., and Karasaki, K. 1980. Automatic visual inspection of LSI photomasks. In *Proc. 5th In. Conference on Pattern Recognition*. Miami Beach, Fla., IEEE Computer Society Press, Washington, D.C., 273–279.

Kahl, D.J., Rosenfeld, A., and Danker, A. 1980. Some experiments in point pattern matching. *IEEE Trans. Systems, Man and Cybernetics*. **10,** 2, 105–116.

Lloyd-Doyle Ltd. 1984. *Trackscan,* Lloyd-Doyle Ltd., Walton-on-Thames, Great Britain.

Mandeville, J.R. 1985. Novel method for analysis of printed circuit images. *IBM J. Res. Dev.* **29,** 1, 73–86.

Okamoto, K., Nakahata, K. Aiuchi, S., Nomoto, M., Hara, Y., and Hamada, T. 1984. An automatic visual inspection system for LSI photomasks. In *Proc. 7th Int. Conference on Pattern Recognition* (Montreal, Canada), IEEE Computer Society Press, Washington, D.C., 1361–1364.

Piironen, T. 1987. Lighting device. U.S. Patent 4,651,262.

Sanz, J.L.C., and Jain, A.K. 1986. Machine-vision techniques for inspection of printed wiring boards and thick-film circuits. *J. Opt. Soc. Amer.* **A, 3,** 9 (Sept.), 1465–1482.

Silven, O., Hakalahti, H., 1985. A method for aligning printed circuit boards with design data. In *Proc. 4th Scandinavian Conference on Image Analysis*. (Trondheim, Tapir.) **1,** 273–280.

Silven, O., Pietikainen, M., Piironen, T., and Elsila, M. 1984a. Performance evaluation of algorithms for visual inspection of printed circuit boards. *Proc. 7th Int. Conference on Pattern Recognition,* vol. 2 (Montreal, Canada), IEEE Computer Society Press, Washington, D.C., 1355–1357.

Silven, O., Virtanen, I., and Pietikainen, M. 1984b. CAD data-based comparison method for printed wiring board (PWB) inspection. *Intelligent robots and computer vision*. (D.P. Casasent, Ed.), *Proc. SPIE* **521,** Cambridge, Mass., 400–405.

Silven, O., Virtanen, I., and Piironen, T. 1985. Experimental system for the inspection of printed wiring boards. *Intelligent robots and computer vision*. (D.P. Casasent, Ed.), *Proc. SPIE* **579,** 554–559.

Silven, O., Westman, T., Huotari, S., and Hakalahti, H. 1986. A defect analysis method for visual inspection. In *Proc. 8th In. Conference on Pattern Recognition,* vol. 2 (Paris), IEEE Computer, Society Press, Washington, D.C., 868–870.

Sterling, W. 1981. Nonreference optical inspection of complex and repetitive patterns. In *Techniques and Applications of Image Understanding,* (J.J. Pearson, Ed.) *Proc. SPIE 281,* Washington, D.C., 182–190.

Thibadeau, R., Friedman, M., and Seto, J. 1982. Automatic inspection for printed wiring. *IPC-TP-428,* IPC, Evanston, Ill.

Tsujiyama, B., Saito, K., and Kurihara, K. 1980. A highly reliable mask inspection system. *IEEE Trans. Electron Devices*. **ED-27,** 7, 1284–1290.

West, M.A., DeFoster, S.M., Baldwin, E.C., and Ziegler, R.A. 1983. Computer-controlled optical testing of high density printed-circuit boards. *IBM J. Res. Dev*. **27,** 1, 50–58.

6
Extracting Masks from Optical Images of VLSI Circuits

HONG JEONG AND BRUCE R. MUSICUS

ABSTRACT: This paper explores line labeling algorithms for extracting the mask layers from a clean line drawing representing the optical image of a VLSI chip. We start by developing a suitable world model for VLSI images, treating a chip as a multilayer sandwich of translucent layers, each of which is composed of planar and rectilinear strips. The arrangement of these strips is interpreted according to a hierarchical description of the chip in which strips combine to form electrical elements, which in turn form gates, which in turn form even higher-level building blocks. We model the optical image of the VLSI chip as a simple 2-D projection of these layers, in which all strip boundaries are preserved but all depth and layer identification is lost. We assume that this image is a perfect line drawing of the chip. Our vision problem is to reverse the image-formation process in order to reconstruct the original scene and extract the original masks. To recover this information, we show that features and design constraints on the layers translate into a natural labeling scheme for the lines, junctions, and regions defined by the line drawing. We present two different algorithms for extracting masks. The first uses a constraint propagation algorithm, exploiting the natural constraints on the junctions to reduce the set of possible interpretations of the lines. The second algorithm attaches a series of labels to the image, building up path fragments from lines, then linking them into paths, assigning paths to layers, labeling the layers, and assigning insides and outsides within each layer. The key issue is to use as much knowledge as possible about VLSI, together with hints from the operator, to reduce the ambiguity of the line drawing, and thereby reduce the number of sets of masks that could possibly form the image. Performance of the system is shown on a typical CMOS gate. We conclude by showing how our approach can be used to generalize previous line

---

This work has been supported in part by the Advanced Research Project Agency monitored by ONR under Contract N00014-81-K-0742, in part by the National Science Foundation under Grant ECS-8407285, in part by AFOSR Grant 86-0164, and in part by OKI Semiconductor Inc.

drawing interpretation methods for projected images of 3-D trihedral blocks worlds with both opaque and transparent surfaces.

1 Introduction

An interesting image-understanding application is using optical inspection of a VLSI chip to estimate the mask layers used to fabricate that chip. This problem is particularly intriguing because quite a bit is known in advance concerning the appearance and structure of such optical images. For example, polysilicon, diffusion, and metal layers are deposited in layers in a fixed order. These layers are thin, and are therefore partially translucent; often the edges of underlying layers can be seen beneath covering layers. Shadow lines cast by the light source reveal the three-dimensional warp of the layers, and this can also be used to infer the position of underlying hidden layers. Despite all this information, however, interpreting VLSI images is generally a difficult task that is inherently ill-posed [Poggio and Koch 1984; Poggio and Torre 1984; Poggio, Torre, and Koch 1985; Poggio, Voorhees, and Yuille 1985].

There are several types of images that might be desirable to analyze during the IC design/fabrication process. For example, we may wish to inspect a *chip image,* a grey-level digitized photograph of the chip taken through a microscope. In other cases, we may wish to inspect a *working mask image,* which is the black-and-white image defining an individual photomask. Yet other "images" of interest might include the pattern generator files (PG files) obtained from a CIF program, stick diagrams, and so forth [Mead and Conway 1980]. We collectively name all such representations *VLSI images*. Given a VLSI chip image, our goal is to extract the individual masks used to create the chip. Further goals might include extracting the circuit or locating defects in the chip; however, we will not discuss these problems in detail.

Our approach is first to segment the given image, extract a line drawing representing the edges of all the segments, and then to use knowledge about the layout process, such as the Mead-Conway rules [Mead and Conway 1980], to interpret the image. To avoid dealing with the extremely difficult problems associated with the segmentation and edge finding in the optical image, we will assume that a front end is available to extract a clean, perfect line drawing representing the segment boundaries of the chip. We will focus primarily on the lines in the projected image and their junctions, following the line-labeling tradition in line-drawing analysis. In addition, we will not exploit color, texture, and brightness cues in the image, though we will point out how such information could be incorporated.

Figure 6.1 shows a typical line drawing generated by a typical CAD system for a pair of CMOS inverters. (We have shown only the four major

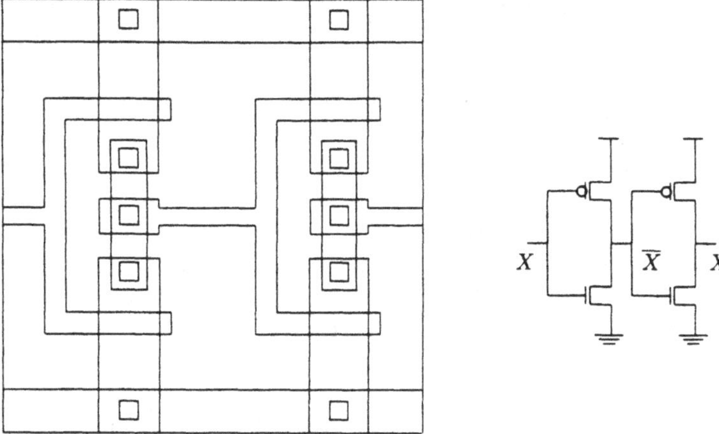

FIGURE 6.1. CMOS logic gates: Line drawing for inverter arrays and its circuit symbol.

layers superimposed.) Figure 6.1 also shows an equivalent circuit symbol. Our mask extractor, written using SKETCH (a Lisp-based operating system for image processing developed in Lincoln Lab), PEARL (package for efficient access to representations in Lisp, developed at University of California, Berkeley), and Franz LISP (a dialect of LISP developed at University of California, Berkeley) under UNIX (a registered trademark of AT&T Bell Laboratories), will convert a superimposed mask image such as Figure 6.1 into the set of individual masks comprising the image shown in Figure 6.2. It would be possible, for example, to feed the masks output by our system into a circuit extraction program, similar perhaps to McCormick's [1984] EXCL, which can extract quantitative information from the masks, in order to generate a circuit description of the chip.

This mask-extraction problem is highly related to other research in vision, particularly to the line-drawing analysis required by blocks world [Cohen and Feigenbaum 1982; Sugihara 1982; Winston 1984]. Such line-drawing analysis exploits physical and geometric laws about three-dimensional objects to interpret the 2-D projection of an image. (In fact, many algorithms combine these two approaches (hybrid methods).) Algorithms in these schemes can be classified into two dual approaches: line-oriented methods and plane-oriented methods. All those methods presume a perfect image for a set of cylinders, cones, spheres, tori, and simple polygonal objects. The line-oriented methods [Chakravarty 1979; Clowes 1971; Guzman 1969; Huffman 1971; Kanade 1978; Roberts 1965; Turner 1974; Waltz 1972] focus on junctions and their legal combinations. The plane-oriented methods, on the other hand, focus on the geometrical foundations of the object surfaces [Kanade 1979; Mackworth 1973; Sugihara 1981]. One interesting extension to line labeling is Kanade [1978]. He considers not only polyhedra but also objects made up of planar faces.

All these methods, however, assume that objects are opaque, contrary to the nature of objects contained in VLSI images. Naturally, they cannot properly explain certain types of lines or junctions that appear in VLSI scenes with overlapping translucent layers. In particular, all these methods cannot deal with edges on lower layers that are visible through translucent upper layers. The other source of difficulty arises when many object edges overlap accidentally so that they appear to be a single boundary segment to the viewers. Unfortunately, such "accidental occlusions" are very common in VLSI layouts and the simple hypothesis of a "general view point" that is adopted in most natural scenes must be discarded. To discriminate such accidental cases, we must know how and why such cases happen, in terms of the physical nature of VLSI circuit fabrication. A key point is that VLSI images are formed from a repertoire of constructs such as transistors and resistors, which are designed according to highly constrained rules. To cope with ambiguous situations or alternative interpretations of features, we exploit the available knowledge about the VLSI layout design process.

In this light, our first strategy is to introduce a new label set, which can be considered an extension of previously developed label sets, and which helps to solve this scene-interpretation problem. To label all the lines with this label set, this scheme propagates constraints between all line labels until they can simultaneously satisfy the natural constraints. We also introduce an alternative approach based upon paths, formed from sequences of line segments. To find masks, we partition the paths into separate mask layers and examine whether or not the particular partition gives a proper mask. Finding all such partitions amounts to searching a decision tree.

We first describe a suitable world model for VLSI images in Section 2. In Section 3, we introduce representation schemes for object features, together with natural constraints these features satisfy. In Section 4, we discuss how to label each junction and how to extract layers from the labeled junctions. Also, we show the overall strategy of the mask extractor. In Section 5, we present an alternative path-oriented method. Finally, Section 6 generalizes our constraint propagation method to more general scenes, which may include sheets, and polyhedral objects, each of whose surfaces may be opaque or transparent.

2 A Multilayer Translucent Scene Model

The problem of extracting the individual masks from a single optical image of a VLSI chip requires that we reconstruct a multilayer, three-dimensional model of the chip from its two-dimensional projection. "Understanding" the optical image implies that we can successfully reconstruct this three-dimensional scene from the observed input image. In order to accomplish this task, we will first need a framework in which we can express both our specific knowledge of the underlying structure of the chip, as well as our general knowledge about constraints imposed by the IC fabrication process. In particular, our first step is to develop syntactic and semantic conventions for representing the multilayer chip.

Two major issues must be confronted: representing objects and features, and defining the relationships between them in 3-D space. Our approach uses a somewhat idealized multilayer model, in which a finite number of well-defined building blocks are organized in hierarchical fashion to represent the chip at various levels of abstraction. Using these conventions, we capture the natural constraints that the "objects" forming the chip must satisfy. Along the way, we incorporate a variety of assumptions about the layout that are not strictly necessary, but that greatly simplify the mask-extraction process and the discussion. Later, in Section 3, we will show how our assumptions about the multilayer structure of VLSI chips can be used to derive constraints on the appearance of the projected 2-D optical image of the chip.

2.1 Representation Hierarchy

An actual VLSI chip is composed of a "sandwich" of multiple layers of material, each fashioned out of highly complex patterns. Typically, the chip is the end product of a top down, hierarchical design procedure, in which the chip is first partitioned into functional modules (CPU, DRAM, bus). Each module is then recursively partitioned into submodules (ALU, registers, flags), each of which in turn is further decomposed (multiplexor, adder), and further decomposed (gates), and so on until we finally reach the level of transistors and wires, which are themselves built from a certain juxtaposition of strips of material at varying layers within the chip. Given the final chip, the key to understanding its functionality is to represent the chip in terms of this hierarchy of "objects." At each level of the hierarchy we need to define the types of objects allowed (simple objects toward the bottom, complex objects at the top), together with their interrelationships.

Table 6.1 depicts some of the levels of objects that can be found in a VLSI image. At the topmost level would be architectural, register-transfer, or logic equation descriptions. At the bottom level are the mask layouts defining the final chip. Depending on the technology being used, various numbers of masks may be used. In this chapter, we assume there are only six layers: metal *(M)*, contact cuts *(C)*, polysilicon *(P)*, diffusion *(D)*, ion implantation *(I)*, and well *(W)*. Each mask is a collection of rectangular strips arranged in various patterns. Note, for example, the masks in Figure 6.2. Strips may or may not connect with each other, and they may or may

TABLE 6.1. Representation hierarchy of VLSI constructs.

Abstraction level	Building blocks	Rules	Coordinate
	More complex objects	Computer architecture, system theory	
Symbol	NAND, NOR	Logic	
	Transistor, resistor, capacitors, inductors	Network theory	
Scene domain	Strip, vertex, edge	IC design	Object-centered
Image domain	Region, junction, line	Natural constraints	Viewer-centered
Function	Pixels	Image formation	

not have bends, forks, or loops. We will call the physical corners of these strips *vertices,* and refer to their boundaries as *edges*. This we call our *object-centered* view of the chip, and it describes what we call the *scene domain.*

We will assume that the optical image is formed by effectively superimposing all these mask layers into a single projected image of the chip. Unfortunately, while we retain the outlines of all the strips, the projection process loses all depth and layer identification information, and removes all the hierarchical description that defines the function of the chip. All that remains is a complicated pattern of squarish patches, or blobs, with various colors and textures, separated by lines. Each patch corresponds to some portion of one or more layers of material. The lines correspond to an actual edge of one of the layers superimposed in one of the adjoining patches. Junctions between lines may correspond to a vertex of one of

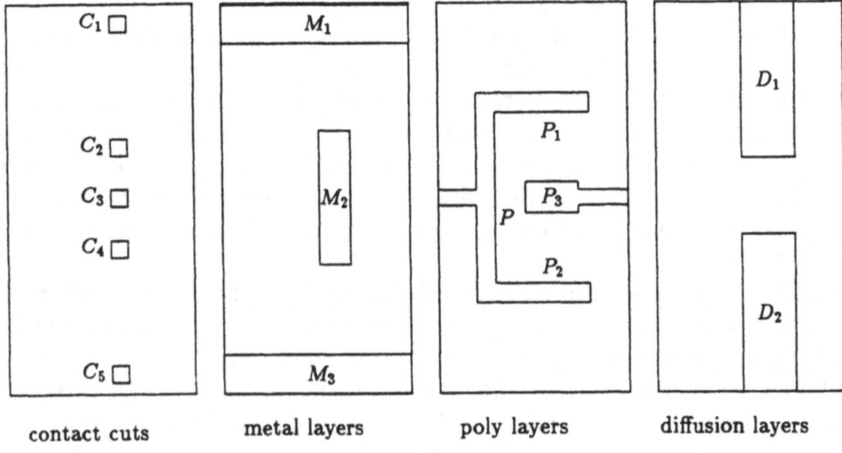

FIGURE 6.2. Four CMOS masks used for the first half in Figure 6.1(a). Each layer is labeled by its associated mask layer name: *C* for contact cuts, *M* for metal layer, *P* for poly layer, and *D* for diffusion layer.

the strips forming the chip, or they may be an artifact of the projection process and may be due solely to the crossing of strips at different layers. In this viewer-centered frame, or image domain, the available features, i.e., pixels, lines, junctions, and regions, obey relationships and satisfy constraints related to those in the object domain. In this section we will develop the object definitions and interrelationships that define the lower levels in the scene domain. In Section 3, we will reinterpret these definitions in terms of the projected image domain.

2.2 Wire Strip Properties

As we have mentioned before, the strips within each layer are the most important building blocks in a VLSI chip. The entire IC process concentrates on accurate registration of layers with precise dimensions. Also, VLSI design rules are in terms of the positioning of strips within the layers. More abstract descriptions of the chip structure are inevitably built on a hierarchical organization of these strips. In this regard, our immediate task must be the recognition of the layer configurations from features derived from the projected image.

In describing the layers in this chapter, we choose to ignore certain physical properties. For example, different layers in a chip often appear to have different colors and textures. However, such properties have been observed to be inconsistent, both between different chips and within the same chip. In this chapter, we focus on understanding images of VLSI chips solely from the arrangement of the lines bounding the segments in the image.

Definition 2.1 We will model a VLSI scene as a multilayer structure formed from a spatially ordered collection of semitransparent objects called wires or strips. Strips within each layer are planar, and their boundaries are assumed to be either horizontal or vertical. Some of the attributes the layers have are listed as follows:

(a) There are six types of strips: contact cuts *(C)*, metal *(M)*, poly *(P)*, diffusion *(D)*, ion implantation *(I)*, and well *(W)*.
(b) Geometric constraints restrict the size of the strip and the distance between adjacent strips.
(c) Strips contained in different layers must be deposited in some fixed order. Let the notation $A > B$ imply that a layer with label A lies directly above another layer of type B. Strips are deposited in the following order: $C > M > P > D > I > W$. Specific combinations of strips are deposited to form electrically active components: (1) electrical connection: $C > M > P$, $C > M > D$, $C > M > D > W$, $C > M > D > I > W$, $C > P > D$, $C > M > P > D$; (2) transistor gate formation: $P > D$, $P > D > I > W$.

The label associated with each layer is simply the material from which it is made. We assume only six possible materials: contact cut, metal, polysilicon, diffusion, ion implantation, and well. The substrate can be viewed as a rectangular background on which the various layer strips are laid, with the boundaries of these strips parallel to the edges of the substrate background. Transistors can be formed only when strips of different materials overlap in a certain fashion. For example, external power is supplied by metal segments; other wires such as diffusion or poly must be electrically connected to the metal power lines through contact cuts $C > M > P$ or $C > M > D$. Such formations form the drain and source of transistors. The other important transistor component is a gate where the electrical potential in a poly strip regulates the current flows in a diffusion strip. Such formations are achieved by crisscrossing poly and diffusion strips and appear as either $P > D$ or $P > D > I > W$, where $P > D$ is a gate for an n-channel transistor and $P > D > I > W$ is a gate of a p-channel transistor in a CMOS inverter.

This definition specifies the basic concept of layers, their geometrical attributes, and some of their relationships. Of course, this definition is somewhat simplified. We have assumed only six major types of layers and buried contacts have been ignored, and we have assumed only a 1-layer metal process. We assumed that layers are only bounded by horizontal or vertical edges, with no diagonal edges. We have omitted detailed descriptions of various geometrical specifications. (For example, contact cuts are almost always rectangular.) We have assumed CMOS technology. Clearly, it would be possible to augment our model to include more knowledge and better reflect the most modern layout packages. However, we will restrict ourselves to these simplified rules in order to focus on the fundamental issue of how to represent and use such knowledge to interpret VLSI images.

2.3 More Complex Objects

Not every layout that follows the rules in Definition 2.1 yields a functional chip. The definition reflects only the minimum requirements for constructing an actual IC chip. In order to represent a legitimate circuit, the arrangement of layers must satisfy restrictions imposed by circuit layout rules. That is, higher level objects (transistors, gates, etc.) formed from the strips must in turn satisfy certain constraints on their interrelationships. (See Table 6.1.)

To describe a particular scene more abstractly, we need some additional descriptive techniques that are sufficiently precise to accurately represent their electrical and functional characteristics. We will use notation similar to a semantic net [Barr and Feigenbaum 1981; Winston 1984]. The syntax of a semantic net consists of objects and the relations among them. In the illustration, objects are denoted by ovals (called nodes) and relations are denoted by arrows and lines (called links). The semantics of this figure is described by the labels on the nodes and links. Note that because the objects are multilayered, the semantics must capture their relative positions in 3-D space. Numerous details concerning the object locations, sizes, and shapes are attached to the nodes and links. To simplify the discussion, however, we will only show and discuss certain of the higher-level characterizations.

Figure 6.3 shows the semantic net which describes the inverter in Figure 1(a). According to this figure, an inverter consists of two higher-level objects, a pull-up transistor *(pu)* and a pull-down transistor *(pd)*, with their diffusion layers connected by a metal bridge segment *(B)*. These objects are further decomposed into simpler objects (*M*, *P*, and *D*) and connected together as the net describes. (The labels, *M*, *P*, and *D*, refer to metal, poly, and diffusion, and should be clear from Figure 2. The objects labeled *G* and *VDD* are the ground and supply lines, and are special cases of label *M*. The other notation in the figure will be explained shortly.)

Higher-level objects are constructed from simple objects arranged in specific geometric patterns. In order to concisely describe this concept, we first introduce notation for representing various spatial relationships.

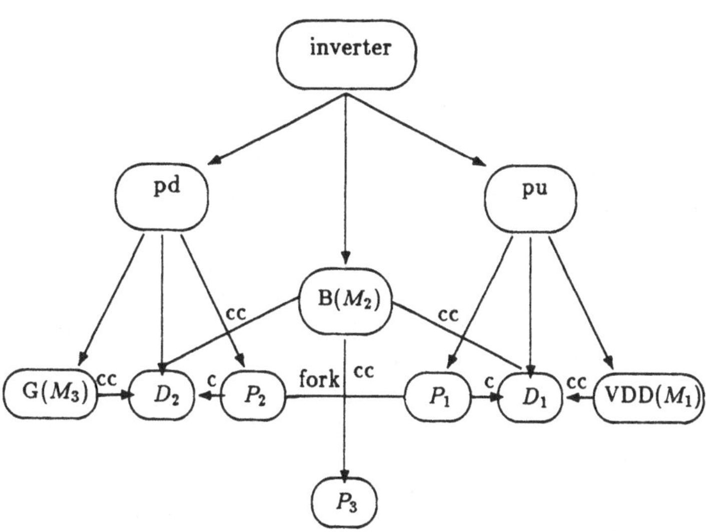

FIGURE 6.3. A semantic net for the inverter in Figure 6.2; the arrows mean "part of" or PART, "c" means CROSS, "fork" means FORK, and "cc" means CONTACT connection.

Definition 2.2 (Spatial Predicates). We define the following predicates, which describe spatial relationships between objects. Given two objects A and B, we define

- *PART(A, B)* means that object B is a part of object A; this is denoted by the symbol $A \rightarrow B$.
- *CROSS(A, B)* means that object A is crossing over object B; this is denoted by the symbol $A \overset{c}{\hookrightarrow} B$.
- *CONTACT(A, B)* means that two objects, A and B, are connected with a contact cut, so that A is over B. This is denoted by $A \overset{cc}{\hookrightarrow} B$.
- *FORK(A, B)* means that A and B connect together to make a single material of fork (or tree branch) shape. This is denoted by $A \overset{fork}{\hookrightarrow} B$.

Note that the order of elements in *PART, CROSS,* and *CONTACT* is important but not in *FORK*. The *PART* relationship indicates how a complex object is built out of simpler objects. The other operators indicate how simple objects connect together to form more complex objects. *CONTACT* is a basic operation primarily used for connecting two strips on a plane via a contact cut. Power is supplied through the contact cut from one object to another. The other important operation is *CROSS* which makes transistor gate *(tgate)*. *FORK* constructs an object with branches.

The meaning of the four operators is most easily understood from Figures 6.2 and 6.3. In this example, we assume a three-level hierarchy of objects: (1) inverter; (2) pull-up *(pu),* pull-down *(pd)* transistors, and bridge *(B)*; and (3) *C, M, P,* and *D*. The inverter consists of a pull-up *(pu)* transistor, a pull-down *(pd)* transistor, a metal bridge connecting the two transistors, and a poly strip connected to the bridge. The *pu* in turn consists of a power supply *VDD* made of *M*, a diffusion layer, and a poly layer. The *pd* is analogous to *pu* except for the ground line *G* made of *M*. The diffusion strips are connected via a metal strip. That is, we have the relationships $CONTACT(M_2, D_1)$ and $CONTACT(M_2, D_2)$. Our illustration shows that $CONTACT(M_1, D_1)$, $CROSS(P_1, D_1)$, $CONTACT(M_3, D_2)$, and $CROSS(P_2, D_2)$ also hold. Finally, we have $FORK(P_1, P_2)$.

In the preceding discussion, we have rather loosely defined these spatial predicates through our example. Nevertheless, properties of these predicates, such as transitivity, are easily derived from these definitions. Dimanzo et al. [1986] deal with such spatial reasoning about scene description in detail. The nodes or arcs in a semantic network can be viewed as alternative notations for the equivalent of predicate calculus predicates.

As the previous example shows, we can define more complex objects and relationships by using the *PART* operation. We will define medium-level objects that must be built from lower objects such as layers *C, M, P,* and *D* and that are building blocks for a variety of higher-level objects such as *AND, OR,* and *NOT* gates. Typical medium-level objects would be *transistor gates (tgates), bridges,* and *ports*. The relationships specify how to combine such blocks to build logic gates.

Remark 2.1 (Transistor Parts). CMOS logic gates are high-level objects composed of medium-level objects arranged in specific patterns, where each medium-level object implements a specific electrical function and is built from an appropriate combination of strips from various layers. Typical medium-level objects include:

- *(tgate)* := *CROSS(P, D)*,
- *(supply)* := *CONTACT(M, D)*,
- *(bridge)* := *CONTACT*(M, D_1) and *CONTACT*(M, D_2),
- *(input port)* := *FORK*(P_1, P_2), and
- *(output port)* := *CONTACT(M, P)*,

where $A := B$ denotes that an object of type A consists of lower level strips arranged as described on the right-hand side. Note that M, P, and D are terminal symbols and *tgate*, *bridge*, and *port* are nonterminal symbols.

A transistor, or *tgate*, is formed whenever a poly strip crosses over a diffusion strip. Voltage for the source and drain of a FET is typically supplied through metal layers connected to the diffusion layer through a contact cut; we call this arrangement a *supply*. A CMOS inverter is formed from two complementary transistors connected through a metal *bridge* through contact cuts. The *input port* and *output port* are the interfaces to the outside world carrying the input and output signals, respectively. For example, the CMOS inverter in Figure 6.3 is built out of the low-level objects M_1, M_2, M_3, P_1, P_2, P_3, D_1, and D_2 arranged into the following medium-level constructs:

$$
\begin{aligned}
(gate1) &:= CONTACT\ (P_1, D_1),\\
(gate2) &:= CROSS\ (P_2, D_2),\\
(supply1) &:= CONTACT\ (M_1, D_1),\\
(supply2) &:= CONTACT\ (M_2, D_2),\\
(bridge) &:= CONTACT\ (D_1, M_3) \text{ and } CONTACT\ (M_3, D_2),\\
(outputport) &:= CONTACT\ (M_2, P_3), \text{ and}\\
(inputport) &:= FORK\ (P_1, P_2).
\end{aligned}
$$

This arrangement of objects in our specific example is a direct consequence of the rules used in typical CMOS design to build inverters. At this level in the hierarchical description of the chip, the rules used to combine objects deal directly with strips in layers. For higher-level objects built from the medium-level objects, yet other rules apply. (See Table 6.1.) We can conceptually hypothesize higher and higher levels of increasingly abstract objects (e.g., multiplexer, ALU, etc.) and conventions for constructing such objects from existing lower-level objects (e.g., NAND, NOR, REGISTERS). Such further abstraction must be used to incorporate more sophisticated circuit reasoning into the image-recognition scheme. In fact, the most abstract description might be a logic equation such as $Y = \overline{AB + C}$, which removes all the details of the image except the logical function of the circuit contained in the scene.

3 Natural Constraints

In Section 2 we considered the objects from which VLSI chips are formed, and their interrelationships in their multilayer space. Unfortunately, the optical image from which we must extract the original masks is only a 2-D projection of the multilayer chip, and we have lost much of the important information about the identity of the layers and the position, size, and shape of objects within layers. A line in this projected image is always caused by an edge of a strip, but a junction in the image may correspond to a strip vertex, or may simply be a projection artifact of overlapping objects. Knowledge of VLSI constraints is critical to properly interpret the lines and junctions in this projected image. Thus we must carefully reinterpret our design constraints from the scene domain in terms of constraints in the projected image domain. In Section 4, we will present these constraints in a form suitable for a constraint-based line-labeling algorithm. In Section 5, we will reinterpret these constraints in terms of a different path-oriented labeling scheme.

3.1 Image Properties

The images we are concerned with are formed by the orthographic projection of a scene onto the (x,y) plane, such that the view point is on the z-axis. Thus, the image gives us direct information about the (x,y) position of edges of objects in the scene, but all direct information about the z-coordinate (or depth) of objects is lost. Because the layers are very thin, the strips are partially translucent. Furthermore, the finite thickness of the strips warps the surface of the chip; overlapping strips in higher layers must ride over the underlying strips, and this causes shadow lines to appear on the borders of overlap areas. The assumptions we have made about the sizes, shapes, and positions of strips in the layers imply that the projected image of the chip appears similar to a Mondrian painting [Horn 1974]. It is composed of rectangular patches of different colors and textures separated by vertical and horizontal lines. Some of these lines mark boundaries of visible layers; others are only shadow lines or partially visible edges of objects seen through overlying translucent layers. We will assume that all edges can be seen in our chip images, and can be cleanly extracted into a line drawing that perfectly represents the chip. (In actuality, this edge-finding task is quite complicated and prone to error. We will not try to solve this image-processing problem in this chapter, however.)

The main problem in interpreting the line drawing is to determine which lines are associated with the same object boundary [Winston 1984]. Once this problem is solved, we can allocate the different objects to the different layers. We will find that restrictions on the layer strips imply that lines in the projected image can come together at junctions in only a few ways. Further restrictions limit which types of junctions may be connected to a given line. Combining all these constraints severely restricts the set of possible interpretations for the lines in the projection; with sufficient information, only one possible labeling will satisfy all the constraints.

An alternative approach that is equally feasible would focus on the regions, or *blobs,* bounded by the lines. Restrictions on the way the layered strips may be laid out map into restrictions on how blobs may abut in the projected image. By combining the constraints imposed by the geometrical arrangement of the neighboring blobs, we can greatly reduce the set of possible interpretations of each blob. Though our approach in this chapter will be junction-based, it should be clear that our basic approach could be applied equally well to build a blob-based method. In general, however, blob-based methods seem harder to implement than junction-based methods.

3.2 Line Features

The image can be modeled as the 2-D projection of all the layers in the chip. Two different types of lines will result. A *boundary line* is one that marks the edge of a strip layer lying on top of the stack of strips. An *interior line* corresponds to a strip edge covered by one or more translucent strips. All these lines are bounded by the *frame boundary,* a rectangle that bounds the field of view. We assume that no boundary or interior edges coincide with the frame boundary.

The Huffman-Clowes-Waltz-Kanade label sets were designed for opaque objects, and therefore do not correctly explain the interior lines that are so important for analyzing VLSI scenes. Mackworth's [1973] gradient approach also missed the depth information. Draper [1981] improved the gradient method by including depth information, but his formulation is intended for projected images of three-dimensional opaque objects. In our multilayer VLSI scenes, every CROSS and CONTACT operation between two objects generates both boundary and interior lines. Clearly labeling interior edges properly, and thereby recovering the depth and layer information, is crucial to interpreting such structures.

We will associate each line with a label *C, M, P, D,* or *F,* indicating whether the adjoining higher-level object, which caused the line, is a contact cut, metal, poly, diffusion, or the frame boundary. In the case of interior lines, this label will reflect the identity of the upper object causing the edge, not the object that covers the edge. Frame boundaries may be labeled *F.* In addition to a label, we need to know which side of the line corresponds to the object at the higher level. To indicate this, we will associate an arrow with each line, so that the object at the higher level is to the right of the arrow.

A feature that greatly complicates the line-labeling mask-extraction processes is the presence of *accidental,* or *double* edges, where edges from two or more different strips exactly align in the (x,y) dimensions, and are thus superimposed in the projected image. Distinguishing such edges from ordinary edges is particularly difficult. There are two types of accidental edges. *Filed* accidentals occur when two strips overlap with their edges aligned, so that the material of both strips is on the same side of the edge. We will attach two labels to such edges, together with an arrow such that both strip materials are to the right of the arrow. *Butted* accidentals occur when two strips abut, with their edges aligned, so that the strip materials are on opposite sides of the edge. We will attach arrows in both directions to this line, and place a label on each side to indicate the strip material. To simplify the line-labeling algorithm, we will assume that no more than two strip edges coincide on any line. We will also assume that strip edges never coincide with the frame boundary. We summarize this as follows.

Definition 3.1 (Edge Representation). In the following notation, a label a or b stands for the mnemonics C, M, P, and so on:

- An ordinary, single, edge is denoted by the arrow, $\xleftarrow{l}$, labeled by a direction and a symbol l. It implies that the region to the right of the arrow has label l.
- A filed accidental is denoted by the arrow, $\xleftarrow{(a,b)}$, where both strips are to the right of the arrow with a above b.
- A butted accidental is denoted by the arrow $\rightarrow {}^{a}_{b} \leftarrow$; this symbol denotes that strip a abuts strip b at this edge.

Once all lines have been labeled correctly, we will be able to peel off the layers in order by simply walking around each object, following the direction of the arrows on the lines labeled with that object's layer in a clockwise direction. If this path runs into the frame boundary, we continue around the frame in a clockwise direction until we reach another edge with this layer's label, then continue on this line.

Other strategies for labeling lines could also be used. For example, we could label each directed line with the names of the layers of the objects on both sides of the line. This method, however, generates many more possible line labelings and complicates the search for a consistent labeling of the entire image.

3.3 Junction Features

Junctions between lines in the projected image reflect the shape and overlapping arrangement of the objects in the multilayer chip. These junctions must be associated with the 3-D scene features. Restrictions on the possible arrangements of the layered objects imply that only certain types of junctions can occur in the projected image. In particular, the lines leading into each junction must be horizontal or vertical. Thus junctions may be formed of either 2, 3, or at most 4 lines.

One circumstance that may cause a junction in the projected image is the convex or concave corner of an object, which may or may not be covered by another object. We call this an L-type junction; it is composed of 2 lines. A junction is also formed at the frame boundary where a strip edge is cut off by the frame. We call this an external T–type junction; it is composed of 3 lines. A junction is also formed where two objects at different layers cross, so that the projection of their edges creates an X-type junction, composed of 4 lines.

More junction types are possible when accidental edges occur. Overlapping strip corners may superimpose in the projection, giving an L-type junction where both legs are actually double edges. An accidental edge may be cut off by the frame boundary, so that the leg of the external T-type junction is a double edge. Crossing strip edges at an X-type junction may be single or double. In addition, new types of junctions may occur. An ordinary T-type junction occurs where one strip corner is superimposed on an edge of another strip. One of the three legs of this T is a double edge; the other two are single edges. Yet other junction types are possible: X-types formed by 2 to 4 superimposed strip corners, and T-types formed by 2 corners superimposed on a third strip edge. We will assume, however, that these occurrences are unlikely and we will not consider them legal labelings. (It would be straightforward to extend our method to include these junctions, but the algorithms would run much longer and would generate many more bizarre labelings of the scene.)

Within each category of junction, there are further restrictions on the directions of the lines forming the junctions, and whether the lines can be boundary or interior. Combining all the restrictions imposed by Definitions 2.1 and 3.1, we obtain the following result.

Theorem 3.1 (Junctions). *Because of our world model, there is only a limited number of junctions that can occur in a projected image* (see Figure 6.4).

- *Ls are convex or concave corners of an object (either single or double).*
- *External Ts are intersections between the frame boundary and an object boundary. Thus, the straight line through the T is the frame boundary and the side branch is the object's occluding boundary. This side branch may be either single or double.*
- *Xs are crossing points where one type of object crosses over another, generating three boundary lines and one interior line. Each pair of crossing lines may be single or double.*

- *The possible (legal) labelings of the lines forming each junction must be chosen from a restricted set, some of which are indicated in Figure 6.4.*

Note that there are only $O(10^2)$ different junction configurations in all, which is substantially fewer than the number $O(10^4)$ one might have expected given that junctions could have 2, 3, or 4 lines, each a boundary or an interior line, each either single or accidental, each with 2 possible directions and 7 possible labels. In fact, it is almost always true that the count of possible combinations of lower-level features in an image is substantially greater than the actual number of combinations that are legal, given higher-level design constraints. It is this observation that allows us to drastically prune the space of possible interpretations of the projected

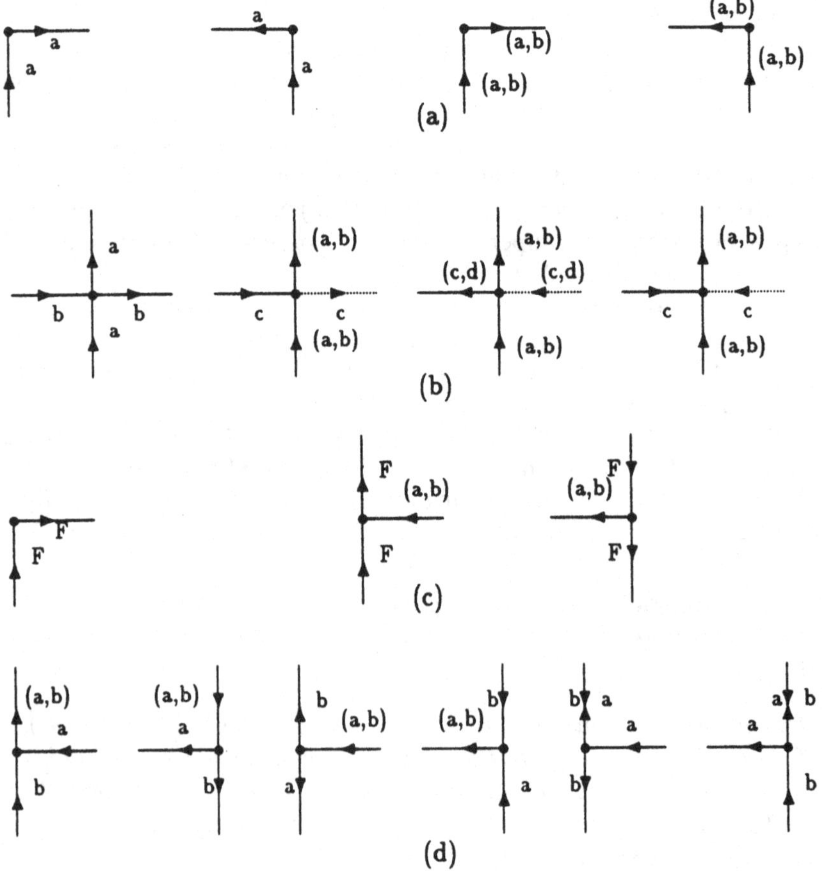

FIGURE 6.4. Representing edges: (a) *ell L*, (b) *cross X*, (c) *frame tee T*, (d) *interior tee T*. Here, $a \neq b, a, b \in \{C, M, P, D, I, W\}$ and $C > M > P > D > I > W$.

image. Note also that although adding 45° diagonal lines would be possible, it would greatly expand the number of possible lines and thus complicate the labeling process.

Note that the labeling of the lines at a junction clearly indicates the identity of at least one adjoining object at some layer in the chip, and it indicates the relative overlapping structure of the objects forming these edges. One difficulty in understanding the image is that even with all junctions properly labeled, the regions bounded by the lines are typically formed from multiple layers of objects superimposed. Labels on the 4 lines adjoining each region may identify one or more layers inside this region, but it is also possible that some or even all the layers in this region cannot be directly inferred from the bounding lines. An L-junction, for example, will identify the upper object whose concave or convex corner caused the junction. However, it will not directly identify the object or objects that are underneath or above. An X-junction can help label the two objects whose edges cross at this point, and specify which object passes underneath the other. However, it will not be able to help identify any objects underneath, between, or above the two objects that cross.

If all junctions and lines have been properly labeled and there are no accidently aligned object edges in the image, then every object in the chip will be bounded in the projected image by a clockwise path labeled with that object's identity. This allows us to peel the layers off the labeled image from top to bottom, by simply following these labeled contours in a clockwise direction.

Of course, the tricky part is to decide, for each junction in the projected image, which line labeling is correct. As we will discuss in Section 4, we use a constraint propagation technique to use the restrictions on possible labelings at each junction to narrow down the set of possible labelings for the entire image.

Figure 6.5 shows a labeled example where a horizontal polysilicon strip crosses over a diffusion strip, forming a transistor gate. The first figure in this illustration contains examples of all three types of junctions. Note that the figure contains no accidental edges. Therefore T-type junctions occur only around the frame boundary. X-type junctions occur whenever one strip crosses over another. An L-type junction marks a corner of a strip. Note that it can be either a convex or concave corner, although this example shows only a convex corner. When all junctions are properly identified, each line will be assigned a unique label.

A region in the projected image is bounded by at least four lines, each of which may have a different name. For example, the center blob in Figure 6.5 has four sides. The left and right sides are labeled with D since they are part of the long boundaries belonging to the diffusion strip. On the other hand, the upper and lower edges of this center blob are labeled P since they belong to the boundary of the polysilicon strip. By examining all the boundaries of this center blob, therefore, we can immediately con-

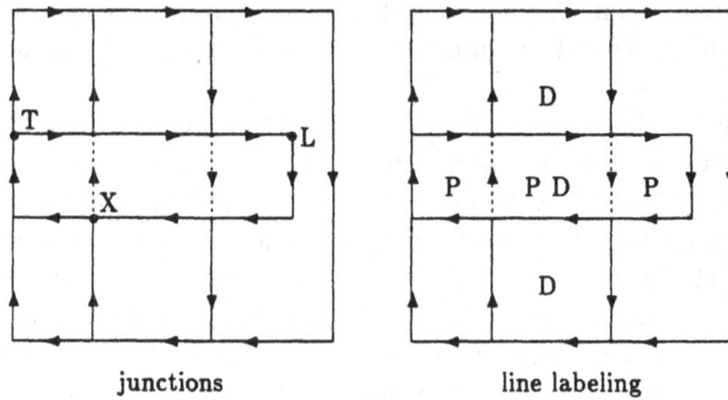

FIGURE 6.5. An example of line labeling: The vertical bar (diffusion) passes under the horizontal bar (poly). The left figure shows the three types of junctions. The right figure shows the result of the proper line labeling.

clude that this region contains a polysilicon layer over a diffusion layer. There may or may not be a metal layer above these, or an isolation well below—to resolve this issue we would have to propagate information from more distant areas of the image.

3.4 Paths

The goal of labeling the lines in the VLSI image is to extract the complete outline of each strip in the projected image. A strip contour must either form a closed loop, or if the strip extends outside the field of view, its contour must run from frame boundary to frame boundary. A strip contour cannot cross over itself, and it cannot cross over any other strip boundary from the same layer. In addition, there are certain minimum size and width constraints on the strip, which depend on the technology used and on the layer.

Because every line in the projected image must be part of one or two strip contours, there are very strong constraints on how the lines in the image can be labeled. A key concept is that of a *path,* which we define as a sequence of connected line segments that satisfies all the requirements to be the edge of a strip in some layer. A path is formed by a sequence of lines joined by various junctions. It may terminate at either end at external T-junctions on the frame boundary, or may simply form a closed loop. It may not cross itself. It may pass through any number of L-junctions. If it enters an X-junction, by assumption it must exit the junction on the opposite leg. It may run through internal T-junctions. Our assumptions about accidental edges imply that no more than 2 paths may run through the same line segment. Every line must belong to 1 or 2 paths. One or two paths may run through an L-junction. Two to four paths may cross at an X-junction (these cases are illustrated in Figure 6.6), and 1 or

FIGURE 6.6. An X-junction (on the left), when displaced, reveals three possible geometrical structures.

2 paths may terminate at a given external T-junction. Finally, exactly 2 paths may run through an internal T-junction. The three possible ways this could happen are shown in Figure 6.7.

One difficulty with extracting all the paths in the image is that it is difficult to trace a path when accidental edges occur. In particular, if we are trying to trace a path that enters an internal T-junction, it could exit on either of the other two legs of the junction. Deciding which direction it goes is a difficult task. A simpler goal is to focus on *path fragments*. These we define as sequences of connected lines that must all belong to the same strip edge, and that only run through L- and X-type junctions. A path fragment either forms a closed loop or runs from an internal or external T-junction to another T-junction. Path fragments must satisfy many of the same restrictions as paths; they never cross themselves, they exit X-junctions in the same direction as they entered, no two path fragments may share a single line, and so forth. As we will discuss in Section 5, path fragments are particularly easy to extract from a line drawing, and therefore form a good basis for an image-labeling algorithm.

The requirement that all lines must belong to 1 or at most 2 paths strongly constrains how we may label the lines in the image. One immediate natural constraint, as discussed in the previous section, is that only a limited number of L-, T-, and X-junction types are feasible. Another natural constraint is that paths that cross at an X-junction or merge at a T must be assigned labels from different layers. We call this a conflict rule. For example, for the right figure in Figure 6.6, the conflict rule guarantees that all four edges must be different. Also in Figure 6.7, the two paths forming an internal T-junction must have different labels.

Another consequence of the path structure is that lines that must be assigned to the same path must always be assigned the same label and direction. In particular, the labeling of junctions connected by a common

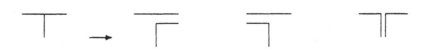

FIGURE 6.7. There are three possible geometrical structures related to a T (on the left). All involved objects are displaced to reveal their relative position.

FIGURE 6.8. Two junctions connected by a path. Dashed lines mean any kind of junctions.

line must be consistent with the labeling of that line. More generally, two junctions connected by a path fragment running through any number of intermediate L- and X-junctions must be consistent with the labeling of the lines on this fragment. This imposes strong restrictions on the labeling of the other lines at each junction, and thereby narrows down the search for a legal labeling of the image. We call these restrictions the coherence rule. For example, if we find two junctions joined by a path fragment as shown in Figure 6.8, then the labeling of the other lines at these junctions must be consistent with the labeling of this fragment. This is a generalization of the coherence rule, which is the basis of Waltz's [1972] concept of constraint propagation.

Finally, if several paths are labeled as belonging to the same layer, then there are additional constraints on the directions of the arrows forming each path. For example, with 2 paths in a layer, either one path surrounds the other, or else neither surrounds the other. Figure 6.9 illustrates the cases. If one path encloses the other, then the arrows must point in opposite directions, implying either that there is a ring of strip material (top second), or a ring-like hole in a strip (top third). If the paths do not enclose each other, then the arrows must be in the same direction, indicating that there are two small strips (top first), or two small holes in the strip (top last). All other cases are illegal. We call this the figure-on-ground rule.

An important point to keep in mind is that if there are no accidental edges in the image, then there are no internal T-junctions, and there is only one way to route paths through the line drawing so that every line

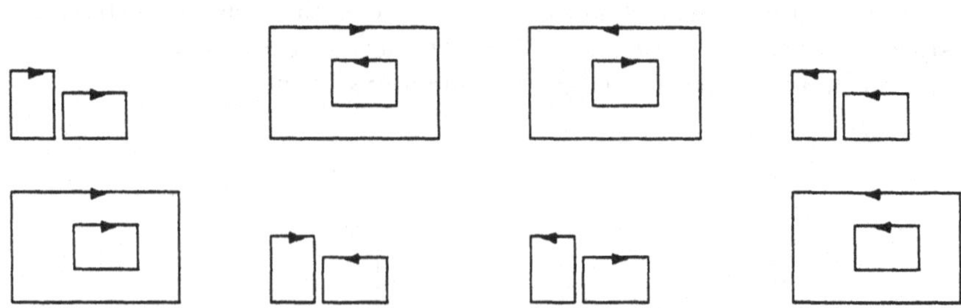

FIGURE 6.9. Among the eight configurations, only the four figures on top are possible.

segment belongs to exactly one path. On the other hand, if there are accidental edges, then there may be two possible routings of a path through an internal T-junction. As a result, there may be several ways to group the lines into paths, and therefore there may be several possible sets of strips that might have generated this image.

Another natural ambiguity we must recognize is that path-crossing information may help determine which paths must be in different layers, but it does not help to determine that a particular path must be the edge of a metal strip, for example. Without additional VLSI knowledge, we could transform any correct line labeling into another correct labeling by, for example, relabeling all *M*s as *P*s and all *P*s as *M*s.

Yet another problem is that, within each layer, the line drawing only supplies edge information for the strips. It is impossible to uniquely distinguish which portion of the image is inside the strip and which is outside without additional VLSI knowledge. This implies that a correct line labeling can be transformed into another correct line labeling simply by reversing the arrows of all the lines in any of the layers.

We do not describe in detail other rules and heuristics here, but they are now beginning to attract our serious attention. For example, certain easily recognized features, such as contact cuts or tgates, provide strong constraints on the interpretation of nearby strips. Further, there are numerous rules governing subtransistor-level and transistor-level building blocks of the VLSI circuits. For a competent mask extractor, all of this high-level knowledge must be represented and used.

4 Relaxation Scheme

Section 3 has shown that there are only a very limited number of legal junction labelings in the projected image compared to the number of possible labelings of lines entering a junction. To analyze the image, therefore, we can start by assigning the set of all possible labelings to each line in the projected image. Because these lines must intersect in junctions, however, the VLSI model imposes strong constraints on the labels that can be assigned to the lines. If we consider pairs of junctions connected by a line, we further constrain the possible interpretations of the pair of junctions and the line in between. If firm knowledge about the label of a particular line or region becomes available, perhaps through operator intervention, then this knowledge can be propagated to adjacent lines, junctions, and regions by using this knowledge to constrain the set of possible labelings on these adjoining features. In this way we can propagate the constraints imposed by junctions on possible line labelings and greatly reduce the number of possible labelings. This section introduces methods for applying such constraints together with other knowledge of the VLSI layout process in order to properly interpret a VLSI image.

4.1 An Inverse Problem

Extracting the masks from the projected 2-D image and reconstructing the original multilayer VLSI chip essentially requires solving an ill-posed inverse problem. Substantial a priori knowledge about layout is necessary to recover a unique set of chip layers. Two kinds of knowledge are relevant:

- Constraints on the features forming the image: lines, regions, and junctions derived directly from the multilayer model.
- Higher-level knowledge concerning the electrical implications of spatial relationships between objects, constraints on the shape or size of an object, and so forth.

Accordingly, it is natural to partition the mask-extraction system into two separate stages: (1) Find a consistent labeling for each junction and each line, and (2) extract layers from the labeled image that obey VLSI rules. The key point for solving the first step is the coherence rule, which specifies natural constraints between the groups of image features.

Draper [1981] formulated a plane-oriented line-drawing interpretation algorithm in terms of solving a set of simultaneous linear equations. We can reformulate our problem in a similar way. We define an image I as a systematic collection of n building blocks. There are three possible approaches we could use for defining these building blocks: strips, junctions, or blobs. With any of these approaches, the ith building block is assigned a label $x_i \in A$, where A is the set of possible object attributes. In our case, if x is a line in the projected image, then its label must be assigned from the set of all possible combinations of layer names and directions. Let m be the size of the alphabet A. (In our specific case, $m = 7 * 2$.) We use the vector $\mathbf{x} = \{x_1, x_2, \ldots, x_n\}^T$ to represent the complete set of labels for all building blocks in the scene. We could view these labels as an unknown label vector whose value must be computed from the available constraints. If no a priori information about line labels is available, then before we begin examining the junctions there are $O(m^n)$ possible values for $\mathbf{x}$ by default.

It is important to observe that not all combinations or intersections of building blocks are legal. We can generalize the coherence rule mentioned in the last section as follows:

Theorem 4.1 (Coherence Principle). *In our world model, in order to assign a label to a building block, then it must be possible to assign labels to adjoining building blocks in such a way that this combination of blocks is legal within the model.*

This coherence rule provides the interaction between the variables, which restricts their values. Hopefully, there will exist only very few solutions that satisfy all the constraints.

Figure 6.10 shows an example where the building blocks are strips. The top left figure contains three strips (thus three variables) and two intersections (thus two equations). The figure shows three possible interpretations of these three strips. For simplicity, assume that we know only that each of the strips has a label chosen from the set $\{M,P,D\}$. Two strips that intersect must be from different layers of the chip, and therefore must have different labels. If we let the symbol "$\neq$" mean "not labeled the same as," and we represent the labels of these three strips by $(x_1x_2x_3)$, then we can represent this example with the following logic equations: $x_1 \neq x_3$ and $x_2 \neq x_3$. Such relationships between objects can be easily stored in a matrix whose rows and columns consist of objects numbers and whose entries are either 0 or 1, depending upon whether the associated objects overlap or not. There are only twelve possible assignments that satisfy these constraints: $(x_1x_2x_3) = \{(PPM), (PDM), (DPM), (DDM), (MMP), (DDP), (MDP), (DMP), (MMD), (PPD), (MPD), (PMD)\}$.

Note that additional information about labels of the blocks can be used to further constrain the set of solutions. In our three-strip example, for instance, if we learned that $x_1 = P$ and $x_2 = D$, then we could infer that $x_3 = M$. On the other hand, if we are initially told that $x_1 = M$ and $x_3 = M$, then this information is inconsistent and there is no solution for x_2. Note that although we have presented this example in terms of strips and intersections between strips, a similar development could also have been

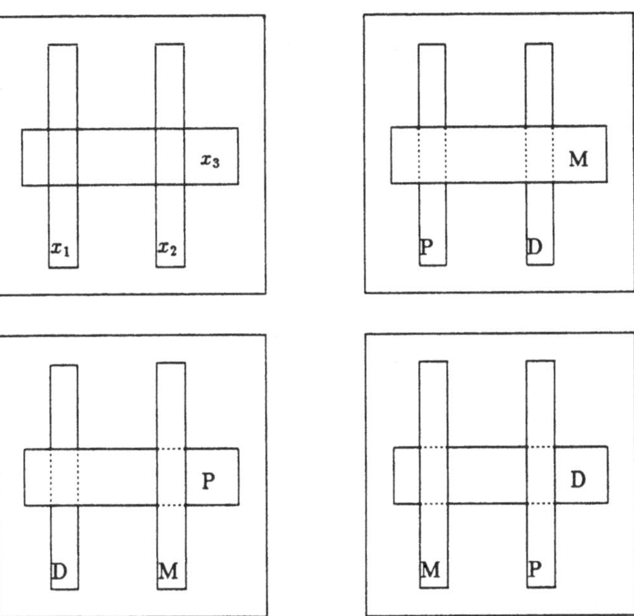

FIGURE 6.10. In the top left, three strips are overlapped. The other figures represent three different interpretations.

provided where the building blocks were lines or regions in the projected image.

4.2 A Mask Extractor

Figure 6.11 shows an overall block diagram of our mask extractor. Our present feature-finder package is programmed in the C language and the remaining portions are programmed in PEARL and Franz Lisp. The two systems are linked by a top-level program written in SKETCH. We have tested several typical CMOS images, including Figure 6.1, and the output of our package has been the desired masks, such as Figure 6.2.

We will describe the overall structure of this program step by step. Internally, the computation revolves around a series of data bases containing all the required information. A junction table lists all legal junctions. A coherence table lists all legal pairs of junctions. A specification table stores all the relevant information about the geometry and physical properties of objects.

The first step requires finding the edges in the chip image and segmenting it into rectilinear regions. In reality, of course, an actual chip image would be noisy and the lines extracted from the image would be highly imperfect. They would not satisfy the rules we have assumed. We would expect that a high-level mask-extraction method, such as the one described in this chapter, could be used to provide feedback to improve the segmentation and edge finding on this original image. In this chapter, however, we will ignore the issues introduced when the initial image is imperfect. The input to our system is assumed to be a very clean line drawing representing the projection of the various layers in the chip in the form shown in Figure 6.1.

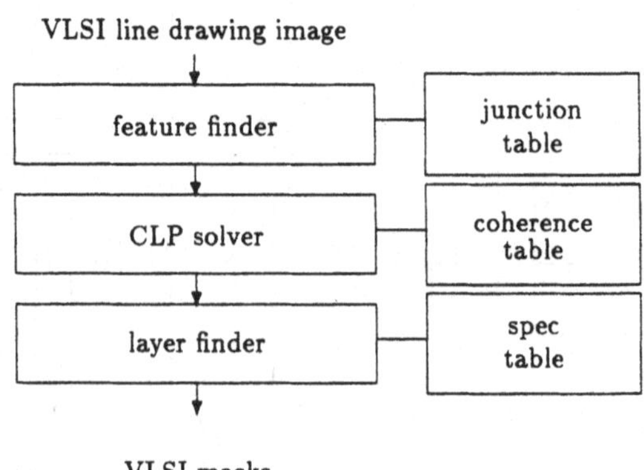

FIGURE 6.11. Outline of the mask extractor.

After line finding, the next step is to find a consistent labeling for all lines in the image. Viewed independently, each individual line could be labeled in a large (though finite) number of ways. However, lines begin and end at junctions, and our world model imposes strong constraints on legal labelings of lines intersecting at junctions. Various efficient algorithms have been proposed for solving constrained labeling problems (CLP) of this type [Haralick and Shapiro 1979]. The strategies that have been proposed include approaches based on filtering, constraint propagation, constraint synthesis, and relaxation of constraint network.

The algorithm we discuss in this section is similar to Waltz's [1972] filtering algorithm, which is especially good at quickly eliminating labels for a vertex that would be impossible given the neighboring vertices and the coherence rule. A practical difficulty is that for most VLSI images, there are too many possible interpretations of the image of which to keep track. A suboptimal strategy, which we have chosen to avoid huge lists of alternative labelings, is to apply the coherence rule only to a small set of adjacent features in the image. Usually we consider pairs of junctions connected by a line. Associated with each junction is a set of possible labels for the junction describing the various labels for the lines connecting at the junction. For each pair of junctions connected by a line, we remove labels from either vertex that would be incompatible with every label in the other vertex. We then iterate such filtering for all pairs of connected junctions. To further speed the algorithm, we use a lookup table of all legal pairs of junctions. Once one line has been narrowed down to only a single possible interpretation, this technique quickly propagates the knowledge to all lines corresponding to edges of the same object and to all edges of objects that cross over this object. After a sufficient number of iterations, we will (hopefully) be left with only a few good interpretations for each junction or line. In general, the operator is required to specify the labelings of various junctions in the image in order to reduce the ambiguity of the image. This step is essential, since otherwise it would be impossible for this technique to positively identify the exact label of any path or to positively identify the inside and outside of the extracted strips in each layer.

For the first figure in Figure 6.5, for example, we will not be able to decide whether the strips are metal, poly, or diffusion. However, if any line within either strip were to be assigned a label due to processing of another part of the image, say poly, then it could immediately be deduced that the other strip was either metal or diffusion.

Note that a VLSI scene is a specific and simple example of the generic blocks world that has been extensively investigated. Line-labeling algorithms in such blocks worlds usually result in a few good alternative interpretations of the image. In this light, it is not surprising that a line-labeling algorithm can greatly reduce the number of possible interpretations of the VLSI scene.

Suppose that only one set of junction labels remains at the end. The next step is to use the labels assigned to the lines to assign labels to the regions in the image. The labels on each line indicate the identity of the uppermost layer in the segment to the right of the arrow that caused the line to appear. Therefore, our strategy is to peel off the layers in order, following the sequence of contact cuts, metal, poly, and finally diffusion layers. We start with lines having the label corresponding to the current layer of interest, then trace out the object at this layer by following the arrows in a clockwise direction. The conflict and coherence rules guarantee that each path must either form a closed loop or run from frame boundary to frame boundary. All edges corresponding to this object are then associated with the extracted object, and are removed from the projected line drawing. The procedure is then repeated for another object at this layer. For example, for the second figure in Figure 6.5, we would start by following the lines labeled P in a clockwise direction, and would extract the uppermost polysilicon object. Since no other poly objects remain, we would next follow the lines labeled D to extract the diffusion layer object.

Extracting these objects from the labeled line drawing is complicated by the fact that the constraint-propagation algorithm may have yielded multiple consistent labelings of the projected image. Each such labeling will lead to different extracted masks. To help resolve these ambiguities, objects whose boundaries have been assigned multiple labelings will be processed through a geometric analyzer. This software checks that the objects satisfy the minimum and maximum size, shape, orientation, and separation rules that the VLSI layout was known to satisfy (see Definition 2.1). Interpretations that violate these rules will be discarded. Object shape, for example, is an important clue for identifying objects such as contact cuts. Additional information obtained by processing the original grey-level image might also be included at this point. (Although color, brightness, and texture are not very reliable indicators of the identity of the regions, they are still useful for resolving any ambiguities remaining in the labeled image.) Note that our strategy relies heavily on the line-labeling task to filter out as many interpretations as possible, leaving only a relatively small amount of work to the final rule-based processing to resolve a (hopefully) small number of remaining ambiguities. Note also that our current software system uses relatively little hierarchical information inferred from the chip layout to resolve ambiguities. To incorporate such information would effectively require adding a circuit and logic gate extractor to the package.

The most difficult situation arises when the relaxation algorithm converges so that each junction has multiple labelings. To cope with this situation, we have augmented this scheme by incorporating two more methods. First, we have allowed substantial operator intervention to reduce the number of layers to a minimum. In most cases, this intervention can substantially reduce the size of the default set of labels used in the constraint-propagation stage. Ultimately, information obtained from other sources such as color, brightness, texture, etc., could partially replace the operator's intervention. Second, we have used some knowledge about the configurations around contact cuts, tgates, etc., to determine the initial guesses for line labelings. Such configurations restrict the possible labelings of the nearby junctions to a small number of possibilities. Eventually, for a fully automated mask extractor, many of the high-level rules and heuristics for VLSI circuits must be used to restrict the set of possible 3-D interpretations to a minimum.

The current program first builds a data base of all legal junction types by rotating, reflecting, and substituting layer symbols into about 15 junction templates. Run time of this stage is proportional to the size of the junction data base. Another slow portion of the program is using pattern matching to build a default set of labels for each junction in the image. Finally, the relaxation algorithm visits each junction between 1 and 4 times on average. Overall run time for the complete constraint-propagation algorithm is nearly proportional to the number of junctions in the image, coming to about half an hour of CPU time on a VAX 750 for a couple hundred vertices.

5 Path-Tracing Algorithm

The line-labeling algorithm in Section 4 has several problems. By treating junctions as the basic object, a large number of labels must be maintained, which is slow. The very low-level focus makes it difficult to incorporate additional VLSI knowledge. The pairwise junction coherence tests cannot easily capture global interactions between multiple strips, which would help reduce the ambiguity of the labeling. By focusing on individual junction labeling, the method never tries to extract entire coherent labelings of the image. Large amounts of operator intervention are required to define a set of junctions, so that the method can come to some decision about the remaining junctions.

There is a faster approach to image labeling, which exploits the structure of the VLSI layout in a more fundamental way. The key is to focus on path fragments as the fundamental objects to be labeled in the image, since all the lines on a path must be assigned the same label and direction. Labels are assigned to path fragments in a 4-stage algorithm. First of all, we find all possible ways in which the path fragments could be interpreted as a set of paths spanning the image. For each such path interpretation, conflict rules are used to find all possible ways of assigning the paths to different layers. For each such assignment, we consider all possible ways of labeling the layers as M, P, D, etc. Finally, for each such assignment we determine which parts of each layer are filled strips and which are holes. A depth-first decision tree structure is used to ensure that every possible labeling of the image is explored, while using only a limited amount of storage.

There are many advantages to this approach. The global perspective gained by considering complete labelings of the image can drastically prune down the number of possible image labelings, even without operator intervention. The 4-stage structure exposes the ambiguities in the labeling process in a systematic way and makes it straightforward to incorporate specific knowledge about the VLSI layout process to prune out impossible interpretations. By separating out the issues of sorting the paths into different layers, from the issues of labeling the layers and assigning inside/outside, we also greatly reduce the ambiguity with which the method must deal at the early stages. The method can also be speedy, since the number of path fragments in an image is considerably smaller than the number of lines. The disadvantage of the path method is that it is only useful for our multilayer strip model, and cannot be extended to projected images of arbitrary 3-D partially translucent objects.

5.1 Extracting Path Fragments

Finding all the path fragments in the image is straightforward. A *path fragment* is defined as a connected sequence of lines that must all belong to a single strip edge. The fragment may run through L- or X-junctions, and will either form a closed loop or else run from T-junction to T-junction. If the fragment enters an X-junction, it must exit on the opposite leg. A path fragment cannot cross itself at an X-junction. Every line must belong to exactly one path fragment, and there is only one way to decompose the image into path fragments. For example, Figure 6.12 contains 6 path fragments.

Extracting the path fragments is straightforward. Start with an external T-junction, and follow the nonframe boundary leg. Continue tracing this path fragment through L- and X-junctions until it terminates at another T-junction. Label each line along the way with this path fragment number. Pick another external T-junction whose leg is not yet assigned and follow this path fragment. Repeat for all external T-junctions. Next, for each internal T-junction, build a path fragment emanating from each unlabeled leg. If any lines remain unassigned after all T-junctions have been pro-

FIGURE 6.12. The left figure contains 6 path fragments as shown on the right. Both ends of a path are marked by filled circles.

cessed, then these must belong to path fragments that form closed loops. Pick an unlabeled line and follow this fragment through L- and X-junctions until it returns to the starting point. Repeat until all lines have been assigned to path fragments.

Several tables of auxiliary connectedness information should be built up as the path fragments are extracted. A line table should list the fragment assigned to each line. A path fragment table should be constructed listing all lines belonging to the fragment. A fragment connection table should list which fragments connect at internal T-junctions. A fragment crossing table should list which fragments cross at X-junctions. Note that in building this crossing table, we should check that a fragment does not cross itself, since this would correspond to an illegal VLSI image.

5.2 Paths

Our goal is to identify the complete boundary of each strip. A path is defined as a connected sequence of path fragments that could form the edge of a single strip. A path may pass through L-, X-, or internal T-junctions, and will either form a closed loop or run from external T- to external T-junction. A path cannot cross itself at an X- or internal T-junction. Every path fragment must belong to at least one path, and by our assumptions about accidental edges, a fragment may belong to at most two paths. No more than two paths may run through an internal T-junction; they enter together on one leg and exit separately on the other two. A path may have to satisfy certain minimum size or distance requirements, depending on from which layer the strip comes. For instance, Figure 6.13 lists all paths constructed from the path fragments in Figure 6.12. There are only six paths in this example. The original circuit described by the line drawing must be composed of some or all of these paths.

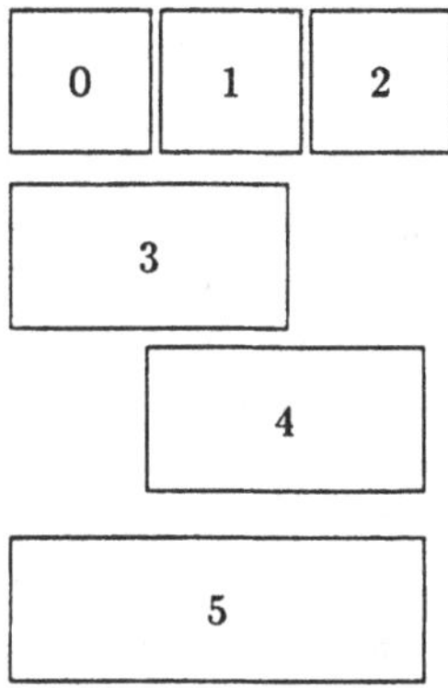

FIGURE 6.13. There are six paths for our example.

Unfortunately, decomposing the line drawing into paths is not straightforward. Path fragments that already form closed loops or run from frame boundary to frame boundary can be immediately classified as paths. Difficulties occur, however, when there are accidental edges and internal T-junctions. The problem is that when a path enters an internal T-junction, it could exit on either of the other two legs. This ambiguity means that, when there are accidental edges, there may be many ways to explain any particular line drawing in terms of paths, and thus in terms of strip edges. A mask-extraction algorithm must derive all possible path routings, then retain only those that correspond to sensible circuits.

5.3 Finding All Paths

There are many possible strategies for extracting paths from the line drawing. We will present one particularly efficient and straightforward approach that first makes a list of all possible paths in the image, then constructs subsets of the paths that could together represent a coherent set of strip edges.

We first must find the set of all possible paths in the line drawing. Path fragments that already form closed loops or run from frame boundary to frame boundary can be immediately classified as paths and strip edges. The remaining fragments connect to internal T-junctions at one or both ends. We will find all possible paths built out of these fragments. Some of these will correspond to strip edges, others will not; we will sort this out later.

Start with the first fragment; at stage n we will find all paths involving fragments numbered n and above. Starting at whichever end or ends terminate at an internal T-junction, we will try concatenating fragments together until we find a path that includes this fragment. At each internal T-junction that we enter, we can consider routing the path through either of the 2 other legs. The fragment on one of these legs may be added to the path, provided that it does not already belong to the path, does not cross any fragments already assigned to this path at an X or a T, and its number is greater than n. These restrictions may leave two, one, or zero choices for routing the path at each internal T-junction. With one choice, we simply follow the next fragment to its end point. With two choices, we consider two possible routings, one through each leg. If the destination is another internal T-junction, we recursively route the path through this junction. Continue in this manner until the fragments are connected into a closed loop or a path running from frame boundary to frame boundary.

If at any point we follow a path to an internal T-junction and discover that neither exit leg is a feasible continuation of the path, then we must back up to the last routing decision made on this path and try the alternative route through that internal T. If no path routing can be found for the fragment we started with, then the line drawing is in error.

Once a legal path is found that contains this segment, we add it to a list of possible paths. After finding this path, back up to the last routing decision made on the path, and try routing the path through the other leg. Continue until we have found all possible paths involving fragment n together with fragments $n + 1$ and higher.

Continue on to stage $n + 1$, and build all possible paths involving fragments $n + 1$ and higher. Repeat until all fragments have been considered. When we finish, we will have a list of all possible paths in the line drawing. Some of these will correspond to actual strip edges. Others will correspond to portions of 2 or more strip edges pasted together. The goal of the next stage is to separate out which combinations of paths might correspond to an actual set of strips, and which can't possibly coexist.

In some images, we may find that the fragments and paths can be grouped into clusters. Let the notation $a\mathsf{x}b$ mean that fragments a and b cross at an X-junction or connect at an internal T-junction. Let the notation $a\mathsf{xx}b$ mean that either $a\mathsf{x}b$ or else there exists a sequence of fragments $a_1, a_2, \ldots, a_n$ such that $a\mathsf{x}a_1, a_1\mathsf{x}a_2, \ldots, a_n\mathsf{x}b$. ($\mathsf{xx}$ is the transitive closure of x.) Then we say that fragments a and b belong to the same cluster if and only if $a\mathsf{xx}b$.

Since it is the crossing and connecting information that constrains path routing, it is easy to see that a cluster of fragments can be assigned to paths independently of the path assignment of a different cluster. It is helpful, therefore, to presort the fragments into clusters and to apply the path-routing algorithm independently to each cluster, generating all possible assignments for each cluster. Path routings for the image are then found by choosing one routing for each cluster.

As we assign fragments to paths, it is very helpful to build several different path tables. One such table includes information such as which fragments belong to this path, which cluster it belongs to, whether it is a closed loop or not, and some size and spacing information. A path crossing table should also be constructed indicating which paths cross at an X or internal T. (Such paths must be assigned to different layers.) A collision table should also be constructed, which lists paths that run through the same internal T and enter and exit on the same legs. (Such paths correspond to hypothetical strip edges that cannot both exist in the actual chip.) These tables will form the data base for the next stages of the algorithm.

5.4 Feasible Subsets of Paths as Strip Edges

The next step is to select subsets of the paths that would correspond to legal sets of strip edges. There may be many such combinations of hypothesized strip edges that would explain this line drawing; our goal is to find all such legal combinations.

There are several key constraints that help to decide which paths really correspond to strip edges and which are only artifacts of accidental edge alignment. Every fragment must belong to at least one strip edge, and by our assumptions about accidental edges, at most two. A fragment that forms a closed loop or runs from frame boundary to frame boundary, and thus never passes through internal T-junctions or accidental edges, must correspond to a strip edge. Internal T-junctions, by assumption, are formed by only two strip edges; one leg has both edges superimposed, the other two are caused by only a single edge. For example, Figure 6.14 lists all possible subsets of paths that satisfy our criteria.

We use a decision tree structure to find all possible subsets of paths that could correspond to strip edges. First, all paths that contain only a single fragment which forms a closed loop or runs from frame boundary to frame boundary can be classified as strip edges. This leaves only paths that pass through internal T-junctions. There are several algorithms for choosing among these; we describe the simplest.

Suppose there are P paths in the cluster of interest that pass through internal T-junctions. We start with path 1 and work through the paths in order. At each stage n, we consider whether or not to add path n to our set of potential strip edges. We may add path n if it contains fragments that are not already on the edges in our set and if it does not collide with any path already marked as a strip edge. (Two paths collide if they pass through the same internal T-junction, entering and exiting on the same pair of legs.) We may not add this path as an edge if any fragment on the path is already on two edges in our set. We must add the path if it contains a fragment not on any edge already in our set, and not on any of the paths $n + 1$ and above. Thus at stage n, we may have to include the path as an edge, we may have to omit it, we may have a choice, or neither choice may be feasible. In the last case, we must back up to the last decision made about a path and try the other choice. Continue backing up and going forward until our set of edges spans all the path fragments, with each fragment on one or two edges, and with no two edges colliding at a T. Record this set, then back up to the last choice made, and try the

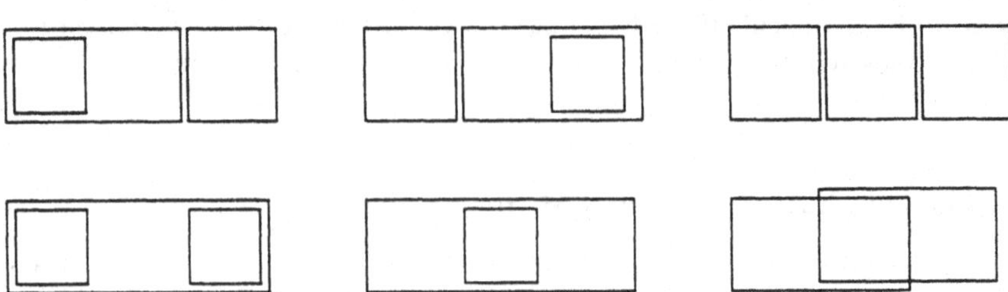

FIGURE 6.14. There are six correct subsets of paths. From left to right, top to bottom, we name A, B, C, D, E, and F. The sizes of paths are slightly changed to show their positions.

alternative. Continue searching in this manner until we find all possible sets of edges for the cluster. Repeat for all clusters.

The overall search structure takes the form of a depth-first search of a P-level binary tree, with 2^P possible sets of strip edges for the cluster. The speed of the algorithm depends on how quickly we can prune the decision tree. This in turn depends on how many accidental edges are in the image, how many total paths there are, the geometry of the image, and the density of the path crossings and collisions. The speed also depends on how the fragments are ordered, since this determines how early we can prune out impossible combinations of paths.

5.5 Assigning Paths to Layers

For each set of hypothesized strip edges in each cluster, we must try assigning the strips to the various layers comprising the chip. Hopefully, we can distinguish incorrect sets of strip edges because they could not be allocated to the available layers or would not form legitimate circuits.

We start by trying to deduce which layers the strips must come from. Rather than try to label the paths immediately as M, P, D, etc., we will first simply try to decide which paths belong to the same layers and which must belong to different layers. Actual labeling will come later.

Assume that there are N different layers in the chip. Two edges that cross each other at an X or a T could only come from strips located on different layers. Two edges that do not cross could be in the same or different layers. Path-crossing information is therefore critical to layer assignment. A cluster of paths can be assigned to layers independently of paths in any other cluster; we therefore process each cluster of paths independently.

We will find all possible ways to assign edges to layers 1 through N. Without loss of generality, we assign the first unlabeled edge to layer 1. The second edge could be assigned to layer 1 if it does not cross the first, or to layer 2. Continuing in this manner, edge n can be assigned to any of the layers 1 through $\min(n,N)$ provided that it does not cross an edge already assigned to that layer. For each possible assignment, we investigate all possible assignments of the remaining edges. If we reach an edge that cannot be assigned to any of the layers, then we must back up to the last layer decision and try something else. Continue backing up as necessary until a complete set of layer assignments is found for all the edges. Record this labeling, then back up and try changing the last layer assignment. Repeat until all possible layer assignments have been found for this cluster of paths. Repeat for all possible sets of edges for this cluster. Repeat for all clusters.

In some cases, we may find that it is impossible to find any legitimate layer labeling for a given set of hypothesized edges. In this case, we can discard this set of edges, and try a different set for this cluster.

Often additional information about the fabrication technology may be available, which might help in the layer assignments. For example, contact cuts can often be easily recognized because they are small isolated rectangles that do not cross or touch any other path. These could be immediately placed into the contact cut layer as they are found; the rest of the edges would then only have to be allocated to the remaining $N - 1$ layers. Distance between parallel sides of the strip edges may also be an important clue for restricting from which layer the strip may have come.

5.6 Labeling the Layers

Once a set of edges has been assigned to N layers, we can try to label each layer as M, P, D, etc. Without additional information, there are $N!$ ways to label the layers. Often, however, knowledge can be used to restrict the ways the layers can be labeled. For example, brightness and texture information are crucial to identifying metal strips. Contact cuts, when recognized, must belong in the contact cut layer. Metal power and ground busses might be directly identifiable by their brightness, length, and width. Finally, the operator may be able to help identify the layers.

5.7 Inside/Outside

Once the layers have been labeled, we need to decide which portion of the layer is filled and which is empty. Since there are two possible choices for each layer, this leads to 2^N possible determinations. Often, however, knowledge about VLSI fabrication can be used to severely restrict this ambiguity. For example, if the frame of view is sufficiently large, then in most cases the filled portion of the layer occupies much less area than the empty portion. Contact cuts provide particularly strong clues. Not only is the interior of the contact cut filled, but also at least two layers underneath each contact cut must be filled. This information alone is often sufficient to fully resolve the inside/outside issue on all layers, and can often be used to invalidate hypothesized strip layer assignments that are incorrect. Metal strips used as wires must have at least two contact cuts, with a contact cut located at the end of each "finger." All filled strips in the M, P, and D layers must be electrically connected to something with at least one contact cut.

Yet other clues, not yet incorporated in our package, can also help resolve the layer labeling and inside/outside ambiguities. Brightness and texture can often be used to identify which portions of the chip are metal. Such brightness, texture, and color cues are often not sufficient to positively identify the other layers, but they can be useful in determining which regions most likely are formed of the same material. Hypothesized strip boundaries that are not consistent with such information could be discarded. Simple electrical circuit constructs, such as transistor gates formed from crossing poly and diffusion, could be recognized, which would provide very strong clues about strip identities and their inside/outside.

5.8 Circuit Extraction

Often considerable ambiguity remains in the strip identification, even after all the simple constraints we have discussed have been applied. One of the strongest tests for whether a hypothesized set of strip labelings is feasible is to extract a crude circuit model from the strip layers and test whether that circuit violates various design rules. Shorts connecting power to ground, meaningless transistor constructs, and so forth can be detected, particularly if the key power and clock busses can be identified. Extending our current software package to include such circuit reasoning is one of our future research goals.

6 Expanded Blocks World

An interesting outcome of previous line drawing research is that the inclusion of more detailed information does not complicate interpretation but, rather, it constrains and facilitates interpretation. For example, researchers prior to Waltz regarded shadows as an annoying complication, but Waltz was able to show that the constraints contributed by shadows make the algorithm converge more quickly and apply to more pictures [Cohen and Feigenbaum 1982].

In the VLSI world model, we started with a model of a multilayer sandwich of translucent planar objects and used rules governing this model to interpret the projected image of the chip. In this section we consider an augmented world model, in which we extend the Huffman-Clowes-Waltz trihedral world model and Kanade's Origami world. We will consider the problem of using a projected 2-D image to reconstruct scenes formed from nonintersecting three-dimensional trihedral objects with both opaque and translucent surfaces. We will show that despite the apparent complexity of such images, strong constraints still remain on the number of legal junction and line interpretations, and these can be used to drastically prune the space of possible image interpretations. The path-oriented algorithm is not easily extendable to a 3-D blocks world, and therefore we will only consider line-labeling methods similar to those in Sections 3 and 4.

6.1 Previous Work

When 3-D objects are projected onto a 2-D image plane, features in the original scene are transformed by such geometric operations as translation, scale, skew, perspective, and zoom. The 3-D shape information about the scene manifests itself in the shading and texture gradients of the image, the contours, and the way the projection changes as we move our viewpoint. In addition, the 3-D structure is reflected in the orientation of the edges in the image, and it implies certain constraints these edges must satisfy. It has been observed that the contour is the minimal representation of intensity discontinuities in a grey-level image that conveys surface structure adequately [Barrow and Tenenbaum 1981]. Much work has been published deriving shape from contour [Barrow and Tenenbaum 1981; Brady and Yuille 1984; Kanade 1981; Stevens 1980; Witkin 1981]. Line-drawing analysis is a special case of this approach.

Previous work attempted to resolve ambiguity in the projected image by using high-level knowledge such as object models [Falk 1972; Roberts 1965], junction catalogs [Huffman 1971; Waltz 1972], or generalized cylinders [Marr and Nishihara 1977]. Since Roberts' [1965] original work, the blocks world has been expanded to more general environments. Huffman [1971] and Clowes [1971] observed that a line in a projected image can be an occluding edge (the regions on either side belong to different objects) or a connect edge (the regions on either side are different facets of the same object). Connect edges may be either convex (+) or concave (−). Focusing on the junctions that can exist in such a projected image, they found that only 16 different types of junctions were possible: six ELLs, 3 ARROWs, 3 FORKs, and 4 Ts. Waltz [1972] extended this idea further to include crack and shadow edges. Turner [1974] needed a catalog many times larger to accommodate solids with parabolic and elliptic surfaces. Kanade [1978] expanded the trihedral world into the Origami world by allowing two- as well as three-dimensional objects in the original scene. Chakravarty [1979] can handle a wide variety of curved objects. His junctions exert remarkably strong local constraints upon the interpretation of lines as extremal, occluding, or intersecting edges.

This previous work was based upon opaque materials. Real-world scenes, however, often contain objects that are translucent or transparent. Such combinations of opaque and translucent materials can create a rather complicated projected image. For example, VLSI chips are constructed of both opaque and transparent materials. In order to deal with projected images of such objects, we must reformulate the previous blocks worlds.

6.2 Line Features

We adopt these researchers' previous assumptions about object shapes, but we introduce a new world model that includes two types of material: opaque surfaces and transparent surfaces. (Some of the assumptions are the following: Objects are formed of planar surfaces meeting at edges. Objects are assumed to be trihedral, with no more than three planar surfaces meeting at any point. Planar surfaces are not allowed to pass through each other. This also implies that objects may not intersect each other, since their intersection would involve more than three planar surfaces meeting at a junction. Edges and vertices are assumed not to be accidentally aligned in the projected image.) Lines in the projected image will be associated with the surfaces that caused the edge and will inherit certain properties due to the optical characteristics of the materials.

A line in the projected image is the result of the intersection of two facets of an object's surface (a connect edge), or is the result of one surface partially occluding another in the projected image (an occluding edge). Connect edges may be either convex (+) or concave (−) relative to the viewpoint. We will say that occluding lines are owned by the adjacent region closest to the viewpoint. To each occluding line we will also assign an arrow such that when we face in the direction of the arrow, the adjoining region that owns the line is to the right of the arrow. The edges corresponding to any given line may be directly visible from the viewpoint, or may be viewed through one or more transparent layers of material. We can therefore assign a depth to each line indicating how many transparent layers are between the viewer and the edge. We will assume that although a transparent surface may not be visible, its intersections with other surfaces and its boundaries always form visible lines. Putting this all together gives:

Definition 6.1 We define the following types of lines:

- An occluding line is the result of a surface on one object partially occluding a surface on another object that is farther from the viewpoint. We indicate such lines by arrows: $\rightarrow$ where the region closer to the viewpoint is to the right of the arrow.
- A connect line is the intersection of two surfaces from a single object. The corresponding edge may be either convex or concave with respect to the viewer; these are indicated by $\xrightarrow{+}$ and $\xrightarrow{-}$, respectively.
- Associated with every line is a depth parameter specifying how many transparent surfaces lie between the corresponding edge and the viewer. As a notational simplification, when drawing junction types, lines whose depth is greater than that of the other lines in the junction will be drawn dotted.

6.3 Junction Features

As in the VLSI world model, the number of different legal junction types is considerably smaller than the number of different ways lines meeting at a point could be labeled. We start by categorizing junctions by their shapes: CROSS, TEE, FORK, ARROW, and so forth. The table of legal junctions will now contain all the junction definitions previously defined for opaque materials by Kanade, as well as new junction types caused by intersections of completely transparent objects, and by mixtures of transparent and opaque objects. We can categorize junctions by their

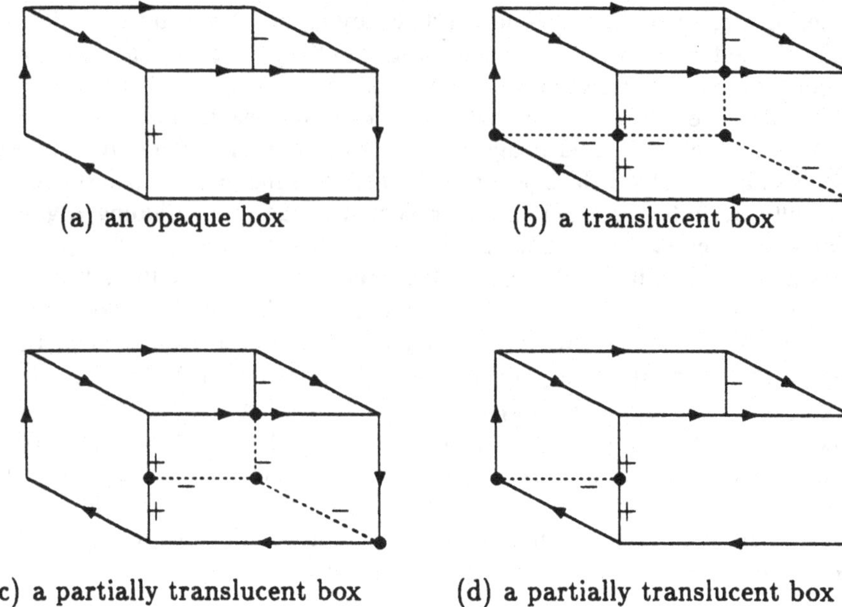

FIGURE 6.15. Labeling boxes: (a) an opaque box labeled by Origami label set, (b) a translucent box, (c)–(d) partially translucent boxes.

branch properties: (1) junctions for opaque objects, (2) junctions for transparent objects, and (3) junctions for mixed objects.

In each category we start with a list of all possible ways that 2-D projections of two- and three-dimensional objects may result in intersecting lines. For each such object juxtaposition, we consider all possible combinations of transparent and opaque surfaces. In all, there are $O(10^2)$ different labelings of these junctions; to save space we will not show these labelings. Instead, Figure 6.15 shows an example of how these legal junction definitions can be used to label line drawings. The first figure is an ordinary opaque box that can be labeled by Kanade's method. The box in the second figure is made entirely of transparent sheets. Our method for line labeling very naturally expresses the shape of the box. The boxes in the third and fourth figures are composed of both opaque and transparent sheets. For example, the front sheet in (c) is transparent and thus the interior lines (dotted) are visible. On the other hand, the front sheet in the fourth figure is opaque. Note again, that our line labeling strategy can correctly categorize these drawings.

The general problem associated with line labeling is ambiguity. The multiplicity of labeling is notorious in Necker's cube [Marr 1982], and the positive and the negative chair of Kanade's [1981] algorithm. In Figure 6.15, drawings (a), (c), and (d) each have only one possible labeling, but drawing (b) has two. In general, transparent surfaces and wire-frame objects can have many ambiguous interpretations.

7 Conclusion

This chapter has explored line-labeling algorithms for extracting the mask layers from a line drawing of a VLSI chip. We assume that the layers in a VLSI chip are thin and translucent, and that the 3-D structure casts shadows in the image. As a result, we assume that the edges of all strips in all layers of the chip are visible, and can be perfectly extracted by an image-segmentation algorithm. Our algorithms start with this line drawing, modeled as the 2-D projection of the strips in the various chip layers and try to use relatively low-level knowledge about VLSI layout to reconstruct the layered structure of the chip.

Our first step was to create a suitable world model for VLSI images that captures the implications of the design rules on legal object sizes, shapes, and spatial interrelationships.

Next, we introduced two different strategies for labeling the strip edges in the projected multilayer image. The first is a line and region labeling strategy, similar to other traditional blocks world line-labeling strategies, but generalized to recognize multilayer translucent objects. Constraints at junctions restrict the possible legal labelings of lines. Propagating these constraints allows us to reduce the set of possible labelings. When we incorporate additional knowledge about sizes, shapes, and permissible arrangements of the layers, and we permit the operator to correctly label selected junctions in the image, then we are often left with a unique labeling for all lines in the image. Regions will then be surrounded by directed, labeled edges; this allows us to label the regions themselves, and peel off the objects, layer by layer.

An alternative approach to the labeling problem is based on a path-oriented method specifically applicable to the multilayer model. We start by identifying path fragments, each corresponding to a portion of a strip edge. From these we build a list of all possible paths, each corresponding to a possible complete strip edge. From this list we hypothesize all possible sets of strip edges that satisfy all the VLSI layout rules and that could explain the projected image. We then find all ways to allocate all strips to the various layers. Next we label the layers with their actual names, and finally we assign which parts of each layer are filled and which are empty. At each stage, we try to use various sources of knowledge about the VLSI fabrication process to prune out ambiguous, incorrect interpretations of the image.

Performance of our labeling algorithms has been demonstrated on simple but representative simulated images such as the CMOS inverter in Figure 6.1. The path-oriented method is still in development; a current version uses no circuit knowledge at all, uses no operator intervention, and generates hundreds of possible interpretations of this image as a result.

We concluded by discussing another application of our approach to interpreting projected 2-D images of a trihedral blocks world incorporating

2- and 3-D objects with both transparent and opaque surfaces. Here our line-labeling strategy could be generalized to this 3-D world, but the path-oriented method could not.

There are at least two major areas of research required to make a complete mask-extraction system feasible. First of all, without operator intervention, and without medium- or high-level circuit knowledge, there are far too many possible explanations of even simple VLSI circuit images. It is crucial to incorporate as much circuit reasoning ability as possible to weed out the patently ridiculous layer reconstructions. Knowledge about contact cuts and about tgates should prove particularly helpful.

The second major problem is that building a perfect image-segmentation system is impossible. In reality, it is quite difficult to find all the edges of all the strips, particularly when strips are deeply buried beneath one or two other strips. Regions near contact cuts are difficult to segment correctly, since many strip edges come very near to each other at these points. Strip edges are often quite ragged, corners are rounded, lighting may be uneven, and so on. It would be nice if the line-drawing-interpretation system could take a faulty line drawing, try analyzing it, then return feedback to the front end suggesting where the line drawing makes no sense and where different image processing should be attempted. Unfortunately, our present system relies heavily on strict rules governing the intersections of lines at junctions and propagates information from these junctions over large distances. As a result, if no explanation of the image can be found, it is difficult to localize exactly where the problem occurred. Better self-analysis will be required in systems where the front end image processing is unreliable. Despite these difficulties, however, this VLSI line-drawing-analysis system shows great promise as the middle stage in a full-scale mask-extraction system.

Acknowledgments. We thank Professors W.E.L. Grimson and Bernard Levy for their helpful ideas.

References

Barr, A., and Feigenbaum, E.A. 1981. *The handbook of artificial intelligence*. Vol. 1, Los Altos, Calif.: Kaufman.

Barrow, H., and Tenenbaum, J. 1981. Interpreting line drawings as three-dimensional surfaces. *Artif. Intell.* **17,** 1–3 (Aug.), 75–116.

Brady, M., and Yuille, A. 1984. An extremum principle for shape from contour. *IEEE Trans. on Pattern Analysis and Machine Intelligence*. **PAMI-6,** 3 (May), 288–301.

Chakravarty, I. 1979. A generalized line and junction labeling scene with applications to scene analysis. *IEEE Trans. on Pattern Analysis and Machine Intelligence*. **PAMI-1,** 2 (Apr.), 202–205.

Clowes, M. 1971. On seeing things. *Artif. Intell.* **2,** 1, 79–116.

Cohen, P.R., and Feigenbaum, E.A. 1982. *The handbook of artificial intelligence*. Vol. 3, Los Altos, Calif.: Kaufman.

Dimanzo, M., Adorni, G., and Gienchiglia, F. 1986. Reasoning about scene descriptions. *Proc. IEEE* **74,** 7 (July), 1013–1025.

Draper, S. 1981. The use of gradient and dual space in line-drawing interpretation. *Art. Intell.* **17,** 1–3 (Aug.), 461–508.

Falk, G. 1972. Interpretation of imperfect line data as a three-dimensional scene. *Art. Intell.* **4,** 2, 101–144.

Guzman, A. 1969. Decomposition of a visual scene into three-dimensional bodies. Ph.D. thesis, M.I.T., Cambridge, Mass.

Haralick, R.M., and Shapiro, L.G. 1979. The consistent labeling problem: Part 1. *IEEE Trans. on Pattern Analysis and Machine Intelligence* **PAMI-1,** 2 (Apr.), 173–184.

Horn, B. 1974. Determining lightness from an image. *Computer Graphics and Image Processing* **3,** 277–299.

Huffman, D. 1971. Impossible objects as nonsense sentences. In Meltzer, B., and Michie, D. (eds.) *Machine Intelligence,* New York: American Elsevier Publ., 295–324.

Kanade, T. 1978. A theory of origami world. *Technical Report CMU-CS-78-144*. Carnegie-Mellon University, Pittsburgh, Pa.

Kanade, T. 1979. Recovery of the three-dimensional shape of an object from a single view. *Technical Report CMU-CS-79-153*. Carnegie-Mellon University, Pittsburgh, Pa., Oct.

Kanade, T. 1981. Recovery of the three-dimensional shape of an object from a single view. *Artif. Intell.* **17,** 1–3 (Aug.) 409–460.

Mackworth, A. 1973. Interpreting pictures of polyhedral scenes. *Artif. Intell.* **4,** 2 (June), 121–137.

Marr, D. 1982. *Vision*. San Francisco, Calif.: W.H. Freeman and Company.

Marr, D., and Nishihara, H. 1977. Representation and recognition of the spatial organization of three-dimensional shapes. *Proc. Roy. Soc. London* **B 200,** 269–294.

McCormick, S.P. 1984. Automated circuit extraction from mask description of MOS networks. Master's thesis, M.I.T., Cambridge, Mass., Apr.

Mead, C., and Conway, L. 1980. Introduction to VLSI systems. Reading, Mass.: Addison-Wesley.

Poggio, T.A., and Koch, C. 1984. An analog model of computation for the ill-posed problems of early vision. *A.I. Memo 783,* M.I.T., Cambridge, Mass., May.

Poggio, T.A., and Torre, V. 1984. Ill-posed problems and regularization analysis in early vision. *A.I. Memo 773,* M.I.T., Cambridge, Mass., Apr.

Poggio, T., Torre, V., and Koch, C. 1985. Computational vision and regularization theory. *Nature* **317,** 26 (Sept.), 314–319.

Poggio, T.A., Voorhees, H., and Yuille, A. 1985. A regularizated solution to edge detection. *A.I. Memo 833,* M.I.T., Cambridge, Mass., May.

Roberts, L. 1965. Machine perception of three-dimensional solids. In Tippett, J.P., et al., (eds.), *Optical and Electro-Optical Information Processing*. Cambridge, Mass.: MIT Press.

Stevens, K. 1980. Surface perception from local analysis of texture. *Technical Report AI-TR-512*. M.I.T., Cambridge, Mass.

Sugihara, K. 1981. Mathematical structures of line drawings of polyhedra. RNS 81-02. Nagoya University, Nagoya, Japan, May.

Sugihara, K. 1986. *Machine interpretation of line drawings*. Cambridge, Mass.: MIT Press.

Turner, K. 1974. Computer perception of curved objects using a television camera. Ph.D. thesis, University of Edinburgh, Edinburgh, Scotland.

Waltz, D. 1972. Generating semantic descriptions from drawings of scenes with shadows. Ph.D. thesis, M.I.T., Cambridge, Mass.

Winston, P.H. 1984. *Artificial intelligence*. 2d ed., Reading, Mass.: Addison-Wesley.

Witkin, A. 1981. Recovering surface shape and orientation from texture. *Artif. Intell.* **17,** 1–3 (Aug.), 17–46.

7
Control-Free Low-Level Image Segmentation: Theory, Architecture, and Experimentation

W.E. BLANZ, J.L.C. SANZ, AND D. PETKOVIC

ABSTRACT: In this chapter, the computer vision problem of segmenting images is addressed. Our approach is based upon the fact that low-level image segmentation is a model-driven operation, conveyed in a way that all relevant knowledge gathered in a supervised learning phase is used in parallel in the segmentation process. Such a control-free image segmentation can be achieved by using a pattern-recognition approach. This method uses a relatively large number of local image features and combines them optimally according to the scene knowledge acquired in a training phase by the use of a supervised classification procedure. In this methodology, training is performed by the user, outlining the image regions belonging to each class. There are two major advantages accrued from this approach. First, the need for expert image-analysis knowledge is minimized, since the user selects what is to be segmented and is not required to determine how this segmentation is to be accomplished. Second, this approach is amenable to parallel pipeline hardware implementation. Extensive experimentation with many different industrial problems demonstrates that this approach is an effective and useful building block for low-level computer vision applications.

1 Introduction

The problem of segmenting images is of key importance in computer vision. Much has been written about the topic and many methods have been described in the literature. It is not the purpose of this chapter to present a survey of image segmentation since the reader can find good review papers such as Fu and Mu [1981] and more information in image-related books such as Rosenfeld and Kak [1982], Nevatia [1982], and Ballard and Brown [1982]. Although much work has been done in image segmentation since the pioneer work of Brice and Fennema [1970] and Roberts [1968], the subject continues to receive an enormous amount of attention. More recently, new interesting paradigms for image modeling and representation have been proposed [Haralick and Watson 1981; Asada and Brady 1984], and several ways of conveying segmentation expertise and related knowledge for image interpretation tasks are known [Hanson and Riseman 1978; Nazif and Levine 1984; Stansfield 1986].

As was pointed out by different authors [Rosenfeld 1984; Haralick 1985; Pavlidis 1986], the computer vision field needs to undergo a significant amount of formalization and theoretical foundation. Today there are four main streams of work aiming at:

- Providing computational models of human visual perception.
- Developing general vision systems.
- Designing realistic, moderately general vision systems.
- Providing cost-effective solutions to specific applications.

The popular goals of having general-purpose vision systems and reproducing basic functions of human vision are still far away. In addition, it is difficult to assess the success of any of these methodologies. The evaluation is hindered by many problems, but among them the lack of consistent experimentation appears as the most serious problem, as pointed out by Price [1985]. However, even in cases for which experimentation shows the usefulness of a system, information involving system performance is often not disclosed due to its proprietary value or lack of research content.

One of the key issues in all segmentation methods is how to convey and apply the a priori (application-dependent) knowledge, i.e., what constitutes the object and background, respectively. As in all automatic decision methods, there are two basic ways of doing it: (1) heuristics (expert-system approach), and (2) statistic (traditional pattern-recognition approach).

The expert-system approach to segmentation [Nazif and Levine 1984] has several disadvantages common to other applications in which control mechanisms are given as inference mechanisms operating on a set of rules. Among others, these problems are that the acquisition of knowledge is complicated, and it is difficult to map the resulting systems onto parallel architectures as pointed out by Forgy et al. [1984] and Fountain [1986].

But expert systems are not the only way to approach decision-making problems, such as segmentation and classification. Statistical pattern recognition is a mature discipline that has been successfully applied in some application domains. The main thrust in statistical pattern recognition consists of assigning a class to a feature vector based on related statistics or probability distributions. Consequently, it constitutes a general approach to decision-making problems based on well-understood mathematical mechanisms. Classification or categorization can be used at several levels of image interpretation like segmentation and object recognition. In these problems, the feature vectors arise from computations carried out on different representations, i.e., pixels, and segmented objects, respectively.

Decision-theoretic methods have been used for both low-level segmentation [Davis and Rosenfeld 1979; Blanz and Reinhardt 1981], and object classification [Besl et al. 1985]. Currently, statistical pattern recognition undergoes significant progress in terms of architectural implementations, efficient algorithms, and the development of systems [Jain 1986].

In the context of these comments, this chapter shows the use of a large number of features computed at the pixel level for image segmentation. The segmentation decision is made by a polynomial classifier that operates on the extracted features. This classifier is trained during a supervised learning phase by presenting to the system typical regions of interest, e.g., object and background. In this training phase, the classifier tunes up its parameters according to a certain optimality criterion. These parameters are then used in the execution phase to classify pixels into one of the trained classes. In addition, we propose a pipeline architecture implementation where segmentation is expected to occur in real time (i.e., TV frame rate).

We find this approach very promising for the following reasons.

- Fast segmentation is an important building block that enables other intermediate-level representations, computations on these structures, and segmentation refinement to be performed on a greatly reduced amount of data. The proposed approach can be used as
  a. a preliminary real-time segmentation that enables the application of more sophisticated intermediate-level processing.
  b. a way to provide convergent evidence, for example, to verify the performance of a certain rule just fired.
- In domain-specific situations, this method can produce strikingly good results. It finds wide applicability in
  a. industrial machine-vision problems, in which images are largely described by local texture composition of data originated by different sensors.
  b. Environments that are sufficiently controlled so that robust training can be guaranteed by showing a number of representative samples of segments.
- It requires simple training, minimizing expert knowledge and intervention.
- The whole approach is amenable to (VLSI) hardware implementation.
- This approach is best suited to objects of amorphous shape distinguished from the background by their texture. One of the limitations of this approach is that it is hard to convey global object shape information. However, this can be done in the subsequent processes that may operate on the results of this low-level segmentation process.

The main thrust of this work is to show the applicability of statistical pattern-recognition techniques to image segmentation. We hope that this approach to image segmentation will be the ultimate answer for a number of domain-specific problems. In this chapter we will show a significant amount of experiments to support this view. In addition, this approach should provide a key input to other control-based segmentation mechanisms. For this reason, the statistical methods should not be thought of as being opposed to expert-systems techniques, but rather complementing and usually preceding them. In fact, we have shown that some simple rules can be approximated by polynomial surfaces [Blanz 1986].

In summary, we hope that vision practitioners will find the results reported in this chapter useful for image applications, and we hope to encourage them to pursue more theoretical work along this line of research.

2 Polynomial Classifiers

Consider the following situation: A certain process creates objects (symbols) that are described by a set of N observations, which we combine to a feature vector $\boldsymbol{f} \in R^N$. We have to automate a decision-making process that groups the objects into one out of C classes. In order to accomplish this task, the decision automaton (classifier) has to be supplied with a certain amount of information concerning the symbol-creating process. This information can be provided in two basically different ways.

- We describe the distribution of each feature in each class to the classifier explicitly, i.e., we map the given specifications into rules and apply them to the extracted features.
- We collect a representative training set where we mark each sample with its appropriate class membership and let the automation derive the information it needs to make the decision.

The first situation is the typical situation for an expert-system or rule-based classifier, while the second is usually connected to probabilistic or statistical approaches. The first needs a knowledge about the symbol-creating process, and is usually bound to intuitively explainable features. The second requires only the information about the class membership of a certain amount of samples and further knowledge about statistical properties of the symbol-creating process. It also deals with any kind of features, although, of course, they have to be specified a priori.

In some image and general decision-making problems, both situations are typical for specific applications. A third situation, however, is also quite common and much more general. In the beginning the only knowledge about a process consists of more or less loosely defined qualitative models (usually rules). The automaton should be able to make decisions without having seen many real samples. As experience grows and more samples are available, the automaton should be able to learn and refine according to the actual outcomes of the process. This can be done automatically because all the information needed comes from the process

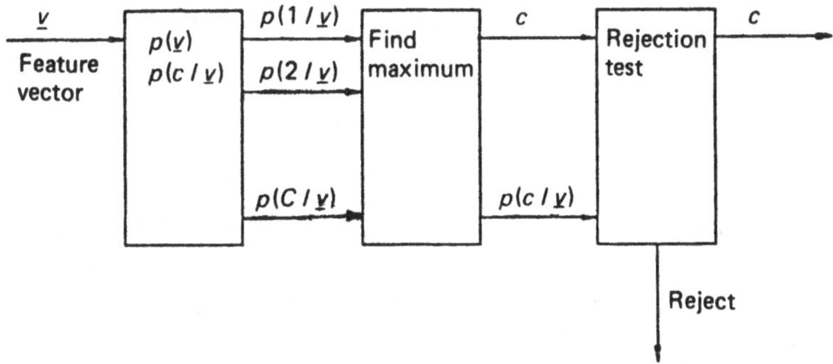

FIGURE 7.1. Bayes' classifier.

itself and the knowledge about the class membership of the objects. Therefore the optimal decision automaton should be able to handle knowledge representations based on both empirical rules and statistical knowledge, or training samples.

We will show that the polynomial classifier [Schuermann 1977] is a good candidate for this approach, due to its nonparametric nature (it does not require knowledge of the type of the process statistics), and due to its real-time hardware amenability. To gain some understanding of a polynomial classifier, we briefly survey the philosophy behind such classifiers. We will return to the topic in more detail in Section 3.

Let's assume the configuration shown in Figure 7.1, where the process is described by the probability distributions $p(\mathbf{v})$, the probability for the occurrence of a certain feature vector **v**; $p(\mathbf{v} \mid c)$, the probability for a certain feature vector **v** given a class c; and the a priori class probability $p(c)$, which creates signs or feature vectors **v**. In that case the Bayes classifier

$$p(c \mid \mathbf{v}) = \frac{p(\mathbf{v} \mid c)\, p(c)}{p(\mathbf{v})}$$

is the optimal classifier and the so-called decision functions $d_c(\mathbf{v})$ are the joint probabilities $p(c \mid \mathbf{v})$ given by Bayes' rule.

The second box in Figure 7.1 simply selects the maximum from among all decision functions and the last box finally checks whether this maximum is large enough to pass the rejection test. If the test is passed, the decision is made in favor for the class with the largest value in the decision function.

In general, however, the probability density distributions are not known. In such cases we use a polynomial approach instead:

$$d_c(\mathbf{v}) = a_{0c} + a_{1c} v_1 + a_{2c} v_2 + \cdots a_{Nc} v_N +$$
$$\cdots + a_{N+1c} v_1^2 + a_{N+2c} v_1 v_2 + \cdots.$$

Or, if we combine the decision functions d_c to a decision vector **d**

$$\mathbf{d} = \mathbf{A}^T\hat{\mathbf{v}}$$

where

$$\hat{\mathbf{v}} = (1\ v_1\ v_2 \cdots v_N\ v_1^2\ v_1\ v_2 \cdots v^g{}_N)^T$$

is the extended feature vector, combined of all the measured features and their combinations up to the degree of the polynomial. The components of **d** are referred to as degrees of object memberships.

If we now introduce for each sample of the training set a target vector **y**, which is one of the spanning vectors of the space of the decision vectors **d** and can be regarded as the optimal decision vector, we can formulate an optimization problem

$$S^2 = E\{\mid \mathbf{y} - \mathbf{d} \mid^2\} = \text{minimum}$$

or

$$S^2 = E\{\mid \mathbf{y} - \mathbf{A}^T\hat{\mathbf{v}} \mid^2\} = \text{minimum}.$$

The optimal solution is given by the equation

$$E\{\hat{\mathbf{v}}\hat{\mathbf{v}}^T\} = E\{\hat{\mathbf{v}}\hat{\mathbf{y}}^T\}.$$

This is a linear equation for the coefficients of the matrix **A.** This equation only includes quantities that can be measured from the training samples, and therefore **A** can be calculated easily from statistical moments of a given training set. See Appendix 1 for a derivation of this formula.

An additional feature makes the polynomial classifier most attractive for decision analysis: it is very easily implemented in special hardware. In the case of a linear classifier, two classes, and N features, the decision is derived from N multiplications, N additions, and one comparison, independent of the input data.

The next four sections contain the main results of this chapter. First we derive the polynomial classifier assuming a given training set that is sufficiently representative, and we discuss some properties of polynomial classifiers in Section 3. We will then show the use of these concepts for image segmentation in Section 4. Architecture concepts will be given in Section 5. Extensive experimentation for various real machine vision problems will be shown in Section 6.

3 Knowledge Representation by Training Sets

In this section, we assume we have a training set of M object samples belonging to C different classes, each represented by a feature vector, and we denote the mth feature vector of the training set by $\mathbf{f}^{(m)}$. In order to have a vector representation of the class membership of our training samples we introduce a target vector $\mathbf{y}^{(m)}$ with the components

$$y_i^{(m)} = \delta_{ic^{(m)}}$$

where Kronecker's symbol denotes that only the cth component of $\mathbf{y}^{(m)}$ is 1, if the mth sample $\boldsymbol{f}^{(m)}$ belongs to class c; all other components of $\mathbf{y}^{(m)}$ are 0. Thus, only C different target vectors exist. These C unity vectors are the spanning vectors of a C-dimensional space R^C, which we call the decision space.

As the target vectors represent the true class membership of the training samples they represent the ideal decision. Therefore, an ideal decision system should produce the target vector $\mathbf{y}^{(m)}$ for each sample of the training set $\boldsymbol{f}^{(m)}$. In the case of the polynomial classifier we approximate the target vectors $\mathbf{y}^{(m)}$ by a decision vector

$$\mathbf{d} = f(\boldsymbol{f}^{(m)})$$

the components of which are given by a polynomial mapping of the feature space R^N in the decision space R^C

$$\begin{aligned} d_c = {} & a_{0c} + a_{1c}f_1 + a_{2c}f_2 + a_{3c}f_3 + \cdots \\ & + a_{(N+1)c}f_1^2 + a_{(N+2)c}f_1f_2 + \cdots . \end{aligned}$$

In order to simplify the notation, we introduce an extended feature vector $\mathbf{v}$ as

$$\mathbf{v} = (1\ \boldsymbol{f}^T\ f_1{}^2\ f_1f_2\ \cdots)^T. \tag{7.1}$$

This is a vector that consists of a 1 in the first place, the original feature vector $\boldsymbol{f}$, and all the combinations of features up to the degree of the polynomial. If we combine the coefficients a_{ic} to a coefficient matrix

$$A = \begin{pmatrix} a_{01} & a_{02} & \cdots & a_{0C} \\ a_{11} & a_{12} & \cdots & a_{1C} \\ \cdot & \cdot & & \cdot \end{pmatrix}$$

we get for the decision vector

$$\mathbf{d} = \mathbf{A}^T\,\mathbf{v}. \tag{7.2}$$

In order to determine the coefficients of $\mathbf{A}$ we use a simple mean square minimization criterion similar to the well-known regression approach. Recall that the $\mathbf{y}^{(m)}$ are the ideal decision vectors. Therefore we use the linear regression technique and make the Euclidean distance from the ideal to the real decision vectors minimal:

$$S^2 = \sum_{m=1}^{M} |\, \mathbf{y}^{(m)} - \mathbf{d}^{(m)} \,|^2 \overset{!}{=} \min_{\mathbf{A}} . \tag{7.3}$$

This optimization criterion is not unquestionable. First the sum goes only over the samples of the training set. Therefore the optimization is only concerned about those samples and nothing is said about future samples, which are not in the training set. But this is true for all statistical approaches, because designers of decision automatons are not prophets and therefore have to rely on the knowledge given by representative training sets.

This criterion gives us the coefficients of **A** for a given degree of the polynomial and a given number of features, but not the optimal degree of the polynomial and not the optimal number of features (which is basically the same thing). If we increase the number of adjustable coefficients arbitrarily we can always force S^2 to 0 without bringing us closer to what we really want: making good decisions not only on the training set but also on future samples produced by the same process. This problem of optimum selection of the number of features could be addressed by the application of Rissanen's [1978] MDL principle.

An additional problem is that we are in general not concerned about the distance to the ideal decision vectors (unless it is not zero) but about the number of right or wrong decisions. This leads to a nonlinear optimization problem that does not yield a closed solution for the coefficients of **A.** We can approach this problem, however, by using the outcome of the approach described in this chapter as a good starting point for another nonlinear optimization problem using, e.g., nonlinear programming techniques [Blanz 1983; Rechenberg 1973].

We will now derive the solution for **A.** This solution is very straightforward and well-known from linear regression theory, where **y** is not a vector but a scalar. We include it here just for the sake of completeness. First we reformulate the optimization criterion with the aid of equation (7.2) and get

$$S^2 = \frac{1}{M} \sum_m \mid \mathbf{y}^{(m)} - \mathbf{A}^T \mathbf{v}^{(m)} \mid^2 \overset{!}{=} \min_{\mathbf{A}} . \tag{7.4}$$

This leads to the formula (see Appendix 1)

$$\sum_m (\mathbf{v}^{(m)} \mathbf{v}^{(m)^T}) \, \mathbf{A} = \sum_m (\mathbf{v}^{(m)} \mathbf{y}^{(m)^T}). \tag{7.5}$$

This is a linear matrix equation for **A,** which only depends on all $\mathbf{v}^{(m)}$ and $\mathbf{y}^{(m)}$, which as an entity represent the training set and therefore are all known. Thus we found a set of linear equations for the coefficients for the mapping polynomial that can be solved by standard numerical methods.

Once **A** is determined during a training phase, it can be applied according to equation (7.2) in a hardware-oriented way to test samples, created by the same symbol-creating process. Due to the nature of **d** as an approximation of **y** the decision is made according to the largest component of **d.**

An important property of this result is that the moment matrices $\Sigma_m(\mathbf{v}^{(m)}\mathbf{v}^{(m)T})$ and $\Sigma_m(\mathbf{v}^{(m)}{}_y{}^{(m)T})$ provide the trainability of the polynomial classifier. If we keep only those matrices we can update them whenever new samples become available and thus we can compute an updated **A** without going through the entire training data set again. We do not explicitly compute the inverse of $\Sigma_m(\mathbf{v}^{(m)}\mathbf{v}^{(m)T})$ but use a (modified) Gauss-Seidel approach to solve the equation system (7.5).

It is a well-known fact that the number of features should be small compared to the number of training samples [Thoussaint 1974], otherwise a classifier overspecification can occur, which means that it will not perform well on future samples. Fortunately, our sample consists of a feature vector associated with each pixel, and consequently the amount of training data is usually large. Nevertheless, the user should make sure that the training data contain the expected variety in sample features.

To end this section, we would like to state an interesting property of the least squares criterion that involves the components of the decision vector; the components of the decision vector (like probabilities) add up to 1. The proof of this important property is shown in Appendix 2.

4 Image Segmentation

The general approach to image segmentation that we use in this section assumes that pixels and their relation to their neighbors are described completely by a set of features; this relationship is usually called texture. A further assumption is that different objects in a given scene differ in either gray-level, or texture, or both. Again, shape information is hard to use in this approach. If we succeed in defining a set of features that describe pixels according to their gray level and/or texture completely, we can, under this assumption, discriminate between pixels of different objects in the feature space using supervised classification methods. A redundant set of features that attempt to describe gray-level and texture is the following.

1. Pixel gray level.
2. Pixel energy.
3. Mean gray level in window.
4. Energy in window.
5. Local minimum.
6. Median value.
7. Local maximum.
8. Gray-level variance in the window.
9. Absolute value of the gradient.
10. Difference of the mean of the right and left neighbors within the window.
11. Difference of the mean of the neighbors in 45°.

12. Difference of the mean of the neighbors in 90°.
13. Difference of the mean of the neighbors in 135°.
14. Value of the gray-level histogram at the value of the pixel.
15. Value of the histogram $f15$ at the value of the pixel.
16. Value of the histogram $f16$ at the value of the pixel.
17. Number of pixels in window with gray level greater than feature 3.
18. Number of pixels in window with gray level less than feature 3.
19. Local experience.
20. Gray-level experience.

All these features are calculated within a window of typically 5×5 pixels and are designed to be easily implemented in hardware. There are other possibilities for designing the set of features.

Histograms $f15$ and $f16$ are calculated like the ordinary gray-level histogram from the whole image before the pixel features are calculated. $f15$ is a modified histogram where the histogram values at a certain gray level are increased whenever a pixel with that gray level is greater than the mean gray level of its window neighborhood. In $f16$ the histogram value is increased whenever the gray level is less than the mean of its neighborhood.

Local and gray-level experience are functions derived from the training set that indicate the probability of a pixel at a certain location or at a certain gray level, respectively, to be an object pixel. The gray-level experience is simply a gray-level histogram of all the pixels belonging to the parts of interest. The local experience function is the probability that the pixel belongs to a specific location. To make this feature translation-invariant, this location is calculated relative to the center of mass of the gray-level image. Obviously if the training set consists of only one image, the values of the local experience function can only be 1 or 0 and the discrimination problem could easily be solved with that feature alone. This of course makes sense only if it is guaranteed that all objects are always presented at the same location with respect to the center of mass of the gray-level image. If that is not so, this feature is automatically suppressed. However, if the parts are presented in similar locations, the local experience function can be blurred, e.g., by a low-pass filter, and used advantageously even if the training set consists of only one image.

One segmentation strategy would be as follows: after the complete set of features is calculated for each pixel in a given scene, look for clusters in the feature space and assign an object number to each cluster. This technique, called *unsupervised learning,* would yield a number of different objects or parts of objects depending on the cluster separation level and the complexity of the objects. This, however, is not the desired outcome of a segmentation process. The optimal solution of the segmentation task would be to mark only the object(s) of interest, however complicated their texture might be, and assign all other objects that might be present in the scene to the background. The definition of objects of interest is application-dependent and may constitute more than one cluster in the feature space. This approach alleviates recognition difficulties for the subsequent recognition process and performs a reasonable amount of data reduction at the same time.

The latter goal can be achieved by using a supervised learning technique. To this end, in a given training set all pixels have to be labeled manually as belonging to the object(s) of interest or the background, which includes all objects that are not of interest. Then, a polynomial classifier is adapted to discriminate between the cluster(s) of pixels labeled as belonging to the object(s) of interest and all other pixels. Once adapted, this classifier makes the decision for each pixel whether it belongs to the object(s) of interest or the background. Of course, other classification methods can be used [Niblack and Blanz 1986].

Thus, this segmentation algorithm is composed of two principal phases.

- Training phase: where the training samples are collected and all pixels of the training set are labeled, e.g., with tablet or joystick, the features are calculated for all pixels of the training set, and the polynomial classifier is adapted.
- Run phase: where the features are calculated for each pixel, and according to the parameters given by the polynomial classifier a decision is made whether the pixel belongs to the object(s) of interest or the background.

We should point out the necessity of gray-level calibration of the extracted features, which is the process of compensating for variations of global scene illumination due to, for example, light source fluctuations. Although some features are invariant to this process, we recommend this calibration. It can be performed either by normalizing the image contrast or normalizing extracted features using some global-correction parameters.

5 Architectural Aspects

To process large quantities of images economically it is essential to have key parts of these algorithms carried out by special processors. This does not necessarily mean that the entire process should be performed by a special processor, but the bottlenecks like the feature calculation and the multiplication of the feature vectors by classification coefficients during the run phase should be carried out by special hardware. The extensive numerical computations during the adaptation phase are still left to standard von Neumann architectures. Since the adaptation phase is conducted only once for each problem, this step does not really affect the overall performance of the suggested algorithm. Figure 7.2 sketches a possible processor architecture to perform the segmentation task. In a first run

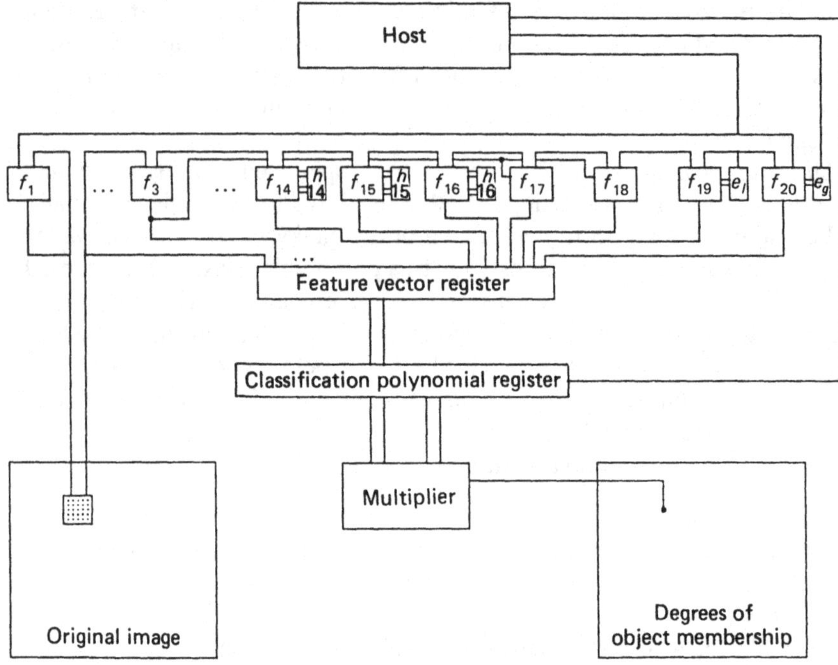

FIGURE 7.2. Architecture for real-Time segmentation.

over the image the histogram processors h_{14} to h_{16} calculate the corresponding histograms. In the next phase, the feature processors f_1 to f_{20} compute one feature each, and put it in the feature vector register. The result of f_3 is needed very fast because this result is used to compute f_{17} and f_{18}. The modules f_1 to f_{20} get the gray values of all pixels of the window by a very broad bus and compute from that the corresponding features f_1 to f_{20}, respectively. (Some modules don't need the entire window information but use only the gray value of the central pixel and get the feature value out of special lookup tables.)

The feature vector register, together with preloaded polynomial coefficients, is used to form the polynomials (degrees of membership). These results can be stored in memory (one image plane for each class) or used for immediate class assignment. This process is done for every pixel of the image. Actually, the degree of membership for the background is not needed and therefore is not computed. This is due to the fact that the degrees of membership add up to one, and therefore one of them is redundant (see Appendix 2). The final segmented image is obtained by taking the maximum among the degrees of membership. Storing the degree of membership is useful if we want to do some additional relaxation relabeling. However, these storage requirements can be eliminated if, for each pixel, we select the class corresponding to the polynomial with maximum output. This can be easily achieved by putting a simple maximum detector with a simple logic at the output of the multiplier in the Figure 7.2, thus immediately generating the class label.

It has been shown [Ruetz and Brodersen 1986] that reasonable approximations of complicated gray-level features like the median value in the window can be carried out by a single VLSI chip that has on-line buffering to save on pin count. Similar methodology can be applied for the proposed architecture. The lookup tables for the local and gray-value experience as well as the classification polynomial registers are loaded directly by the host after the training phase.

The system should use only the set of selected features for particular application, which is controlled by appropriate polynomial coefficients obtained in the training phase.

6 Applications

In this section, we demonstrate the performance of the proposed methodology by applying it to several different industrial problems. The tasks have been selected so that the variety and breadth of possible applications of the suggested approach could be demonstrated. Although we do not claim that any of these vision problems is completely solved by the segmentation procedure, in each of these cases our approach leads to a reasonable segmentation of the given scene. This makes further processing at a higher level feasible. Furthermore, this segmentation was achieved without any special development or manual tuning of parameters. The built-in automatic training and adaptation capabilities of the algorithm were sufficient to adapt to all these different applications. In addition, the training and testing phases were performed in a very short time (on the order of hours) making this approach an excellent vehicle for speeding up the application development.

In all the examples we show a mask produced as a result of the segmentation decision for each pixel. For further processing we can, according to the specific problem, either process these masks alone, e.g., to derive some shape information, or we can use them to mask out some of the original gray-level image information if we are more interested in textural features of the segmented objects. The segmentation parameters of all the experiments together are shown in Table 7.1.

As training areas, we manually selected representative regions in the training image by means of a mouse and an IBM 7350 image-processing system. The sizes of the training areas are given in the second column of the table. The software was written in FORTRAN and was running on an IBM 4341 computer.

The size of all the images in this example was 512 × 512 pixels. The average training time per task depended on the number of training pixels and was on the order of a few minutes of CPU time. Similarly, the running

TABLE 7.1

Experiment	Number of training pixels	Window size	Number of classes	Polynomial degree	Rank order of selected features
PCBs	18,993	5×5	3	2	3, 4, 6, 8, 1, 2, 5, 7, 13, 20
Plated through holes	7,335	5×5	3	2	6, 1, 2, 20, 5, 3, 4, 14, 15, 16
Disk heads	10,241	5×5	3	2	6, 3, 1, 2, 4, 7, 5, 16, 15, 14
IC solder balls	27,500	5×5	2	1	6, 2, 1, 20, 4, 3, 7, 5, 16, 19, 14, 15, 8, 9, 13, 12, 10, 11, 17, 18
Contamination of dark-field images	258,064	5×5	4	2	7, 4, 3, 6, 1, 2
Conductors on a substrate	4,740	3×3	5	2	3, 4, 7, 6, 5, 2, 1, 16, 14, 15

phase was less than half a minute. These numbers are merely given for the sake of completeness because our segmentation scheme is definitely tailored to run on a special processor, as pointed out in Section 2.3.

In the first experiment we addressed the task of segmenting the conducting copper portions in printed circuit board images. Numerous publications [Thibadeau 1985; Sanz and Jain 1986] deal with the problem of detecting defects on printed circuit boards. They typically assume that a binary image of the conducting parts exist. In practice, however, such binary images are not easily obtained, due to the fact that the gray-level distributions of the copper conductors and the board partially overlap and

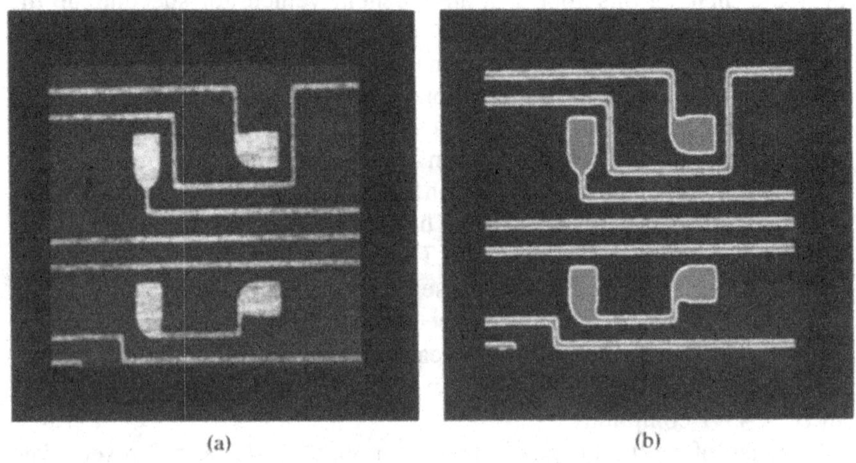

(a) (b)

FIGURE 7.3. (a) Training PCB image; (b) segmented image.

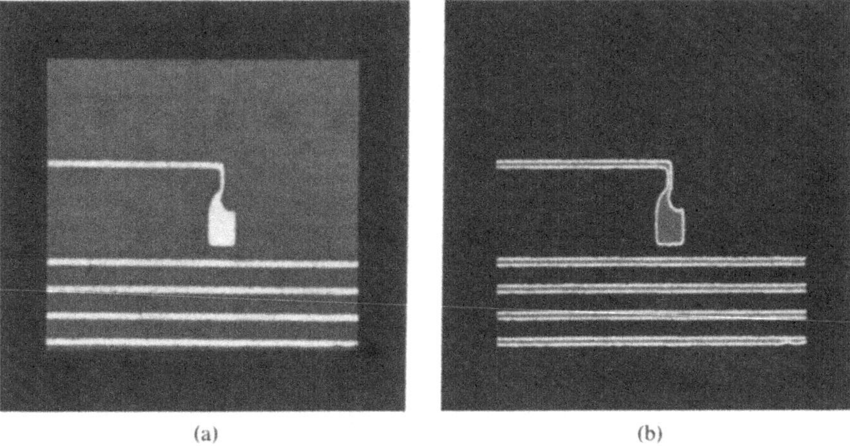

FIGURE 7.4. (a) Original PCB image; (b) segmented image.

therefore texture features should be applied to make the binarization more robust and more insensitive to changes in illumination. The system was trained on a small portion of one image and tested on five images. Figure 7.3(a) shows the original image from which the training area has been taken, and Figure 7.3(b) shows the corresponding segmentation result. Figures 7.4(a), (b), 7.5(a), (b), 7.6(a), (b), and 7.7(a), (b) show the originals and segmentation results. The borders of the conductors are considered a separate class since they have different statistics. They can later be merged with the main body of the conductor by using a lookup table before assignment of a final class tag. This way of treating each cluster as a

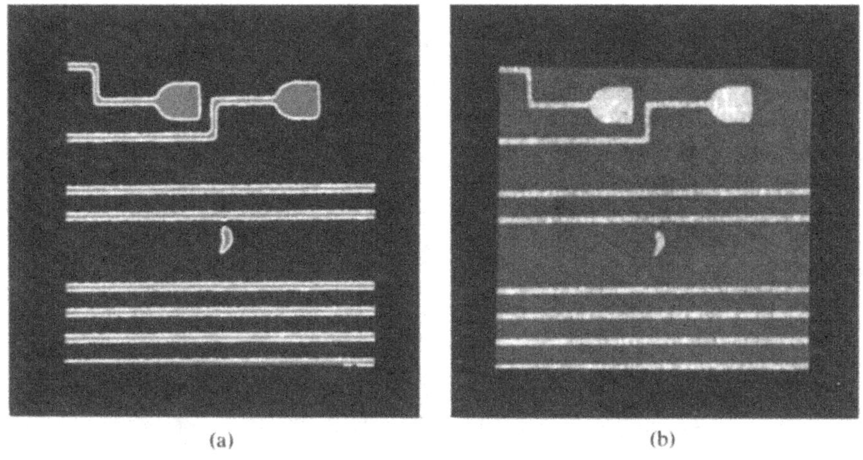

FIGURE 7.5. (a) Original PCB image; (b) segmented image.

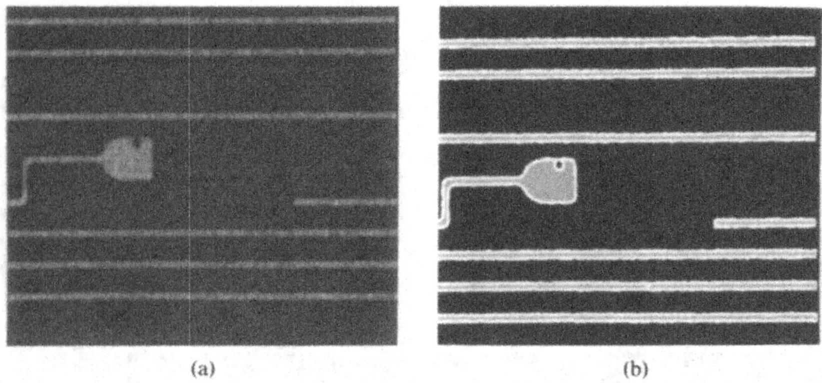

FIGURE 7.6. (a) Original PCB image; (b) segmented image.

separate subclass makes the derivation of decision surfaces easier and more robust.

The next example shows an X-ray image of plated through holes in multilayer boards. The system was trained on one periodicity element, including a defect that shows as a discontinuity in the cigar-formed bright areas. Figure 7.8(a) shows the original image and Figure 7.8(b) shows the segmented image. The defects are easily detected in the segmented image since they show as bright regions in the cigar shapes.

In another experiment we segmented the contaminations on the air-bearing surface of a disk head. For details regarding this inspection problem and possible solutions, see Petkovic et al [1986]. In this case, the system was trained on a portion of one head and tested on two images. Figures

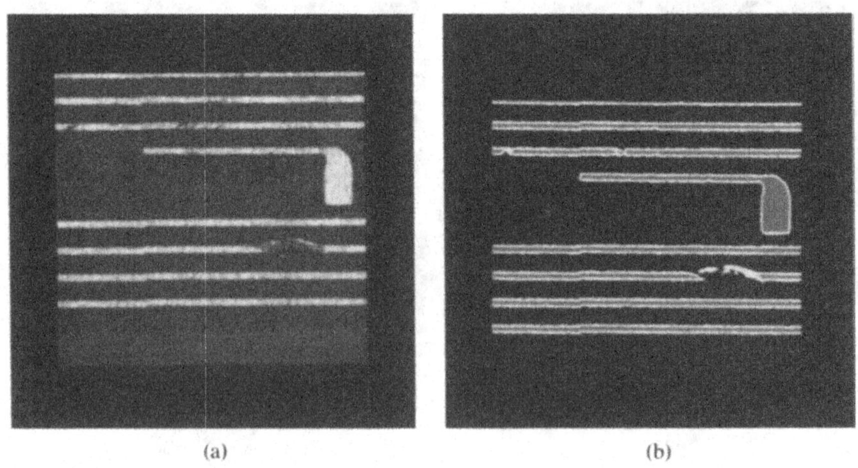

FIGURE 7.7. (a) Original PCB image; (b) segmented image.

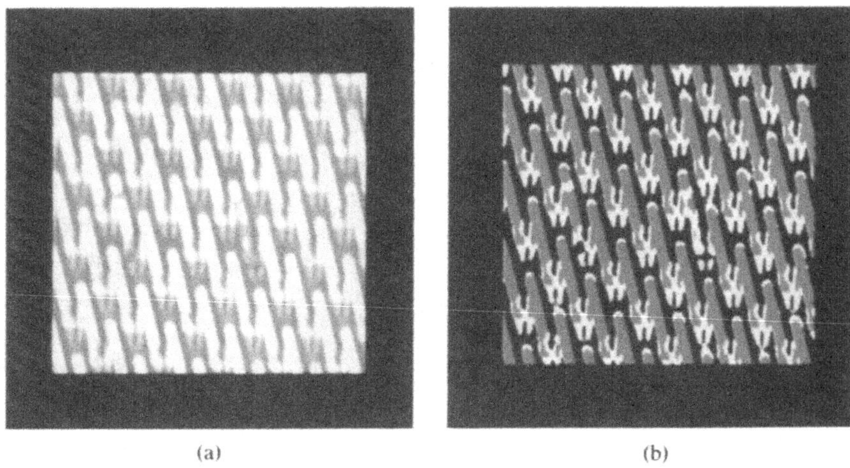

(a) (b)

FIGURE 7.8. (a) Training X–image; (b) segmented image.

7.9(a), (b), and 7.10(a), (b) show the original scenes and segmentation results. In this case the degree of contamination is easily determined by measuring the area of dark portions on the upper part of the head surface.

Figures 7.11(a) and (b) show a training dark-field microscopy image and its segmentation result. The goal was to segment surface contamination [Sanz et al. 1985]. We trained on the entire image and tested on this one and two other images. Figures 7.12(a), (b) and 7.13(a), (b) show the test originals and corresponding segmentation results, which match very well the results obtained using a specifically designed algorithm [Sanz et al.

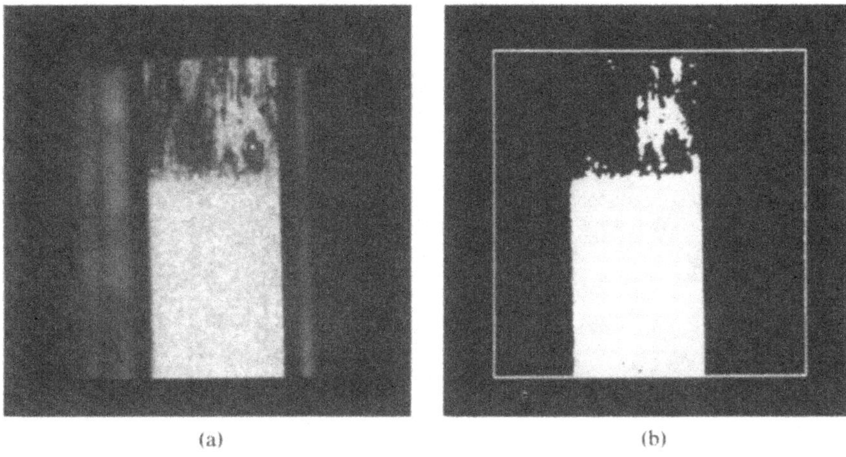

(a) (b)

FIGURE 7.9. (a) Training surface contamination image; (b) segmented image.

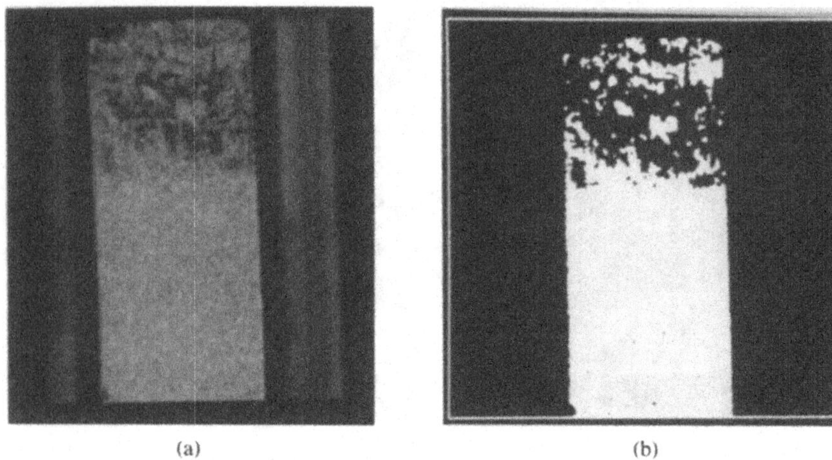

FIGURE 7.10. (a) Original surface contamination image; (b) segmented image.

1985]. In segmenting other air-bearing defects we also obtained results similar to the ones reported in Petkovic et al. [1986].

In the next experiment we segment shadows of solder balls on a semiconductor chip [Chastang and Koener 1983; Blanz et al. 1988]. We trained on three periodicity elements of one image and tested on four images. Figures 7.14 and 7.15 show four originals and the segmentation results. Defects are visible as slightly smaller blobs in the segmented images.

In the last experiment we tried to segment conductors on a substrate.

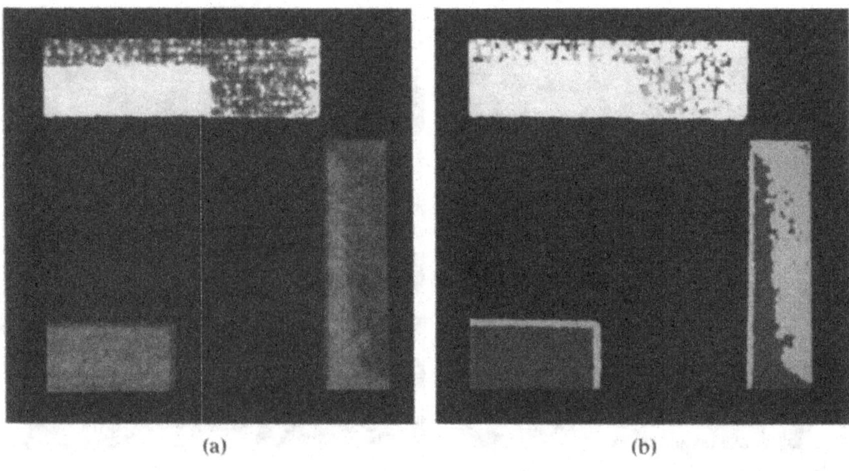

FIGURE 7.11. (a) Training contamination darkfield image; (b) segmented image.

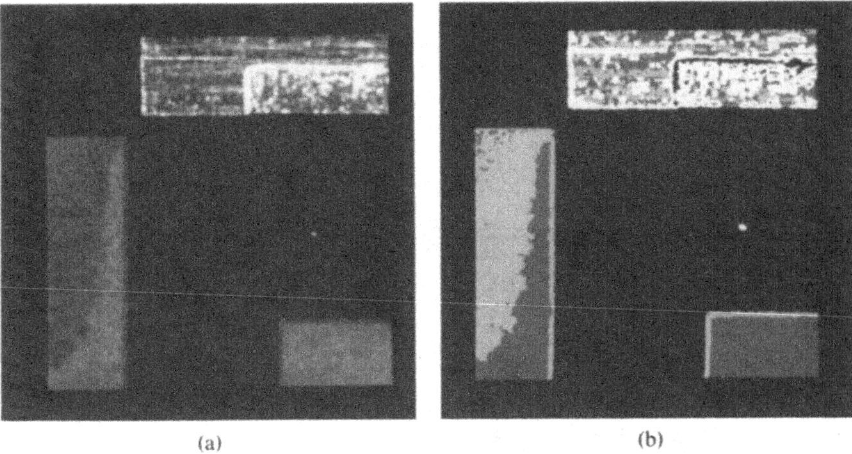

(a) (b)

FIGURE 7.12 (a) Original contamination darkfield image; (b) segmented image.

We trained on a small portion of the image and segmented the entire image. Figures 7.16(a) and (b) show the original and segmentation result.

These results show that for a large variety of different industrial machine vision applications the suggested approach yields reasonable segmentation results, which enables further intermediate-level processing. The performance in the biomedical field of applications has been demonstrated earlier [Blanz and Reinhardt 1982]. The applications from both fields together show the robustness and reliability of this approach. It is obvious that 20 pixel and texture features together with the built-in adaptability of the method and its hardware amenability provide enough flexibility to cover

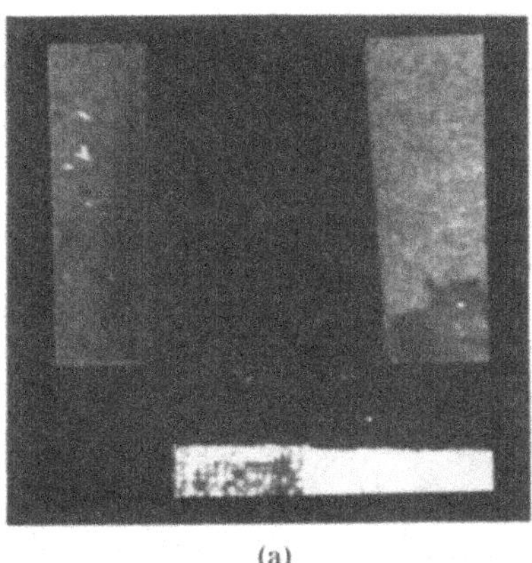

(a)

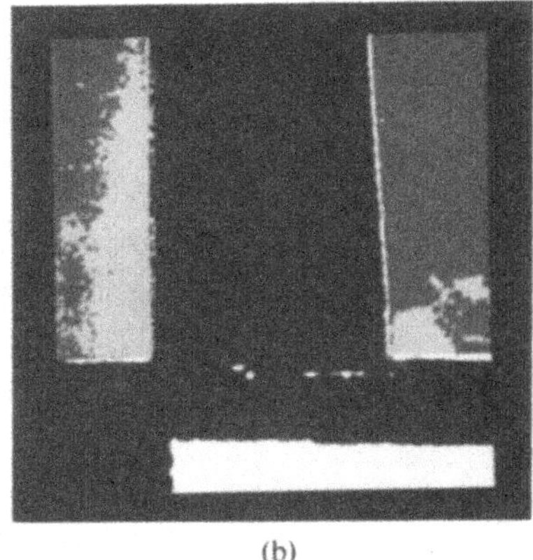

(b)

FIGURE 7.13. (a) Original contamination darkfield image; (b) segmented image.

FIGURE 7.14. Training, original, and segmented solder-ball images.

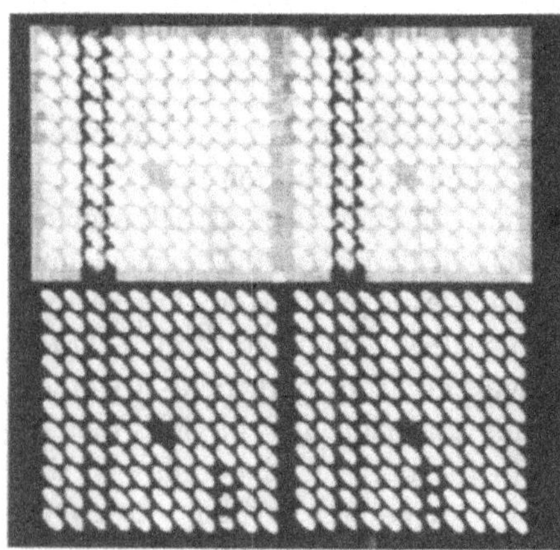

FIGURE 7.15. Training, original, and segmented solder-ball images.

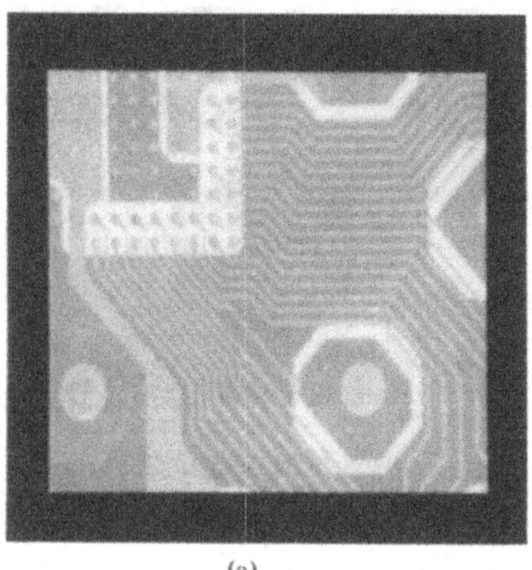

(a)

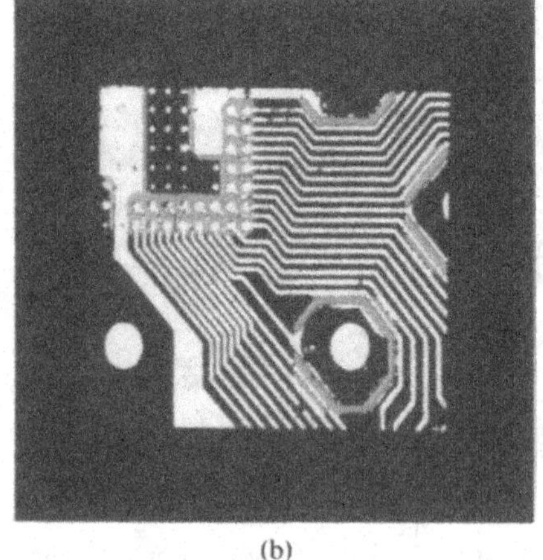

(b)

FIGURE 7.16. (a) Training conductor image; (b) segmented image.

a wider field of applications. In addition, this method requires minimal image-analysis expertise and can be performed in a very short time to lead to quick solutions. These characteristics seem to surpass most segmentation schemes proposed in the literature [Haralick and Shapiro 1985].

7 Conclusions

In this chapter, a pattern recognition–based image-segmentation scheme has been shown. This technique is based upon the fact that low-level segmentation can be accomplished, in certain environments, by providing image models in terms of multidimensional feature vectors. These models can be conveyed in such a way that all relevant knowledge gathered in a supervised learning phase is used in parallel in the segmentation process. This method uses a relatively large number of local image features and combines them optimally according to the scene knowledge acquired in a training phase by the use of a supervised classification procedure. A polynomial classifier is used to discriminate among classes. There are two important advantages to this approach. First, the need for expert-image analysis is minimized. Second, it is amenable to parallel pipeline hardware implementation. This characteristic makes the method very appealing as a building block for low-level image segmentation. Our extensive experimentation with many different industrial problems demonstrates that this approach is an effective and useful building block for applied computer vision systems.

References

Asada, H., and Brady, M. 1984. The curvature primal sketch. *IEEE Workshop on Computer Vision: Representation and Control.* (Apr.), IEEE, New York.

Ballard, D., and Brown, C. 1982. *Computer vision.* Englewood Cliffs, N.J.: Prentice-Hall.

Besl, P., Delp, E., and Jain, R. 1985. Automated visual solder joint inspection. *IEEE J. Robotics and Automation.* **1** (Mar.), 42–56.

Blanz, W.E., and Reinhardt, E.R. 1981. Image segmentation by pixel classification. *Pattern Recognition.* **13,** 4, 293–298.

Blanz, W.E., and Reinhardt, E.R. 1982. General approach to image segmentation. *Intl. Conference on Pattern Recognition.* (Munich, Oct.).

Blanz, W.E. 1983. Bildsegmentation durch Texturanalyse. Ph.D. dissertation. University of Stuttgart, Department of Electrical Engineering, Stuttgart, Germany.

Blanz, W.E. 1986. Feature selection and polynomial classifiers for industrial decision analysis. *IBM Research Report RJ 5242 (54242),* IBM, San Jose, Calif., July.

Blanz, W.E., Sanz, J.L.C., and Hinkle, E.B. 1988. Image analysis methods for solder ball inspection in integrated circuit manufacturing. *IEEE J. Robotics and Automation.* **4,** 2, 129–139.

Brice, C., and Fennema, C. 1970. Scene analysis using regions. *Artif. Intell.* **1** (Fall), 205–226.

Chastang, J.C., and Koener, R. 1983. Oblique viewing attachment for microscope. In *Proc. SPIE.* **339** (Apr.), 239–245.

Davis, L., and Rosenfeld, A. 1979. Some experiments in image segmentation by clustering of local feature values. *Pattern Recognition,* **11,** 1, 19–28.

Forgy, C., Gupta, A., Newell, A., and Wedig, R. 1984. Initial assessment of architectures for production systems. In *Proc. Natl. Conference on Artificial Intelligence.* (Aug.), 116–120.

Fountain, T.J. 1986. Array architectures for iconic and symbolic image processing. In *Proc. Intl. Conference on Pattern Recognition.* (Paris, Oct.), 24–33.

Fu, K.S., and Mui, J.K. 1981. A survey on image segmentation. *Pattern Recognition.* **13,** 1, 3–16.

Hanson, A., and Riseman, E. 1978. *Computer vision systems.* New York: Academic Press.

Haralick, R., and Watson, L. 1981. A facet model for image data. *Computer Graphics and Image Processing.* **15,** 2, 113–129.

Haralick, R. 1985. Computer vision theory: The lack thereof. In *Proc. 3d Workshop on Computer Vision: Representation and Control.* (Bellaire, Mich.), 113–121.

Haralick, R., and Shapiro, L. 1985. Image segmentation techniques. *CVGIP,* **29,** 1, 100–132.

Jain, A.K. 1986. Advances in statistical pattern recognition. In *Proc. NATO Advanced Study Institute on Pattern Recognition Theory and Applications.* NATO, Belgium (June).

Nazif, A.M., and Levine, M.D. 1984. Low level image segmentation: An expert system. *IEEE Trans. on Pattern Analysis and Machine Intell.* **PAMI-6,** (Sep.), 555–578.

Nevatia, R. 1982. Machine perception. Englewood Cliffs, N.J.: Prentice-Hall.

Niblack, W., and Blanz, W.E. 1986. A comparison of polynomial and parametric Gaussian maximum likelihood classifiers. *IBM Research Report, RJ 5418 (55369).* IBM, San Jose, Calif., Dec.

Pavlidis, T. 1986. A critical survey of image analysis methods. In *Proc. Intl. Conference on Pattern Recognition.* (Paris, Oct.), 502–511.

Petkovic, D., Sanz, J.L.C., Moidin, K., et al., 1986. An experimental system for disk head inspection. In *Intl. Conference on Pattern Recognition.* (Paris, Oct.).

Price, K. 1985. I've seen your demo; so what? In *Proc. 3d Workshop on Computer Vision: Representation and Control.* (Bellaire, Mich.), 122–124.

Rechenberg, I. 1973. Evolutionsstrategie—Optimierung technischer Systeme nach Methoden der biologischen Evolution. *Friedrich Frommann Verlag,* Stuttgart.

Rissanen, J. 1978. Modelling by shortest data description. *Automatica.* **14,** 5, 465–471.

Roberts, L. 1968. Machine perception of three-dimensional solids. In Tippett, J., et al. (eds.), *Optical and electro-optical information processing.* Cambridge, Mass.: MIT Press, 159–197.

Rosenfeld, A., and Kak, A. 1982. *Digital image processing.* New York: Academic Press.

Rosenfeld, A. 1984. Image analysis: Problems, progress and prospects. *Pattern Recognition.* **17,** 1, 3–12.

Ruetz, P., and Brodersen, R. 1986. A custom chip set for real-time image processing. *Proc. ICASSP.* (Tokyo).

Sanz, J.L.C., Merkle, F., and Wong, K.Y. 1985. Automated digital visual inspection with darkfield microscopy. *J. Opt. Soc. Amer.* **2,** 11 (Nov.), 1857–1862.

Sanz, J.L.C., and Jain, A.K. 1986. Machine vision methods for inspection of printed circuit boards and thick-film circuits. *J. Opt. Soc. Amer.* **3,** 9 (Sept.), 1465–1482.

Schuermann, J. 1977. Polynomklassifikatoren fuer die Zeichenerkennung. *R. Oldenbourg.* Munich, Vienna.

Stansfield, S. 1986. ANGY: A rule-based expert system for automatic segmentation of coronary vessels from digital subtracted angiograms. *IEEE Trans. on Pattern Analysis and Machine Intell.* **PAMI-8,** 2 (Mar.), 188–200.

Thibadeau, R. 1985. Automated visual inspection as skilled perception. *Vision 85,* Soc. Manuf. Eng., Detroit, Mich., Mar.

Thoussaint, G.T. 1974. Bibliography on estimation of misclassification. *IEEE Trans. on Inf. Theory.* **IT-20,** 4 (July), 472–479.

Appendix A

PROOF

$$MS^2 = \sum_m (\mathbf{y}^{(m)} - \mathbf{A}^T\mathbf{v}^{(m)})^T (\mathbf{y}^{(m)} - \mathbf{A}^T\mathbf{v}^{(m)})$$

$$MS^2 = \sum_m \text{trace} \left[(\mathbf{y}^{(m)} - \mathbf{A}^T\mathbf{v}^{(m)})(\mathbf{y}^{(m)} - \mathbf{A}^T\mathbf{v}^{(m)})^T \right].$$

Because of the basic vector arithmetic

$$(\mathbf{a} - \mathbf{b})(\mathbf{a} - \mathbf{b})^T = \mathbf{a}\mathbf{a}^T - \mathbf{a}\mathbf{b}^T - \mathbf{b}\mathbf{a}^T + \mathbf{b}\mathbf{b}^T,$$

we get

$$MS^2 = \sum_m \quad \text{trace} \left[(\mathbf{y}^{(m)}\mathbf{y}^{(m)^T}) - \mathbf{y}^{(m)}(\mathbf{A}^T\mathbf{v}^{(m)})^T - (\mathbf{A}^T\mathbf{v}^{(m)})\, \mathbf{y}^{(m)^T} + (\mathbf{A}^T\mathbf{v}^{(m)})\, (\mathbf{A}^T\mathbf{v}^{(m)})^T \right];$$

$$MS^2 = \sum_m \quad \text{trace}\, (\mathbf{y}^{(m)}\mathbf{y}^{(m)^T})$$

$$- \sum_m \quad \text{trace} \left[\mathbf{y}^{(m)}\, (\mathbf{A}^T\, \mathbf{v}^{(m)})^T + (\mathbf{A}^T\mathbf{v}^{(m)})\, \mathbf{y}^{(m)^T} \right]$$

$$+ \text{trace} \sum_m \quad (\mathbf{A}^T\mathbf{v}^{(m)})\, (\mathbf{A}^T\mathbf{v}^{(m)})^T. \tag{7.6}$$

As for arbitrary vectors **a** and **b**, it holds that

$$\mathbf{ab}^T = (\mathbf{ba}^T)^T$$

and therefore

$$\text{trace}(\mathbf{ab}^T) = \text{trace}(\mathbf{ba}^T),$$

and we get from equation (7.6)

$$MS^2 = \sum_m \text{trace}(\mathbf{y}^{(m)}\mathbf{y}^{(m)^T}) - 2\sum_m \text{trace}(\mathbf{A}^T\mathbf{v}^{(m)})\mathbf{y}^{(m)^T}$$
$$+ \text{trace} \sum_m (\mathbf{A}^T\mathbf{v}^{(m)})\,(\mathbf{A}^T\mathbf{v}^{(m)})^T;$$

$$MS^2 = \sum_m \text{trace}(\mathbf{y}^{(m)}\mathbf{y}^{(m)^T}) - 2\sum_m \text{trace}(\mathbf{A}^T\mathbf{v}^{(m)})\mathbf{y}^{(m)^T}$$
$$+ \text{trace} \sum_m (\mathbf{A}^T\mathbf{v}^{(m)})\,(\mathbf{v}^{(m)^T}\,\mathbf{A});$$

$$MS^2 = \sum_m \text{trace}(\mathbf{y}^{(m)}\mathbf{y}^{(m)^T}) - 2\,\text{trace}\,\mathbf{A}^T \sum_m (\mathbf{v}^{(m)}\mathbf{y}^{(m)^T})$$
$$+ \text{trace}\,\mathbf{A}^T \sum_m (\mathbf{v}^{(m)}\mathbf{v}^{(m)^T})\,\mathbf{A}. \tag{7.7}$$

$\mathbf{y}^{(m)}\,\mathbf{y}^{(m)^T}$ is a matrix that has only one element in the main diagonal, which is 1. All others are 0, therefore, if we sum over all M elements of the training set, we have the following

$$\sum_{m=1}^{M} \text{trace}(\mathbf{y}^{(m)}\mathbf{y}^{(m)^T}) = M.$$

Therefore equation (7.7) becomes

$$MS^2 = M - 2\,\text{trace}\,\mathbf{A}^T \sum_m (\mathbf{v}^{(m)}\mathbf{y}^{(m)^T}) + \text{trace}\,\mathbf{A}^T \sum_m (\mathbf{v}^{(m)}\mathbf{v}^{(m)^T})\mathbf{A}$$

or

$$S^2 = 1 + \frac{1}{M}\,\text{trace}\,\mathbf{A}^T \sum_m (\mathbf{v}^{(m)}\mathbf{v}^{(m)^T})\mathbf{A} - \frac{2}{M}\,\text{trace}\,\mathbf{A}^T \sum_m (\mathbf{v}^{(m)}\mathbf{y}^{(m)^T}), \tag{7.8}$$

and with that, equation (7.4) becomes

$$1 + \frac{1}{M}\,\text{trace}\,\mathbf{A}^T \sum_m (\mathbf{v}^{(m)}\mathbf{v}^{(m)^T})\mathbf{A} - \frac{2}{M}\,\text{trace}\,\mathbf{A}^T \sum_m (\mathbf{v}^{(m)}\mathbf{y}^{(m)^T}) \stackrel{!}{=} \min_{\mathbf{A}}.$$

This is a matrix equation, which is to be minimized. There are different ways to calculate the minimum of this with respect to **A**. One is to introduce $\Delta\mathbf{A}$ with

$$\forall_{\Delta\mathbf{A}}\; S^2(\mathbf{A} + \Delta\mathbf{A}) \geqslant S^2(\mathbf{A}). \tag{7.9}$$

Therefore, from (7.8), we get for S^2

$$S^2(\mathbf{A} + \Delta\mathbf{A}) = 1 + \frac{1}{M}\text{trace}(\mathbf{A} + \Delta\mathbf{A})^T \sum_m(\mathbf{v}^{(m)}\mathbf{v}^{(m)^T})\ (\mathbf{A} + \Delta\mathbf{A})$$

$$- \frac{2}{M}\text{trace}(\mathbf{A} + \Delta\mathbf{A}) \sum_m(\mathbf{v}^{(m)}\mathbf{y}^{(m)^T})$$

$$S^2(\mathbf{A} + \Delta\mathbf{A}) = 1 + \frac{1}{M}\text{trace}\mathbf{A}^T \sum_m(\mathbf{v}^{(m)}\mathbf{v}^{(m)^T})\mathbf{A}$$

$$+ \frac{1}{M}\text{trace}\Delta\mathbf{A}^T \sum_m(\mathbf{v}^{(m)}\mathbf{v}^{(m)^T})\Delta\mathbf{A}$$

$$+ \frac{1}{M}\text{trace}\mathbf{A}^T \sum_m(\mathbf{v}^{(m)}\mathbf{v}^{(m)^T})\Delta\mathbf{A}$$

$$+ \frac{1}{M}\text{trace}\Delta\mathbf{A}^T \sum_m(\mathbf{v}^{(m)}\mathbf{v}^{(m)^T})\mathbf{A}$$

$$- \frac{2}{M}\text{trace}\mathbf{A}^T \sum_m(\mathbf{v}^{(m)}\mathbf{y}^{(m)^T})$$

$$- \frac{2}{M}\text{trace}\Delta\mathbf{A}^T \sum_m(\mathbf{v}^{(m)}\mathbf{y}^{(m)^T}). \tag{7.10}$$

Because of basic matrix transformations,

$$\begin{aligned}\mathbf{D}^T\mathbf{a}\mathbf{a}^T\mathbf{E} &= (\mathbf{a}^T\mathbf{D})^T(\mathbf{E}^T\mathbf{a})^T \\ &= ((\mathbf{E}^T\mathbf{a})(\mathbf{a}^T\mathbf{D}))^T \\ &= (\mathbf{E}^T(\mathbf{a}\mathbf{a}^T)\mathbf{D})^T,\end{aligned}$$

and therefore

$$\text{trace}(\mathbf{D}^T\mathbf{a}\mathbf{a}^T\mathbf{E}) = \text{trace}(\mathbf{E}^T\mathbf{a}\mathbf{a}^T\mathbf{D}).$$

We get

$$\text{trace}(\Delta\mathbf{A}^T \sum_m \mathbf{v}^{(m)}\mathbf{v}^{(m)^T}\ \mathbf{A}) = \text{trace}(\mathbf{A}^T \sum_m \mathbf{v}^{(m)}\mathbf{v}^{(m)^T}\ \Delta\mathbf{A}),$$

and hence equation (7.10) becomes

$$S^2(\mathbf{A} + \Delta\mathbf{A}) = 1 + \frac{1}{M}\text{trace}\mathbf{A}^T \sum_m (\mathbf{v}^{(m)}\mathbf{v}^{(m)^T})\mathbf{A}$$

$$+ \frac{1}{M}\text{trace}\Delta\mathbf{A}^T \sum_m (\mathbf{v}^{(m)}\mathbf{v}^{(m)^T})\Delta\mathbf{A}$$

$$+ \frac{2}{M}\text{trace}\Delta\mathbf{A}^T \sum_m(\mathbf{v}^{(m)}\mathbf{v}^{(m)^T})\mathbf{A}$$

$$- \frac{2}{M}\text{trace}\mathbf{A}^T \sum_m(\mathbf{v}^{(m)}\mathbf{y}^{(m)^T})$$

$$- \frac{2}{M}\text{trace}\Delta\mathbf{A}^T \sum_m(\mathbf{v}^{(m)}\mathbf{y}^{(m)^T}).$$

So the inequality (7.9) becomes

$$
\begin{aligned}
1 &+ \frac{1}{M}\text{trace}\mathbf{A}^T \sum_m (\mathbf{v}^{(m)}\mathbf{v}^{(m)^T})\mathbf{A} \\
&+ \frac{1}{M}\text{trace}\Delta\mathbf{A}^T \sum_m (\mathbf{v}^{(m)}\mathbf{v}^{(m)^T})\Delta\mathbf{A} \\
&+ \frac{2}{M}\text{trace}\Delta\mathbf{A}^T \sum_m (\mathbf{v}^{(m)}\mathbf{v}^{(m)^T})\mathbf{A} \\
&- \frac{2}{M}\text{trace}\mathbf{A} \sum_m (\mathbf{v}^{(m)}\mathbf{y}^{(m)^T}) \\
&- \frac{2}{M}\text{trace}\Delta\mathbf{A} \sum_m (\mathbf{v}^{(m)}\mathbf{y}^{(m)^T}) \\
\geqslant 1 &+ \frac{1}{m}\text{trace}\mathbf{A}^T \sum_m (\mathbf{v}^{(m)}\mathbf{v}^{(m)^T})\mathbf{A} \\
&- \frac{2}{M}\text{trace}\mathbf{A}^T \sum_m (\mathbf{v}^{(m)}\mathbf{y}^{(m)^T})
\end{aligned}
$$

$$
\begin{aligned}
&\frac{2}{M}\text{trace}\Delta\mathbf{A}^T \sum_m (\mathbf{v}^{(m)}\mathbf{v}^{(m)^T})\mathbf{A} \\
&\quad + \frac{1}{M}\text{trace}\Delta\mathbf{A}^T \sum_m (\mathbf{v}^{(m)}\mathbf{v}^{(m)^T})\Delta\mathbf{A} - \frac{2}{M}\text{trace}\Delta\mathbf{A} \sum_m (\mathbf{v}^{(m)}\mathbf{y}^{(m)^T}) \geqslant 0
\end{aligned}
$$

$$
\begin{aligned}
&\frac{1}{M}\text{trace}\Delta\mathbf{A}^T \sum_m (\mathbf{v}^{(m)}\mathbf{v}^{(m)^T})\Delta\mathbf{A} \\
&\quad + \frac{2}{M}\text{trace}\left[\Delta\mathbf{A}\left(\sum_m (\mathbf{v}^{(m)}\mathbf{v}^{(m)^T})\mathbf{A} - \sum_m (\mathbf{v}^{(m)}\mathbf{y}^{(m)^T}\right)\right] \geqslant 0. \qquad (7.11)
\end{aligned}
$$

Because of

$$
\begin{aligned}
\text{trace}\Delta\mathbf{A}^T \sum_m (\mathbf{v}^{(m)}\mathbf{v}^{(m)^T})\Delta\mathbf{A} &= \sum_m \text{trace}\Delta\mathbf{A}^T\, \mathbf{v}^{(m)}\, \mathbf{v}^{(m)^T}\Delta\mathbf{A} \\
&= \sum_m \text{trace}(\Delta\mathbf{A}^T\mathbf{v}^{(m)})\,(\mathbf{v}^{(m)^T}\Delta\mathbf{A}) \\
&= \sum_m \text{trace}(\Delta\mathbf{A}^T\mathbf{v}^{(m)})\,(\Delta\mathbf{A}^T\mathbf{v}^{(m)})^T \\
&= \sum_m (\Delta\mathbf{A}^T\mathbf{v}^{(m)})^T\,(\Delta\mathbf{A}^T\mathbf{v}^{(m)}) \\
&= \sum_m |\,\Delta\mathbf{A}^T\,\mathbf{v}^{(m)}\,|^2 \geqslant 0.
\end{aligned}
$$

Thus, the first expression in equation (7.11) is always nonnegative, whatever $\mathbf{\Delta A}$ we choose, and so inequality (7.11) holds for arbitrary $\mathbf{\Delta A}$ if and only if the expression in bold parenthesis vanishes, or

$$\sum_m (\mathbf{v}^{(m)}\mathbf{v}^{(m)^T})\mathbf{A} - \sum_m (\mathbf{v}^{(m)}\mathbf{y}^{(m)^T}) = 0.$$

This concludes the proof. □

Appendix B

PROOF. In this proof we follow the argumentation of Schuermann [1977]. Assume a vector $\mathbf{e}$, the components of which are all 1, that is,

$$\mathbf{e} = (1\ 1\ \cdots\ 1)^T.$$

With this vector the condition to be proven reads

$$\mathbf{e}^T\mathbf{d} = \sum_{c=1}^{C} d_c = 1. \tag{7.12}$$

Because of equation (7.2), we get

$$1 = \mathbf{e}^T\ \mathbf{A}^T\ \mathbf{v}.$$

We remember that

$$\mathbf{v} = (1\, f_1\, f_2\, \cdots f_1^2\, \cdots)^T$$

and write

$$\mathbf{v} = (1\ \mathbf{v}^{*T})^T.$$

According to that separation, we separate $\mathbf{A}$ in the row vector of the first line $\mathbf{a}_0^T$ and the rest of $\mathbf{A}$, which we call $\mathbf{A}^*$:

$$\mathbf{A} = \begin{pmatrix} \mathbf{a}_0^T \\ \mathbf{A}^* \end{pmatrix}.$$

With this we get

$$1 = \mathbf{e}^T\mathbf{a}_0 + \mathbf{e}^T\mathbf{A}^{*T}\mathbf{v}^*.$$

This is a sum of two parts, the first of which is independent of $\mathbf{v}^*$, the second is not. This sum is equal to 1 for all $\mathbf{v}^*$ if and only if

$$\mathbf{a}_0^T\mathbf{e} = 1$$

and

$$\mathbf{e}^T\mathbf{A}^{*T} = \mathbf{A}^*\mathbf{e} = 0$$

or if we take both conditions together

$$\mathbf{Ae} = \begin{pmatrix} 1 \\ \mathbf{0} \end{pmatrix}. \tag{7.13}$$

This is nothing but a reformulation of the initial condition. We have transformed a certain property of the decision vector **d** into a property of the matrix **A**, i.e., the sum of the elements of the first row of **A** is 1, the sum of the elements of all other rows is 0:

$$\sum_{c=1}^{C} a_{0c} = 1$$

and

$$\forall_{m \neq 0} \sum_{c=1}^{C} a_{mc} = 0.$$

If we multiply equation (7.13) by the invertible matrix $\Sigma(\mathbf{v}^{(m)}\mathbf{v}^{(m)^T})$, we get

$$\sum_m (\mathbf{v}^{(m)}\mathbf{v}^{(m)^T})\ \mathbf{A}\ \mathbf{e} = \sum_m (\mathbf{v}^{(m)}\mathbf{v}^{(m)^T}) \begin{pmatrix} 1 \\ \mathbf{0} \end{pmatrix}$$

and from that, because of equation (7.5), we get

$$\sum_m (\mathbf{v}^{(m)}\mathbf{y}^{(m)^T})\ \mathbf{e} = \sum_m (\mathbf{v}^{(m)}\mathbf{v}^{(m)^T}) \begin{pmatrix} 1 \\ \mathbf{0} \end{pmatrix}.$$

If we again write **v** as $\begin{pmatrix} 1 \\ \mathbf{v}^* \end{pmatrix}$, we get

$$\begin{pmatrix} \sum \mathbf{y}^{(m)^T} \\ \sum (\mathbf{v}^{*(m)}\mathbf{y}^{(m)^T}) \end{pmatrix} \mathbf{e} = \begin{pmatrix} 1 & \sum \mathbf{v}^{*(m)T} \\ \sum \mathbf{v}^{*(m)} & \sum (\mathbf{v}^{*(m)}\mathbf{v}^{*(m)T}) \end{pmatrix} \begin{pmatrix} 1 \\ \mathbf{0} \end{pmatrix}. \tag{7.14}$$

Because of the inherent properties of the target vector **y** it is obvious that

$$\mathbf{y}^T\mathbf{e} = 1$$

in all cases. Therefore we get easily from equation (7.14)

$$\begin{pmatrix} 1 \\ \sum\limits_m \mathbf{v}^{*(m)} \end{pmatrix} = \begin{pmatrix} 1 \\ \sum\limits_m \mathbf{v}^{*(m)} \end{pmatrix}$$

and therefore the initial condition equation (7.12) is fulfilled. (Note that unlike probabilities the components of **d** are not restricted to the interval [0,1].) □

This result allows us to reduce the amount of computational effort, because for C classes we have only to evaluate $C - 1$ polynomials, as the last component of **d** is given as the difference between 1 and the sum of all other components of **d**.

8
Computer Vision: Algorithms and Architectures

CONCETTINA GUERRA AND STEFANO LEVIALDI

ABSTRACT: Ever since computers were used for pattern recognition, image processing, and more generally for vision, a number of special-purpose algorithms and architectures have been developed. As new architectures reached the construction stage, different classes of algorithms emerged in order to produce more effective and efficient solutions to the new, heavy burdens of color and moving images, stereo vision, and real-time performance. The multiprocessor machines (including a variety of interconnection patterns, memory organization, control structures, and input-output management) stimulated algorithm designers to develop suitable data structures, choice of appropriate primitive operations, adequate sequencing of input image data, use of concurrency of local computations, etc. This chapter presents a review of some basic image-processing algorithms implemented on different multiprocessor machines. Algorithms for connected component labeling, line detection, and stereo matching are considered on the systolic, mesh, tree, and pyramid machines. The analysis and evaluation of these algorithms may hopefully lead to their use in real applications in a cost-effective way.

1 Introduction

Algorithms for image processing are becoming a crucial point in obtaining an efficient performance from a vision system that must work in a real environment where time, noise, and quantity of data may prevent it from being cost-effective. Both low- and high-level vision tasks require suitable algorithms, possibly well matched to the new computer architectures, generally making use of multiple processor computers to enable program execution at the fastest possible rate. A number of discussions and papers have dealt with the general problem of which algorithm is better suited to which architecture and how to evaluate nonconventional architectures with benchmarks [Uhr et al. 1986] and there is no single way to standardize and test algorithm-architecture performance (in terms of time-dependency, machine cycle, processed pictorial data throughput, etc. [Cantoni et al. 1983]).

For these reasons, most authors have decided to categorize the classes of algorithms (a) using a neighborhood classification (point-local-global operation); (b) using statistics (operations involving few elements–all elements); and (c) using the number and complexity of required operations (single, multiple, arithmetic, logical, set, or others). Generally, after one classification is chosen, one task per class is selected and the best algorithm to achieve this task is evaluated on a number of architectures. The architectures range from the classical Von Neumann model (one single processor) to those having more processors operating in SIMD, multi-SIMD, and MIMD mode. In turn, the SIMD mode can be further broken down into other architectures, like systolic, meshes, and trees.

The tasks we have selected to give a broad view of the problems (and advantages) obtained by restructuring the algorithms for particular architectures are the detection of connectivity, shape, and depth. There is an open discussion as to how high- and low-level vision should be defined (some insight may be gained from Duff [1986]) but a consensus may be reached in considering the first two tasks belonging to low-level vision and the last one more likely as a high-level vision task.

The first task, connectivity analysis, is a classical one related to the fact that it is in general impossible to have only the interesting objects present in the image and therefore the connected components extraction is mandatory. The second uses the Hough approach, capitalizing on the power of having a relevant number of processors; the third one, essentially a matching problem, may be conveniently solved by overlapping the scanning process to the computation as we will see later.

It is in general difficult to reformulate sequential algorithms in view of the different computational structures, as already shown by some authors [Duff 1986; Uhr et al. 1986]. The communication issue (between processors and memory and between processors) of the task may become so important in the overall time evaluation as to predominate with regard to the computation time so that a well-designed algorithm should allow the data to reach the available processors. Unfortunately, not all algorithms are so regular in terms of their operations on data as to enable synchronized data feeding (all processors receiving data at the same time), and when this condition of regularity is not met, delays are inevitable.

2 Connectivity Analysis

Separating objects from background is a fundamental operation in any vision system. Connectivity analysis has been suggested for this task since the 1960s [Rosenfeld and Pfaltz 1986] and has been widely used for industrial systems. The SRI vision module [Agin 1980] performs connectivity analysis first and then attaches a description to each extracted component in terms of such features as perimeter, area, moments of inertia, etc., to be used in the subsequent recognition step. The SRI module has been applied to a variety of problem domains, such as recognition of parts on a conveyor belt and robot manipulation.

We now describe three serial algorithms for labeling connected components in images; in the next section their parallel versions will be reviewed. Labels, usually integer numbers, are assigned to image pixels so that pixels belonging to the same connected component have the same label, and different components have distinct labels.

A simple approach [Rosenfeld and Pfaltz 1986] is based on a two-pass algorithm: During the first scan of the image, in a top-bottom left-to-right raster fashion, for each new assigned label, typically an integer, a propagation through its connected component is performed. Conflicting situations may arise in which a pixel can be given two different labels, since for a given row a new component may be discovered (and labeled), while in a later row a connected path between these components is revealed and therefore the second label should be replaced by the first one. Equivalence classes of labels are constructed and stored to be used in the second pass of the algorithm to disambiguate such conflicts: in the second scan of the image, each label is replaced with its smallest equivalent. This algorithm requires a large number of memory locations for storing equivalence classes, which is unacceptable in many cases.

An alternative approach [Lumia et al. 1983] consists of repeatedly scanning the image by alternating top-down and bottom-up scans: For each scan the label assigned to a pixel either remains unchanged or is updated according to the following rules.

Step 1 (top-down left-to-right scan). Assign to each nonzero pixel $a_{i,j}$ a new label $l_{i,j}$.

Step 2 (top-down left-to-right scan). Assign to each pixel a label that is the minimum of the set of labels including the pixel's own label and the nonzero labels of neighboring pixels already examined in the same scan sequence.

Step 3 (bottom-up right-to-left scan). Like step 2 with a different scan sequence, bottom-up instead of top-down.

A cycle is made by steps 2 and 3 and is iterated until no changes occur in the labeling of the image with a number of iterations dependent upon the contents of the image. After termination of the algorithm, each object will have a unique label.

In Lumia et al. [1983] the results of applying this algorithm to real images are presented and compared with other strategies. It is shown that as the image size increases this algorithm works better than the classical algorithm

[Rosenfeld and Pfaltz 1986]. However, the number of iterations, and consequently, the CPU time are still quite high and a function of the tortuosity of the image.

A serial-labeling algorithm has been presented [Selkow 1972; Kung and Webb 1986; Schwartz et al. 1987] that labels an image in only two scans (top-down and bottom-up) and yet uses few memory locations for storing equivalence classes. The algorithm works in two passes. The first pass processes the image in raster-scan fashion and produces a partially labeled image and a label-mapping table for each row. The partially labeled image has the property that in any processed row any two pixels that can be connected using paths above or on the row are assigned the same label. The label-mapping table translates labels on one row into labels on the previous row that correspond to the same connected component. During the second scan the image is processed in reverse order to obtain the final labeling. Information from the label-mapping table is crucial to this final step.

2.1 The Mesh Architecture

Consider an $n \times n$ mesh with processors connected by the nearest neighbor connection (4 or 8 neighbors). Assume an image size $n \times n$ so that each processor contains a single image pixel. A simple algorithm for connected component extraction is based on propagation. Each 1-pixel is labeled initially with a different value and, at each new iteration, each pixel is labeled with the minimum value of the labels of its adjacent pixels. The algorithm stops if no changes have occurred during the last iteration. In general, the algorithm can be set to run in $O(d + c)$ time, where d is the diameter of the largest connected component, i.e., the maximum length of a path between any pair of pixels in the component, and c is the communication diameter of the machine, i.e., the maximum interprocessor distance. Unfortunately, in the worst case the diameter of a component can be $O(n^2)$ as for an image of a spiral. It can be expected, however, that for industrial applications this worst case is very unlikely, and that the diameter of an object in an image is $O(n)$.

An optimal algorithm for a mesh that always runs in $O(n)$ can be designed using the well-known technique of divide-and-conquer. This technique has been applied to the connectivity problem on images in Nassimi and Sahni [1980] and Stout [1985]. The algorithm works as follows:

1. Assign each pixel a different label.
2. If the image size is 1×1 then stop. Otherwise, recursively divide the image into quadrants and label each quadrant independently.
3. Merge information from adjacent quadrants by forming equivalent classes of labels at the boundaries between the quadrants. Propagate equivalent classes to individual quadrants to adjust the labels.

It has to be noticed, however, that in order to obtain this performance the machine should be able to individually mask PEs so that only certain PEs would execute certain instructions (for example, only the PEs at the boundaries between quadrants operate during step 3 on adjacent pixels to form equivalent classes). Such masking capability is, for example, available on the MPP and on most existing meshes [Batcher 1980].

The connected component algorithm based on Levialdi's shrinking algorithm also requires $O(n)$ time but appears to be more practical than the divide-and-conquer algorithm. It is shown in Sanz et al. [1987] that the shrinking-based algorithm requires $15n \log n + 3n$–bit operations while the other algorithm requires $1760n \log n$ bit operations. The only drawback of the algorithm is that $O(n)$ space is required at each PE. The shrinking-based algorithm consists of two stages (a backward and a forward one); during the forward one in $2n$ steps every component is shrunk to a single isolated 1-element (at, say, the left bottom corner of the rectangle circumscribing the object).

This process is achieved by the sequential application of parallel local operations on a 2 by 2 neighborhood of every pixel. The new value of pixel $a_{i,j}$ is obtained from the previous values of neighboring pixels according to the following expression:

$$a_{i,j} = h[h[a_{i,j-1} + a_{i,j} + a_{i+1,j} - 1] + h[a_{i,j} + a_{i+1,\, j-1} - 1]]$$

where $h[t] = 0$ for $t \leqslant 0$, $h[t] = 1$ for $t > 0$.

At any step t of the process, the current value of pixel $a_{i,j}$ is stored in the local memory of the PE at address t to be used in the backward phase. In this phase, image pixels are labeled using the results of the previous phase in the reverse order. At any step t, with t from $(2n - 1)$ to 0, an isolated 1-pixel generates a new label, which is thereafter propagated to adjacent pixels. Precisely each PE (i,j) which has a 1 at time t obtains a label from the PEs (i,j), $(i + 1,j)$, $(i, j - 1)$, and $(i + 1, j - 1)$ if they have a 1 in memory location $t + 1$.

2.2 The Pyramid Architecture

Consider a pyramid with an $n \times n$ mesh as its base and $\log_2 n$ levels of meshes. A generic PE at level k is connected to four PEs at the same level, four children at level $k - 1$, and one parent at level $k + 1$. Pyramids for image processing are described in Cantoni and Levialdi [1986]. A number of image-processing algorithms have been designed for pyramids and others for mesh computers have been adapted to pyramids with slightly better performance. An algorithm for connected-component determination was given in Tanimoto [1982]; this algorithm is based on propagation detecting convex objects in $O(n)$ time by successively labeling neighbors of already labeled pixels. Another algorithm with time performance of $O(\sqrt{n})$ for all the components in the image is presented in Miller and Stout

[1987]. Similarly to the second mesh algorithm, it uses the divide-and-conquer technique but is significantly faster. The computations for the divide-and-conquer solutions proceed in a bottom-up fashion. The first stage involves analyzing and labeling subimages of size 4^3 using a standard connected components algorithm on squares of PEs of size 4^3. For any pair of neighboring 1-pixels on the boundaries of such subimages, a data record containing the current labels of the two pixels is created to be used in the next stage of the processing. Stage i, with i from 1 to log$n$, labels subimages of size 4^{3+i} using square blocks of PEs of size $4^{3+\lceil i/2 \rceil}$ at level $\lfloor i/2 \rfloor$. The data records to be used at stage i (generated at stage $i - 1$) are already available to the PEs at level $\lfloor i/2 \rfloor$ or must be moved from the previous level depending on whether i is odd or even, respectively. In either case, a generic PE will contain at any given stage, at most, one data record. After log$n$ stages, all the correct labels are available at some level of the pyramid and need to be moved back to the base. Not all pyramid levels are involved, i.e., only up to level (1/2)$\log_2 n$. The overall time for this operation is $O(\sqrt{n})$.

2.3 The Systolic Array Architecture

We describe now the systolic implementation of the Lumia et al. [1983] algorithm (based on alternate top-bottom scanning) presented in the previous section. This algorithm can be implemented on an array of linearly connected PEs whose size is equal to the size of the considered neighborhood $S_{i,j}$ of a pixel $a_{i,j}$.

The flow of data through the systolic array is similar to that required by other serial local operators [Guerra 1986]; i.e., input and output of data move along opposite directions, one processor every other cycle.

Generally, the set $S_{i,j}$, over which the value of label $1_{i,j}$ is minimized, consists of the values of the labels of adjacent pixels. However, if a sufficiently large number of cells is available, the set $S_{i,j}$ can be extended to a larger neighborhood of $a_{i,j}$ without significantly increasing the throughput of the array, reducing at the same time the number of iterations.

For example, $S_{i,j}$ can be chosen to contain all the pixels on the previous row to the right of $a_{i,j}$ plus $a_{i-1,j}$ and $a_{i-1,j-1}$. Since in this case $S_{i,j}$ also includes pixels not adjacent to the examined pixel labeled $1_{i,j}$, a preliminary test must be done for each value $1_{r,s}$ in $S_{i,j}$ to ensure that there is a connected path consisting of only 1-elements between the two pixels in the original image. Only if this condition is satisfied the value $1_{r,s}$ will enter in the computation of $1_{i,j}$. With a preliminary scan of the image, to each pixel $a_{i,j}$ is assigned a pair of integers $r_{i,j}$ and $t_{i,j}$ representing the number of 1s on row i to the right and to the left of $1_{i,j}$, respectively. Thus at each step, to check a possible connection between labels $1_{i,j}$ and $1_{r,s}$, a single comparison between column positions s-j and r-i is needed. The systolic algorithm thus consists of three steps.

Step 1 (compute $r_{i,j}$ for each pixel). The image pixels (input data) traverse the array and count the number of 1s to the right of each pixel.

Step 2 (compute $t_{i,j}$ for each pixel). Similar to the previous step, except that the 1s to the left of each pixel are counted.

Step 3 (compute $1_{i,j} = \min_{S i,j} (l_{i,j}, 1_{r,s})$). This step is iterated until no changes occur.

A parallel implementation of the third algorithm for connected component labeling is considered in Kung and Webb [1986] on the WARP machine, a linear systolic array built at CMU that consists of powerful programmable cells. The input image is partitioned into equal-sized horizontal regions that are labeled independently. Each cell in the array executes the serial labeling algorithm presented earlier. At the end of this step, all partial outputs have to be recombined. The cost of recombining the outputs is negligible, thus a considerable speed-up is obtained.

A similar strategy was proposed in Fisher and Highnam [1985] for a scanline array processor, a linear array of cells, each associated with a single pixel on a scan line. The image is divided into vertical strips that are labeled independently. Information from separated strips is combined in the same way as between regions within a strip.

In conclusion, elegance and practicality favor the first algorithm for connected components mentioned in the discussion, i.e., Rosenfeld and Pfaltz [1986].

3 The Hough Transform

The Hough transform [Hough 1962; Ballard 1981; Duda and Hart 1972] is a powerful technique for the detection of lines and, more generally, curves in an image. Although computationally intensive it is very useful when, as in the case of industrial applications, other techniques fail due to the amount of noise. The method consists of a preliminary conversion of the cartesian space into a new parameter space. A line can be parameterized by two values θ and ρ according to the following expression:

$$\rho = x \cos \theta + y \sin \theta \tag{8.1}$$

The parameter space is quantized into "accumulator" cells (θ_i, ρ_j), $i = 1, \ldots, k; j = 1, \ldots, m$. Boundary pixels (x,y) in the image space, which are determined by standard edge-detection techniques, "vote" for the parameter values of possible lines passing through them: the θ- and ρ-values satisfying equation (8.1) are computed so that the contents of the corresponding cells in the accumulator array are incremented.

After all boundary pixels have been treated, the cell with most votes is found. Thus, the Hough transform consists of two steps: (1) incrementing the contents of the cells in the accumulator array, and (2) determining the cell containing the maximum value in the accumulator array. We denote by:

$k \times m$ the size of the accumulator array.
b the number of boundary pixels.
v number of votes of each pixel.
h^2 the size of the image array.

The sequential implementation of this algorithm requires $O(km + bv)$. Because of the heavy computation requirements, a number of different implementations on multiprocessor machines have been proposed for the Hough transform. Despite the global nature of the operations involved in such a transform, the algorithm is amenable to an optimal implementation on a mesh that only requires linear time in terms of the dimension h of the image. Such implementation has been independently obtained by Guerra and Hambrusch [1987] and Sanz et al. [1987].

In the following, we first give a straightforward implementation on a mesh that uses a processor allocation scheme and data movements common to other image-processing operations, for instance, in histogramming. Similar allocation schemes and data movements are also used on a systolic array. Next, the linear time algorithm is reviewed. The algorithm, based on the idea of projections, makes intensive use of pipelining and involves only simple data movement operations so that it can also be expected to be practical.

3.1 The Mesh Architecture

An implementation of the Hough transform on a mesh was first proposed in Silberberg [1985]. Both the image array and the accumulator array reside in the processor array, one entry per PE or one block of data if the processor array is not large enough. For simplicity, the method described here is designed for one pixel (x_i, y_j) and one accumulator cell (θ_i, ρ_j) in PE (i,j). This mapping method, which consists of spreading the output data among the PEs is advantageous when, as in the case of the Hough transform, the output depends on the entire input data set.

Step 1 of the algorithm, the voting part, is carried out in the following manner: for a given value of θ_i (i = 1 to k) each PE evaluates expression (8.1), i.e., determines the ρ_j-value corresponding to its (x,y) values. Then the (θ_i,ρ_j) values are moved to the appropriate cells in the accumulator. This operation is similar to histogramming [Kushner et al. 1982]. It is obtained by first accumulating along the rows and then totaling the columns. Accumulating along the rows involves passing the ρ-values cyclically around the cells in a row. A slightly more complicated procedure computes the total along each column. Both phases require time $O(\max(k,h))$. After the votes for a particular θ have been accumulated in the appropriate row of the array, the process is repeated for the next θ-value.

As far as the second step, i.e., finding the maximum, this is obtained by first determining the maximum in each row (by a series of shifts) and then the maximum of maxima in a similar way. This operation requires time $O(s)$. A different implementation of the first step of the Hough transform on a mesh that results in a slightly different time complexity is now presented because of its similarity with the systolic implementation later. In both implementations boundary points move across the processing elements and accumulation is done along one dimension only. At each iteration the cells compute a ρ-value corresponding to their stored (x,y) and θ-value. Then histogramming along each row is obtained. After each iteration, the (x,y) values are shifted down by one position. Such implementation requires the addition of variable θ to each cell, which gives the θ-value of the cell in the Hough array. It is easily seen that the time requirement is $O(\max(km,h^2)$. Notice that in this time expression h^2 can be replaced by b if we assume that only boundary points are stored in the array.

3.2 The Systolic Array Architecture

The Hough transform can be cast into a systolic network that consists of two arrays: one that computes the ρ-values and the other that accumulates the (θ,ρ) values at the appropriate cells in the Hough array [Chuang and Li 1985]. Each cell in the second array corresponds to a pair (θ,ρ). Boundary points enter at the first cell of the first array and move along this array only. The time dependency for this step is $O(b + s)$. The determination of the maximum in the Hough array requires the addition of feedback and vertical links along one column. But it is not different from the one previously discussed.

3.3 The Tree Machine

Two algorithms are presented in Ibrahim et al. [1985] for the Hough transform on a tree machine. The first one is similar to the previous implementations on a systolic array and on a mesh, in that processing elements correspond to accumulator cells (θ,ρ) and boundary points move across the cells and increment a cell count when appropriate. Thus the tree implementation requires a number of processing elements equal to the array size $k \times m$ and a number of steps $O(b)$. Since the association between PEs and (θ,ρ) pairs is not obvious for a tree as in the previous array (a row of the accumulator array in each linear array of PEs), expression (8.1) needs to be evaluated at each node in the tree.

The second algorithm uses a completely different approach. Boundary points concurrently generate all the (θ,ρ) pairs and cast them into separate subtrees. Note that this implies redundancy in the accumulator data. The number of PEs is equal to bv, in which v is the number of votes by all boundary points. To determine the maximum in the accumulator array, time O (s log v) is spent. In fact, for each pair (θ,ρ), all the counts from different subtrees must be added. The interest of this implementation is essentially in proving the feasibility of the transform on such a machine rather than as a significant alternative to the previous machines. Little is gained from the tree structure organization in the first implementation, and the reduction of time complexity in the second implementation is at the expense of the number of processors.

3.4 The Hough Transform Based on Projection

It has been pointed out that the Hough transform can be regarded as based on projections of the digital image along many different directions [Rosenfeld and Kak 1982]. The projection of a picture in a direction θ is obtained by adding up the gray levels (or gradients) of the image along the family of lines perpendicular to θ. A straight line in the image is detected if one of these projections results in a high count or sum.

Based on this idea, an implementation of the Hough transform on a linear pipeline was presented in Sanz and Dinstein [1985]. A similar idea can be used on a scanline array processor [Fisher and Highnam 1985]. An optimal $O(h + k)$ implementation on a mesh is in Guerra and Hambrusch [1987] and Sanz et al. [1987]. This latter consists of tracing lines on a mesh in a pipelined fashion. The tracing of a line (θ,ρ) starts at a border processor crossed by the line, where a triple (θ,ρ,s) is created. The variable s counts the 1-pixels on the line and is initialized to zero. Such triple is then sent to the next adjacent processor crossed by the line. In $O(n)$ steps the final value s reaches the other border processor on the mesh crossed by the same line (either the adjacent side or the opposite side of the mesh, depending on the θ-value). All parallel lines are traced simultaneously. Assuming that no two parallel lines cross the same processor, this operation does not cause any congestion. Nonparallel lines are traced in separate stages. During a stage, the tracing of lines with θ-values in a 45° range is started at consecutive time steps from the same side of the mesh. In eight stages all lines can be traced, thus obtaining $O(n + k)$ time.

4 Stereo Analysis

The stereo vision problem is the recovery of 3-D depth information of a scene, given two-dimensional images taken from two different view points. The main difficulty in stereo vision is in the so-called "correspondence problem," which consists of identifying corresponding points in the two images. A fundamental problem is whether simple or complex descriptions extracted from the images are to be used as basic elements in the correspondence problem. Early experiments by Julesz on random-dot stereograms indicated that the human visual system is able to determine correspondences using primitive descriptions available at early stages of the processing. Based on those experiments, many algorithms have been developed that attempt to emulate the human visual system. Most of these algorithms, referred to as area-based algorithms, match small areas or windows surrounding pixels in the images and use a relaxation technique.

One of the most attractive features of relaxation for area-based stereo matching is the way it is naturally suited to parallel hardware. In the general formulation of relaxation labeling, the way processors of the network interact is completely determined by the relaxation; but there is still the problem of how to set up the configuration of processors and the interconnection network for a specific instance of the problem. In the area-based stereo matching, however, the configuration of processors and the corresponding interconnection is not dependent on the images, but is fixed and regular. Therefore an SIMD machine appears appropriate for such a task.

Another approach to vision uses features instead of areas as basic elements of the correspondence problem. This approach follows recent psychological experiments, which seem to suggest that it is necessary to match more complex descriptions. Edge-based techniques represent a move in that direction. An edge carries, along with position information, a number of other attributes such as contrast on both sides of the edge, slope, intensity, etc.

Feature-based matching offers the advantage of greater performance than area-based matching; there are obviously fewer feature points than pixels. However, when it comes to parallel implementation there are other factors that affect the performance of an algorithm. Regularity of data and computation is as important as input size. While windows are fixed in size and location, the position and orientation of edges or any other feature may change for different images. Thus, in the feature-based approach the data structures and data movement are dependent on the particular images being analyzed, and cannot be determined a priori.

A systolic algorithm for edge-based stereo, which uses dynamic programming was presented in Guerra and Kanade [1985]. The algorithm assumes that the left and right projective lines (epipolar lines) are coincident with the horizontal scan lines. This assumption drastically reduces the combinatorics involved in the correspondence process: The two-dimensional search space for the corresponding element of a given feature is limited to a one-dimensional space. The line-by-line matching translates into an optimal path finding on a 2-D search plane. Let (i_k, j_k) represent a node in the 2-D search plane, where i_k, j_k are indices of the left and right image edges on a scanline.

Let $d(R_{i,\,k-1}\, L_{j,k-1} -\, R_{i,k}\, L_{j,k})$ denote the cost of the segment from point $(R_{i,k-1},\ L_{j,k-1})$ to point $(R_{i,k},\ L_{j,k})$ according to a suitable measure. The optimal-cost path $g\ (R_{i,k}, L_{j,k})$ from the origin of the plane, involving the first k pairs of edges, can be defined as:

$$G(R_{i,k}, L_{j,k}) = \min[g(R_{i,k-1}, L_{j,k-1}) + d(R_{i,k-1}\ L_{j,k-1}, R_{i,k}\ L_{j,k})]. \quad (8.2)$$

In a systolic implementation of dynamic programming, the points on the search plane can be processed on a diagonal-by-diagonal basis starting from the origin. A structure, which implements the systolic algorithm, is an array of n linearly connected cells, where n is the number of edges in a scanline. Right features are preloaded to the cells and stay there throughout the computation. Data move through the array in two opposite directions: During the first phase of the algorithm, left input features move along the array from cell to cell starting from the leftmost cell. As they traverse the array, the partial scores are computed. When the last input data reaches the rightmost cell the final score is obtained at that cell. Then a backtracking procedure starts. By means of pointers that traverse the array from right to left the path is traced that produced the minimum score.

The overall performance of the systolic algorithm is improved by having the computations performed on a 2-D network of processors connected with vertical and diagonal links. The number of PEs in the network is dependent upon the number of neighboring points of a given point examined in equation (8.2). The computation steps involved in the matching process can be very efficiently pipelined along the processors of the network.

The systolic algorithm only solves the line-by-line matching. This procedure has to be followed by a process in which the partial results from individual pairs of scanlines are checked for consistency. Those corresponding points that violate some global criterion have to be removed and possibly replaced by other pairs of feature points. Baker [1982] suggested a procedure to solve the consistency problem. The procedure appears to be quite reliable; however it is unlikely to be as highly parallelizable as the line-by-line matching procedure.

Recently, a 3-D dynamic programming technique has been proposed to solve the matching problem simultaneously on scanlines and between scanlines [Otha and Kanade 1985]. Because of its regularity, the 3-D dynamic programming can be performed on a systolic machine in much the same way as the 2-D dynamic programming. However, the number of required processors makes it unattractive for real implementation.

5 Conclusions

Computer vision requires a number of sophisticated algorithms using different neighborhoods, primitive operations, iterative mechanisms, communication paths, and control structures so that no single multiprocessor architecture may turn optimal for achieving practical results. This explains the interest in studying, evaluating, and choosing the adequate computing system in terms of classes of tasks. The purpose of this work was to navigate through a selected set of representative algorithms on each architecture so as to give some insight into the general problem of multicomputer vision.

References

Agin, G.J. 1980. Computer vision systems for industrial inspection and assembly. *Computer*. **13,** 5, 11–20.

Ballard, D.H. 1981. Generalizing the Hough transform to detect arbitrary shapes. *Pattern Recognition*. **3,** 2, 11–22.

Baker, H.H. 1982. Depth from edge and intensity based stereo. Tech. Rep. AIM-347. Stanford University, Stanford, Calif.

Batcher, K.E. 1980. Design of a massively parallel processor. *IEEE Trans. on Comp*. **C-29,** 9, 836–840.

Cantoni, V., Guerra, C., and Levialdi, S. 1983. Evaluation of an image processing system. In Duff, M.J.B. (ed.), *Computer structures for image processing*. London: Academic Press.

Cantoni, V., and Levialdi, S., Eds. 1986. *Pyramidal systems for computer vision*. NATO ASI Series F, Vol 25, Heidelberg: Springer-Verlag.

Chuang, H.Y., and Li, C.C. 1985. A systolic array for straight line detection by modified Hough transform. In *IEEE Workshop on Computer Architecture for Pattern Analysis and Image Data Base Management*. IEEE, New York, 300–304.

Duda, R.O., and Hart, P.E. 1972. Use of the Hough transformation to detect lines and curves in pictures. *Commun. ACM*. **15,** 1.

Duff, M.J.B., Ed. 1986. *Intermediate level image processing*. New York: Academic Press.

Fisher, A.L., and Highnam, P.T. 1985. Real time image processing on scan lines array processors. In *IEEE Workshop on Computer Architectures for Pattern Analysis and Image Data Base Management*. IEEE, New York, 484–489.

Guerra, C., and Hambrusch, S. 1987. Parallel algorithms for line detection on a mesh. *J. Parallel and Distributed Computing*.

Guerra, C., and Kanade, T. 1985. A systolic algorithm for stereo matching. In *Proc. Conference on VLSI Algorithms and Architectures*. North-Holland.

Guerra, C. 1986. Systolic algorithms for local operations on images. *IEEE Trans. Comput*. **C-35,** 73–77.

Hough, P.V. 1962. Methods and means to recognize complex patterns. U.S. patent 3.069.654.

Ibrahim, H.A.H., Kender, J.R., and Shaw, D.E. 1985. The analysis and performance of two middle level vision tasks on a fine grained SIMD machine. In *Proc. IEEE Comp. Society Conference on Computer Vision and Pattern Recognition,* IEEE, New York, 248–256.

Kung, H.T., and Webb, J. 1986. Mapping image processing operations in a linear systolic machine. *Distrib. Comput*. 246–257.

Kushner, T., Wu, A.Y., and Rosenfeld, A. 1982. Image processing on MPP. *Pattern Recognition*. **15,** 3, 121–130.

Levialdi, S. 1972. On shrinking of binary patterns. *Commun. ACM.* **15,** 1, 7–10.

Lumia, R., Shapiro, L., and Zumiga, O. 1983. A new connected components algorithm for virtual memory computers. *Computer Vision, Graphics and Image Processing,* 287–300.

Miller, R., and Stout, Q. 1987. Data movement techniques for the pyramid computer. *SIAM J. Comput.* **16,** 1, 38–60.

Nassimi, D., and Sahni, S. 1980. Finding connected components and connected ones on a mesh connected parallel computer. *SIAM J. Comput.* 734–757.

Otha, Y., and Kanade, T. 1985. Stereo by intra and inter-scan line search using dynamic programming. *IEEE Trans. on PAMI.* **PAMI-7,** 7, 139–154.

Rosenfeld, A., and Kak, A. 1982. *Digital picture processing.* New York: Academic Press.

Rosenfeld, A., and Pfaltz, J.L. 1986. Sequential operations on digital picture processing. *J. ACM.* 471–494.

Sanz, J.L.C., Cypher, R.E., and Schneider, L. 1987. SIMD mesh array algorithms for image component labeling. TR-RJ5515. IBM.

Sanz, J.L.C., and Dinstein, I. 1985. A new approach to computing geometric features of digital objects for machine vision, image analysis and image processing: Algorithms in pipeline architectures. TR-RJ4561. IBM.

Schwartz, J., Sharir, M., and Siegel, A. 1987. An efficient algorithm for finding connected components in a binary image. Robotics Research TR-38. Courant Institute, New York University, New York.

Selkow, S. 1972. One pass complexity of digital picture processing. *J. ACM.* **19,** 283–295.

Silberberg, T.M. 1985. The Hough transform on the geometric arithmetic parallel processor. In *IEEE Workshop on Computer Architecture for Pattern Analysis and Image Database Management.* 387–391.

Stout, Q. 1985. Properties of divide and conquer algorithms for image processing. In *Proc. Workshop on Computer Architectures for Pattern Analysis and Image Database Management.* 203–209.

Tanimoto, S.L. 1982. Programming techniques for hierarchical parallel image processing. In Preston, K., Jr., and Uhr, L. (eds.), *Multicomputers and image processing.* New York: Academic Press.

Uhr, L., Preston, K. Jr., Levialdi, S., and Duff, M.J.B., Eds. 1986. *Evaluation for multicomputers for image processing.* New York: Academic Press.

9
Image Understanding Architecture and Applications

DAVID B. SHU, GREG NASH, AND CHARLES WEEMS

ABSTRACT: We describe in this chapter how various image-understanding problems can be mapped onto an architecture and associated implementation specifically designed for such problems. This parallel architecture, which has been funded as part of the DARPA Image Understanding Program, provides a hierarchical, heterogeneous structure to support the wide granularity of processing encountered in the image-understanding domain. In addition, it has an associative capability that allows rapid feedback of global and local summary information to facilitate knowledge-directed processing. We present several applications of this architecture, which span a considerable space of potential use.

1 Introduction

This chapter is intended to describe an image-understanding architecture (IUA) effort under way at Hughes Research Labs and the University of Massachusetts to build a prototype vision-specific parallel computer. The broad scope of this activity is reflected in this chapter, which is presented in the form of an overview. We use the term "image understanding" here to imply vision-related processing that depends heavily upon techniques from the domain of artificial intelligence (AI) to classify objects in an image. For example, various AI-related concepts, such as frames, rules, and evidential reasoning, combined with image-processing algorithms, can be mapped efficiently onto the IUA to provide a more robust vision capability. The goal of the IUA effort is a flexible, powerful machine that will support general vision research and provide a basis for the real-time processing needs of sensor-driven intelligent machines capable of adapting to their environment. Since the IUA details are available elsewhere [Weems et al. 1987], the purpose here will be to indicate the salient architectural features and how they can be efficiently applied to some representative image-understanding problems.

The IUA can be differentiated from other parallel vision architectures in that it is designed with the goal of being able to support the entire range of vision algorithms. Architecturally, this requires efficient mating of a numeric processor with a symbolic processor at a fine grain as shown in Figure 9.1. From the point of view of software, this can be viewed as combining an expert system with traditional image-processing techniques. This must be done in a way that minimizes the possibilities of serial bottlenecks during the course of the computation.

In Section 2, we provide a brief introduction to the IUA and its important features. Among these is the heterogeneous architecture, consisting of three different types of processing elements. For high-level, coarse-grained operations, there is an array of commercial microprocessors available. For medium grained, numerically intensive calculations, there is an array of arithmetic-oriented processors. Finally, for the processor per pixel and low-level symbolic operations, there is an array of fine-grained bit-serial type processors. These arrays are organized in a hierarchical fashion, in that a processor at any level has associated with it an array of elements beneath it. Since the types of computations associated with image understanding are typically performed in a hierarchical way with variable granularity in going from raw imagery to higher levels of abstractions, the basic IUA represents a very efficient match to the problem.

Another key feature of this architecture is its associative processing capability in the bit-serial array. Associative processing represents a significant departure from other signal/image-processing techniques in that it provides a way of processing data without data shuffling. Conventional techniques often rely on very fast preprocessors, such as convolution engines to do the fast pixel-level processing. This is appropriate only for the case where one knows a priori what operations should be applied to the data. If the results of lower-level processing are used to alter front-end processing, as, for example, in resegmentation or use of finer matched filters in selected areas, then the conventional approach is inefficient. The reason for this is that the host processor must inefficiently examine on a pixel-by-pixel basis the entire image to ascertain the results of preprocessing. After this, the entire image must be shuffled back to the preprocessor to fine-tune the processing; consequently, data bandwidth limitations slow the processing. Alternatively, associative techniques permit data to remain in place during processing. Information about the image, such as region statistics, can be gathered by queries to the entire pixel array. The IUA has special adder tree hardware to speed up this process. For a 512×512 per pixel processor system, the use of associative techniques provides an effective bandwidth of approximately 10^{11} bytes/sec.

The associative capabilities have been designed in such a way that they can be either local, e.g., to a region, or global. Both are necessary to efficiently process an image. For example, it is often necessary to obtain global statistics (e.g., histograms) on an image during the initial stages of computation. However, after the region segmentation process, only local

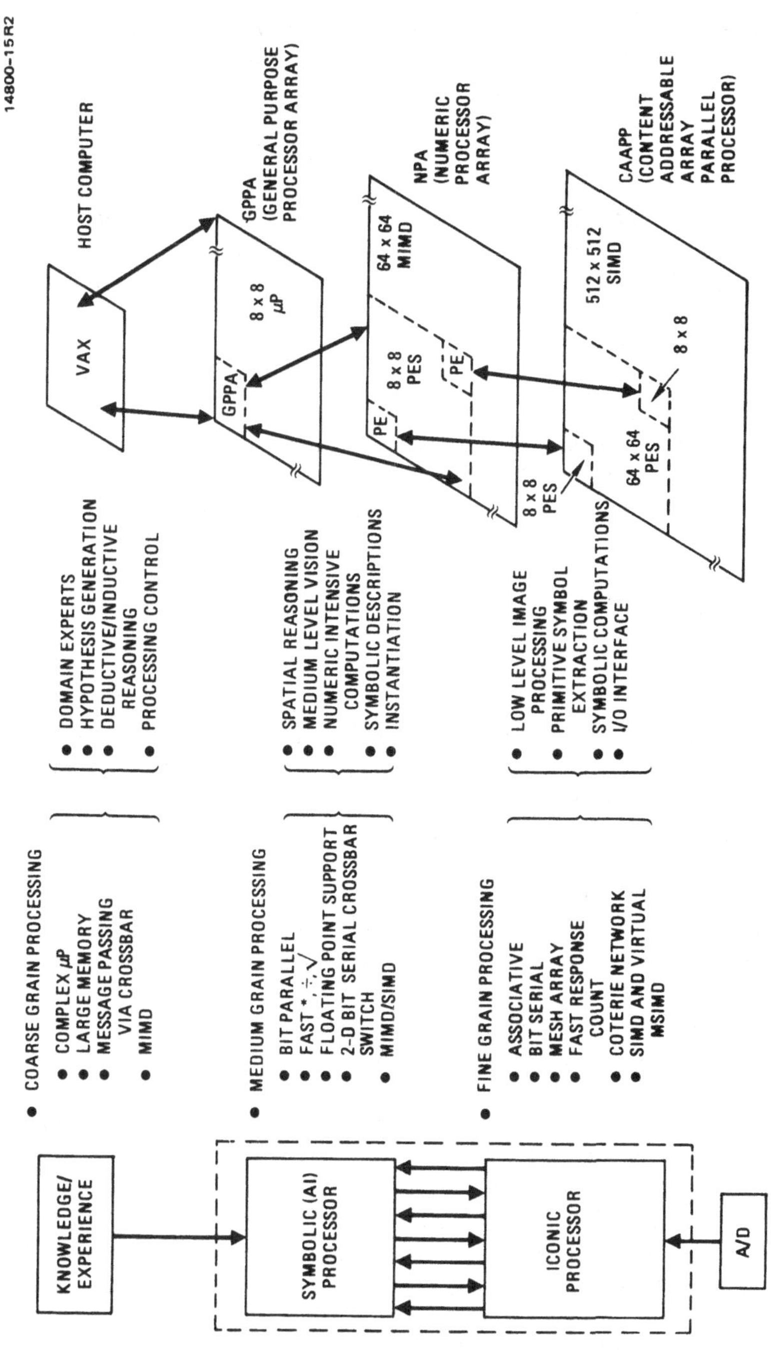

FIGURE 9.1. Image understanding architecture.

feedback might be necessary to process each region separately. In the bit-serial processor array these two modes of operation are equivalent to pure single-instruction, multiple data stream (SIMD) and multiple SIMD (MSIMD). As will be seen later, the latter capability has considerable implications for a variety of important algorithms.

Section 3 provides examples of how the IUA can be used from the point of view of high-level image-understanding software and computationally intensive algorithms. As an example of the former, we describe the parallel mapping of some representative AI-based object-recognition software onto the IUA. In order to illustrate the capability of the IUA for performing some complex algorithmic computations, mapping examples are provided for connected component labeling, large window convolutions, the Hough transform, and graph matching.

Section 4 addresses some future concerns, specifically the issue of a parallel Lisp-based language that would provide the appropriate language constructs to effectively abstract the IUA for the user, provide for coding efficiency and portability, and still maintain a conventional Von Neumann uniprocessor programmer's model of the IUA.

2 Architecture

2.1 Introduction

The basic IU architecture is a four-level hierarchical, heterogeneous parallel processor, organized as shown in Figure 9.1. Each level provides a processing capability different from the others; levels and communications have been chosen to provide for efficient parallel transfer of data between and within layers. At the lowest level is the 512 × 512 content-addressable array parallel processor (CAAPP) [Weems 1985], which is a mesh-connected array of bit-serial processing elements (PEs) having an associative or content-addressable parallel processing capability. At a level above this is a 64 × 64 numeric processor array (NPA), which provides a fast word parallel processing capability. The general purpose processor array (GPPA) level is an 8 × 8 array of powerful 32-bit microprocessors. Finally, at the highest level is the host computer, possibly a VAX or high-performance workstation. Ideally, the host would be a much higher performance version of one of of the GPPA PEs.

Control over the hierarchical architecture would occur through user programs residing in the host. The GPPA level would be available to run coarse-grained tasks, such as performing the functions of a domain expert, which might be called upon to analyze some aspect of an image region. Presumably there would be a large number of these domain expert routines running simultaneously in an MIMD mode. One of the GPPA PEs would also be assigned any task associated with system-level functions such as peripheral I/O. The GPPA PEs communicate via message passing rather than through shared memory. The interconnection scheme associated with this array is planned to be a crossbar switch with 32-bit parallel data paths. This interconnection network provides maximum flexibility for the message-passing paradigm of communications. Each GPPA PE can also communicate with other GPPA PEs using a global bus, although this would only be used in special cases.

The NPA level consists of a 64 × 64 array of processors suited to high throughput numeric computations, in particular floating point computations supported by parallel arithmetic units. Processing in an NPA PE would typically be that associated with intermediate-level vision operation, where the per pixel processing of the CAAPP and high-level processing associated with the GPPA PEs is much less efficient. The NPAs have sufficient onboard control capabilities to provide for MIMD operation. Also, each NPA PE can communicate with the 8 × 8 array of CAAPP PEs in the level beneath it using the hierarchical bus structure. This layer is also needed to provide computational support to keep the powerful CAAPP layer busy. The NPA PEs can communicate between themselves in a bit-serial fashion using a crossbar network constructed of the same elements as the GPPA-level crossbar switch.

The 512 × 512 CAAPP will function as both an efficient pixel-level SIMD numeric processor (primarily fixed-point operations) and as a symbolic processor. Symbolic operations often involve manipulations of data consisting of short strings, as, for example, simple Boolean operations. Examples that will be described later are graph matching and connected-component labeling. These types of operations are performed inefficiently for processors with only word parallel processing capabilities. The principal ingredient of the bit-serial CAAPP PE is the activity bit, which controls whether or not the PE will respond to instructions. An associative query would simply result in the activity bits being set such that only PEs with data matching the query would be left in the active state. Consequently, it is possible to selectively process data after the activity bit has been set. The CAAPP PEs are connected together in a mesh to facilitate neighborhood operations as in a conventional cellular architecture.

With the organization just described, various levels are available for processing, depending on the granularity of the problem. In general, as the level of abstraction in the analysis process increases, the center of activity moves up the hierarchy. This is facilitated by the use of three dual-port memories that act as conduits of information between the different levels, as shown in Figure 9.2. Each of these RAMs is distributed in such a way that there is one block of each of the three types associated with one NPA PE and an 8 × 8 CAAPP array. The dual-port RAM feeding the CAAPP can be considered an intelligent frame buffer since it is distributed among the CAAPP PEs. While data is being loaded into it, the CAAPP level can be performing operations on the previous frame of data.

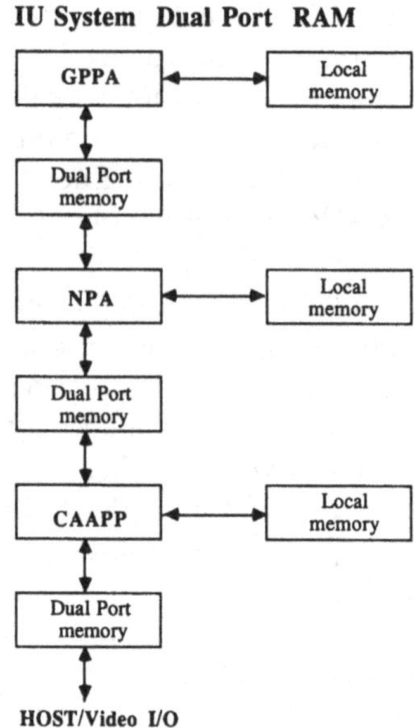

FIGURE 9.2. IUA memory organization.

There are two sources of associative feedback at the CAAPP level: the some/none response and the count responders. Each CAAPP PE has a single some/none conditional output. Logically these some/none responses are wired OR together with special hardware, so that within a single clock cycle the system controller will know whether any PEs responded to a query. In addition, there is special adder tree hardware that provides a count to the controller of the number of responders. An example of usage of this circuitry would be rapid construction of a histogram. All PEs with pixel intensities within the prescribed range would set their some/none lines, and the count responder circuitry would provide rapid feedback on the number of pixels in this histogram bin. Sometimes local rather than global information is needed. For example, if it is desired to obtain statistics simultaneously on a large number of regions, then feedback would only be necessary over the region being processed. This facility is available through a novel "Coterie" network, which will be discussed later. Having a local feedback capability provides a form of data-dependent computation within the framework of the SIMD CAAPP control structure.

2.2 System Prototype

In the previous section the overall image-understanding architecture was described in a relatively generic fashion. Currently only a prototype 1/64th slice of the system is being constructed. In this section we provide a summary of this design and implementation. The full system would be designed in basically the same way, although we would expect some changes resulting from differences in available technologies. For example, wafer-scale integration might have matured sufficiently to allow mapping the entire system onto a stack of wafers [Little et al. 1985].

The prototype IUA slice, organizationally described in Figures 9.3 and 9.4, consists of 64 custom-designed CMOS CAAPP/glue chips, 64 commercially available TI digital signal-processing (DSP) chips (TMS320C25) for NPA PEs, and a host processor (68020 based), which is intended to function as the GPPA for the prototype slice. There will also be a controller, whose basic function is to provide an uninterrupted stream of instructions to the CAAPP-level PEs. The custom chip also contains various glue components, so that the implementation is straightforward.

Physically the three arrays (GPPA, NPA, and CAAPP) are partitioned into two basic board types, a motherboard and a daughterboard. There are 64 3-in. × 4-in. daughterboards, each containing the custom CAAPP/glue, memory, and the DSP. The motherboard provides 64 sockets for these daughterboards. A full system, built using today's technology, would therefore contain 64 of these motherboards. The motherboard also has two additional slots, one for a "concentrator" board, which receives the some/none feedback and associated count, and one for an interconnect board for the NPA crossbar switch. This modular organization allows for ease of upgrade. For example, a user could use whatever interconnection network he desired by changing interconnect boards. A separate VME chassis associated with the motherboard provides for the controller and various I/O interfaces.

The abstracted view of the daughterboard, shown in Figure 9.5, shows that there are only four different chip types being used: the custom CAAPP/glue chip, a dual-port dynamic RAM, a static RAM, and a DSP chip. The static RAM is intended only for storing programs and data specifically for the DSP. There are three different dual-port RAMs, one associated with each of the memories shown in Figure 9.2. Dual-port RAM 2, accessible by the host via the VME bus and by the DSP via the daughterboard bus, is the basic means of large data communication between the GPPA level and the NPA/CAAPP levels. Dual-port RAM 1, which is accessible by the DSP from the daughterboard bus and from the CAAPP directly, is intended primarily as a backing store for the CAAPP PEs (32 kbits per PE) and, second, as a means of communication between the CAAPP and DSP.

Dual-port RAM 3 is a distributed frame buffer providing each daughterboard with raw image data. It is interfaced to an I/O unit having access to the VME bus so that data can be taken from hard disk peripheral or to other buses such as the MAXbus. Since there are 64 of these frame buffer RAMs they can supply the CAAPP with data at a rate of 640 MBytes/sec. Consequently, the CAAPP can load an entire image (512 × 512, 8-bit pixel) in less than 0.5 msec.

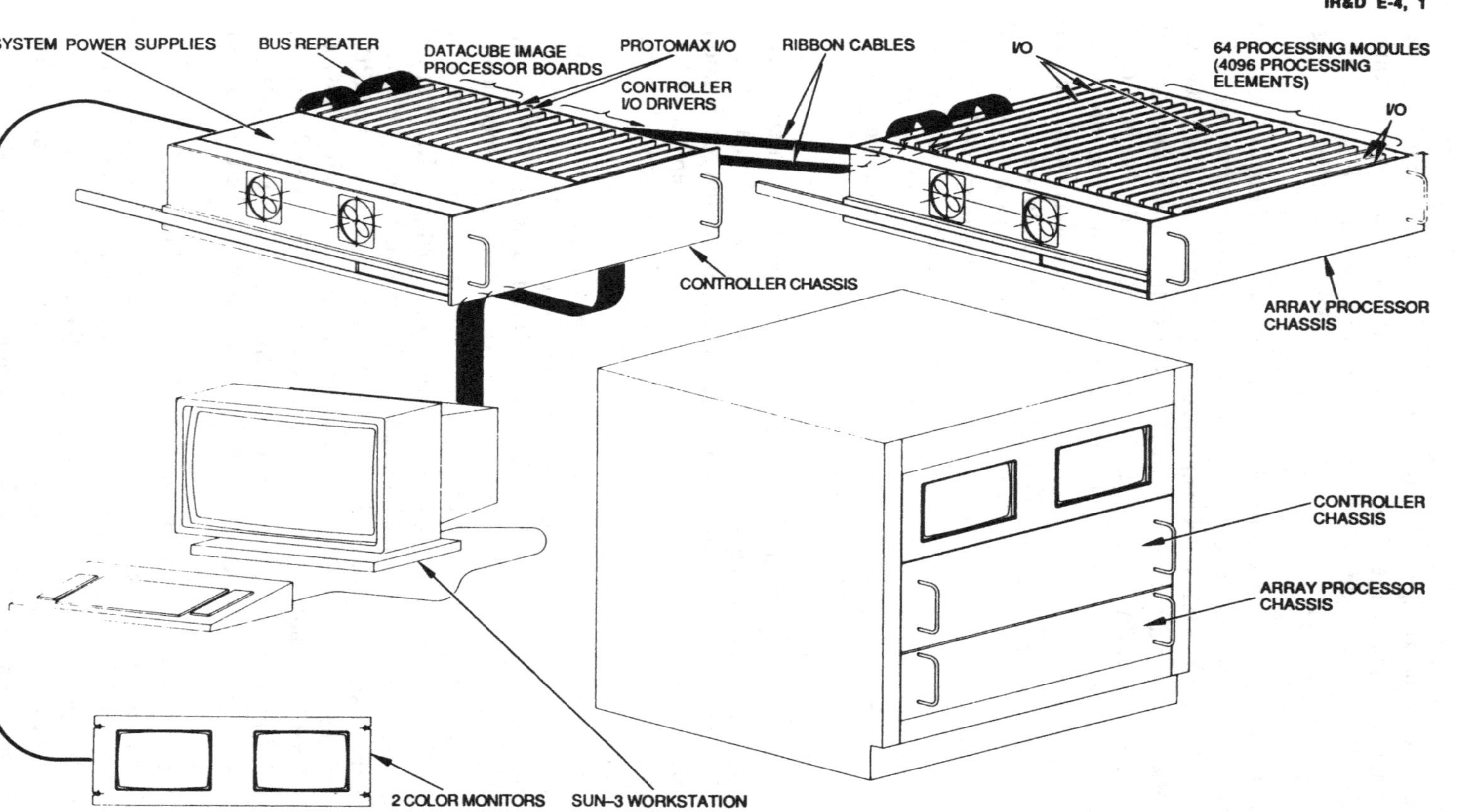

FIGURE 9.3. IUA 1/64th prototype slice.

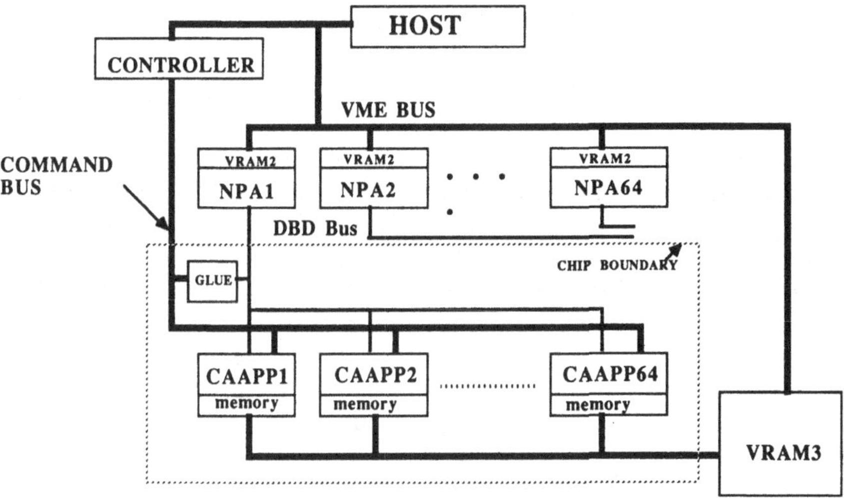

FIGURE 9.4. IUA prototype bus organization.

Since the purpose of the prototype slice was not simply demonstration of a concept, but rather to produce a research machine, it was decided to pay special attention to providing sufficient memory to deal with full image arrays. Clearly, a machine with the computing power of 64 10-MIP DSP chips and 4096-bit serial processors, could not be used efficiently without large amounts of memory. Therefore, enough chips were put on the daughterboards to provide 44 MBytes of memory for the entire prototype.

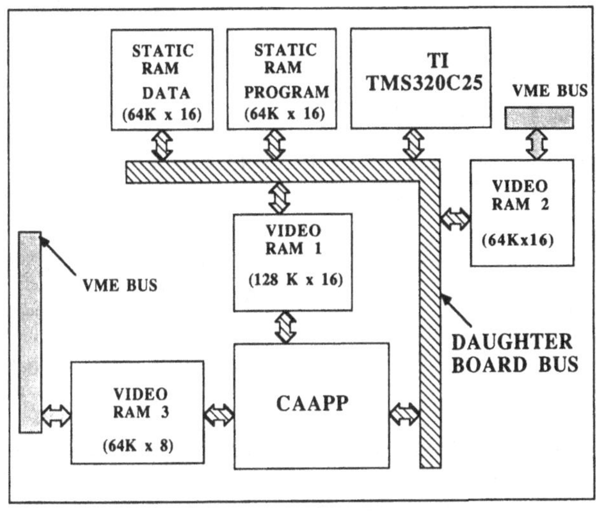

FIGURE 9.5. High-level organization of daughterboard.

2.3 Custom CAAPP/Glue Chip

The custom chip contains the 8 × 8 array of bit-serial processors, associated memory, and the necessary "glue" circuitry for the daughterboard.

The glue circuitry on the chip serves several relatively independent purposes. First, it provides the controller access to the DSP chip for initialization and interface. For example, the static DSP program and data RAM shown in Figure 9.5 can be loaded and the DSP initialized or interrupted through this glue. There are also video RAM controllers associated with the three sets of dual-port memories shown in Figures 9.2 and 9.5. The interface between video RAM 1 and the CAAPP requires some special circuitry, because data must be converted from 16-bit word parallel form to the bit-serial form. Finally, there are various status and data registers that must be accessible from either the controller or the DSP chip.

The CAAPP circuitry, which is separate from the glue, represents 80% of the circuit area. Each CAAPP PE has 320 bits of RAM, five one-bit registers *(A,B,x,y,z)*, an ALU, and routing circuitry allowing north, east, south, and west communications to neighbors in the cellular mesh. The *A* register is the activity register, which controls whether or not the associated PE is active. This plays a crucial role for associative processing because it allows selective operations on data sets. For example, the following code is an example of a program that turns off all PEs except those containing the label ID in their RAM memory:

```
1  A:=1!                               ;turn all PEs on ("!" means the
                                       ;instruction is executed on all PEs
                                       ;regardless of present activity bit
                                       ;setting)
2  M(reslt):=1                         ;initialize M(reslt) in all PE RAM
3  For I:=0 to ID_length do
   begin
4    M(reslt):=(M(label+I) XOR M(ID+I)) AND M(reslt)
                                       ;each PE compares its label beginning
                                       at M(label) with the prestored ID
                                       beginning at M(ID) and leaves the
                                       result in M(reslt)
   end
5  A:=M(reslt)                         ;store result of comparison in A
```

At the end of this computation the PEs that have a "1" in M(reslt) will be active. Then it is possible to perform selective processing on just those PEs with the correct activity label. Processing by a suitable label is a key element of associative techniques.

Although processing is on a bit-serial basis, data can be moved around in the CAAPP memory in byte units. There is also double buffering between the backing store and the CAAPP to minimize processor interruption during loading of new data.

On each CAAPP PE the "x" register is loaded with a 1 when it is desired to indicate globally that it is responding. This output is wired OR with the same output of all the other PEs to form the some/none response. This output is also an input to an adder tree contained on each CAAPP/glue chip. The adder tree provides a seven-bit register with a binary count of the number of responders on that chip. This register is accessible by the controller or the DSP chip.

The some/none responses of all the daughterboards are routed to the concentrator board where the 64 inputs are wired OR together. Similarly, the response count can be serially clocked out of the on-chip response-count register to the concentrator board where the total response count for the motherboard is accumulated. Both the some/none response and the response count from the concentrator board are then available to the controller.

2.4 CAAPP Coterie Network

The SIMD character of fine-grain cellular architectures represents a serious limitation for all but the first level of image processing performed. Typically, an image is processed to the point where segmentation has occurred and it is necessary for region-dependent analysis. This might begin with simple data-dependent operations, such as region labeling, followed by extraction of primitive symbolic information (area, perimeter, minimum bounding rectangle) and gathering of other statistics (moments, histograms). Later these activities would be followed by higher-level symbolic operations intended to extract features that ultimately lead to object recognition. In all cases it is necessary to process each region separately in some way. If there are many regions in an image, then a purely SIMD approach to such processing will be relatively inefficient for per pixel–based architectures, because each region will have to be dealt with separately.

The desirability also exists of simultaneous data-dependent processing of element groups for a variety of transform and symbolic calculations. For example, we will see in Section 3 that for the Hough transform it would be convenient to group pixels along lines associated with certain directions. Many simple symbolic operations, such as boolean matrix operations, finding the minimum spanning tree [Shu and Nash 1988], or minimum cost path of a graph [Shu and Nash 1988], can be performed very efficiently in a bit-serial fashion if appropriate groupings are possible.

In order to perform local region-based computations efficiently it is necessary to provide for a communication capability above and beyond that of the mesh-connected array. In this section we describe a coterie network that allows relatively arbitrary communication networks to be created in a very simple way. This network consists of a mesh array of six simple transmission gates per PE, as shown in Figure 9.6. A PE output to this array is via the x-register and the input to a PE is via the some/none line. Communication among PEs is determined by the switch settings on the gates. In Figure 9.6, if PE 1 wants to send a message to PE 2, then the appropriate gate connections are made and the two PEs now have an electrical connection between them. The gate settings are determined by a six-bit register that resides in the memory space of each CAAPP PE.

The coterie network is precharged before using, so that the communication occurs by having the source PE place a 1 or a 0 into its x-register. A 1 will pull down the precharge network, and a 0 will leave it unchanged. In either case the result is sensed by the some/none input to the destination PE and the network is precharged again. Clearly, under certain conditions it appears that a single pull-down transistor will have to provide enough current-sinking capability to pull down a large network. For this reason the network has been designed with a number of hardware and software features to enable a single transistor to pull down an entire 512 × 512 network in less than 2 μsec. On each CAAPP chip there is special circuitry associated with each PE that only requires it to pull down the network associated with eight-column PEs. Also, there is special circuitry at the CAAPP chip edge that effectively buffers connections with other chips. We have also added special software instructions to facilitate usage of the coterie network. There are CAAPP PE instructions to control the precharging of the network to allow time for propagation. In addition it is possible to have those PEs that neighbor the source PE sense the network

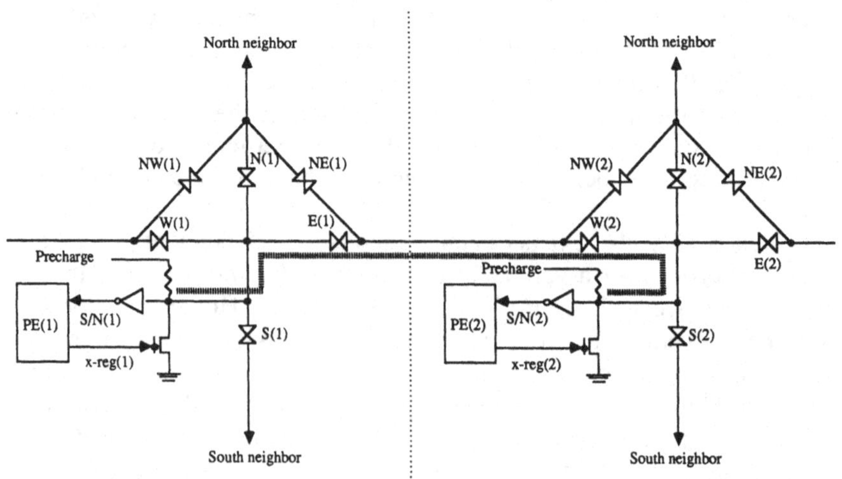

FIGURE 9.6. Coterie network.

voltage and aid in pulling it down. The number of PEs performing this function will grow in proportion to the number already aiding the pull-down operation, so that there is exponential growth in the coterie network-sinking capability.

Communication between PEs can be of three types: broadcast, point to point, and many to one. To illustrate how these work consider the case where one PE needs to broadcast to others within its coterie network a data value of length *N*. We assume that the source PE keeps a source active flag in *M*(src) and the destination active flag is stored in *M*(dest). The broadcasting procedure, then, is as follows:

```
1  x-reg: =0!                  ;isolate x-reg output from Coterie
                               ;network
2  For I: =0 to N-1 do
   begin
3    A-reg: =M(src)!           ;source flag M(src) is 0 for other PEs
4    x-reg: =M(msg+I)          ;source PE puts data in x-reg
5    A-reg: =M(dest)!          ;activate all receiving PEs
6    M(msg+I): =some/none      ;destination PEs save some/none into
                               ;memory
   end
```

For point-to-point communications the source PE would have an identification tag (ID_DEST) for the destination PE. The source PE first broadcasts the ID_DEST to all PEs connected in the coterie network, so that the destination PE can be found. The appropriate code here is

```
1  x-reg: : =0!                ;isolate all x-reg of PEs in Coterie
                               ;network
2  M(dest): =1!                ;present M(dest)
3  A-reg: =M(src)!             ;activate the source PE
4  For I: =0 to ID_length-1 do
   begin
5    x-reg: =M(ID_DEST+1)      ;broadcast the ID_DEST tag
6    M(dest): =(M(ID+I) XOR some/none) AND M(dest)!
                               ;each PE compares ID_DEST with its
                               ;own ID and saves the result in M(dest)
   end
7  A: =M(dest)!
```

At the end of this computation the PE having *M*(dest) = 1 is the destination PE. All other PEs will turn themselves off.

Multiple sources can also send wired OR messages to the same PE. This can be useful when it is desirable to only let the minimum value pass through. This is very useful in finding the minimum-cost path of a graph, since one of the objectives for a given node is to receive multiple messages from all the possible sources and select the smallest value. With the coterie this can be done in an on-the-fly fashion.

2.5 Control

The control of the prototype slice will be organized hierarchically in order to maximize the efficiency of the overall architecture, in particular that of the CAAPP layer. The NPA and GPPA PEs have their own local control plus storage for memory and data; therefore, they do not present such a problem. It is only necessary for the controller to provide start addresses for stored routines. On the other hand the 64 × 64 CAAPP array functions in a purely SIMD mode. Because the IUA recognizes the necessity of fast associative feedback of information from the CAAPP layer, the controller must be able to act rapidly on this information in order to keep the CAAPP PEs busy. In order to provide for this need it is necessary to divide overall control into three parts. At the highest level the host computer will be directing processing; however, it is only able to respond very slowly (~10 μsec) to new information. On the other hand, a high-speed controller with the appropriate response time (0.1 μsec) would be difficult to program and would not have sufficient intelligence to provide all the desired capabilities. For this reason we have added another layer in between so that the controller consists of two parts, a macrocontroller and a microcontroller, as shown in Figure 9.7. The overall goal of the controller is to maximize the ratio of CAAPP instructions generated by the microcontroller to the number processed by the macrocontroller.

The macrocontroller will be a 68020 tightly coupled to the microcontroller through dual-port and status registers. For example, this will enable it to efficiently pass subroutine parameters to the microcontroller. Because it is a general-purpose processor, it will also provide the desired software-development environment. The microcontroller is basically a sequencer having a large program memory, various status register, data registers,

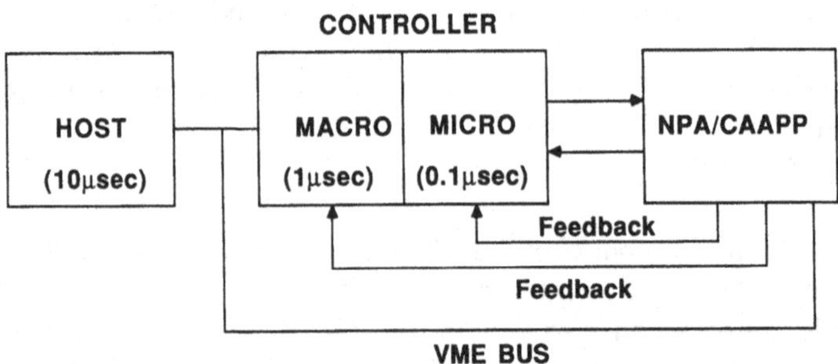

FIGURE 9.7. IUA controller organization.

and an address-generation capability suited specifically to the needs of the IUA. Feedback to the controller consists of the some/none response line, the response count, and status bits from the DSP indicating it is finished processing.

3 Application Examples

3.1 Introduction

In this section we illustrate how some representative problems would map onto the IUA. The goal has been to choose various algorithms and software that collectively use most of the relevant features of the parallel architecture and tend to span the range of the types of problems that might be encountered. There are three basic parts to this section. The first deals with the issue of defining a suitable structure that serves as a means of representing objects in a way that can bridge the pixel and symbol-based needs of the interpretation process. Second, we describe a possible scenario for the high-level procedures involved in object recognition, and finally we describe a few computationally intensive algorithms. A summary of performance estimates for some algorithms we have look at are provided in Table 9.1, based on the overall system in Figure 9.1 running at a 10 MHz rate.

3.2 Hierarchical Symbolic Pixel Array

A spatial blackboard plays an important role in the translation of raw imagery into discrete identified objects. It is capable of representing information at both the pixel and the object levels without loss of the relationship between scene objects and the pixels from which they originated. The symbolic pixel array is a data structure introduced by Payton [1984] to satisfy the need for this kind of blackboard representation. It makes use of separate representations for scalar properties and scene objects. Scalar properties such as intensities are represented by numeric arrays the size of the image. Scene objects are represented with binary masks, which identify where in the image each scene object is thought to exist.

One obvious disadvantage of using image-size binary masks to represent each small object in an image is the potentially large memory that would be required. By replacing the binary mask with a structure called a virtual array, which uses the concept of an offset for each object, memory use is minimized [Payton 1984]. The virtual array uses only enough memory to hold the smallest possible binary array necessary to represent an object. However, the virtual array adds overhead and makes it difficult to simultaneously control multiple objects of the same class randomly distributed in the image using parallel processors.

TABLE 9.1 IU Algorithms.

Benchmark	Time	Critical path	CAAPP PE	CAAPP Coterie	NPA	GPPA	Problem
Connected component labeling	80 μs	CAAPP	Yes	Yes	No	No	Provide each pixel in a 512 × 512 array with a label unique to its own region.
Hough transform	40 ms	CAAPP	Yes	Yes	Yes	No	Transform 512 × 512 image to a 512 × 180 array in hough space.
Convex hull	4.7 μs * h	NPA	No	No	Yes	Yes	For 1,000 real coordinate pairs in a plane, find the bounding polygon.
Minimal spanning tree	0.6 ms	CAAPP	Yes	Yes	No	No	For 100 real coordinate pairs in a plane, find minimum spanning tree.
Visibility	57.6 ms	NPA	No	No	Yes	No	For 1,000 triangles in space, generate a list of vertices visible from a given point.
Graph matching	7.5 μs * h	CAAPP	Yes	Yes	Yes	No	Find match(es) between graph G (100 vertices, 10 edges/vertex) and graph H (30 vertices, 3 edges/vertex).
Minimum-cost path	70 μs * h	CAAPP	Yes	Yes	Yes	No	For a random 1,000 vertex graph, each vertex joined randomly by a weighted edge to 100 other vertices, find the minimum path between two vertices.

With our hierarchical architecture, it is possible to replace the virtual array with a structure we call the hierarchical symbolic pixel array (HSPA). In HSPA, each object has three levels of binary mask representations, the *G*_mask, *N*_Mask, and *C*_mask, corresponding to processor levels at GPPA, NPA, and CAAPP, respectively. Each binary bit of the mask corresponds to one PE at that level. The content of the bit at any level can be obtained by a some/none test on the 8 × 8 PE array on the level beneath it. A value of 1 indicates a portion of the object resides in the subimage (sector) corresponding to that PE. The bit positions within a bit array for a given PE are called the mask index. The collection of these bit arrays is called the mask cube, as shown in Figure 9.8. For example, if the *N*_Mask index (NMI) for an object *A* is equal to 3 (i.e., NMI*(A)* = 3), then the corresponding binary mask of the NPA-level representation resides somewhere in the third layer of the *N*_mask cube. The layer sizes of the GPPA, NPA, and CAAPP mask cubes are 64, 4096, and 512 × 512 bits, respectively. The mask bit at each level controls the value of the 8 × 8 memory tile on the level beneath it. In other words, the smallest possible binary mask needed to represent an object at any level is always a multiple of 64 (i.e., 8 × 8). Figure 9.8 shows the HSPA representations for three objects. Object 1 occupies the third layer of the *G*_mask cube (i.e., GMI(1) = 3). Since only two *G*_mask bits are set to 1 at G_{ij} and $G_{(i+1)j}$, it occupies 128 (i.e., 2 × 64, of which *n* bits are set to 1) bits at the fifth layer of the *N*_mask cube. Consequently, the mask at CAAPP level has a size of 8 × 8 × *n*, and resides in the second layer of the *C*_mask cube (CMI(1) = 2). Usually, the three mask indices are different for an object.

Object 2 has the same *G*_mask as object 1 (GMI(1) = GMI(2)); therefore, it is possible to accommodate more objects than the number of layers in the *G*_mask cube. As a result, the *N*_mask of object 2 must occupy a different cube layer from that of object 1. It may reside in the same layer as that of object 3 because their *G*_masks are nonoverlapping. Similarly, the *C*_masks of all three objects may occupy the same mask layer, based on whether their corresponding *N*_masks overlap (e.g., CMI(1) = CMI(2) = CMI(3) = 2, as shown in Figure 9.2). Two objects *A* and *B* may have overlapping *C*_masks since some pixels can belong to two different hypotheses associated with objects *A* and *B*. In this case, their CMIs have to be different. Therefore, mask cubes enable individual pixels to hold multiple hypotheses.

The board/chip selection can be controlled by the *G*_mask/*N*_mask in order to focus attention on particular objects. For example, to process object 3 (e.g., runway) only, the controller will specify *G*_mask and *N*_mask indices (GMI(3) and NMI(3)) on the address bus, and send CAAPP a command through the data bus, which will load the CAAPP activity bit (*A*-register) with the *C*_mask index. Any subsequent CAAPP instructions will only affect object 3. Thus, any object can be uniquely

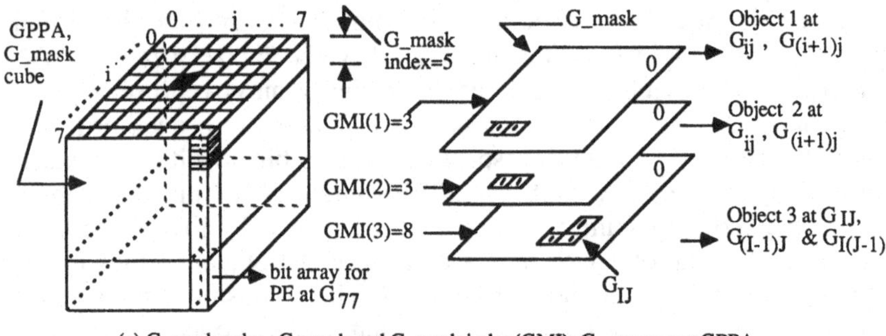

(a) G_mask cube, G_mask and G_mask index(GMI); G_{ij} represent GPPA PE at the board address of row i, column j.

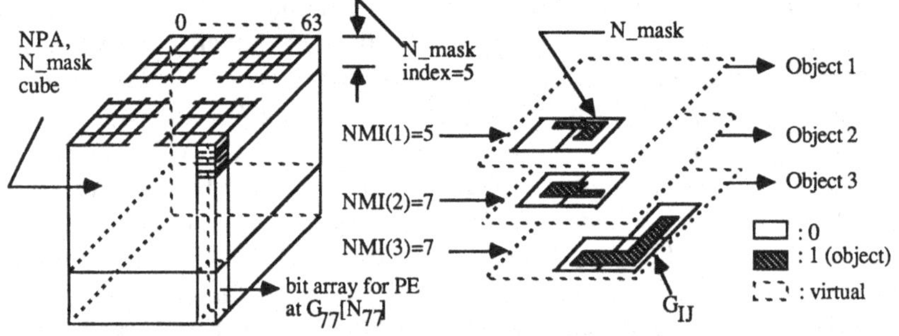

(b)N_mask cube, N_mask and N_mask index(NMI); $G_{ij}[N_{kl}]$ represent NPA PE at chip address row k, column l within G_{ij} board.

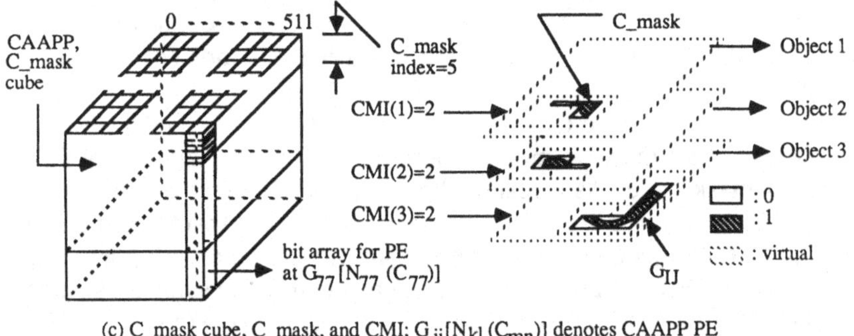

(c) C_mask cube, C_mask, and CMI; $G_{ij}[N_{kl}(C_{mn})]$ denotes CAAPP PE at row m, column n in chip $G_{ij}[N_{kl}]$.

FIGURE 9.8. HSPA representations for three objects.

accessed/processed by specifying its corresponding three mask indices. To simultaneously control multiple objects of the same class dispersed in the image, an HSPA can be easily created to represent the union of them. The HSPA of the union can then be treated as a single entity as far as the controller is concerned, without destroying the original identities of the individual objects.

An important feature of the HSPA is that it provides a structure to facilitate a virtual MSIMD capability on the IUA, with a control structure that maintains the simplicity of an SIMD architecture. If there is an HSPA associated with each object, and a coterie network to allow data-dependent processing at the CAAPP level, then with a measure of local control it would be possible for each HSPA to be processed separately. With the current prototype this is not possible because there is a single controller associated with the 1/64th system slice, as shown in Figure 9.4. Thus, the command bus could only serve one HSPA at a time. However, for the full-size prototype, we plan to migrate the microcontroller shown in Figure 9.7 to each daughterboard or possibly onto the CAAPP chip itself, so that the command bus wouldn't have to be tied up.

Fortunately, we can take advantage of the fact that CAAPP is a bit-serial machine and most image-processing routines require byte or word parallel operation. The basic idea is to have an instruction queue associated with the microcontroller on each daughterboard. The CAAPP PEs associated with an HSPA representing a particular object would receive their instructions from this microcontroller. The microcontroller would internally expand word level instructions into a large number of microcode-level bit-serial instructions. For example, from one multiple-assembly-level instruction the microcontroller can keep a CAAPP PE busy for at least 256 clock cycles for 256 bit-serial operations.

The routines run by the microcontroller would be determined by a GPPA PE acting as a domain expert for the particular object represented by the HSPA. During the latter stages of image analysis there would be many active domain experts in various GPPA PEs and each of these would be issuing small sets of instructions over the command bus to the appropriate microcontrollers, which in turn would expand them into much longer streams of bit-serial code. By specifying a unique set of HSPA mask indices, the instruction queue of every object can be loaded in turn with a different set of programs and processing can occur simultaneously. If the queue is empty, the PEs would be idle and, therefore, disabled. Since each object cannot fetch its own instruction using a program counter, it is not a true MSIMD architecture in the conventional sense, but a virtual MSIMD operation.

The *G*_mask controls the synchronization of GPPA PEs, and the *N*_mask controls the loading of instruction queues at each object daughterboard. Thus, the combined features of HSPA and microcoded instruction queues make the physical board/chip boundaries invisible to the object-processing routines, so that the scene object can assume any shape and size without concern with regard to microcontroller synchronization.

There are other research issues to resolve in this future plan to achieve a virtual MSIMD capability. For example we expect that time slicing will play an important role in synchronizing processing associated with objects having overlapping *G*_masks. For such cases it might be appropriate to have a time slice index (TSI) along with the HSPA masks to arbitrate the necessary processing associated with each object. Even if objects have nonoverlapping *G*_masks, it might be desirable to synchronize processing of each. Special hardware would dynamically select the TSI for each object at run time. A time slice index could also resolve contentions among multiple objects having the same *G*_masks for global resources such as response counts and some/none tests.

3.3 Object Recognition Expert System Mapping

The principal interest in image understanding involves the automatic transformation of the image to symbolic form, effectively providing a high-level description of the image in terms of objects, their attributes, and their relationships to other objects in the image. For nontrivial images it is necessary to incorporate schemes for including a priori knowledge about the possible objects and context in the image. The VISIONS system, developed at the University of Massachusetts [Hanson and Riseman 1978], is an example of such a system, and considerable work has already been done on mapping this system onto the IUA [Weems and Levitan 1987].

Another software paradigm we have looked at is that of the Context Cueing system, developed at the Hughes Artificial Intelligence Center [Silberberg 1987], which uses scene knowledge in the form of object models and relationships to aid in the interpretation of the image. The approach is object oriented so that hypothesized scene objects are responsible for gathering their own evidence for establishment, along with an appropriate confidence level. Domain experts exist to direct usage of more conventional image-processing algorithms to aid in the evidence-gathering effort. In the following discussion we describe how generic software of this type might be mapped onto the IUA. The emphasis will be on how parallelism might occur rather than on details of an interpretation strategy.

We start with the initial set of regions produced by an appropriate general segmentation algorithm. Unconditionally, each region is initially classified as a scene object, the most generic object class that subsumes all object classes in the image domain. Note that the classification of a region as a scene object does not involve any ambiguities or uncertainties. As the inference process proceeds, each object is hypothesized as each of its subclasses, and evidence is gathered to confirm or refute these hypotheses. The split/merge operation may also be performed by using the semantically directed feedback for resegmentation. This cycle of hypothesis generation, evidence gathering, and confirmation or refutation is repeated for each confirmed hypothesis until each region is classified as a terminal object class of the object hierarchy, or no further subclassification is possible because of low confidence for the current classification.

In the end, the symbolic description of the entire scene is constructed and stored in the NPA/CAAPP PE memories in the form of a semantic network with each node represented by one or more instance frames. The scalar properties and binary masked scene objects are stored in the CAAPP memories. The instance of an object frame and its associated slot values, super/subclass, and member/component relationship pointers are stored in the NPA memories. The host/GPPA memories stores knowledge that is contextual, domain specific, and picture specific. There are two roles played by GPPA PEs, local controller for NPA/CAAPP, and domain expert for a particular set of objects. As a local controller, GPPA stores primitive image-operation routines such as convolution, histogramming, and so on for the CAAPP and primitive rule-matching routines for NPA. The host will store complex image-processing routines in terms of GPPA primitive operations if the GPPA is constrained by memory size. As a domain expert, GPPA will be equipped with object models, knowing its stable states and the most likely segmentation strategy, etc.; it also performs housekeeping for sets of objects of the same class, as will be seen in the following example.

3.4 Example of Scene Interpretation

Here we provide an example of how a highly idealized scene-interpretation process might evolve. Using the hypothetical scene in Figure 9.9, the initial general region segmentation result would be as shown in Figure 9.10. For the sake of explanation, it is assumed that the image size is 64 × 128 and

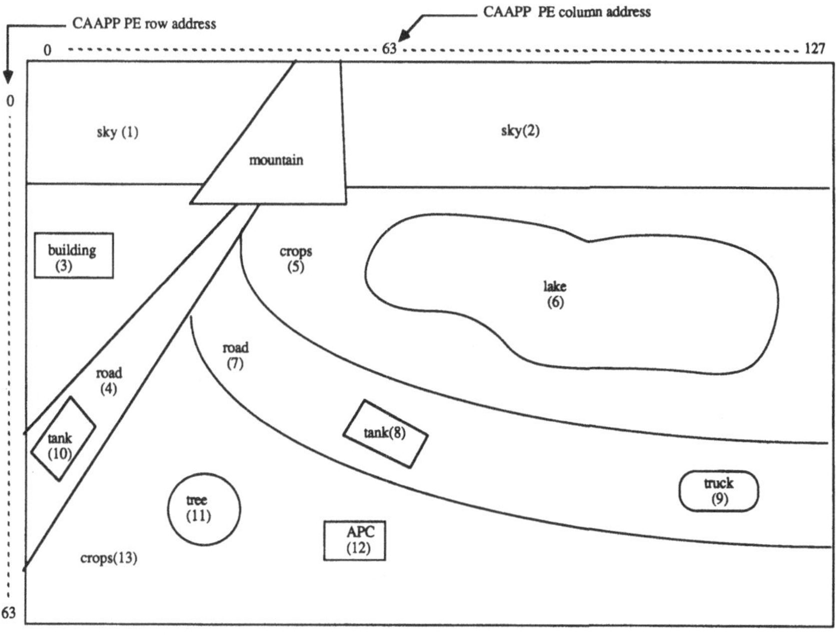

FIGURE 9.9. Hypothetical scene containing 13 objects.

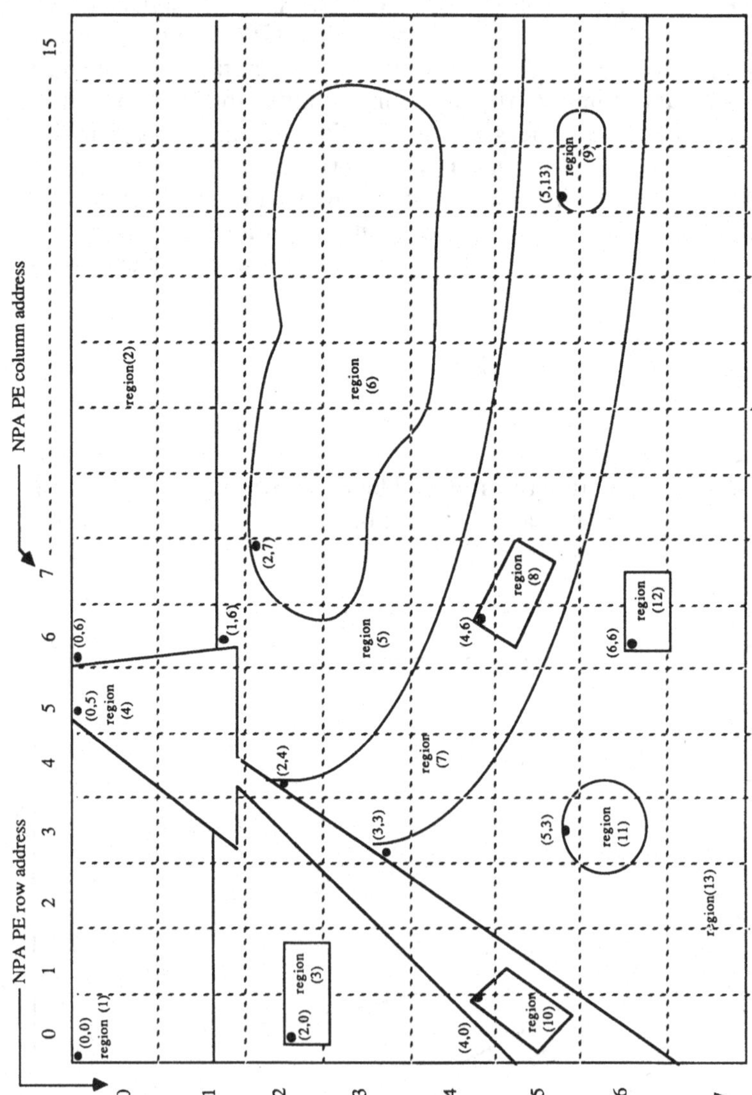

FIGURE 9.10. Dominant region cells (•) and their corresponding NPA PEs as indicated by NPA row, column address (r, c).

occupies two GPPA boards at (0,0) and (0,1), and that local microcontrol is available for virtual MSIMD operation. The row and column address ranges for NPA and CAAPP are (0–7, 0–15) and (0–63, 0–127), respectively. To extract connected components, we use the coordinates of the PEs in the region to determine the component labels (see Section 3.5.2). Collisions between adjacent PEs having the same region properties are resolved by letting the one with the least (row,col) coordinate be the dominant region label. The particular region PE having the least (row,col) component is called the dominant region PE. In the IUA, the NPA PE corresponding to this dominant CAAPP PE is where the instance frame, which contains various attributes of this scene object, is stored. Figure 9.11 shows the coordinates of those NPA PEs that correspond to 13 scene objects found. Initially, these NPA PEs contain the instance frame with empty slots. These slots can be filled by stepping sequentially through each extracted scene object using a "find first responder" operation of the CAAPP. By broadcasting the region label, it is straightforward to compute simple region properties, such as area, perimeter length, minimum bounding rectangle, and so forth, for the corresponding region. The HSPA representations for an object are also generated at this stage by latching the some/none test results at each appropriate level. The corresponding HSPA mask indices are stored in the slots of individual instance frames as part of attribute lists.

As the inference process proceeds, the established objects will attempt to generate hypotheses to subclassify themselves into more specific classes based on the object hierarchy shown in Figure 9.12(a). In this hierarchy, the scene object is automatically assumed established; therefore, its three subclassification hypotheses, tactical, terrain, and space, are generated accordingly. To achieve efficiency, we may proceed with two computational steps. In the first step, hypotheses are filtered by computationally simple tests. Highly unlikely hypotheses are quickly eliminated by simple binary, true/false, tests. Only the hypotheses that pass this screening test will receive further evaluation. In the second step, each piece of evidence is carefully weighed, integrated into the existing body of evidence, and a confidence level is updated.

In the first computational step, Figure 9.11 shows that each of the 13 scene object frames, before the screening test, contains three NIL pointers corresponding to three hypotheses generated: tact (tactical), terr (terrain), and space. Figure 9.13 shows that after a screening test for tactical objects, five tactical hypotheses are successfully instantiated, as indicated by the values stored in the tact pointer slots, which point to the corresponding empty tactical object instance frames residing in the neighboring physical NPA PEs. The tact pointer slots of other scene objects will remain NIL to manifest the fact that the hypotheses are generated but not instantiated, through reserving NPA PEs for storage due to failure of the screening test. For example, at the upper left corner in Figure 9.13, the tact pointer

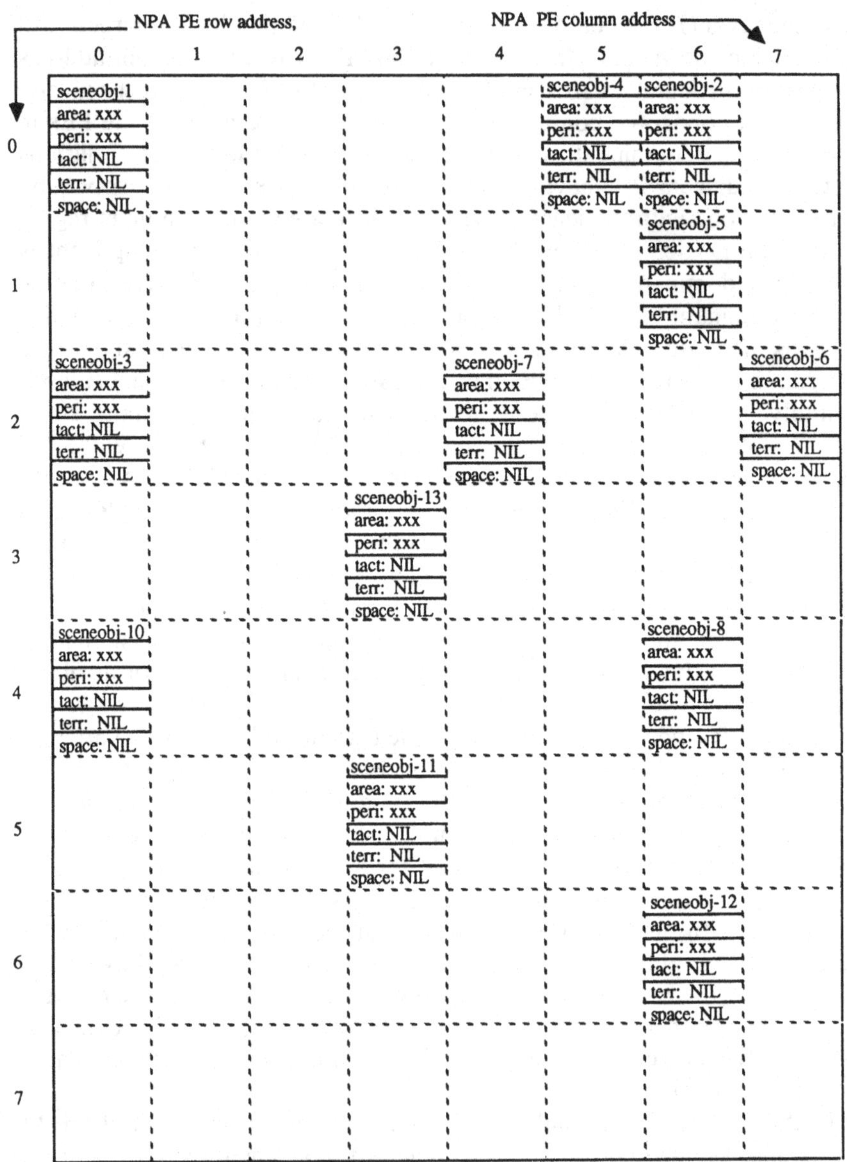

FIGURE 9.11. Various attributes stored in the instance frames of scene objects that touch the GPPA PE at (0, 0).

of scene object 3 contains (2,1) and points to the instance frame with the identification tactical-3 at the neighboring NPA PE (2,1). Note that scene object 3, which is a building in Figure 9.9, relates to region 3 in Figure 9.10, and stores its general attributes in NPA PE (2,0) in Figure 9.11. Even though only the forward pointer is shown, all the links in the object

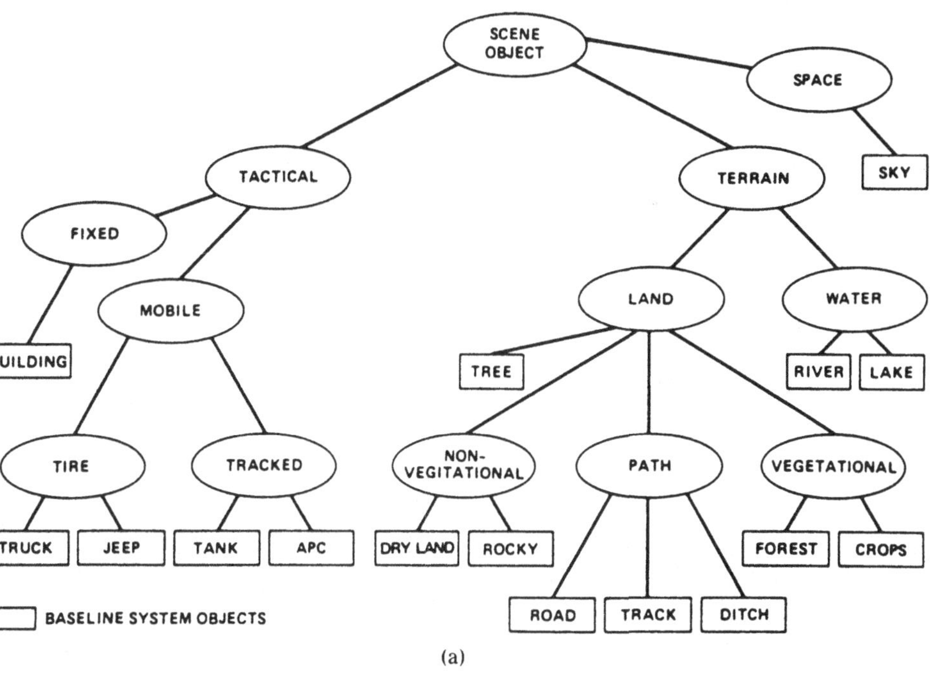

(a)

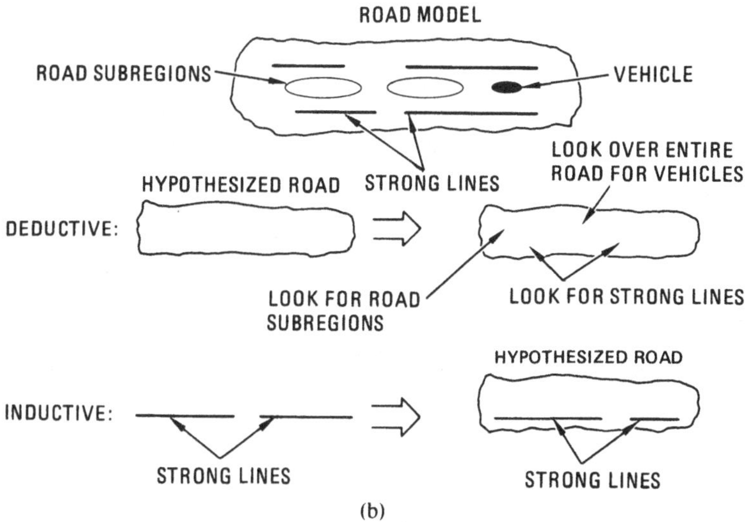

(b)

FIGURE 9.12. (a). Scene object hierarchy; (b) model-driven hypothesis generation.

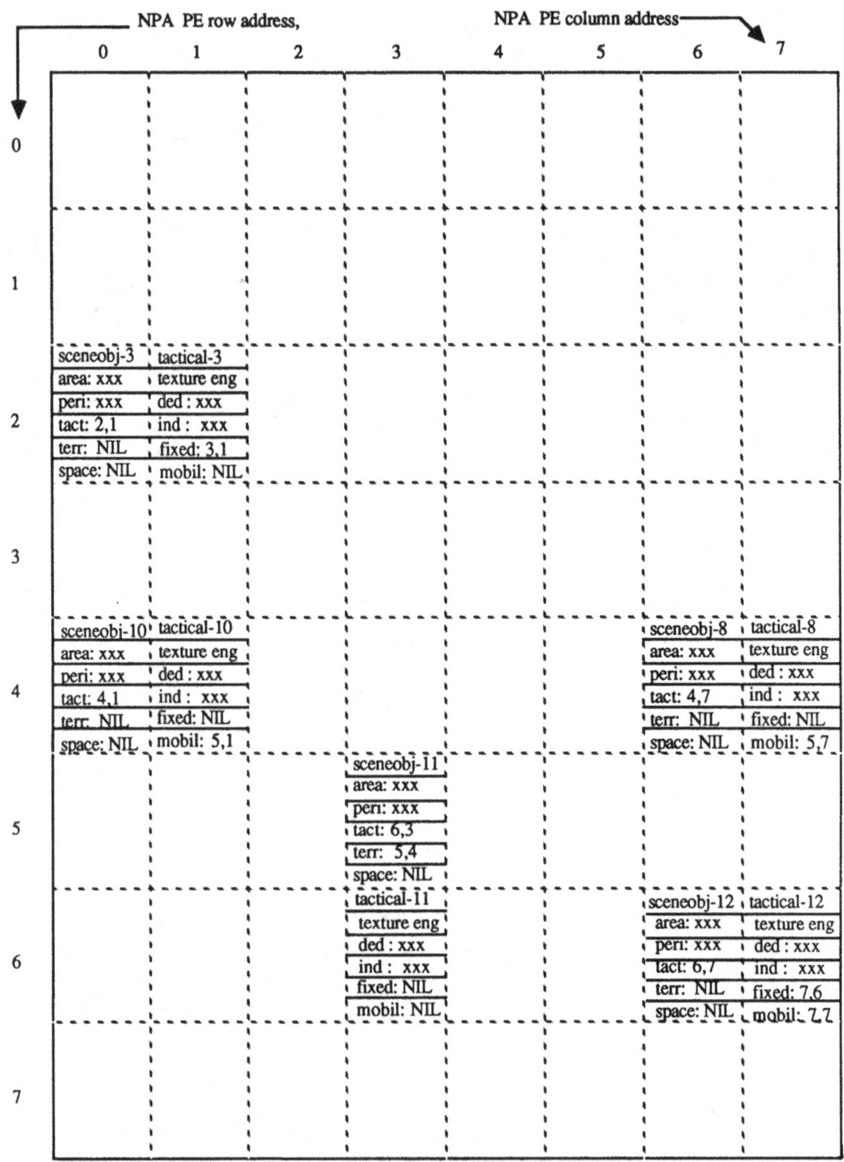

FIGURE 9.13. Five established (confirmed) tactical objects and their corresponding scene object instance frames.

hierarchy are doubly linked. (Note that we are only showing objects that touch the board (0,0) in the figures.)

There are two ways to obtain a new pointer for reserving an empty instance frame. The first is through the host/GPPA, which may perform garbage collection and maintain free storage lists. This approach is most effective when the NPA array is highly populated. The second method is through message passing through the NPA crossbar network concurrently/locally by all objects passing the screen test. This approach is very efficient when most of the neighboring NPA PEs are free. To see how the first approach works, consider the previous five tactical hypotheses. At the beginning, the host (or a GPPA PE when acting as a domain expert at the lower levels in the object hierarchy) sent screening tests to all 13 scene objects, only five of which passed. The host steps through each of them using the find-first-responder operation, and delivers one pointer extracted from the free storage list to the corresponding tact pointer slot. Before proceeding to the second computational step, the host will filter all 13 objects by terrain- and space-screening tests in case multiple hypotheses for an object are necessary.

To establish an instantiated hypothesis, evidence needs to be gathered and weighed in the second computational step. In addition to delivering empty frame pointers to five potential tactical objects, the host will gather the corresponding HSPA mask indices and form the union of them. This information will be passed to the appropriate domain expert to control all five objects simultaneously if possible.

Assuming host, GPPA PE(0,0), and GPPA PE(0,1) are experts on space, terrain, and tactical, respectively, then GPPA PE(0,0) will receive relevant information about instantiated terrain hypotheses and supervise the execution of image-processing routines on these dispersed objects (i.e., the corresponding CAAPP PEs), by sending routine pointers over the command bus. The operations performed on tactical and terrain objects can be concurrent if their HSPA masks are nonoverlapping. Unfortunately, in Figure 9.13 scene object 11 (tree) is instantiated both as a tactical and a terrain object as can be seen by the non-NIL pointers. By performing set difference operations on HSPA masks, GPPA PE (0,1) will be able to initiate activity on the other four tactical objects while doing the housekeeping chores for object 11 and waiting for its resources to be free. With just one object, there is a better chance to find nonoverlapping HSPA masks next time around. When the image processing on the four tactical objects is finished the results can be sent, using the scene object pointer, to the destination slot in the tactical instance frame, or further down the hierarchy as more subclassification is instantiated. All four objects can do this concurrently or pipelined, depending on the availability of global resources, to obtain the result. Since the processing routines for terrain and tactical objects are different, their results will be sent at different times. Consequently, there is less chance for contention for the NPA interconnection network. It should be noted that HSPA mask indices are the bridge between the nonspatial symbolic representation of instance frames, which are linked through pointers, and the spatial scene objects where the physical location and image scalar properties are important for image processing.

To gather evidence for a given hypothesis in part there are two slots, ded (deductive) and ind (inductive), in the tactical instance frame in Figure 9.13, which store results of deductive and inductive reasoning about context. In the corresponding slots in the model frame, the domain expert stores pointers to the deductive and inductive reasoning procedures in the host. Figure 9.12(b) shows a road model and its corresponding deductive and inductive reasoning methods. It is referred to as model-driven reasoning, since these procedures may all be defined relative to the model itself; they may be tuned specifically to operate over a defined domain. After all the slots for a given instance frame are filled if possible, the confidence will be weighed by NPA/GPPA according to some rules. If the confidence score is low, the hypothesis will be discarded and the corresponding NPA PE storage space for the instance frame will be returned to the free storage list. The pointer slot of its superclass will be NILed. If the confidence score is high enough, then the instantiated hypothesis will be established. A new cycle of subclassification hypothesis will be generated. This is referred to as data-driven reasoning, because new hypotheses are being generated through evidence gathering. The NPA will perform complex symbolic processing, and medium-level vision analysis. Since the NPA can access CAAPP memory, a CAAPP PE can be treated as a content-addressable memory for the NPA when image-processing operations are idling.

After a few cycles of hypothesis generation, scene object 10 at the middle left corner in Figure 9.14 failed to be classified as a terminal object (tank in this case). Just as human beings would refuse to classify an object into a specific class unless sufficient information were available, the last instance frame of mobile-10 says "That is definitely a moving object but I don't know whether it is a tank or truck." (Pointers for "tire" and "tracked" are NIL, meaning insufficient evidence for any further subclassification.)

In part, the fact that mobile-10 is a moving object is strongly supported by the evidence that it has a wheel, as indicated by the value (5,2) in the "ded" pointer slot, which points to the "wheel-14" instance frame at NPA PE (5,2), and was obtained through a deductive reasoning method as follows: The wheel hypothesis is first generated and the CAAPP image routine of "wheel finder" is then invoked. Since the routine is defined relative to the vehicle itself, it has been tuned to much higher-sensitivity levels because of the reduced amount of misleading clutter within the domain of object 10. The attributes list, including HSPA mask indices, of the newly segmented region 14, is gathered and stored in the scene object instance frame at NPA PE (6,1). After passing the screening test for wheels, the hypothesis is instantiated by storing (5,2) in the "wheel" pointer slot of scene obj-14. The wheel-14 instance frame is established by further processing. For example, based on the orientation of mobile-10, the projection of the modeled wheel can be compared with the observed wheel.

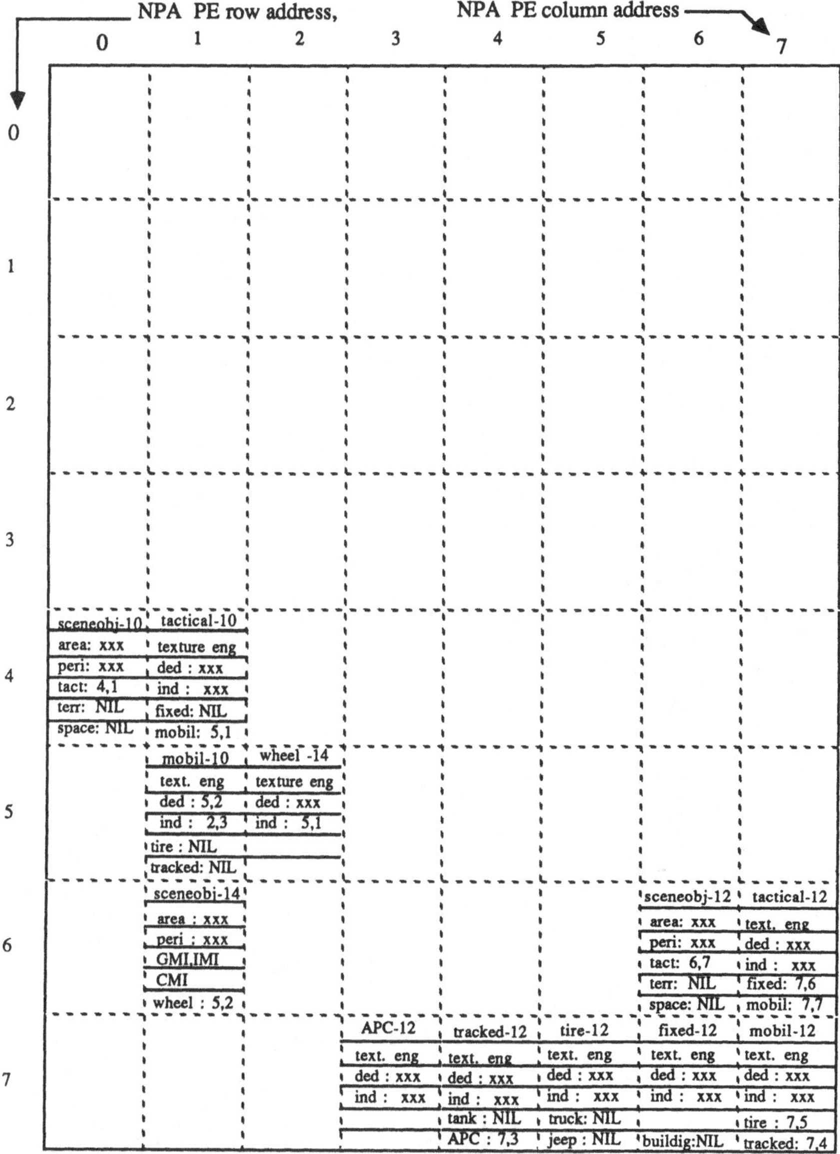

FIGURE 9.14. Scene object 12 is successfully classified as a terminal object of APC of the object hierarchy.

The pointer to the established wheel instance is returned to the ded pointer slot of mobile-10 along with the confidence score of the wheel. Therefore, mobile-10 can know its wheel location by retrieving HSPA mask indices through the pointer threads. In the end, the confidence score of mobile-10 is further increased by the fact that it is on road-4 as indicated by the ind pointer slot, which has a value of (2,3) and points to road-4 instance frame at NPA PE (2,3) (Figures 9.9, 9.15). Consequently, object-10 is definitely a moving object.

Scene object 12 at the lower right corner in Figure 9.14, is successfully classified as an APC with appropriate pointer threads. If it is desired to

NPA PE row address, NPA PE column address

	0	1	2	3	4	5	6	7
0	sceneobj-1 area: xxx peri: xxx tact: NIL terr: 0,1 space: 1,0	terrain-1 text. eng ded : xxx ind : xxx land : NIL water: NIL		land-4 text. eng ded : xxx ind : xxx tree: NIL path: 1,3	terrain-4 texture eng ded : xxx ind : xxx land : 0,3 water: NIL	sceneobj-4 area: xxx peri: xxx tact: NIL terr: 0,4 space: NIL	sceneobj-2 area: xxx peri: xxx tact: NIL terr: NIL space: 0,7	space-2 texture eng ded : xxx ind : xxx sky : NIL
1	space-1 texture eng ded : xxx ind : xxx sky : 1,1	sky-1 texture eng ded : xxx ind : xxx		path-4 texture eng ded : xxx ind : xxx road : 2,3 track: NIL			sceneobj-5 area: xxx peri: xxx tact: NIL terr: NIL space: NIL	
2	sceneobj-3 area: xxx peri: xxx tact: 2,1 terr: NIL space: NIL	tactic-3 text.eng ded:xxx ind:xxx fixed:3,1 mobil:NIL		road-4 texture eng ded : xxx ind : xxx	sceneobj-7 area: xxx peri: xxx tact: NIL terr: 2,5 space: NIL	terrain-7 texture eng ded : xxx ind : xxx land : 3,5 water: NIL		sceneobj-6 area: xxx peri: xxx tact: NIL terr: NIL space: NIL
3		fixed-3 texture eng ded : xxx ind : xxx building:3,2	building-3 texture eng ded : xxx ind : xxx	sceneobj-13 area: xxx peri: xxx tact: NIL terr: NIL space:-NIL	path-7 text. eng ded : xxx ind : xxx	land-7 texture eng ded : xxx ind : xxx tree: NIL path: 3,4		
4	scenobj10 area: xxx peri: xxx tact: 4,1 terr: NIL space: NIL	tactic10 text.eng ded:xxx ind:xxx fixed:NIL mobil:5,1					sceneobj-8 area: xxx peri: xxx tact: 4,7 terr: NIL space: NIL	tactic-8 text eng ded:xxx ind:xxx fixed:NIL mobil:5,7
5		mobil-10 texture eng ded : 5,2 ind : 2,3 tire : NIL tracked: NIL	wheel-14 text. eng ded : xxx ind : 5,1	sceneobj-11 area: xxx peri: xxx tact: 6,3 terr: 5,4 space: NIL	terrain-11 text. eng ded : xxx ind : xxx land : 5,5 water: NIL	land-11 text. eng ded : xxx ind : xxx tree: 5,6 path: NIL	tree-11 texture eng ded : xxx ind : xxx	mobil-8 text. eng ded : xxx ind : xxx tire : NIL tracked: 6,5
6		sceneobj-14 area : xxx peri : xxx GMI,IMI CMI wheel: 5,2		tactic-11 text. eng ded: xxx ind: xxx fixed:NIL mobil:NIL		tracked-8 text. eng. ded : xxx ind : xxx tank : NIL APC : NIL	scenobj-12 area: xxx peri: xxx tact: 6,7 terr: NIL space: NIL	tactic-12 text. eng ded: xxx ind: xxx fixed:7,6 mobil:7,7
7				APC-12 text. eng ded : xxx ind : xxx	tracked-12 texture eng ded : xxx ind : xxx tank : NIL APC : 7,3	tire-12 text. eng ded : xxx ind : xxx truck: NIL jeep : NIL	fixed-12 text. eng ded : xxx ind : xxx buildig:NIL	mobil-12 texture eng ded : xxx ind : xxx tire : 7,5 tracked: 7,4

FIGURE 9.15. Symbolic description of a given scene in terms of semantic network of instance frames.

find an APC in an image, simply broadcast APC to the NPA array, and NPA PE (7,3) will initiate backward tracing and reach the scene object instance frame at NPA PE (6,6). The HSPA mask indices (i.e., object physical location) will be retrieved along the way with other pertinent information required. It also contains multiple hypotheses for this object. Figure 9.15 shows the full semantic network representation for the scene. If tactical objects are of interest, all the corresponding NPA PEs will flag and retrieve physical locations. If closest tanks are of interest, all the tanks will initiate image processing, and the one closest to certain pixels will be tagged. This is possible due to the bridging role of the HSPA between nonspatial and spatial information.

3.5 Algorithmic Mapping Examples

3.5.1 Large Window Convolutions. A discrete two-dimensional convolution is based on a mask of multipliers that each PE applies to its local neighborhood, forming the sum of products of the PE's neighbors with their corresponding mask values. There are two different ways of approaching the problem of examining the neighborhood. In one case each PE gathers what information it needs to perform an update. This can involve a complex problem to determine an optimal set of data-collection paths as the neighborhood's diameter varies. Alternatively, instead of each PE collecting all the data from its neighborhood, each PE distributes its own data to every PE in the neighborhood [Weems 1984]. The problem of establishing an optimal distribution path is trivial for a square array of odd diameter: it is simply a rectangular spiral out from the center PE. For even diameter square neighborhoods the problem is only slightly more difficult because the center PE is actually half of a PE width off center in two directions. In this case the appropriate choice of start direction and spiral direction must be made to select the optimal path.

Because this is a distribution process rather than a collection process, the convolution mask value, $h(\varepsilon,\eta)$, which is broadcast by the controller, must be mirrored across the central PE. For example, when the PE's value is being stored in its north neighbor, the south mask multiplier must be applied. The mirroring of the convolution mask can be easily accomplished, as shown in Figure 9.15, by simply stepping through the mask array in exactly the opposite direction from the distribution path through the neighborhood array.

This process is shown in the following detailed example. Assume the function mask, $h(\varepsilon,\eta)$, is a 5×5 array of multiplier values that will be used to weight the values stored in the neighbors. Let us first define two variables, "SUM" and "TEMP," which are stored in all CAAPP PEs. SUM stores the cumulative sum of the pairwise products of the PE's neighbors with their corresponding mask values, and TEMP stores the value traveling through the distribution path. Throughout the convolution algorithm the controller shown in Figure 9.7 will broadcast the appropriate mask value, $h(\varepsilon,\eta)$, on the command bus to every CAAPP PE, while each PE performs the appropriate multiplication, summation, and shifting operations. At the outset, all PEs receive $h(0,0)$ and multiply this by their image values; for example, PE (i,j) will store the resulting product $h(0,0) * f(i,j)$ in variable SUM. This PE then shifts its image value $f(i,j)$ to the TEMP variable of west neighbor PE $(i - 1,j)$ as shown in the distribution path of Figure 9.16(b). This action is simultaneously performed by all of the PEs. In the next step the controller, following the broadcasting sequence shown in Figure 9.16(a), issues the mask value $h(1,0)$ to all the PEs, and instructs every PE to multiply this by the value stored in the variable TEMP and accumulate it in the variable SUM. In the case of PE (i,j), the TEMP variable contains $f(i + 1, j)$ and variable SUM contains $h(0,0) * f(i,j) + h(1,0) * f(i + 1, j)$. Before the central controller broadcasts the next mask value $h(1,1)$, each PE will shift its TEMP value to the TEMP variable of the north neighbor, as shown in Figure 9.16(b) so that TEMP (i,j) contains $f(i + 1, j + 1)$. In the last step, TEMP of PE $(i - 2, j + 2)$ will receive $f(i,j)$ and the controller will broadcast the last mask value $h(2,-2)$.

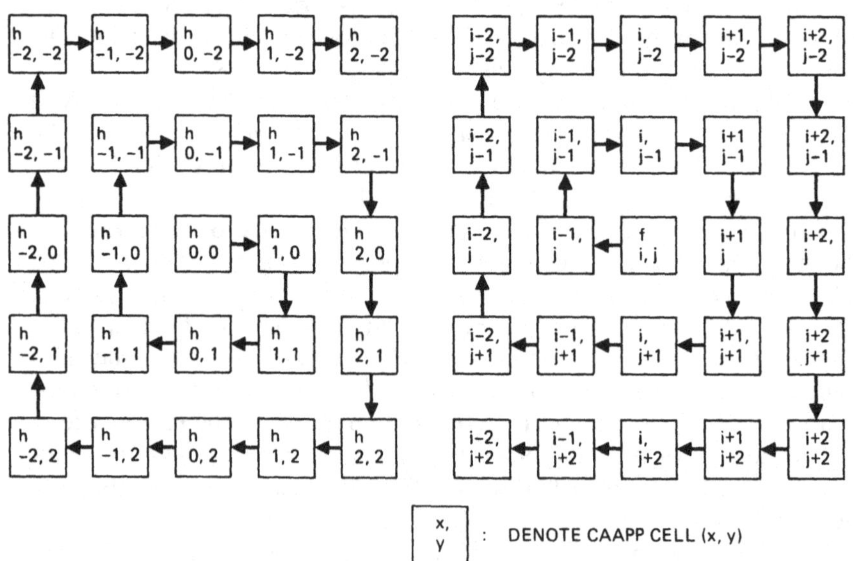

(a) Broadcast sequence used by CAAPP central controller for the 5 x 5 convolution mask h(ε,η).

(b) Distribution path for image data f(i,j) at CAAPP cell (i.j).

FIGURE 9.16. Data distribution path for convolution.

3.5.2 Large Area Convolution Using B-Splines. It should be noted that the time required to perform a convolution as described is independent of the size of the image (assuming the image is no larger than the array) and only dependent upon the area of the convolution mask. Therefore, for large enough convolution masks, this algorithm becomes slow. Using a B-spline approximation developed by Ferrari et al. [1986] for large-area convolution masks, an order of magnitude speed improvement can be obtained over the method described earlier. And by using the NPA, another order of speedup can be obtained.

Given the general case of a spatially varying convolution mask $h(\varepsilon,\eta : x,y)$, let the function $h_a(\varepsilon,\eta : x,y)$ be the B-spline approximation to $h(\varepsilon,\eta : x,y)$:

$$h_a(\varepsilon,\eta{:}x,y) = \sum_{i=1}^{M} \sum_{j=1}^{N} h(\alpha_i,\beta_j{:}x,y)\ \phi^{1,1}\ (\varepsilon,\{\varepsilon_r\},\eta,\{\eta_s\}) \tag{9.1}$$

where ϕ is a first-order B-spline and the sets $\{\varepsilon_r\}$ and $\{\eta_s\}$ are sample locations. If the exact output of image g is given by

$$g(x,y) = \int\int h(\varepsilon,\eta{:}x,y)f(\varepsilon,\eta)\ d\varepsilon d\eta, \tag{9.2}$$

where f is the input image, then we can find an approximate output image $g_a(x,y)$ using

$$g_a(x,y) = \int\int \mathbf{h}_a(\varepsilon,\eta{:}x,y)f(\varepsilon,\eta)d\varepsilon d\eta. \tag{9.3}$$

Ferrari's theorem 2 then leads to

$$g_a(x,y) = \sum_{i=1}^{M} \sum_{j=1}^{N} h(\alpha_i,\beta_j{:}x,y) \cdot S_{2,2}(x-\varepsilon_i,\ y-\eta_j) \tag{9.4}$$

where $S_{2,2}$ is

1. $$\begin{aligned} S_{2,2}(x-\varepsilon_1,\ y-\eta_j) = {} & [F_{2,2}(x-\varepsilon_{i-1},\ y-\eta_{j-1}) - 2F_{2,2}(x-\varepsilon_i,y-\eta_{j-1}) \\ & + F_{2,2}(x-\varepsilon_{i+1},y-\eta_{j-1}) - 2F_{2,2}(x-\varepsilon_{i-1},y-\eta_j) \\ & + 4F_{2,2}(x-\varepsilon_i,y-\eta_j) \\ & - 2F_{2,2}(x-\varepsilon_{i+1},y-\eta_j) + F_{2,2}(x-\varepsilon_{i-1},y-\eta_{j+1}) \\ & - 2F_{2,2}(x-\varepsilon_i,y-\eta_{j+1}) + F_{2,2}(x-\varepsilon_{i+1},y-\eta_{j+1})]. \end{aligned}$$
2. $$\begin{aligned} F_{2,2}(I,J) = {} & F_{2,2}(I-1,J) + F_{2,2}(I,J-1) \\ & - F_{2,2}(I-1,J-1) + F_{1,1}(I,J). \end{aligned}$$
3. $$F_{1,1}(I,J) = \sum_{m=1}^{I} \sum_{n=1}^{J} f(m,n).$$

and $h(\alpha_i,\ \beta_j : x,y)$ are the (MN) appropriate sample values of $h(\varepsilon,\upsilon : x,y)$.

It should be noted that $F_{2,2}$ is independent of $h(\varepsilon,\eta)$ and could be computed prior to the time that the input image is first loaded into the CAAPP, and may be used over several different h-masks for a given image (each CAAPP PE stores its corresponding $F_{2,2}$-value). Each point $h(\alpha_i,\beta_j : x,y)$ given in equation (9.4) uses one value $S_{2,2}$ $(x - \varepsilon_i, y - \eta_j)$ based on the nine support points of $F_{2,2}$. Obtaining $S_{2,2}$ is equivalent to the convolving of $F_{2,2}$ terms with the 3 × 3 mask as shown in Figure 9.17.

As an example we assume $h(\varepsilon,\eta : x,y)$ is a 128 × 128 mask with its one-dimensional profile through the origin shown as a sine function in Figure 9.18. There are 11 equally spaced ($\Delta\varepsilon = 15$) sample points in the profile, with two endpoints having sample values of zero; hence, as far as the computation is concerned, there are nine sample values used to reconstruct the $h_a(\varepsilon : x_c)$. In other words, the original 128 × 128 convolution is reduced to the convolution of the 9 × 9 sample values of $h(\varepsilon,\eta)$ and their corresponding $S_{2,2}$-values, each of which is obtained through another 3 × 3 convolution shown in Figure 9.17.

To perform the required computations using the CAAPP processor alone, we proceed as follows: Using the basic convolution algorithm described in Section 3.5.1, all CAAPP PEs perform the 3 × 3 convolution by applying the mask shown in Figure 9.17 to the $F_{2,2}$-values instead of the image values f. Because the support points are 15 PEs (pixels) apart, the distribution path takes 15 times longer to travel.

After this convolution, every CAAPP PE has its $S_{2,2}$-value ready for the 9 × 9 convolution in the next step. The controller will broadcast the

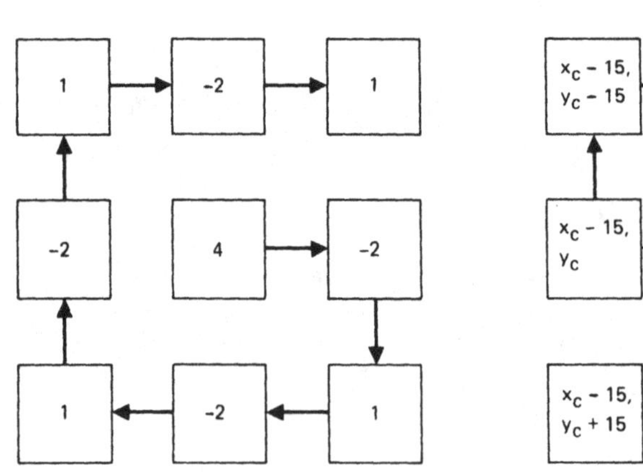

(a) 3x3 mask used to compute the support for each sample point.

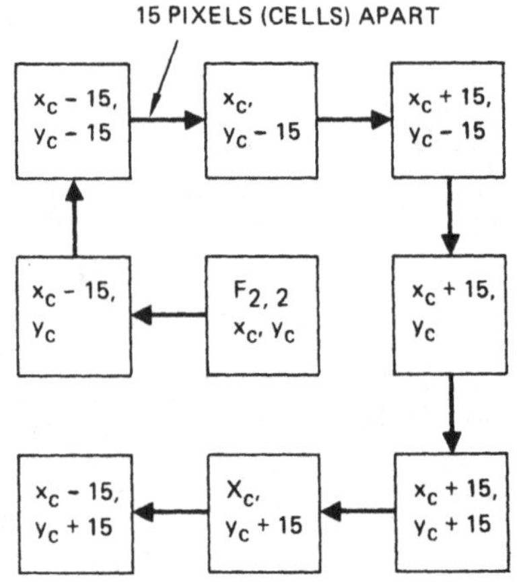

(b) 3x3 support points used by CAAPP cell (x_c, y_c).

FIGURE 9.17. Computation of $S_{2,2}$ support at CAAPP PE (x_c, Y_c).

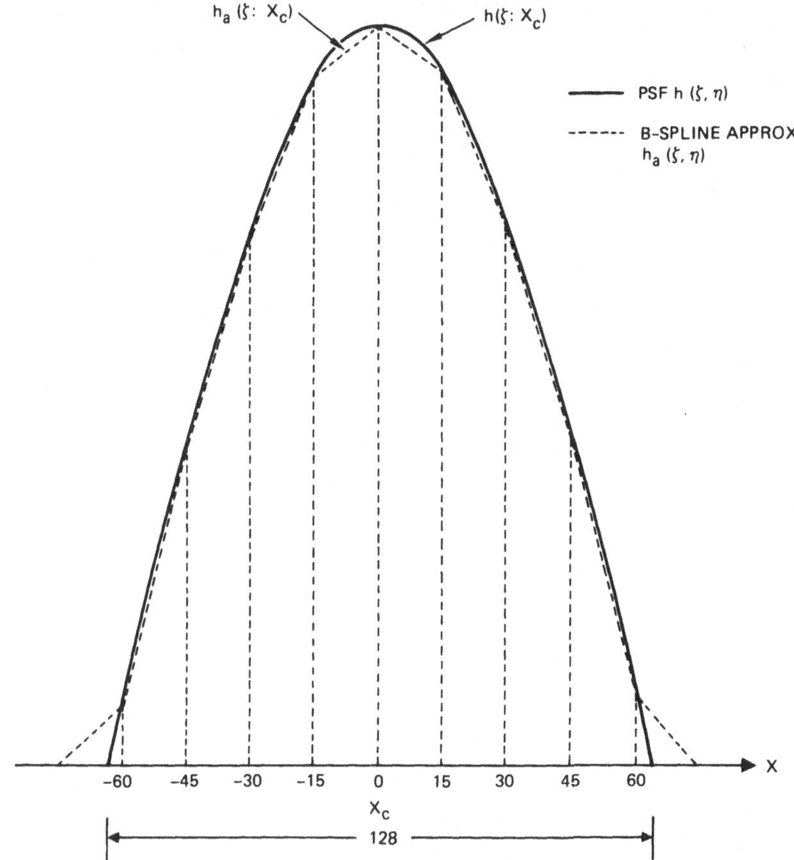

FIGURE 9.18. Profile of a 128 × 128 sine mask with its associated B-spline approximation.

sparsely sampled 9 × 9 values of $h(\varepsilon,\eta : x,y)$ based on the sequence shown in Figure 9.19, while all the CAAPP PEs distribute the $S_{2,2}$-values by shifts of 15 at each step (Figure 9.20). Note that each pixel has its own unique set of 9 × 9 $S_{2,2}$-values and every PE's $S_{2,2}$-value has been used, even though it travels in 15-PE increments.

A rough estimate of the time required for 128 × 128 convolution using the approach described in Section 3.5.1 is proportional to

$$128 \times 128(M + D + A) = 16K(M + D + A)$$
$$= 16K(M + A) + 16KD$$

where M is the time required for multiplication, D is the time for distribution of data to adjacent PEs, and A is the time for addition. Using the B-spline approach, the time required for the same convolution is

$$3 \times 3(15D + A) + 9 \times 9(M + 15D + A) \simeq 81(M + A) + 1.2KD.$$

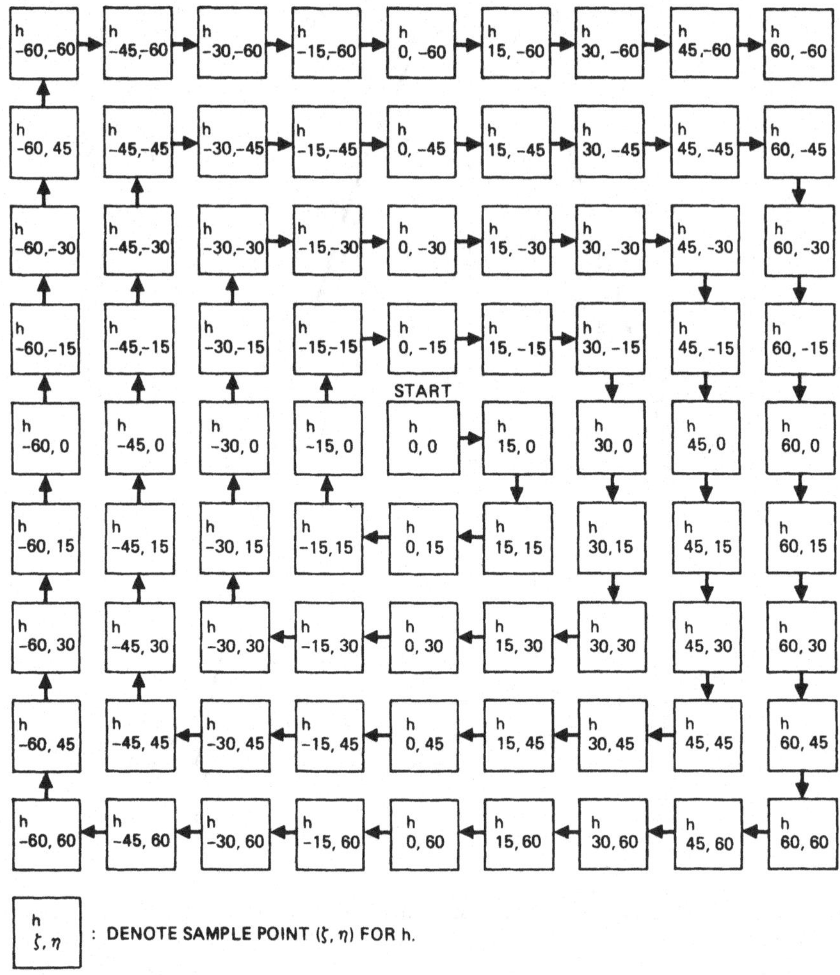

FIGURE 9.19. Broadcasting sequence used by CAAPP controller for the 9 × 9 sample values of 128 × 128 *h* mask.

The first term is the time used to perform the 3 × 3 convolution for $S_{2,2}$, and is negligible with respect to 9 × 9 convolution. The new algorithm thus achieves two orders of magnitude improvement in multiply-add time ($16K$ versus 81), while obtaining one order of magnitude improvement in the distribution time ($16KD$ versus $1.2KD$). Since the CAAPP nearest-neighbor communication is bit-serial, the resulting distribution time is larger than the multiply-add time for the B-spline approach. To see this assume the number of bits in $S_{2,2}$ is 32, since $S_{2,2}$ is the result of convolution with the integral of the input image. The number of bits in the mask value h is typically 8 (comparable to image value). Therefore, $D \propto 32$ and $M \propto 32 \times 8$, so that $M/D \simeq 8$ and $1.2\ KD/81(M + A) \simeq 2$.

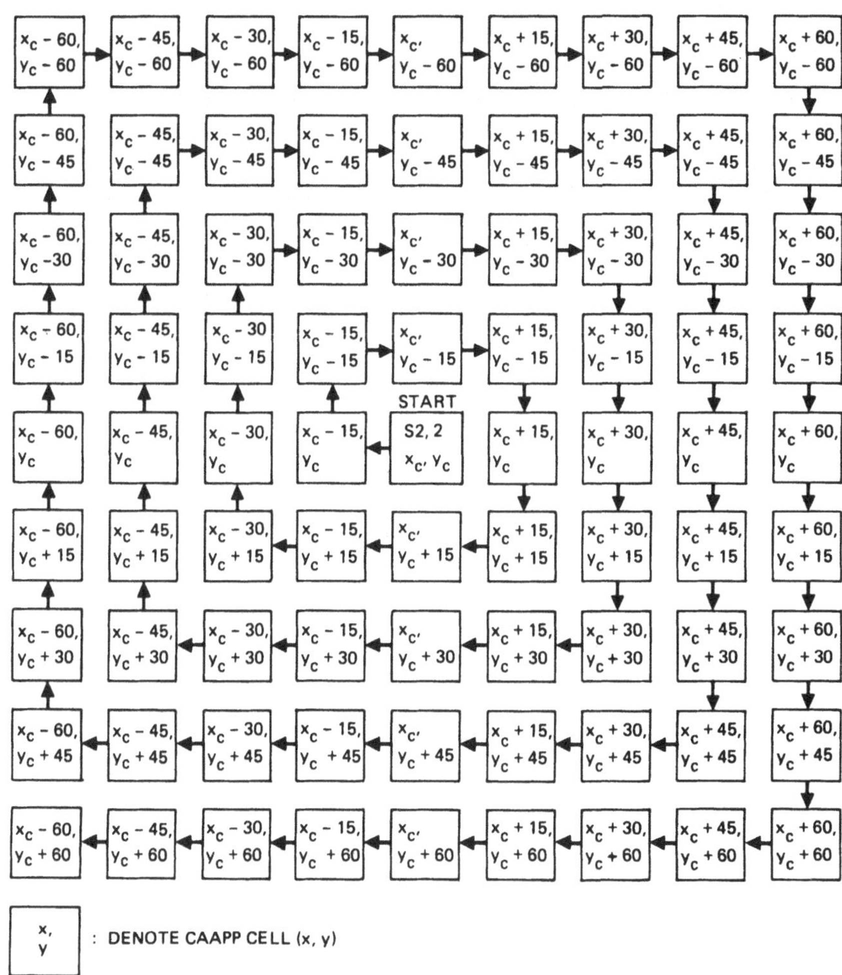

FIGURE 9.20. Distribution path for support data $S_{2,2}$ (X_c, Y_c) at CAAPP PE (X_c, Y_c).

3.5.3 B-Spline Approach Including NPA. By using the NPA level concurrently with the CAAPP array, the distribution time can be totally eliminated. Instead of having each CAAPP PE within the same NPA accumulating different sets of 9×9 $S_{2,2}$-values, while receiving the same set of sample values of mask h, we have each PE accumulate the same set of 9×9 $S_{2,2}$-values while using a different set of sample values of mask h. For a given mask function $h(\varepsilon,\eta : x,y)$, at the same sampling rate, there are many different phased B-spline approximations to h. As long as the sampling rate is greater than the Nyquist rate, the approximation errors should all be tolerable. Figure 9.21 shows two different phased B-spline approximations to a sine function $h(\varepsilon : x)$ 128 pixels wide. Here $h_{a0}(\varepsilon : x)$

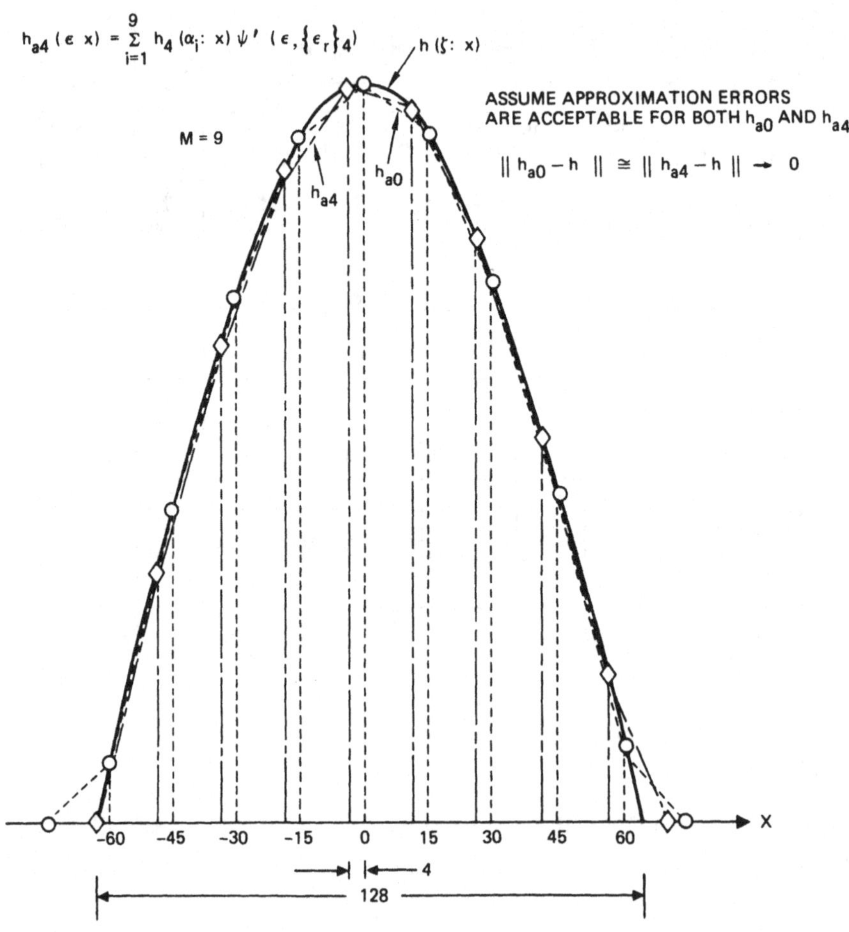

FIGURE 9.21. Different phased B-spline approximations of mask h with same sampling rate.

is the zero-phased approximation based on dotted sample points with values of $h_o(\alpha_i : x)$ and $h_{a4}(\varepsilon : x)$ is the result of phase shifting to the left by 4; the coordinates of its sample points, with sample values of $h_4(\alpha_i : x)$, are 4 units less than those of h_{ao}.

The approximations are given by

$$h_{a0}(\varepsilon{:}x) = \sum_{i=1}^{9} h_0(\alpha_i{:}x)\psi^1(\varepsilon,\{\varepsilon_r\})$$

$$h_{a4}(\varepsilon{:}x) = \sum_{i=1}^{9} h_4(\alpha_i{:}x)\psi^1(\varepsilon,\{\varepsilon_r\}_4).$$

If the pixel at $x = x_c$ is using h_{a0} as the approximation for h, while the pixel located at $x = x_c + 4$ is using h_{a4} instead, then they will share the same set of $S_{2,2}$-values for their corresponding but different sample points as shown in Figure 9.22. Assuming the 64 CAAPP PEs in a given chip have in-chip coordinates of the range of $\{(-3,-3), \ldots (0,0), \ldots (4,4)\}$,

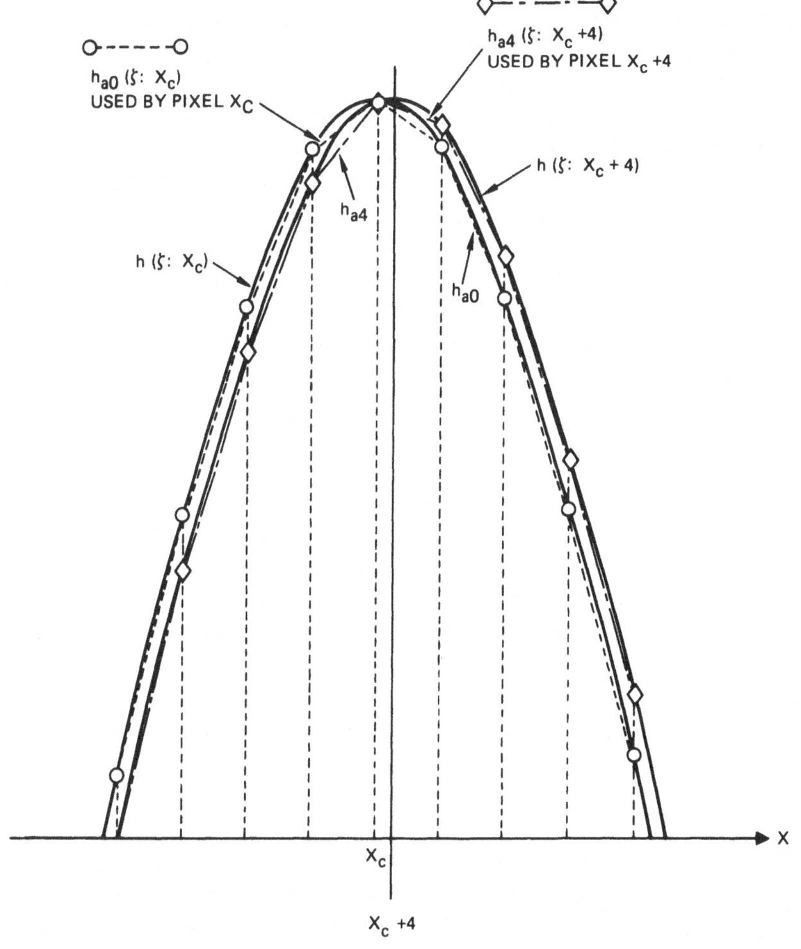

FIGURE 9.22. Two pixels, X_c and $(X_c + 4)$, using different approximations for the same PSF, share the same nine supports.

if the PE *(i,j)* uses the corresponding B-spline approximation $h_{ai,j}$, then all 64 PEs in a chip will share the same set of 9 × 9 $S_{2,2}$-values. Also, the set of h_a sample values is the same for every chip in the system.

Since the CAAPP memory is dual ported with the NPA, the CAAPP PEs can be using the current set of *h*-values while the next set of *h*-values is being loaded. Since each NPA has only one $S_{2,2}$ to transmit at each distribution step, the time it takes for communication is much smaller compared with the multiplication that occurred at the CAAPP level. Therefore, the theoretical computation time for the large-window B-spline convolution, which is faster than the conventional approach by the square of the ratio of data points to control points, is achieved.

3.5.4 Connected Component Labeling. Component labeling is an important task in many applications, the goal of which is to derive a unique label for each region in an image. For example, if the input image were a 1-bit digital image of size 512 × 512 pixels, then the output would be a 512 × 512 array of nonnegative integers in which pixels that were 0s in the input image have value 0 and pixels that were 1s in the input image have positive values. Two such output pixels would have the same value if and only if they originally belonged to the same connected set of 1s in the input image. The approach we follow is to determine which PE in the region has the minimum concatenated (row,col) coordinate and then to use that coordinate as the unique label for all of the PEs in that particular region. This approach guarantees the uniqueness of the label since each pixel coordinate is unique. This is done simultaneously on all regions by setting up a coterie network for each.

The initial gate settings for object pixels (i.e., value = 1) is

$$<N, E, W, S, NW, NE> = <*, *, *, *, 0, 0,>,$$

where the * indicates to be determined. In the example here we describe the 4-connected case, although the method is straightforward for the 8-connected case. Using the image in Figure 9.23 as an example, it takes four steps to set up the $<N, E, W, S>$ set of gates. (Background pixels (i.e., value = 0), have all gates set open.) For a given direction, the gates are closed towards a PE having the same value, but opened when the neighboring PE has a different value, as can be seen in Figure 9.23 for the two regions. After this initial set procedure all pixels within a region have their some/none inputs electrically connected.

The procedure to find minima using some/none responses is well known [Weems 1984]. Here, a simple local minimum example is given, adapted to the coterie network. Consider five gate-connected PEs having values of 2, 3, 4, 5, and 6, respectively, as shown in Figure 9.24. We want to find the local minimum 2 and store it in the label field of each PE. The procedure is as follows:

```
1  for I := 2 down to 0 do
2  begin
3     x-reg := -M(V+I)             ; x-reg of active PEs (i.e.,
                                   ; A-reg=1) are updated
4     if some then                 ; A-reg of active PEs will be
         A-reg := x-reg            ; updated only if some/none signal
                                   ; on Coterie net indicates "some"
5     M(LBL+I) := -some/none !     ; All PEs will store the some/none
                                   ; result in its label field
6  end
```

In this example, V is the starting bit position of the row/column value field and LBL is the starting bit position of label field. Again, an operation with a trailing exclamation point (!) will ignore the value of the activity bit (i.e., A-reg) and take place on all PEs.

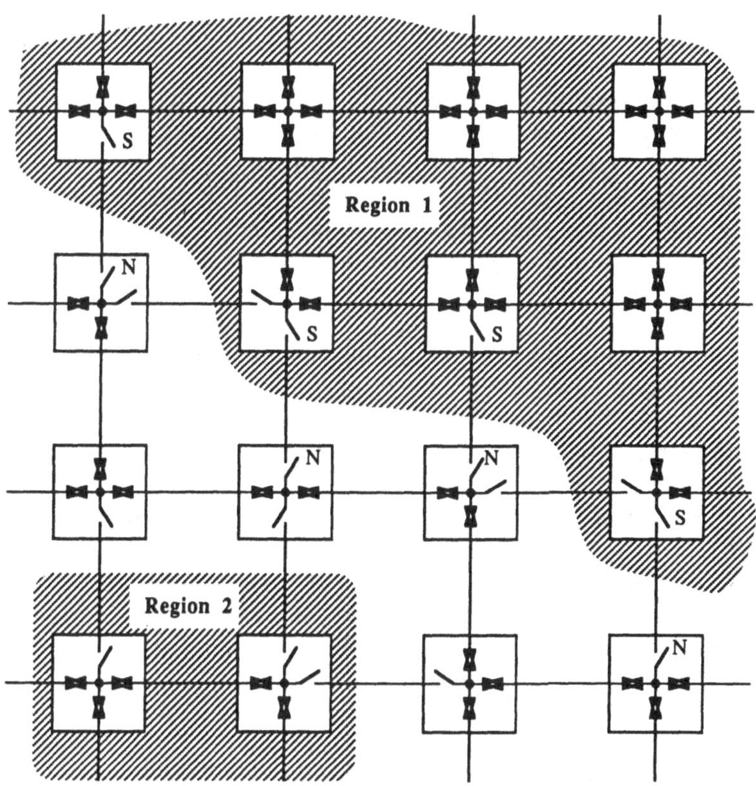

FIGURE 9.23. Coterie network applied to regions 1 and 2.

Steps	Index I	PE data binary →	2 010	3 011	4 100	5 101	6 110
0	Start	X	1	1	1	1	1
		A	1	1	1	1	1
		M(LBL)	0	0	0	0	0
1	2	X	1	1	0	0	0
		A	1	1	0	0	0
		M(LBL)	0	0	0	0	0
2	1	X	0	0	-	-	-
		A	1	1	-	-	-
		M(LBL)	1	1	1	1	1
3	0	X	1	0	-	-	-
		A	1	0	-	-	-
		M(LBL)	0	0	0	0	0

FIGURE 9.24. Connected component labeling.

Figure 9.24 shows the contents of x-reg, A-reg, and label field of each PE at each step in the loop. Initially, the x-reg and A-reg are set to 1. At step 1 (i.e., $I = 2$), the most significant bit (MSB) of the value is inverted and loaded into the x-reg. This is shown in step 1 in Figure 9.24 where the x-reg of PEs 2 and 3 have the value 1 (since their MSB = 0), whereas the other PEs (4, 5, and 6) have their x-reg set to 0. In such a manner, it is possible to eliminate PEs 4, 5, and 6 as potential candidates for the label.

Then a some/none test is made to determine if some or none of the x-regs in the coterie network PEs have been set to the value 1. The contents of the A-reg will be changed or updated to reflect the contents of their associated x-reg only if the some/none test is positive. Since in Step 1 the test was positive, the A-regs are set to 1 for those PEs with $MSB = 0$. In step 2, the shrinking process continues to the second significant bit for those PEs that are active. The x-regs of PEs of 2 and 3 are again set to the inverse of the second significant bit and thus equal to zero. A some/none test is conducted again. In this case, none of the active PEs have their x-reg at a 1 level. Consequently, their A-regs remain the same. Statement 4 of the code prevents turning off all the PEs if all x-regs are zero; this is the purpose of performing the some/none test in the first place. In addition, the label field for the second significant bit of all of the PEs is set to 1 (the inverse of the some/none test result). This is correct since the ultimate objective is to set the binary value 010 as the label field. The some/none result of other PEs in the image will not affect this group since they are electrically isolated.

In loop step $I = 0$, line 3, the x-reg are set to the inverse of the least significant bit (LSB). In this case, the x-reg of PE 2 is set to 1 since its LSB is a 0 whereas the x-reg of PE 3 equals 0 since the LSB of PE 3 equals 1. Again, a some/none test is conducted to narrow down PE 2 as the only active PE with A-reg = 1 at the end. At the same time, the LSB of the label field is set to the inverse of the some/none test, i.e., 0. Thus, all connected PEs in this group will have their label fields set to the minimum row/column binary value 010.

The time to perform connected component labeling is only proportional to the row/column word size, or 18 bits for a 512 × 512 image. Thus, to first order there is only a logarithmic dependence on the size of the regions in the image; however, there is no dependence on the number of regions. The estimate shown in Table 9.1 was based on regions of approximately 2,000 pixels.

An important consideration is the pull-down time of the coterie network. We use special hardware and software techniques to aid in this task. For example, one software technique we use is called the wavefront, and the associated procedure is

```
1  x-reg_PC := value;
2  for I :=0 to delay do
       begin
3         x-reg := some/none !
       end.
```

The first line precharges (_PC) the network and sets the initial value of x-reg to value. For an extreme case, there may be only one transistor activated by one x-reg to sink all the gates in the network. Due to the resistive nature of the x transistor, it can only sink the charges associated with neighboring pixels. Statement 3 does not permit precharging (i.e., no postfix _PC) and enables the neighboring PEs having the right some/none value to group together to help pull down the network by updating their x-reg. This wavefront will propagate exponentially because more PEs will be included in the process. The delay in statement 2 depends on the expected size of the local network.

3.5.5 Hough Transform. The Hough transform is an example of an algorithm that is as expensive in terms of computational complexity as it is useful in analyzing images. This occurs because the purpose of a large fraction of image-understanding efforts arise as a result of the need to identify man-made objects, which typically are built with some geometric structures. To perform this computation we use the CAAPP layer, where the pixel data and the coterie network reside. The basic idea is to set up parallel linear networks of pixels for each possible direction, and then to count the number of possible edge pixels associated with each line. This information can then be transformed into the traditional polar coordinates. We begin with the counting network.

The coterie net can dynamically support a degenerate binary tree so that grouped counts may be obtained in logarithmic time. Figure 9.25 schematically shows a degenerate binary tree for the case of eight PEs linked through a column net. Step 0 shows the net configuration for the lowest level of the binary tree, and steps 1 and 2 for the second and third levels of the tree, respectively. Since all levels of the tree time share the same net, the binary tree is a degenerate one. There are three types of leaf nodes at a given step: source (src), destination (dest), and idle. The

	"src" flags								"dest" flags							
	PE 0	PE1	PE2	PE3	PE4	PE5	PE6	PE7	PE 0	PE1	PE2	PE3	PE4	PE5	PE6	PE7
Step 0	1	0	1	0	1	0	1	0	0	1	0	1	0	1	0	1
Step 1	0	1	0	0	0	1	0	0	0	0	0	1	0	0	0	1
Step 2	0	0	0	1	0	0	0	0	0	0	0	0	0	0	0	1

(a) Contents of "src" and "dest" flags of every PE at each step

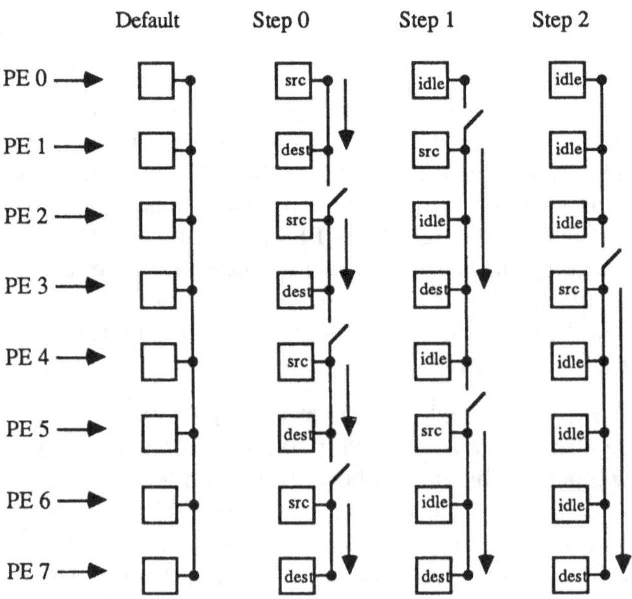

(b) Binary tree at various steps

FIGURE 9.25. Degenerate binary tree Coterie networks.

source PE is the transmitter of the count value, while the destination PE accumulates the received value with its own count and becomes source candidate in the next level. The idle PE is disabled from the net. To convert the default net into a tree at a given level, all the source PEs will open their upstream gates. For example, at step 0 in Figure 9.25(b), PE 2 will open its north gate to disconnect the tree of PE 0 and 1 and the tree of PE 2 and 3. Each PE contains two flags src, dest, and a count field to determine these settings. Figure 9.25(a) shows the contents of these flags of every PE at each step. The code to do the accumulation for step *k* is:

```
<net_gates> : = M[default]!       ;setup default net;: = [ ] loads
                                  ;a byte
x-reg, A-reg : = M(src) !         ;enable source PEs and turn off
                                  ;x-regs of other PEs so they
                                  ; won't sink net.
                                  ;M(src) contains the "src" flag.
<net_gates> : = M[UpStream]       ;source PEs open their upstream
                                  ;gates
z-reg : =0 !                      ;clear the carry registers
for I : =0 to length-1 do         ;operations performed bit-serially
begin
  x-reg : = M(count + I)          ;source transmit one bit of count
                                  ;via net
  A-reg : = M(dest)!              ;enable destination PEs to latch
                                  ;some/none result
  M(count + I) : = M(count + I) + some/none + z-reg
                                  ;dest. PE's accumulate Ith bit of
                                  ;counts of PE pairs.
  A-reg : = M(src) !              ;reactivate the source PEs.
end
M(count + length) : = z-reg       ;MSB of the count is equal to
                                  ;carry.
```

It takes 5 + 4 × length cycles to accumulate counts at a given level.

The src and dest flags and associated upstream-gate patterns can be prestored for a fixed mesh-of-trees network or can be dynamically computed during run time. For example, if consecutive sequential ID numbers, starting from 0, can be assigned to all gate-connected PEs, then the induced tree can be generated. In other words, based on the ID, each PE can know its position in the degenerate binary tree at each level.

To illustrate the Hough transform computation we use the simple 9 × 9 image example shown in Figure 9.26(a) and (b) and consider only one line orientation. Extrapolation to other array sizes and orientations is straightforward. Assume, for example, that there are eight 45° digital lines, $j, 1 \leq j \leq 8$, and the pixels PEs(x,y) associated with each line are shown in Figure 9.26(a), $0 \leq x,y \leq 8$. For the sake of clarity, all the PEs that

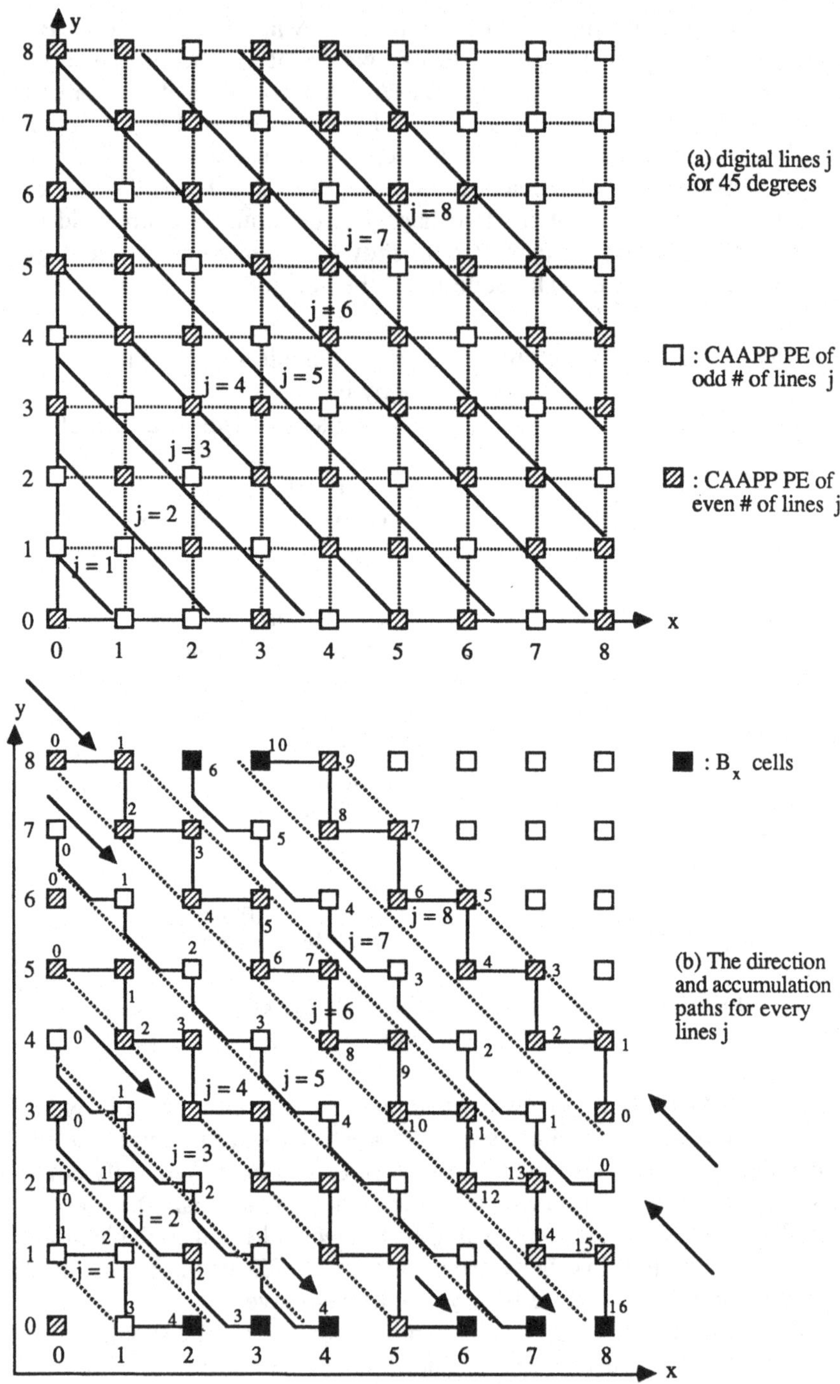

FIGURE 9.26. Coterie nets for Hough transforms.

belong to lines with an even number j (i.e., $j = 2,4, \ldots, 8$) are shaded. Associated with each value of j will be a coterie network that connects pixels along the 45° diagonals, as shown in Figure 9.26(b) and a degenerate binary tree mask supplied by the NPA. To isolate line $j = 7$ from line $j = 6$, we use the diagonal <*NW*> and <*NE*> gates shown in Figure 9.6. The direction for gathering counts is indicated. For example, at the upper right-hand corner, line $j = 8$ has 11 pixels from index 0 to 10, so that it takes 4 levels of the degenerate binary tree to accumulate the number of pixels having the image value of 1. The sum is accumulated at the edge of the array in the black boxes according to the directions shown by the arrows.

At this point the transform values have been found for one angle and the results in polar coordinates reside in the black boxes. The desired output is a rectangular array corresponding to the angle on one axis (y) and distance on the other (x). This can be achieved by using the coterie net to transfer all results in the black boxes to the left-hand column as shown in Figure 9.27(a).

To transfer the polar summation values in the black PEs to the correct row requires first that they move their contents to the left column of edge pixels. The transfer from the bottom row can take place in one step, as shown in Figure 9.27(a) (full line). The top two black PEs must move their sum in two steps, with an intermediate stop on the right-hand side (full line followed by dashed line). (Each movement, of course, involves correct prior setup of the coterie gates.)

After the polar values have moved to the left PE column, they are moved to the appropriate row according to the nets shown in Figure 9.27(b). The top four PEs are able to perform this movement in one step (full line), whereas the bottom five PEs make this move in two steps (dashed line followed by full line).

There is a well-defined algorithmic procedure for performing these computations for any angle and any size array, choosing the accumulation sites and transforming the results to rectangular presentation form. While this is occurring, the degenerate binary tree patterns for a given line direction can be generated concurrently by the second-level NPA of the IUA as mentioned. There are a variety of ways of generating these patterns, depending on various constraints. These patterns are passed via the dual-ported video RAM under dedicated hardware control and double buffering from the NPA to the CAAPP. Thus, when the CAAPP finishes accumulating the current direction, the patterns for the next direction can be swapped with just one instruction.

3.5.6 Graph Matching. Since graphs play an important role in the codification of information relevant to images, it is natural that a capability to try to match graphs or subgraphs would be highly desirable. This particular problem unfortunately falls into the category of those with exponential time complexity. In other words, the difficulty in comparing all

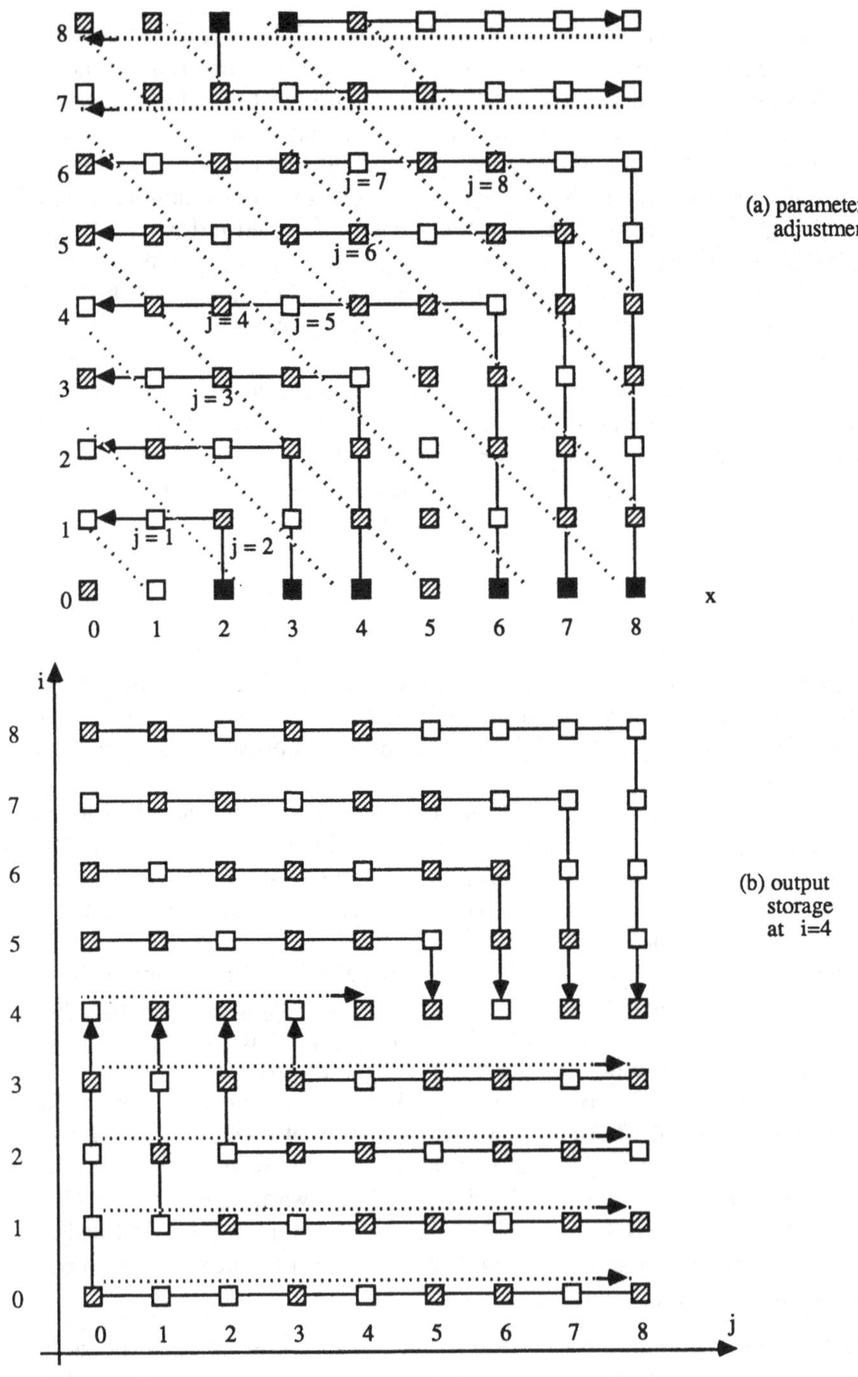

FIGURE 9.27. Coterie nets for parameter adjustment.

the possibilities of one graph with those of another increases exponentially with the size of the graph. There are a variety of search techniques and heuristics used to deal with this complexity. Here we describe one approach for the subgraph isomorphism problem that use Boolean matrix operations to support a refinement procedure that eliminates paths not leading to isomorphisms during tree search [Moldovan and Nudd 1983]. By using the CAAPP layer with its massive parallelism and efficient capability for simple Boolean operations, the iteration time of the procedure can be made very small. Thus, at least for relatively small graphs, all possible isomorphisms can be determined in reasonably short times.

The graph-matching algorithm is based on manipulations of adjacency matrices. We first define a $u \times v$ permutation matrix $M = [m_{ij}]$ whose elements are all 1s initially to contain all existing isomorphisms. The permutations of rows and columns of one adjacency matrix to match another is equivalent to a tree search. Moldovan used a refinement procedure due to Ullman [1976], which improves upon the brute-force method of testing all possible row and column permutations. This procedure tests the following necessary condition: if vertex i in graph G_g corresponds through an isomorphism to vertex j in graph G_h, then all vertices in graph G_g adjacent to vertex i must have corresponding vertices in graph G_h adjacent to vertex j. This means that for any $m_{ij} = 1$ in matrix M for which this condition is not satisfied, $m_{ij} = 1$ is changed to $m_{ij} = 0$. This simple idea can be translated into the following Boolean matrix equations:

$$R = M(k) \times G$$

$$S = H \times R'$$

$$M(k + 1) = M(k) \cdot S'$$

where $\times$ indicates Boolean product, $\cdot$ indicates logic AND, and k is the iteration number. Here, G and H are adjacency matrices of graphs G_g and G_h with u and v nodes, respectively. The equations are used in an iterative manner with $M(k)$ simplified to $M(k + 1)$ during iteration k. $M(k + 1)$ is then tested for isomorphism, which requires that each row of matrix M contain one 1 and no column containing more than one.

With the coterie network we can perform Boolean matrix multiplication so that the result R of first product is readily available for the second product to obtain S. To illustrate how this is done, we show in Figure 9.28 the wavefront used to compute the product of the $u \times v$ matrix M and $v \times v$ matrix of G for the case $u = 4$, $v = 6$. We assume that matrix M is assigned to CAAPP PEs(i,j), $0 \leq i \leq 5$, $0 \leq j \leq 3$ and call this group the left block. Matrix G will occupy CAAPP PEs(i,j), $0 \leq i \leq 5$, $4 \leq J \leq 9$ in the central block, and the product matrix R has CAAPP PEs(i,j), $6 \leq i \leq 9$, $4 \leq j \leq 9$ in the bottom block. During the operation, matrix M is shifted to the right at each time step while matrix G remains in place.

The product is obtained in the diagonal waves at the bottom of Figure 9.28(b). The nearest-neighbor communication network, used by the shift operation, shares the same mesh connection with the coterie net through time multiplexing. The coterie net is set up to connect all PEs in the same column, as shown in Figure 9.28(b). The logical AND operation is performed by the individual PE's ALU, while the OR operation is performed by the vertical coterie net using a wired-or pull down. The inner product result can be latched by any PE in a given column under control of the activity bit (A-reg).

At time step $t = 1$ shown in Figure 9.28(b), the inner product of the first row of matrix M and the first column of G is latched by PE(6,4) as r_{11}; of course as mentioned earlier, it can be latched by any other PEs in column 4, as will be useful later. At time step $t = 2$, the inner product of first row of M and second column of G is latched as r_{12} through the column 5 net while column 4 is used to latch r_{21} for the product of the second row of M and first column of G. At time step $t = 5$, column 4 of the net could be idling since all rows of M have been consumed. However, it is faster to start to compute the second matrix product $S = H \times R'$ as shown in Figure 9.29. Here the H matrix is substituted for the M matrix to be accessed by left block PEs for the shift operation into column 4 PEs after $t = 4$. However, unlike the earlier case, the result of first product is not stored in the bottom block, but instead in the top of the central block and complemented as r'_{11}, r'_{21}, etc. (The elements $g_{i,j}$ of matrix G are not shown for clarity.) The bottom block is used to store the result of the second product. At $t = 5$, the complement of the inner product of h_{11}, h_{12}, h_{13}, h_{14}, and r'_{11}, r'_{21}, r'_{31}, r'_{41} is stored as s'_{11} at PE(6,4) using column 4 net, while wavefront r'_{15}, r'_{24}, r'_{33} and r'_{42} at the central block are computed using the net in columns 5, 6, 7, and 8.

Since the CAAPP is an SIMD machine, and can only access the same memory location in every PE, values of $r'_{i,j}$ will be written over those of $g_{i,j}$. For example, at $t = 1$, r'_{11} occupies the memory where g_{11} was stored so that at $t = 5$, r'_{11} can be retrieved to compute s_{11} from the same memory address as those used by g_{15} to compute r'_{15}. This is an efficient procedure because the third operation, $M(k + 1) = M(k) \cdot S'$, requires ALU to perform logical AND. To support the third operation, we need to insert one more step before computing the R matrix. During the right shift operation of the $M(k)$ matrix, we add one more wavefront at the bottom block to store the $M(k)$ matrix. Therefore, at $t = 1$, PE(6,4) will store m_{11} and PE(0,4) will store r'_{11}. At $t = 2$, PE(7,4), PE(6,5) will save m_{21} and m_{12}, respectively, while PE(1,4) and PE(0,5) will latch r'_{21} and r'_{12}, respectively. These two wavefronts would be time shared on the same coterie net. After $t = 13$, both the S' and $M(k)$ matrices are in place and one logical AND will generate $M(k + 1)$ at the bottom block, ready for the next iteration.

At the next iteration, the left and bottom blocks will exchange roles,

$$R = M \times G = \begin{pmatrix} m_{11} & m_{12} & \cdots & m_{1v} \\ m_{21} & m_{22} & \cdots & m_{2v} \\ \cdots & \cdots & \cdots & \cdots \\ \cdots & \cdots & \cdots & \cdots \\ m_{u1} & m_{u2} & \cdots & m_{uv} \end{pmatrix} \times \begin{pmatrix} g_{11} & g_{12} & \cdots & g_{1v} \\ g_{21} & g_{22} & \cdots & g_{2v} \\ \cdots & \cdots & \cdots & \cdots \\ \cdots & \cdots & \cdots & \cdots \\ \cdots & \cdots & \cdots & \cdots \\ g_{v1} & g_{v2} & \cdots & g_{vv} \end{pmatrix}$$

$$= \begin{pmatrix} r_{11} & r_{12} & \cdots & r_{1v} \\ r_{21} & r_{22} & \cdots & r_{2v} \\ \cdots & \cdots & \cdots & \cdots \\ \cdots & \cdots & \cdots & \cdots \\ r_{u1} & r_{u2} & \cdots & r_{uv} \end{pmatrix}$$

(a) Boolean Matrix Multiplications

At $t = 1$, $r_{11} = m_{11} \bullet g_{11} + m_{12} \bullet g_{21} + m_{13} \bullet g_{31} + m_{14} \bullet g_{41} + m_{15} \bullet g_{51} + m_{16} \bullet g_{61}$

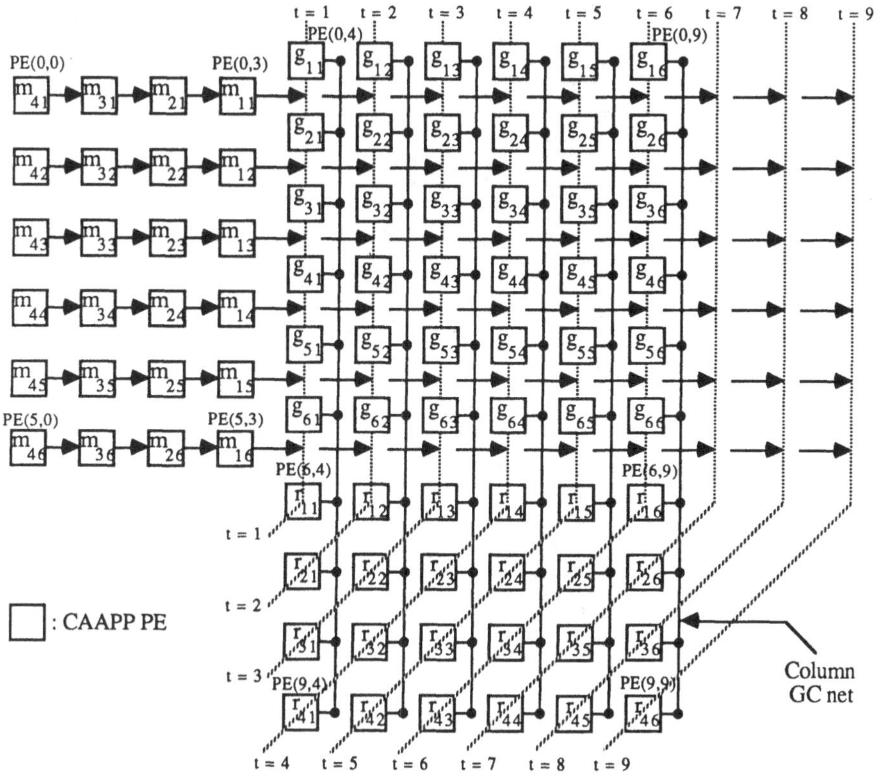

(b) Wavefront for the case u = 4, v = 6.

FIGURE 9.28. Coterie net for Boolean operation.

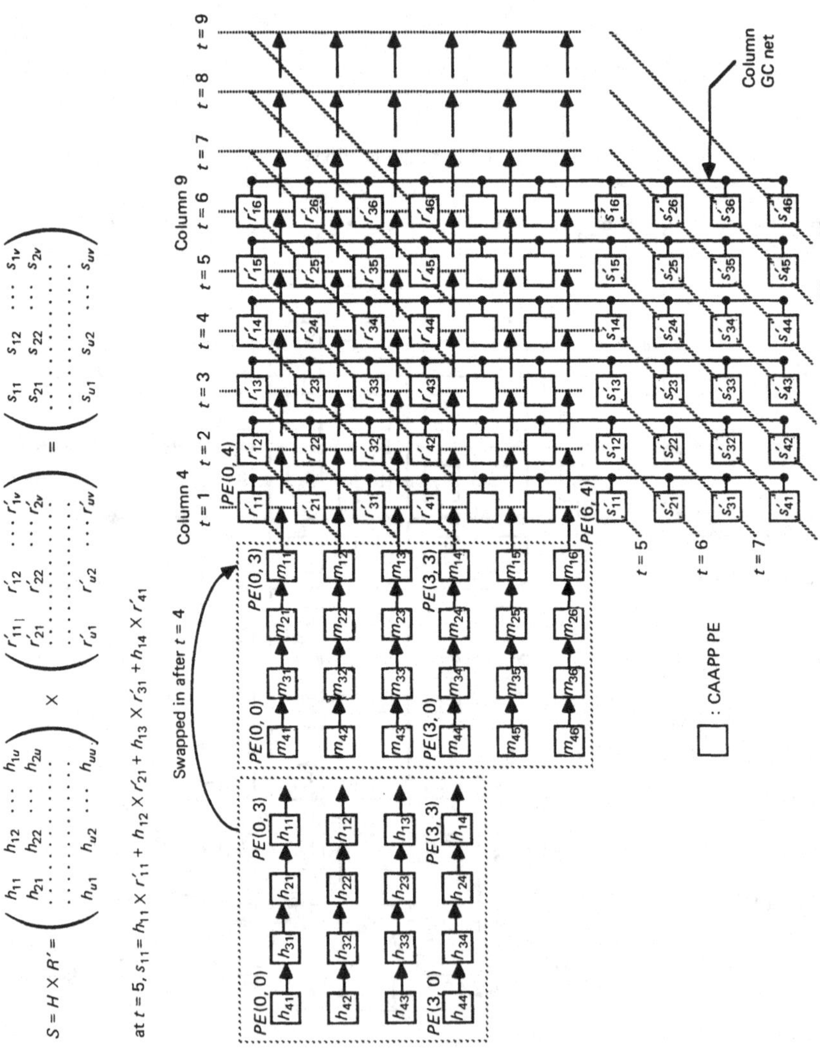

FIGURE 9.29. Wavefront for the case $u = 4$, $v = 6$.

and the counterclockwise rotated version of the G matrix will be used. In other words, instead of proceeding from left block($M(k)$) to central (R) and then to the bottom block(S), the operation will start from the bottom block($M(k+1)$) then to central (R) and left block(S). Iterative operations would be oscillating back and forth between left and bottom block. Thus, Ullmann's refinement procedure can be implemented with great efficiency.

Each iteration requires $(u + v - 2)2$ CAAPP PEs and the PEs need 12 cycles per wavefront time step. It is also possible to have several problems active if the CAAPP array is big enough. This could be useful because some iterations will generate siblings so that multiple-search paths in the tree could occur simultaneously as a result of a splitting operation.

4 Future Directions: High-Level Language Support

The programmer's view of the IUA depends ultimately on how he plans to use it. Having three different processor types and a busing hierarchy, the IUA could provide a relatively complex, if rich, programmer's model. Our ultimate goal, however, is to provide a more conventional programmer's model, in which the machine is a standard Von Neumann serial processor with intelligent memory. To access this intelligent memory the programmer would have available a few powerful, high-level language constructs that contain embedded parallelism to abstract the machine. An example of how we might proceed is based on using CmLISP from *The Connection Machine* [Hillis 1985]. To this it would be necessary to add multiple SIMD (MSIMD) and MIMD processing constructs such as Fork, Join, and Assign.

The three most important abstractions from CmLISP are xector representations and the α,β operators. A xector is a kind of generalized vector in which the elements are distributed across a large number of processors. Then, when operations are performed on a xector all processors can contribute simultaneously. For example, when two xectors are added together, processors take local values associated with them and add them to form a third xector. The α operator provides the capability to perform operations in parallel on a xector in a simple way. For example, the expression

$$(\alpha + '[a\ b\ c]\ '[d\ e\ f])$$

returns the result

$$[a + d, b + e, c + f]$$

where the bracket [] indicates the xector domain is a sequence of integers starting from zero. In addition to collective operations it is necessary to perform summations or grouping operations on elements of a xector. For example, to determine the number of regions in an image with particular characteristics the β operator could be used. Examples of β operations are

$$(\beta+\ [5\ 7\ 8]) \quad \text{returns} \quad (20)$$

and

$$(\beta\text{MIN}\ [13\ 2\ 9]) \quad \text{returns} \quad (2).$$

The α,β constructs and xectors are more complex and powerful entities than indicated here, but these simple examples illustrate the basic concepts. The remainder of this section provides examples of possible usage of these constructs modified for the IUA.

DEFSTRUCT is the common Lisp mechanism for defining structures with named components. It is important for programming the IUA. IUALisp would add three additional features to DEFSTRUCT to provide three options—:CAAPP, :NPA, and :GPPA. This would allow the programmer to specify that all structures of a particular type are to be stored on the CAAPP, NPA, or GPPA layer of the IUA, as, for example:

```
(DEFSTRUCT (PIXEL :CAAPP)
   GRAY-SCALE(8)
   LABEL(18)
   BINARY(1)
   DOMINATE(1)
   CMASK(4)
   TEMP(1)
   NEIGHBORS)
```

This causes MAKE-PIXEL to store new pixel structures on the CAAPP layer of the IUA. The components of this pixel structure can be accessed and modified as in standard Lisp. The only difference is that each pixel structure is stored in its own CAAPP PE/memory cell. This allows parallel xector operations to be performed on the structures or their components, as, for instance, the xector of all pixels or the xector of all labels. The statement

```
(DEFSTRUCT (SCENEOBJ :NPA)
   HSPA          ; Point to a xector consists of CAAPP-PIXEL,
                 ; NPA-HSPA & GPPA-HSPA
                 ; set representation is HSPA
   AREA
   LABEL
   ATTRIBUTES
   BBR)          ; Best bounding rectangle
```

causes MAKE-SCENEOBJ to store new scene object frame structures on the NPA layer of the IUA. A third example:

```
(DEFSTRUCT (GPPAHSPA :GPPA)
   ROWCOL
   GMASK(4)
   BINARY(1)
   TEMP(1))
```

causes MAKE-GPPAHSPA to store top HSPA structures on the GPPA layer of the IUA.

The following function statement:

```
(DEFUN make-array-x (dim0 dim1 start STRUC)
   ; x ε {C, N, G}
   ; C denotes CAAPP structure
   ; N and G denote NPA, GPPA
. . . . . . . . . . . . . . . . . . .
. . . . . . . . . . . . . . . . . . .)
```

where *x* is in *C, N* or *G* for CAAPP, NPA, and GPPA, sets aside storage space. Function make-array-*C* will make an array (xector) of size dim0, dim1 of structures (STRUC) with starting CAAPP memory address equal to start. The set of ROW,COL addresses of the CAAPP PE is the xector domain with STRUC as the range. For example, evaluating

```
(SETQ IMAGE (make-array-C 512 512 img 'PIXEL))
```

sets the value of IMAGE in the host to point to a newly created image xector of PIXELs residing in the CAAPP and

```
(SETQ S-N-MASK (make-array-C 512 512 0 'SOME-NONE))
```

reserves the space for a xector of some/none mask patterns required by the connected component labeling.

Parallel operations using the α operator are very efficient. For example,

```
α (setf (PIXEL-BINARY •IMAGE)
   (cond ((< (PIXEL-GRAY-SCALE •IMAGE) threshold) 0)
   (T 1)))
```

thresholds the image xector of the GRAY-SCALE component of PIXEL to separate object from background. The resulting binary image xector of the BINARY component of PIXEL will have 1 for the object and 0 for the background. The CmLisp symbol, •, cancels the effect of α, and indicates that the IMAGE xector does not need to be alpha converted. Similarly, the S-N-MASK xector in the following is not to be converted by α:

```
α (setf (SOME-NONE-NORTH •S-N-MASK)
   (cond ((= (PIXEL-BINARY •IMAGE) (PIXEL-NEIGHBORS-
```

```
NORTH-BINARY
        •IMAGE)) 1)
        (T 0)))
```

This expression sets up the NORTH gate of each PIXEL to configure the coterie network used to extract the minimum ROW,COL for each object as the object region label. The gate setup is based on comparing the BINARY component of the neighboring PIXEL to that of itself. If they are the same, then the gate will be closed. Evaluating similar expressions for SOUTH, EAST, and WEST directions will complete the coterie network for region labeling. The IUA kernel function extmin will extract the minimum value within all coterie-connected components. For example,

```
α (extmin 'PIXEL-BINARY 'PIXEL-LABEL •IMAGE
                'COORD-ROWCOL •coordinates)
```

assigns the LABEL slot of each PIXEL to the minimum ROW,COL such that all the connected regions will have one distinct label.

Alpha notation can also be used by xectors in the NPA layer of IUA. Assuming the range of NPA xector sceneobjs is made of the SCENEOBJ structure defined before; the domain is the row, column coordinates *(r,c)*, as indicated in Figure 9.30.

Thus, the expression

α(terrain-screen 'SCENEOBJ-ATTRIBUTES •sceneobjs)))
  $==>$ {$(r,c)_1$ ->pass $(r,c)_2$ ->pass $(r,c)_3$ ->fail $(r,c)_4$ ->pass
  . . . .
  $(r,c)_{n-3}$ ->pass $(r,c)_{n-2}$ ->fail $(r,c)_{n-1}$ ->pass $(r,c)_n$ ->unknown}

causes all the scene objects to go through the terrain-screen test according to their attributes. The range of the result is {pass, fail, unknown}.

The general form of β takes as arguments a combining function and two xectors. It returns a third xector whose values are created from the values of the first xector and whose indexes are taken from the values of the second xector. The combining function specifies how collisions are handled. It is used to reduce colliding values into a single value, as for example:

(β+ '[1 2 5] '[*X Z Z*]) ==> {*X* ->1 *Z* ->7}
(β* '[1 2 5] '[*X Z Z*]) ==> {*X* ->1 *Z* ->10}.

In IUA, β can be used to group all the scene objects passing the terrain-screen test mentioned earlier into one xector, group the failed ones into another, and unknown the third. The combining function merge-xector used will merge two colliding values (xectors) into a single xector. For example,

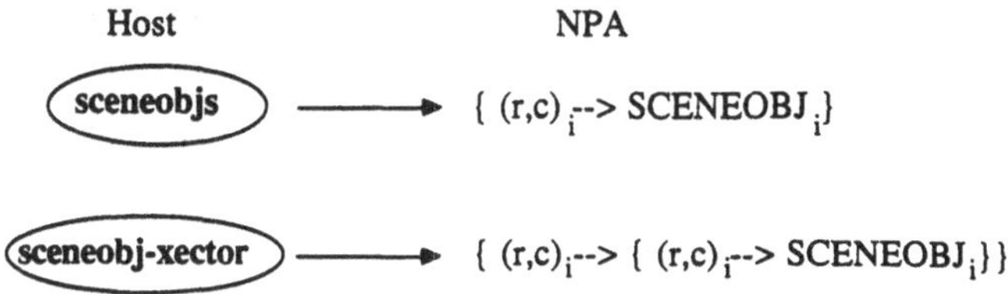

FIGURE 9.30. Scene objects xector.

(merge-xector '{(r,c)$_1$ -> obj$_1$ (r,c)$_2$ -> obj$_2$} '{(r,c)$_4$ -> obj$_4$})
==>
{(r,c)$_1$ -> obj$_1$ (r,c)$_2$ -> obj$_2$ (r,c)$_4$ -> obj$_4$}

The resulting β operation is stored in a xector called test-result according to

(setq test-result
    (βmerge-xector sceneobj-xector
    α(terrain-screen 'SCENEOBJ-ATTRIBUTES ·sceneobjs)))
==>
  {pass -->{(r,c)$_1$ -> obj$_1$ (r,c)$_2$ -> obj$_2$ (r,c)$_4$ -> obj$_4$ .....
        (r,c)$_{n-3}$ -> obj$_{n-3}$ (r,c)$_{n-1}$ -> obj$_{n-1}$}
  fail --> {(r,c)$_3$ -> obj$_3$ ..... (r,c)$_{n-2}$ -> obj$_{n-2}$}
  unknown --> {(r,c)$_n$ -> obj$_n$}}

Where sceneobj-xector is equal to

{(r,c)$_1$ -> {(r,c)$_1$ -> obj$_1$} (r,c)$_2$ -> {(r,c)$_2$ -> obj$_2$} ....
(r,c)$_n$ -> {(r,c)$_n$ -> obj$_n$}}

To extract the set (xector) of terrain objects that pass a screening test, the function XREF can be used or

(setq terrain-objs (XREF test-result 'pass))
==>
{(r,c)$_1$ -> obj$_1$ (r,c)$_2$ -> obj$_2$ (r,c)$_4$ -> obj$_4$ .....
(r,c)$_{n-3}$ -> obj$_{n-3}$ (r,c)$_{n-1}$ -> obj$_{n-1}$}.

Similarly, xector of nonterrain objects can be accessed or

(setq non-terrain (XREF test-result 'fail))
==>
{(r,c)$_3$ -> obj$_3$ ..... (r,c)$_{n-2}$ -> obj$_{n-2}$}.

Clearly, the issue of programming the IUA is a research issue. The purpose of this section is to indicate that the possibility of programming in a Von Neumann style is a reasonable one given an appropriate choice of language constructs. This feeling is based on written code in this IUA version of CmLisp that performs the object-recognition tasks outlined in Section 3.3. This activity is currently being pursued parallel to the IUA development.

5 Summary

We have attempted to give a broad overview of the IUA with particular emphasis on how it might be used. Tentative plans are to have a working 1/64th prototype slice running towards the middle of 1988 with various enhancements to be added periodically after that. While this machine effort will provide an important capability for real-time vision systems, we feel that it also represents a powerful tool for IU research. It will provide the throughput to run problems at rates up to 1,000 times faster than possible with conventional minicomputer-based systems. At the same time it provides the large memories and fast I/O required to support IU analysis.

Although we have described the IUA system in terms of supporting the IU problem, we feel that its applicability to real-world problems is much broader than this. For example, planning systems in autonomous land and air vehicles require a similar breadth of algorithmic requirements. They need a high-level, knowledge-based, expert system component as well as a capability to perform fast numeric and structured symbolic computations like our parallel versions of the minimum spanning tree and minimum cost path computations in Table 9.1. This is not surprising, because, as systems become more complex and sensor data arrive at ever-increasing rates, it will ultimately be very important to include knowledge-based reasoning capabilities to form correct interpretations. Thus, a parallel computer system with a tightly integrated numeric and symbolic processing capability would be highly desirable.

References

Ferrari, L.A., Sankar, P.U., Sklansky, J., and Leeman, S. 1986. Efficient two dimensional filters using B-spline representations. *Computer, Vision, Graphics and Image Processing*. **35** (Aug.), 152–169.

Hanson, A.R., and Riseman, E.M., Eds. 1978. VISIONS: A computer system for interpreting scenes. *Computer vision systems*. New York: Academic Press, 303–333.

Hillis, W.D. 1985. *The connection machine*. The MIT Press Artificial Intelligence Series, 31–48.

Little, M.J., Nash, J.G., Etchells, R.D., Grinberg, J., and Nudd, G.R. 1985. A three-dimensional computer for image and signal processing. *Proc. 1985 Custom Integrated Circuit Conference*. (Portland Ore.), IEEE, New York, 119–123.

Moldovan, D.I., and Nudd, G.R. 1983. A VLSI algorithm and architecture for subgraph isomorphism. *Phoenix Conference on Computers and Communications*. (Phoenix), IEEE, New York.

Payton, D.W. 1984. A symbolic pixel array for representation of spatial knowledge. *Proc. 3d Annual Intl. Phoenix Conference on Computers and Communications*. (Phoenix), IEEE, New York, 11–16.

Shu, D.B., and Nash, G. 1988. Minimum spanning tree algorithm on an image understanding architecture. SPIE, Orlando, Fla., Apr.

Shu, D.B., and Nash, G. 1988. The gated interconnection network for dynamic programming. In Tewksburg, S.K., et al. (eds.), *Concurrent Computations: Algorithms, Architecture and Technology,* New York: Plenum Press.

Silberberg, T.M. 1987. Context dependent target recognition. *Proc. 1987 IU workshop*. (Los Angeles), DARPA/ISTO, Los Angeles, 313–320.

Ullman, J.R. 1976. An algorithm for subgraph isomorphism. *J.ACM*. **23,** 1 (Jan.), 31–42.

Weems, C.C. 1984. Image processing on a content addressable array parallel processor. Ph.D. Thesis, University of Massachusetts, Amherst, Mass.

Weems, C. 1985. The content addressable array parallel processor: Architectural evaluation and enhancement. *Proc. 1985 International Conference on Computer Design*. (Portchester N.Y.), IEEE, New York, 500–503.

Weems, C.C., and Levitan, S.P. 1987. The image understanding architecture. *Proc. 1987 IU workshop*. (Los Angeles), DARPA/ISTO, Los Angeles, 483–496.

Weems, C., Riseman, E., Hanson, A., Shu, D., and Nash, G. 1987. Image understanding architecture. Technical Report 87-76, Computer and Information Science, University of Massachusetts, Amherst, Aug.

10
IDATEN: A Reconfigurable Video-Rate Image Processor

SHIGERU SASAKI, TOSHIYUKI GOTOH, AND
MASUMI YOSHIDA

ABSTRACT: This chapter describes a reconfigurable real-time image-processing system, IDATEN, that can process time-varying images at video rate. The development goal was to devise a system that could process and analyze dynamically moving objects in a scene, while also being able to process images at high speed. The basic design concept of this system is to improve the overall processing efficiency, from input to output of image data. We present a reconfigurable pipeline architecture for the image-processing system. In this architecture, multiple-processing modules are interconnected via a network. Each processing module can execute basic functions for image processing at video rate. The network is based on a Benes multistage switching network, and its configuration is extended such that multiple branching is supported for image processing. Based on this architecture, we have developed a prototype system named IDATEN, a video-rate image processor. The system was made up of a 16 × 16 network unit and a processor unit that consisted of 15 high-speed processing modules and video input/output modules. To process a time-varying image, the system programmers have only to determine the connection of pipelines and set parameters for processing modules in order to specify pertinent connection information in the network unit and to select the function of each processing module.

1 Introduction

One goal of present-day researchers in the image-processing field is the direct processing of moving objects. A moving object–processing system, as referred to here, should allow flexible responses to various types of image-processing request at the regular scanning speed of a TV camera, the video rate, which is normally 30 images per second.

In various fields, the need for digital image processing has been rapidly increasing. Some systems, using digital image-processing techniques, have already been developed for specific fields. However, conventional image-processing systems cannot always satisfy the demands made of them. For applications in a wide variety of fields, it is desirable to develop a high-speed flexible image-processing system that not only processes an image statically, but also processes multiple images continuously input from a TV camera at video rate.

To date, various kinds of image-processing architectures have been presented, including a fully parallel processor, multiprocessor, and pipeline processor. A fully parallel processor is one that performs parallel processing on a two-dimensional array of simple processing elements associated with the respective pixels of an image. Processors of this type include CLIP-4 [Duff 1976; Fountain and Goetcherian 1980], DAP [Batcher 1980], and MPP [Reddaway 1973]. A multiprocessor usually consists of more than one microcomputer that perform parallel processing on segments of an image. Processors of this type include PASM [Siegel 1981] and ZMOB [Kushner et al. 1981]. A pipeline processor is one that performs parallel processing on simpler processing elements connected in series, while data passes each of the component-processing elements. Processors of this type include SPARC [Allen and Juetten 1979], CYTOCOMPUTER [Lougheed and McCubbery 1980], and FLIP [Gemmar et al. 1981].

These fully parallel processors and multiprocessors are characterized as systems in which images are temporarily stored in memory and then processed at high speed. From the viewpoint of total system throughput, these architectures do not exploit the maximum performance available from the processors because it takes a rather long time to input or output to the storage from the peripheral devices. On the other hand, the pipeline processor enables the whole process, from data input to output, to be simultaneously achieved at high speed, although this architecture lacks flexibility.

To solve the problem of inflexibility while keeping the high speed of a conventional pipeline architecture, we propose a reconfigurable pipeline architecture in which a number of high-speed image processors are coupled via a network unit. The high speed is achieved by connecting the processors to form a pipeline at execution time. The problem of inflexibility is solved by switching the network unit under the control of a host computer, even though the processing modules have specified functions. To confirm the advantages of this architecture, we developed the prototype system IDATEN (IDATEN is the name of a Japanese fleet-footed god).

IDATEN consists of 15 processing modules and a 16 $\times$ 16 network unit and can continuously process time-varying images (512 $\times$ 512 $\times$ 8 bits) at video rate. The processing modules were constructed with dedicated hardware that have specific functions for image processing. To achieve video-rate processing, we designed each module so that it is capable of handling one pixel in 100 nanoseconds in pipelining. To achieve a flexible connection with small-scale hardware, we enhanced the Benes-type multistage switching network to enable image data from a processing module to be transferred to more than one module. The multistage switching network consists of a lot of 2 × 2 switching elements. To obtain the desirable connection using the multistage switching network, the state of each switching element has to be determined. We have also developed the efficient setting algorithm for the network. Therefore, to process a time-varying image, we have only to determine the connection of processing modules and specify pertinent connected information in the network unit using the setting algorithm.

In this chapter, Section 2 presents the architecture. Section 3 describes the prototype system IDATEN, including a network unit and processing modules in detail. Section 4 contains examples of image processing by this system and describes the program. In Section 5, we summarize our proposal.

2 Architecture

2.1 Conventional Pipeline Processor

The major advantage of a conventional pipeline processor architecture is that the processing modules (PMs) can simultaneously input, process, and output data. Figure 10.1 shows the configuration of a conventional pipeline processor. This architecture can process algorithms at high speed, but have lacked flexibility because the flow of processing cannot be changed. For this reason they have been used only in dedicated systems for special purposes in which high speed was required.

To solve the problem of inflexibility, a pipeline structure was proposed where the processing modules are connected through a ring bus [Temma et al. 1980]. It is shown in Figure 10.2. However, with this system, the maximum capacity of the processing modules cannot always be used, because the single data bus results in waiting and data collisions.

2.2 Reconfigurable Pipeline Processor

Figure 10.3 illustrates the proposed reconfigurable pipeline architecture, which overcomes the problem of inflexibility while making full use of the high processing speed. The enhanced Benes permutation network (BPN) provides mutual communication between the processing modules, enabling

FIGURE 10.1. Configuration of a pipeline processor with multiple processing modules (PMs).

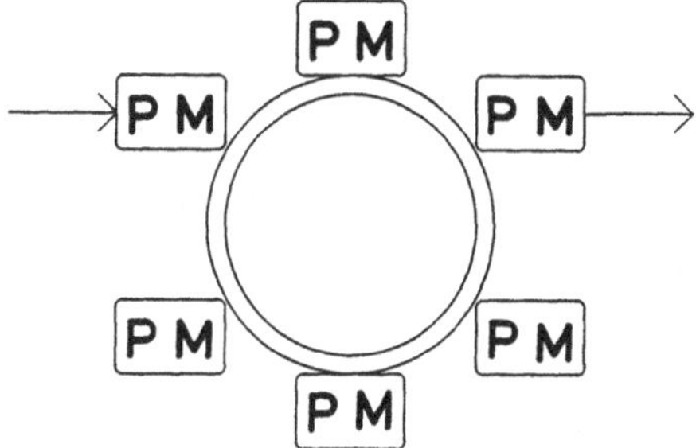

FIGURE 10.2. Pipeline structure, connected with multiple-processing modules through a ring bus.

the handling of complex image-processing algorithms. The pipeline configuration, consisting of multiple processing modules linked by the network, can execute image processing at high speed. Digital image data is input from port *A*, processed by PMs through the network unit, and then the processed data is output to port *B*.

Figure 10.4 shows an example of the processing flow for a system that is extracting only moving object in time-varying images. As shown in this figure, parallel pipeline streams must be able to be implemented on the

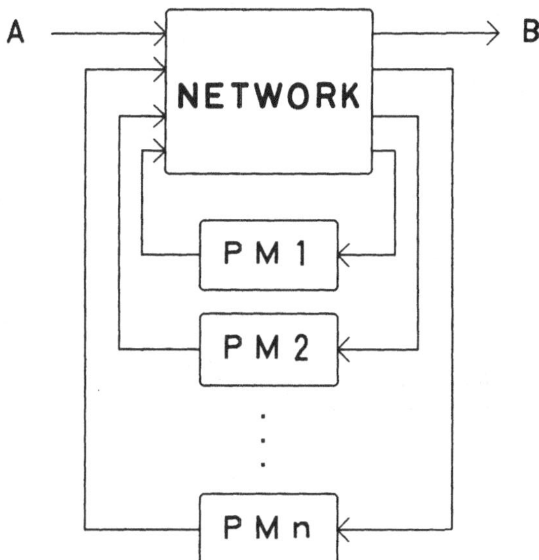

FIGURE 10.3. The proposed reconfigurable pipeline architecture, constructed with multiple-processing modules through a network.

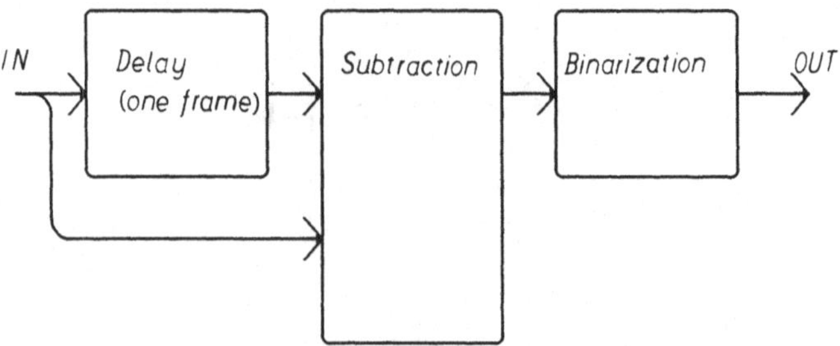

FIGURE 10.4. An example of the processing flow graph for the reconfigurable pipeline architecture.

system. We can support image-processing including parallel pipeline streams using the enhanced BPN.

A PM does not have simple arithmetic functions such as addition, subtraction, multiplication, and division, but does have basic image-processing operations such as filtering. By connecting the basic operations of modules through the network unit, the flexibility is achieved even though each PM only has one specific function. This will be explained in detail in the next section.

Another advantage of this architecture is its ability to handle colored image processing by interconnecting three processor units via the network, as shown in Figure 10.5. A binocular vision–oriented system is also realized by interconnecting two processing units. Thus, this architecture allows the connection and configuration of PMs in each processor unit, as well as unit interconnections, to be changed freely, so that various types of image processing can be flexibly supported at video rate.

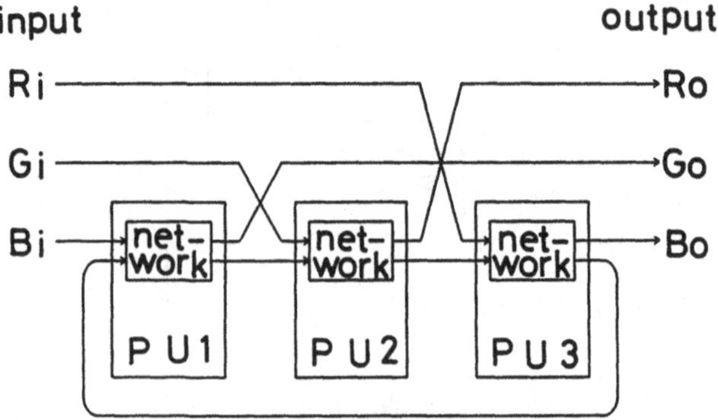

FIGURE 10.5. An example of system configuration for color image processing, with one processing unit (PU) each for red, green, and blue.

3 IDATEN

3.1 System Configuration

Figures 10.6 and 10.7 show the reconfigurable pipeline image-processing system IDATEN. The host computer consists of a 16-bit 68000 CPU, and 2M bytes of main storage. The IEEE 796 standard bus of the host CPU is connected to the processor unit via the bus adapter. All the control registers in the processor unit are assigned to the CPU's main memory-addressing area. The software for controlling the unit is written in the C-language.

The processor unit consists of a 16 × 16 network unit, 15 processing modules, and video I/O modules (VIM/VOM). The image data bus has 12 bits, 4 for video signals, and 8 for the image data. This system can

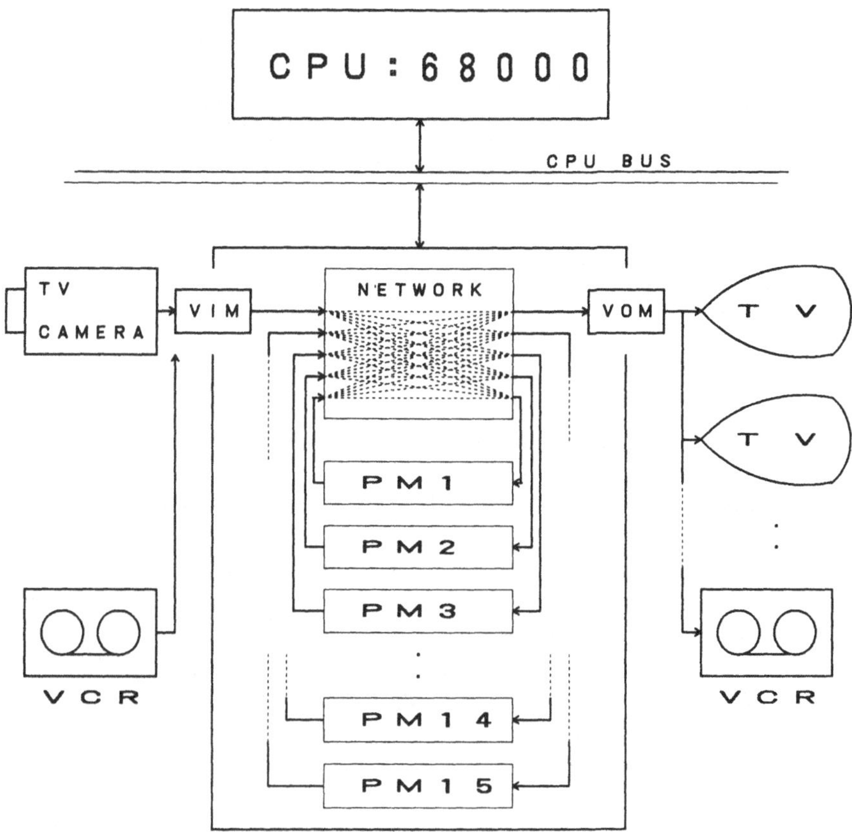

FIGURE 10.6. Configuration of the reconfigurable video-rate image-processing system, IDATEN.

FIGURE 10.7. Overview of the prototype system, IDATEN.

input and output a video signal that conforms to the EIA RS-170A standard.

The input image data streams are processed according to the following sequences: In VIM, the input analog composite video signal is separated into interlace horizontal and vertical synchronous signals and an interlace digital image with a size of 512 × 512 × 8 bits. The interlace image data and the synchronous signals are converted into noninterlace image data and synchronous signals. The converted signals and image data are sent to the network unit, and are processed in processing modules according to the network connections in pipeline. The control signals are delayed in each processing module to synchronize the control signals and image data. After processing, in VOM, the image data is transformed into interlace image data, and then converted back to an analog video signal. This configuration provides high-speed image processing, at video rate, of time-varying images from a TV camera or a VCR. The processed image data and extracted feature data can also be referred by the host through the CPU bus.

3.2 Video I/O Modules

To interface between video input/output devices and the processor unit, video I/O modules (VIM and VOM) convert the analog video signal into noninterlace digital data and the processed data into the analog video signal. Figure 10.8 shows the configuration of the VIM and the VOM.

The VIM consists of a timing generator, an analog-to-digital converter (ADC), and a scan-converter-1 (SC1). The timing generator generates two kinds of clocks ($\Phi 1 = 81.5$ and $\Phi 2 = 120$ nanoseconds) and an external synchronous signal (ES). To keep the aspect ratio of the pixel one to one, the video signal (VSi) is sampled and converted by the ADC every 81.5 nanoseconds. The synchronous signals are also separated in the ADC. Then, digitized interlace signals are converted into noninterlace signals by SC1. Each scanning line of the video signal consists of actual image data with a duration of 63.5 microseconds and a horizontal blanking time of 1.9 microseconds. To use this blanking period effectively for image processing, the SC1 also changes the clock rate and outputs the converted synchronous and image data every 120 nanoseconds.

The VOM consists of a scan-converter-2 (SC2) and a digital-to-analog converter (DAC). The SC2 converts the processed noninterlace data back into interlace format. Then, the data is converted in the DAC to obtain the analog composite video signal (VSo) every 81.5 nanoseconds.

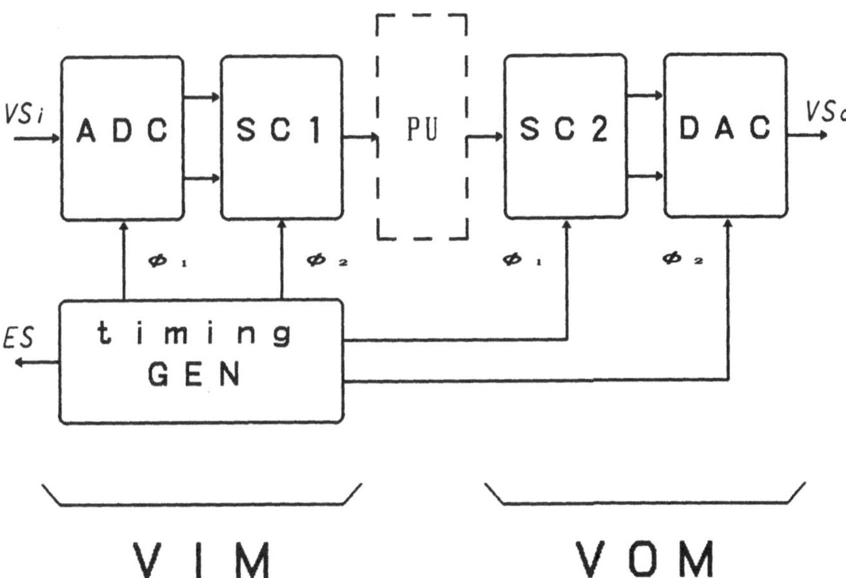

FIGURE 10.8. The configuration of video input/output modules (VIM/VOM).

3.3 Processing Modules

3.3.1 Interface. Each PM has an input video bus, an output video bus, and a CPU bus, shown in Figure 10.9 A video bus has 12 bits. Eight bits are for image data, and four bits for the control signals: vertical synchronous signal, horizontal synchronous signal, masking bit for the image, and parity. These video buses are internally linked between PMs through the network unit. The image data is input from the input video bus. Then each pixel of the image is processed in the dedicated processing circuit when the masking bit is 0. The processed data is output to the video output bus, or is stored in internal short-term memory in processing circuits. Since each PM has a different function and the number of pipeline delays depends on the kind of PMs, the four control signals are synchronized to the processed data by adjusting the delay time. The processed data can directly be accessed through the CPU bus as if the data were stored in the main storage of the host CPU.

3.3.2 Functions. For the prototype system IDATEN, we have developed 7 kinds of processing modules: a spatial filter module, logical filter module, median filter module, interimages operation module, feature extraction module, image memory module, and delay module. Each processing module can process one pixel in 100 nanoseconds. All modules are connected via the network unit, and 15 processing modules are implemented on IDATEN. To obtain high-speed processing, these modules are designed based on a local parallel architecture. A local parallel processor can input image data sequentially, generate a window in which the entire area sur-

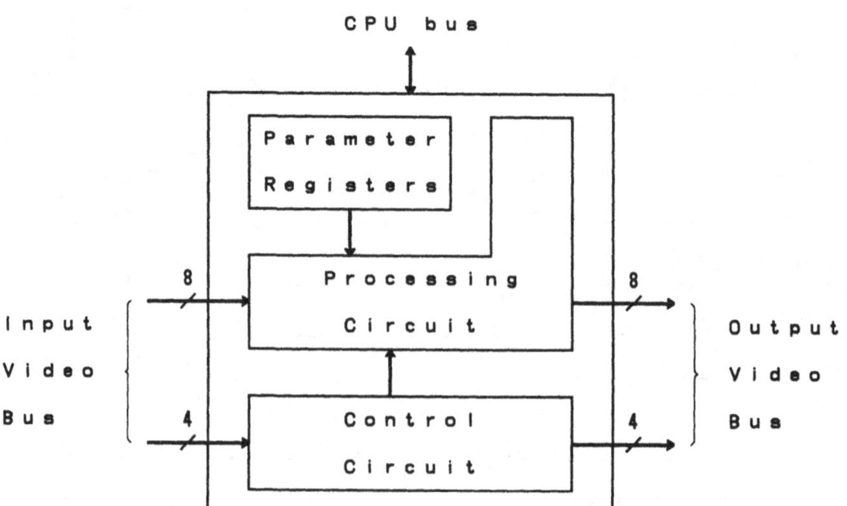

FIGURE 10.9. The interface specification of the processing module.

rounding an image pixel can be referenced at one time, perform parallel operations on the pixels in this window, and output the processed data simultaneously. These modules can also be combined in pipeline through the network unit.

The functions of the processing modules are as follows. Here, $g(x,y)$ denotes input gray-level image; $G(x,y)$ denotes processed gray-level image; $b(x,y)$ denotes input binary image; $B(x,y)$ denotes processed binary image; $m(x,y)$ denotes masking data for input image; where x is horizontal address, and y is vertical address of image throughout.

1. Spatial filter module. This module calculates the convolution in a 3 × 3 window, expressed by the following equation:

$$G(x,y) = \{\sum_i \sum_j g(x+i,\ y+j) * c(i,j)\} \cdot m(x,y)$$

where i and j are offsets in window $i, j \in (1, 0, 1)$, and $c(i, j)$ represents the weight coefficients.

Figure 10.10 is a block diagram of the spatial filtering module. The two line buffers constitute a local two-dimensional window inputting sequential image data. The weight coefficients $c(i, j)$ were previously stored in the registers from the ports (A to I).

2. Logical filter. This module inputs binary image data $b(x,y)$ and processes them with the following 3 × 3 window functions F.

$$\begin{aligned} B(x,y) = F\{&b(x-1,y-1),\ b(x,y-1),\ b(x+1,y-1),\\ &b(x-1,y),\ b(x,y),\ b(x+1,y),\\ &b(x-1,y+1),\ b(x,y+1),\ b(x+1,y+1)\} \cdot m(x,y) \end{aligned}$$

and

$$\begin{aligned} B(x,y) = F\{&B(x-1,y-1),\ B(x,y-1),\ B(x+1,y-1),\\ &B(x-1,y),\ B(x,y),\ B(x+1,y),\\ &b(x-1,y+1),\ b(x,y+1),\ b(x+1,y+1)\} \cdot M(x,y) \end{aligned}$$

where window function F can be defined arbitrarily by a 512-bit look-up table.

This module can be used for contour extraction, thinning, skeletonizing, or noise reduction for binary images.

3. Median filter. This module selects a pixel with median value in a 1 × 3, 1 × 5, 1 × 7, or 1 × 9 horizontal window, and is used to reduce noise in the image.

$$\begin{aligned} G(x,y) = \text{med}\ \{&g(x-4,y),\ g(x-3,y),\ g(x-2,y),\ g(x-1,y),\\ &g(x,y),\ g(x+1,y),\ g(x+2,y),\ g(x+3,y),\\ &g(x+4,y)\} \cdot M(x,y) \end{aligned}$$

where the function med { | } calculates the median of its argument.

Vertical median filtering can be performed by combining this module

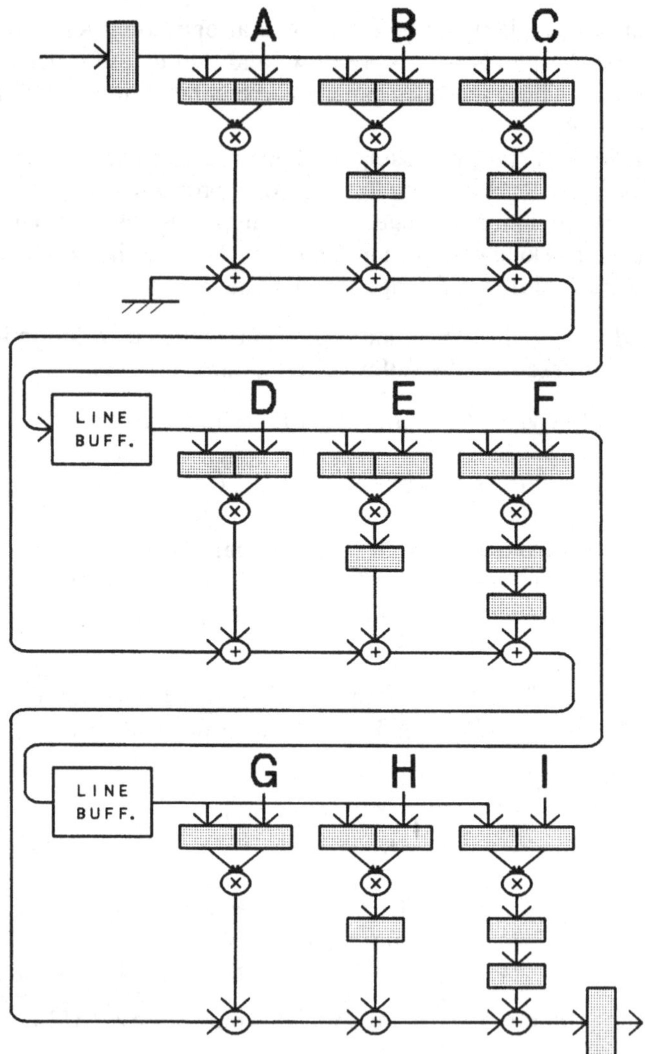

FIGURE 10.10. Block diagram of a 3 × 3 spatial filtering module based on the local parallel pipeline architecture. The symbols A-I are filtering weighting coefficients.

and image memory module, and rotating the image data 90 degrees in an image memory module.

4. *Interimage operation module.* This module inputs a set of two images and performs arbitrary operations using a 64-kilobytes look-up table.

$$G(x,y) = F\{g_1(x,y), g_2(x,y)\} \cdot m(x,y)$$

and

$$B(x,y) = F\{b_1(x,y), b_2(x,y)\} \cdot m(x,y).$$

This module can also be used for gray-level transformation for one image.

$$G(x,y) = F\{g(x,y)\} \cdot m(x,y)$$

and

$$B(x,y) = F\{g(x,y)\} \cdot m(x,y)$$

where the function F is defined arbitrarily by the host CPU. This module has a 64-kilobits look-up table and a $512 \times 512 \times 1$ bit masking image to generate dynamic or static masking data. The dynamic masking data is made from the set of two images using this look-up table, and output it as the masking signal. The static masking data is output from the masking image storage synchronizing to the processed image.

5. *Feature extraction module.* This module extracts features and stores them in internal memory at each frame. The extracted results can be referenced by the host through the CPU bus. This module has four functions. The first is a histogram measurement for gray-level images. The second is a horizontal projection calculation for gray-level image as shown by the following equation. The results of the projection $R(y)$ are given by

$$R(y) = \{\sum_x g(x,y)\} \cdot m(x,y)$$

The third is the histogram measurement for local properties in a binary image. This detects each shape in a 3×3 window, and counts the number of the shapes in a image. The fourth is the detection of local properties. This detects the specific shape representing 3×3 binary pixels, and outputs the coordinates of the image.

6. *Image memory module.* The image memory module is a kind of processing module. This module also has an input and an output video bus, as do other processing modules, and is connected to the network unit. This module has the following two major functions.

The first function is the rotation and scaling transformation of an image, at video rate, expressed by the following equation.

$$\begin{bmatrix} X' \\ Y' \end{bmatrix} = C \cdot M \cdot \begin{bmatrix} X \\ Y \end{bmatrix}$$

$$M = \begin{bmatrix} \cos\theta & \sin\theta \\ -\sin\theta & \cos\theta \end{bmatrix}$$

where X' and Y' denote the coordinates of a pixel after a rotation and scaling: X and Y are the coordinates of the input image, C is the scaling factor, and M is a matrix defining the rotation angle θ.

In order to transform images at a video rate, we had to solve the problem that random memory access might result in a low processing efficiency. To resolve this, we expanded the rotational matrix into the following expression:

$$M = T_1 \cdot T_2 \cdot T_3 \cdot T_4$$

where

$$T_1 = \begin{bmatrix} \sec\theta & \tan\theta \\ 0 & 1 \end{bmatrix}$$

$$T_2 = \begin{bmatrix} 0 & 1 \\ -1 & 0 \end{bmatrix}$$

$$T_3 = \begin{bmatrix} \cos\theta & \sin\theta \\ 0 & 1 \end{bmatrix}$$

$$T_4 = \begin{bmatrix} 0 & -1 \\ 1 & 0 \end{bmatrix}.$$

According to this expression, we can construct the rotation with diagonal transformations (T_1 and T_3) and rotation by 90° and −90° (T_2 and T_4). This expression enables memory addressing to be simplified and rotation transformation is possible at video rate with hardware.

The second function is the generation of a one-frame pipeline delay for time-varying images. This function can be used for detection of movement in time-varying images.

This image memory module can also freeze the time-varying images and we can directly transfer the frozen data by host computer through the CPU bus.

7. Delay module. As this architecture allows more than one parallel pipeline at the same time, it is important to synchronize the parallel pipelines. This module generates the pipeline delay of the video bus from 0 to 1.63 milliseconds to adjust the delay of the parallel pipeline. Figure 10.11 shows the use of the delay module (DM). When the pipeline delay is $d1$ for path A, and 0 for path B, we have to set a delay module with a delay of $d1$ in path B to synchronize the image data. The output video bus of this module is connected directly to one of the input buses of an interimage operation module without going through the network unit.

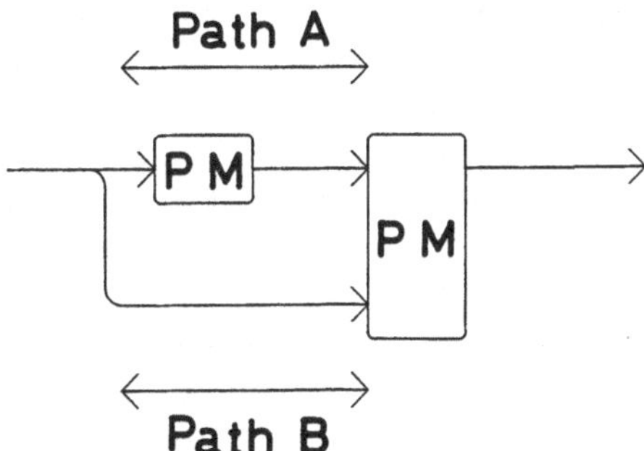

FIGURE 10.11. An example of delay module (DM) application. The pipeline delay is $d1$ for path A, zero for path B.

In this prototype, 15 processing modules are implemented. Table 10.1 summarizes the number of implemented PMs.

3.4 Network Unit

A flexible network unit is necessary to implement the image-processing algorithm in a system based on a reconfigurable pipeline architecture. Various types of switching logic have been proposed as a means of enabling information to be transferred at high speed for distribution [Siegel et al. 1979]. The Benes [1964] permutation network (BPN) is the most promising of the proposed network structures; the BPN is now able to connect every input node to any output node, while the hardware size remains small. However a conventional BPN can not provide multiple connection from an input node to multiple output node, which are necessary to implement various kinds of image processing. The BPN cannot connect an input node to multiple output nodes. To produce any desired combination of processing modules, we improved the BPN by enhancing the switch elements from dual to quad states.

TABLE 10.1. Summary of the implemented processing modules.

	Name of PM	Number of implemented PM	Nickname of PM
A.	Spatial filter	2	PM1, PM2
B.	Logical filter	1	PM3
C.	Median filter	2	PM4, PM5
D.	Interimage operation	3	PM6, PM8, PM10
E.	Feature extraction	1	PM12
F.	Image memory	3	PM13, PM14, PM15
G.	Delay	3	PM7, PM9, PM11

Figure 10.12 shows the states of the switching elements. In addition to the conventional straight and cross states, we introduced upper branch and lower branch for image data distribution. Moreover, we provided each switching element with three programmable logic arrays (PAL20X8) and obtain high-speed transfer. Our 16 × 16 (× 12 bits) network is composed of 56 switching elements, and its transfer speed is 20 megawords per second by interelement pipeline.

To connect the processing modules as required, it is important to develop a setting algorithm for determining the state of each switching element. Waksman proposed a setting algorithm for the BPN using a binary tree multigraph approach, whereby the number of operations to determine each state in the network are on the order of $O(N\log N)$, where N is the number of nodes in the network [Waksman 1968].

We developed a setting algorithm for our network by modifying Waksman's algorithm. Figure 10.13 is an example of image processing, which we are going to implement. The notation in each box represents the kind of processing module, and the number indicates the node on which the module is implemented. To implement this image-processing algorithm, the network unit has to be set as shown in Figure 10.14. Here, we represent the network connections using array $S(i)$, where address i means the output node, and $S(i)$ means the input to which output is connected. Using this

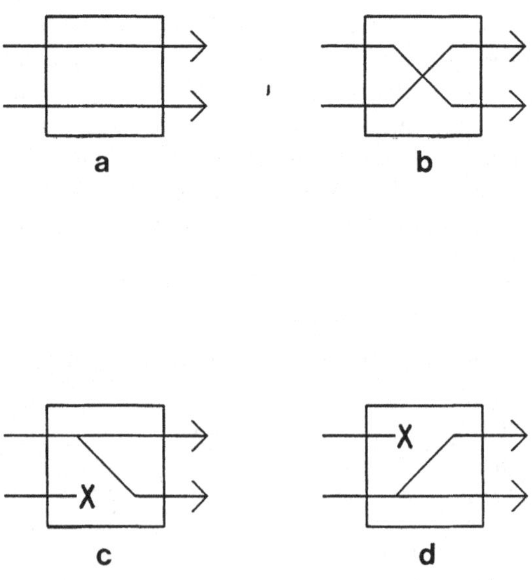

FIGURE 10.12. States of the switching elements in the multistage switching network, including the (a) straight, (b) cross, (c) upper-branch, and (d) lower-branch states.

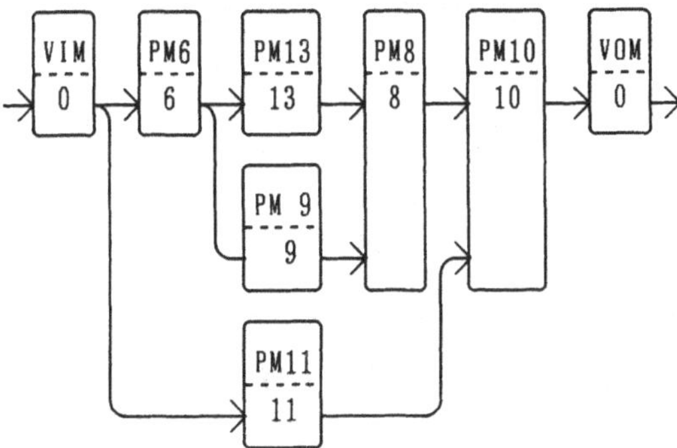

FIGURE 10.13. Sample flow graph for the established network; each number corresponds to a processing module or node number of the network.

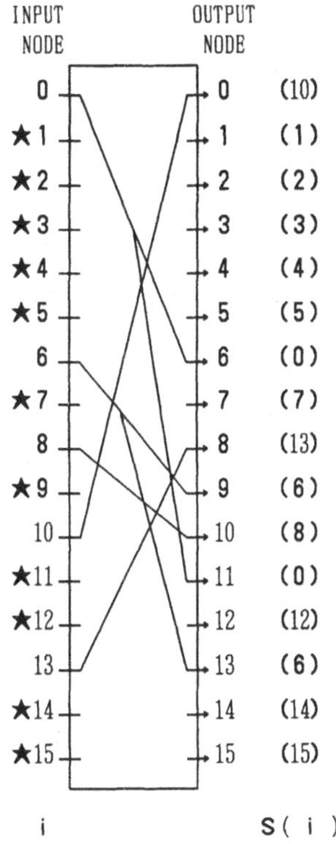

FIGURE 10.14. Connection relationship between the input and output modes; the symbol *i* is an input node, and *S(i)* means the input to which that of output is connected.

representation, the network connection in Figure 10.14 is expressed as follows:

$$S = \{S(0),S(1),S(2),S(3),S(4),S(5),S(6),S(7), S(8),S(9),S(10),S(11),S(12),S(13),S(14),S(15)\}$$
$$= \{10, 1, 2, 3, 4, 5, 0, 7, 13, 6, 8, 0, 12, 6, 14, 15\}.$$

Our setting method is explained here using the representation.

Step 1. Determine dummy nodes. Dummy nodes are source nodes that need not be connected to any destination. In the case of Figure 10.14, the star-mark nodes are dummies.

Step 2. Substitute the dummy nodes with the duplicated source nodes. For example, the connections represented by expression are exchanged by the connection represented by the following expression:

$$S' = \{10, 11, 2, 3, 4, 5, 1, 9, 13, 7, 8, 0, 12, 6, 14, 15\}.$$

Step 3. Determine the state of each switching element using Waksman's setting algorithm enabling one-to-one communication to be established. In this step, each switching element is tentatively set to either the straight or cross state.

Step 4. Find the switching element whose inputs are connected to the duplicated source node and the corresponding substituted dummy node. If the switching element is not found, substitute the dummy nodes with other duplicated source nodes, and go to step 2.

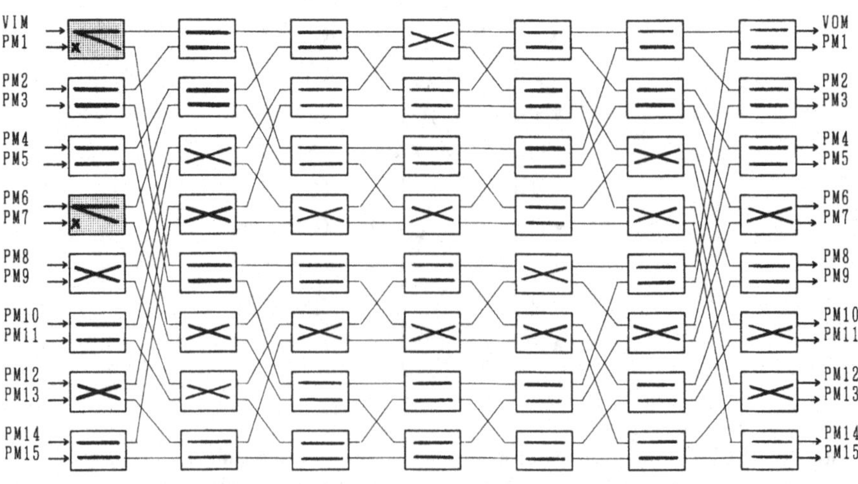

FIGURE 10.15. Status of each switching element in the network, determined on the basis of our setting algorithm.

Step 5. When the switching element is found, change the state of the switching element to either upper branch or lower branch.

Figure 10.15 shows the states of each switching element in the network determined by the algorithm. The system expansion shown in Figure 10.5 can be constructed by interconnecting more than one network.

4 Experiments and Results

To verify the high speed of the reconfigurable pipeline architecture, we performed the following experiments. Time-varying TV images were input to IDATEN. After being processed, the output images were displayed on a TV monitor. The input image is shown in Figure 10.16. The train was the only moving object in the scene.

4.1 Experiment 1

Figure 10.17 shows an example flow of binary image processing. The grey-level image from the TV camera was converted to a binary image at a predetermined threshold using the grey-level transformation module (PM6). The contours were then extracted using the 3 × 3 logical filtering

FIGURE 10.16. Original image of a moving object; the only moving object in the scene is the train.

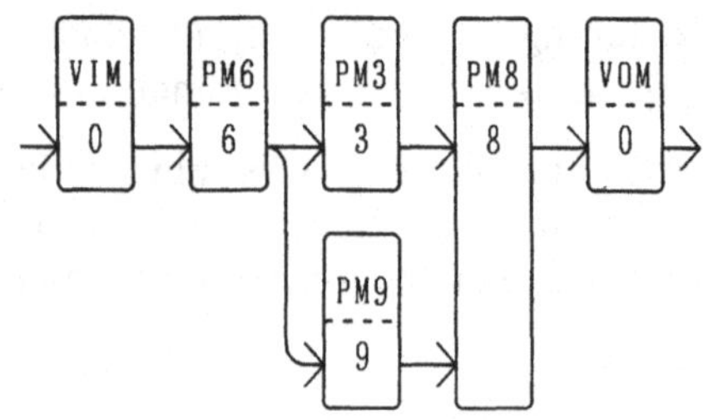

FIGURE 10.17. Flow graph for experiment 1.

module (PM3), and were superimposed on the original image using interimage operation module (PM8). The PM9 is the delay module to synchronize the input of the interimage operation module, the PM connections and the parameter setting for the related modules for this system are obtained by the following commands.

```
network (8 1 2 6 4 5 0 7 3 6 10 11 12 13 14 15)
binary 30 -> PM6
contour -> PM3
or -> PM8.
```

Such command strings, consisting of network, binary, contour, and or, as expressed in the form of the expression, are usually coded in C-language and input by operators via a host terminal. The network command determines the states of each switching element in the network unit to implement the flow graph, and this command is also provided adaptively to set the delay time into the delay module (PM9). Other commands are provided to set parameters in each PM. Figures 10.18 and 10.19 show the processing results for PM6 and PM3 at the instants shown in Figure 10.17.

4.2 Experiment 2

Input images represented by unsigned numbers were transformed into signed images using the interimage operation module (PM6). After detecting the edges using the 3 × 3 spatial filtering module (PM1), the processed image was transformed into unsigned values using the interimage operation module (PM8) superimposed on the original image using the interimage operation module (PM10). PM11 is the delay module to synchronize the input images of interimage operation module. Figure 10.20 shows the flow. The connections are obtained using the following commands:

```
network (10 6 2 3 4 5 0 7 1 8 1 12 13 14 15)
sign -> PM6
filter 1 1 1 0 0 0 −1 −1 −1 -> PM1
unsign -> PM8
addition -> PM10.
```

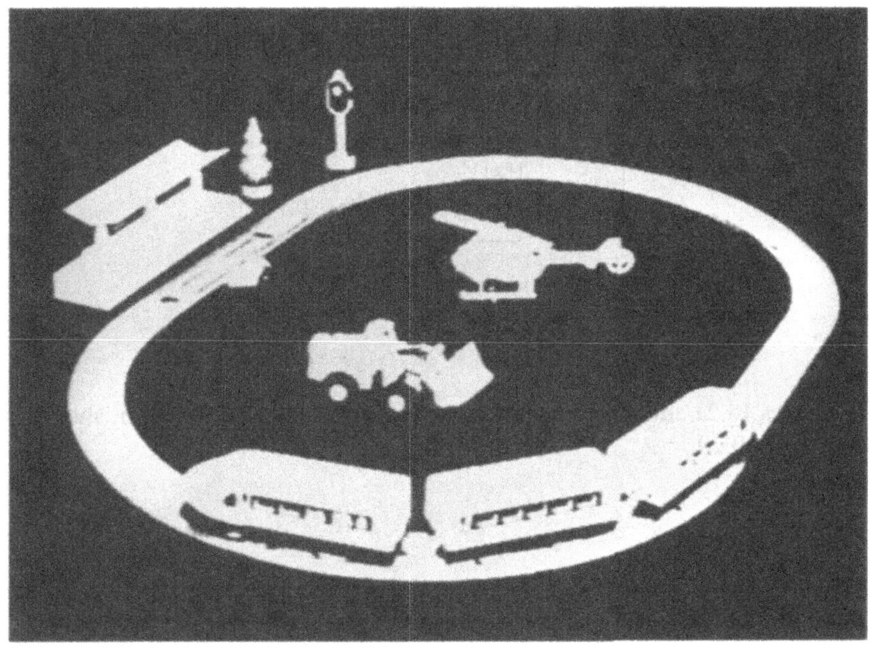

FIGURE 10.18. Binary image at threshold level 30.

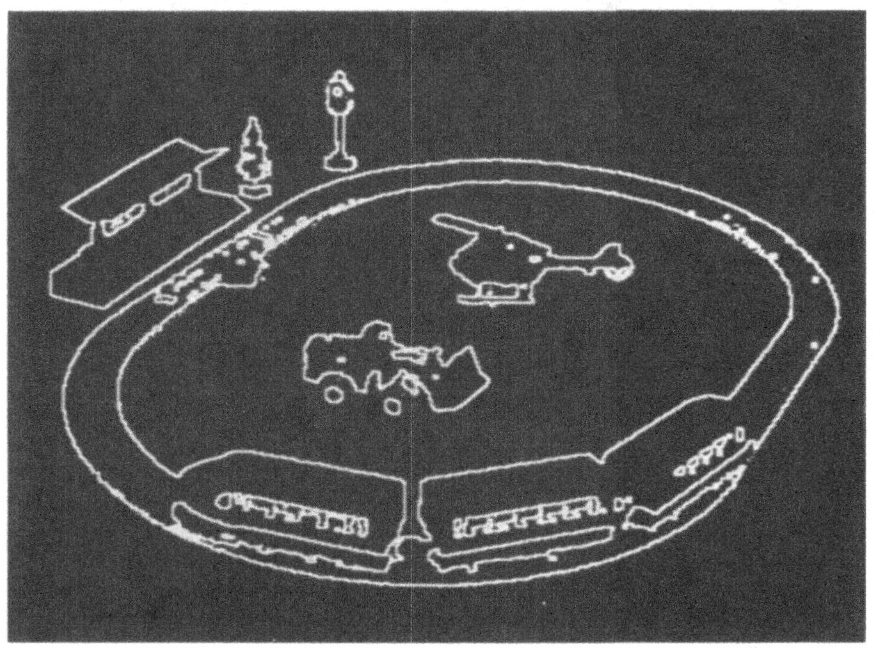

FIGURE 10.19. Contour of Figure 10.18, extracted using PM3.

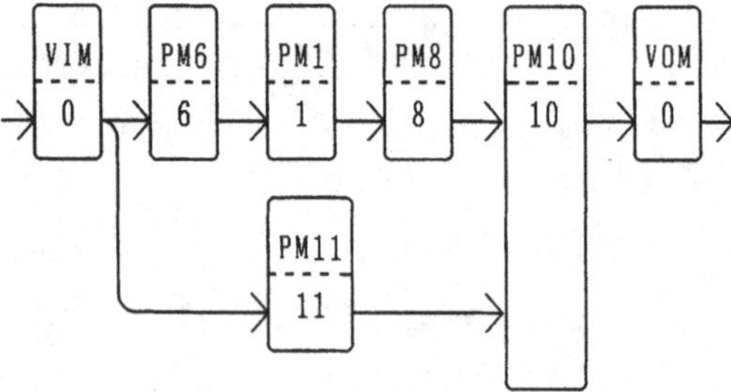

FIGURE 10.20. Flow graph of experiment 2.

Figures 10.21 and 10.22 show the processing results for the point shown in Figure 10.20.

4.3 Experiment 3

The moving parts were extracted from the input image. The original image was overlaid with the extracted image, allowing the velocity and accel-

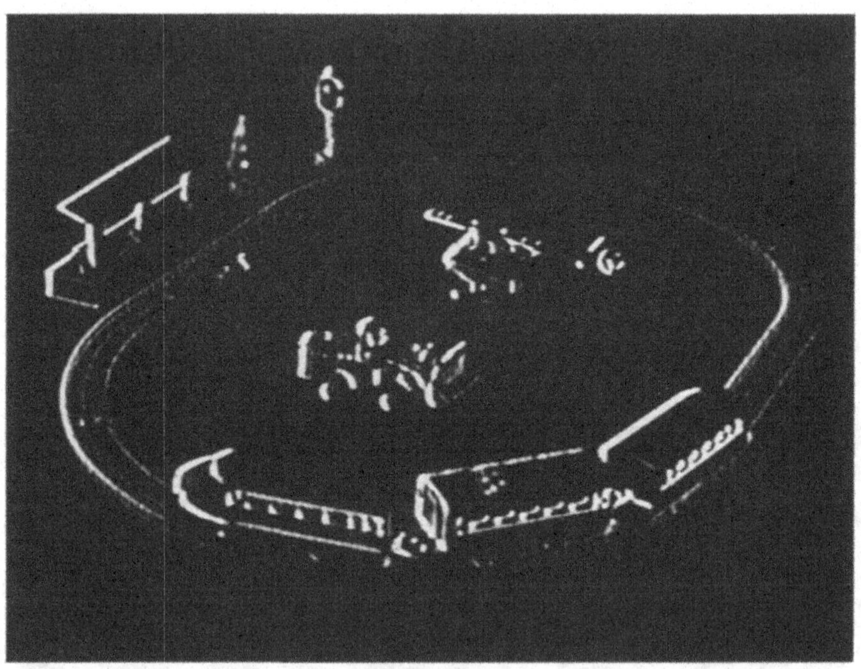

FIGURE 10.21. Vertical edges, which were extracted using the PM1 3 × 3 spatial filtering module.

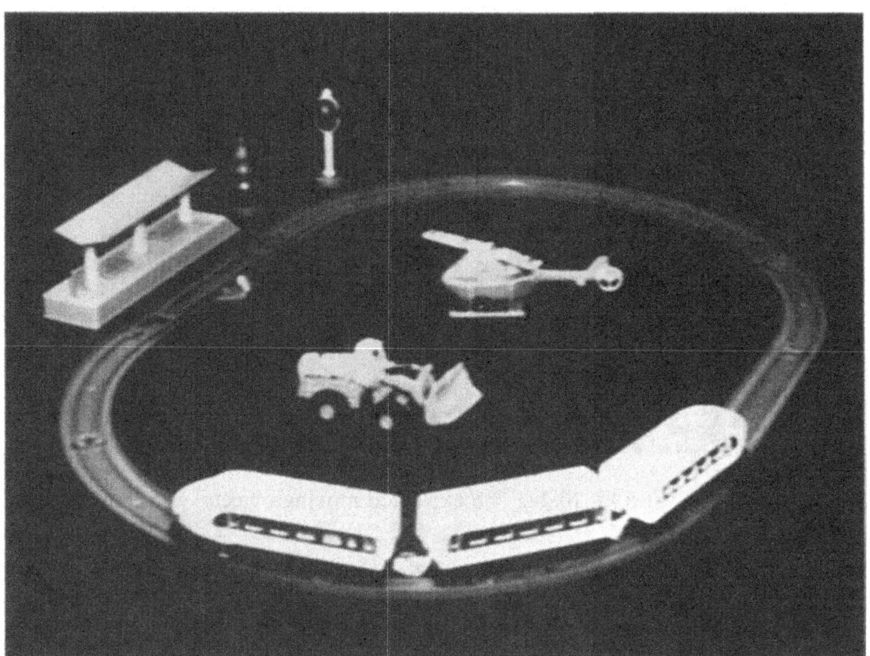

FIGURE 10.22. Edge-emphasized image, output from PM10.

eration of any moving object to be measured. Figure 10.23 is the flow graph. The connections are obtained by the following command:

network (10 6 2 3 4 5 0 7 1 9 8 1 12 13 14 15)
subtraction -> PM6
binary 40 -> PM8
or -> PM10.

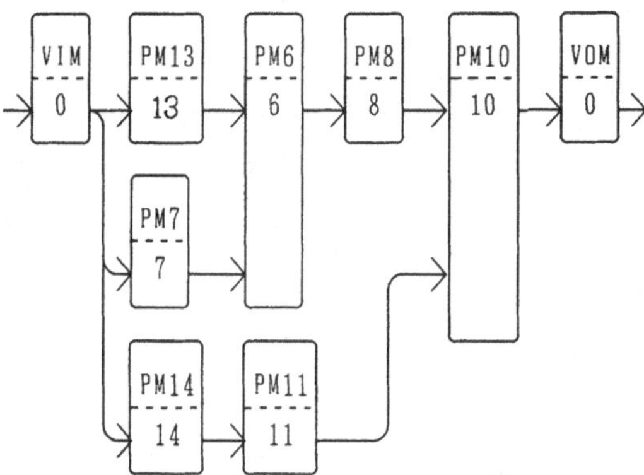

FIGURE 10.23. Flow graph of experiment 3.

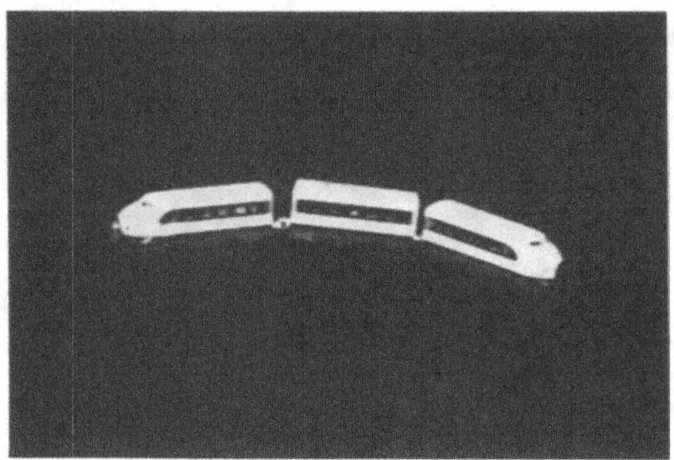

FIGURE 10.24. The extracted moving objects.

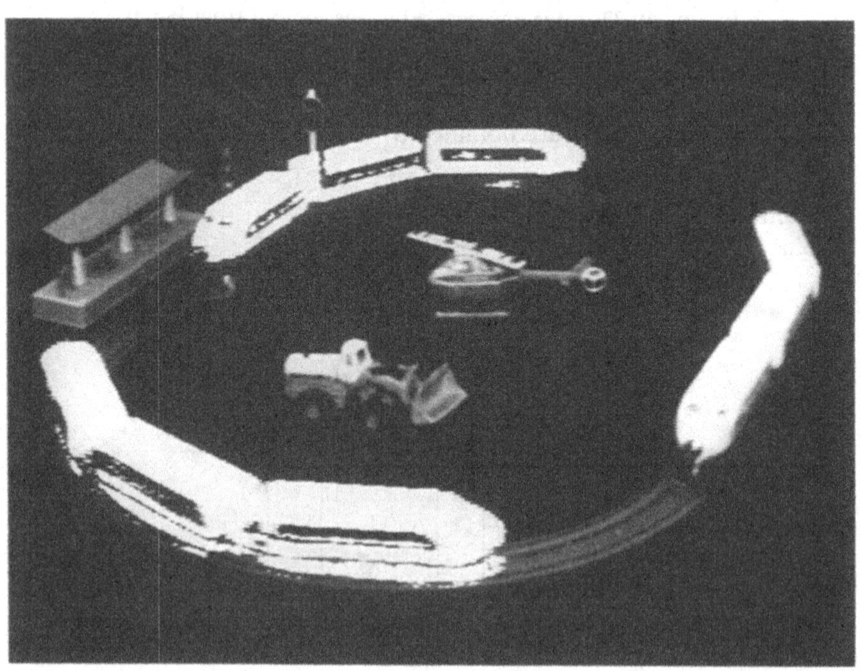

FIGURE 10.25. Overlaid images of a moving object at several instances, output from PM10.

Figures 10.24 and 10.25 show the processing results for a certain frame of time-varying images shown in Figure 10.23.

The results of these three experiments verify that this architecture enables video-rate processing, which has not been possible using conventional architectures. We cannot compare the processing speed of this system with that of general-purpose computers. However, if we consider basic arithmetic and logical operations as single instructions, we find that the processing speed is higher than 500 MIPS for a simple process like that of experiment 1.

The ease with which software can be coded is an important aspect of this parallel architecture. As shown in the experiments, image-processing algorithms can be implemented easily. The order in which processing modules are connected via the network is defined, and the function of each processing module is selected by setting its parameters.

5 Conclusion

We have presented the reconfigurable pipeline architecture, which solves the problem of inflexibility of conventional architectures while making full use of the available speed of processing modules. In this architecture, multiple-processing modules are interconnected via a network. Each processing module can execute basic functions for image processing at video rate. The network is based on the Benes multistage switching network, its configuration being extended such that multiple branching is supported for image processing. We also developed a setting algorithm of the network. To cope with complex image-processing algorithms, the network provides mutual communication between processing modules, and the pipeline configuration provides high-speed capabilities. Based on this architecture, we have developed a prototype system named IDATEN, a high-speed image processor. As a result, we found that this system could continuously process time-varying images at video rate. The system effectiveness and ease of software operation were verified experimentally.

Acknowledgments. We thank Mr. M. Minejima, Mr. T. Ozaki, Mr. Y. Ohta, and Mr. M. Komeichi for giving us support during the development of this project.

References

Allen, G.R., and Juetten, P.G. 1979. SPARC—Symbolic processing algorithm research computer. In *DARPA Image Understanding Workshop*. 171–174.

Batcher, K.E. 1980. Design of a massively parallel processor. *IEEE Trans. Comput.* **C-29**, 9, 836–840.

Benes, V.E. 1964. Optimal rearrangeable multistage connecting networks. *Bell Syst. Tech. J.* **43,** 4, 1641–1656.

Duff, M.J.B. 1976. CLIP4: A large scale integrated circuit array parallel processor. In *Proc. 3rd IJCPR*. IEEE, Calif., 728–733.

Fountain, T.J., and Goetcherian, V. 1980. CLIP4 parallel processing system. *IEEE Proc.* **127E,** 5, 219–224.

Gemmar, P., Ischen, H., and Luetjen, K. 1981. FLIP: A multiprocessor system for image processing. Duff, M.J.B., and Leuialdi, S. (eds.), New York: Academic Press, 245–256.

Gotoh, T., Sasaki, S., and Yoshida, M. 1985. Two image processing systems challenging the limits of local parallel architecture. In *Proc. CAPAIDM*. IEEE, New York, 272–279.

Kushner, T., Wu, Y., and Rosenfeld, A. 1981. Image processing on ZMOB. In *IEEE CAPAIDM*. IEEE, New York, 88–95.

Lougheed, R.M., and McCubbery, D.L. 1980. The cytocomputer: A practical pipelined image processor. In *Proc. 7th Symposium on Computer Architecture*. IEEE, Calif., 271–277.

Reddaway, S.F. 1973. DAP—A distributed processor array. In *Proc. 1st Symposium on Computer Architecture*. IEEE, New York, 61–65.

Sasaki, S., Gotoh, T., Satoh, T., and Iwase, H. 1985. High speed pipeline image processor with a modifiable network. In *Proc. 1st International Conference on Supercomputing Systems*. IEEE, New York, 476–484.

Siegel, H.J. 1979. A model of SIMD machines and a comparison of various interconnection networks. *IEEE Trans. Comput.* **C-28,** 12, 907–917.

Siegel, H.J. 1981. PASM: Reconfigurable multimicrocomputer system for image processing. M.J.B. Duff and S. Levialdi, Eds. New York: Academic Press, 257–265.

Temma, T., Mizokuchi, M., and Hanaki, S. 1980. Data flow processor for image processing. *Proc. Mini Micro Comput.* **5,** 3, ACTA, 52–56.

Waksman, A. 1968. A permutation network. *J. ACM.* **15,** 1, 159–163.

11
Applying Iconic Processing in Machine Vision

ROBERT M. LOUGHEED, DAVID MCCUBBREY, AND RAMESH JAIN

ABSTRACT: Shape-based (iconic) approaches play a vital role in the early stages of a computer vision system. Many computer vision applications require only 2-D information about objects. These applications allow the use of techniques that emphasize pictorial or iconic features. In this chapter we present an iconic approach using morphological image processing as a tool for analyzing images to recover 2-D information. We also briefly discuss a special architecture that allows very fast implementation of morphological operators to recover useful information in diverse applications. We demonstrate the efficacy of this approach by presenting details of an application. We show that the iconic approach offers features that could simplify many tasks in machine vision systems.

1 Introduction

One of the major goals of a computer vision system is to recognize objects in an image. Ideally, a recognition system should be able to identify an object from an arbitrary viewpoint, under varying illumination conditions, and possibly from only partial views. Since objects are usually 3-D, their projections in an image may differ significantly, depending on the viewpoint. As shown by Besl and Jain [1985], the general object recognition problem is very complex, even when explicit surface information is available. There is no existing system that comes close to solving the general object recognition problem. Most existing systems work in a constrained environment. Some of the common constraints placed on the environment are: uniform illumination, planar objects, completely visible objects, and a limited number of objects. Even in a constrained environment, an approach based on exhaustive matching of intensity values to a model of the object is computationally a hopeless task. Early researchers in pattern recognition believed that the only hope to solve the object-recognition problem was to use features of objects in matching. Features allow simpler models for the objects to be recognized and thus reduce the computational complexity of the recognition problem.

Early systems used statistical pattern classification methods for recognizing objects [Duda and Hart 1973]. Statistical methods generally use global features for object recognition. A global feature depends on the full image of an object. This makes the use of global features unsuitable in applications requiring recognition of objects that may be occluded by other objects. Because in most applications objects are occluded, the techniques based on global features are only of limited use. This realization by researchers led to the use of local features for object recognition. A local feature depends on a limited spatial neighborhood of a point in an image. For an object, a local feature captures information about a small segment of its image. An object is represented as a concatenation of its local features, or as a graph showing the spatial relationship between different features of the image. Local features allow recognition of objects from their partial views; but the partitioning of an object into local features has proven to be a very difficult problem, especially when confronted with the limited tools available for representing features in a computer vision system. Research efforts of several groups have resulted in the success of these methods in only very constrained environments containing a small number of different objects [Knoll and Jain 1986; Perkins 1978].

A common approach, almost universally accepted by the computer vision community, to object recognition from partial views is to partition the silhouette of an object into several disjoint boundary segments and then to use these segments as features [Perkins 1978]. Most techniques try to represent each boundary segment by components that are straight lines, circular arcs, or some other regular curve. The quest for these regular curves seems to be influenced by analytical geometry. Analytical geometry gives us tools for representing geometric objects using compact algebraic equations. Such curves have compact representation and can be manipulated easily. Because in the early days of pattern recognition and computer vision one had to use sequential computers with limited power, these representations were very desirable, if not mandatory. Unfortunately, such representations alone do not solve the general problems, since extraction of boundary segments in real-world images is difficult and error-prone. Also, many 3-D objects present a nearly infinite number of 2-D boundary segments given all possible viewpoints.

Other researchers have approached the problem of attempting to use symbolic, or highly abstracted, features to represent objects. Recognition of 3-D objects from 2-D views will certainly be facilitated by using symbolic features [Besl and Jain 1985]. However, the detection of those symbolic features is still a formidable task. Another alternative is the use of small local features that are shape-based. This has been commonly termed *iconic representation*. The features used in iconic representation can contain elements of both the object and the background. In many cases, the description of features as shapes or patterns is more direct than boundary segments or global features. On the other hand, iconic features are not as abstract as symbolic features that represent whole symbolic objects or major components of scenes.

In this chapter we present an iconic approach for early processing in vision systems. This approach, called morphological image processing, was pioneered by Serra [1982] and has started attracting researchers in computer vision [Haralick 1987]. The morphological approach uses local logical operations to transform images, with the aim of removing noise or detecting features for recognizing objects. Though in their basic form these operations can be applied only to binary images, a clever extension to gray images was suggested by Sternberg [1980] using the concept of umbras. As will be shown later, these operators have some properties that make them very attractive in many applications. Moreover, a special multiprocessor architecture has been designed and extensively used in our group [Lougheed and McCubbrey 1980; Lougheed and Tomko 1985] for several years. This architecture, called the Cytocomputer, allows a very fast implementation of the morphological operators, which are discussed briefly in Section 3. The basic architecture of the Cytocomputer and the most recent implementation, the Cyto-HSS, are discussed in Section 4. The efficacy of this approach is discussed in Section 5 using several examples. The examples are chosen to show the potential and limitations of this approach. Section 6 presents some ideas to extend the applicability of these concepts for size and rotation invariant shape matching using complex log mapping. Finally, we discuss several aspects of this approach in comparison with conventional approaches.

2 Iconic Processing

Consider Figure 11.1. This figure contains two objects of approximately equal size. The first object is a square; what is the second object? Analytical geometry favors regularly shaped objects. If an object does not have a regular shape, it is partitioned into objects that have regular shapes. The second object in Figure 11.1 can be described as a combination of a square, a triangle, and a circle. Note that the complexity of the description increases with the departure of the object's shape from a regular shape. A regular shape is one that can be compactly described in analytical geometry. For example, a regular curve is a curve that can be represented using a polynomial equation to represent it with acceptable accuracy.

An arbitrary shape, in general, cannot be represented exactly using regular shapes; some kind of approximation is required. The approximation tries to identify the closest regular shape in some sense. In fact, one may

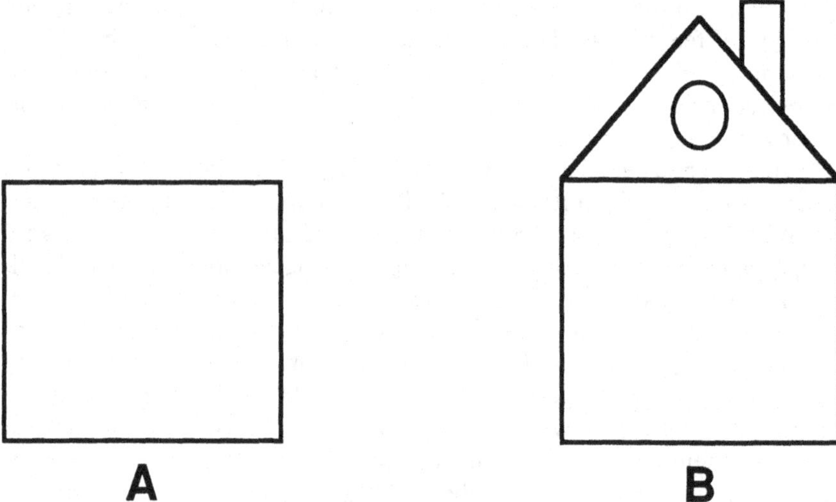

FIGURE 11.1. A "simple" and a "complex" object.

view the process of approximation as a model-based approach that tries a fixed set of models to represent an arbitrary curve. Thus, geometrical representations are symbolic representations. A given shape is represented using symbols corresponding to predetermined shapes. These predetermined shapes can be selected based on either regularity or frequency. In analytical geometry these shapes are selected based on regularity or simplicity of their representation using algebraic tools. If the aim is to describe a shape in order to reproduce it, these primitives offer a compact representation of the shape.

Unfortunately, regularity is not necessarily a good criterion for differentiating one object from another. In object recognition, one is usually interested in the most discriminating features, because these features allow recognition with minimal matching. However, it has been a difficult problem to select appropriate primitive shapes, or features, for recognition of objects. The experience of researchers has shown that the most discriminating features for an object depend not only on its shape, but also on the shapes of other objects in the domain of application.

It is interesting to note that most object-recognition approaches that use local features have used boundary features. This may be due to the fact that it is easier to characterize and recognize curves than regions. Also, it is easier to partition, or segment, an arbitrary curve than an arbitrary region. These factors have resulted in most approaches for object recognition to focus on boundaries of object images, rather than regions. It is well known that boundaries and regions in an image contain the same information in an ideal case. However, due to the relatively simpler partitioning of boundaries, most research has ignored region-based approaches. An important advantage in working with regions is their robustness with respect to noise and other distortions. A few erroneous points may affect the behavior of a curve descriptor significantly more than that of a region descriptor. Cross correlation and template matching are used for matching regions and have been applied for object recognition in some cases. Not much attention has been given, however, to the partitioning of a region into component shapes that may be used as local features.

It appears that most researchers implicitly assumed that the features should be regular. The last few years have seen approaches that work with irregular curves, but most approaches still assume that analytical features are good for object recognition. In many real applications good distinguishing features are irregular. These features can be easily represented in pictorial or iconic form rather than model-based symbolic form. If the objects are 3-D and can appear in an arbitrary orientation, the iconic features may be difficult to use; symbolic features may be more robust in such cases. On the other hand, if the images are obtained so that only a particular view of the object is visible, making the object essentially 2-D for this application, then iconic features will be robust and useful. Now that the cost of memory is no longer prohibitive and processing speed is ever increasing, it may be worth considering working in the iconic domain, rather than limiting ourselves to approaches that were restricted due to von Neumann architecture and limited computing resources.

By representing a shape in a pictorial form some problems in representation may be simplified significantly. An arbitrary shape may be represented exactly by storing a bit mask corresponding to the points on the object. The information lost due to approximation in this case is due to the spatial quantization alone; in the approximation of the boundary, there is additional information loss due to the approximation using standard primitives. Thus, if the same resolution is used, the size of the bit masks used to represent the various shapes shown in Figure 11.1 are all the same. If these shapes are represented using analytical geometry, the exact shape of the objects cannot be recovered from their representations using only a few symbolic descriptors. Another very interesting aspect of the pictorial, or iconic, representation is the fact that for partitioning an object into its local descriptors, one does not have to use a complex process. A mask can be partitioned into any number of disjoint submasks, depending on the applications. The partitioning process does not depend on any model fitting and is a local process. The partitioning of a boundary to obtain local segments requires a best-fit approach and hence is computationally expensive. Moreover, due to the nature of approximation, that approach is also sensitive to the starting point. Iconic representations do not encounter any of these problems.

3 Morphological Operators for Iconic Processing

Mathematical morphology gets its name from the study of shape. This approach exploits the fact that in many machine vision applications, it is natural and easy to think in terms of shapes when designing algorithms, which is not always the case when using linear arithmetic operations. A morphological approach facilitates shape-based, or iconic, thinking. The history of morphological image processing has followed a series of developments in the areas of mathematics and computer architecture. Minkowski [1903], Matheron [1975], and Serra [1982] used set-theoretic approaches to develop the mathematical foundations of morphology. Ulam [1957] developed theories dealing with cellular automata that provide computational underpinnings for the morphological approach to image processing. A number of researchers are extending morphological concepts to develop image algebra [Ritter 1984; Haralick 1987].

3.1 Language for Parallel Image Processing

An image algebra is the formulation of computer image-processing algorithms into algebraic expressions whose variables are images and whose operations logically or geometrically combine images. The *binary image* is the fundamental unit of pictorial information of our image algebra.

Let E^n denote the set of all points in Euclidean n-space and let $p = (x_1, x_2, \ldots, x_n)$ represent a point of E^n. With each set A belonging to E^n is associated a binary image, an n-dimensional composition in black and white, where a point p is black in the binary image if and only if $p \in A$, otherwise p is white. A binary image in E^2 is a silhouette, a composition in black and white that partitions the plane into regions of foreground (black) and background (white). A binary image in E^3 is a partitioning of a volume into points belonging to the surface and interior of objects (black) and points belonging to the space surrounding those objects (white). The notion of a binary image augments the usual notion of a black-and-white picture by specifying a coordinate system for the picture.

The intersection of any two binary images A and B in E^n, written $A \cap B$, is the binary image which is black at all points p, which are black in both A and B. Thus,

$$A \cap B = \{p \mid p \in A \text{ and } p \in B\}.$$

The union of A and B, written $A \cup B$, is the binary image that is black at all points p, which are black in A or black in B (or black in both). Symbolically,

$$A \cup B = \{p \mid p \in A \text{ or } p \in B\}.$$

Let Ω be a universal binary image (all black) and A a binary image. The compliment of A is the binary image that interchanges the colors black and white in A. Thus

$$\overline{A} = \{p \mid p \in \Omega \text{ and } p \notin A\}.$$

Next, denote two points $(x_1, x_2, \ldots, x_n)$ and $(y_1, y_2, \ldots, y_n)$ of E^n by p and q, respectively. The vector sum of p and q is the point

$$p + q = (x_1 + y_1, x_2 + y_2, \ldots, x_n + y_n),$$

while the vector difference $p - q$ is the point

$$p - q = (x_1 - y_1, x_2 - y_2, \ldots, x_n - y_n),$$

both in E^n.

If A is a subimage of E^n, then the translation of A by p is a subimage of E^n given by

$$A_p = \{a + p \mid a \in A\}.$$

Translation of a binary image A by a point p shifts the origin of A to p. If $A_{b^1}, A_{b^2}, \ldots, A_{b^n}$ are translations of the binary image A by the black points of the binary image $B = \{b_1, b_2, \ldots, b_n\}$, then the union of the translations of A by the black points of B is called the dilation of A by B and is given by

$$A \oplus B = \bigcup_{b_i \in B} A_{b_i}.$$

Figure 11.2 shows the dilation operation. Dilation has both associative and commutative properties. Thus, in a sequence of dilation steps the order of performing operations is not important. This fact allows breaking a complex shape into several simpler shapes, which can be recombined as a sequence of dilations.

The operational dual of dilation is erosion. The erosion of a binary image A by a binary image B is black at a point p if and only if every black point in the translation of B to p is also black in A. Erosion is given by

$$A \ominus B = \{p \mid B_p \subseteq A\}.$$

Figure 11.3 shows the erosion operation. Often the binary image B is a regular shape used as a probe on image A and is referred to as a structuring element. Erosion plays a very important role in many applications. Erosion of an image by a structuring element results in an image that gives all locations where the structuring element is contained in the image. This operation is the same as template matching. The only difference is that erosion represents binary template matching; most other methods give a score that represents how well the template matches at a location in the image.

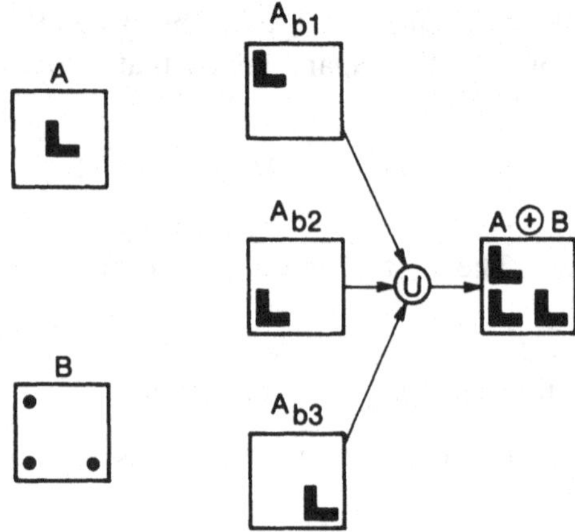

FIGURE 11.2. Dilation of image *A* by image *B*.

While thresholded correlation is equivalent to erosion, and while thresholded convolution can produce equivalent results to dilation, the duality of erosion and dilation expressed as set-theoretic operations has a number of benefits. One of the most important is the concept that any shape generated by a series of dilations can be detected with a series of erosions using the same structuring elements. Another important concept is that dilations of the foreground in an image are equivalent to erosion of the background. This is shown in the example of Figure 11.4.

The dual nature of dilation and erosion is geometric rather than logical and involves a geometric compliment as well as a logical compliment. The geometric compliment of a binary image is called its reflection. The reflection of a binary image B is that binary image B', which is symmetric with B about the origin, that is

$$B' = \{-p \mid p \in B\}.$$

The geometric duality of dilation and erosion is expressed by the relationships

$$\overline{A \oplus B} = \overline{A} \ominus B'$$

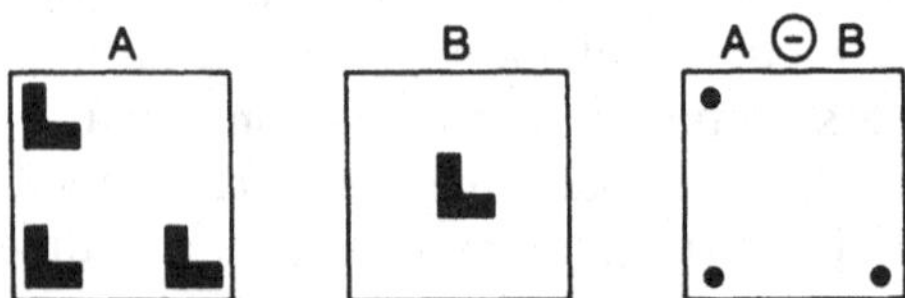

FIGURE 11.3. Erosion of image *A* by image *B*.

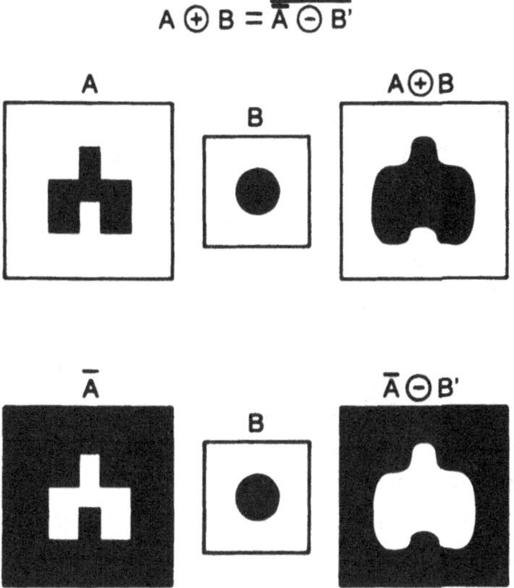

FIGURE 11.4. Duality of dilation and erosion.

and

$$\overline{A \ominus B} = \bar{A} \oplus B'.$$

Geometric duality contrasts with logical duality (DeMorgan's law);

$$\overline{A \cup B} = \bar{A} \cap \bar{B}.$$

and

$$\overline{A \cap B} = \bar{A} \cup \bar{B}.$$

This formalism allows representing images as sets and defines operations on them using a set-theoretic approach. In this formalism, images may be considered as variables, and algorithms are a sequence of well-defined operations expressed in algebraic terms using the preceding and other operators. This image algebra can be used to express algorithms for recovering information from images. Algorithms are represented as well-formed strings of primitives that are either variables representing binary images or binary image operations. The image being processed is referred to as the active image. Other images referred to in an image algebraic expression are reference images. An image-processing algorithm then consists of modifying the active image by logically or geometrically combining it with reference images or with previously modified active images. This approach has already resulted in the development of languages for image processing using this morphological approach [Lougheed and McCubbery 1985; Svetkoff et al. 1984]. Some interesting mathematical developments using this approach are also taking place in image algebra [Ritter 1984].

Erosion and dilation are often used in filtering images. If the nature of noise is known, then a suitable structuring element can be used and a sequence of erosion and dilation operations applied for removing the noise. Such filters affect the shape of the objects in the image in nonlinear ways. We will discuss this in more detail in the following paragraph.

The basic operations of mathematical morphology can be combined into complex sequences. For example, erosion followed by a dilation with the same structuring element will remove all of the pixels in regions that are too small to contain the probe, and it will leave the rest. This sequence is called *opening*. As an example, if a disk-shaped probe image is used, then all of the convex or isolated regions of pixels smaller than the disk will be eliminated. This forms a filter that suppresses positive spatial details. The remaining pixels show where the structuring element is contained in the foreground. The difference of this result and the original image would show those regions that were too small for the probe, and these could be the features of interest, depending on the application.

The opposite sequence, a dilation followed by an erosion, will fill in holes and concavities smaller than the probe. This is referred to as closing. These operations are shown in Figure 11.5 with a disk-shaped structuring element. Again, what is removed may be just as important as what remains. Such filters can be used to suppress spatial features or discriminate against objects based upon their size. The structuring element used does not have to be compact or regular, and can be any pattern of points. In this way features made up of distributed points can be detected.

In some cases, erosions, dilations, and morphological filters are overly sensitive to small distortions in the object's image. Also, in some cases the order of applying openings and closings can make an undesired difference in the result. Iterative filters were developed to solve this problem. These filters are characterized by a sequence of alternating openings and closings, each with a progressively larger version of the structuring element. This process will gradually remove larger amounts of the noise and distortion without biasing the result either toward the foreground or the background. This is shown in Section 5. Other sequences of morphological operations can be used to find patterns in images (e.g., ends of lines), to extract the central skeletons of regions, to form the convex hulls of regions, and to relate features spatially for recognition of objects [Lougheed and Tomko 1985; Serra 1982]. The key to these operations is a compound pattern match that identifies specific configurations of foreground and background points. When the configuration of interest is detected, the addition or removal of foreground points is made. This transformation requires a pattern of foreground points and a nonoverlapping pattern of background points to be specified (with all other points being don't-care values) and both patterns have to match for the transformation to take

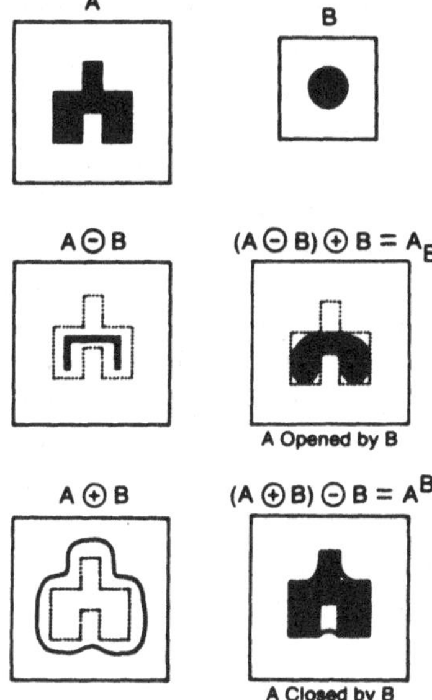

FIGURE 11.5. Image *A* closed and opened by image *B*.

place. (This operation has been called a hit-or-miss by some researchers [Serra 1982] even though it is a hit *and* miss.) This type of pattern-matching capability can be derived from the primitive operations presented earlier and gives iconic processing a more powerful tool for complex shape recognition.

4 Architecture

The processing of images with digital computers was first done over 30 years ago using general-purpose uniprocessors. To overcome the limitations of a single processor when operating on images, Unger [1959] proposed the first two-dimensional array (or mesh) of processors with each processor interconnected to its neighboring processors. This basic idea formed the foundation for such machines as the ILLIAC 3 [McCormick 1963], the CLIP series [Duff 1973], the MPP [Batcher 1980], and several others. These machines are optimized for local transformations in which each pixel is replaced by a new value computed from the original values of the pixel and its nearest neighbors. These are often referred to as cellular transformations. All of these machines have the advantage of being flexible in the types of cellular operations they can perform on images through sequences of microinstructions, but have a number of serious limitations. These include the I/O bottlenecks of image acquisition and storage devices, extensive hardware resource requirements leading to high cost and low reliability, and tedious programmability.

Another approach to the design of special-purpose architectures for image processing includes the translation machines. Translation machines implement local cellular transformations by shifting a copy of the image in accordance with the set of translations specified by a structuring element [Serra and Klein 1972; S.R. Sternberg, personal communication 1984]. A structuring element is represented as a list of points, representing translation vectors, as shown in Figure 11.6. The shifted versions of the original image, as specified by the structuring element, are successively combined using logical operators to form the result image.

A third category of special-purpose image-processing architectures includes the raster subarray machines, which implement cellular transformations by accessing the data in a raster scan format and buffering enough data to have a complete neighborhood of pixels available for the computations. Since most local transformations can be effectively implemented through sequences of 3 × 3 operations, most of these processors have limited the window reconstructed by the processor to this size. Examples of this type of architecture include the Diff3 and the Picap [Danielsson and Levialdi 1981].

A final category is raster pipeline processors. These function in a manner similar to the raster subarray machines in that each processing unit reconstructs a subarray (generally 3 × 3) from an incoming serial data stream. Unlike those machines, however, they are composed of multiple

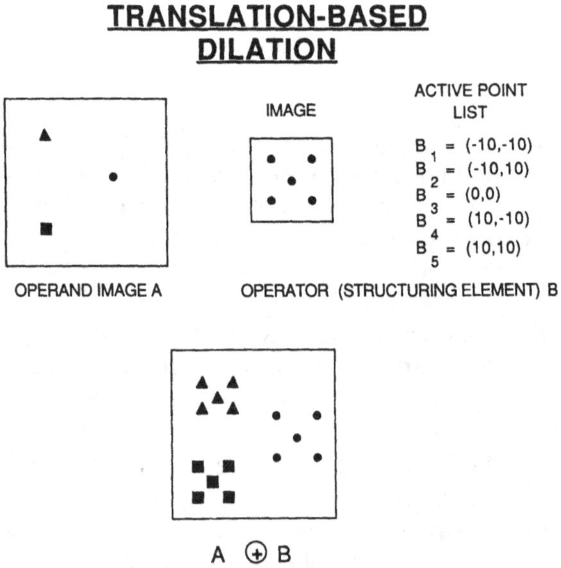

FIGURE 11.6. A structuring element represented as an image and as a set of points.

processing units which connect in a cascaded or pipelined fashion. Some were formed by a small number of special-function hardware units, each dedicated to a single function. The Cytocomputer [Lougheed and McCubbery 1980] and the Warp [Gross et al. 1985] are composed of identical hardware units (stages), each programmable for a wide variety of functions. Warp is optimized for floating-point arithmetic operations while the Cytocomputer is intended for morphological neighborhood operations.

4.1 Cyto-HSS Image-Processing System

The shortcomings of parallel array image processors led researchers to develop an alternative parallel architecture, the Cytocomputer. The name Cytocomputer is derived from *cyto,* the Greek word for cell, referring to its cellular architecture. First proposed by Sternberg [1980], it consists of a serial pipeline of neighborhood-processing stages, with a common clock, in which each stage performs a single transformation of an entire image. Images are entered in the pipeline as a stream of pixels in sequential line-scanned format and progress through the pipeline of processing stages at a constant rate. Neighborhood logic transformations are performed within the data-transfer clock period, allowing the output of a stage to appear at the same rate as its input. In this architecture, since the data format is serial and overlaps processing, there is no overhead involved with image I/O. The details of this architecture are given in Lougheed and McCubbery [1980].

The newest Cytocomputer high-speed system (Cyto-HSS) is a greatly enhanced version of the previous generations of special-purpose ERIM cellular image processors [Lougheed and McCubbery 1985]. In addition to executing a very large and powerful set of cellular transformations for implementing local operations, it includes special-purpose processors for efficiently performing the other major types of operations required for image analysis. It also supports real-time image input and output. The Cyto-HSS operates under the control of a host microcomputer. Figure 11.7 shows the main components and a typical host system. Cellular processing is performed in the pipeline of raster subarray neighborhood processors. Combinations of multiple images are performed in the combiner unit at the right, which has four input and two output image paths. Other types of image processing may be performed by the host or in the additional pixel processors, as shown at the right of Figure 11.7. The image data paths have been designed to accommodate a variety of devices with different data rates. An example of this is the video digitizer also shown in Figure 11.7, which allows direct asynchronous loading of video data into the image memory.

The system has the following basic capabilities:

- Circulates images through the Cytocomputer stages for neighborhood processing, each stage operating at a continuous 10,000,000 pixels/second, independent of image size.

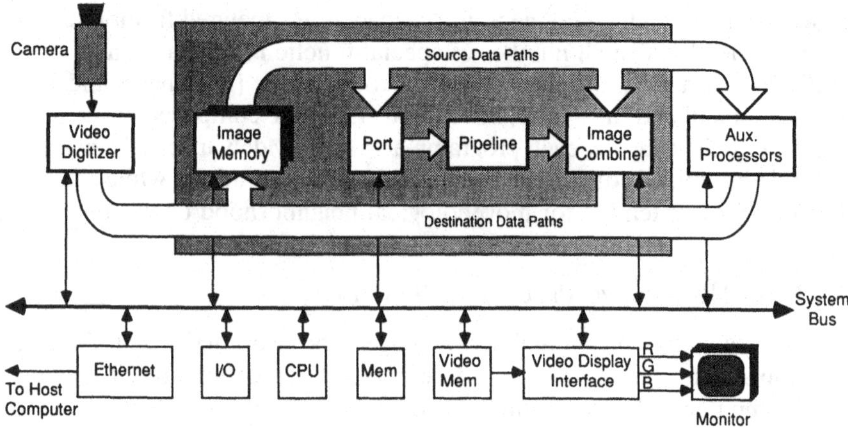

FIGURE 11.7. Cyto-HSS block diagram.

- Performs arithmetic, multiplication, Boolean, morphological, and comparison operations on multiple images at 10,000,000 (resulting) pixels/second.
- Processes 8-bit images (gray-scale or 3-D) up to 4 megabytes in size.
- Loads Cytocomputer-stage programs in less than 80 microseconds per stage.
- Detects memory and data-path parity errors and data-synchronization faults.
- Allows the host computer random access to image memory at all times.
- Includes multiple, independent hardware windowing (subregions) along with up-sampling and down-sampling image access.
- Acquires and processes image data at any rate up to 10,000,000 pixels per second (video digitizing), simultaneously with processing.

The architecture is open and elastic, permitting long pipelines, multiple-image memories, and repeating series of pipelines and combiners. There are four major sections of the Cyto-HSS. These include the pipeline of Cytocomputer neighborhood processing stage(s), an image memory, a control port, and a combiner.

4.2 Neighborhood Processor Pipeline

The pipeline consists of one or more Cytocomputer stages. Each stage performs a preprogrammed 3×3 neighborhood transformation on incoming raster-scan ordered 8-bit pixels, producing a raster-scan stream of processed pixels at its output. Images with line lengths up to 2,048 pixels may be processed. The stages directly execute all 2-D binary and 3-D umbra neighborhood transformations and are described in Lougheed and McCubbery [1980].

The neighborhood operation capability of the stage gives the Cyto-HSS the ability to efficiently perform many fundamental shape-analysis operations, such as skeletonization, convex hull determination, and others. The Cytocomputer stage is capable of treating 8-bit images in several different ways.

First, images may be treated as binary bit-planes. Neighborhood erosion and dilation may occur independently in up to 8 planes in parallel. These binary images may also be combined directly by the stages in any way through an efficient look-up table built into each stage. This supports complex feature detection based upon patterns of simple features.

Second, operations may occur based on multiple bit-plane encoding of states. This capability allows so-called conditional dilations and erosions to occur. Useful in segmentation and region-labeling operations, it allows information to be propagated only until predetermined boundary pixels are encountered. In addition, nonoverlapping image features may be encoded using multiple bit-planes to allow as many as 256 features to be simultaneously accommodated.

The third capability of the stages allows them to interpret the 8-bit data three-dimensionally as height or range. In this case, the stages operate within a $3 \times 3 \times 256$ volume for their neighborhood transformations. This capability is particularly useful for such operations as nonmaxima suppression in gradient edge images, dimensional measurement on two-dimensional shapes, and range-image analysis [Massone et al. 1985].

One potential liability of a cascaded pipeline of processors is the latency of unneeded stages. When only a short sequence of transformations is required, the extra stages are bypassed automatically, avoiding any wasted time. The stages also allow reprogramming for the next transformation sequence to be overlapped with the execution of the image-processing operation.

4.3 Image Memory

The memory section consists of two or more memory units. Each unit is capable of supplying pixels to any one of three available image source data paths. Read circuitry on each memory unit accesses a programmably defined region of memory (i.e., a window) and delivers it onto an image source path in raster-scan order. Independent write circuitry receives raster-scan ordered pixels from either of two image destination paths and stores them into a programmably defined region of memory. Memory boards can act as sources, destinations, or both simultaneously. Each memory can store 256 Kbytes using 64K RAM chips, extendable to 1 Mbyte.

Translation is a fundamental operation of morphological image analysis since it forms the basis for pointwise erosion and dilation operations. The Cyto-HSS system supports translations in two ways: small translations using the stages, and large translations using the image memories. The large translations are implemented by accessing a shifted window directly from the larger image, clipping at the image boundary. This is shown in Figure 11.8.

These capabilities can be used either independently or together. For example, dilating an image by a hexagon of radius 24 would require only two frame times in a system with 12 stages. In this case, each stage would be programmed to expand hexagonal wavefronts one pixel in a cellular space. Dilating an image by a hollow hexagon of radius 16 would employ both the image memory and the stages. In this case, four frame times would be required for a system with 16 stages. During the first three frames, the stages would construct a single 16-pixel facet of the hexagon. The memory scan controllers and image combiner would be used to translate the segment into the correct position in the resultant image. The fourth frame would translate a reflected result of the first three frames to complete the hexagon.

The image memory read and write region controllers support the changing of resolution for simulating pyramid operations, pumping pixels at the full rate while sparsely sampling and/or writing in the memory space. There are separate programmable sampling intervals for both the X- and Y-axes.

4.4 Port Controller

The port acts as the central control for initiating, monitoring, and halting high-speed hardware operations. It can initiate a host system interrupt to signal completion of an image-processing cycle or detection of an error

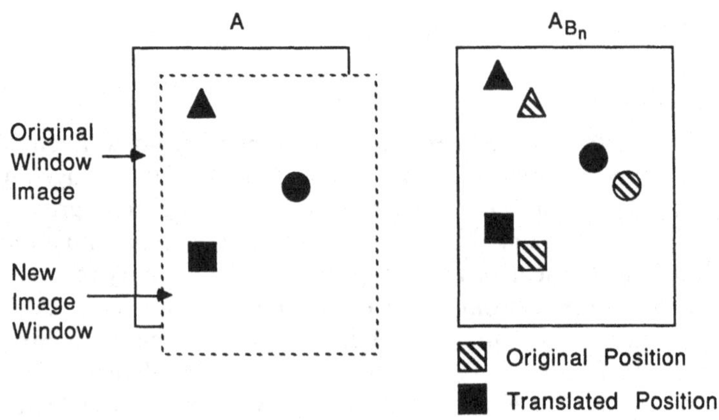

FIGURE 11.8. Translation implemented with windowing.

condition. The port contains a data-storage queue that can be loaded with port commands and stage program data for the next cycle while the current image-processing cycle is in progress. When the current cycle is over, integral port logic unloads the queue at 10 megabytes/second to program the stages. Thus, the queue allows the relatively slow transfer of program data to be overlapped (i.e., hidden) during image processing. The port incorporates a two-channel DMA controller, one channel of which is designed for efficient loading of the queue from host memory. Using another channel of its DMA controller, the port can load control registers on all cards, thus minimizing the CPU overhead for starting an image-processing cycle.

4.5 Combiner

The combiner performs multiple-image comparison, arithmetic, morphologic, and logical operations. Up to three image operands can be used, selectable from the pipeline output and the three source image data paths. The computed results can be placed on the image destination paths. The combiner contains two calculation units, which can each be used for performing image-to-image operations. The results from one can be used to select the operations performed by the second, or the results can be a full 16-bit image.

For erosion and dilation of 2-D binary images with an arbitrary structuring element, the combiner performs the logical AND and OR functions between image pairs. For operations on 3-D or gray-scale images, it performs the analogous MIN and MAX operations. It can also form a 16-bit product of two images.

4.6 Feature Extraction

Feature extraction capability is crucial for image analysis. A machine vision system spends a significant part of its processing efforts on feature extraction. By implementing feature extraction in hardware, the speed of processing of a machine vision system can be increased to realize real-time performance.

Global features are easily extracted in raster-scan architectures because the entire image is always accessible during each scan. Feature extraction is simply a matter of routing the pixel stream through the serial feature extraction hardware. If this operation can be pipelined with other image operations (as is the case in the Cyto-HSS), then features can be extracted essentially without any time penalty.

The presence of any pixel(s) of a specified state in the image is simple to detect but has a variety of important uses. For instance, features detected in the image domain could be placed in a specific state as part of the image-transformation sequence. The presence of any such features would easily be detected as a nonzero count of pixels in that state.

Another important use of pixel state counting is in image comparison. Two separate images can be tested for identity by subtracting them and testing for the presence of any nonzero pixels. Besides the obvious utility in matching images, this capability can be used to detect completion of many cellular image transformations, such as skeletonization and convex hull formation.

Another fundamental type of feature is a pixel's position coordinates. Any machine vision system that must locate objects will generally have some sort of pixel coordinate extraction mechanism. A histogram memory array is easily adapted to also serve as an *X-Y* coordinate list accumulator. Due to advances in semiconductor memory technology, it is not expensive to accumulate several thousand coordinates during a scan of an image. This amount is sufficient for many purposes, particularly those involving higher-level feature coordinates, since the number of high-level features is generally small relative to the original image size.

4.7 Error Detection

One topic that has rarely been discussed in the literature dealing with the architecture for machine vision is that of reliability. We feel that, given the complexity of the systems, automatic error detection is critical for all image processors.

Automatic error detection is designed into the Cyto-HSS to ensure reliability. During image processing, six types of errors will be detected: data-path parity, memory parity, data synchronization, data overrun, data underrun, or data latency. Parity and timing errors from all modules are collected and indicated on a central status register located on the port card. An interrupt to the host can be generated if any error occurs. The port contains an error counter, which can be programmed to indicate how many errors occurred or when the first error occurred in an image-processing cycle. Each module in the system has a set of LED (light emitting diode) status indicators along the top edge of the cards. They indicate the module's status during an image-processing cycle (selected, active, etc.). Each error bit in the unit's status register has a corresponding LED, which will light if that error is detected. In this way, a visual indication of the location and nature of any error is available.

5 Examples Using Morphological Operations

As discussed earlier, iconic processing is a shape-based approach to image analysis. This section illustrates the use of iconic processing at various levels in image-processing algorithms, from the point following image acquisition to object recognition. The generic types of operations in an algorithm are shown in Figure 11.9. Not all algorithms will have all of these steps, and some operations do not easily fall into a single category, but this breakdown is useful for discussing many types of image-analysis and machine-vision functions.

The use of iconic versus symbolic processing is not an either-or choice. As has been observed by many researchers, the transition from an image of pixels representing some physical property of the scene (e.g., brightness) to a decision based on (at least partial) scene understanding is a concentration of information. At some point the representation becomes symbolic, so it is partially a question of how detailed the symbols that we use are.

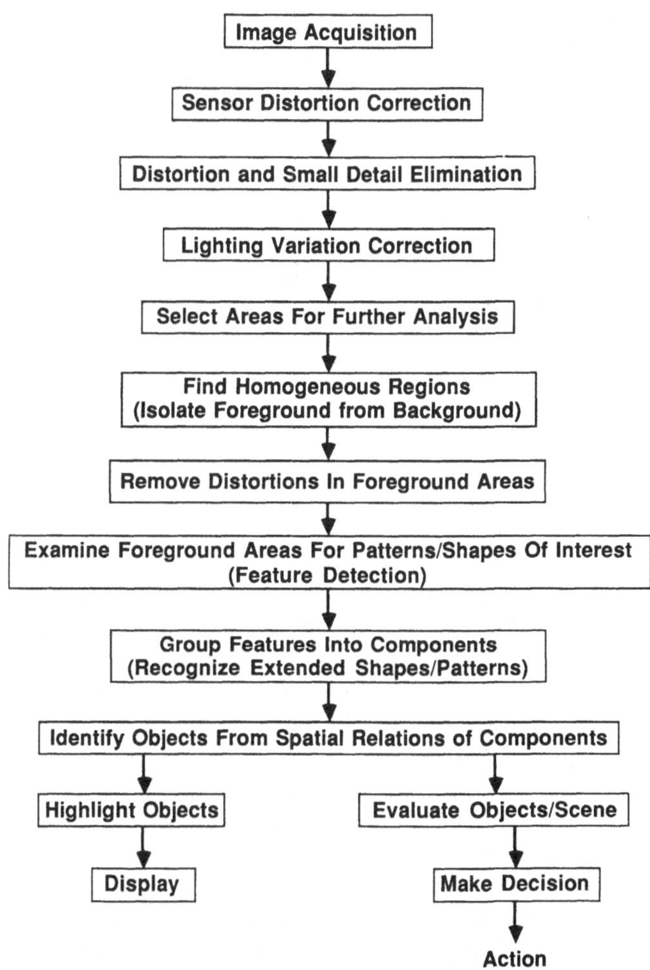

FIGURE 11.9. Flow chart of image-analysis algorithm.

Also, at some point the iconic representation of the image becomes so abstract that one could argue it is symbolic.

Our goal here is not to argue semantics but instead to show the importance of both types of processing, and to illustrate the uses of iconic operations for image analysis. Shape-based tools are valuable at many of the steps in an image-analysis algorithm. Later we will discuss each of the major steps and, where appropriate, illustrate the use of iconic operations.

5.1 Correction of Sensor Distortions

The first step following image acquisition is sensor-distortion correction, which is application- and sensor-specific. Examples of the types of distortions encountered are dropouts (dark isolated points), saturated or stuck points, point noise (additive or subtractive), bands of uneven response, etc. Iconic processing using shapes specific to the types of noise can be quite effective for these needs. For example, an open ring-shaped probe will detect isolated irregularities and allow them to be replaced by a neighboring value, for instance, the maximum or minimum of the values near it. This type of nonlinear filter is also known as a weighted-median filter, but picturing it as an iconic-based operation allows us to discuss similar operations with more complex probes for the different distortions. Obviously, for distortions that are linear in nature, linear functions may be the most appropriate for making corrections, and we do not intend to imply that iconic processing should be used exclusively.

5.2 Filtering

The operations just described are a type of filtering, but more generally one desires to eliminate details in the scene or objects that fall outside the size range of interest. Iconic processing using a sequence of small probes can be used to remove such details without losing important information. An example of this is shown using the image in Figure 11.10, which is a 256×256 image of 8-bit grey-scale values. There is a thin line of interest (a seam) running down the image, along with an uneven brightness gradient (shadow) across the image; added to this is random noise, which has a Gaussian distribution.

The goal is to remove the noise without disturbing the underlying scene. As can be seen by examining a histogram of the values in the image (Figure 11.11) and a profile of one line of the image (Figure 11.12), a simple thresholding operation cannot be used to extract the line of interest. In the morphological/iconic approach to this problem, the image is treated as a surface in three dimensions, with brightness represented by height. The image can be filtered by conceptually moving a hemisphere of specified size over and under this surface and filling in spaces where the hemisphere

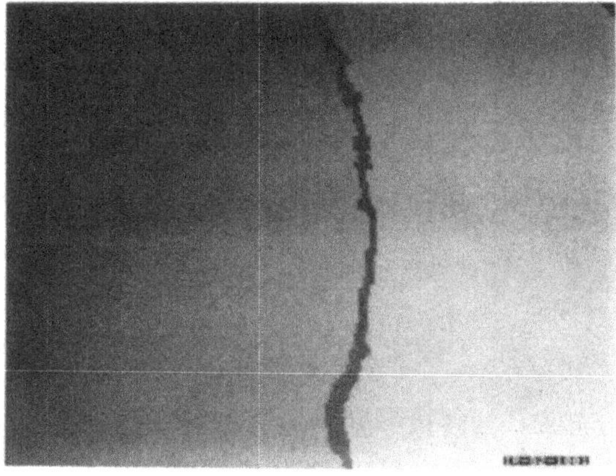

FIGURE 11.10. Original image of seam with distortions.

will not fit. This is the effect produced by closing and opening as discussed earlier.

The first step in this processing sequence is to remove the noise from the image. This is done by progressively opening and closing with hemispheres of increasing radii, up to radius 2. The result of this operation can be seen in the smoother profile shown in Figure 11.13. The next step will be removal of the shadow.

5.3 Correction for Lighting Variations

The image shown in Figure 11.10, as mentioned, has an overall illumination gradient, which prevents us from using a thresholding technique for seg-

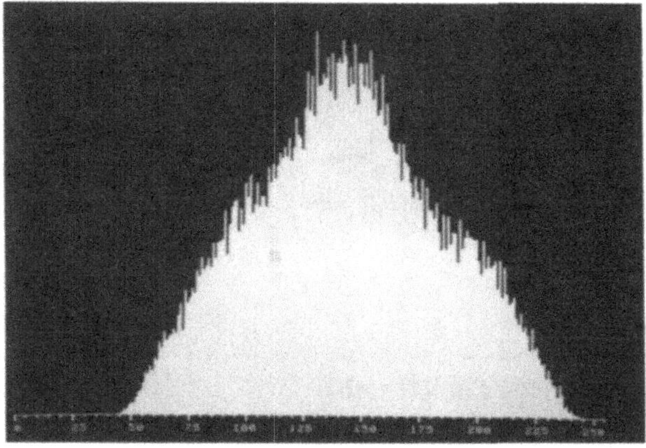

FIGURE 11.11. Histogram of original image.

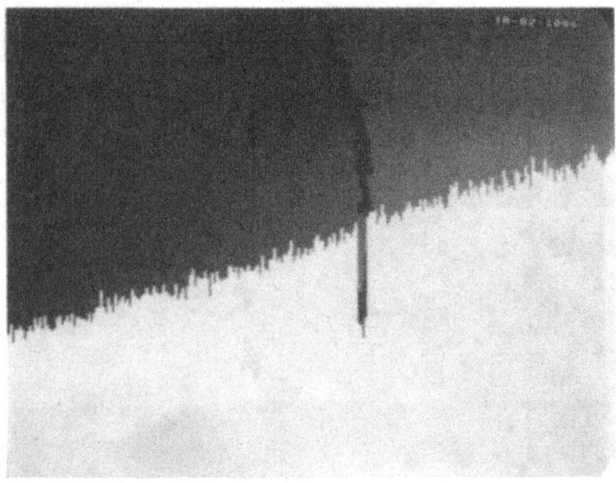

FIGURE 11.12. Profile of one line of original image.

menting the seam from the background. In this case, the background in some areas is darker than the seam near the bottom of the image. To remove the shadow, we iteratively open and close with hemispherical structuring elements, progressing up to a radius of 8. This eliminates the line of interest, producing an image in which only the background (the shadow) remains (Figure 11.14), a profile of which is shown in Figure 11.15. This background image is now subtracted pixel by pixel from the noise-filtered image, the difference being the line of interest on a uniform background (Figure 11.16). Both the histogram (Figure 11.17) and profile (Figure 11.18) of the difference image show that this image may now be easily thresholded to result in a clean binary image containing only the line (Figure 11.19). Note that by using a hemisphere this technique will be rotationally invariant and will detect seams at any orientation.

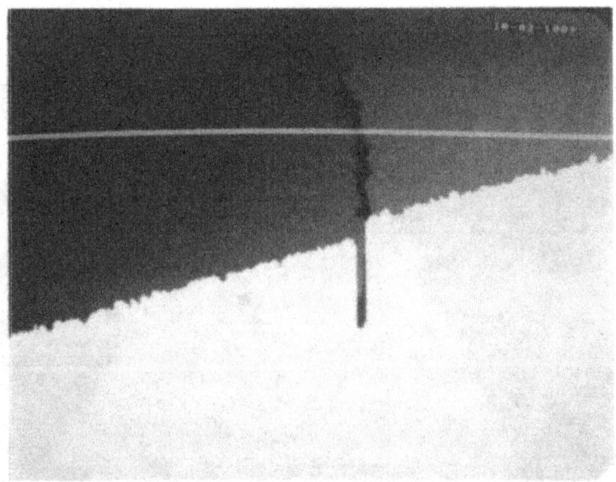

FIGURE 11.13. Profile of noise-filtered image.

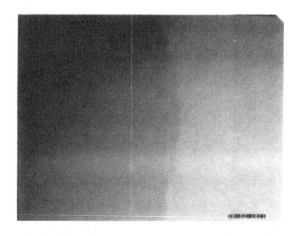

FIGURE 11.14. Background extracted.

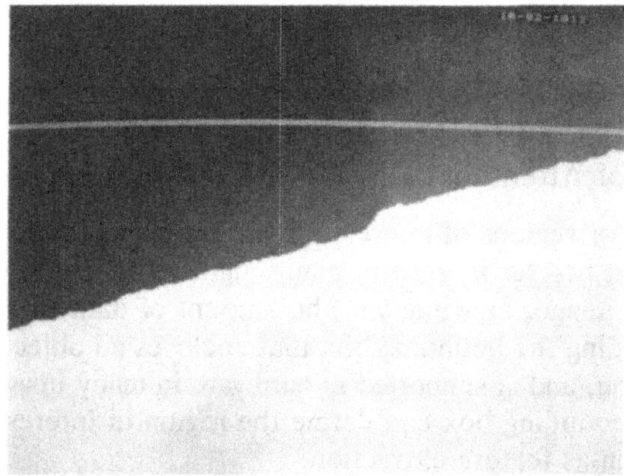

FIGURE 11.15. Profile of extracted background.

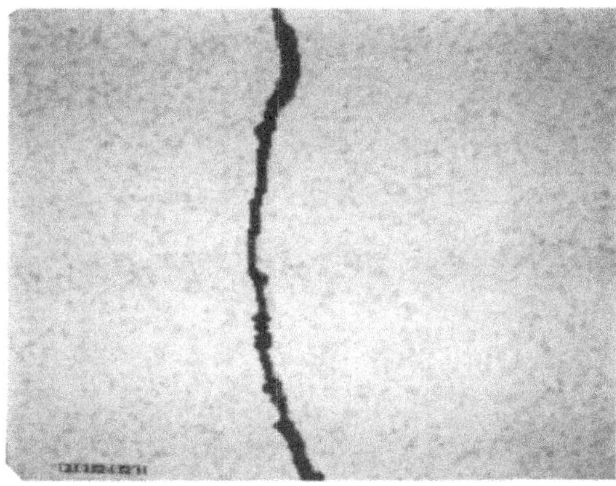

FIGURE 11.16. Background subtracted from noise-filtered image.

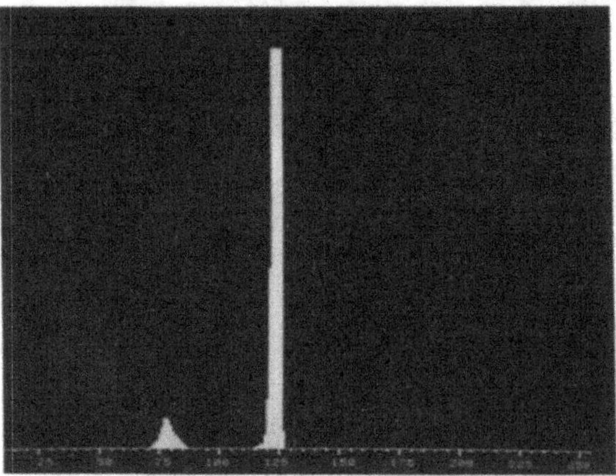

FIGURE 11.17. Histogram of difference image.

5.4 Focusing of Attention

Selecting areas or regions of interest for further processing, while not an iconic operation per se, is used in many algorithms. By selecting small sections of the image, or windows, the amount of data to be processed is reduced. Finding the bounding box that encloses an object is a type of feature extraction, and is supported in hardware in many image-processing systems. This bounding box can define the region of interest for further processing, such as feature extraction.

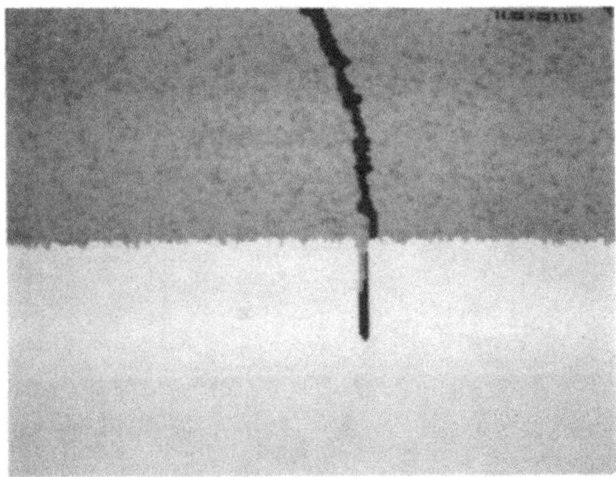

FIGURE 11.18. Profile of difference image.

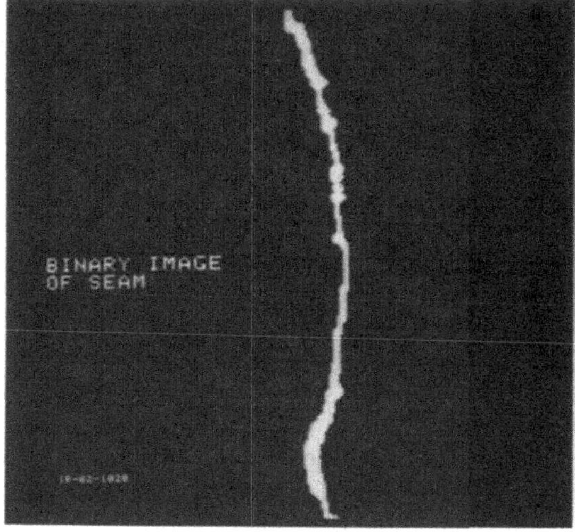

FIGURE 11.19. Thresholded image of seam.

5.5 Segmentation

Segmentation is the grouping of homogeneous regions, attempting to identify surfaces or objects separated by demarcations. Smooth regions can be differentiated from transitions by using flat (in the 3-D sense) structuring elements, for example, disks or upright cylinders. If opening and closing operations are performed, the smooth regions will fit the structuring element better and be identifiable, as in the preceding example.

Alternatively, one can use a structuring element that has a 3-D parabolic shape to detect the brightness transitions in an image and use these as region boundaries. In addition, both techniques can be used together to find areas of change, homogenity, and not-sure regions. These not-sure regions can be labeled with a relaxation technique, working from the known smooth regions but not crossing the known boundaries. This technique was used in identifying multiple types of inks in a printed circuit inspection application, and is described in detail in Lougheed [1985].

5.6 Filtering Regions

Since segmentation will not be perfect, we need to remove small regions, fill in small holes in blobs, and smooth the outlines of the regions. The same techniques used earlier can be applied with two-dimensional structuring elements, such as a disk. As always, structuring elements specific for the application (i.e., matching a shape of interest) can be used to better discriminate against or for the objects or features of interest. Iconic domain processing avoids the data-structure and graph-searching problems of most state-space approaches to region labeling, since all information remains imbedded in the images.

5.7 Feature Detection

While exhaustive identification of objects in all orientations under all conditions is too computationally complex for most real-world needs, small features can be used that are simpler and more consistent. Using features instead of matching whole objects is simpler due to the fact that smaller features can be picked, which require fewer computations to detect, and which are often more invariant to changes in the scene. The features can be simple geometric shapes, or can be some attribute of a region, such as size, shape, length, etc. A detailed example of this is given in the following example, which was part of a robot guidance project.

As this section has shown, the transition from pixels to object recognition is not characterized by a sudden shift from pixels to symbols. The overall flow is to reduce information that is not needed and to recognize features that are part of the objects of interest. Iconic processing offers an attractive set of tools for doing this in an efficient and straightforward fashion.

5.8 A Robot Guidance Application

In this section we discuss a specific application of the proposed approach. Our aim is to show how morphological operators are used to solve an image-analysis problem. A more detailed discussion of this is given in Coleman and Sampson [1985].

5.8.1 Description of the Application. The aim of this project was to extract a part from a compartmentalized tray, determine the location and position of the grasped part, and then assemble the part to a housing. The parts were white plastic end plates of automobile heater blower motors, shown in Figures 11.20(a), (b), and (c). The process begins with the parts in a tray, also made of white plastic, at the pick-up station. Each compartment has a single part, but the position and orientation of the part is unconstrained. At this point in the manufacturing process, the end plates contain a bearing and holding plate on the outside of the part, as shown in Figure 11.20(c). Figure 11.20(a) shows the inside surface with two contact springs and two electrical pick-up assemblies inserted. The subassemblies each consist of a connector tab attached to a braided copper wire that attaches to a brush. The pick-up station is located within the robot work envelope and under an ERIM 3-D laser scanner. Using the data from the 3-D laser scanner, the image-analysis system determines the location of a grippable point on each end plate [Coleman and Sampson 1985]. The grip-point location is communicated to the robot control computer, which directs the robot arm to extract the part.

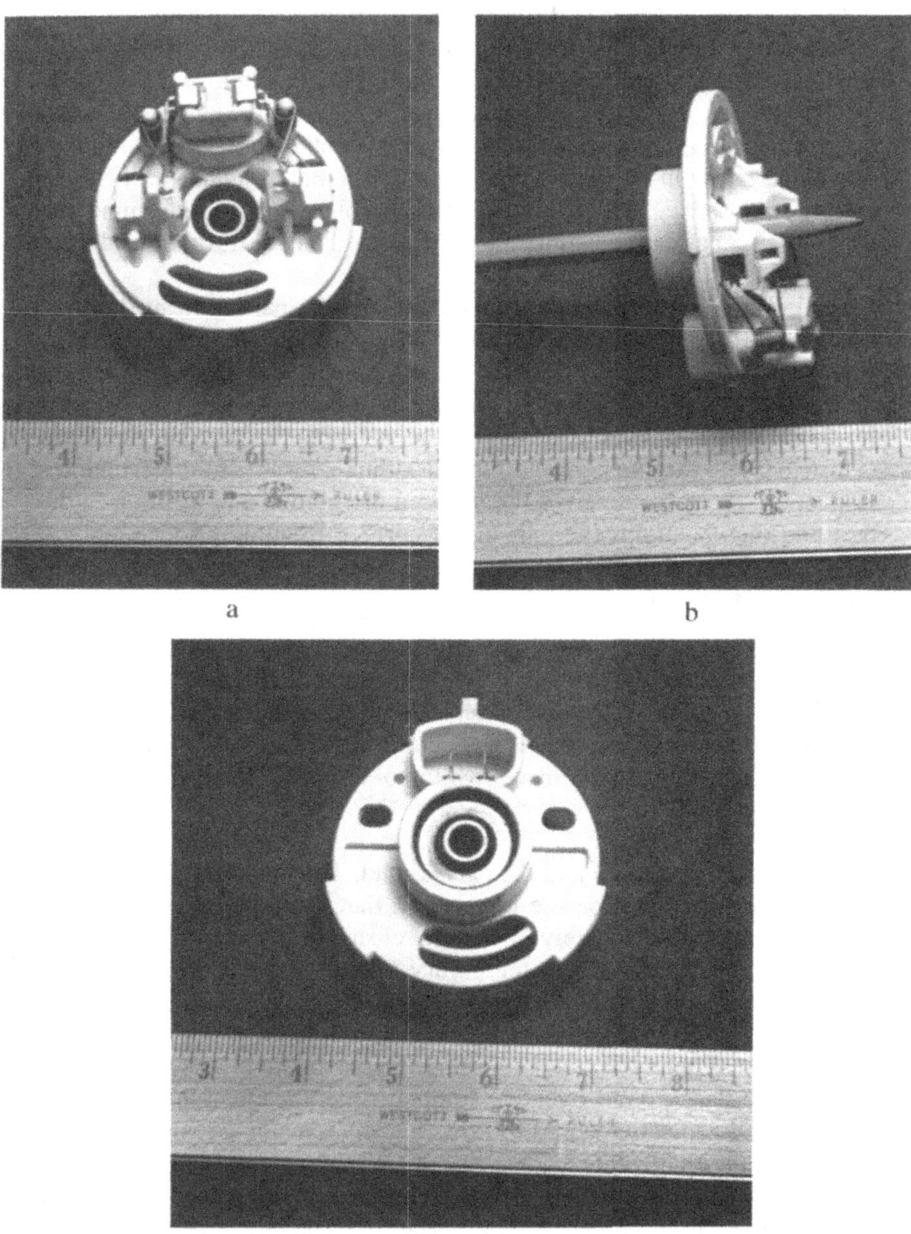

FIGURE 11.20. Motor end plate: (a) front view; (b) side view; (c) back view.

The part is held between the robot gripper fingers after extraction from the tray, but the absolute location and orientation of the part may have changed. This may be due to one or more effects, such as the gripper moving the part during the grasping, interference with container side walls during extraction, slippage due to gravity, or vibration during robot motion. This uncertainty in the part's position and orientation makes critical assembly impossible. Our solution to this problem was to determine the part's position after acquisition and to disregard any perturbations during acquisition and transit.

To find the orientation, the robot positions the part in front of a TV camera and the image-analysis system determines the location of the part with respect to the gripper fingers. The system also determines if the correct side of the part is facing the camera and if so, then inspects the part for flaws. If the incorrect side of the part is facing the camera, the robot is instructed to flip the part and the algorithm is rerun. If the part passes inspection, the robot receives the updated orientation and location of the part and then positions the part in the correct orientation for assembly. If the part fails inspection, it is placed in a reject bin. This procedure is repeated until the tray is empty.

5.8.2 Tab Finder. In this section, we discuss one part of the algorithm in detail. This part of the algorithm determines the location of an orienting tab that projects from the circumference of the part. The first phase of the tab-finder procedure locates the center of the tab in a low-resolution image, which is the approximate position of the tab in the high-resolution image.

The tab-finder procedure is given a down-sampled image segmented into the part (foreground) and the background. The first step is an iterative disk-filtering operation on the foreground that smooths the edges of the part. A disk filter alternately opens and closes the image by disks of increasing radii. Next, using a temporary state, the foreground is dilated over the background with a large-diameter disk to fill in any holes in the part (Figure 11.21). This will remove any tabs located inside holes in the part. Next, the temporary state around the part perimeter is removed by dilating the background over the temporary state. Finally, the filled-in holes are merged with the part by covering any remaining temporary state with the foreground state.

After the interior tabs have been eliminated, small projections of the foreground must be removed. The image foreground is eroded by a disk of the MinimumTabSize. Next, the foreground is eroded further by a disk with a radius equal to the difference in the MaximumTabSize and MinimumTabSize, placing a label state on the eroded pixels (Figure 11.21(h)). An opening sequence is completed by dilating the foreground back over the labeled pixels by the same amount (Figure 11.21(i)). This isolates the projections smaller than the MaximumTabSize. The labeled pixels are then skeletonized down to a single pixel (Figure 11.21(k)). This is the location of the tab in the down-sampled image, which is the approximate location in the high-resolution image.

The second phase of the tab-finder procedure determines the exact location of the center of the tab. A small window is selected in the high-resolution image around the location found in the previous steps. The algorithm is repeated on the window image to determine the exact location of the tab. The coordinates of the center of the tab are then sent to the coordinate transformation program, which in turn passes them to the robot controller.

This system has been functioning in our laboratory with rare mistakes in determining grip points. The tab-finder procedure discussed herein has been functioning without any problems.

6 Rotation and Scale Changes

The applicability of morphological operators for matching templates using a special architecture is useful in those applications where the instances of the template to be recognized appear in an image in the same orientation and size as the template. The fact that a shape or template can be recognized in real time is very important in many industrial applications. The applicability of these approaches can be increased significantly by making the recognition process invariant to orientation and size of the template.

Complex log mapping (CLM) has been advanced as a method to implement invariant topological mapping [Messner and Szu 1985; Schenker et al. 1981; Jain et al. 1987; Schwartz 1977; Weiman and Chaikin 1979]. It has been shown that in the transformed image, both rotation and scale changes of an object result in translation of the CLM representation of the object. It is possible to use iconic processing on the transformed images. For fast recognition of 2-D shapes in arbitrary orientation and sizes the approach shown in Figure 11.22 may be used. As shown in Figure 11.22, by using iconic matching on an image and its transformed version, translation, rotation, and size invariances may be achieved. The results of iconic matching in the image domain and transformed domain may be combined to detect all instances of objects. Since these operations may be implemented in hardware (NBS system [Jain et al. 1987]) the 2-D shape recognition may be achieved fast. In Massone et al. [1985], a template-matching approach in the cortical space is discussed for recognizing industrial objects.

There is a problem, however, in using CLM for obtaining size and rotation invariance in most real applications. The transformation is shift-variant. The shape of the image in the transformed domain depends on its location in the image. The invariances can be obtained if the scaling

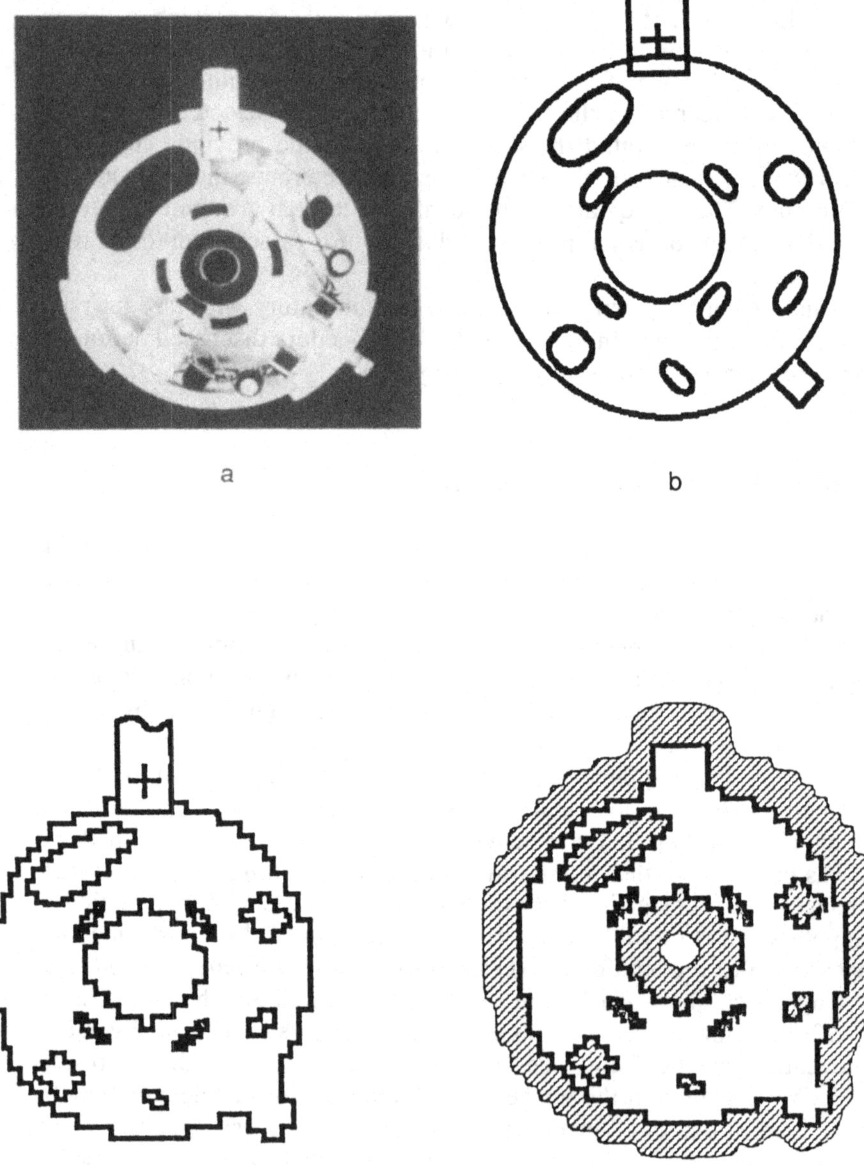

FIGURE 11.21. Sequence of operations in the tab-finder algorithm.

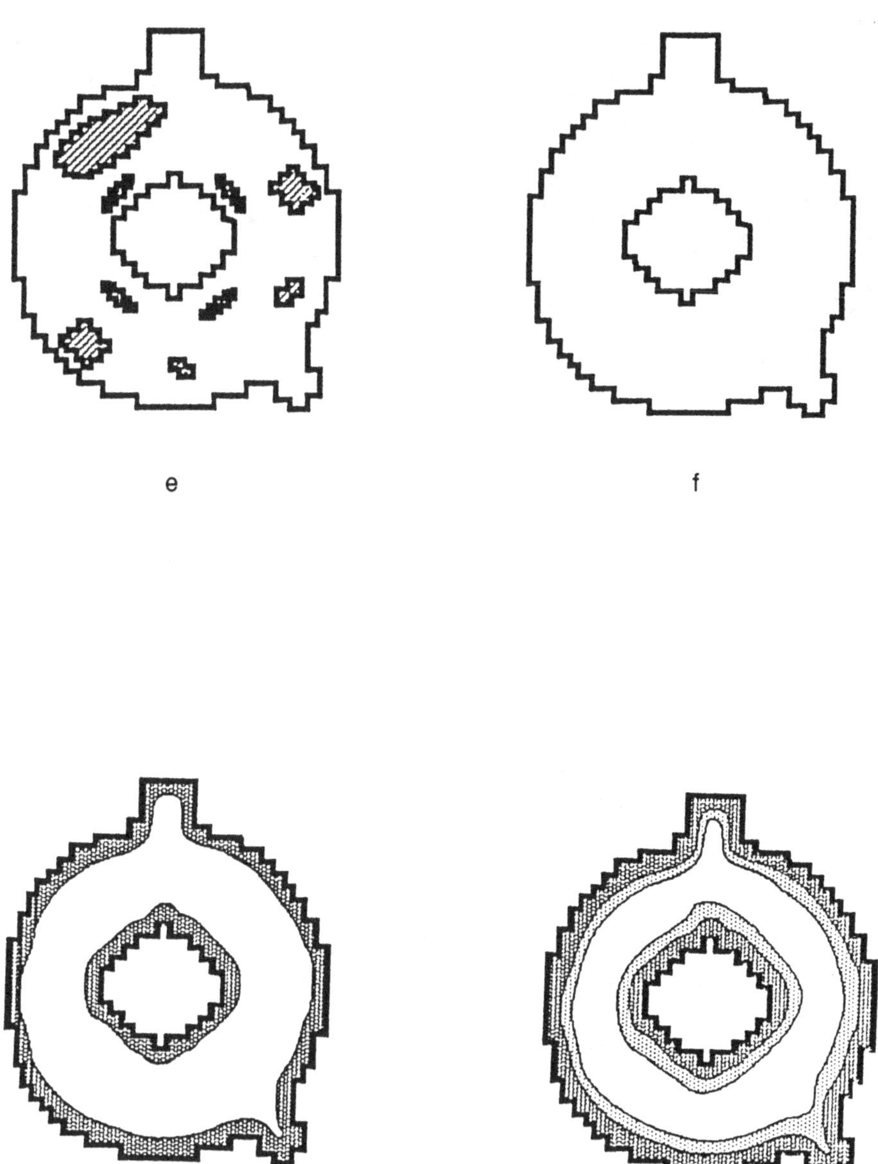

FIGURE 11.21. *Continued.*

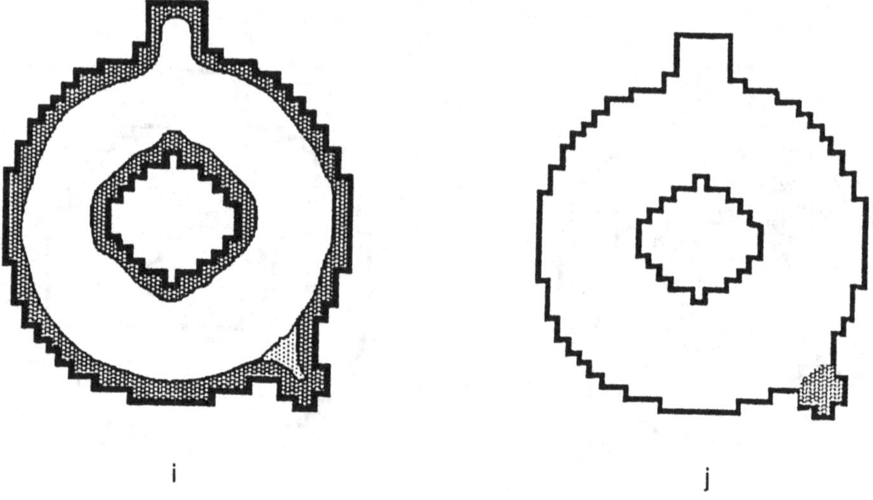

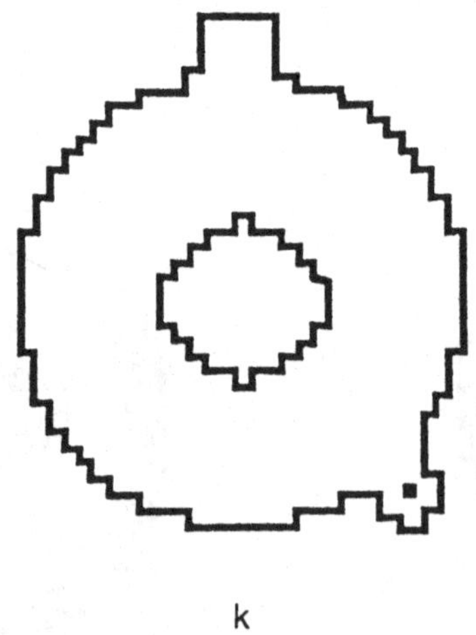

FIGURE 11.21. *Continued.*

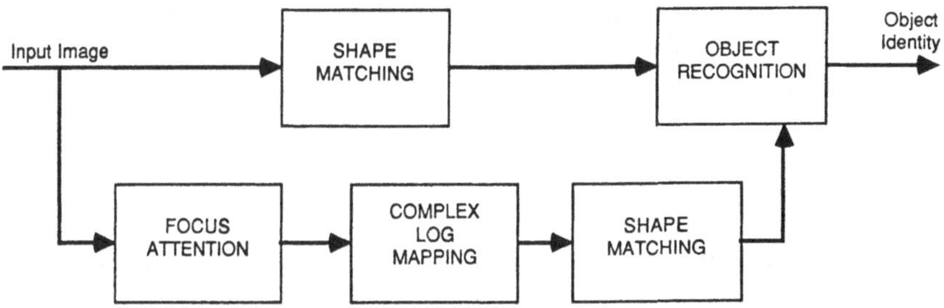

FIGURE 11.22. Enhanced algorithm using iconic processing with CLM.

and/or rotation of the template are with respect to the optical axis or the origin of the image. That means the object has to be at the center of the image to use this method. In most applications, the rotation and scale changes may not be with respect to the center of the image. In such cases, one may find regions corresponding to objects in an image and then obtain the transformation with respect to the center of those regions or some predetermined feature points on the object. Template matching, then, can be used in the transformed domain, as shown in Massone et al. [1985], and is effectively supported by image-processing systems that can efficiently extract and process regions (windows) within the image.

7 Conclusion and Discussion

Shape-based (iconic) approaches play a vital role in many applications of computer vision. Such techniques can detect shapes easily and help in object recognition and other early processing tasks in an application. Morphological approaches have been developed to analyze 2-D shapes. These techniques can be applied very fast using special architectures. This chapter discussed advantages of iconic approaches and briefly presented mathematical aspects of morphology. We also discussed an architecture that allows efficient implementation of morphological and other image-processing operators in real time for many applications. There is a rich software environment developed to use this architecture. We considered discussion related to the software environment beyond the scope of this chapter.

The approaches discussed in this chapter have been applied in several industrial applications. The Cyto-HSS is being used in several industrial and government organizations. Our experience with assorted applications suggests that iconic methods can solve many difficult low-level image-understanding problems. Until recently, not much attention was given to these approaches. We believe that with increasing processing power and availability of memory, iconic approaches will become increasingly popular for low-level operations. However, this field is in its early stages; much remains to be done.

References

Batcher, K. 1980. Design of a massively parallel processor. *IEEE Trans. Comput.* **C29,** (Sept.), 836–840.

Besl, P.J., and Jain, R. 1985. Three-dimensional object recognition. *Comput. Surv.* **17,** 1 (Mar.), 76–145.

Coleman, E.N. Jr., and Sampson, R.E. 1985. Acquisition of randomly oriented workpieces through structure mating. In *Proc. IEEE Conference on Computer Vision and Pattern Recognition.* IEEE, New York, 350–357.

Danielsson, P.E., and Levialdi, S. 1981. Computer architectures for pictorial information systems. *IEEE Comput.* **14,** 11 (Nov.), 53–67.

Duda, R.O., and Hart, P.E. 1973. *Pattern classification and scene analysis.* New York: Wiley.

Duff, M.J.B., et al. 1973. A cellular logic array for image processing. *Pattern Recognition.* **5,** 3 (Sept.), 229–247.

Gross, T., Kung, H.T., Lam, M., and Webb, J. 1985. Warp as a machine for low-level vision. In *Proc. IEEE Intl. Conference on Robotics and Automation.* (St. Louis, Mar. 25–28), IEEE, New York, 790–800.

Haralick, R.M., Sternberg, S.R., and Zhuang, X. 1987. Image analysis using mathematical morphology. *IEEE Trans. on Pattern Analysis and Machine Intelligence.* **9,** 4, (July), 532–550.

Jain, R., Bartlett, S.L., and O'Brien, N. 1987. Motion stereo using ego-motion complex logarithmic mapping. *IEEE Trans. on Pattern Analysis and Machine Intelligence.* **PAMI-9,** 3 (May), 356–369.

Knoll, T.F., and Jain, R. 1986. Recognizing partially visible objects using feature indexed hypotheses. *IEEE J. Robotics and Automation.* **RA-2,** 1, 3–13.

Lougheed, R.M. 1985. Application of parallel processing for automatic inspection of printed circuits. In Duff, M.J.B., Levialdi, S., Preston, K., and Uhr, L. (eds.), *Computing Structures and Image Processing.* New York: Academic Press.

Lougheed, R.M., and McCubbrey, D.L. 1980. The Cytocomputer: A practical pipelined image processor. *Proc. 7th Annual Intl. Symposium on Computer Architecture.* (LaBaule, France, May, 6–8). IEEE, New York, 271–278.

Lougheed, R.M., and McCubbrey, D.L. 1985. Multiprocessor architectures for machine vision and image analysis. *Proc. IEEE Workshop on CAPAIDM.* (St. Charles, Ill., Aug. 20–23), IEEE, New York, 493–497.

Lougheed, R.M., and Tomko, L.M. 1985. Robot guidance using a morphological vision algorithm. *Intelligent Robots and Computer Vision,* SPIE, **579** (Sept.), 367–376.

Massone, L., Sandini, G., and Tagliasco, V. 1985. Form invariant topological mapping strategy for 2-D shape recognition. *Computer Vision, Graphics, and Image Processing.* **30,** 2 (May), 169–188.

Matheron, G. 1975. *Random sets and integral geometry.* New York: Wiley, xxiii–261.

McCormick, B.H. 1963. The Illinois pattern recognition computer ILLIAC III. *IEEE Trans. Electronic Comput.* **EC-12** (Dec.), 791–813.

Messner, R.A., and Szu, H.H. 1985. An image processing architecture for real time generation of scale and rotation invariant patterns. *Computer Vision, Graphics, and Image Processing*. **31,** 1 (July), 50–66.

Minkowski, H. 1903. Volumen und Oberflaeche. *Math. Ann.* **57,** 447–495.

Perkins, W.A. 1978. A model-based vision system for industrial parts. *IEEE Trans. on Computers*. **C-27,** (Feb.), 126–143.

Ritter, G.X., and Gader, P.D. 1985. Image algebra implementation on cellular array computers. In *IEEE Computer Society Workshop on Computer Architecture for Pattern Analysis and Image Database Management*. (Miami Beach, Fla.), IEEE, New York, 430–438.

Schenker, P.S., Wong, K.M., and Cande, E.L. 1981. Fast adaptive algorithms for low-level scene analysis: Application of polar exponential grid (PEG) representation to high-speed scale and rotation invariant target segmentation. *Techniques for Applied Image Understanding*. SPIE, **281,** 47–57.

Schwartz, E.L. 1977. Spatial mapping in the primate sensory projection: Analytic structure and relevance to perception. *Biological Cybernetics*. **125,** 4, 181–194.

Serra, J. 1982. *Image analysis and mathematical morphology*. Academic Press, New York.

Serra, J., and Klein, J. 1972. The texture analyzer. *J. Microscopy*. **995** (Apr.), 349–356.

Sternberg, S.R. 1980. Language and architecture for parallel image processing. In Gelsema, E.S., and Kanal, L.N., (eds.), *Pattern Recognition in Practice*. Amsterdam: North Holland.

Svetkoff, D.J., Leonard, P.F., Sampson, R.E., and Jain, R. 1984. Techniques of real time 3D feature extraction using range information. *Intelligent Robots and Computer Vision*. SPIE (Nov.), 302–309.

Ulam, S.M. 1957. On some new possibilities in the organization and use of computing machines. IBM Research Report RC 68. May.

Unger, S.H. 1959. Pattern recognition and detection. *Proc. IRE*. **47,** 1737–1739.

Weiman, C.F.R., and Chaikin, G.M. 1979. Logarithmic spiral grids for image processing and display. *Computer Graphics and Image Processing*. **11,** 3 (Nov.), 197–226.

Index